New Courts in Asia

This book discusses court-oriented legal reforms across Asia with a focus on the creation of 'new courts' over the last 20 years. Contributors discuss how to judge new courts and examine whether the many new courts introduced over this period in Asia have succeeded or failed. The 'new courts' under scrutiny are mainly specialist courts, including those established to hear cases involving intellectual property disputes, bankruptcy petitions, commercial contracts, public law adjudication, personal law issues and industrial disputes.

The justification of the trend to 'judicialize' disputes has seen the invocation of Western-style rule of law as necessary for the development of the market economy, democratization, good governance and the upholding of human rights. This book also includes critics of court building who allege that it serves a Western agenda rather than serving local interests, and that the emphasis on judicialization marginalizes alternative local and traditional modes of dispute resolution.

Adopting an explicitly comparative perspective, and contrasting the experiences of important Asian states – China, Japan, Korea, Malaysia, Vietnam, Brunei, Thailand and Indonesia – this book considers critical questions including:

- Why has the 'new-court model' been adopted, and why do international development agencies and nation-states tend to favour it?
- What difficulties have the new courts encountered?
- How have the new courts performed?
- What are the broader implications of the trend towards the adoption of judicial solutions to economic, social and political problems?

Written by world authorities on court development in Asia, this book will not only be of interest to legal scholars and practitioners, but also to development specialists, economists and political scientists.

Andrew Harding holds the Chair in Asia-Pacific Legal Relations at the University of Victoria BC Canada, where he is also Director of the Centre for Asia-Pacific Initiatives. He is the author of *Law, Government and the Constitution in Malaysia,* co-editor of *Comparative Law in the 21st Century*, and co-editor of the series *Constitutional Systems of the World.*

Penelope (Pip) Nicholson is Associate Professor at the Melbourne Law School and is also the Associate Director (Vietnam) and Director of Comparative Legal Studies in the Asian Law Centre, University of Melbourne, Australia. She is the author of *Borrowing Court Systems: The Experience of Socialist Vietnam* and co-editor of *Examining Practice, Interrogating Theory: Comparative Legal Studies in Asia.*

Routledge law in Asia
Series editor Randall Peerenboom

1 **Asian Discourses of Rule of Law**
Theories and implementation of rule of law in twelve Asian countries, France and the U.S.
Edited by Randall Peerenboom

2 **Human Rights in Asia**
A comparative legal study of twelve Asian jurisdictions, France and the USA
Edited by Randall Peerenboom, Carole J. Petersen and Albert H.Y Chen

3 **Support for Victims of Crime in Asia**
Edited by Wing-Cheong Chan

4 **Administrative Law and Governance in Asia**
Comparative perspectives
Edited by Tom Ginsburg and Albert H.Y. Chen

5 **Regulation in Asia**
Edited by John Gillespie and Randall Peerenboom

6 **New Courts in Asia**
Edited by Andrew Harding and Penelope (Pip) Nicholson

7 **Legal Education in Asia**
Edited by Stacey Steele and Kathryn Taylor

New Courts in Asia

Edited by
Andrew Harding and
Penelope (Pip) Nicholson

Routledge
Taylor & Francis Group
LONDON AND NEW YORK

First published 2010 by Routledge
2 Park Square, Milton Park, Abingdon, Oxon, OX14 4RN

Simultaneously published in the USA and Canada
by Routledge
270 Madison Avenue, New York, NY 10016

Routledge is an imprint of the Taylor & Francis Group, an informa business

Typeset in Times New Roman by
Glyph International
Printed and bound in Great Britain by TJ International, Padstow

British Library Cataloguing in Publication Data
A catalogue record for this book is available
from the British Library

Library of Congress Cataloging in Publication Data
New courts in Asia / edited by Andrew Harding and
Penelope Nicholson.
p. cm. — (Routledge law in Asia)
Includes bibliographical references and index.
1. Courts—East Asia. 2. Justice, Administration of—East Asia. 3. Courts—Southeast Asia. 4. Justice, Administration of—Southeast Asia. I. Harding, Andrew, 1950- II. Nicholson, Penelope.
KNC459.N49 2010
347.5'01—dc22 2009025649

ISBN 10: 0-415-47005-6 (hbk)
ISBN 10: 0-203-86284-8 (ebk)

ISBN 13: 978-0-415-47005-6 (hbk)
ISBN 13: 978-0-203-86284-1 (ebk)

Contents

List of contributors

Kent Anderson, Professor, has a joint appointment with The Australian National University (ANU) College of Law and College of Asia and the Pacific, where he is Director of the Faculty of Asian Studies. He convenes a variety of courses on Japanese law for both the Law and Asian Studies faculties. His research has largely focused on comparative law, particularly with regards to Japan; private international law; commercial law, particularly insolvency and recently the introduction of Japan's quasi-jury system (*saiban-in seido*). Before joining ANU, Kent worked as an airline manger in Alaska, commercial lawyer in Hawaii, and associate professor at Hokkaido University Law School. He is Co-director of the Australian Network for Japanese Law (ANJeL) and Associate of the Asian Law Centre at Melbourne Law School.

Adriaan Bedner is a Senior Lecturer at the Van Vollenhoven Institute (Leiden University). He has been active in the field of Indonesian law and governance since 1992, which led among others to a PhD-thesis on administrative courts in Indonesia (2000). He has also published on Indonesian environmental law, constitutional law, land law and family law, and is currently in charge of a major research project on access to justice in Indonesia.

Ann Black received a BA, B.SocWk and LLB (Hons) from the University of Queensland and was admitted as a barrister. She completed an LLM (University of Queensland) and a SJD (Bond University). Ann is a lecturer-in-law at the University of Queensland and on the Board of the Centre for Public, International and Comparative Law. She is the current Director of the JD program. Ann's current research focuses on Brunei Darussalam and also on the role of Shari'a law in Australia and in South East Asia.

Mark Cammack is Professor of Law at Southwestern Law School where he teaches in the areas of criminal procedure, evidence and comparative law. Prior to entering teaching Professor Cammack was an assistant district attorney in New York City. His comparative law research has focused primarily on Indonesia where he spent a year researching the Islamic courts with a Fulbright grant. In addition to articles and book chapters, he is co-author with Norman Garland of *Advanced Criminal Procedure in a Nutshell* (2004) and co-editor with Michael Feener of *Islamic Law in Modern Indonesia: Ideas and Institutions* (2007).

Connie Carter is Professor of Law at Royal Roads University in Canada. She earned her PhD and her LLB degree at the School of Oriental and African Studies (SOAS), University of London. She is a qualified Barrister, having graduated from the Inns of Court School of Law in London and been called to Lincoln's Inn in London. Her first degree was a BEd from the University of Cambridge. Dr Carter has worked in the business and academic worlds in Europe and Asia. Before joining Royal Roads University, she spent five years in China, partly as Professor of Law at Xiamen University, partly as Human Resources and Public Affairs Director at a German-owned manufacturer of heavy machinery. While practising law as a barrister in London, she also taught intellectual property on the LLM programme and law and development on the undergraduate programme at SOAS, University of London. She has taught international trade law and intellectual property law as a visiting professor at several universities, including Chulalonghorn University in Bangkok. Her publications include: *Eyes on the Prize: Law and Economic Development in Singapore* (2002) and *Fighting Fakes in China: The Legal Protection of Trademarks and Brands in the PRC* (1996).

Minh Duong is a lawyer in the Ho Chi Minh City branch office of the international law firm Allens Arthur Robinson. Minh has been practising in Vietnam for more than three years. He advises on a range of foreign investment law issues in Vietnam including capital markets, mergers and acquisitions, and banking and finance transactions. Minh is a LLM candidate at The University of Melbourne and his thesis is on contract disputes in Vietnamese courts. Minh has a LLB (Honours) degree from the The Australian National University and is a lawyer admitted to the New South Wales Supreme Court.

Tom Ginsburg is a Professor at the University of Chicago Law School. He previously taught at the University of Illinois, and has served as a visiting professor at Seoul National University, Tokyo University, Kyushu University and Trento University. He received a BA in Asian Studies, a JD and a PhD from the University of California at Berkeley. His books include *Judicial Review in New Democracies* (2003*), Rule By Law: The Politics of Courts in Authoritarian Regimes* (2008) and *Administrative Law and Governance in Asia* (2009).

Andrew Harding received a MA (Oxon) in 1974, a LLM (Singapore) in 1984, a PhD (Monash) in 1987, and is currently Professor of Asia-Pacific Legal Relations, University of Victoria, Canada. Professor Harding joined the Faculty of Law at the University of Victoria in 2004 and works half-time with the Centre for Asia-Pacific Initiatives as its Law Chair. He teaches Law and Society in Southeast Asia and Law, Governance and Development. He is a former Head of Department and Professor of Law in the Law School, School of Oriental and African Studies (SOAS), University of London, and Chair of SOAS' Centre of South East Asian Studies. Professor Harding previously taught at the Faculty of Law, National University of Singapore, and as a Visiting Professor at Harvard Law School. He is co-General Editor of the Hart

Publishing book series entitled Constitutional Systems of the World. Professor Harding's interests include Southeast Asian legal studies, comparative public law, law and development, comparative law theory and environmental law. Recent publications include *Access to Environmental Justice: A Comparative Study* (2007), *Constitutional Landmarks in Malaysia: the First 50 Years, 1957–2007* (2007) and *Comparative Law in the 21st Century* (2002).

Hendrianto received his LLB from Gadjah Mada University, Yogyakarta, Indonesia in 1997. At the Utrecht University, Netherlands he received a LLM degree in comparative public law in 2003. In 2008, he earned his PhD at the University of Washington, School of Law. The title of his dissertation was, "From Humble Beginnings to a Functioning Court: The Indonesian Constitutional Court, 2003–8".

David T. Johnson is Professor of Sociology at the University of Hawaii. He received a PhD in Jurisprudence and Social Policy in 1995 from the Boalt Hall School of Law at the University of California at Berkeley. His first book, *The Japanese Way of Justice: Prosecuting Crime in Japan* (2002), received awards from the American Society of Criminology and the American Sociological Association. *The Next Frontier: National Development, Political Change, and the Death Penalty in Asia* (with Franklin Zimring), was published in 2009.

Hoong Phun ('HP') Lee, Professor holds the Sir John Latham Chair of Law at Monash University since 1995 and currently is the Deputy Dean of the Faculty of Law. He is the Vice-Chairman of the Australian Press Council and an Adjunct Professor of the School of Law, City University of Hong Kong (2009–10). Professor Lee's publications include *Constitutional Conflicts in Contemporary Malaysia* (1995) and *The Australian Judiciary* (2001) (coauthor).

He is the co-editor of *Australian Constitutional Landmarks* (2003), *The Constitution of Malaysia: Further Perspectives and Developments* (1986), *The Constitution of Malaysia: Its Development 1957–1977* (1978) and *Australian Administrative Law: Fundamentals, Principles and Doctrines* (2007). He recently co-edited with Professor Andrew Harding *Constitutional Landmarks in Malaysia – The First 50 Years 1957–2007* (2007).

Peter Leyland is Professor of Public Law at the London Metropolitan University and Visiting Professor at the School of Oriental and African Studies. His specialist interests include United Kingdom constitutional and administrative law, and comparative constitutional law with a special emphasis on Italy and Thailand. His publications include *The Constitution of the United Kingdom: A Contextual Analysis* (2007), *Public Law in a Multi-Layered Constitution* (2003) and *Textbook on Administrative Law* (2008). On Thai constitutional and administrative law he has written "Thailand's Constitutional Watchdogs: Dobermans, Bloodhounds or Lapdogs?," "Droit Administratif Thai Style: A Comparative Analysis of the Administrative Courts in Thailand," and "The Ombudsman Principle in Thailand". Professor Leyland teaches in Italy,

Thailand and Canada and contributes to international conferences. His recent public lectures include "Constitutionalism in Thailand: When Red Shirt Turn to Yellow," at John Hopkins University, Bologna.

David Linnan is a scholar of comparative, economic and public international law with a special interest in Asian law. He is Associate Professor of Law at the University of South Carolina School of Law, an associated faculty member at the University of South Carolina School of the Environment, and an Associate of the Asian Law Centre at the University of Melbourne. He studied humanities at Emory University (BA 1976) and law at the University of Chicago (JD 1979), where he was comment editor of the law review. He has held research or teaching appointments elsewhere at the University of Washington-Seattle, The Australian National University in Canberra (RSPAS and Faculty of Law),the University of Indonesia Faculty of Law and Graduate Law Programme in Jakarta (separately), and the Max-Planck-Institut (Strafrecht), Freiburg i.Br., Germany. From 2000 he has been the Programme Director for the Law and Finance Institutional Partnership, a legal and financial sector reform project run from Jakarta now as an academic consortium of Indonesian and foreign universities.

Shigenori Matsui is a Professor of Law at the University of British Columbia, Faculty of Law, in Canada. He received his LLB from Kyoto University in 1978, an LLM from Kyoto University in 1980, a JSD from Stanford Law School in 1986, and an LLD from Kyoto University in 2000. He worked as a research associate at Kyoto University (1980–83), as an Associate Professor at the Osaka University (1983–94), as a Professor at the Osaka University (1994–2005) before joining the University of British Columbia, Faculty of Law, in 2006. He is an expert in Japanese constitutional law, comparative constitutional law, mass media law and cyberspace law.

Pip Nicholson received a BA/LLB (Melbourne Law School) in 1988, a MPP (Australian National University) in 1993 and PhD (Melbourne Law School) in 2000. Pip is an Associate Professor at the Melbourne Law School, Australia and is also the Associate Director (Vietnam) and Director of Comparative Legal Studies of its Asian Law Centre. Pip's most recent publications include: *Borrowing Court Systems: The Experience of Socialist Vietnam* (2007) and a co-edited publication *Examining Practice, Interrogating Theory: Comparative Legal Studies in Asia* (2008). Pip's current research focuses on the impacts of donor-funded court-oriented legal reform in Vietnam.

Michael Palmer is Professor of Law at the University of London, and Chair of both the Centre of Chinese Studies the Centre for East Asian Law at the School of Oriental and African Studies, the University of London. He has published a very substantial corpus of work on Chinese law, played an important role in the development of practical legal training programmes for Chinese lawyers, judges and others, and also co-authored the principal text in Europe on alternative dispute resolution (with Simon Roberts: *Dispute Processes: ADR and*

Primary Forms of Decision-Making (2005)). Professor Palmer is Joint Editor for the *Journal of Comparative Law*. He is also Co-editor (with Professor Anthony Dicks) of a new monograph series on Law in East Asia. Professor Palmer's contributions to the field of comparative law were acknowledged in 2006 by his election as an Associate Member of the International Academy of Comparative Law. In recognition of his publications' record and standing in the field of East Asian and comparative law, Palmer was appointed an overseas Panel Member for Law, Hong Kong Research Assessment Exercise, 2005–6. He is also the holder of a Higher Doctorate in Law (LLD) at the University of London, and Honorary Professorships in China at Renmin University, and the South West University of Politics and Law. Professor Palmer is a barrister, practising at Serle Court Chambers, Lincoln's Inn.

Raul Pangalangan is a Professor of Law and former Law Dean at the University of the Philippines. He received his SJD from the Harvard Law School and holds a Diploma from The Hague Academy of International Law. He was a Philippine delegate to the Rome Conference that drafted the Statute of the International Criminal Court and sat on its Drafting Committee. He appeared before the Philippine Supreme Court as court-designated amicus counsel in the case on the impeachment of the Chief Justice. He has worked in various capacities in legal education and bar examination reform. He has taught at Harvard Law School, The Hague Academy of International Law, Hong Kong University, The University of Melbourne and Duke University's Asia-America Institute in Transnational Law.

Pitman Potter is a Professor of Law and Hong Kong Bank Chair in Asian Research at the University of British Columbia. His teaching and research focus on the People's Republic of China and Taiwan law and policy in the areas of foreign trade and investment, dispute resolution, intellectual property, contracts, business regulation and human rights. Dr Potter has published several books, including most recently *A Guide to Business Law in Asia* with Ljiljana Biukovic (2008), as well as numerous articles for such journals as *Law & Social Inquiry*, *The China Quarterly* and *The International Journal*. Dr Potter is admitted to the practice of law in British Columbia, Washington and California, and serves as a consultant to the Canadian national law firm of Borden Ladner Gervais LLP. He has served on the boards of directors of several public institutions, including the Canada-China Business Council and the Asia Pacific Foundation of Canada.

Mr Benjamin Tahyar is a lawyer and development specialist. He was born in Indonesia and speaks Indonesian fluently. By the time of the conference, Mr Tahyar had spent a total of more than six months in Indonesia studying the country's judicial reform process, including the Anti-Corruption Court. He is in the process of completing his PhD thesis (to be submitted to the School of Oriental and African Studies, University of London). Mr Tahyar also has previous expertise relating to Indonesia's Commercial Court through his master's dissertation (submitted to the London School of Economics and Political Science) – "The Political Content of Economic Laws: The Case of Indonesia's Bankruptcy Law Reforms," in which he examined the early performance of Indonesia's Commercial Court.

Veronica L. Taylor was the Dan Fenno Henderson Professor of Asian Law and Director, Asian Law Center at the University of Washington from 2001–2010. In 2010 she takes up the positon of Director, Regulatory Institutions Network (RegNet) in the College of Asia Pacific at Australian National University and remains an Affiliate Professor of Law at Washington: vtaylor@u.washington.edu. Professor Taylor specializes in comparative law and society in Asia, commercial law and regulation, and law reform in transition economies. She directs the *Afghan Legal Educators Project*, a U.S. State Department initiative to train Afghanistan's law deans and law professors and with Professor Susan Whiting (UW Political Science) she directs a U.S. State Department-funded multi-year project on *Empowering Rural Communities: Legal Aid and the Rule of Law in Rural China*, which both delivers and studies the effects of legal aid in some of China's poorest provinces.

Recent publications include *Rule of Law Promotion: Global Perspectives, Local Applications* (edited with Per Berling and Jenny Ederlöf) (Iustus, Uppsala: in press) and 'From Manners to Rules: the Reregulation of Japan' in John Gillespie and Randy Peerenboom (eds) *'Pushing Against Globalization: Regulation in Asia'*, Routledge (2009)

Preface

On 14–15 July 2007, 25 scholars came together in Victoria, British Columbia, Canada to debate 'New Courts in the Asia-Pacific Region' at the invitation of the Centre for Asia-Pacific Initiatives (CAPI) and the Faculty of Law at the University of Victoria, and the Asian Law Centre (ALC) at Melbourne Law School, Australia. The workshop was held to enable the debate of papers by a geographically dispersed group of scholars who had established credentials in the investigation and research of Asian courts: some from the region and some as external commentators. The conviviality of the workshop did not preclude robust debate. The issues discussed included: the catalysts for Asian court reform; the diverging internal dynamics producing reform; the relationships courts have with other state institutions; the role of actors in court reform; the relevance of legal transfers to court reform processes; how we assess the success or failure of court reform; and what is meant by 'effective court reform'. Many of these issues are canvassed in each of these papers; however, the breadth of the papers delivered at the workshop has also required the preparation of succinct chapters for this book.

So-called 'new' courts have mushroomed in Asia with little comparative analysis of their experience. This publication brings together scholars writing about and reviewing comparatively the experience of many different species of Asian courts. Most of the courts studied here have been operative for between 10 and 30 years, enabling a retrospective and reflective review of the record. This book is therefore an attempt to assess these recent experiences of court innovation in Asia and to spark debate about the desirability of these innovations; the nature of the political processes and choices leading to their adoption; and techniques for enabling them to succeed as legal institutions.

There are many people to thank. We would like to thank the Social Sciences and Humanities Research Council of Canada for a workshop grant and the International Centre for Excellence in Asia Pacific Studies at the Australian National University and the Centre for Asian Law at the University of Washington for assisting with travel and other expenses. We also thank our respective centres, CAPI and the Faculty of Law at the University of Victoria, and ALC at Melbourne Law School, for their unstinting support and for contributing to the funding. In particular we wish to thank Heidi Tyedmers of CAPI and Kathryn Taylor of

ALC for their wonderful organisation of the workshop and Philippa Duffy of ALC for her extraordinarily assiduous efforts on the copy-editing. We are also very grateful to Philippa and Sonja Zivak for managing the geographically dispersed editors and contributors with such grace and organizational flair. Finally we would like to thank the participants at the workshop and the authors of the various chapters for being such a pleasure to work with.

Andrew Harding, Victoria, and
Pip Nicholson, Melbourne,
March 2009

1 New courts in Asia

Law, development and judicialization

Andrew Harding and Pip Nicholson[1]

As we have stated in the Preface, 'new courts' have mushroomed in Asia, with little comparative analysis of their experience.[2] While country-specific studies of Asian courts, including monographs, increase almost daily, this publication brings together scholars writing about and reviewing the experience of Asian courts to enable a timely, comparative analysis of the new court phenomenon.[3]

Determining critically to investigate new courts produces fundamental questions with which a comparative analysis of court construction must engage. More particularly, an analysis of 'new courts' must at the outset consider what is meant by this term. It must also reflect upon how we judge the success or failure of courts generally, and new courts in particular. Even those authors claiming not to judge the record of a new court, implicitly do so, as a discussion of court construction or reform inevitably produces normative assessments from a particular perspective. Essentializing somewhat, these are the two critical questions with which the authors had to grapple, producing diverging assessments of what could be called a new court and what constituted a successful or failed court.

In this chapter we introduce key issues arising from this comparative study. We do not presume to give final answers to the issues and questions we raise. Instead, it is hoped that through explicitly identifying challenges to the analysis of new courts, we will spark further and more robust debate of these issues. The new court 'project', both in the 'field' and as a scholarly inquiry is a work in progress, and what we offer here is a reflective account of these experiments, albeit an account limited to Asia.

A note on the literature

Within Asia, the publishing on courts in English is very uneven. Both the Chinese and Japanese court systems and their reforms have attracted substantial scholarly interest over a long period.[4] Indonesian court reforms have also sparked sustained interest from commentators.[5] However, the courts of much of Southeast Asia have been relatively ignored.[6] And while there is much very insightful writing on courts, there is a dearth of literature that engages comparatively with the increase in the number and experience of courts introduced more recently to resolve conflicts or pursue particular policy agendas within Asia. The literature that does exist largely approaches the issue of courts from a rule of law or governance perspective, which is not strictly our project.[7]

This publication, rather, seeks to look at new courts comparatively to assess, in light of the documented experience, a court's reach, impact and reception – but more later about what is to be assessed. There was agreement at the workshop in Victoria that the comparative legal study of courts demands a socio-legal and/or historical scrutiny of the record to enable meaningful analysis.[8]

Can we talk of new courts?

The use of the term 'new courts' is problematic. After all, what is a 'new' court? For example, is a court new if it is refashioned from a pre-existing court? Does it have to have been established within the last 10 years? Can a court established 20 or 30 years ago still be new? Or do we mean by 'new', judging cases within a new jurisdiction or using new procedures? In designing this collaborative project we were acutely aware of the ambiguity and flexibility afforded by the descriptor 'new courts'. Rather than confine our comparative investigation either to courts recently established or to specialized courts with new jurisdictions, we opted for the less definitive 'new courts', precisely to enable a broader comparative canvas to consider the judicialization of dispute resolution in Asia. Put simply, 'new court,' as the phrase is used here, refers either to the introduction of a court not already in existence (or a new chamber within the existing court structure) having a specially defined jurisdiction (e.g. the Indonesian Commercial Court), or to a judicial innovation which does not relate to jurisdiction as such (e.g. the restructuring of the *Syariah* Courts in Brunei). In the main, the 'new' institutions considered here have been introduced in the last 30 years, but most of them much more recently than that.[9] Much as it would be useful, it is beyond the scope of this publication to compare judicial innovations with non-judicial innovations, such as new forms of alternative dispute settlement, and thus we make no attempt to do so.

Why have disputes been judicialized?

Two contextual questions, given a study of new courts in Asia, are 'have we experienced the judicialization of disputes in Asia?' and 'if so, why?'. Without doubt there has been a move across the region to establish new courts. In this publication, when we talk of judicialization we are not claiming that the numbers of disputes going to courts in Asia have increased. Rather, we are studying the phenomenon of establishing new courts, and therefore the project of providing judges and courts as arbiters of disputes. The question of why one should judicialize disputes is all the more prescient, given the long-standing alleged aversion to formal dispute resolution mechanisms in Asia. However, we do not seek to answer the ongoing dispute about whether there is an 'Asian' approach to dispute resolution based on customary, Confucian, consensus-based, or similar approaches to disagreement, or whether dysfunctional institutions could equally drive disputing parties to broker their own resolutions to disputes.[10] That is a debate for another place.[11]

In general terms the justification for the trend towards 'judicialization' has been that 'rule of law reforms' or 'rule of law implementation' or 'legal certainty' is necessary for the development of the market economy, democratization, good governance or the enforcement of human rights.[12] Thus both economic development and good governance are thought to be strengthened by 'judicialization'.[13] For example, in Indonesia a condition of the World Bank bailout loan in 1997–8 was the establishment of the Indonesian Commercial Court.[14]

The internationalization of Asian economies, with pressures for membership of multilateral organizations and to deliver on bilateral agreements, has also prompted much court reform, including the establishment of new courts. World Trade Organization (WTO) membership has proved a particular incentive for many Asian states to establish or reform existing courts into 'new' courts. In Vietnam, for example, recent Politburo policy papers on judicial reform invoke WTO membership and international integration in support of reforms to civil and economic laws: ultimately reforms that affect the jurisdiction and role of the courts in the resolution of economic cases.[15] Concurrently, some Asian states have, for various reasons, set up new courts of their own volition and for their own reasons; for example, the Special Court for cases involving traditional rulers in Malaysia.

Yet, as Thomas Carothers and others remind us, the casual relationship between democratization and the rule of law is not unequivocally made out.[16] Further, as Katharina Pistor and Phillip Wellons and others argue, the nexus between economic growth and rule of law is also unclear.[17] Recently, Tom Ginsburg has argued that constitutional courts or judicial review has emerged in Asia as a result of political players seeking to set up checks and balances on political power and courts, strategically and incrementally increasing their hold on judicial review.[18] Despite the scepticism, the trend to judicialize in the name of the rule of law continues.[19]

Indeed, judicialization in Asia comes at a price; for example, the World Bank extended loans totalling US$6,383.9 million for rule of law development projects in the period 1990–2007.[20] Both multilateral and bilateral donors invest considerable funds in promoting and facilitating court-based reforms with the avowed aim of contributing to the construction or spread of the rule of law; again, this is rationalized either on the basis of supporting economic development or on the spread of rights.[21] And yet, as Erik Jensen reminds us, this substantial investment does not generally produce positive results: rather, 'rule of law through court-centric programs founder'.[22]

This publication does not position its study of new courts and their development from a rule of law perspective; although some authors invoke this lens when assessing the efficacy of reforms, particularly when they talk of the independence of courts and their judges. Instead it asks, 'given the current focus and investment in and on new courts in Asia, what is the experience of these new courts?' This is a broader question inviting socio-legal and historical readings of court reform to elicit what has happened by way of court construction in diverse locations, and what we can learn from this experience generally, without tying the inquiry to the question of whether or not the reforms have heralded an export of the (notoriously hard to define) rule of law.[23] Putting this another way, in general terms disputes have been judicialized for all the reasons listed here, but that leaves the more interesting question, 'what has this judicialization produced'?

At what cost privileging the study of courts?

Critics have alleged that court-building is a Western agenda serving non-local economic and/or human rights agendas, rather than meeting a local concern about dispute resolution. It has been argued that nuanced reform of alternative dispute resolution, for example, might produce better dispute resolution mechanisms in a range of locations; particularly when compared with the results of donor reforms driven by ideological commitments to independent courts.[24] If this argument is right, then further studies of (new) courts that fail to embrace the logic of disputes, and their resolution beyond courts, could undeservedly privilege courts. It is not the intention of this project to reduce the importance of research into dispute resolution – the wider inquiry of 'naming claiming and blaming', as William Felstiner *et al.* put it.[25] Rather, as noted above, our interest lies in investigating what has been introduced as a new court, why and with what effect, including where possible and relevant the effect on alternative practices. As Michael Palmer demonstrates in his contribution, there exists a reassertion of mediation of administrative disputes in China, despite its apparent prohibition.

Nevertheless this study, taking courts as its focus, inevitably privileges courts. But in so doing, does it overstate the significance of courts? Does it marginalize effective non-court dispute resolution methods, which should be the focus of scholarship? These questions are legitimate, but require answers elsewhere.

Success or failure: assessing court reform

As is noted above, one of the issues confronting any investigation of new courts is whether the new courts are assessed as 'a success' or 'a failure'. However, there is no agreement concerning what constitutes success or failure. At the meeting in Victoria there was consensus that any benchmark for making these judgments ran the risk of a normative assessment reached from a particular perspective, and moreover, that the kind of consistency required for comparative purposes might well prove elusive, given the rather different purposes for which these courts have been set up. More particularly, the contributors did not necessarily share any common notion as to how to assess success or failure. However, amid the disagreement several matters emerged as critical.

First, the decision was made in Victoria that no one method of assessing the success and failure of courts would be adopted in the publication. The variety in approaches and assessments around 'success' and 'failure' of courts was considered beneficial to the investigation. In short, it was deemed inappropriate to insist on a particular mode of assessment from contributors, as this closed debates about how to assess court performance. So, for example, Shigenori Matsui asks whether the establishment of the Japanese Intellectual Property High Court has met the objectives articulated when it was introduced. H. P. Lee, in an analysis of the Special Court in Malaysia, claims that this court should be assessed in light of the context and challenges, legal and political, in which it must operate. Pip Nicholson and Minh Duong argue the need to assess the Vietnamese Economic Court from the vantage point of particular stakeholders to see what legitimacy the new institution has garnered locally.

Second, as David Linnan and Mark Cammack argue, all too often assessments of court performance emanate from stakeholders: donors for example, or local players whether supporters or detractors of a particular institution's reform. This can cloud the assessment. As Linnan argues, Indonesian courts are consistently given 'good marks for institutional improvement' (better procedure laws, more cases, better technically qualified judges, for example), yet this obscures an analysis of whose disputes are being resolved by whom, and why, and to what overall effect.

Moving from reflections on who makes the assessment and from what perspective, the use of statistics – while indicative of use rates and perhaps therefore local acceptance of courts – can be helpful and unhelpful in equal parts. Linnan argues that court-use rates are not indicative of actual court use by particular litigants. He argues that unless the researcher investigates the profile of court users and seeks to explain their dispute-resolution practices in and beyond courts there is a risk of fundamentally inaccurate assessments of court performance. Turning to the Korean constitutional experience, the alleged success of the Korean Constitutional Court results from an assessment of its cautious and incremental advance into topical and difficult cases, as Ginsburg suggests, rather than from a statistical assessment of the cases.

Other bases of assessment of court performance proposed included the transparency or efficiency of courts. While no one argued that 'successfully' reformed courts could be inefficient or lacking in transparency, there was disagreement about the critical nature of these factors as criteria by which to assess the efficacy of new courts. Certainly, at best, they were seen as a part of the mix involved in any assessment process, rather than determinative, particularly given the lack of agreement about what might constitute either of these criteria. For example, what is a transparent court system? Is it one that must publish all its decisions; or is it enough to have open hearings? What of cases that are dealt with through mediation, rather than in open court? Again a set of uniform criteria for assessing the success of a new court proved fraught with difficulty.

There was also robust debate about how to assess court failure. As Ginsburg reminds us, it might be the strategic use of local values and ideals by the courts that give the court local credibility and standing and therefore power. Does the lack of political will to support a court, as in the case of the Indonesian Human Rights Court, mean that the court has failed? Or, as Cammack suggests, can courts struggling with political enemies emerge as relative successes given the ways in which they challenge the state?

Several participants at the meeting in Victoria argued that one of the ways to gauge a new court's success was critically to assess the legitimacy or credibility the court had with its local constituents (perhaps, but not necessarily, synonymous with its users). As Lee reminds us, legitimacy might be manufactured by perceptions of courts, either by the press or by political powers, or by some potent combination of forces. The attitude of the state to the court, it was said, is not a reliable indicator of its acceptance, as states periodically set out to sabotage their own courts: the experience of the Indonesian Human Rights Court emerged as a case in point. Further, as Ginsburg and Tamir Moustafa note,

> authoritarian rulers may also attempt to make up for their questionable legitimacy by preserving [or instituting] judicial institutions that give the image, if not the full effect, of constraints on arbitrary rule.[26]

Court users, on the other hand, as commentators on the credibility of a court, might include: litigants; lawyers; judges; the government; prosecutors; and non-governmental organizations. While turning to see how each of these groups might evaluate the performance of new courts arguably overcomes the issue of normative judgments about transparency, efficiency and independence, how to judge legitimacy still remains problematic.[27] For example, H. P. Lee in his analysis suggests that while the introduction of the Malaysian Special Court to hear suits against the traditional Rulers in the nine Malay states is an imperfect reform (Malaysians cannot institute proceedings without the permission of the Attorney-General, and foreigners only if there are reciprocal arrangements), it might be that it is better seen as a successful innovation, precisely because its constraints enabled its introduction. In another sense, the paucity of cases before the Special Court might indicate that it has fulfilled its purpose of changing royal behaviour. In other words, even 'legitimacy' does not offer a simple solution to assessing the success or failure of a court. But perhaps a context-based assessment of court legitimacy can elicit not only how the court appears to multiple stakeholders, but also an appreciation of the contextual challenges to any court reform rather than pre-established criteria (such as those that exist when the rule of law paradigm is adopted).

A court's writing and contribution to legal discourse and understandings of law (different in the context of civil and common law systems) was also identified as a means by which to assess court performance. Andrew Harding suggested that logically structured discourse might afford insight into a court's standing and impact on its relationship with the broader public. In other scholarship, socialist courts' propagandist roles have been well documented.[28] In the former, the language of judgments is the suggested study; in the latter, the educational/propagandist work of the courts has also been nominated for analysis. These are but two illustrations of the potential for discourse analysis of new and emerging courts to reveal aspects of court development or change.[29]

The analysis of court discourse is varied in the chapters presented here. Several contributors looked closely at case readings: sometimes interpreting the subject matter with the benefit of a political science interpretative framework (Ginsburg assessing the decisions of the South Korean Constitutional Court); at other times noting the jurisprudential continuum historically to see what it revealed (Harding analysing the Thai Constitutional Court). This produces but one of many possible approaches to interpreting court change, albeit also a welcome shift from the much commented-upon weakness, noted in this collection, of 'institutional profiles'. The latter refers to studies of judges trained, dollars spent on infrastructure and law redrafted that does little to reveal the causes and consequences of actual reforms.

Contrasting new courts with reformed courts

Some have suggested that constructing new courts, rather than reforming those that already exist, is not necessarily 'good reform'. It is argued that whatever advantages there may be in setting up a new court, these are offset by the disadvantages accruing from deterioration or downgrading of the reputation of pre-existing 'ordinary' or 'traditional' courts. In these studies various views emerge. More particularly, Cammack's study suggests that the fact that the Indonesian Human Rights Court was 'new' was part of whatever success it enjoyed. In the case of Vietnam, Nicholson and Duong do not see that the Economic Court's designation as a new chamber within an existing court has radically constrained its performance. Adriaan Bedner warns that a new court may not necessarily perform better than the 'ordinary' courts, with the added problem of jurisdictional conflicts to consider, which may become severe. Indeed it would appear that many more factors than the institutional model adopted for introducing 'new courts' are at play.

Patterns and pathways: 'species' of new courts

Almost all of the new courts investigated here are specialist courts, that is, courts with highly focused jurisdictions. To enable comparisons of courts that share a jurisdictional focus, we have grouped the studies and take this opportunity to summarize the chapters, commenting on their significance for the general issues we raise in this introduction, and relating them to each other.

Part I comprizes two studies of economic courts in Southeast Asia. In the first of these, Pip Nicholson and Minh Duong consider Vietnam's Economic Court, established in 1994 as part of the rapid transition from collectivism to a socialist-oriented market economy, asking whether the Economic Court has emerged as an 'effective' forum for the resolution of economic disputes. Noting that usage rates remain low, they judge effectiveness in terms of legitimacy considered from the perspectives of its users (lawyers and enterprizes), its employees, and the party–state it serves. While by no means neglecting the broader context of dispute settlement and, in particular, that courts remain party–state led and directed, these contributors emphasize the many daunting internal and other challenges the Court faces in establishing itself as a reliable and reputable avenue for dealing with contractual issues. Principal among these are the lack of adequate laws and legal information, training, and other resources available to judges. The chapter proceeds to balance this picture against user responses to the Court on a number of relevant issues, noting in particular the delay, the complexity of procedure, and problems in obtaining evidence and enforcing judgments. 'Even assuming the judicial will to reform', they conclude,

> substantial impediments to trusted decision-making exist, some of which are largely beyond judicial control ... [The Court] has not developed a well of supporters ... while legal reforms may be enabling, institutional and cultural inertia will make court legitimacy aspirational rather than real.

The study does not, however, indicate total failure or lack of hope for the Economic Court, noting the comparatively good performance of the Court in Ho Chi Minh City, where usage rates have increased significantly. One can conclude from this study that more attention to the practical needs of judges, lawyers and litigants, in combination with political will to reduce party leadership of courts, would have been required to entrench the Court more successfully after 15 years of operation.

In his chapter on the Indonesian Commercial Court, David Linnan inquires into the apparent 'success' of the intellectual property jurisdiction of the Court as against the apparent 'failure' of its insolvency jurisdiction. He finds the resolution of this paradox in factors outside an analysis of the Court alone itself, which although a preference among Western lawyers and donors, may be misleading. Linnan refers to the 'political necessity of donors and non-governmental organizations to demonstrate "success" in relatively expensive rule-of-law programmes,' finding that politics underlies much of the praise for the Commercial Court's record in the intellectual property area, which may mask actual Court performance. He counsels against misconceiving the importance of courts in dispute resolution for a legal system still evolving in rule-of-law terms, which may distract attention from still existent problems in those institutions linked to actual dispute resolution (in this case the shadow role of the police and the settlement of disputes outside the Commercial Court). Interestingly for our question about assessing success and failure, while Linnan looks at litigation rates, he finds that a better approach is to focus on the still-limited place of courts in Indonesian dispute resolution, and that the clearest understanding of what goes on institutionally requires attention to where disputes go and how they are resolved; more often than not, outside the courts.

Instructive also at a general level is Linnan's discovery of an

> open mismatch between concepts such as specialized courts and the general organization and career paths of the Indonesian judiciary ... attempts to meld common law and civil law institutional approaches have not fully succeeded as a result ... [and] most judges are subject to transfer just about the time they develop some degree of expertise.

Thus,

> statistics only make sense when properly interpreted in the broader context of what is going on also with substantive law, the nature of litigants, the police, ... that lawyers looking at courts have a tendency to view courts formalistically as free-standing institutions, while their function (at least in the commercial setting) is really dispute settlement.

In his conclusion, Linnan leaves us with another consideration which was extensively discussed in Victoria: namely, whether there is a distinction between public law and private law in this context; one which, given 'the [smaller] number of Asian jurisdictions seeking to establish functioning constitutional courts [as opposed to commercial courts] as part of the standard governance rubric', argues for 'a more nuanced view of the true roles and expectations concerning new courts'.

We are here offered two quite different assessments of economic court performance. Linnan's analysis is compelling because it insists on seeing courts work as part of the landscape of dispute resolution only, and not as formative of dispute resolution. Further, he reviews analyses of court development made by donors and their consultants, critiquing the analytical assumptions upon which such assessments are made. Nicholson and Duong augment this by insisting that local legitimacy (traced through users, functionaries and lawyers' perceptions) is telling of whether there has been actual reform. Given the continuing socialist constraints on court reform (e.g. courts directed by the party–state in major litigation) in Vietnam, they suggest that the Economic Court may ultimately be treated as a special species of court in Vietnam, attracting particular freedoms to develop law as a result of the need to keep investors and multilateral agencies placated. However, to date, the Economic Court remains marginal at best; although the authors do not rule out effective reforms into the future.

Part II comprises two studies of Northeast Asian intellectual property courts introduced to reinforce efforts to improve the protection of intellectual property rights (IPRs).

First, Shigenori Matsui introduces the specialized Intellectual Property High Court in Japan. In a manner reminiscent of many 'new court' stories that we discussed at the Victoria workshop, this Court has its origins in the need to protect IPRs in a more obviously concerted manner (Matsui uses the phrase 'showcase the government's commitment to protect intellectual property rights'), given the average duration of court cases in Japan and the specialized nature of intellectual property (IP) and especially patent cases. The Court is in fact a division of an existing court (the Tokyo High Court) that brings together pre-existing Courts (IP divisions) under one banner, having its own 'grand panel' comprising all the division heads, and therefore falls clearly within our loose definition of a new court as adumbrated above. The reason for this particular arrangement, influenced by the United States' Court of Appeals for the Federal Circuit dealing with IP cases, was the need to avoid raising the complex jurisdictional issues which would be raised by a completely separate court. Matsui's chapter suggests that the Japanese experience of specialized courts[30] may be instructive for court reform in other locations and jurisdictions.

While careful to admit that it is hard to evaluate a court as young as the 4-year-old Intellectual Property High Court, Matsui tentatively suggests that analysts must be alert to the distinction between rhetorical statements of institutional change and substantive doctrinal change. Despite the introduction of an ostensibly new and independent court that is able to deliver authoritative decisions and shorter trials (although these were becoming shorter before the introduction of the Intellectual Property High Court), he discerns comparatively little shift in practice towards the greater protection of IPRs in Japan, conceding only that they have become more stable and predictable. In this he offers a salutary reminder of the need to look beyond the rhetoric of institution-building to the real causes and effects of new courts. He assesses the success of this innovation on the basis not of the extent to which Intellectual Property High Court cases upheld patent office registration and ruled that an infringement had taken place; rather, he notes that 'excessive protection of patent might hinder the development of new inventions. The Intellectual Property High Court might be looking for proper balance between the protection of IPRs and progress and new development'.

In a chapter which is highly comparable with Matsui's,[31] Connie Carter discusses the intellectual property divisions of the courts in the People's Republic of China (PRC),[32] originally introduced in 1981 but now of great importance in view of the PRC's accession to the WTO, which requires enhanced protection of IPRs. The IP Appellate Division in the Beijing Higher People's Court is vested with the exclusive IP appellate jurisdiction for the entire country. Despite publicity about the creation of a new IP court, it is now clear that this is a misrepresentation and is in fact 'merely a firmer implementation of China's ongoing policy to have specific judges rule on IP cases and thereby develop greater knowledge and expertise in IP issues'. Reflecting on more general analyses of new courts, Carter opposes, on the one hand, the need for new knowledge and expertise, consistency, predictability, speed and effectiveness to, on the other hand, the dangers of intimacy between the IP courts and IP litigators, lack of effective access for, and bias against, one-time litigators, and the sheer cost of the undertaking. She indicates that the development of expertise is the crucial factor in the PRC context. However, she also notes that any analysis must include a critical appraisal of the law in action, rather than attributing success for reform on the basis of laws introduced. More significantly, Carter suggests that until there are endogenous pressures for the protection of IPRs there will only be limited, and largely ineffective steps, taken to protect them, despite the loud and long-standing calls internationally for reform.

Part III, moving to the field of public law, contains studies of emerging constitutional courts[33] in Asia and a parallel analysis of the role of the Indonesian Human Rights Court.

In his chapter on the Constitutional Court of Thailand 1998–2006, which has now been replaced with a new version of the Court under the 2007 *Constitution of Thailand*, Andrew Harding sets the discussion in the broader context of Thailand's evolving but problematic version of constitutionalism. Judging the Court against the principles implemented by the constitution-makers of 1997, he notes the general failure of the Court to display genuine independence and to act as a counterweight to the authoritarianism of the Thaksin regime. He does so by examining the Court as part of the evolving political and constitutional process, but also (as do Ginsburg and Hendrianto, see below) by looking at key cases which indicate an ambivalent position. Inquiring as to what should appear on the Constitutional Court's tombstone, Harding points out that the reason for the Court's demise was not its indifferent performance, but rather the fact that the coup leaders of 2006 were compelled to abolish the Court by the prospect of their actions being ruled illegal. Like Lee (see below), Harding emphasizes that the study does not prove that the idea of a specialist court is defective, but that the design of later versions of the Court can benefit from the experience of 1998–2006. One conclusion to Harding's study which could be considered at a more general level is this: 'the reasoning and interpretive process should be open, explanatory, and represent a continuous and logically structured discourse'. This phrase sparked some discussion in Victoria: while the quality of a court's jurisprudence might contribute to its legitimacy (this is reflected in Matsui's and Ginsburg's chapters too, for example), what does such a logically structured discourse mean in practice and is this factor crucial as Harding maintains, or is it merely the perception of lawyers?

In his examination of 'new Asian constitutionalism', Tom Ginsburg argues that the 20-year-old Constitutional Court of South Korea – whose creation was inspired by and modelled closely on the German Federal Constitutional Court, and in turn inspired Thai and Indonesian lawmakers – has been an effective 'new court' and the most successful example among the five constitutional courts in East Asia. This is attributed to its structure: its credibility, stemming from politically prudent judgments responding to political crises, with judges demonstrating acute sensitivity to their responsibilities and making good use, for example, of different levels of constitutionality; and the role granted the nascent institution at its establishment by competing political parties in South Korea's emergent democracy of the 1980s. Ginsburg's chapter offers yet another approach to assessment: an analysis of Constitutional Court judgments dealing with issues of economic rights, retroactive justice, social issues, national security, and key issues arising in the political process. In addition, he notes public responses, which consistently rate the Court as one of the most effective institutions, and the most effective among state institutions in the country. This example runs counter to several other chapters in the book, in that it tells a story of successful, rather than deeply problematic, judicialization.

Adverting to a common problem with regard to specialist courts – their relationship to the ordinary courts – Ginsburg argues that the Constitutional Court has also established its supremacy over the Supreme Court, while ensuring that it has not abandoned traditional values through the careful endorsement of Confucian/Korean values in certain highly topical decisions. He posits that it is the combination of impartiality and independence with politically savvy handling of political tensions that have catapulted the Constitutional Court into centre stage of South Korean socio-political and economic decision-making.

Taking the Indonesian Constitutional Court as his subject, Hendrianto argues that in large part the Court's design is based on its Korean 'role model' (especially with regard to the selection of judges). There are telling comparisons here with Ginsburg's and Harding's chapters, both in method and conclusions. The three chapters analyse the politics of the Court's design and also its case law (Hendrianto analyses four prominent cases covering different areas of jurisdiction).

This chapter also examines Ginsburg's idea that the design of a Constitutional Court is determined by the varied needs of political parties to either protect themselves from challenges or to create opportunities for challenge in a politically fragmented environment: Hendrianto, extending Ginsburg's idea, notes that a sitting President of Indonesia secured a design which would place obstacles in the way of her easy impeachment. However, critical differences in Korean and Indonesian politicians' aspirations for their courts have produced an Indonesian Constitutional Court that operates in very different ways from the Korean example. In particular, Hendrianto argues that that restrictive bases of jurisdiction adopted in Indonesia (where the Court may only review a statute enacted by Parliament and not administrative decisions or implementing laws or edicts) has radically curtailed its accessibility. In turn, he argues this has produced low case numbers and decisions of only limited impact. In effect, the Court has been kept insulated from achieving a large role in many of the contentious issues facing the Indonesian people in the twenty-first century.

In his chapter on the Indonesian Human Rights Court, Mark Cammack insightfully argues that any evaluation of the Court, approved in November 2000 and commencing its first trial in March 2002, ought not focus on whether it exposed the 'truth' and 'imposed accountability' for Indonesian-sanctioned violence in East Timor. Rather, he suggests, a close examination of the court record reveals a 'new' institution, some of the members of which sought to act independently and give effect to 'real' trials of highly contentious politico-military issues. Some judges, writes Cammack, were stymied in their work by an uncommitted prosecution and witnesses speaking more for the defence than the prosecution. By revisiting the ways in which the number of convictions are calculated and closely scrutinizing judicial performance, Cammack contends that as a new court the

Human Rights Court was 'less compliant than originally anticipated'. He makes plain, as does Linnan, the need to assess new courts not simply on the basis of judicial performance, but also to include other related institutions (the police and prosecution service, for example) and their impacts in an evaluation.

In each of these three analyses of constitutional courts and Cammack's study of the Indonesian Human Rights Court, the power devolved to the court has been critical to its functionality and the continuing politico-legal landscape that has (re)shaped the courts' roles. As Harding explains, the Thai Constitutional Court's ascendancy put political power at risk and thus it was 'decommissioned,' as it were. Similarly, Ginsburg tells us that the South Korean model works precisely because the political parties seek an arbiter of their struggles; and the arbiter has invoked values strategically to win-over the public. In Indonesia, the powers not given to the Constitutional Court very much hamper its capacity, as Hendrianto explains. Cammack reiterates the significance of inclusion of the political landscape to analysis of court performance, when he posits that the Indonesian Human Rights Court was remarkably effective given its operational constraints. This is not to state the obvious: that the powers given to these courts will determine their strengths. Rather, the point made is that the political landscape (as manifest in frustrations and allowances of court authority) continues to shape courts' performances in fundamental ways, despite the powers they have been ascribed. Put another way, where courts have challenged the political organs of the state, those political institutions have proved either vindictive (Thailand), or determined to quash any potential ascendancy (Indonesia). However, as each contributor to the section also notes, the development of public law architecture has also 'played out' in unanticipated ways.[34]

In Part IV, continuing with the theme of public law and good governance, three analyses of administrative courts are offered. Indonesia has to date introduced no less than nine different sets of specialist courts, and seems about to introduce a tenth (land and environment courts). Adriaan Bedner studies the Indonesian Administrative Courts, which unlike the other Indonesian courts (and indeed most of the courts of any kind) discussed in this book, were not introduced during a passage of political and legal reform but in the middle of a period of authoritarian government – the New Order period of President Suharto. While their introduction since the late 1980s might seem a paradox (why would a highly authoritarian government seek to create legal checks on administrative power?[35]), Bedner finds the explanation is an attempt to avoid the adverse publicity of unsuccessful public-interest cases and a desire to bolster the legitimacy of the government (by a 'rhetorical device' as he calls it), alloyed with significant advocacy from individual justice ministers. Interestingly, in view of some of our general questions, the Dutch government was instrumental in assisting the introduction of a court based squarely on the Dutch example (i.e. a court with narrow jurisdiction).

The Administrative Courts were set up in such a way as to avoid them having real teeth, and have encountered many obstacles, particularly jurisdictional issues and problems of enforcement. Like Leyland (see below), Bedner engages in some statistical analysis but also examines the grounds of review, the remedies available, and the relationship with the ordinary courts. However, through an analysis of how and why these Courts sought to extend their authority beyond the tight jurisdictional limits originally set, he concludes that the combination of jurisdictional ambiguity and constraint prompted them to break out of the jurisdictional limits, creating great complexity and instability for the new administrative laws. The verdict is that while having separate Administrative Courts entails some advantages in terms of accountability and opening up of the judiciary to new ideas and skills, problems of uncertainty and jurisdictional conflict, especially with the Supreme Court, make them little better than the ordinary courts were, as a device available to the citizen to correct administrative actions. Bedner advises that those creating new courts should pay special attention to the harmonizing of jurisdiction with that of the ordinary courts.

In a strikingly different chapter on a similar theme, Peter Leyland discusses the Administrative Courts of Thailand, which were introduced together with the Constitutional Court under the 1997 *Constitution of Thailand* in order to provide for judicial remedies for abuse of powers, as part of an ambitious attempt to provide the institutional basis for democracy and good governance; here this chapter may also be compared to Harding's. This reform is nonetheless located historically by Leyland in a long process around creating administrative accountability, which began with the reforms of Rama V and became salient after the 1932 coup against the absolute monarchy. At several points in his chapter, Leyland finds relevance or explanation in the French *droit administratif* and *conseil d'etat* origins of Thai administrative justice. The Administrative Courts make sense as part of the grievance chain or hierarchical system of justice which includes, the Constitutional Court, the ordinary courts, the Office of the Thai Ombudsman as well as other less formal methods of grievance resolution.

In assessing the Administrative Courts' performance Leyland chooses to use both statistics and an analysis of important cases. His conclusion is in general much more positive than Harding's with regard to the Constitutional Court. The Administrative Courts appear to have resolved satisfactorily the inevitable jurisdictional questions relating to the public/private distinction, and not to have become ensnared in the politics of the Thaksin and post-Thaksin periods. Leyland lays emphasis here on the quality and independence of the administrative judges, and concludes that 'the introduction of the Administrative Courts has resulted in the strengthening of the judicial branch as part of a constitutional order embodying checks and balances', noting that these courts 'have continued to function as an accepted part of the Thai legal system despite the collapse of their constitutional foundations'. In short, they have achieved the legitimacy which has eluded the Thai Constitutional Court.

Michael Palmer's chapter, which follows Leyland's, looks at certain aspects of the position and work of the administrative chambers of the people's courts in the PRC. These were established in various areas of China on an experimental basis in the 1980s, in order to give greater effect to provisions in Article 41 of the 1982 *Constitution of the People's Republic of China*, empowering aggrieved citizens to seek compensation from the state when their civil rights had been infringed by a state organ or functionary. The administrative chambers became nationwide with the introduction of a special administrative litigation process provided for in the 1989 *Administrative Litigation Law of the People's Republic of China*. Particular attention is given in this chapter to the question: what is the nature and significance of the robust provision in Article 50 of the 1989 Law prohibiting a people's court from using mediation in its decision-making in administrative suits? In answering this question Palmer considers both judicial practice and the jurisprudence of administrative litigation in China, and contextualizes the changes that have been taking place in the system of administrative suits in the shifting institutional and ideological post-Deng environment. The chapter chronicles the use of mediation by the administrative chambers and the relatively unsuccessful attempt of the central administration to curb this practice, arguing that the party–state commitment to a 'socialist harmonious society' appears to *encourage* mediatory practices. Again we can see that politics (in this case the unrelentingly centralist politics of a one-party state) can steer a new court in a desired direction – in this instance in a manner that actually directly contradicts the stated law.

This triptych of papers suggests that administrative courts (in each of these case studies at least) are innately more resilient than their constitutional counterparts, where they exist. Why? Perhaps the administrative court judges understand the governmental need for these courts (because of the rhetorical use made of them by administrations to indicate citizen-focused reform?) which, in turn, affords these 'new courts' certain institutional space to develop; albeit not always as intended. Further, perhaps it is precisely because administrative courts deal in the main with individual complaints, rather than critical constitutional issues, that they are able to survive unscathed. The relatively low profile of many administrative cases enables the courts to deal with individual cases with less risk of governmental interference. These case studies also demonstrate the many ways in which court reform can be unanticipated, producing both beneficial features (such as resilience) and complications (such as uncertainties about procedures and jurisdiction).

In Part V we present an analysis of two anti-graft courts in Southeast Asia.

Through an analysis of the Indonesian Anti-Corruption Court ('*Tipikor*'), Benjamin Tahyar argues that fundamental to the success of new specialized courts are adequate funding, rigorous selection procedures, insulation from existing courts and the introduction of a structure that is realistically able to survive in the politico-economic context in which it must operate. Tahyar also points to the court's design, which saw prosecution launched by the anti-corruption agency, rather than the general prosecution service, as contributing to the quality of briefs brought before the Court: this is a weakness, as Cammack notes, of the Indonesian Human Rights Court, which was dependent on state prosecutors. While acknowledging criticism of the *Tipikor*, Tahyar argues it to be a most effective institution when its performance is measured against its objectives. With a 100 per cent 'success' rate in terms of convictions, this example spawned some discussion as to the proper definition of 'success' at the Victoria workshop. Here we can compare to Pangalangan's study of the Philippines Anti-Graft

Court below. Yet the future of *Tipikor* remains uncertain, the Court having been declared unconstitutional in late 2006 by the Constitutional Court. In explaining the inaction of the government to 'save' the *Tipikor* as a legal institution (the Constitutional Court gave the government three years in which to rectify its lack of constitutionality), Tahyar explains that the tenacity of the Court may be its own undoing. Ironically, Tahyar's is a chapter about a 'successful' court, the future of which is not assured.

Raul Pangalangan's chapter, which follows, deals with the *Sandiganbayan* (Anti-Graft Court) in the Philippines, although noting that the *Sandiganbayan* is just one body among many dealing with corruption. Pangalangan maintains that the *Sandiganbayan* has a 'dismal record', which he ascribes to both the Court's institutional weakness (particularly its vulnerability to appeals to the Supreme Court and its dependence on the Ombudsman to prosecute), and also a 'frailty of political and normative commitment to stop corruption itself'. Again, the political landscape is invoked to explain the near-absolute power of the executive. However, Pangalangan places no faith in rule of law or formal constraints on power, arguing that the level of detail required would effectively hamper the administration. Further, he states that formal resort to an anti-corruption court has not supplied adequate, or indeed any effective, prosecution of corruption cases. With the exception of the conviction of Imelda Marcos, Pangalangan argues through five case-studies that the *Sandiganbayan* and the Ombudsman have failed to punish corruption, owing to 'inaction or manipulation'. Following his indictment of the *Sandiganbayan*'s performance, Pangalangan states that the normative and political landscape itself must undergo reform, and the only hope for such fundamental revisionism is normative shifts made real by an active civil society; including the press and non-governmental organizations.

Here again we have two very different assessments of courts having a similar purpose. While Tahyar calls for constitutional recognition and the escalation of bedrocks such as funding and training to shore up the *Tipikor*, Pangalangan offers a damning analysis of the Philippine *Sandiganbayan*. Ultimately, Pangalangan's frustration drives him to advocate political and cultural changes premised on convictions about the transformative power of civil society activity within the press and non-governmental organizations.

In Parts VI and VII we move from a jurisdictional classification of new courts to critically analyse what we here call 'special courts and related issues'. Part VI contains studies of a regional court: Xinjiang in the PRC, the Special Court for cases involving the traditional Rulers in Malaysia, and the restructuring of the *Syariah* Courts in Brunei.

H. P. Lee chronicles the establishment of the Special Court in Malaysia in 1993 for the hearing of civil and criminal cases brought against any of the hereditary Rulers existing in the Malay states (nine of the 13 Malaysian states). This Special Court also has jurisdiction to hear a claim against the *Yang Di-Pertuan Agong*, the King selected from among the nine Rulers. The Special Court was introduced in light of incidents creating profound public concern about the legal immunity of the Rulers which entailed a lack of accountability for their behaviour.

Lee includes an analysis of the jurisdiction of the new court, its procedural rules and a study of the nascent jurisprudence. He concludes by canvassing the rationale for the Court's establishment, noting that it falls short of ensuring substantive equality of treatment of citizens: the Special Court involves special rules for particular litigants, hears only those matters brought against the Rulers, and proceedings require the consent of the Attorney-General. However, Lee implicitly supports the view that the introduction of the special court is contextually responsive and politically realistic in the Malaysia's federal structure and constitutional monarchy in the twenty-first century.

In the next chapter Ann Black chronicles the reform, since 2000, of the Islamic courts in Brunei Darussalam. She argues that the Sultan of Brunei seeks to assure the status and expertise of the Islamic courts, as part of a more general policy of Islamicization of the state; in turn reiterating the sovereignty and cultural particularity of a country that only regained independence from its colonial rulers in 1984. Black analyses the structural changes, notes the introduction of appellate review within the Islamic court system, details the increasing jurisdiction of these courts and the increased technical qualifications required for judicial appointments. These reforms, coupled with the potent symbolism of replacing the *Kadis*' Courts with the *Syariah* Courts, give effect to the pronounced *Melayu Islam Beraja* (Malay Islamic Monarchy) ideology espoused by the incumbent Sultan. The result, argues Black, is the introduction of largely new courts, not the re-establishment of a pre-colonial institution. However, ironically (as has been noted elsewhere) the process of re-Islamicization invokes Western strategies used to legitimize secular courts, such as the introduction of a court hierarchy and technical qualifications for judges. This has also been done in Malaysia.[36]

Pitman Potter's chapter shifts the traditional focus in the court-oriented literature on the development of large urban courts in China to those located in the Xinjiang Uighur Autonomous Region. Potter argues that courts located in China's 'regional borderland', largely 'offer a counterpoint' to the tales of 'impressive developments' emanating from large urban areas and investment nodes throughout China, often exemplified through studies of coastal courts. In assessing the performance of the courts in the Xinjiang Uighur Autonomous Zone, Potter explores their political context, and particularly the pressures upon them from the central party–state, echoing here Palmer's chapter discussed above. He combines this highly telling socio-economic and political background with an assessment of the institutional capacity of the courts, predicated on an investigation of (i) their institutional purpose ('ways in which goals of institutions reflect material and ideological contexts'); (ii) location (central–local relationships); (iii) orientation ('priorities and habitual practices that inform institutional performance'); and (iv) cohesion (linkage between individuals working within institutions and expectations of them from leadership). Potter concludes that the institutional capacity of the courts in this area is compromised by the tensions between ill-informed party demands for implementation of its agenda and local legitimacy – only securable if the courts track and reflect local mores and political and economic concerns.

Part VII presents two chapters concerning Japan, which can also be read with Matsui's chapter on the Intellectual Property High Court to give a unique insight into court reform in Japan.

The chapter by Kent Anderson and David Johnson probes the remarkable recent revival of the jury or lay judge system in Japan, abolished in 1943, which, although it does not create a new court as such, remakes the criminal courts in a manner approximating to the creation of a completely new trial system. The reform is remarkable because nothing as extensive as this form of 'penal populism' has been undertaken since the early 1950s in relation to Japan's very conservative and elitist legal community. Indeed India, Singapore and Malaysia have all abolished the jury system for criminal trials; nonetheless the authors see the jury system as possibly being encouraged by developing democratization in East Asia, and Taiwan and the PRC have been discussing a similar innovation. At the time of writing, the new system was not yet in effect, making it impossible to assess its effect as distinct from its prospects. Instead, the authors concentrate attention on the politics of the creation of the new system. As with other reforms discussed in this book, this one is not unrelated to general governance reform processes, being an

> effort to improve the quality of Japanese law and democracy by increasing the size of the legal profession and the availability of legal services, improving the quality of legal services through changes in legal education, and by instituting other 'huge' and 'extensive' reforms that 'relate to the very foundation of all aspects of the justice system'.

Part of this process is to secure greater civic engagement with the criminal justice system, and liberalize the trial system, which exhibits some dysfunctional features such as procedural rules systematically favouring state interests. Nonetheless, as the authors point out, the reforms do not address the rights of accused persons or the police. The jury system should not be understood as a wholesale adoption of a common-law device, but is in fact a hybrid of the jury and mixed-court systems. In moving to this new system, Japan, although not directly influenced by international pressures, has nonetheless been influenced by the processes of internationalization and the related factor of the impact of the views of Japanese business and political classes.

In her chapter on the Japanese civil courts, Veronica Taylor focuses on corporate governance in a new regulatory climate with reference to damage liability. This is not a study of a new court as such, but reminds us of the context of, and also reasons for, reform in Anderson and Johnson's discussion of criminal justice, and poses interesting issues for any discussion of 'newness' in courts in Asia, being concerned with the influence of new factors. The newness in Japan's legal system has however, in a development exactly mirroring Matsui's discussion, resulted in new court divisions in Tokyo and Osaka dealing with bankruptcy matters. Taylor argues that while a court system can remain stable and relatively unchanged in terms of, for example, staffing, structure and procedure codes, still the determinations it makes can change in character substantially; particularly, it is suggested, in response to economic and regulatory changes affecting its milieu. Through an analysis of the recent Japanese original and appellate court decisions in two cases (*Duskin* and *Daiwa Bank*), Taylor suggests convincingly that regulatory impacts can have as great an impact on the work of courts as other changes, and these need to be critically addressed when undertaking an analysis of court development.

Perennial questions

In this final section of the introductory chapter we pose, without attempting to finally answer, some of the questions that were raised in discussion sessions at the Victoria workshop. Some of these (what counts as 'new'? how should we assess these new courts?) have already been dealt with above.

One issue we discussed was whether the new courts in Asia evinced any Asian characteristics. This, in turn, raises the issue of what counts as 'Asian' for these purposes; after all, development, transition, innovation and pluralism are themselves characteristic of Asia in the early twenty-first century. The question is more likely to refer to traditional modes of dispute settlement or communitarian or religious values or political discourse. Clearly, several instances discussed in this book are directly concerned with these issues, which would not arise, for example, in Western legal systems (*Syariah* court reconstruction) or are not likely to do so (anti-graft courts). Most of the contributions see the 'Asian-ness' not so much in the design of the court or its decision-making, but rather in the relevant context of dispute settlement, and (it is often alleged: *sed quaere*) the Asian preference for informal rather than court-based dispute settlement; or in responses to purely localized factors.

For example, Potter's analysis of remote Chinese courts and Lee's study of royal courts take particular features of a community: in China its vastness and the challenges this produces for one court system; and in Malaysia the long-standing immunity of royalty from criminal or civil suit. The authors investigate how these challenges have been met by courts recently introduced. In Brunei, Black asks whether the *Kadi* Courts have been substantively refashioned when they were relaunched as *Syariah* Courts, an innovation based upon a state-promoted ideology.

Since we have not had space to consider alternatives to litigation in this book, the comparison of new courts with such alternatives is not an issue to be judged here, but clearly it needs careful handling. This is very much the case in the context of economic dispute resolution, where multiple options exist for dispute resolution including: international arbitration, formal and informal mediation, and state-based and private arbitration in-country. There are less obvious court alternatives in the constitutional arena, although administrative and anti-graft reforms are often part of a package of legal institutional changes.

Returning to the economic court examples, Nicholson and Duong indicate a strong preference among commercial enterprises (90 per cent), both local and foreign, not to go to court. This finding could well be replicated in most world legal systems, where we know that litigants bargain in the shadow of the law rather than in necessarily taking their disputes to legal institutions.[37] However, Nicholson and Duong are not suggesting that Vietnamese entities necessarily bargain in the shadow of court-based resolution of disputes.[38] Rather, they note that Vietnamese and foreign companies eschew courts and seek out other institutions such as foreign alternative dispute resolution or informal mediation – the latter at least, to date, not shaped by court determinations. Linnan, speaking of the Indonesian context, also notes that particular commercial institutions have developed strategic responses to court development.

The best answer we feel able to give is that, with scarcely an exception, the authors of this volume advert to the local context in which the courts operate, and this applies even to those who seem most focused on the details of the design and operation of the court itself, not just those who set the court in its broader legal and political context. Nonetheless, readers may want to consider some instances where elements of what looks like Asian culture seem to emerge in relation to court performance. So, for example, Nicholson and Duong and also Linnan are pointing not to culture as the necessary cause of avoiding economic courts, but to commercial strategy as an equally likely explanation. In other jurisdictions, Ginsburg writes about the Confucian nature of some Constitutional Court decisions in South Korea. In the same vein Harding writes about the Thai Constitutional Court's attention to contemporary cultural attitudes to disabled judges and monks holding office; he also points out ways in which the court machinery has only operated when prompted to do so by the King. Lee's chapter, on the other hand, shows a clear and opposite reaction to an element of traditional Malay culture – the unquestioned authority of the traditional Ruler. Perhaps in each case the emerging court discourse has recognized values and ideals to legitimate its reasoning. And again this is not unique to Asia. Arguably judges of the Australian High Court, for example, have variously and very differently invoked values when developing constitutional law and legal doctrine.[39]

In the discussions, the issue of Asian-ness was also related to the issue of what was continuously referred to as the 'politics of legitimacy'. Although politics is very apparent in all of the contributions, and not least in relation to legitimacy, there seems little evidence here that there is anything peculiarly or characteristically Asian about the nature of the legitimacy or lack of it which we find in relation to these new courts. The factors referred to (impartiality, independence, consistency, and actual usage, for example) seem to be of general relevance in relation to courts, not just in Asia; as is the broader and sometimes hard-to-define issue of legitimacy in the eyes of the public; in part perhaps reflecting what has been identified above, but also, perhaps, including something vaguer like public acceptance or favourable predisposition. To turn once again to the Australian context, bitter arguments about who should defend the Australian High Court from attack by politicians when it resolved that native title extended to pastoral leases emerged.[40] The Court contended that the Attorney-General had a duty to protect the legitimacy of judicial law-makers; at least in as far as explaining that they were doing their job. The Attorney-General declined this role, although it had been largely the practice since the introduction of the High Court in 1901.[41] The example illuminates how the public/court interface, as a part of the matrix of influences merging in notions of legitimacy, is also not necessarily exclusive to Asia or an 'Asian way'.

Another area of discussion was the public/private distinction. It was even mooted whether the considerations and approach were so different that two volumes might be needed: one on private law, and one on public law. Readers will judge for themselves, but will see that although there are differences, and although we have grouped the courts partly according to this criterion, the differences between them arguably do not amount to a distinction in principle that requires a different approach or mode of comparison. For example, although constitutional courts and administrative courts deal with political questions and much politics surrounds their introduction, the same is often true of the introduction of economic courts, if not their actual case-load. At the same time many issues, such as legitimacy and resourcing, cut across the public/private divide. Not only did we see no reason to separate these two kinds of court, but we saw every reason to place them side by side.

Perhaps the sharpest disagreement among the contributors related to the issue of legal transfers or legal transplants. While one contributor saw the debate on this as outmoded and 'done to death', another saw genealogy at least as fundamental to the project. Discussion revolved around whether 'models' were determinative; relevant but not determinative; or irrelevant and non-determinative. The evidence of the studies presented here is ambiguous. Some of these, such as Hendrianto's, Leyland's, Bedner's, and both of the studies of intellectual property courts (Carter's and Matsui's), lay some, or even heavy, emphasis on the importance of available models, whereas other chapters do not, partly because the issue does not arise (e.g. Lee's and Palmer's).

Is specialization the weapon of choice for court reform?

Harding said at the beginning of the workshop that Asia exhibits a considerable degree of specialization. Citing the recently established Indonesian Fisheries Court (2007) as an extreme example of specialization,[42] he then noted that the Japanese had gone one stage further in specialization by creating a Tuna Court![43] Nonetheless, despite these examples and an obvious tendency towards specialization, it can be seen that Asian legal systems do not tend to go beyond familiar forms of specialization. All the types of court considered here can be seen in non-Asian jurisdictions (except perhaps the Special Court in Malaysia discussed in Lee's chapter). In Japan's case, Matsui points out that no country has a totally separate intellectual property court, and that this weighed at the design stage.

The individual authors (apart from Bedner) did not extensively discuss the issue of whether the creation of a specialist court was preferable to giving the same jurisdiction to ordinary courts, understandably preferring on the whole to examine what was there rather than speculate on what might have been; and in some cases the issue did not arise. In general terms, however, it does look as though there is some scepticism abroad as to the viability of having specialist courts in the sense of courts enjoying jurisdiction separated from that of the ordinary courts.

The reasons for specialization are quite consistently evident in the studies. The ordinary courts are slow, expensive, lacking in competence and resources. A special court can be designed more effectively to deal with a particular policy objective, such as reassurance of foreign investors or insulation from political influence. To judge by the case studies, not just national governments and parliaments seem to favour specialized courts: donors too seem to favour them. Obvious difficulties with special courts are, however, revealed by the studies: jurisdictional uncertainties and even open conflicts and hostility are encountered, especially in early stages of development; the problem of training and keeping judges (and lawyers) with the relevant speciality; and the implicit or even explicit demotion of the ordinary courts with consequent loss of legitimacy and even, perhaps, resources, with international development aid being channelled into creating the new court. One is left wondering if any form of emphasis on judicial specialism requires a proportionate de-emphasizing of the project of reforming the ordinary courts. To take an example, Leyland points to the ring-fencing of the Thai Administrative Court budget, the recruitment of qualified candidates, and the adequacy of judges' remuneration – but why do other courts not deserve this kind of treatment? Is there an element of unreality even where specialist courts are seen to be successful (as in Leyland's study), given that a broader study of the performance of the entire judiciary might reveal no overall improvement (see Bedner's chapter), despite all the efforts being made? On the other hand, does this concentration of effort have the beneficial effect of showing us how improvement can be achieved, which might lead to adoption of best practices, attracting of new talent and ideas, and so to general improvement? These questions remain to be answered.

To conclude, if there is one lesson to be learned from the study of new courts in Asia, it would be that where a specialist new court is to be introduced there are many issues which require careful assessment. A specialist court is not necessarily a good solution, attractive as it might be to reformers, with time scales and limited budgets to consider. The ultimate goal must be to improve the delivery of justice in all areas. As to whether these 'new courts' in any form actually serve this end remains uncertain. It looks, however, as if the obsession with new courts will remain a notable feature of law reform in Asia.

Notes

1. Professor of Asia–Pacific Law, University of Victoria, Canada; Associate Professor, Melbourne Law School, The University of Melbourne, Australia.
2. Several recent publications have commenced comparative publication in this emerging field: Tom Ginsburg and Tamir Moustafa, eds, *Rule by Law: The Politics of Courts in Authoritarian Regimes* (New York: Cambridge University Press, 2008); *Albert Chen*

and Tom Ginsburg, eds, Administrative Law and Governance in Asia: Comparative Perspectives (London: Routledge, 2008); Tom Ginsburg, *Judicial Review in New Democracies: Constitutional Courts in Asian Cases* (New York: Cambridge University Press, 2003); Michael Pryles, ed., *Dispute Resolution in Asia*, 2nd edn (The Hague: Kluwer Law International, 2003).

3. See, for example of country-specific publications: Bee Chen Goh, *Law Without Lawyers, Justice Without Courts: On Traditional Chinese Mediation* (Aldershot, UK: Ashgate, 2002); Institute of Law, Chinese Academy of Social Science, Beijing, *Dispute Resolution Process in China, IDE Asian Law Series*, Vol. 15 (Beijing: Institute of Developing Economies, 2002); Yasunobu Sato, *Commercial Dispute Processing and Japan* (The Hague: Kluwer Law International, 2001); Joseph W. S. Davis, ed., *Dispute Resolution in Japan* (The Hague: Kluwer Law International, 1996); Sharifah Zaleha Syed Hassan and Sven Cederroth, *Managing Marital Disputes in Malaysia: Islamic Mediators and Conflict Resolution in the Syariah Courts* (Surrey, UK: Routledge Curzon, 1997).
4. On Japan and in reverse chronological order: Carl F. Goodman, *The Rule of Law in Japan: A Comparative Analysis* (The Hague: Kluwer Law International, 2003); Mark J. Ramseyer and Eric B. Rasmusen, *Measuring Judicial Independence: The Political Economy of Judging in Japan* (Chicago: University of Chicago Press, 2003); Malcom M. Feeley and Setsuo Miyazawa, *The Japanese Adversary System in Context: Controversies and Comparisons* (Houndmills, UK: Palgrave Macmillan, 2002); Yasunobu Sato, *Commercial Dispute Processing and Japan* (The Hague: Kluwer Law International, 2001); Joseph W. S. Davis, ed., *Dispute Resolution in Japan* (The Hague: Kluwer Law International, 1996); Hiroshi Itoh, *The Japanese Supreme Court: Constitutional Policies* (New York: M. Wiener, 1989); Dan Fenno Henderson and John Owen Haley, *Law and the Legal Process in Japan: Materials for an Introductory Course on Japanese Law* (1978). On China and in reverse chronological order: Albert H. Y. Chen, *An Introduction to the Legal System of the People's Republic of China* (Singapore: LexisNexis Butterworths, 2004); Bee Chen Goh, *Law Without Lawyers, Justice Without Courts: On Traditional Chinese Mediation*; Gui Guo Wang, "The Legal System of China," in *Business Law in Hong Kong*, ed. D. K. Srivastava (Hong Kong: Sweet & Maxwell, 2007), 67–82; Karen Turner, James V. Feinerman and R. Kent Guy, eds, *The Limits of the Rule of Law in China* (Seattle: University of Washington Press, 2000); Institute of Law, Chinese Academy of Social Science, *China's Judicial System and its Reform, IDE Asian Law Series*, Vol. 2 (Beijing: Institute of Developing Economies, 2001); Ronald C. Brown, *Understanding Chinese Courts and Legal Process: Law with Chinese Characteristics* (The Hague: Kluwer Law International, 1997). See also: Fu Yulin and Randall Peerenboom, "A New Analytic Framework for Understanding and Promoting Judicial Independence in China," http://ssrn.com/abstract = 1336069; Julie Lewis, "China's Courts Gain Credibility," *Law Society Journal* 45 (2007): 22; Benjamin L. Liebman, "China's Courts: Restricted Reform," *China Quarterly* 191 (2007): 620–38; Hualing Fu, "Putting China's Judiciary into Perspective: Is it Independent, Competent, and Fair?," in *Beyond Common Knowledge: Empirical Approaches to the Rule of Law*, ed. Erik Jensen and Thomas C. Heller (Stanford, CA: Stanford University Press, 2005): 193–219; Molly Riley, "On the Rule of Law and the Role of Courts in China," *International Company and Commercial Law Review* 16 (2005): 151–6; Colin Hawes, "Seeds of Dissent: The Evolution of Published Commercial Law Court Judgments in Contemporary China," *Australian Journal of Asian Law* 5 (2003), 1–41; Margaret Y. K. Woo, "Law and Discretion in Contemporary Chinese Courts," in *The Limits of the Rule of Law in China*, ed. Karen Turner, James Feinerman and R. Kent Guy (Seattle: University of Washington Press, 2000), 163; Jerome A. Cohen, "Reforming China's Civil Procedure: Judging the Courts," *American Journal of Comparative Law* 45 (1997): 793–804; Susan Finder, "The Supreme People's Court of the People's Republic of China," *Journal of Chinese Law* 7 (1991): 145–223.

5. Adriaan Bedner, *Administrative Courts in Indonesia: A Socio-legal Study* (The Hague: Kluwer Law International, 2001); Daniel S. Lev, "Judicial Unification in Post-Colonial Indonesia," in *Legal Evolution and Political Authority in Indonesia: Selected Essays*, ed. Daniel S. Lev (The Hague: Kluwer Law International, 2000), 33; Daniel S. Lev, "Judicial Authority and the Quest for an Indonesian Rechtsstaat," in *Legal Evolution and Political Authority in Indonesia: Selected Essays*, ed. Daniel S. Lev (The Hague: Kluwer Law International, 2000), 215; Daniel S. Lev, "Judicial Institutions and Legal Culture," in *Legal Evolution and Political Authority in Indonesia: Selected Essays*, ed. Daniel S. Lev (The Hague: Kluwer Law International, 2000), 161; Daniel S. Lev, "The Supreme Court and Adat Inheritance Law in Indonesia," in *Legal Evolution and Political Authority in Indonesia: Selected Essays*, ed. Daniel S. Lev (The Hague: Kluwer Law International, 2000), 99; Daniel S. Lev, "The Politics of Judicial Development in Indonesia," in *Legal Evolution and Political Authority in Indonesia: Selected Essays*, ed. Daniel S. Lev (The Hague: Kluwer Law International, 2000), 71; Timothy Lindsey, ed., *Indonesia: Bankruptcy, Law Reform and the Commercial Court* (Sydney: Desert Pea Press, 2000); Erman Rajagukguk, "Judicial Reform: A Proposal for the Future of the Commercial Court," in *Indonesia: Bankruptcy, Law Reform and the Commercial Court*, ed. Timothy Lindsey (Sydney: Desert Pea Press, 2000), 57–60; S. Butt, "The Eksekusi of the Negara Hukum: Implementing Judicial Decisions in Indonesia" in *Indonesia: Law and Society*, ed. Timothy Lindsey (Sydney: Federation Press, 1999), 247–57; P. Lotulung, "Judicial Review in Indonesia," in *Comparative Studies on the Judicial Review System in East and Southeast Asia*, ed. Yong Zhang (The Hague: Kluwer Law International,1997), 167–82; Adriaan Bedner, "Administrative Courts in an Executive-Dominated State: The Case of Indonesia," in *Comparative Studies on the Judicial Review System in East and Southeast Asia*, ed. Yong Zhang (The Hague: Kluwer Law International,1997), 183–210; R. Rohdewohld, *Public Administration in Indonesia* (Melbourne: Montech Pty Ltd, 1995); Keebet von Benda-Beckman, *The Broken Stairways to Consensus: Village Justice and State Courts in Minangkabau* (Dordrecht, The Netherlands: Foris Publications, 1984); Daniel S. Lev, "Judicial Institutions and Legal Culture in Indonesia," in *Culture and Politics in Indonesia*, ed. C. Holt (Ithaca, NJ: Cornell University Press, 1972), 246–318; Daniel S. Lev, *Islamic Courts in Indonesia* (Berkeley, CA: University of California Press, 1972).
6. See generally, Pryles, *Dispute Resolution in Asia*. For example, the publication on Thai courts in English is limited (Central Intellectual Property and International Trade Court, *The Judicial System in Thailand: An Outlook for a New Century, IDE Asian Law Series* [Bangkok: Institute of Developing Economies, 2001]). And although the publication of the Vietnamese court system is relatively more voluminous, it remains slight compared with that in Indonesia: Pip Nicholson, "Legal Culture 'Repacked': Drug Trials in Vietnam," in *Examining Practice, Interrogating Theory; Comparative Legal Studies in Asia*, ed. Pip Nicholson and Sarah Biddulph (Leiden, The Netherlands: Martinus Nijhoff Publishers, 2008), 71–108; Pip Nicholson, *Borrowing Court Systems: The Experience of Socialist Vietnam* (The Hague: Martinus Nijhoff, 2007); John Gillespie, "Rethinking the Role of Judicial Independence in Socialist Transforming East Asia," *International Comparative Law Quarterly* 4 (2007): 837–70; Pip Nicholson, "Vietnamese Courts: Contemporary Interactions Between Party–State and Law," in *Vietnam's New Order: International Perspectives on the State and Reform in Vietnam*, ed. Mark Sidel and Stephanie Balme (New York: Palgrave Macmillan, 2007), 178–97; Gary Chan, "Judicial Immunity and Independence of Vietnamese Judges," *Australian Journal of Asian Law* 7 (2005): 143–68; Pip Nicholson, "Vietnamese Jurisprudence: Informing Court Reform," in *Asian Socialism and Legal Change: The Dynamics of Vietnamese and Chinese Reform*, ed. John Gillespie and Pip Nicholson (Canberra: Asia Pacific Press, 2005), 159–90; Brian J. M. Quinn, "Vietnam's Continuing Legal Reforms: Gaining Control Over the Courts," *Asian-Pacific Law and Policy Journal* 4 (2003): 432–68; Brian J. M. Quinn, "Legal Reform and its Context in Vietnam,"

Columbia Journal of Asian Law, 15 (2002): 219–93; Pip Nicholson, "Judicial Independence and the Rule of Law: The Vietnam Court Experience," *Australian Journal of Asian Law* 3 (2001): 37–58.

7. See, for example, Erik Jensen and Thomas C. Heller, *Beyond Common Knowledge, Empirical Approaches to the Rule of Law* (Stanford, CA: Stanford University Press, 2003); Thomas Carrothers, ed., *Promoting the Rule of Law Abroad: In Search of Knowledge* (Washington DC: Carnegie Endowment for International Peace, 2006); Per Bergling, *Rule of Law on the International Agenda: International Support to Legal and Judicial Reform in International Administration, Transition and Development Cooperation* (Oxford: Intersentia, 2006). See also, Edgardo Buscaglia and Maria Dakolias, *Comparative International Study of Court Performance Indicators* (Washington DC: The World Bank, 1999); Legal and Judicial Reform Unit Legal Department, *Initiatives in Legal and Judicial Reform* (Washington DC: The World Bank, 2000); James Anderson, David Bernstein and Cheryl W. Gray, *Judicial Systems in Transition Economies* (Washington DC: The World Bank, 2005).
8. See Pip Nicholson and Sarah Biddulph, eds, *Examining Practice, Interrogating Theory; Comparative Legal Studies in Asia* (Leiden, The Netherlands: Martinus Nijhoff Publishers, 2008); Nicholson, "Legal Culture 'Repacked': Drug Trials in Vietnam," 71–108; Annelise Riles, "Casting Off, and Reclaiming, the Weberian Tradition: Comparative Law and Socio-Legal Studies," Cornell University, Legal Studies Research Paper Series No. 05–33, http://papers.ssrn.com/sol3/papers.cfm?abstract_id = 850165
9. The exception to this is the work by Veronica Taylor on Japan in this book, where neither a 'new' court or new jurisdiction or procedure law is under scrutiny. Taylor suggests 'newness' can also be extended to include new regulatory approaches and argues the transformative impacts these have had on Japanese courts.
10. In the case of Vietnam this argument is run by Nguyen Hien Quan, "The Social Structures of Contracts: A Case Study of the Vietnamese Market" (PhD diss., The University of Melbourne, 2006). Nguyen Hien Quan argues that many local Vietnamese businesses, particularly in Ho Chi Minh City, are disinterested in courts, at this stage, preferring informally to resolve their disputes, because so doing is more efficient and a culturally familiar approach. Compare with John O. Haley, "Litigation in Japan: A New Look at Old Problems," *Willamette Journal of International Law and Dispute Resolution* 10 (2002): 121.
11. See, however, the comments of David Linnan, in this book.
12. See, for example, Erik G. Jensen, "The Rule of Law and Judicial Reform: The Political Economy of Diverse Institutional Patterns and Reformers' Responses," in *Beyond Common Knowledge: Empirical Approaches to the Rule of Law*, ed. Erik Jensen and Thomas C. Heller (Stanford, CA: Stanford University Press, 2003), 336–81; Kenneth W. Dam, *The Law-Growth Nexus: The Rule of Law and Economic Development* (Washington DC: Brookings Institution Press, 2006); Bergling, *Rule of Law on the International Agenda*.
13. Compare with Stephen Golub, "A House without Foundation," in *Promoting the Rule of Law Abroad: In Search of Knowledge*, ed. Thomas Carrothers (Washington DC: Carnegie Endowment for International Peace, 2006), 104–36.
14. William A. W. Neilson, "The Rush to Law: IMF Legal Conditionalities Meet Indonesia's Legal Realities," in *Indonesia After Soeharto*, ed. T. Lindsey and D. Duncan (Victoria, Canada: Centre for Asia–Pacific Initiatives, 1999), 4–15; Timothy Lindsey and Veronica Taylor, "Rethinking Indonesian Insolvency Reform: Contexts and Frameworks," in *Indonesia: Bankruptcy, Law Reform and the Commercial Court*, ed. Timothy Lindsey (Sydney: Desert Pea Press, 2000), 2–14. See, further David Linnan in this book.
15. *Resolution Number 48 – NQ/TW*, 24 May 2005 of the Central Committee Communist Party of Vietnam on the Strategy for the Development and Improvement of Vietnam's

Legal System to the Year 2010 and Directions for the Period up to 2020, 24–25 (UNDP translation, 2006).

16. Thomas Carrothers, "Promoting the Rule of Law Abroad: The Problem of Knowledge," *Rule of Law Series: Democracy and the Rule of Law Project* 34 (2003): 1–14; Golub, "A House without Foundation," 104–36.
17. K. Pistor and P. Wellons, *The Role of Law and Legal Institutions in Asian Economic Development 1960–1995* (New York: Oxford University Press, 1999). See also Carrothers, "Promoting the Rule of Law Abroad: The Problem of Knowledge"; Lawrence Tshuma, "The Political Economy of the World Bank's Legal Framework for Economic Development," in *Governance Development and Globalization*, ed. Julio Faundez, Mary E. Footer and Joseph Norton (London: Blackstone Press Limited, 2003), 20–24.
18. Ginsburg, *Judicial Review in New Democracies*. See also Andrew Harding and Peter Leyland, Tom Ginsburg in the *Journal of Comparative Law* 2 (2008).
19. Faundez reminds us that the use of the term 'rule of law' is deliberately opaque thus enabling donor agendas. Julio Faundez, "The Rule of Law Enterprises: Promoting a Dialogue Between Practitioners and Academics," *Democratization* 12 (2005): 569, 573.
20. World Bank, "IBRD and IDA Cumulative Lending Since Fiscal 1990 by Theme and Sector and by Region," http://go.worldbank.org/UKQ5JPQB30. Of this total, US$4,708.96 million was provided by the International Bank of Reconstruction and Development and US$6,383.9 million was provided by the International Development Association.
21. The rhetoric used to rationalize court-based aid-supported reforms (called rule-of-law aid by Thomas Carrothers) does vary, even among the bilateral agencies. For example, Pip Nicholson argues that the Swedish International Development Agency in Vietnam justifies its aid on the basis of public international law and human rights, while the Australian Agency for International Development cites economic development in support of is interventions. See Pip Nicholson, "Vietnamese Court Reform: The Discourse(s) of Aid?," in *Rule of Law Promotion: Global Perspectives, Local Applications, eds* Per Bergling, Jenny Ederlöf and Veronica Taylor, (Uppsala: Iustus Forlag, 2009). Thomas Carrothers, "The Problem of Knowledge," in *Promoting the Rule of Law Abroad: In Search of Knowledge*, ed. Thomas Carrothers (Washington DC: Carnegie Endowment for International Peace, 2006), 15–16.
22. Jensen and Carrothers, *Beyond Common Knowledge*, 336.
23. On the question of definition, see: Brian Z. Tamanaha, *On the Rule of Law, History, Politics, Theory* (Cambridge: Cambridge University Press, 2004); Rachel Kleinfeld, "Competing Definitions of the Rule of Law," in *Promoting the Rule of Law Abroad: In Search of Knowledge*, ed. Thomas Carrothers (Washington DC: Carnegie Endowment for International Peace, 2006), 31–74; Stephen J. Troope, "Legal and Judicial Reform through Development Assistance: Some Lessons," *McGill Law Journal* 48 (2003), 367–69; Randall Peerenboom, *Asian Discourses of Rule of Law: Theories and Implementation of Rule of Law in Twelve Asian Countries* (London: Routledge Curzon, 2004).
24. Stephen Golub, "A House without Foundation," in *The Rule of Law Abroad: Search of Knowledge*, ed. Thomas Carothers (Washington DC: Carnegie Endowment for International Peace, 2006), 109.
25. William L. F. Felstiner, Richard L. Abel and Austin Sarat, "The Emergence and Transformation of Disputes: Naming, Blaming and Claiming," *Law and Society Review* 15 (1980–1): 631.
26. Tom Ginsburg and Tamir Moustafa, eds, "Introduction: The Function of Courts in Authoritarian Regimes," in *Rule by Law: The Politics of Courts in Authoritarian Regimes*, ed. Tom Ginsburg and Tamir Moustafa (New York: Cambridge University Press, 2008), 5. See also, Clark B. Lombardi, "Egypt's Supreme Constitutional

Court: Managing Constitutional Conflict in an Authoritarian, Aspirationally 'Islamic' State," *Journal of Comparative Law* 3:2 (2008): 234.
27. Yash Ghai, "The Rule of law, Legitimacy and Governance," *International Journal of the Sociology of Law* 14 (1986): 178–208.
28. Nicholson, *Borrowing Court Systems*, 129–32, 184, 252–5.
29. See also the work of Gillespie, "Rethinking the Role of Judicial Independence in Socialist Transforming East Asia,".
30. See further, Kent Anderson and David Johnson, and Veronica Taylor, in this book.
31. See also David Linnan's chapter in this book, which discusses the IP function of Indonesia's Commercial Court.
32. Here readers can compare Michael Palmer's chapter on administrative divisions in this book.
33. For a contemporary journal special issue on constitutional courts in general, but including articles on new Asian courts, see the *Journal of Comparative Law* 3 (2008).
34. See literature on unanticipated developments arising from law reform generally: See generally, R. K. Merton, "The Unanticipated Consequences of Purposive Social Action," *American Sociological Review* 1 (1936): 894–904; See with respect to evaluations of court development initiatives: B. Garth, "Rethinking the Process and Criteria for Success," in *Comprehensive Legal and Judicial Development: Toward an Agenda for a Just and Equitable Society in the 21st Century*, ed. R. V. van Puymbroek (Washington DC: World Bank, 2001); Linn Hammergren, "Assessments, Monitoring, Evaluation, and Results: Improving the Knowledge Base for Judicial Reform Programs," http://www.undp-ogar.org/publications/judiciary/linn1/knowledge.pdf.
35. pp 2–4 for discussion of this issue.
36. D. L. Horowitz, "The Qur'an and the Common Law: Islamic Law Reform and the Theory of Legal Change," *American Journal of Comparative Law* 42 (1994): 233–93; D. L. Horowitz, "The Qur'an and the Common Law: Islamic Law Reform and the Theory of Legal Change," *American Journal of ComparativeLaw* 42 (1994): 543–80.
37. See for example, the pioneering work done in this field by Robert Cooter, Stephen Marks and Robert Mnookin, "Bargaining in the Shadow of the Law: A Testable Model of Strategic Behaviour," *Journal of Legal Studies* 11 (1982): 225. See also, the literature on private ordering that suggests extra-legal mechanisms for particular sectors or industries: L. Bernstein, "Opting out of the Legal System – Extra-legal Contractual Relations in the Diamond Industry," *Journal of Legal Studies* 21 (1992): 115; Lisa Bernstein, "Private Commercial Law in the Cotton Industry: Creating Competition Through Rules, Norms and Institutions," *Michigan Law Review* 99 (2001): 1724.
38. See also, Quan Nguyen, *The Social Structures of Contracts: A Case Study of the Vietnamese Market*.
39. *Nationwide News Pty Ltd v. Wills* (1992) 177 CLR 1, 31, 72–5; *Australian Capital Television Pty Ltd v. Commonwealth (No. 2)* (1992) 177 CLR 106, 183; *R v. L* (1991) 174 CLR 379, 390.
40. *Wik People v. Queensland* (1996) 187 CLR 1.
41. *The Highest Court*, Video, directed by Daryl Dellora (Canberra, ACT: Ronin Films, 1998).
42. Indonesia has no less than nine different types of special, new court, with a tenth possibly in the offing (land and environment).
43. E. Feldman, "The Tuna Court: Law and Norms in the World's Premier Fish," *California Law Review* 94 (2006): 313–70. See also, E. Feldman, "Suing Doctors in Japan: Structure, Culture, and the Rise of Malpractice Litigation," in *Fault Lines: Tort Law as Cultural Practice*, ed. Michael McCann and David Engel (Stanford, CA: Stanford University Press, 2009).

Part I

Introducing economic courts in Asia

2 Legitimacy and the Vietnamese Economic Court

Pip Nicholson with Minh Duong

Introduction

Vietnam first established an Economic Court in 1994 as part of its transition to a socialist-oriented market economy. Since its introduction, there has been substantial reform of the court system generally and Economic Court-related reform initiatives more particularly. Nearly 15 years on it is time to ask whether the Economic Court has emerged as an 'effective' forum for the resolution of economic disputes. Noting that the very notion of 'effective' is problematic, we argue that the best way to explore this issue is to ask what legitimacy the Court has to resolve economic disputes at the beginning of the twenty-first century. Legitimacy will be considered from the multiple perspectives of its users (lawyers and enterprises), its employees and the party–state it serves.

This chapter analyses the history, development and reform of the Vietnamese Economic Court drawing upon Communist Party of Vietnam policy, legislation, court decisions, commentary and use rates to portray the Economic Court as a functioning institution, striving for legitimacy. In answering why it is that Vietnamese Economic Court use rates remain so low, the chapter argues that substantial challenges remain for the Economic Court and its reformers.

Framing the inquiry

In 1994, and with much fanfare, the Vietnamese party–state[1] introduced an Economic Court in Vietnam, a mere eight years after the introduction of the *doi moi* (renovation) policies aspiring to give effect to a socialist-oriented market economy.[2] Fifteen years later it is timely to investigate the role of this institution. Some may quibble about categorizing the Vietnamese Economic Court as a 'new' court – it is technically the establishment of a new 'chamber' or division within the existing court system.[3] Yet when introduced, the Economic Court was given a new and specific jurisdiction and a few staff were exclusively appointed to that division of the Court. In terms of this publication, therefore, it would seem reasonable to classify the introduced Economic Court as a 'new' court, albeit under the auspices and management of the Supreme People's Court.

This analysis does not debate the independence of the Vietnamese Economic Court.[4] This question has been extensively discussed.[5] Further, as a socialist court, the Vietnamese Economic Court is accountable to the National Assembly and led by the Communist Party of Vietnam (the party). Although increasingly self-managed, the court system is not designed to be independent from government and would inevitably 'fail' if this were the benchmark by which it is assessed. As one Vietnamese scholar notes, 'their [the party's] promise of delegating more powers to independent courts does not seem to be a credible commitment'.[6] Additionally, analysis using such a fundamentally Western-created benchmark risks obscuring the actual context and reality of the Vietnamese court system generally, and the Economic Court in particular.[7]

Instead, we suggest that evaluating the Economic Court's legitimacy in the eyes of stakeholders such as the party–state (including its judges), practitioners, and actual and potential users, affords insights into receptivity towards, and traction of, this new institution.[8] We posit that 'legitimacy', as an evaluative tool, may better capture the diverse challenges facing new courts. More particularly, in a socialist system, the concept of legitimacy enables an analysis of the Court as an organic institution in a particular context, rather than resorting to a chronicle of how it is that the court system might fail to operate in a Western tradition – be that a common or civil law tradition.[9] However, this is not an analysis of all economic courts in Vietnam. It takes as its focus the Hanoi and Ho Chi Minh City Economic Courts and the appellate division of the Supreme People's Court.

To analyse the Vietnamese Economic Court's 'legitimacy' we ask the following questions in order to understand better the Court's role, its reach and its reputation:

- How was the Court established and what reforms have subsequently taken place, particularly in light of its ideological and political environment?
- What is the status of its decisions?
- What do judges think of how the Economic Court operates?
- Is the Court used by claimants and what are their attitudes to it?
- What does the legal profession, domestic and international, think of the Court?

In effect, we undertake a short history of the Economic Court and its reforms to ascertain how the party–state envisions its role. Court personnel and the party–state are not necessarily aligned on the role of the Court, and we investigate the extent of the tension between central reform policies and their impact within courts. We also ask whether the Economic Court has been accepted as an emerging legal institution in Vietnam by actual and potential court users, primarily businesses. And then we explore lawyers' perceptions of the Court. In answering the questions set out above we draw on Communist Party of Vietnam policy, legislation, court decisions, commentary, interview data and use rates.

A note on the context

The extent of reforms to the Vietnamese court system has attracted great comment.[10] As already explained, the Vietnamese court system is subservient to party and state institutions; this is a reflection of the dominance of the doctrine of 'concentration of state power', which is a key tenet of the Vietnamese politico-legal context.[11] This doctrine provides that the four pivotal organs of the state (the National Assembly, the government, the courts, and the Fatherland Front), operate as individually managed institutions that are concurrently highly interlocked.[12] In consequence, the notion of the separation of powers is not currently a relevant doctrinal bedrock for the Vietnamese court system, although independent judicial review of government action and an enforceable constitution have all been debated within Vietnam.[13]

Court history

Establishment

There is insufficient space here to recount the history of the socialist court system of Vietnam.[14] However, put briefly, the Democratic Republic of Vietnam established a highly localized ad-hoc court system through the period 1945–59, introducing a formal court system in the late 1950s. This formally unified court system of the 1960s and 1970s had to operate within the constraints of an ongoing civil war, during a period when there was little time for legal development as a major policy priority. Following the unification of Vietnam in 1976, the party–state established a national court system, subsequently the target of many waves of reform. Most recently, three party policies and an action plan of the Standing Committee of the National Assembly have made mention of the need for ongoing court reform,[15] canvassing such issues as the technical capacity of judges, resources for courts, restructuring the court hierarchy and revisiting the role of the procuracy; these debates are largely driven by a wish for public faith from domestic and international stakeholders in the Vietnamese dispute resolution system, noting that World Trade Organization compliance is a great catalyst for reform.[16]

Adhering to the socialist ideology that economic matters should be managed by the state, economic disputes up to the early 1990s were resolved by state economic arbitration tribunals established by the government. These economic arbitration tribunals were established as an arm of the central and provincial governments and were solely responsible for resolving disputes involving economic contracts (see below).[17] Economic contracts involving foreigners had to be resolved by these tribunals, which had the effect of disallowing any choice of a foreign dispute resolution venue.

From 1994, the state economic arbitration tribunals were disbanded[18] and replaced with the Vietnamese Economic Court (*Toa an Kinh te*).[19] *Law No. 29-LTN on Amendment and Supplement to the Law on the Organisation of the People's Court* (*LOOPC 29*), establishing the Economic Court, made it explicit that the People's Courts were able to hear economic matters and, as noted, that the Economic Court was to be part of the structure of the Supreme People's Court and the People's Courts in the provinces and centrally-run cities (i.e. Ho Chi Minh City and Hanoi).[20]

In implementing *LOOPC 29*, the Chief Justice of the Supreme People's Court broadly stated in a decision that the role and responsibility of the Economic Court of the Supreme People's Court includes:

- adjudicating and reviewing economic matters from the provincial level in accordance with the law on civil procedure;
- assisting the Chief Justice to resolve matters that are within the authority of the Economic Court;
- reporting to the Council of Judges of the Supreme People's Court on decisions issued; and
- drafting official letters of the Supreme People's Court to provide judgment guidelines on economic matters and bankruptcy.[21]

Jurisdiction

The Economic Courts were empowered to hear economic and bankruptcy matters in accordance with relevant, fairly restrictive, procedure laws.[22] More specifically, the Economic Court was introduced to hear 'economic disputes' in accordance with the now defunct *Ordinance No. 31-L-CTN of the Standing Committee of the National Assembly on Procedures for Resolution of Economic Disputes* (*Procedure Ordinance No. 31*)[23] which, together with the *LOOPC 29*, came into effect on 1 July 1994.

While replaced recently (see below), *Procedure Ordinance No. 31* generated some confusion that arguably continues to impact on the perception of the Economic Courts today. In 1994, under *Procedure Ordinance No. 31* the Economic Courts had jurisdiction to hear:

- disputes relating to economic contracts entered between corporate entities;
- disputes between corporate entities, or between a corporate entity and an individual with a registered business;
- disputes between a company and its members, or between the members of the company on matters which relate to the establishment, operation, and dissolution of the company;
- disputes relating to the purchase and sale of shares and bonds; and
- all other economic disputes pursuant to law.

Determining what amounted to an economic contract became a commonly argued legal issue in Vietnam.[24] This debate coupled with the complications introduced by the *Ordinance No. 24-LCT/HĐNN8 of the State Council on Economic Contracts* (*Ordinance on Economic Contracts No. 24*),[25] created jurisdictional and substantive law issues that militated against widespread use of the Court.

Practice within jurisdiction

As a matter of practice, the Economic Courts became the body responsible for resolving economic contract disputes, a special category of contract created by *Ordinance on Economic Contracts No. 24*.[26] This special category of contract law was originally developed to govern contracts made by state-owned enterprises, which in 1989 were the only type of enterprises legally existing in Vietnam. The *Ordinance on Economic Contracts No. 24* exemplifies the Vietnamese party–state's policy of micromanaging the economy through adjudging economic activity at all levels, including at the micro-contractual level.[27] *Ordinance on Economic Contracts No. 24* specified the form of the contract to be used in certain economic transactions, capped damages arising from a contract breach and prescribed a short statutory limitation period of six months.[28] If the economic contract was not in the prescribed form, courts would frequently strike down the contract as being non-effective.

The privileging of form over substance frustrated lawyers and businesses alike.[29] For example, courts will invalidate a contract if the legal representative does not execute an agreement, even though the contract has been performed by the parties.[30] When asked why this is the case, a Ho Chi Minh City lawyer explained that courts find it easier to find fault by testing whether there has been compliance with the form required for contracts.[31] This reflects the reality that Vietnamese law is structured to prescribe the procedures and formalities for conduct and does not necessarily set out substantive tests. In author Minh's experience, when a particular requirement for form is not met, courts will rarely examine other substantive elements of law.[32]

Snapshot of the court in the twenty-first century

Implemented reforms: current law

On 2 April 2002, the National Assembly passed the new *Law No. 33–2002-QH10 on the Organisation of the People's Court* (*LOOPC 33*).[33] This law did not affect the structure of the Economic Courts continuing, at least officially, as separate divisions at the central and provincial court levels.[34] However, the Chief Justice of the Supreme People's Court was given greater control in the appointment and termination of judicial officers at the provincial and centrally-run city court level.[35] Previously, this was a decision made by provincial governments. In addition, the Chief Justice was given greater power to manage the operational budget of the court system.[36]

On 15 June 2004, the National Assembly passed *Civil Proceedings Code No. 24–2004-QH11* (*Law No. 24 on Civil Proceedings Code*) combining all the ordinances that prescribed procedures for civil, labour, economic and administrative matters.[37] *Procedure Ordinance No. 31* was repealed,[38] although allowing a transitional period for existing disputes to be resolved under the old civil procedure system until 1 July 2009.[39]

The Adjudication Council of the Supreme People's Court implemented Articles 29 and 30 of *Law No. 24 on Civil Proceedings Code*[40] by widening the jurisdiction of the Economic Court to hear all business and commercial matters, without limiting the jurisdiction of the Economic Courts to certain types of economic contracts or economic entities. Shortly thereafter, the troublesome law governing economic contracts, which had produced court decisions giving effect to form rather than substantive agreements between parties, was abolished with effect from 1 January 2006.[41] These changes were celebrated for ridding the Vietnamese law of an outdated and unnecessary category of contract which had failed to serve the changing Vietnamese market.[42] With the abolition of economic contracts, contract law in Vietnam is now governed generally by the new *Civil Code* of 2005,[43] with particular contracts subject to specific legislation. For example, purchase and sale of goods and services contracts are governed by *Law No. 44 on Commerce*.[44] The *Civil Code* is an umbrella law and will apply to matters that are not specifically legislated under a special subject matter law. As a result of these changes, the Economic Court may now hear contract disputes relating to the purchase and sale of goods, securities, financing, banking and construction.

Despite the list of new matters which have been assigned to the Economic Court, it appears that the civil court (civil division of the People's Court) may also hear economic disputes. For instance, the Ho Chi Minh City People's Court will allocate matters on the basis of case-load.[45] More particularly, if the Economic Court has a high case-load, these cases will be reallocated to the civil court. The decision to reallocate is an internal court administration policy which is set by the Chief Justice of the Ho Chi Minh City People's Court. Therefore, in practice the jurisdictional delineation between the courts is less clear. There are currently 40 provincial economic courts within the existing 64 provincial courts (not all provincial courts yet have an economic court).[46]

A note on hierarchy

As noted, the Vietnamese court system currently comprises three levels: district courts, provincial level courts, and the Supreme Court. Both the Supreme Court and provincial courts have dedicated economic court divisions, staffed by judges on five-year terms, but the district court judges are appointed to a court and not a division and can potentially hear all types of cases. A reform to the current hierarchy was announced in *Resolution No. 48 of the Politburo*, foreshadowing the introduction of a regional court, although the form regional courts might take remains a matter of debate.[47] As of mid-2008, no regional court had been introduced.[48]

Court use statistics

As we will show, the variability of the role of the Economic Court is brought home through statistics. Thus, while the legislation suggests a story of institutional renewal, the actual experience is of an institution that is only, really active in Ho Chi Minh City and used little nationally.

Table 2.1[49] makes plain that the overall number of cases received (this table does not distinguish heard, settled and discontinued cases) in the Economic Court is low. With a population of 81.5 million, there was only 1.1 economic cases per 100,000 population in 2004.[50] Further, there is a low rate of new cases across the Vietnamese court system, which is almost half that of China when calculated

Table 2.1 Comparison of number of cases received by Economic Courts at first instance

Year	*Number of cases received by Economic Court at first instance throughout Vietnam*	*Number of cases received by Economic Court at first instance in Ho Chi Minh City*	*Percentage of national economic cases received at Ho Chi Minh City courts*	*Number of cases received by Economic Court at first instance in Khanh Hoa*
2001	690	377	54.6 %	4
2002	724	210	29.0 %	12
2003	638	246	38.5 %	10
2004	885	304	34.3 %	26
2005	1260	487	38.6 %	10
2006	2233	1065	47.6 %	13

per head of the population.[51] Moreover, Table 2.1 highlights that most economic case activity takes place in Ho Chi Minh City. In 2006, 47.6 per cent of economic cases received nationally were lodged with the Ho Chi Minh City courts. In the past, the percentage of Vietnamese economic cases lodged in Ho Chi Minh City has been even higher, the figures suggesting that other regional centres may be beginning to attract a consistent, albeit small, number of cases.[52]

Enforcement

While difficult to prove, it is logical to assume that critical to the use rate of a court system is its capacity to enforce its judgments. Enforcement has been a long-standing thorn in the side of the Vietnamese court system. As recently as 2002, anonymous bureaucrats suggested informally to author Pip Nicholson that only 15 per cent of Vietnamese judgments were enforced by the Ministry of Justice, tasked with the responsibility of enforcement of judicial decisions through provincial and district enforcement agencies.[53]

More recent survey work, where 11 Economic Court judges from six localities (Hanoi, Ho Chi Minh City, Ha Tay, Nghe An, Lam Dong and Khanh Hoa) were interviewed in 2006–7 and a further 50 questionnaires were distributed, again to Economic Court judges (the *DANIDA Survey*), suggests enforcement issues continue.[54] The *DANIDA Survey* also sent questionnaires to 260 enterprises and 90 lawyers in the same six localities to ascertain their attitudes to commercial dispute resolution generally and, within that, the role of the Economic Court more particularly.[55] The *DANIDA Survey* reported widely diverging estimates of enforcement. Businesses suggested that only 48.7 per cent of judicial decisions were effectively enforced.[56] Judges claimed that 67.8 per cent of judgments 'are able to be' enforced, and lawyers suggested only 24.2 per cent of judgments were executable.[57] The judges cite 'insufficient conditions to execute' (presumably a reference to lack of funds or assets on the part of the judgment debtor) as the main reason why judgments are not enforced.

Compounding the lack of enforcement are the delays associated with enforcement of contracts in Vietnam. For example, research suggests that it takes 404 days to enforce a contract in Vietnam, compared with 241 days for contract enforcement in China and only 69 days in Singapore.[58] The reasons for the low rates of effective enforcement vary, depending on the interviewee. Each group of interviewees, judges, lawyers and businesses attribute delays to the execution agencies. Additionally, unclear judgments, debtor evasion (particularly delays sufficient to disburse assets before enforcement), and vulnerability of the execution agency to pressures are cited as frustrating the process.[59]

Lack of effective enforcement of judgments is an institutional problem. Vietnamese courts do not have the power to enforce their judgments. Under *Law No. 24 on Civil Proceedings Code*, once a court issues its decision, the court judgment enforcement agency under the Ministry of Justice is responsible for enforcing that decision. Some lawyers are of the view that the separation of the enforcement agency from the courts establishes the policy that power and authority should not be concentrated in one body.[60] Therefore, the enforcement agency remains under the auspices of the Ministry of Justice, not the courts. This structure creates an additional layer of red-tape, as the aggrieved party needs to apply to the enforcement agency to enforce a judgment. As it is not uncommon for Vietnamese agencies to operate in silos, with the enforcement agency often not communicating with the courts, this process tends to be drawn out. Payment to officials to quicken the process is not uncommon.[61]

The Economic Court cases and its decisions

Contextualizing jurisprudence

Whereas judicial decisions in the common law system are a source of law and their capacity to bind lower courts determined according to the doctrine of precedent, judgments by Vietnamese courts currently make little contribution to the interpretation of Vietnamese law.[62] The traditional role of the courts under the *Constitution of Vietnam*, as amended in 1992, is not to interpret the law but to apply the law. Legal interpretation is a power given to the Standing Committee of the National Assembly.[63] As a result, the Vietnamese court decision is, as in other civil law systems, a statement of applicable law for a particular case, rather than a significant source of law. That said, the importance of judge-made law is changing as the party–state recognizes the importance of circulating interpretations publicly to increase the currency and traction of law.

In 2008, there were four categories of legal instruments. Of highest authority were Orders of the President, followed in second place by Resolutions and Decrees of the Government and Directives of the Prime Minister.[64] In 2008, a decision of a Vietnamese court ranked fourth in the second-category of legal instruments that served to give effect to National Assembly resolutions and laws, which, as noted, were first-category legal instruments. Decisions of Vietnamese courts were ranked below Decisions, Directives and Circulars of Ministers and

Government agencies, which ranked third.[65] As a result of this hierarchy, courts could not strike down a Decision of a minister, nor could a court determine that a ministerial Decision was contrary to a Decree of the Government or a law of the National Assembly. The result was that government officials could write to the People's Courts to suggest how a particular case should be resolved and how the law should be applied.[66] Not infrequently, judges deferred to administrative agencies, seeking their advice on the proper application and interpretation of law.[67]

From 1 January 2009, a new hierarchy of legal documents became effective, making decisions of the Adjudication Council of the Supreme People's Court and Circulars of the Chief Justice of the Supreme People's Court superior to both Circulars of the Procuracy (to be ranked seventh) and Circulars of ministers (to be ranked eighth).[68] This reform elevates the decisions of the ultimate appellate body of the Supreme People's Court substantially. It remains to be seen how the changes will be taken up in practice.

Decisions of the Economic Court, as with other judgments, are short and usually lack legal reasoning.[69] The judgments are presented as joint judgments with no record of dissent. Under Vietnamese law a judgment must have a preamble (which contains details of the parties and their legal representatives), the contents of the case/summary of the record (*nhan thay*), and the remarks of the court/assessment of the facts (*xet thay*) and its decision (*quyet dinh*).[70] The 'summary of the record' section of the judgment must include a description of the claim brought by the plaintiff, their submissions and any counterclaims by the defence and any independent claims or related party claims. The 'remarks' section of the judgment contains the legal instruments used as the basis for the court's decision and any offered analysis. The judgment must also detail court fees and the right of the parties to appeal against the court's decision. According to law, courts only have an obligation to provide their decisions to the disputing parties.[71]

In recent work, John Gillespie argues that Vietnamese judicial decision-making reflects the diverse texts and influences shaping the work of judges. In particular, Gillespie concludes that judicial discretion, as given effect in court decisions, reflects four narratives: party policy; the legislative text; local situational reasoning; and adopting legal fictions – the latter two strategies enabling greater creativity in the application of law.[72] With the exception of the citation of relevant laws, these influences are rarely explicitly, or even implicitly, recorded in the judgments, although party influence of court judgments has long been recognized.[73]

Reading cases comparatively

Focusing on how it is that the law is technically analysed in Economic Court judgments, the authors note that in the 15 years since the establishment of the Economic Court there has been a noticeable increase in the technical reasoning offered by all courts, perhaps with the Ho Chi Minh Economic Court spearheading this development nationally.

Below we have reviewed two cases: Decision No. 64/64-KT/PT of the Hanoi Appellate Court of the Supreme People's Court in the matter of Hanoi Bus Company and SUDEMEX dated 16 March 1995 (the *Hanoi Bus Case*); and Decision No. 82/2007/KDTM-PT of the Ho Chi Minh City Appellate Division of the Supreme People's Court in the matter of United Concord International Co. Ltd and Radiant Investments Co. Ltd dated 28 August 2007 (the *Park Hyatt Case*). The *Hanoi Bus Case* heralded from the Supreme People's Court appellate division based in Hanoi, in 1995. The *Park Hyatt Case* emanated from the appellate division of the Supreme People's Court sitting in Ho Chi Minh City in 2007. The cases can be compared to consider whether the Supreme-People's-Court-level of the court system has exhibited any changes in its written determinations over a 10-year period. Although one decision comes from Hanoi and one from Ho Chi Minh City, the authors take the view that in each jurisdiction the courts are bound to apply the same law and so they remain comparable. In each case the authors obtained copies of these unpublished judgments from colleagues working around the courts, although the latter case is now also published on a free-access website.[74]

Though the format of the court judgments remains the same, as described above, there is a clear attempt in the *Park Hyatt Case* to give a more detailed analysis of the application of law. We will first explain the decisions and how they illustrate changes in the ways court decisions are presented and then suggest explanations why the courts have shifted to a slightly more detailed, if not more analytical, judgments.

The *Hanoi Bus Case* demonstrates how a literal application of the law precludes the Court from questioning the substance of legal provisions and reduces the prospect of an analytical basis to judgments. In the *Hanoi Bus Case*, the Supreme People's Court invalidated a joint venture contract between the Hanoi Bus Company and SUDEMEX on the basis that the purpose of the contract was unlawful. The Court concluded that allowing SUDEMEX to use part of the land allocated to the Hanoi Bus Company was in effect a transfer of land use rights from the Hanoi Bus Company to SUDEMEX. At law, the Hanoi Bus Company was prohibited from transferring the land use rights. However, the Court failed to provide reasons for the finding that the contract was unlawful, only referring to a provision of the land law to support its determination. The Court did not explain how, on the facts or at law, the Hanoi Bus Company's decision to allow SUDEMEX to use part of the land was a transfer of land use rights. On the facts apparent to a reader, the ownership of the land use rights appeared to remain with the Hanoi Bus Company; there was no agreement to transfer ownership to SUDEMEX.

The *Hanoi Bus Case* also demonstrates how courts resolve legal questions by privileging form over substance. In the *Hanoi Bus Case*, it was easier for the Court to take the conservative view that the contract was illegal on the basis of an illegal transfer of land use rights, rather than to consider the substance of the transaction between the Hanoi Bus Company and SUDEMEX, a business joint venture to develop a property where both parties were to use land; however, no title to land needed to be transferred.

The 2007 *Park Hyatt Case* is one of the first cases involving allegations of the oppression of minority interest holders of companies in Vietnam. It also arose at a time when joint venture enterprises were caught between two legislative regimes: those joint venture enterprises established on or after the effective date (1 January 2006) of *Law No. 60 on Enterprises of the National Assembly* dated 29 June 2005 (*Law on Enterprises*) and the old regime which governed the establishment and governance of joint venture enterprises, *Law No. 52-L/CTN on Foreign Investment* of the National Assembly dated 12 November 1996. There is continued uncertainty about the interaction between the two regimes, which unfortunately the Court did not analyse or resolve.

In the *Park Hyatt Case*, eight of the ten members of the Board of Management of the Grand Imperial Saigon Limited Liability Company (Grand Imperial) (similar to a board of directors which is the highest decision-making body of Grand Imperial) agreed under three separate circular resolutions to appoint a new chairman and general director and to proceed with the re-registration of the company to be governed under the *Law on Enterprises*. There were three owners of Grand Imperial: Radiant Investments Ltd (RIL), Saigon General Construction Company (SGC) and United Concord International Ltd (UCI). The members who passed the circular resolutions were appointed by RIL and SGC. UCI members did not agree with the circular resolutions. UCI applied to the Court disputing the validity of the circular resolutions. The circular resolutions effectively terminated Mr Nguyen Van Hao as chairman and general director of Grand Imperial. Mr Hao had been UCI's nominee for those positions.

UCI argued, and its argument is recorded in the judgment, that the circular resolutions were inconsistent with the *Law on Enterprises*, the charter of Grand Imperial and the joint venture agreement between the owners of Grand Imperial. UCI argued that according to the charter and joint venture agreement, matters requiring special resolution, such as the matters which were the subject of these circular resolutions, require an unanimous decision at a meeting of the Board of Management and cannot be replaced by a circular resolution. The *Law on Enterprises* has set the minimum ratio for passing a circular resolution of a limited liability company to be members holding 75 per cent of the charter capital of such a company, though the law provides that this may be higher if the charter specifies otherwise, as is the case here.[75] SGC and RIL, the defendants, argued that members of Grand Imperial had acknowledged and agreed in the circular resolutions that the resolutions were passed as though they had been passed at a properly convened meeting and that therefore the Court should respect the resolutions. In particular, the defendants argued that 81 per cent of members voting in favour of the circular resolutions was sufficient to meet the requirements of the *Law on Enterprises*. The defendants' position, also recorded in the judgment, was that since the charter and joint venture agreement of Grand Imperial were made pursuant to the old investment law, and were not constituent documents under the new regime of the *Law on Enterprises*, the Court should defer to the statutory limits prescribed by the *Law on Enterprises* vis-à-vis the 75 per cent voting ratio.

The Court ruled in favour of the applicant UCI. In its recorded *xet thay* and *nhan thay* the Court indicated that although the *Law on Enterprises* requires members representing 75 per cent of the charter capital of the company to pass a circular resolution, the charter of Grand Imperial and the joint venture agreement stipulated a higher threshold, which was binding on the owners of Grand Imperial. The Court referred to *Decree 101/2006/ND-CP of the Government* dated 21 September 2006 and noted that that the charter of Grand Imperial is effective because enterprises which do not re-register under the new *Law on Enterprises* may continue to exercise rights that are stipulated in their charter and investment license. The Court invalidated the circular resolutions and reinstated Mr Nguyen Van Hao to the positions of general director and chairman of Grand Imperial. The *Park Hyatt Case* also gives comfort to minority shareholders or interest holders in Vietnamese enterprises who have agreed to certain veto rights in either company charters or joint venture agreements, that they will be respected and enforced by the Courts. It also demonstrates that a charter, which is governed by the laws that predate the *Law on Enterprises*, will continue to operate.

In the *Park Hyatt Case* the Court provided a more detailed commentary on the applicable law than in the *Hanoi Bus Case*, in both the *xet thay* and *nhan thay*. The *Park Hyatt Case* is a lengthier judgment with about 3,200 words in the *xet thay* section as opposed to 1,200 words for the *Hanoi Bus Case*. The *Park Hyatt Case* also provided an analysis of the *Law on Enterprises* as opposed to merely citing the relevant legal provisions, as had been the case in the *Hanoi Bus Case*.

The increased technical grasp evident in the later judgment may be attributable to many factors here grouped under two heads: increased judicial expertise and political sensitivity of cases. First, the comparison of judgments indicates that there are today more expert judges writing Economic Court judgments. This expertise may be attributable to judicial qualifications. It may also reflect the fact that judges have also become more familiar with commercial cases and now have experience upon which to draw. The increase in the number of commercial disputes and the slowly increasing breadth of litigation may also contribute to enhancing judicial capacity. This is particularly true in Ho Chi Minh City as commercial and court activity in this part of Vietnam has (exponentially) grown over the last 15 years. Alternatively, judicial expertise may have been developed by the rapidly expanding capacities of lawyers appearing in the courts. The parties to the *Park Hyatt Case* had legal representation from prominent lawyers who were able to assist the Court in its deliberations.[76] As noted above, lawyers play an important role in the education of judges.[77] Therefore, at its most basic, the prominent lawyers in the *Park Hyatt Case* may well have contributed to a better reasoned decision than the *Hanoi Bus Case*, where the judgment only records SUDEMEX as having legal representation. Finally, greater judicial expertise may also flow from an increase in the passage of relevant laws, some of which have made clearer the really ambiguous areas of the law.

Secondly, the *Park Hyatt Case* received a great deal of media attention, as it involved a dispute among the owners of the Park Hyatt Hotel, an icon within Ho Chi Minh City.[78] This high level of media scrutiny meant that the Court was on 'show' and sought to prove that it is a functional institution, well able to give sensible and reasoned judgments.

Debating publication

Despite the relative insignificance of court determinations, when compared with common law legal systems, there are calls from the profession in particular, and judges, for the publication of judgments.[79] Donors also actively support this reform.[80] Further, there is increasingly a momentum locally to debate and analyse existing cases. This emerging jurisprudential analysis occurs in part to try and distil the law – an effort, largely undertaken by the profession, to determine how judges will determine cases.[81] However, academics are also calling for the publication of judgments to enable students to be taught to interpret legal provisions.[82] These study groups and debates are mentioned to illustrate the growing interest in courts generally and their jurisprudence more particularly. While the judgments frequently attract robust criticism, the very fact of this debate is new and demonstrates an energy and interest in doctrinal development almost unheard of even five years ago in Vietnam. The escalating interest by the profession in court decisions is telling of a profession motivated to see courts deliver consistent and more analytical decisions.

The Court, on the other hand, is concurrently keen to see the increased circulation of judgments and wary of over-committing to publication before judges are themselves adequately equipped to write.[83] Moreover, the Court does not speak with one voice on this topic. Generalizing somewhat, the Hanoi-based courts appear more wary of rushing to publish, while the courts based in Ho Chi Minh City are, at least in part, feeding judgments to private searchable websites, such as that allegedly supported by lawyer Le Cong Dinh and published in Ho Chi Minh City.[84] These websites have recently been approved by the Ministry of Informatics and Communication under Licence 199/GP-CBC dated 5 May 2008. To date, the only officially sanctioned hard-copy publication of judgments is the publication of decisions of the of the Supreme People's Court (*Toa An Nhan Dan Toi Cao*) Justice Council's (*Hoi Dong Tham Phan*) cassational reviews (*giam doc tham*), which has now published cassational decisions for the periods 2003–4 and most recently 2005–6.[85] However, what this debate about publication indicates is that court leadership, based in Hanoi, seeks to increase its legitimacy through the provision of judgments (albeit slowly), in turn making judges more accountable for their decisions.

Some may inquire why publication is debated in this chapter, when as a civil court there ought be no assumption that publication of judgments is fundamental to the court's work. Going further, some may allege that the common law bias of the authors has shaped the analysis. We take the time to include the debate on publication because it illustrates the interface between the conservatism of the Hanoi-led court leadership and the proactive agitation of groups, particularly lawyers, in Vietnam. The extent of the call for publication suggests an endogenous call for accountability for the court system to escalate its local and international legitimacy: both foreign and local lawyers are active in this debate. It also makes plain that decisions of the court to date remain highly criticized for lack of reasoning and the resultant lack of transparency, corruption[86] and lack of technical expertise.[87]

Attitudes to reforms

The establishment and subsequent raft of reforms aimed at the Economic Court (such as changing its procedure rules, jurisdictional limits and slowly increasing transparency) makes clear that the party–state seeks a forum for the resolution of economic cases that is well regarded. Yet the *DANIDA Survey* suggests a different story. When the DANIDA data is analysed alongside earlier survey work,[88] interesting trends emerge. Generally, Economic Court use is trending up (see above), and there is now a suggestion that in some localities the Economic Court is a viable forum for the resolution of *some* disputes. However, there remain substantial constraints on resources, technical capacity and transparency that preclude the Court being celebrated as a popular, or indeed widely used, forum for the resolution of commercial disputes. Its legitimacy is not established; rather, it remains under construction and the result of the substantial investment in reform to date remains unclear, with the possible exception of the increasing standing of the Court in Ho Chi Minh City.

Party–state

As noted, party–state visions for reform and the ways judges experience reforms ought not be conflated. In large part the reforms set out above indicate the commitments of the party–state to reform the court system. There has been a preparedness, made explicit by Politburo policy statements, to reform the socialist courts, moving towards more self-managed and better, technically competent institutions. For example, the reform of the ways in which judges are appointed, ceding more power to the Chief Justice of the Supreme People's Court, and the requirement, at least in theory, that all new judges have law degrees, exemplify these commitments.[89] However, the official statements about court reform not infrequently misrepresent the actuality of the lived court reform experience. Hence our decision, in this chapter, to disaggregate how the reforms are experienced and note the insights afforded from users (lawyers and their clients) and functionaries.

Challenges reported by Economic Court judges

Vietnamese Economic Court judges report real challenges to their judicial work. In particular, judges are under-resourced and call for more training.[90] In terms of resources, judges interviewed in the *DANIDA Survey* noted that only about a third (29.0 per cent) had access to the Internet, only 12.9 per cent had access to the Supreme People's Court Official Gazette (a publication ostensibly aiming to disseminate court policy and case notes), 38.7 per cent had access to personal computers, and reference materials (undefined) were only available to 48.4 per cent of economic judges interviewed.[91] Judges of the busiest Economic Court in Vietnam, in Ho Chi Minh City, reported in the *DANIDA Survey* that although they had internet access from mid-2006 they had to self-fund usage.[92] These findings are broadly consistent with a much more extensive United Nations Development Programme *Report on Survey of Needs of District People's Courts Nationwide* (the *District Court Survey*), which found that only 15.4 per cent of district court judges accessed laws and legal commentary through computers, with a preponderance (58.9 per cent) having to access laws through their own personal libraries/endeavours.[93] The *District Court Survey* documents that district court judges seek a higher frequency of more relevant training.[94] Judges also note 'difficulties' in the courtroom.[95] More particularly, they recount fundamental challenges to their capacity to resolve disputes including: lack of evidence, lack of legal reference documents and conflicting laws (Table 2.2). [96]

Each of these challenges alone would make the job of judging cases hard. In combination, judges face great difficulties in the court room. Putting to one side accusations of corruption, inconsistency and lack of technical expertise, it is clear that judges are seriously challenged in undertaking their assigned tasks: to resolve economic cases. All too often the Vietnamese court system is criticized without regard for the conditions judges face and the very low rate of pay they earn. For instance, despite recent attempts to increase judicial pay, judges currently earn amounts that vary according to their experience (number of years service), added to which is a responsibility allowance and a hearing allowance.[97] At law, judges are also potentially personally liable for judicial errors.[98]

Table 2.2 Explanation of challenges faced by judges when resolving business or commercial cases[97]

Cause of difficulty	*Percentage of judges nominating difficulty*
Lacking necessary legal documents	77.4 %
Lacking reference materials from Vietnamese courts	77.4 %
Defence not providing sufficient evidence	74.2 %
Lack of reference material on foreign experience	61.3 %
Conflicting legal documents	54.8 %
Refusal of third party to provide evidence	54.8 %
Plaintiff not providing sufficient evidence	45.2 %

These comments are not offered as a defence of the courts, but rather to make explicit the challenges facing those within the courts to increase their own standing. Even assuming the judicial will to reform, substantial impediments to trusted decision-making exist, some of which are largely beyond judicial control. For example, if government agencies are restricting the supply of evidence that is fundamental to economic cases, this undermines the capacity of potential litigants to bring cases. As Mark Cammack also notes in this book it is important to see how court work is affected by the work of other agencies, rather than to evaluate the courts in isolation from their context.[99]

Attitude of business court users

Given the low volume of cases and the difficulties faced by the courts, what are the attitudes of court users, businesses and lawyers, to the Economic Court in Vietnam? In the late 1990s the general consensus emanating out of several business surveys was that the courts were to be avoided. Writing in 1997, Per Bergling noted that 90 per cent of the 46 businesses he interviewed advised it was best to avoid courts.[100] In a similar vein, in 1999 John McMillan and Christopher Woodruff reported that most businesses preferred relational mechanisms for the resolution of disputes over courts.[101] Nguyen Hien Quan's doctoral research, although based on a smaller sample, confirmed these results in Ho Chi Minh City over the period 2005–7.[102] Finally, the *DANIDA Survey* restates this aversion to using the courts to resolve disputes reporting that 'most enterprises brought their disputes to court after all other methods [of dispute resolution] had failed'.[103] Negotiation, commercial arbitration and conciliation, whether by organization or individual, were all cited as alternatives to be explored before going to court (Table 2.3).[104]

The three most significant factors creating an unfavourable impression of the courts included: time consuming (cited by 59.8 per cent of businesses); ineffective execution of judgments (cited by 46.7 per cent of businesses) and complicated procedures (cited by 46.4 per cent of businesses). Further, the *DANIDA Survey* and the study by Nguyen both note that businesses see litigation as 'negatively affecting' their business reputation.[105] Additionally, 31.7 per cent of businesses identified economic court judges as 'not qualified' to resolve their disputes.[106] Finally, if government actively 'advises' courts on decisions, there is little incentive to go to a court to determine a case.

Although the use of the Economic Court is increasing and there has been a three-fold increase in the number of economic cases notified in the period 2001–6 nationally (see Table 2.1), the general aversion to use of the Economic Court remains. The reasons for this mistrust of courts are largely unchanged: time-consuming, unenforceable judgments, bad for firms' reputations and risking decisions from those not qualified to provide them. In addition, the *DANIDA Survey* elicited that businesses see great challenges in the collection of evidence, reporting that witnesses refuse to cooperate, government departments refuse to supply information, and case dossiers held at the courts are inaccessible.[107] It seems both

Table 2.3 Explanation of challenges faced by businesses when resolving business or commercial cases[97]

Cause of difficulty	*Percentage of businesses nominating difficulty*
Time consuming	59.8%
Ineffective execution of judgments	46.7%
Complicated procedures	46.4%
Lack of transparency	36.0%
Negative impact on business reputation	34.3%
Judges not qualified to resolve disputes	31.7%
High procedural costs	25.5%
Other	5.6%

judges and businesses see effective litigation as challenged by the difficulties in collection of evidence.

Lawyers' perceptions

Lawyers are similarly critical of the Economic Court as a forum for dispute resolution. Lawyers are on the record robustly criticizing judges for lack of competence and lack of transparency.[108] Yet lawyers based in Ho Chi Minh City have observed an increasing use of the Economic Court in recent times, probably attributable to the introduction of the *Law on Commerce* in 1999 and its subsequent amendment (see earlier discussion) and other legal instruments that confer rights to commercial parties. More specifically, the *DANIDA Survey* records lawyers' perceptions of the types of matters that might be taken to the Economic Court, highlighting that some matters are considered better able to be litigated in that forum than others. For instance, 32.8 per cent of interviewed lawyers suggested that they might take a purchase and sale of goods dispute to the Economic Court, whereas only 13 per cent of lawyers suggested they would see service agreements litigated in the Economic Court.[109]

It is well known that the nature of the dispute alone does not guide a lawyer in whether or not to use the Court. Other factors, such as the value of the dispute and the legal status of the parties, impact on decisions whether to use the Economic Court. It has often been said by practising lawyers that when acting for a state-owned enterprise (SOE) it may be strategically beneficial to sue in the courts, whereas if one's client is not an SOE, and the defendant is, there may be a disadvantage in invoking the authority of the court to resolve a dispute. Certainly, bias towards resolution of a dispute in favour of state instrumentalities, reflecting the governmental and party interference and influence on court decisions, is well documented.[110]

As previously noted, informal dispute resolution methods are commonly used in Vietnam and routinely cited as the best way to resolve disputes. There is, however, a difference of opinion about the value of international arbitration.[111] Vietnamese and foreign lawyers give different advice to clients on the relative benefits of Vietnamese courts when compared to foreign arbitration. Vietnamese lawyers (even those lawyers working in foreign law firms) recommend Vietnamese courts to resolve contracts between a local Vietnamese party and a foreign party. The majority of foreign lawyers advising clients investing in Vietnam have a pessimistic view of Vietnamese courts as a venue for resolving disputes, because of the inexperience of judges and the complexity of transactions, perceived bias towards the Vietnamese parties and particularly towards state-owned enterprises.[112] However, many Vietnamese lawyers are more practical in their approach. They suggest that Vietnamese courts have rarely enforced and recognized foreign arbitral awards, despite Vietnam being a member of the 1959 *Convention on the Recognition and Enforcement of Foreign Arbitral Awards*.[113] Therefore, to avoid the potential cost and time associated with two hearings, many of the Vietnamese lawyers advise that it is better to hear an economic dispute in Vietnam. Additionally, domestic arbitration is seen as a likely growth area for the resolution of economic disputes.[114]

There are also extra-judicial methods of dispute resolution invoked by disputants; sometimes on the advice of a lawyer. These can involve the police in a dispute sometimes to recoup assets, on other occasions to criminalise what has hitherto been a civil/economic matter into a criminal prosecution. Widespread use of debt collection agencies is also reported; some agencies existing within law firms and some as independent businesses.[115] One of the down sides of this approach is that debt collection agencies, of which there are 126 formally registered in Hanoi alone, expect to recover 30–35 per cent of the amount sought in fees.[116]

Functional while striving for legitimacy

This brief analysis suggests that the 15-year-old Vietnamese Economic Court has slowly increased its case numbers, while having had its procedure laws rewritten and its jurisdiction overhauled. Despite this radical reform of the legislative foundation of the Court, the capacity of its personnel to deliver impartial and well-informed judgments attracts a great deal of criticism. It has not developed a well of supporters. At best, canvassing the attitudes of lawyers (both international and domestic) and businesses, it is suggested that the Ho Chi Minh branch of the Economic Court might be the most dynamic and house the most technically able of the judges practising in this jurisdiction. Yet, in large part this comment is supported by anecdotal evidence and not by any systemic review of judgments from the Economic Courts nationally. Certainly, the case management systems and access to case tracking made available to the public, coupled with the availability of judgments, from the Ho Chi Minh Court distinguishes it from other courts in the country. It has developed a higher level of trust with its users than exists anywhere else. Yet, we must not overstate this. There is some developing confidence in the Ho Chi Minh Economic Court, but it remains fragile and evolving rather than entrenched.

It is premature to describe the Vietnamese Economic Court as having either widespread appeal or legitimacy. Its hold on the public's imagination as a forum for the effective resolution of economic disputes is tenuous at best. That said, the Economic Court is arguably in a marginally stronger position than it was in 1994, when introduced. Put another way, the Economic Court has managed to slightly better its reputation, particularly in the south, over the last 15 years, which is a trend in the right direction for the increasing number of private businesses now active in Vietnam. Regrettably, the improvements taking hold in the south will not spread quickly nationally while the Hanoi Supreme People's Court is the only court the party–state endorses to lead reform of the Economic Courts. Whether wary of ceding power to the south or losing power out of Hanoi, the party–state has consistently refused suggestions that court reform be led by or at least shared with the more progressive Ho Chi Minh People's Court. Given that this situation will continue, while legal reforms may be enabling, institutional and cultural inertia will make court legitimacy aspirational rather than real.

Notes

1. We contend that it is best not to conceive of the state as separate from the party: hence the use of the term party–state. Party membership leading state organs (such as courts and the National Assembly) hovers at around 90 per cent, functionaries are accountable to the party as well as the state blurring any ostensible separation of the two, and every court has a Communist Party of Vietnam (the party) cell which reports on its activities. See Pip Nicholson and N. H. Quang, "The Vietnamese Judiciary: the Politics of Appointment and Promotion," *Pacific Rim Law and Policy Journal* 14 (2005): 1–34.
2. For a discussion of economic reforms, see for example, Brian Van Arkadie and Raymond Mallon, *Viet Nam: A Transition Tiger?* (Canberra: Asia Pacific Press, 2003).
3. For a discussion of the term Economic Court see Pip Nicholson, *Borrowing Court Systems: The Experience of Socialist Vietnam* (Leiden, Boston: Martinus Nijhoff Publishers, 2007), 32–3.
4. See Nguyen Quoc Viet, "Explaining the Transition to the Rule of Law in Vietnam: The Role of Informal Institutions and the Delegation of Powers to Independent Courts" (PhD diss., University of Kassel, 2006).
5. See Van-Hoa To, *Judicial Independence: A Legal Research on its Theoretical Aspects, Practices from Germany, the United States of America, France, Vietnam, and Recommendations for Vietnam* (Lund: Juristforlaget i Lund, 2006); Nguyen Quoc Viet, "Explaining the Transition to the Rule of Law in Vietnam: The Role of Informal Institutions and the Delegation of Powers to Independent Courts"; Nicholson, *Borrowing Court Systems: The Experience of Socialist Vietnam.*
6. Nguyen Quoc Viet, "Explaining the Transition to the Rule of Law in Vietnam: The Role of Informal Institutions and the Delegation of Powers to Independent Courts," 148.
7. See Pip Nicholson, "Legitimising Legal Reform: Dialogical Law Making and the Rule of Law" (paper presented at the Hague Institute for the Internationalisation of Law, Law Future Series, the Hague, October 26–27, 2007). See also John Gillespie, "Rethinking the Role of Judicial Independence in Socialist Transforming East Asia," *International Comparative Law Quarterly* 4 (2007): 837–70.

8. See Yash Ghai, "The Rule of law, Legitimacy and Governance," *International Journal of the Sociology of Law* 14 (1986): 178–208, on the many meanings of legitimacy.
9. See also Pitman Potter's chapter in this publication. Potter argues that assessments of Chinese regional courts need to consider "institutional capacity."
10. See Brian J. M. Quinn, "Legal Reform and its Context in Vietnam," *Columbia Journal of Asian Law* 15 (2002): 221; Brian J. M. Quinn, "Vietnam's Continuing Legal Reforms: Gaining Control Over the Courts," *Asian-Pacific Law and Policy Journal* 4 (2003): 432–68; Pip Nicholson, "Vietnamese Jurisprudence: Informing Court Reform," in *Asian Socialism and Legal Change; The Dynamics of Vietnamese and Chinese Reform*, ed. John Gillespie and Pip Nicholson (Canberra: Asia Pacific Press and Australian National University, 2005), 159–90; Pip Nicholson and Nguyen Hung Quang, "The Vietnamese Judiciary: The Politics of Appointment and Promotion," *Pacific Rim Law and Policy Journal* 14 (2005): 1–34; Nicholson, *Borrowing Court Systems: The Experience of Socialist Vietnam*; Gillespie, "Rethinking the Role of Judicial Independence in Socialist Transforming East Asia," 837–70.
11. Nguyen Van Quang, "A Comparative Study of the Systems of Review of Administrative Action by Courts and Tribunals in Australia and Vietnam" (PhD diss., Latrobe University, 2007), 66.
12. For a detailed analysis in English of the constitutional principles of parliamentary supremacy, peoples' sovereignty and party leadership, see To Van Hoa, *Judicial Independence: A Legal Research on its Theoretical Aspects, Practices from Germany, the United States of America, France, Vietnam, and Recommendations for Vietnam*, 366–70.
13. Nguyen Van Quang, "A Comparative Study of the Systems of Review of Administrative Action by Courts and Tribunals in Australia and Vietnam"; Mark Sidel, *Law and Society in Vietnam* (Cambridge: Cambridge University Press, 2008), 18–73.
14. See Pip Nicholson, *Borrowing Court Systems: The Experience of Socialist Vietnam*.
15. *Resolution No. 8 – NQ/TW*, 2 January 2002; *Resolution No. 48 – NQ/TW*, 24 May 2005 (*Resolution No. 48 of the Politburo*); *Resolution No. 49 – NQ/TW*, 2 June 2005; *Resolution No. 900/UBTVQH11*, 21 March 2007.
16. For a detailed analysis of *Resolution No. 8 – NQ/TW*, 2 January 2002 see Nicholson, "Vietnamese Jurisprudence: Informing Court Reform," 159–90.
17. LEADCO, *Research on Role of Current Formal and Informal Commercial Dispute Resolution Bodies*, (Hanoi: LEADCO, 2007), 19.
18. *Resolution No. 166-NQ-UBTVQH9*, 2 February 1994 disbanded the State Economic Arbitration Tribunals as of 30 June 1994 and established the Economic Courts after that date.
19. *Law No. 29-LTN on Amendment and Supplement to the Law on the Organisation of the People's Court*, 28 December 1993.
20. Ibid.
21. *Decision No. 94-TCCB of the Chief Justice of the Supreme People's Court* dated 11 August 1994.
22. *Ordinance No. 31-L-CTN of the Standing Committee of the National Assembly on Procedures for Resolution of Economic Disputes*, 29 March 1994.
23. *Ordinance No. 31 L CTN of the Standing Committee of the National Assembly on Procedures for Resolution of Economic Disputes*, 29 March 1994.
24. Interview with Lawyers A (Hanoi), May 2008 and G (Ho Chi Minh City), June 2008.
25. *Ordinance No. 24-LCT/HĐNN8 of the State Council on Economic Contracts*, 29 September 1989.
26. *Ordinance No. 24-LCT/HĐNN8 of the State Council on Economic Contracts*, 29 September 1989.

27. Phong Tran, "Vietnam's Economic Liberalization and Outreach: Legal Reform," *Law and Business Review of the Americas* 9 (2003): 146.
28. *Ordinance No. 24-LCT/HĐNN8 of the State Council on Economic Contracts*, 19 September 1989, arts 12, 29(2). See also *Ordinance No. 31-L/CTN of the Standing Committee of the National Assembly on Resolution of Procedures for Economic Legal Proceedings*, 29 March 1994, art. 31(1).
29. Interview with Lawyer H (Ho Chi Minh City), March, 2008.
30. Interview with Lawyer J (Ho Chi Minh City), March, 2008.
31. Ibid.
32. Ibid.
33. *Law No. 33–2002-QH10 on the Organisation of the People's Court*, 2 April 2002.
34. Not all provincial courts have been able to establish separate divisions of judges to staff the Economic Courts. A lack of technically qualified judges (and the limited need for judges in many provinces) has meant differences in practices among the provinces. Interviews with judges and bureaucrats (Hanoi, Ho Chi Minh City and Danang), January 2004.
35. For a detailed discussion of court appointments, see Nicholson and Quang, "The Vietnamese Judiciary: The Politics of Appointment and Promotion," 1–34.
36. Nicholson, *Borrowing Court Systems: The Experience of Socialist Vietnam*, 251.
37. *Civil Proceedings Code No. 24–2004-QH11*, 15 June 2004 (*Law No. 24 on Civil Proceedings Code*).
38. *Resolution No. 32–2004-QH11*, 15 June 2004 with effect from 1 January 2005.
39. *Resolution No. 32–2004-QH11*, 15 June 2004 with effect from 1 January 2005.
40. *Resolution No. 01/2001-NQ-HDTP*, 31 March 2005.
41. *Resolution No. 45/2005/QH11*, 14 June 2005.
42. See Freshfields Bruckhaus Deringer, *Vietnam – Amended Civil Code* (Hanoi: Freshfields Bruckhaus Deringer, 2006), 2; Phillips Fox, "Death of Economic Contracts," *Vietnam Legal Update* 13 (2005): 7–14; Ngo Quy Linh, "Economic Contracts Only in the Name," *Vietnam Investment Review*, January 11, 2006, http://www.vir.com.vn/Client/Dautu/dautu.asp?CatID = 56&DocID = 9309.
43. *Law No. 33/2005/QH11 on Civil Code of the National Assembly*, 29 June 2005 (*Civil Code*).
44. *Law No. 35/2005/QH11 on Commerce*, 14 June 2005.
45. Interview with Lawyer H (Ho Chi Minh City), March, 2008.
46. LEADCO, *Report on the Diagnostic Study on the Functioning of the Existing Commercial Dispute Resolution System: Judicial and Non-Judicial* (Hanoi: Danish International Development Agency (DANIDA), 2007), 29.
47. *Resolution No. 48 – NQ/TW*, 24 May 2005, 21.
48. Interview with Lawyer I (Hanoi), June, 2008.
49. This table collates statistics from LEADCO, *Report on the Diagnostic Study on the Functioning of the Existing Commercial Dispute Resolution System: Judicial and Non-Judicial*, 54–57. These figures differ from those Nicholson had extracted from the Supreme People's Courts' annual reports over the period 2005–7. The divergence in case numbers was not great, and all Vietnamese statistics are ultimately compilations from official sources, whether published or obtained from the court in answer to specific queries.
50. Population Reference Bureau, "2004 World Population Data Sheet," http://www.prb.org/pdf04/04WorldDataSheet_ENG.pdf
51. Gillespie, "Rethinking the Role of Judicial Independence in Socialist Transforming East Asia," 842.
52. See Quinn, "Legal Reform and its Context in Vietnam," 221; Quinn, "Vietnam's Continuing Legal Reforms: Gaining Control Over the Courts," 432–68; Statistics obtained by Nicholson in interviews with judges, January 2004 and June 2008.

53. Interviews with bureaucrats (Hanoi), February, 2002.
54. LEADCO, *Report on the Diagnostic Study on the Functioning of the Existing Commercial Dispute Resolution System: Judicial and Non-Judicial*, 5–6.
55. Ibid., 7.
56. LEADCO, *Report on the Diagnostic Study on the Functioning of the Existing Commercial Dispute Resolution System: Judicial and Non-Judicial*, 63.
57. Ibid.
58. World Bank, "World Development Indicators," quoted in Gillespie, "Rethinking the Role of Judicial Independence in Socialist Transforming East Asia," 864.
59. Ibid., 63–4.
60. Interview with Lawyer H (Ho Chi Minh City), March, 2008.
61. Ibid.
62. Compare with the situation in other civil law countries where judicial decisions are accorded highly persuasive value under the doctrine of *jurisprudence constante* when there is agreement in multiples cases on a single issue or point. See Vincy Fon and Francesco Parisi, "Judicial Precedents In Civil Law Systems: A Dynamic Analysis," George Mason School of Law, Law and Economics Research Paper No. 04–15 and University of Minnesota Law School legal Studies research Paper No. 07–19, 6–8, http://ssrn.com/abstract = 534504
63. *Constitution of the Socialist Republic of Vietnam* (as amended in 1992) art. 91(3).
64. *Law No. 12 QH on Promulgation of Legal Instructions*, 12 November 1996, art. 2.
65. *Law No. 12 QH on Promulgation of Legal Instructions*, 12 November 1996, art. 2.
66. Information made known to Duong in the course of commercial practice in Ho Chi Minh City in 2006.
67. Quan Hien Nguyen, "Cross-Border Transactions in Vietnam and the Vietnam–US Bilateral Trade Agreement," *International Trade and Business Law Annual* 8 (2003): 170. See also United Nations Development Programme, *Report on Survey of Needs of District People's Courts Nationwide* (Hanoi: Judicial Publishing House, 2006), 250–2 where it is reported that 58.03 per cent of district court judges explain that they seek 'court leaders' advice on how to handle a case' where they face problems determining a case.
68. *Law No. 17QH on Promulgation of Legal Instruments*, 12 June 2008, art. 2.
69. This is not unique to Vietnam. Nicholson, in the course of comparative study of court reasoning, notes that many French court decisions are similarly lacking in analysis. See for example, *Bulletins des Arrets, Chambres Civiles Cour de Cassation*, No. 1 January, 2008.
70. *Civil Proceedings Code No. 24–2004-QH11*, 15 June 2004, arts 238 and 279 for first instance for judgments and appellate judgments, respectively. Interview with Lawyer A (Hanoi), May–June, 2008.
71. *Civil Proceedings Code No. 24–2004-QH11*, 15 June 2004, art. 241.
72. Gillespie, "Rethinking the Role of Judicial Independence in Socialist Transforming East Asia," 861–2.
73. See N. H. Quang and Kerstin Steiner, "Ideology and Professionalism: The Resurgence of the Vietnamese Bar," in *Asian Socialism and Legal Change; The Dynamics of Vietnamese and Chinese Reform*, ed. John Gillespie and Pip Nicholson (Canberra: Asia Pacific Press and Australian National University, 2005), 191–211.
74. Digest of Case Law, "Case No. 82/2007/KDTM-PT, 28 August 2007," http://e-law-review.com/Default.aspx?tabid = 213&ctl = Detail&mid = 695&ArticleID = ARTICLE08060001
75. *Law No. 60 on Enterprises of the National Assembly*, 9 June 2005, art. 52(3).
76. Phan Anh, "Park Hyatt bị xé ruột vì thủ đoạn và sự bội ước," (Infighting at the Park Hyatt due to factionalism and dishonesty), *Vn Express*, July 10, 2007, http://www.vnexpress.net/GL/Kinh-doanh/2007/07/3B9F842B/. Phan Anh records that Vilf Hong Duc, a top tier Vietnamese law firm, represented RIL. According to the Park

Hyatt Judgment UCI also had legal representation, although it was not recorded who the lawyers were.

77. Interview with Lawyer J (Ho Chi Minh City), March, 2008.
78. Nguyen Sa, "Park Hyatt Hotel Matter and Development of Vietnamese Law," *Vietbao*, July 18, 2007, http://vietbao.vn/Kinh-te/Vu-khach-san-Park-Hyatt-va-buoc-tien-cua-luat-Viet-Nam/20719601/87/
79. VNA, "Court Verdicts for 2005–6 to be Made Public," http://www.nhandan.com.vn/english/lofe/170508/life_co.htm; Interviews with Lawyers A (Hanoi), B (Hanoi), C (Hanoi), D (Hanoi), E (Hanoi) and F (Hi Chi Minh City), May-June, 2008. See also LEADCO, *Report on the Diagnostic Study on the Functioning of the Existing Commercial Dispute Resolution System: Judicial and Non-Judicial*, 61 where it is reported that 77.4 per cent of interviewed judges cited 'lack of reference materials on the experience of Vietnamese courts' as a difficulty faced by Economic Court judges.
80. For example, the Danish International Development Agency (DANIDA), Japanese International Cooperation Agency and United States Agency for International Development have each had programmes to assist the Supreme People's Court publish its decisions. Consultations with STAR (USAID) and DANIDA personnel, May–June, 2008. See Project of Technical Assistance for Judicial and Legal System Reforms, "Technical Cooperation Program," http://www.jica.go.jp/vietnam/activities/TCP_list.html
81. Interviews with Lawyers A (Hanoi) and G (Ho Chi Minh City), May–June, 2008. Nicholson was advised of regular meetings of lawyers in large firms in Ho Chi Minh City to discuss cases. Further, there is a movement to establish regular discussion to debate cases in Hanoi also, and not restricted to members of large firms.
82. Interview with Lawyer E (Hanoi), May–June, 2008.
83. Nicholson was a consultant to a DANIDA project on the publication of judgments in 2008 and witnessed first-hand the tension internal to the court on the issue of how much ought to be published how soon.
84. See Digest of Case Law, http://suutamanle.vn/ or http://e-lawreview.com/Default.aspx?tabid = 36
85. Toa An Nhan Dan Toi Cao (Supreme People's Court), *Quyet Dinh Giam Doc Tham Cua Hoi Dong Tham Phan Toa An Nhan Dan Toi Cao 2006* (Cassational Review Decisions of the Supreme People's Court Justice Council 2006) (Hanoi: Toa An Nhan Dan Toi Cao, 2008), l; Toa An Nhan Dan Toi Cao (Supreme People's Court), *Quyet Dinh Giam Doc Tham Cua Hoi Dong Tham Phan Toa An Nhan Dan Toi Cao 2005* (Cassational Review Decisions of the Supreme People's Court Justice Council 2005) (Hanoi: Toa An Nhan Dan Toi Cao, 2008); Toa An Nhan Dan Toi Cao (Supreme People's Court), *Quyet Dinh Giam Doc Tham Cua Hoi Dong Tham Phan Toa An Nhan Dan Toi Cao 2003–2004, Quyen 1 va 2* (Cassational Review Decisions of the Supreme People's Court Justice Council 2003–4, Vols 1 and 2) (Hanoi: Toa An Nhan Dan Toi Cao, 2004).
86. Pip Nicholson, "The Vietnamese Courts and Corruption," in *Corruption in Asia: Rethinking the Good Governance Paradigm*, ed. T. C. Lindsey and H. W. Dick (Annandale, NSW: Federation Press, 2002), 201–18.
87. Interviews with Lawyers A, B, C, D, E, F, and G (Hanoi and Ho Chi Minh City), May–June, 2008.
88. See Per Bergling, *Legal Reform and Private Enterprise: The Vietnamese Experience* (Umea, Sweden: Department of Law, Umea University, 1999), Vol. 1; John McMillan and Christopher Woodruff, "Dispute Prevention without Courts in Vietnam," *Journal of Law, Economics and Organization* 15 (1999): 637–58; Nguyen Hien Quan, "The Social Structures of Contracts: A Case Study of the Vietnamese Market" (PhD diss., The University of Melbourne, 2006).

89. For a fuller discussion of judicial appointments, see Pip Nicholson and Nguyen Hung Quang, "The Vietnamese Judiciary: The Politics of Appointment and Promotion," 1–34.
90. LEADCO, *Report on the Diagnostic Study on the Functioning of the Existing Commercial Dispute Resolution System: Judicial and Non-Judicial*, 61.
91. Ibid., 53.
92. Ibid., 52.
93. United Nations Development Programme, *Report on Survey of Needs of District People's Courts Nationwide*, 243.
94. Ibid., 269–78.
95. LEADCO, *Report on the Diagnostic Study on the Functioning of the Existing Commercial Dispute Resolution System: Judicial and Non-Judicial*, 61.
96. Ibid.
97. United Nations Development Programme, *Report on Survey of Needs of District People's Courts Nationwide*, 307–8. A district court judge who has served for nine years, for example, could earn a base salary of 1755,000 *dong*/month (roughly US$110/month).
98. See Gary Chan, "Judicial Immunity and Independence of Vietnamese Judges: Reflections on the Ordinance on Judges and Jurors and the Law on the Organisation of the People's Courts," *Australian Journal of Asian Law*, 7 (2005): 143–68.
99. See Mark Cammack's chapter in this publication.
100. Bergling, *Legal Reform and Private Enterprise: The Vietnamese Experience*.
101. McMillan and Woodruff, "Dispute Prevention without Courts in Vietnam," *Journal of Law, Economics and Organization*," 637–58 and see also J. McMillan and C. Woodruff, "Interfirm Relationships and Informal Credit in Vietnam," 1285.
102. Nguyen Hien Quan, "The Social Structures of Contracts: A Case Study of the Vietnamese".
103. LEADCO, *Report on the Diagnostic Study on the Functioning of the Existing Commercial Dispute Resolution System: Judicial and Non-Judicial*, 65.
104. Ibid., 61.
105. Ibid., 68; Nguyen Hien Quan, "The Social Structures of Contracts: A Case Study of the Vietnamese".
106. LEADCO, *Report on the Diagnostic Study on the Functioning of the Existing Commercial Dispute Resolution System: Judicial and Non-Judicial*, 68.
107. Ibid., 69.
108. Interviews with Lawyers A (Hanoi), C (Hanoi), D (Hanoi) and F (Ho chi Minh City), May–June, 2008.
109. LEADCO, *Report on the Diagnostic Study on the Functioning of the Existing Commercial Dispute Resolution System: Judicial and Non-Judicial*, 57.
110. Gillespie, "Rethinking the Role of Judicial Independence in Socialist Transforming East Asia," 849–53.
111. See generally James S. Finch and Harold P. Fiske, "Vietnam's Evolving Arbitration System," *East Asian Executive Reports* 17 (1995): 9; Kazuo Iwasaki, "Arbitration of Foreign Investment Disputes in Vietnam," in *Commercial Legal Development in Vietnam: Vietnamese and Foreign Commentaries*, ed. John Gillespie (Singapore: Butterworths Asia, 1997), 177–86; Binh T. T. Ha, "Arbitration as a Means of Resolving Business-Related Disputes in Vietnam: The Present Situation and Prospective Development," *Journal of international Arbitration* 19 (2002): 337–48; Richard Garnett and Kien Cuong Nguyen, "The Enforcement of Arbitration Awards in Vietnam," *Asian International Arbitration Journal* 2 (2006): 137–45; Michael Pryles, ed., *Dispute Resolution in Asia*, 3rd edn (Leiden: Kluwer Law, 2006).
112. Insight from Duong as a practitioner working in Ho Chi Minh City for the last three years.

113. Opened for signature 10 June 1958, 330 UNTS 38 (entered into force 7 June 1959).
114. LEADCO, *Report on the Diagnostic Study on the Functioning of the Existing Commercial Dispute Resolution System: Judicial and Non-Judicial*, 21–23.
115. Ibid.
116. Ibid.

3 'Reading the tea leaves' in the Indonesian Commercial Court

A cautionary tale, but for whom?

David K. Linnan

The *Pengadilan Niaga* or Indonesian Commercial Court was initially created as an insolvency forum in 1998, at the height of the Asian Financial Crisis, arguably under International Monetary Fund pressure. But it was also part of a longer term discussion concerning the creation of specialized courts, and by 2000–1 its jurisdiction had been expanded to include intellectual property matters. The Commercial Court is commonly viewed as having failed in mastering Indonesia's widespread insolvency problems brought on by the Asian Financial Crisis, and bankruptcy case filings declined precipitously by 2003–4 as potential litigants voted with their feet. But in the same general timeframe, intellectual property cases filed in the Court began to increase in number. The same Court (and often the same judges) who were criticized for their insolvency case decisions then garnered relative praise and increased case filings in the intellectual property area. Thereafter, what few outsiders have realized is that intellectual property cases levelled off around 2004–5, while insolvency cases have resurged, even while their composition changed.

What is the explanation for the perceived differing performance of the Commercial Court in different substantive areas, the rise and fall of case-loads over time, and what does it tell us about judicial reform and court creation processes in Asia? Is the performance differential more perceived than real, or does it lie with the judges or the lawyers or the character of litigants? How much is the mix of perceptions more a product of donor expectations, and possibly politically-influenced hype, as opposed to fact? This is indirectly a story not only about a new court, but also about how local and international perceptions may mislead more than they inform some legal development debates in Asia.

Answers to the above questions are mixed and take us into an examination of what lies behind the court statistics cited below. They show an increase in intellectual property case filings, even as bankruptcy filings in the Commercial Court declined, then a new pattern visible in filings and dispositions commencing 2004–5. On one level, the differing nature of the cases and litigants is a primary factor. More importantly, they highlight that to approach the question of the success or failure of the Commercial Court based upon case filings, or even dispositions without more background analysis, is misleading. Instead, the better approach is to focus on the still limited place of courts in Indonesian dispute resolution.[1] The clearest understanding of what goes on institutionally requires attention to where disputes go and how they are resolved; more often than not outside the courts and also in countries with a stronger rule of law tradition (drawing an implicit comparison to prior legal scholarship in areas like plea bargaining and criminal justice comparing approaches in the United States and continental European legal systems).[2]

There is something disjointed otherwise in the attitudes of those who pursue, somewhat formalistically, rule of law efforts in the developing world, while seeming to ignore how (party controlled) dispute resolution works at the practitioner level, even in Western jurisdictions with strong legal systems. Even in the West, comparatively few sophisticated commercial disputes are disposed of at trial, for cost reasons if nothing else, and only lawyers 'like' litigation. The object lesson is that formalism can mislead, and courts are both more and less important in rule of law efforts than is sometimes thought.

There is also probably a hidden difference of emphasis between Western, often common law-oriented donors, who may be focused on courts generically in the public law setting as restraints on government, and mostly civil law-oriented developing Asia, where states envision courts, more often than not, as private law dispute resolution fora to support economic development. The overlap between, and differences of opinion concerning, general concepts at the level of modernization, governance, economic development, democracy, and the rule of law are part of the hidden agenda concerning courts, but our focus in this chapter is more on the use and abuse of court statistics, rather than the broader issues on which Western donors and Asian developing countries sometimes differ.

Misleading statistics: whose and why?

Insiders familiar with Indonesian court reform and donor law reform documentation post-1998 have probably seen some version of the following juxtaposed statistical tables *c.* 2004–5 comparing the performance of the *Pengadilan Niaga* in insolvency versus intellectual property cases (Tables 3.1 and 3.2).[3]

The pitfalls of Indonesian insolvency law have been documented elsewhere,[4] but the basic development in insolvency filings, according to donors through 2004–5, was that an initial surge was visible from 1998–2000, then by 2001

Table 3.1 Indonesian Commercial Court bankruptcy petitions 1998–2003 re donor

Petitions	*1998**	*1999*	*2000*	*2001*	*2002*	*2003*	*Total*
Registered	31	100	84	61	39	38	353
Petition granted	13	31	32	17	9	12	114
Petition declined/ refused	13	60	42	40	25	25	205
Settlement reached	3	7	8	1	4	1	24
Suspension of payment	2	2	2	3	1	–	10

* Commenced in September 1998.

Table 3.2 Indonesian Commercial Court intellectual property rights petitions re donor

Petitions	*2001**	*2002*	*2003*	*Total*
Registered	11	63	84	158
Trade mark	11	59	79	149
Patent	–	2	3	5
Industrial design	–	2	2	4

* Commenced in November 2001.

filings were already dropping off, and by 2002–3 that drop-off was precipitous. The Commercial Court as an insolvency venue was pronounced a failure (a somewhat misleading conclusion even in its own terms, since voluntary or negotiated reorganisations had been diverted largely to an administrative venue referred to as the Jakarta Initiative modelled in large part on the London approach).[5] In the same time frame, however, donors celebrated surging intellectual property petitions in the Commercial Court (although less attention is usually paid to the idea that the intellectual property cases were overwhelmingly trademark cases, so the substantive distribution of intellectual property right (IPR) cases was skewed). This curious juxtaposition, and assertions that the *Pengadilan Niaga* succeeded with IPR cases even where it failed with insolvency cases, lies at the heart of this chapter. But first, let us examine in more detail, directly from the Commercial Court logbooks, more recent intellectual property law and bankruptcy proceeding statistics, as well as parallel statistics concerning voluntary debt compromise proceedings, which were omitted from the previously recited donor statistics (Tables 3.3 to 3.5).

More recently, there seems to be a change in the composition of insolvency proceedings to the extent that domestic creditor and even debtor use have replaced the initial generation of predominantly international creditors, who initiated petitions in the immediate aftermath of the Asian Financial Crisis. The first generation reached back to the Financial Crisis and de facto depression accompanying what Indonesians refer to as the 'multidimensional crisis', reflecting political as well as economic turmoil in the aftermath of the end of over 30 years of President Suharto's New Order government. It commenced in 1998 and lasted 5–6 years. The statistical chronology, it bears note, matches up with donor views as visible *c.* 2004–5, but also shadows certain technical amendments to Indonesian insolvency law in 2004 (particularly granting voting rights to secured creditors in voluntary debt compromise proceedings).[6] The mystery for interpretation then becomes how did the donors see things so darkly, also on the insolvency side, just before a relative dawn? And meanwhile, things have not changed significantly for IPR cases, to the extent that the vast majority are trademark cases involving appropriation of (consumer) trademarks, whether it be the case of a well-known foreign automobile manufacturer's trademark (Ferrari) being used without permission for a different category of goods (cosmetics),[7] or the use of

Table 3.3 Indonesian Commercial Court bankruptcy petitions 1998–2007*

Petitions	*1998***	*1999*	*2000*	*2001*	*2002*	*2003*	*2004*	*2005*	*2006*	*2007*	*Total*
Commenced (*masuk*)	31	100	84	61	39	38	52	44	59	64	572
Order accepted (*putus dikabulkan*)	14	33	37	19	12	14	22	20	29	30	230
No order issued, rejected (*putus ditolak*)	4	34	15	25	15	13	18	13	20	23	180
No order issued, none received (*putus tidak dapat diterima*)	2	9	4	2	1	3	1	–	2	–	24
Order withdrawn, party action (*putus dicabut*)	3	8	17	9	8	8	11	10	8	9	91
Order withdrawn for lack of legal interest (*putus gugur*; for example, a debt is successfully challenged)	4	4	1	2	–	–	–	–	–	–	11
Settlement by parties (*putus damai*)	4	4	6	2	–	–	–	–	–	–	16
Temporary 45-day postponement for party discussions (*penundaan*)	–	8	4	2	3	–	–	1	–	2	20

*Detailed court statistics are from the logs of the Jakarta Commercial Court. Branches of the Commercial Court were established relatively recently outside Jakarta in several major commercial cities, but no attempt has been made to cover these and their development for the purposes of this chapter. In fact, there have been very few cases outside Jakarta to date, and the few such cases outside Jakarta in the new regional branches have been brought seemingly for tactical reasons (forum shopping for a less experienced court).

**Commenced September 1998.

Table 3.4 Indonesian Commercial Court voluntary debt compromise petitions 1998–2006*

Petitions	*1998***	*1999*	*2000*	*2001*	*2002*	*2003*	*2004*	*2005*	*2006*	*2007****	*Total*
Commenced (*masuk*)	10	15	21	8	7	4	2	5	3	N/A	75
Temporary order, like standstill (*sementara*)	6	3	2	2	–	–	1	–	–	N/A	14
Final order (*tetap*)	4	3	5	2	–	1	1	–	1	N/A	17
Settlement by parties (*damai*)	–	4	6	4	4	1	–	3	1	N/A	23
Withdrawn, party action (*dicabut*)	–	2	–	–	2	1	–	1	1	N/A	7
Rejected (*ditolak*)	–	3	–	–	–	–	–	–	–	N/A	3
Bankruptcy determination, automatic conversion (*pailit*)	–	–	7	–	–	–	–	1	–	N/A	8
No order issued, received and other (*tidak diterima*)	–	–	1	–	1	1	–	–	–	N/A	3

* Detailed court statistics are from the logs of the Jakarta Commercial Court. Branches of the Commercial Court were established relatively recently outside Jakarta in several major commercial cities, but no attempt has been made to cover these and their development for the purposes of this chapter. In fact, there have been very few cases outside Jakarta to date, and the few such cases outside Jakarta in the new regional branches have been brought seemingly for tactical reasons (forum shopping for a less experienced court).

**Commenced September 1998.

***Complete statistics not available past 2006 because of proceeding duration (statutory maximum of 270 days, which has been exceeded in practice; retained for comparability to bankruptcy petitions table).

Table 3.5 Indonesian Commercial Court intellectual property case petitions 2001–7*

Petitions	*2001***	*2002*	*2003*	*2004*	*2005*	*2006*	*2007*	*Total*
Commenced (*masuk*)	11	63	84	74	72	90	83	477
From ancillary proceeding (*masuk perlawanan*)	–	–	–	–	–	–	2	2
Order accepted (*putus dikabulkan*)	8	35	48	41	46	43	44	265
No order issued, rejected (*putus ditolak*)	1	11	18	21	8	11	16	86
No order issued, received (*putus tidak diterima*)	1	11	10	11	10	25	19	87
Order withdrawn, party action (*putus dicabut*)	1	6	8	1	8	10	5	39
Settlement by parties (*putus damai*)	–	–	–	–	–	1	1	2
Substantive law applied: Trademark (merek)	11	61	75	61	60	65	64	397
Industrial design (*desai industri*)	–	1	3	10	3	14	9	40
Patent (*paten*)	–	1	4	1	1	1	4	12
Copyright (*hak cipta*)	–	–	2	2	8	10	6	28

*Detailed court statistics are from the logs of the Jakarta Commercial Court. Branches of the Commercial Court were established relatively recently outside Jakarta in several major commercial cities, but no attempt has been made to cover these and their development for the purposes of this chapter. In fact, there have been very few cases outside Jakarta as yet, and the few such cases outside Jakarta in the new regional branches have been brought seemingly for tactical reasons (forum shopping for a less experienced court).

**Commenced November 2001.

similar sounding but slightly different internationally well-known clothing marks such as Couture Balenciaga (infringer Balencio).[8] So what is happening in parallel with copyright, patent and similar non-trademark intellectual property cases, notable mostly by their absence?

Intellectual property law's civil–criminal overlap: substantive criminal law, police and politics

The fact of the matter is that parallel criminal justice institutions, such as the police carrying out investigations, affect civil filings. The civil IPR case filings in the Commercial Court (*Pengadilan Niaga*) largely involve trademark cancellation cases,[9] which are brought after matters fail to be resolved in informal settlement negotiations. These negotiations most often occur between private parties under the pressure of police criminal investigations (in IPR cases as so-called *delik aduan* or complaint offence), which would be heard in the ordinary district courts (*Pengadilan Negeri*), if a criminal case went to trial. Technically speaking, *aduan* delict cases are brought under criminal complaints requiring the injured party's agreement to prosecute, a statutory matter under Indonesian law, but seemingly following the civil law tradition of relatively minor 'honour' crimes, such as defamation requiring the victim's application for prosecution.[10] To that extent, the IPR civil cases actually filed by private parties in the *Pengadilan Niaga* are a second or third order side-effect of unsuccessful dispute resolution pursued elsewhere, with many of the real issues being why and how different kinds of intellectual property disputes are pursued outside the Commercial Court.

The Commercial Court has shown some success in the IPR area, but donor claims about its general 'success' in the intellectual property area post-2000 looked good chiefly in comparison to its generally admitted 'failure' in the insolvency area post-1998.[11] They are probably best interpreted as reflecting a combination of politics and simpler cases in substantive terms. Where IPR cases are more complex substantively and procedurally (e.g., patent cases), there has been no apparent surge of cases in the *Pengadilan Niaga*. The bulk of the cases cited as the basis for claiming that the *Pengadilan Niaga* is an IPR success story are trademark cases, with a bias towards trademark cancellation proceedings (considered relatively simple by judges and IPR lawyers). Digital video disc (DVD) and similar relatively simple piracy cases involving pirated software or entertainment industry products (movies and music recordings) are largely noticeable by their absence, however, despite the fact that such cases also may start as police investigations (more typically of copyright or similar violations). Thus, there is a hidden issue when evaluating IPR performance in the *Pengadilan Niaga* concerning why piracy copyright cases should be different from trademark cases (and chiefly prominent by their absence in the court statistics).

So where does politics enter the picture, or why do we see foreign, mostly Western, donors spending generously to support rule of law initiatives, particularly aimed at court reform as part of institutional development? Asian developing countries have embraced institutional development as the engine for economic development and modernization. But it is a political necessity of donors and non-governmental organizations (NGOs) to demonstrate 'success' in relatively expensive rule of law programmes pursued since the 1990s in Indonesia. It is hard to justify the short-term costs of institutional development initiatives from donor perspectives (foreign aid is famously problematic in terms of domestic donor politics) as longer-term undertakings, so positives are naturally accentuated in the shorter term. Current, broader development plans may play a role, to the extent of the success in anticorruption and rule of law programmes, as it would seem to be necessary to render Indonesia eligible to participate in more selective bilateral development assistance programmes involving threshold qualifications. Think of the United States government's Millennium Challenge Corporation or MCC programme, for which developing countries need to pre-qualify. Inclusion pressure on the donor side was again in part political, related to Indonesia's status as the world's most populous Muslim country, and moderate in its politics relatively speaking. Finally, claiming success in dealing with IPR cases may be particularly attractive to donors, to the extent that IPRs are a special concern to developed-country donors due to domestic pressure groups (as witnessed by introduction of the topic into the trade law world of World Trade Organization in the Uruguay Round in the form of the entire *Agreement on Trade-Related Aspects of Intellectual Property Rights* [*TRIPs Agreement*][12] complex of issues).

To the extent that politics underlies much of the praise for the Commercial Court's record in the IPR area, it masks actual court performance (given that judging or measuring success in legal development is already a difficult exercise). It also misconceives the importance of courts in dispute resolution to a legal system still evolving (in rule of law terms), and distracts attention from still-existent problems in those institutions linked to actual dispute resolution; for example, the shadow role of the police and the settlement of IPR disputes outside the Commercial Court. Similarly, donors may approach court improvement projects with problematic concepts more suited to their own judicial systems than Indonesia's; we shall review this problem in greater detail subsequently.

Following donor claims of intellectual property 'success' versus insolvency 'failure' *c.* 2004–5, Commercial Court intellectual property cases stabilized in terms of case filings, even as insolvency case filings resurged (calling into question the entire prior donor interpretation of plunging insolvency versus soaring intellectual property case filings). But a real understanding of what is happening requires closer attention to the relationships between and changes within, varieties of filings and procedural niceties, which arguably reflect the development of an experienced bar and businesses that are now beginning to use litigation tactically and strategically. Indonesian business parties do not simply lay their disputes before courts for Delphic disposition, but by the same token neither do litigants in the West. Whereas pre-1998 sophisticated Indonesian private parties of all stripes conscientiously avoided the courts, now the private sector views the courts as one more area for commercial contests where a party may be surprised or pursued by its competitors. So now Indonesian business persons must develop a view about how to use and defend court actions as part of a changing business environment. This frames the use of law and courts instrumentally rather than in terms of a search for justice, the view behind most invocations of the rule of law. Recognition of the differences between pristine rule of law concepts and an appraisal of the strategic/instrumental use of courts opens up a more nuanced assessment of courts.

Substantive IPR law background and sociology of intellectual property versus insolvency law parties and legal counsel

Both the donor-created statistical table and the more detailed statistics above overwhelmingly contain trademark cases, so that some background in Indonesian trademark law and institutions is necessary to interpretation. We are less interested in substantive law than procedural/institutional aspects, and the implicit comparison with insolvency law stands in the background. Both Indonesian insolvency and intellectual property law have a pre-1998 history, but in practical terms, the bankruptcy concept was new in 1998. Initially, there was no experienced Indonesian insolvency bar, and uncertainty generally surrounded the concept of bankruptcy in Indonesian business circles. Thereafter, a practice grew up, in which lawyers solely represented either debtors or creditors. Meanwhile, arguments abounded that bankruptcy was either incompatible with social mores, or represented a foreign scheme to dominate Indonesia economically (since the then current perception in Jakarta was that only foreigners had cash available to purchase assets owned by the insolvent, domestically owned businesses). Within Indonesian insolvency law there were two approaches to judicial proceedings, namely liquidation in bankruptcy (*kepailitan*) as well as a voluntary debt compromise procedure (*penundaan kewajiban pembayaran utang* or deferment of the duty to pay debt), amounting to a relatively weak tool for corporate reorganizations. In real terms, the economic condition of Indonesian enterprises post-1997 was so bad that for all practical purposes insolvency proceedings were understood commonly in terms of liquidation as opposed to the typical understanding of a reorganization process in which the business itself might survive on a reorganized basis, even while ownership of the entity changed.[13] This common view is crucial in understanding the initial general Indonesian antipathy to insolvency proceedings (based also in social concerns like unemployment).[14]

By comparison, Indonesian intellectual property law was much more firmly established with a small, specialized bar by the early 1990s.[15] There were a significant number of intellectual property statutes passed in 2000–2,[16] but they are best described as updating efforts to bring Indonesian IPR law into compliance with *TRIPs Agreement* requirements post-1994 Uruguay Round. There was some nationalistic rhetoric associated with political claims that strengthening IPRs benefited only developed countries, but on the whole such rhetoric was calm by comparison with nationalism-inspired attacks on insolvency law following the Asian Financial Crisis.[17] In consequence, insolvency cases and intellectual property cases grew out of disparate sources, and the economic situation of potential litigants was also different. Economically speaking, it appears that IPR cases were not conceived of as 'bet the company' exercises, as was commonly the case with judicial insolvency proceedings in the aftermath of the Asian Financial Crisis.

Both insolvency and IPR law were procedurally distinctive, with special court procedures and accelerated deadlines inserted into the substantive statutes.[18] Insolvency law post-1998 incorporated a system of trustees or administrators, depending upon whether liquidation or reorganization proceedings were at stake; but in practice, existing company management typically was left in control of the debtor in possession, and largely deferred to by the judiciary concerning management of the insolvent enterprise (despite possessing the authority to run the business independently). On the other hand, a distinctive aspect of IPR law is that several different agencies or branches of Indonesian government are involved in the IPR filing and enforcement system.

IPR law's administration is under the Directorate General for Intellectual Property (*Direktorat Jenderal Hak atas Kekayaan Intelektual, Dirjen HAKI*). The Directorate General for Intellectual Property is nominally a department head in the Indonesian Ministry of Justice, but in fact maintains a semi-autonomous presence in his or her own intellectual property directorate's office in Tangerang in the Jakarta suburbs (as opposed to the central Justice Ministry building in the downtown Kuningan section of Jakarta). In effect, the Directorate General for Intellectual Property is the functional equivalent of the independent United States Patent and Trademark Office, despite being formally a department head within the Ministry of Justice. The Directorate General for Intellectual Property is responsible for various IPR filings, including making a variety of substantive determinations concerning matters such as novelty of inventions, etc.

Intellectual property also has a criminal law aspect involving the police and public prosecution, typically investigating and pursuing alleged IPR violations (due to parallel criminalization of IPR violations, e.g. under Sections 90–95 of *Law No. 15/2001* on trademarks). The criminal law trademark option, however, still treats IPR violations as quasi-private matters to the extent of trademark violations, which, for example, are designated as *delik aduan* under Section 95 of *Law No. 15/2001*. This limits law enforcement action to commencing criminal investigations only at the victim's request, and as a procedural matter it is not possible to continue such an investigation if the victim's permission is withdrawn. Thus, the injured private party is given a significant degree of formal control over criminal proceedings, while having incentives to lay off initial efforts in enforcing trademark rights via the state's criminal apparatus in the normal District Court's (*Pengadilan Negeri*'s) criminal jurisdiction, as opposed to the Commercial Court's (*Pengadilan Niaga*'s) specialized civil jurisdiction.

'Formal' control and the state criminal law apparatus are stressed, to the extent that going to the police for a criminal investigation in practical terms typically requires payment of informal levies (it is generally acknowledged that such informal payments are still customary, even when making a well-grounded request for an investigation).[19] But in practice, this allows private parties to use the criminal justice system in the first instance to pressure alleged intellectual property violators, which is different from insolvency proceedings solely on the civil side.[20]

Civil proceedings are also available in IPR cases since 2000–1 before the *Pengadilan Niaga*, which is precisely the source of the statistics showing a steady increase in IPR filings, largely on the trademark side. The problem in just focusing on the court filings in the *Pengadilan Niaga*, however, is the extent to which it ignores all the alternate dispositions available to potential litigants. There is some administrative recourse via the Directorate General for Intellectual Property. There is also criminal recourse via the *delik aduan* in the *Pengadilan Negeri* for trademarks, and under a normal criminal complaint for copyright and patent law. In practice, however, trademark cases start as police investigations, which may never make it to court, because the injured party will withdraw its legally required request to prosecute the *delik aduan* if a settlement is reached in direct negotiations between the private parties commenced under pressure of the criminal proceedings. There is also civil recourse in the Commercial Court, but IPR practitioners note that the trademark cases that make it to the *Pengadilan Niaga* are typically cases which started out as criminal police investigations of the *delik aduan*, but in which the parties never reached agreement in settlement discussions.[21]

To form a clearer, statistically-based picture of what actually occurs in IPR dispute settlement in terms of private party behaviour, it would be necessary to trace alleged IPR violations within the system, and compare statistics from several different government agencies and branches: namely, the police and prosecutor's office on the criminal side, the Directorate General for Intellectual Property on the administrative side, the *Pengadilan Niaga* and *Pengadilan Negeri* on the judicial side of proceedings, whether civil or criminal, and ultimately, non-public settlement negotiations between the private parties, which typically follow commencement of a criminal investigation but precede the filing of a civil action. Collecting all the above statistics probably would not resolve the hidden issue visible in the substantively skewed statistics of civil filings in the Commercial Court; namely, why do we effectively only see trademark proceedings in any significant numbers? What happens to patent cases, much less piracy, understood as copyright cases? For preliminary answers recourse was made to members of the Jakarta intellectual property bar and judges for clarification not only on trademark law's apparent success visible in the *Pengadilan Niaga* statistics, but equally important, what accounts for the skewed statistics in terms of why certain kinds of cases are not visible there. This is the classic problem of explaining the mystery of the 'dog that did not bark'.

Hidden institutional frameworks as limitations

The Indonesian intellectual property bar is a relatively small group of specialized practitioners, who typically are well-schooled enough in underlying IPR law questions that both the judiciary and IPR lawyers stress how *Pengadilan Niaga* judges often rely on their opinions of the applicable law in deciding cases. Some intellectual property case litigants in the Commercial Court do employ normal, non-specialized litigation counsel, but judges stress that the relatively high quality of specialized practitioner arguments is of great assistance to them in deciding cases. But here distinctions should be drawn also as to how different intellectual property cases are tried, according to whether they involve patent law versus trademark cases.

Both the judiciary and specialized IPR counsel stress that complex intellectual property law matters, such as a patent case, which are largely tried via expert witnesses, are still very difficult for *Pengadilan Niaga* judges to decide owing to their relative complexity, and so these cases are relatively rare (as borne out by the statistics, showing that the Commercial Court overwhelmingly deals with trademark cases that are consistently on the intellectual property law side). Compared to bankruptcy law, however, the judiciary and specialized practitioners have also identified the relatively straightforward nature of intellectual property legal theory as an aid to a decision. It allows cases to be decided typically on doctrinal grounds, as opposed to the problems of judges in the insolvency law area who have to understand economically based concepts like valuation. So one ground for differentiating the *Pengadilan Niaga*'s performance is not really intellectual property versus insolvency law, but rather simple versus complex cases.

The judiciary's positive performance where simpler cases are involved is easily understood, but appraising the complexity of cases does not fully explain the performance of the Commercial Court. This allows us to reflect on an underlying problem with specialized courts that in the judiciary's opinion has continuing special relevance to the *Pengadilan Niaga*. The institutional issue is that Indonesian judges are trained as civil law judges drawing on Dutch models inherited from its colonial past. Meanwhile, much donor assistance for the court system comes from common law countries under rule of law programmes (e.g. Australia or the United States). The difference is that common law judges are typically in their second careers, having first been successful litigators. They enter their judicial systems at a relatively high level and typically stay at a single court. On the other hand, civil law judges typically enter the judiciary straight out of law school and then are rotated through positions of increasing responsibility in several different courts. To adopt a sports analogy, Indonesian judges start in the minor leagues and theoretically advance according to performance, although in practice seniority still rules over ability within the Indonesian judiciary.

There have been repeated efforts since 1998 to introduce non-career judges (meaning lawyers entering the judiciary laterally at a relatively senior level) into the Indonesian judiciary, but most attempts have met with limited success. Instead of attracting the kind of leading lawyers who become judges in common law jurisdictions based upon legal ability, Indonesian non-career judges are seemingly more often office-seekers drawn from a lower level of legal practice. Non-career judges are also supported by the broader Indonesian public, seemingly due, more than anything else, to suspicion of corruption being endemic among career judges This is the judicial mafia or *mafia peradilan* claim, in Indonesian terms (the view that many, if not most, career judges, particularly those who entered the judiciary prior to 1998,[22] are ethically challenged). So, there is an open mismatch between concepts such as specialized courts and the general organization and career paths of the Indonesian judiciary, and attempts to meld common law and civil law institutional approaches have not fully succeeded as a result.

The institutional problem at the *Pengadilan Niaga* level involves what is referred to as the *mutasi* (mutation) system, which is Indonesian judicial shorthand for the typical civil law practice of rotating judges through many different courts as career pattern.[23] Depending upon seniority upon arrival, the typical Commercial Court judge probably does not expect to spend more than 18–42 months at the Court. Conditions at the *Pengadilan Niaga* are considered generally positive (because living in Jakarta or another major city with a Commercial Court branch is more desirable than living in a small provincial city housing with an ordinary court). However, the failure to be transferred beyond the Commercial Court would typically mean that the judge in question would be stopped mid-career from further advancement. So, potential 'high flyers' cannot and do not aspire to remain too long at the Commercial Court.

As a result, the institution of the Commercial Court as a specialized court created its own problems, because most judges are subject to transfer just about the time they develop some degree of expertise in the specialized commercial cases funnelled into the *Pengadilan Niaga*. Thus, one underlying rationale for why simpler (IPR) cases may be better processed reflects the reality that specialized courts without specialized judges are problematic. There is an argument to be made that simpler cases are just easier for any judge to resolve adequately, but the hidden problem is with the concept of concentrated commercial expertise. Donors expended considerable resources training Commercial Court judges, particularly in the insolvency area, immediately following the *Pengadilan Niaga*'s 1998 creation. The problem is that the benefit of the training was largely lost within a relatively short period as the trained judges were rotated out of the *Pengadilan Niaga* under the *mutasi* system. Constantly training new Commercial Court judges to a high standard in specialized substantive areas of law is simply not possible given limited resources.[24] Meanwhile, the current judiciary at the Commercial Court seems to stress prior familiarity with intellectual property law in explaining relatively favourable views of its IPR law performance, and its relatively limited scope compared to insolvency law, given limited resources for continuing judicial education.

To the extent that insolvency law expertise is now concentrated anywhere in Indonesia, it is probably in those law firms involved in significant insolvency matters regularly since 1998. Unlike the intellectual property bar, however, the Indonesian insolvency bar is not a homogeneous group. Serious splits and apparent antipathy exists among leading debtor and creditor lawyers. Recently, a leading lawyer known to represent debtors alleged a conflict of interest against a prominent lawyer who frequently acted for creditors. This was either a 'hardball' litigation strategy, or, alternatively, action premised on personal animosity.[25] Insolvency law is seemingly a more 'rough and tumble' practice than intellectual property law.

Parties' differing character, or why 'the dog did not bark'

Does corruption affect the perception of the Commercial Court's performance? By way of example, some of the most criticized Indonesian cases in the past decade involving suspicion of judicial corruption, arose under the insolvency jurisdiction of the Commercial Court (e.g., the infamous *Manulife* case[26]). In a procedural nicety lost on outsiders, many of these cases involved foreign creditors' bankruptcy petitions, which were changed into voluntary debt compromise proceedings at the behest of local debtors. Involuntary procedures provided that, in theory, a 'voluntary' debt compromise could not be approved over creditors' objections. However, the perceived abusive practice was for fictive creditors to be found who would then outvote foreign creditors to confirm a debt compromise plan providing for minimal creditor recovery (as in the *Panin Overseas* case[27]).

Meanwhile, much judicial-reform energy in the NGO community was, and is, currently expended in Indonesia on court-watch projects – examining judicial decisions with an eye to corruption claims in the context of claims about the so-called judicial mafia.[28] However, the generally positive reception of the Commercial Court's intellectual property law jurisprudence seems to imply that corruption is not an issue, at least under normal circumstances, since cases are perceived as being decided correctly (meaning in accordance with the law). Some theorize that the generally higher quality of the specialized intellectual property bar, linked with the idea that they do not customarily represent just one side in IPR disputes, has led to what Indonesians characterize as more ethical behaviour at the level of legal counsel. However, there are alternate explanations. Voices in the bar complain otherwise about corruption in intellectual property matters beyond the *Pengadilan Niaga*.

Here the focus shifts to the nature of defendants and their behaviour in (mostly trademark law) proceedings before the Commercial Court and parallel explanations for the lack of anti-piracy copyright cases before that same Court (linked with a different characterization of the defendants in such anti-piracy cases). The explanation offered is that the defendants in the trademark cases are largely rational business people who perhaps cut a few corners but view any individual case as typically not about such large amounts of money that a 'win at all costs' approach would be justifiable. This must be understood in opposition to defendants' 'bet the company' view of insolvency proceedings in the Commercial Court *c*. 1998–2003, when losing in bankruptcy would have meant loss of control of their company or business empire. 'Anything goes' was how their attitude was described when involved in judicial insolvency proceedings. Those seeking a negotiated workout or reorganization had already bypassed the courts in favour of such venues as the Jakarta Initiative.[29] The idea was simply that to appropriate a trademark presupposed a certain magnitude of business to do related manufacturing, etc., and so involved a relatively visible defendant as a real business person.

The explanation most commonly offered for IPR cases (largely trademark cases) is that it was simply not worth engaging in expensive corruption payments for the amounts involved. However, that explanation must be understood in conjunction with the chief reason offered for defendants not already settling in private negotiations at the police investigation stage of the prior (trademark) *delik aduan* criminal proceedings which, as already explained, may lead to a civil case in the *Pengadilan Niaga*. The view espoused by practitioners was that the alleged intellectual property infringement was sometimes sufficiently lucrative, so that trademark violators were not willing to settle (and instead tried to continue activity pending a judicial determination). The opinion was also offered that, in the absence of a resolution to their liking, many trademark law plaintiffs (who were often foreign enterprises asserting marks well known on an international basis) would pursue a civil action before the *Pengadilan Niaga* in an attempt to build a reputation for toughness in protecting their marks.[30] But the real corruption problem in intellectual property law practice was claimed to exist at the level of the police.

As noted above, the basic practice in the trademark area saw injured parties first attempting to pressurize those violating their intellectual property via police investigation of a *delik aduan* claim. One technical distinction between Indonesian trademark, copyright and patent law's criminal provisions (under Sections 90–95 of *Law No. 15/2001* on trademarks, Sections 130–35 of *Law No. 14/2001* on patents and Sections 72–73 of *Law No. 19/2002* on copyright) is that the criminal copyright and patent law violations are not *delik aduan*, and so formal prosecution does not require the injured party's authorization. But it is doubtful whether in practice the formal control vested in private parties over the trademark prosecution via the *delik aduan* is decisive. IPR practitioners do not stress the formal *delik aduan* aspect of trademark law, instead pointing to the different nature of defendants in piracy cases, and informal arrangements that render it practically impossible to prosecute criminally those with control over counterfeiting operations. Meanwhile, as noted, patent cases are generally rare, perhaps because of their complexity (also as a reflection of lower technology levels) and because they tend to involve industrial products and processes rather than consumer goods.

The view expressed is that intellectual property counterfeiting operations actually involve the Indonesian equivalent of organized crime, at least insofar as counterfeiting operations were transferred from areas like Hong Kong to Indonesia five to ten years ago as a result of increased anti-piracy police action in Northeast Asia. These 'foreigners' allegedly brought a new *modus operandi*, including ensuring police tolerance if not support for their illegal activities, with the result that it is very difficult to even get the police to undertake actions against them. On the one hand, they do not shy away from organizing counteractions if street-level enforcement actions are undertaken against sellers of pirated DVDs. For example, riots were sparked in the Kota section of Jakarta as the fate of one donor-sponsored IPR protection activity, when mid-level police were inspired to try out their intellectual property protection skills acquired in a just-completed, donor-sponsored course (by confiscating pirated DVDs and similar materials that Jakarta residents know are openly sold on the street in that area). On the other hand, should any major figures be mistakenly taken by the occasional police actions against sellers of counterfeited materials, according to the IPR bar they will be represented by certain lawyers and quickly disappear from any prosecution for IPR piracy.

It is difficult for injured parties owning copyrighted materials to pursue police investigations for two reasons. First, dealing with the police in the criminal justice system is always difficult (the informal levy problem). Additionally, the police may be worried about maintaining public order, and what might happen in the case of a raid, so there will be ample reasons to forego enforcement (the riot problem). Second, the police do not subject major copyright violators to any realistic law enforcement sanctions in a practical sense. In any case, law enforcement's anti-piracy actions traditionally tend to be directed at the street vendor retail level, rather than the sophisticated machinery of counterfeiting at the wholesale production level.

Conversely, injured parties owning copyrighted materials also hardly make use of their ability to bring a civil action for copyright violation directly in the Commercial Court under the very detailed Sections 42 and 56–63 of *Law No. 19/2002* on copyright. So, the apparent explanation for the lack of copyright as opposed to trademark cases in the *Pengadilan Niaga* statistics probably lies more in the nature of the defendants tending towards organized crime at the upper level in piracy cases, versus 'ordinary' business people in trademark cases, rather than the technical issue of any *delik aduan* character of the underlying criminalized intellectual property violation. And if one speaks with Indonesian business association officials about intellectual property compliance questions generally, they are quite explicit, even if they hesitate to explain why, that they can work on negotiating compliance in trademark violation disputes between foreign and domestic businesses, but simply cannot touch the piracy problem.

Exploring insolvency law performance and changes

Understanding insolvency proceedings' development requires understanding changes in parties and practices over time. These proceedings involve not only bankruptcy or liquidation proceedings, but also voluntary debt compromise or weak reorganization proceedings. It is difficult to tell whether 2004–5 donor performance evaluations of the Commercial Court utilizing statistics only from bankruptcy (rather than including also debt compromise statistics) occurred out of ignorance, or conviction that only liquidations mattered for creditors. And as previously noted, initial use of the debt compromise proceedings was often perceived as abusive, since it was typically linked with fictive creditors being used to outvote real (foreign) creditors' opposition to debt compromise plans limiting recovery.

However, that is not the only story. That procedure peaked in 2000, which is clear from the debt compromise statistics. What is less clear is that many of those debt compromises ultimately involved the Indonesian government as a creditor, through its bank restructuring agency (IBRA), or otherwise often involved negotiated workouts in the Jakarta Initiative that amounted to pre-packaged bankruptcies only brought to court at the end of the restructuring process. A quick look at the bankruptcy conversion statistics illustrates the change from earlier abuses (7 of 21 in 2000, or 33 per cent of such filings, were automatically converted to bankruptcy or liquidation proceedings when voluntary debt compromise failed). The bankruptcy or liquidation determination applied as a matter of law if creditors rejected a voluntary debt compromise plan.

What is even more striking is the apparent drop off in voluntary debt compromises post-2000, particularly by 2003–4, which may be why the donor statistics did not include them. But comparing rising bankruptcy or liquidation filings from 2004 forwards, what explains the discrepancy? The explanation lies in substantive bankruptcy law amendments in 2004, which gave voting rights to creditors in voluntary debt compromise proceedings (which they had lacked previously as a matter of Dutch and civil law bankruptcy tradition). That gave (mostly local) secured creditors the power to kill voluntary debt compromises they opposed,[31] which is probably the best explanation for the apparent decrease in voluntary debt compromises. In fact, they typically offered all creditors lower recoveries compared to liquidation. As creditor positions were strengthened, the voluntary debt compromises decreased.

Recently a new phenomenon has appeared on the scene, namely, voluntary debt compromises initiated by debtors as initial filing (as opposed to the traditional procedural posture post-1998 that debtors typically used: the voluntary debt compromise procedure in opposition to creditors filing bankruptcy or liquidation proceedings). Debtors are apparently using the voluntary debt compromise procedure's temporary bar on even secured creditor enforcement, that is to say, they are using it tactically for the Indonesian equivalent of a United States bankruptcy law temporary stay order. But things had changed already at a certain level by 2003–4, since the rough comparison of creditor success rates in bankruptcy proceedings 1998–2002 typically approached 33 per cent, while creditor success rates climbed almost to 50 per cent by 2003. So, just as donors left the Commercial Court for dead, insolvency proceedings results also began to improve.

Revisiting what the Commercial Court's insolvency versus intellectual property law performance tells us about newer courts in Asia

I now revisit the question of how to account for the perceived vastly different Commercial Court performance in the insolvency and intellectual property spheres. The apparent donor view in 2004–5 was misplaced, to the extent that it assumed that the *Pengadilan Niaga* itself (meaning its judges and the Court as an institution) was responsible for the visible differences in performance. Instead, the Commercial Court statistics only make sense when properly interpreted in the broader context of what is going on with substantive law, the nature of litigants, the police and other factors. Nonetheless, there is a tendency for any apparent improvement in court performance to be played up for political or other purposes by donors, which actually masks what is going on with dispute resolution and particular segments of the Indonesian legal system (as witnessed by our analysis surrounding IPR cases, including the problem of the relative absence of patent and copyright cases as the 'dog that did not bark'). But what can we say more broadly about the expectations of newer courts in Asia, if we do try to generalize from our understanding of what is actually happening with the Indonesian Commercial Court?

The first caution is one of proper orientation: that lawyers looking at courts have a tendency to view them formalistically as free-standing institutions, while their function (at least in the commercial setting) is really dispute settlement. Further, they exist in context, as part of a legal system, rather than being free-standing institutions. The problem is that dispute settlement is more properly viewed as the provenance of sociologists or anthropologists, while lawyers usually pose their inquiry in terms of court character and performance (rather than in terms of broader dispute resolution). In effect, the lawyers considering these issues were arguably asking the wrong question initially.

Those familiar with the Indonesian legal system post-1998 would recognize that important changes have occurred in the behaviour of (Commercial) Court users during the past ten years or so.[32] At a very basic level, Indonesian courts still may not be highly efficient, much less paragons of virtue in rule of law terms. However, they are now viewed as having a role to play by potential local users. At the level of commercial dispute settlement generally, the upper level of Indonesian business is still suspicious of courts, but thinks that they must be taken into account because business counterparts may use them for tactical purposes. So, whereas pre-1998 business people would not even think of going to court, now the courts are regarded as a tactical option, albeit mostly as a trap for the unwary. The problem is that this is really separate from any inference that courts like the *Pengadilan Niaga* are on a path of rapid improvement and so the rule of law has triumphed. And it also infers that the courts may still not be viewed really as the primary forum for dispute resolution by potential litigants, notwithstanding received wisdom in terms of donor-sponsored rule of law efforts. The hidden issue is whether users in practice approach courts instrumentally, as opposed to entertaining idealistic assumptions embedded in rule of law discourse.

There was some improvement in performance apparent in the Commercial Court intellectual property law area as opposed to the insolvency area by 2001–4. Here the differing nature of the cases and litigants seems important. Abstracting at a relatively high level, it would seem that where cases are of relatively low value, and are not viewed as difficult in substantive doctrinal terms, the Commercial Court may be able to deal with them. Problematically, anything that looks too much like a complex commercial dispute may be beyond current judicial capacity. Organizational aspects of the judicial system render it unlikely that this can be changed just by pouring more money into training at the *Pengadilan Niaga* as an isolated court.

So, what has been gained to date in establishing a specialized court specifically for complex commercial disputes? It appears this question can only be analysed by looking at the (potential) litigants. If they are ordinary business people and the case is not particularly important to them in business terms, they will not be tempted as rational business people to pull out all the stops, particularly in terms of potential corruption (because such a case is simply not worth it). To that extent, the Commercial Court seems more to resemble a voluntary arbitration-like forum rather than being pictured as a coercive judicial institution implementing the rule of law as commonly understood. This is also consistent with the view that in the insolvency area, the Commercial Court may increasingly be a tactical venue for disputes between domestic creditors and debtors, but arguably is still not a coercive judicial institution, the formal existence of which is assumed by rule of law views.

On the other hand, if potential defendants are not ordinary business people the cases probably do not reach the court in the first place, because rational business people would not waste time or money trying to bring them to court. The courts themselves are not the only locus of dispute settlement, and the problem of cases not being brought points to continuing concerns about broader legal system performance. But the practical difficulty is what to do when faced with the argument that all segments of the legal system need significant upgrading in Indonesian terms before any individual one works. This is the problem of context, that courts do not exist in isolation, much as we also implicitly emphasize that dispute resolution is not solely, or even primarily, the province of courts (as may be implied often in rule of law discussions).

One common answer might seem an argument that non-judicial dispute resolution only works with the implicit threat of litigation. However, in the case of the Commercial Court, it would still be the case that the non-judicial dispute settlement mechanisms proceed via pressure on the criminal justice side, rather than follow ordinary civil litigation. Certainly, the trademark case experience suggests that piggybacking on the criminal justice system avoids hidden problems of enforcement anyway. So, on the intellectual property side, the basic dispute resolution approach still seems to rely more on police pressure that is steered by private parties under the *delik aduan* in criminal trademark cases, rather than by private parties litigating civil disputes. Post-2004, the picture is still too new to be completely clear. Otherwise, patent and copyright cases are few and far between as a result of general problems with complex cases, corruption issues outside the courts, and the sociology of different kinds of defendants, producing the low volume of such cases in the Commercial Court.

On the one hand, the general rise in insolvency filings compared with the fall in voluntary debt compromise proceedings during the past two to three years allows an inference that giving secured creditors a vote in voluntary debt compromise proceedings in the 2004 bankruptcy law amendments has affected practice. If substantive law changes like that apparently have such a clear effect on outcomes, local court users seemingly think that at least sometimes going to (insolvency) court is now a viable tactic, although a wide variety of caveats may still apply. On the other hand, the still existing voluntary debt compromise proceedings reflect changes in debtor statistics, to the extent that local debtors are now initiating voluntary debt compromise proceedings, at least through the preliminary stage of proceedings (but apparently for the tactical benefit of a stay to stop secured creditors claiming their collateral, as in the *Ciputra Development* case[33]).

The difference in perspective between formalistic treatments of courts under common rule of law approaches and what we see here is the difference in viewing courts as truth-seeking fora where disputes are judged, versus courts being used, more often than not, as ancillary levers for a dispute resolution process anchored outside the courts. The characteristic is the parties' sometime use of the state in the form of its criminal justice system as a lever, in a still largely private dispute resolution process, versus Western lawyers' public-law-influenced view of courts as places for the neutral determination of rights (where enforcement is typically assumed).

This situation may itself reflect a hidden institutional bias on the part of donors, under which courts are often viewed *sub silentio* as developed for public law purposes in terms of establishing restraints on the state's reach against citizens (the human rights view of what courts do), while recipient countries may seek specifically targeted courts such as the Commercial Court as part of economic development efforts (the view that courts exist to settle economic disputes between private parties). In Asia, every country seemingly aspires to the creation of something like an effective commercial court as part of economic development efforts, and it now constitutes part of the standard institutional development playbook. By opposition, the number of Asian jurisdictions seeking to establish functioning constitutional courts as part of the standard governance rubric is rather more limited. This distinction would argue for a more nuanced view of the true roles and expectations concerning new courts in Asia.

Notes

1. See D. Linnan, "Commercial Law Enforcement in Indonesia: The *Manulife* Case," in *Indonesia: Law and Society*, ed. T. Lindsey (Sydney: Federation Press, 2008), 596.
2. See, for example, J. Langbein, "Land Without Plea Bargaining: How the Germans Do It," *Michigan Law Review* 78 (1979): 204; J. Langbein, "Understanding the Short History of Plea Bargaining," *Law and Society Review* 13 (1979): 261; J. Langbein, "Torture and Plea Bargaining," *University Chicago Law Review* 46 (1978): 4; J. Langbein and L. Weinreb, "Comparative Criminal Procedure: 'Myth' and Reality," *Yale Law Journal* 87 (1978): 1549; J. Langbein, "Controlling Prosecutorial Discretion in Germany," *University Chicago Law Review* 41 (1974): 439. The plea bargaining controversy, which engaged American comparative law scholarship particularly in the 1970s, is a particularly good model for understanding why interpreting courts' success or failure in terms of filings or even disposition statistics taken out of context can be extremely misleading. The problem there was understanding how a legal system's broader problems or incentives can skew apparently neutral statistics, which themselves become a subject of politically motivated debate. In the end, examination of both plea bargaining and the Commercial Court is less doctrinally oriented in lawyers' terms than bordering on criminology as an empirical exercise.

3. These particular statistics are draw from Economic Growth Office of USAID/Indonesia, *Scope of Work: Specialized Court Reform and Strengthening Activity (SCORSA)* (Jakarta: Economic Growth Office of USAID/Indonesia, 2005), 8. There are some small discrepancies compared with the more detailed and recent statistics from the *Pengadilan Niaga* logbooks reviewed in this chapter, but the discrepancies are minor, relating primarily to dispositions. The more detailed statistics presented here also break out a variety of dispositions lumped together in the earlier statistics employed by *SCORSA*.
4. See, for example, D. Linnan, "Insolvency Law and Institutions in Indonesia," in *Insolvency Law in East Asia*, ed. R. Tomasic (Aldershot, UK: Ashgate, 2006); D. Linnan, "Insolvency Reform and the Indonesian Financial Crisis," *Bulletin of Indonesian Economic Studies* 35 (1999): 107; D. Linnan, *Indonesian Bankruptcy Policy and Reform: Reconciling Efficiency and Economic Nationalism* (Singapore: Institute of Southeast Asian Studies, 1999).
5. In fact, Indonesian insolvencies were largely resolved in non-judicial proceedings like the Jakarta Initiative, if at all, based upon the debtors' perception that speedy resolution offered its own advantages in areas like renewed access to international capital markets. Linnan, "Insolvency Law and Institutions in Indonesia," 360–61. Judicial filings were pursued largely in cases of debtors unwilling to settle their debts, although 'pre-packaged' filings were also possible later.
6. See Linnan, "Insolvency Law and Institutions in Indonesia," 359.
7. *Ferrari S. P. A.*, Putusan No. 04/Merek/2001/PN.Niaga.Jkt.Pst, reproduced in 1 *Himpunan Putusan-Putusan Pengadilan Niaga dalam Perkara Merek* (Compilation of Decisions by the Commercial Court on Cases involving Trademarks) (Jakarta: Tatanusa, 2002), 97.
8. *Balenciaga*, Putusan No. 66/Merek/2004/PN.Niaga.Jkt.Pst, reproduced in 10 *Himpunan Putusan-Putusan Pengadilan Niaga Dalam Perkara Merek* (Compilation of Decisions by the Commercial Court on Cases involving Trademarks) (Jakarta: Tatnusa, 2007), 239.
9. Technically speaking, Indonesian law distinguishes between deletion and cancellation, with the difference being that *cancellation* involves filing an action in the Commercial Court under Articles 4–6 of *Law No. 15/2001* on trademarks, proof of the prior registrant's bad faith, similarity of marks for goods or services of the same kind, or an otherwise unregisterable mark by the owner of an unregistered mark within five years of the original registration, after the said owner submits a registration request to the Directorate General for Intellectual Property as a independent United States Patent & Trademark Office (PTO) equivalent. *Deletion* on the other hand can be done on the Directorate General for Intellectual Property's own initiative, or upon application of the mark owner, or by a third party's application to the Commercial Court based upon non-use under Articles 61(2) and 63 of *Law No. 15/2001* on trademarks, whether involving similar or non-similar goods (as in the *Ferrari* case above). Deletion may be perceived as easier because no distinction is made between trademark usage for similar or dissimilar goods (because non-use is the underlying concept). Non-use is a term of art because token sales are not recognized.
10. So-called *Privatanklagedelikte* are characterized in continental European doctrinal terms by the protected legal interests (*Rechtsgueter*) chiefly concerning individual rather than 'public interests', with the result that prosecution is not mandatory (recalling the *Legalitaetsprinzip*, or mandatory prosecution as the default rule). The concept commonly encompasses equally criminal offences at the level of insult, but also certain IPR offences in the German-speaking part of the civil law world. Presumably, they entered Indonesian law via Dutch sources.
11. As witnessed by the SCORSA RFP itself, which this chapter takes as a point of departure in looking at Commercial Court statistics.

12. Opened for signature 15 April 1994, 1869 UNTS 299 (entered into force 1 January 1995). The *TRIPs Agreement* reflected industrialized countries' determination to create an enforcement mechanism for intellectual property violations via trade law, given their economic interests. It was in that sense a *quid pro quo* for developing countries' focused on the export of goods, which pursued further liberalization of trade in goods during the Uruguay Round as a means to enable an export-led development strategy.
13. As an economic matter, the economic interests of deeply underwater debtors resembled options more than common stock. See Linnan, "Insolvency Reform and the Indonesian Financial Crisis," 113–14. This is important to the extent that debtors conceived of insolvency proceedings as a threat to their businesses' very existence. As a result, many elected for non-cooperation and pursued all available means to vitiate judicial insolvency proceedings. Those who saw a business advantage in settling their debts instead tended to pursue voluntary negotiations in fora such as the Jakarta Initiative.
14. Meanwhile, the failure of insolvency law in practical terms saddled the Indonesian government with large debts under which it suffers to this day (because contrary to public perceptions most debts were owed by domestic debtors to domestic creditors, which the Indonesian state largely assumed through responsibility for the insolvent banking system, see Linnan, "Insolvency Law and Institutions in Indonesia").
15. As discussed subsequently, however, current IPR litigants before the *Pengadilan Niaga* are not all represented by legal counsel who specialize in intellectual property law.
16. These included *Law No. 19/2002* on copyright, *Law No. 15/2001* on trademarks, *Law No. 14/2001* on, *Law No. 30/2001* on trade secrets, *Law No. 32/2000* on integrated circuit design and *Law No. 31/2000* on industrial design. Legislation was enacted also in this timeframe to protect biodiversity in the form of *Law No. 29/2000* on protection of (biological) riches, but it would not normally be considered intellectual property legislation for private party purposes.
17. See Linnan, *Indonesian Bankruptcy Policy and Reform: Reconciling Efficiency and Economic Nationalism.*
18. It would appear that the short-fused deadlines were more often followed in the IPR than insolvency areas, since it is generally admitted that courts often simply ignored such (unrealistic) deadlines as a 270-day case disposition deadline in the insolvency area.
19. The problem of informal police levies and corruption is a much broader topic, but for our purposes it suffices to note that participating in such an IPR criminal investigation is a money-making activity for the police, so that they have all the right incentives to pursue such investigations actively, even while disposition of the eventual criminal case is subject to the private party's control due to the *delikt aduan* character of the alleged criminal act.
20. As a formal matter, Indonesian law recognizes potential criminal law sanctions for directors and commissioners in insolvencies, following the civil law pattern. However, the criminal law sanctions are essentially never applied in insolvency proceedings. See Linnan, "Insolvency Law and Institutions in Indonesia," 371–2.
21. It would seem that the *delik aduan* case might still have to be dismissed to proceed in the Commercial Court to escape the general problem under Indonesian procedural law that civil cases should be delayed pending resolution of a criminal case covering the same subject matter. Presumably, an injured party must make a choice, but the hidden issue addressed subsequently is best characterized as why the private party settlement negotiations under pressure of criminal sanctions failed to reach a result.
22. See, for example, The RAB Experience, "Judicial Reform in Indonesia," http://therabexperience.blogspot.com/2008/09/judicial-reform-in-indonesia.html.
23. The *mutasi* system was itself the subject of much discussion post-1998, mostly focused on judicial independence claims that led to responsibility for judges'

promotion and training being moved out of the Ministry of Justice and into the Supreme Court or *Makamah Agung*. But the *mutasi* system remains in force.

24. This mismatch results in part from the unwillingness or inability to organize or fund system-wide judicial training, with donors instead trying to produce a model functioning court by investing disproportionate resources in the chosen court. That represents alternatively a lack of understanding about differences between the career patterns and training of civil law as opposed to common law judiciary, resource limitations, or otherwise politics in terms of choosing a single court of special interest to the donor. This is presumably part of the background for claims that the *Pengadilan Niaga* is an IPR success story. But the pitfalls of general judicial reform in Indonesia exceed the limited scope of this chapter addressing special issues in the *Pengadilan Niaga* context.
25. The reference is to leading commercial lawyer and human rights activist, Todung Mulya Lubis, who was the target of well-known bankruptcy lawyer, Hotman Paris Hutapea, see "Mulya Lubis diberhentikan," (Mulya Lubis Dismissed) *Kompas Online*, May 17, 2008, http://cetak.kompas.com/read/xml/2008/05/17/01322470/mulya.lubis.diberhentikan; "Todung Lubis, Hotman Hutapea, Otto Hasibuan," *BlogBerita.net*, May 27, 2008, http://blogberita.net/2008/05/27/todung-lubis-hotman-hutapea-otto-hasibuan/; Mathew Moore, "Hotman's World of Smoke and Mirrors," *The Age*, July 9, 2005, http://www.theage.com.au/news/general/hotmans-world-of-smoke-and-mirrors/2005/07/08/1120704552967.html; Wayne Arnold, "International Business; An Advocate for Indonesia's Debtors," *New York Times*, July 6, 1999, http://query.nytimes.com/gst/fullpage.html?res = 9E04E7D6113DF935A35754C0A96F958260&sec = &spon = &pagewanted = all.
26. See Linnan, "Commercial Law Enforcement in Indonesia: The *Manulife* Case".
27. See Linnan, "Insolvency Law and Institutions in Indonesia," 358.
28. For example, Masyrakat Pemantau Peradilan Indonesia (MAPPI), or the Indonesian Judicial Watch Society, is based at the University of Indonesia's Faculty of Law. See content at http://www.pemantauperadilan.com. Similarly, Gadjah Mada University's Center for Anti-corruption Research or *PuSKAT Korupsi* is located in the UGM Faculty of Law and focuses in part on judicial corruption; see Irawaty Wardany, "Guest Speaker's Forum: Corruptors Buy Time to Delay Corruption Court Law," *The Jakarta Post*, October 20, 2008.
29. See Linnan, "Insolvency Law and Institutions in Indonesia," 360–1.
30. In fact, there are at least four distinct categories of cases visible in the ten volumes of *Pengadilan Niaga* trademark cases published as of mid-2008. The first involves Western enterprises typically asserting protection of consumer product trademarks, as with the previously noted *Ferrari* and *Balenciaga* cases. Initially, these represented a very significant majority of the reported cases. The second largest group of cases involved non-Indonesian Asian enterprises asserting protection for what might be regarded as pan-Asian brands, as with the *100 Plus Power* case, Putusan No. 11/Merek/2004/PN.Niaga.Jkt.Pst, reproduced in 8 *Himpunan Putusan-Putusan Pengadilan Niaga dalam Perkara Merek* (Compilation of Decisions by the Commercial Court on Cases involving Trademarks) (Jakarta: Tatanusa, 2006), 107 (Singapore company Frazer and Neave Limited's isotonic drink). They are a significant and still-growing group involving trademarks for both consumer and industrial goods, including also People's Republic of China-based trademarks, but still lag behind Western trademarks in the number of reported cases. The third largest group of cases involve a small but still growing group of domestic consumer product trademarks, as with the *So Klin* case, PT Wings Surya, Putusan No. 13/Merek/2003/PN.Niaga.Jkt.Pst, reproduced in 4 *Himpunan Putusan-Putusan Pengadilan Niaga dalam Perkara Merek* (Compilation of Decisions by the Commercial Court on Cases involving Trademarks) (Jakarta: Tatanusa, 2005), 215 (So Klin detergent, perhaps Indonesia's most popular domestic detergent brand). The fourth, final and smallest

group of the reported cases involve services, often involving educational or similar institutions with some foreign connection, as with the *Gandhi School* case, Putusan No. 26/Merek/2002/PN.Niaga.Jkt.Pst, reproduced in 3 *Himpunan Putusan-Putusan Pengadilan Niaga dalam Prekara Merek* (Compilation of Decision by the Commercial Court on Cases involving Trademarks) (Jakarta: Tatanusa, 2004), 153 (involving English language international school operated by the expat Indian community in Jakarta).

31. Procedural aspects make things a bit more complicated still, since the 2004 bankruptcy law amendments do not provide for a separate class vote for secured creditors. Instead, they vote together with unsecured creditors in a single class, so that secured creditors only enjoy 'veto' power if they constitute a sufficiently large portion of the class. The problem has already arisen of divergent secured and unsecured creditor interests, since on a technical level liquidation in bankruptcy commonly means that the going concern value of the business is lost to unsecured creditors (as compared to corporate reorganizations where the problems of a 'fire sale' of assets are avoided). So secured creditors are comfortable seeking liquidation as long as their own collateral covers the value of their secured claim, even if it leads to bigger losses at the level of unsecured creditors (but secured creditors also count as unsecured creditors to the extent their claims exceed the value of the collateral). There is simply no cram down or similar provision under current Indonesian bankruptcy law to force secured creditors to leave their collateral in the hands of reorganized debtors after the expiration of the 270-day stay period applicable to Indonesian law's form of voluntary debt reorganizations.
32. For broader purposes, we note that public law courts are established typically more with a view to binding the government itself under various views of the rule of law (e.g. a constitutional court). This chapter concerns only what are essentially civil law disputes between private parties, but the question would be to what extent a government might regard substantial restraints on its actions on the public law side to be more like 'bet the company' litigation on the insolvency side, which the *Pengadilan Niaga* is generally regarded as not having successfully addressed, as opposed to not terribly important trademark litigation which it could successfully address. So the problem is that the inference that a court like the *Pengadilan Niaga* may now be able to function in substantively simple, low value cases may simply not carry over to the higher stakes public law side.
33. *PT Ciputra Development Tbk*, Putusan No. 02/PKPU/2005/PN.Niaga.Jkt.Pst reproduced in 19 *Himpunan Putusan-Putusan Pengadilan Niaga Dalam Perkara Kepailitan* (Jakarta: Tatanusa, 2008), 319.

Part II

Introducing intellectual property courts in Asia

4 The Intellectual Property High Court of Japan

Shigenori Matsui

Introduction

On 1 April 2005, Japan established a new court: the Intellectual Property High Court (IPHC). Although established within the Tokyo High Court, its independence is apparent from its unique name and independent status inside the hierarchy of judicial courts. This was the first time that the government, during its 60 years of post-war history under the *Constitution of Japan* (*Constitution*), established a court specializing in resolving specific types of legal issues, aside from the Family Court.[1]

The establishment of the IPHC is part of the post-2000 judicial reform taking place in Japan. It is also a result of the call for the introduction of a judicial system by which more effective protection of intellectual property can be afforded.

This chapter will outline the judicial structure in Japan, and trace the historical background for the establishment of the IPHC. The chapter will also examine the organization and jurisdiction of the IPHC and some of its noteworthy decisions. Furthermore, the chapter will evaluate the establishment of the IPHC against its stated goals. Although an assessment of the IPHC may seem premature, at this stage, it proves to be a useful exercise, as I shall argue.

The judicial system

Article 76 of the *Constitution* enacted in 1946 provides that '[t]he whole judicial power is vested in a Supreme Court and in such inferior courts as are established by law',[2] and that '[n]o extraordinary tribunal shall be established, nor shall any organ or agency of the Executive be given final judicial power'.[3]

Therefore, with the establishment of the Supreme Court, the Diet has discretion to establish lower courts. Yet, the prohibition on the establishment of the extraordinary tribunal prevents the Diet from establishing special courts outside of the hierarchy, which is under the leadership of the Supreme Court. This prohibition was inserted into the *Constitution* based on experience with the former *Meiji Constitution*. Under the *Meiji Constitution*, the judicial courts were supposed to exercise judicial power in the name of the Emperor. However, the judicial power was defined as a power to adjudicate on civil and criminal matters only, and was to exclude administrative cases. With respect to the exercise of administrative power, a citizen can file an objection to the Administrative Court. The Administrative Court was thus believed to be the administrative organ, as its power of adjudicating administrative cases was perceived as administrative and not civil. A citizen could not file a suit over the exercise of administrative power in the judicial courts, or file an appeal from the Administrative Court to the Supreme Court of Judicature, the supreme judicial court at the time. Moreover, there was only one Administrative Court in the entire country, and citizens could file objections based on listed grounds only. The availability of legal redress against the improper exercise of administrative power was severely restricted. In addition, there was the Imperial House Court, which had jurisdiction on matters within the Imperial House, and the Court Martial which had jurisdiction on crimes committed by military personnel. There was no way to appeal to the Supreme Court of Judicature from either of these courts.

The *Constitution* attempted to change the above-mentioned system. As a result, the judicial power in the *Constitution* is generally believed to extend to all legal issues, including civil, criminal, as well as administrative cases. The *Constitution* explicitly prohibited the establishment of an extraordinary court, and any organ or agency of the executive branch from receiving final judicial power. Therefore, the establishment of the Administrative Court, the Imperial House Court, or Court Martial, which is not subject to the jurisdiction of the Supreme Court, is prohibited.

The Diet passed the 1947 *Judicial Organization Act* and established eight High Courts and 50 District Courts as well as 438 Summary Courts. The hierarchy of judicial systems in Japan is as follows.[4] The District Court is the court of general jurisdiction, and if the parties are not satisfied with the decision of the District Court, they can appeal to the High Court. If the parties are still dissatisfied with the decision of the High Court, they can file an appeal to the Supreme Court. The reasons for appeal to the Supreme Court are limited and often the Supreme Court rejected appeals on the ground that the reason for appeal was not appropriate. The Summary Court has jurisdiction over small claim civil cases and criminal cases involving petty offenses. If the parties are not satisfied with the decision of the Summary Court, they can appeal to the District Court, and then to the High Court.

The only exception to this general hierarchy was the Family Court. The 1947 *Judicial Organization Act* established 50 Family Courts alongside the District Courts and gave them jurisdiction on civil cases of a domestic nature, juvenile delinquency cases and child protection cases.[5] The status of the Family Court was subsequently challenged before the Supreme Court. It was asserted that the Family Court was an 'extraordinary tribunal' prohibited by the *Constitution*. Yet, the Supreme Court of Japan upheld the constitutionality of the Family Court, noting that the *Constitution* merely prohibited the establishment of the court independent and outside of the hierarchy and control of the Supreme Court of Japan.[6] The Family Court was established as a lower court, and its decisions can be challenged before the High Court, and ultimately before the Supreme Court.

The Supreme Court thus held that the Family Court was not an 'extraordinary tribunal' as prohibited by the *Constitution*.

Establishment of the IPHC[7]

Special treatment of intellectual property cases began in November 1950, when a civil litigation special division (fifth special division) was created inside the Tokyo High Court. Since the Tokyo High Court handles many different cases, it has established divisions consisting of four judges (currently, there are 24 civil litigation divisions and 12 criminal litigation divisions) and hears a case by the panel of three judges of one of its divisions. This special division was created in order to deal with patent cases and appellate cases involving intellectual property. This became necessary when the *Patent Act* was amended in 1948, which gave the Tokyo High Court exclusive jurisdiction over suits seeking revocation of patent adjudication by the Japan Patent Office (JPO). However, the Tokyo High Court assigned these cases to one of the ordinary civil litigation divisions instead of the special division. In 1953, the sixth civil litigation division was thus assigned to deal with intellectual property cases. Thereafter, the thirteenth, eighteenth and third civil litigation divisions were similarly assigned to adjudicate intellectual property cases. On 1 April 2004, the names of these divisions were changed to the first, second, third, and fourth 'intellectual property divisions', and a new grand panel consisting of five judges was created as the sixth intellectual property special division, in accordance with an amendment made to the *Code of Civil Procedure*.

In April 2005, these divisions were reorganized into the IPHC consisting of one to four ordinary divisions and the grand panel special division. The noteworthy aspect of the IPHC is that it was established inside the Tokyo High Court, even though it has a separate name and organization. It is not, therefore, a new court wholly independent from the existing court hierarchy.

Intellectual property cases, especially patent cases, are believed to necessitate special treatment, because of the technicality involved in these cases. That was one of the reasons why the Tokyo High Court set up a special division to deal with such cases in 1950. The Tokyo District Court similarly set up a special division for intellectual property cases in 1961, and the Osaka District Court followed suit in 1964. The Osaka High Court similarly established a special division for intellectual property cases in 1990.

However, the number of lawsuits involving intellectual property grew rapidly.[8] It was pointed out that the adjudication of intellectual property cases in Japan takes too much time,[9] and a more effective judicial regime to adjudicate such claims was needed. It is often claimed that if it takes more than five or six years to resolve a patent infringement case, the patent would be worthless because speedy judicial protection is vital for patents. This criticism was especially fuelled by the growing concern that the progress of technological innovations would suffer if there were no adequate protection of intellectual property. Pro-patent lawyers thus called for the establishment of an intellectual property high court similar to the Court of Appeal for the Federal Circuit in the United States.[10] In June 2001, these criticisms led the Council for Judicial Reform, which was assigned the task of proposing specific measures to be adopted in order to strengthen the judicial system in Japan, to call for comprehensive strengthening of the judicial system that handles intellectual property cases in its final report.[11]

The government then decided to implement a policy that promotes technology development by providing more comprehensive protection of intellectual property rights. Prime Minister Junichirou Koizumi made his intention of protecting intellectual property rights clear to the nation during his address before the Diet in February 2002.[12] The government then decided to establish the Strategic Council for Promotion of Intellectual Property, headed by Prime Minister Koizumi.[13] The Council published the Strategic Outline for Promotion of Intellectual Property in July 2002,[14] in which Japan proclaimed to aspire to be a 'country built on protection of intellectual property' and indicated that the establishment of a patent court was necessary. In December 2002, the *Basic Act for Protection of Intellectual Property*[15] was enacted,which implemented the government's policies for the protection of intellectual property rights. The Act took effect on 1 March 2003. At the same time, the Strategic Headquarters for Protection of Intellectual Property was established inside the Cabinet Office.[16] The Headquarters then published a report on its plan to facilitate the protection of intellectual property rights in July 2003.[17] The report also called for the establishment of an intellectual property high court as a means to facilitate the adjudication of intellectual property cases, as well as to showcase the government's commitment to protect intellectual property rights.[18]

The Headquarters for Promotion of Judicial Reform, which was established in 2001 to follow up on the final report of the Council for Judicial Reform,[19] set up a study group on intellectual property litigation.[20] Based upon the discussions in the study group, the Cabinet submitted a bill to the Diet and subsequently the Diet passed the *Act to Establish the Intellectual Property High Court* (*IPHC Act*) in June 2004.[21] The *IPHC Act* took effect on 1 April 2005, and the IPHC went into operation the same day.

It is noteworthy that during the debate on the establishment of the IPHC, the most heated discussions revolved around whether to establish the IPHC as a ninth High Court, or to establish it as a branch inside the Tokyo High Court. Looking at the past experiences of the United States, which established the Court of Appeal for the Federal Circuit to deal with intellectual property cases, it would have made sense to establish an independent high court. However, the establishment of the IPHC as the ninth High Court was opposed, mainly because of the difficulty in limiting jurisdiction, which would cause unnecessary jurisdictional disputes.[22] This was the fundamental reason why the IPHC was established as a branch inside the Tokyo High Court.[23]

Organization of the IPHC[24]

Although the IPHC was established as a branch of the Tokyo High Court,[25] it has a distinctive name, its own Chief Judge, its conference of judges and its own administrative office. It is therefore a unique, independent body inside the Japanese judicial system.[26]

The IPHC consists of four divisions; in addition, there is the grand panel, which consists of five judges. The first division is staffed with a Chief Judge in addition to two other judges. The remaining three divisions are staffed with five judges.[27] Each case will be heard by the panel of three judges of one of the four divisions. The total number of judges in the IPHC is currently 18. These judges will hear exclusively intellectual property cases. The current Chief Judge is Judge Tomokatsu Tsukahara.

The grand panel was introduced in order to provide authoritative decisions on controversial issues and to provide stability and predictability. The grand panel consists of a Chief Judge (head judge of the first division), three head judges from the second to fourth divisions and one judge who is specifically assigned to the case. The Chief Judge presides over the panel. The grand panel sits when a case contains important issues, and therefore it is appropriate to provide a unified opinion of the Court without delay. Only civil appellate cases on patent rights, utility model rights, the rights of the layout design of integrated circuits, copyrights on program work and administrative cases on patent rights can be heard by the grand panel.[28] The grand panel cannot thus hear the regular copyright or trademark infringement cases.

In addition to judges, judicial research officials assigned by the Court investigate technical matters relevant to intellectual property. They can question parties during the trial, when an order to do so is granted by the presiding judge.[29] Currently, there are 11 judicial research officials working in the IPHC. Most of them are former adjudicators of the JPO,[30] but one is appointed from among patent attorneys. Once a case is filed, one judicial research official will be assigned to the case. The most senior judicial research official, customarily called the head judicial research official, makes an assignment based on the expertise of the judicial research officials: four of them have expertise in mechanical fields, four in chemical fields and three in electrical fields.

A unique system utilized by the IPHC is the appointment of technical advisors on intellectual property issues.[31] They are appointed by the Supreme Court as part-time officials. Most of these technical advisors are university professors or researchers who are expected to offer expert knowledge on intellectual property to the Court. Technical advisors can participate by giving expert opinions during preparation for trial, the trial itself, an evidentiary hearing or through participation in settlement procedures.[32] Yet, in most cases, technical advisors only participate in the proceeding of the IPHC in order to give an expert opinion during preparation of trial or the trial itself.[33]

Jurisdiction of the IHPC[34]

The IPHC has exclusive jurisdiction on administrative suits over the adjudication decisions of the JPO, which was originally assigned to the jurisdiction of the Tokyo High Court.[35]

According to the *Patent Act*, the head of the JPO orders the examiner to review the patent application.[36] The examiner must grant the patent unless he or she finds some reasons for refusing to do so.[37] The patent will take effect upon registration,[38] and the patent holder can seek damages as well as an injunction against any infringement.[39] The *Patent Act* allows the applicant for a patent to file an objection to the examiner's rejection of the patent application.[40] The *Patent Act* also allows anyone to file an objection to a patent grant made by the JPO seeking invalidation.[41] A panel of administrative law judges would hear such objections.[42] One can also file a lawsuit in the Court to challenge the decision of the panel.[43] The decision by the JPO to grant a patent can be invalidated by an objection and subsequent litigation seeking revocation of such a grant. Unless the patent is declared invalid by the Court, one cannot invoke the invalidity of the patent as a defence in an infringement case. That used to be the principle. However, the Supreme Court substantially modified this principle and allowed a defendant in an infringement case to claim the invalidity of a patent when the patent is clearly invalid.[44] Furthermore, a 2004 amendment to the *Patent Act* explicitly recognized this defence as a limitation on the exercise of patent rights, and removed the clarity requirement.[45] As a result, the invalidity of a patent can now be invoked as a defence in infringement cases.[46]

The IPHC also has exclusive jurisdiction over civil appellate cases on patent rights, utility model rights, the rights of the layout design of integrated circuits and copyrights on program work.[47] In short, the IPHC hears all appeals from decisions of the District Court all over Japan in these matters.[48]

The IPHC also has jurisdiction over civil appellate cases on trademarks, copyright (other than the authors' copyright on program work), and infringement of trade interests by unfair competition, that arise out of the decisions by the District Courts, which are under the jurisdiction of the Tokyo High Court.[49] The IPHC thus has the same jurisdiction compared to other High Courts on appellate cases in these matters.

Finally, the IPHC has jurisdiction over civil and administrative appellate cases which require special knowledge on intellectual property issues arising out of the decisions of the District Courts, for which the Tokyo High Court has appellate jurisdiction.[50]

The IPHC thus does not have exclusive jurisdiction on all intellectual property cases. Yet, because its jurisdiction covers cases against the JPO, civil appellate cases involving the patent rights, and civil appellate cases involving intellectual property cases arising in the Tokyo area (where most of the head offices of the major Japanese companies are located), the IPHC hears the great majority of intellectual property cases in Japan.[51]

Court Proceeding[52]

Traditionally, administrative cases brought to the High Court as the court of first instance on trademark or design rights, as well as the appeals from District Courts on civil or administrative cases, are heard at oral proceedings in the court-room by a panel of three judges from the first date of the trial. On the other hand, cases relating to patents or utility model rights are left, from the outset, to the judge assigned to each specific case for the preparatory proceedings, where the allegations and presentation of evidence are fully completed, and regularly left to the oral proceedings for final conclusion after the submission of the report and the completion of the draft decision.

Because of the rapid increase in the number of cases brought to the Court, the introduction of the intensive hearing method was proposed and came into effect in 2003. This method allows the judge to have a clearer understanding of the allegations and the issues in dispute during preparatory proceedings by requiring the parties to submit preparatory documents.

Also in 2003, the *Code of Civil Procedure* was amended (the amendment came into effect on 1 April 2004), which introduced a planned hearing method. The judges are supposed to talk with parties to specify the issues and evidence to be examined during the preparatory proceedings and make a plan for trial and the day for announcing a judgment.

The IPHC has now published its procedural guideline for an administrative suit seeking revocation of the JPO's panel decision. According to this guideline, parties are now required to submit preparatory pleadings, which provide the cause of revocation up until a week before the date of the first preparatory proceedings. During a first preparatory proceeding, the judge will clarify the points in dispute, notify the parties of the subsequent due date for all preparatory documents, and lay out the approximate schedule for rendering judgment. The Court will then specify the date for second preparatory proceedings of the intensive hearing. The assigned judge will form his or her opinion on the issues, while relying on the report prepared by the judicial research official, and notify the parties of the date for oral hearing and date of rendition of judgment. At the oral hearing, the results of the preparatory proceeding will be reported before the three-judge panel, and the Court will render its judgment on the date specified at the end of the oral hearing.

Notable decisions of the IPHC

To what extent is the IPHC giving protection to intellectual property rights? Has the establishment of the IPHC brought any significant changes to the protection of intellectual property rights?

In its first three years, the IPHC has handed down several significant and newsworthy decisions. The first significant decision was a grand panel decision on Ichitarou.[53] In this case, the Matsushita Electric Industrial Company sued the JustSystems Corporation, which distributes the popular Japanese word-processing software, Ichitarou, and graphic design software, Hanako, for patent infringement. The Matsushita Electric Industrial Company held a patent on an information processing system that allowed a user to click one icon for help and another for explanation. The plaintiff asserted that JustSystems infringed its patent by using a help menu whereby after a user clicks on help, a question mark pointer appears on the screen, and the user can move this pointer to various function menus for explanation. This lawsuit attracted a great deal of attention in Japan because the Matsushita Electric Industrial Company is one of the largest electronics companies in the world, and the JustSystems Corporation is one of the leading software companies in the country. The Tokyo District Court concluded that the defendant infringed the plaintiff's patent and gave an injunction against the defendant. The IPHC reversed that decision and held that the plaintiff's patent was invalid, since the plaintiff's technology was obvious to a person skilled in the art based on the information available at the time; therefore, there was no inventive step in its creation.

The other noteworthy decision was a grand panel decision involving Canon Inc.[54] In this case, the plaintiff, Canon Inc., one of the world's leading companies in manufacturing computer printers, sued the Recycle Assist Company for patent infringement. The defendant company distributed the so-called recycled ink tank. Traditionally, ink tanks are thrown away after all the ink in them has been used. The plaintiff urged users to return the used ink tank for recycling; it then collected these used ink tanks and manufactured other products from them. In contrast to this practice, the defendant collected these used ink tanks, punctured a small hole in them, cleaned the inside of the tank, dried it, refilled it with new ink, and manufactured recycled ink tanks. The defendant then distributed them at a much lower price than the new ones from the original manufacturer. The plaintiff argued that the distribution of these recycled ink tanks was an infringement of its patent.

The Tokyo District Court rejected the plaintiff's claim but the IPHC reversed that decision and concluded that the defendant did infringe the plaintiff's patent. Among the various defences raised, it was argued that the first sale doctrine should prevent the plaintiff from asserting patent infringement. In addition, there should be no liability because the defendant merely repaired the used ink tank and refilled them with ink. The IPHC held, however, that the first sale doctrine is not a bar for asserting patent infringement after the normal use of goods, and neither is it a bar for asserting violation of technological invention. The Court also held that the defendant should not be immune from liability merely by describing its conduct as a repair instead of a manufacture. This case also attracted a wide range of attention because the defendant raised two important issues: (1) the acceptability of preventing recycling in the name of patent infringement; and (2) the issue of whether the business model of the plaintiff, who distributes computer printers with low prices but charges high prices for ink tanks, is appropriate. The IPHC concluded that patent infringement cannot be justified in the name of recycling, and also that the plaintiff's business model is not unreasonable, since it spent a considerable amount of money in developing suitable ink tanks.[55]

The IPHC also upheld the decision of the JPO to reject the invalidation claim in a suit filed by Tamura Kaken Corporation against Taiyo Ink MFG Co. Ltd.[56] In this case, the plaintiff filed a request to the JPO for a decision to invalidate the patent on '[p]hotosensitive thermosetting resin composition and method of forming solder resist pattern by use thereof' that the defendant holds. The JPO made a decision in favour of patent invalidation and the defendant filed an action to seek cancellation of the decision. The defendant then filed a request for a review based on correction, and the IPHC thus ordered cancellation of the decision. Following this judgment, the JPO approved the correction and the plaintiff sought revocation of this decision. At issue was whether the correction was within the 'scope of the matters stated in the description or drawings'. The IPHC held that the correction should be allowed unless the correction does not add any new technical matters to the technical matters that a person skilled in the art can understand, taking into account all statements in the description or drawings, thus upholding the decision of the JPO.[57]

The IPHC also handed down many other significant decisions. For instance, it held that the three-dimensional trademark of a Japanese sweet called Hiyoko (Chick) was invalid, since the shape of the sweet is not unique and can be found in many places, thus rejecting a trademark infringement action filed by the plaintiff against a competitor who sold the sweet under different names.[58] On the other hand, it admitted that the bottle of Coca-Cola is entitled to a three-dimensional trademark, thus overturning the decision of the JPO to refuse its registration.[59]

The IPHC also held that the service provided by Maneki TV is not an infringement of copyright where the defendant, Maneki TV, installed a 'location free television set' which enabled users to watch television programmes on computer screens outside of their homes via Internet connection.[60] The TV stations in this case filed an action alleging an infringement of enabling right to public transmission under the *Copyright Act*. The Tokyo District Court held that there was no infringement because the defendant merely allowed individual owners to install their sets and it was not transmitting a programme to the public. The IPHC affirmed this decision.

In another decision, the Court rejected an injunction sought by motion picture companies such as Paramount Motion Pictures against distributors of discount DVDs.[61] The case traces its origin to an amendment to the *Copyright Act* passed by the Diet that extended the term for copyright protection on motion pictures from 50 years to 70 years after publication. The amendment took effect on 1 January 2004. However, the terms for many famous movies published in 1953 were due to expire on 31 December 2003. Insisting that their copyright term on these movies were extended by the aforementioned amendment for an additional 20 years, the movie companies sought injunctive relief to prevent the distribution of such movies by other distributors. The Head of the Cultural Agency supported this interpretation, but the Tokyo District Court rejected it and the IPHC affirmed this judgment. The Court held that the copyright protection for movies whose term expired on 31 December 2003, should not be given another 20 years of protection by the amendment, which took effect on 1 January 2004.

In yet another decision, the Court upheld a damages award for Yomiuri Shinbun, the largest newspaper company in Japan, which brought a copyright infringement action against Digital Alliance, an online headline services provider.[62] The defendant provided online services that allowed users to read the news headline of the plaintiff's newspaper and get access to the text of these newspaper articles.

The Tokyo District Court held that the particular headlines of the newspaper are not copyrightable and rejected the suit. The IPHC agreed with the District Court in that the particular newspaper headlines lacked originality and were thus not copyrightable. But it found that the plaintiff spent substantial effort and money to report newspaper articles, which the defendant took advantage of. The Court thus ordered the defendant to pay tort damages to the plaintiff.

Overall, the IPHC overturned the decisions of the JPO in a substantial number of cases; remarkable in light of the general tendency of the Japanese courts to defer to the judgments of administrative agencies and to refrain from interfering with them. While the majority of JPO's decisions refusing patent registration or invalidating patents have been sustained, a considerable number of the JPO's decisions to grant patents have, however, been reversed. In addition, in a considerable number of cases the IPHC has refused injunctions or damages awards against those infringing patents, holding the patent invalid.

Was the establishment of the IPHC a success?

It is still too early to comprehensively evaluate the activities of the IPHC and to pass judgment on whether its establishment was a success or not. However, there is now sufficient data from the Court to afford preliminary assessment.

There were two main reasons for the establishment of the IPHC: (1) to provide more effective protection of intellectual property rights by offering speedy judicial remedies; and (2) to showcase the government's commitment to protect intellectual property rights. Has the IPHC accomplished these goals?

As to the first goal, the establishment of the IPHC, especially its grand panel, should surely be welcomed, since the new Court now has almost exclusive jurisdiction on cases involving intellectual property, and it could, especially through its grand panel, hand down authoritative decisions on controversial issues more quickly.[63] In this sense, it has contributed to the stability and predictability of intellectual property protection in Japan.[64] And, as the case studies mentioned illustrate, the IPHC has had its fair share of contentious issues to determine in the short period since its establishment.

The average trial length has been reduced.[65] The establishment of the IPHC, with concentration of intellectual property cases into a single dedicated court staffed with experts on intellectual property issues, arguably contributes, at least in part, to the efficient handling of intellectual property cases as well as reducing trial length. Of course, the reduction of trial length has already been brought up as an urgent issue in Japanese courts, and the Diet passed a statute calling for the reduction of trial length and the facilitation of speedy trial (the *Act for Facilitation of Speedy Trial*). As a result, the average trial length for intellectual property cases had been declining, even before the establishment of the IPHC. It is thus somewhat unclear to what extent the establishment of the IPHC has contributed to further shortening of the trial length of intellectual property cases. Yet, the introduction of the IPHC definitely contributed, at least in part, to the further speedy resolution of intellectual property cases. In this sense, the IPHC has accomplished the first goal.

As to the second goal, the establishment of the IPHC illustrates the commitment of the Japanese government to promote the country's image as one that is based on the protection of intellectual property.[66] Yet, pro-patent lawyers argue that the Japanese courts are not enthusiastic enough in protecting patent rights. The Japanese courts, including the IPHC, they argue, tend to reject patent infringement cases by finding the patent to be invalid. Thus, although they welcome the establishment of the IPHC, they argue that the IPHC has not drastically changed this tendency.[67]

The Japanese *Patent Act* allows patent registration on new inventions.[68] There are three basic requirements for an invention to be granted a patent: novelty, an inventive step, and industrial applicability.[69] If the invention was already publicly known or publicly implemented in Japan or abroad before the application, then the application will be rejected for lack of novelty. Moreover, if a person with standard knowledge in the given area of technology (an ordinary person skilled in the art) could have easily made such an invention, then the application will not be accepted for lack of inventive step. It has been pointed out that the requirement of novelty and inventive step as construed by the courts, especially by the IPHC, is unduly demanding.[70]

In this sense, although the establishment of the IPHC can be said to have symbolized Japan's commitment to the protection of intellectual property, it may not have contributed to any substantive strengthening of intellectual property rights.

Of course, we cannot expect the IPHC to uphold patent registration by the JPO and the infringement suit filed by patent holders in every case. Excessive protection of patent might hinder the development of new inventions. The IPHC might be looking for a 'proper' balance between the protection of intellectual property rights and progress and new development.

Alternatively, the IPHC may still not be confident enough to embark on giving stronger protection to intellectual property rights. In order for the IPHC to obtain public trust and confidence, there are several problems to overcome. First, there are some concerns about the way in which the IPHC handles its cases. The IPHC usually holds a preparation hearing for trial only once or twice; thus there are questions raised as to whether the parties have sufficient opportunities to present their case before the Court.[71] In addition, even though the parties do have an opportunity to explain technological matters during the preparation proceedings, the judges tend to rely upon briefs and documentary evidence and are not eager to engage in oral argument with parties during trial.[72] Furthermore, since the case is assigned to a particular judicial research official, his or her opinion is very important to the outcome of the case. For the parties, it might be desirable to avoid a certain judicial research official if there is a potential conflict of interest; however, they have no say on this matter. Moreover, the judicial research official's report is not disclosed. Thus the parties cannot know to what extent the decision of the Court was influenced by the report. Since most of these judicial research officials are JPO adjudicators (on secondment to the Court and they will return to JPO after several years of work in the IPHC) questions are raised about their impact on the decision of the IPHC.[73] Finally, there are complaints about transparency in the decision-making process of the IPHC. Unlike the Court of Appeal for the Federal Circuit in the United States, the decision of the IPHC does not allow inclusion of dissenting opinion. It is thus hard to know what kinds of opinions were held by individual judges and whether the decision was unanimous or not.[74] It is thus imperative for the IPHC to alleviate these concerns to acquire public trust and confidence and to start giving more protection to intellectual property rights.

Conclusion

The establishment of the IPHC is a symbolic event for the protection of intellectual property in Japan. Although some countries have patent courts, such as Germany[75] and the United Kingdom,[76] and although there has been a proposal to set up a European Patent Court,[77] no country in the world has a court that specializes in intellectual property. Even though the Court of Appeal for the Federal Circuit in the United States is often referred to as a symbol of patent protection, it does not exclusively deal with intellectual property cases. Although Thailand has an Intellectual Property and International Trade Court,[78] it is not a court which has exclusive jurisdiction in intellectual property cases. In this sense, the IPHC of Japan is a unique institution and deserves attention.

Although the case studies suggest that the substantive doctrines employed by the courts may not have changed much, its establishment has contributed to a reduction of trial length and rendition of authoritative decisions on intellectual property issues. We need to watch the new Court's development closely to see whether the introduction of such a specialty court is a success and could becomes a model to follow.

Notes

1. There have been some arguments for the establishment of the Administrative Court under the jurisdiction of the Supreme Court. See Itsuo Sonobe, "Sihou no Gyousei nitaisuru Check no Arikata nitsuite" (Possible Checks against Executive Power by the Judiciary [paper presented to the Council for Judicial Reform]) http://www.kantei.go.jp/jp/sihouseido/dai41/41bessi1.html. Some have also argued for the establishment of a labour court and introduction of citizen participation, in order to protect the rights of workers. See Japan Federation of Bar Association, "Roudoukankeijiken eno Sougoutekina Taioukyouka nitsuiteno Chukantorimatome nitaisuru Iken," (Opinion on the Interim Summary of Means to Improve Handling of Labour Related Cases) http://www.nichibenren.or.jp/ja/opinion/report/2003_46.html. There are also some proposals for the establishment of the Court Martial under the jurisdiction of the Supreme Court together with a proposal for a constitutional amendment to Article 9 of the *Constitution* in order to legitimize the self-defence force. See Liberal Democratic Party, "Shinkenpou Souan," (A Draft of New Constitution) http://www.jimin.jp/jimin/shin_kenpou/shiryou/pdf/051122_a.pdf. But none of these arguments has attracted wide support.
2. *Constitution of Japan* art. 76(1).
3. Constitution of Japan art. 76(2).
4. Hiroshi Oda, *Japanese Law*, 2nd edn (Oxford: Oxford University Press, 1999), 62–9, 71–3.

5. Ibid., 69–71.
6. Supreme Court (Grand Bench), 30 May 1956, *Keishu* 10 (1956): 756.
7. Katsumi Shinohara, "Outline of the Intellectual Property High Court of Japan," *AIPPI Journal* 49 (2005): 131–3; IPHC, "History," http://www.ip.courts.go.jp/eng/aboutus/history.html
8. The number of lawsuits seeking revocation of adjudication of the Japan Patent Office (JPO) was 285 in 1994, but it reached 527 in 2004. Similarly, the number of appellate cases involving intellectual property was 48 in 1994, but reached 113 in 2004. See Judge Shuhei Shiotsuki, "Zadankai: Tizaikousai no Setti to Kongo no Tizaisoshou no Arikata," (Roundtable Discussion: The Establishment of the Intellectual Property High Court and the Future of Intellectual Property Litigation) *Jurist* 1293 (2005): 11, 19.
9. According to the statistics filed by the Supreme Court of Japan, the average trial on civil cases dealing with intellectual property issues took about 25.7 months in the District Court in 1998, and another 18.5 months in the High Court in 1997. The average trial of administrative cases on patent also took 18.6 months in the Tokyo High Court in 1997. See IPHC, "Statistics," http://www.ip.courts.go.jp/aboutus/statistics.html
10. The Court of Appeals for the Federal Circuit was established in 1982 by combining the United States Court of Customs and Patent Appeals and the appellate division of the United States Court of Claims. The Court of Appeals for the Federal Circuit is unique among the 13 federal Courts of Appeals. Unlike other Courts of Appeals, it has nation-wide jurisdiction in a variety of subject areas, including patents and trademarks, and it also takes appeals of certain administrative agencies' decisions, including the Board of Patent Appeals and Interferences and the Trademark Trial and Appeals Board. It is sometimes said that its establishment was symbolic of the pro-patent policy of the United States.
11. Council for Judicial Reform, "Final Report," http://www.kantei.go.jp/jp/sihouseido/report/ikensyo/index.html. Another issue regarding the infringement suit of the intellectual property cases was the protection of trade secrets during trials. Article 82 of the *Constitution* mandates that the '[t]rials shall be conducted and judgment declared publicly' and that the court can close its trial only '[w]here a court unanimously determines publicity to be dangerous to public order or morals', but 'trials of political offences, offences involving the press or cases wherein the rights of people as guaranteed in Chapter III of this Constitution are in question shall always be conducted publicly'. '[P]ublic order or moral' had been construed narrowly to mean public safety and sexual morality. Therefore, even in a suit seeking damages or injunction against infringement of a trade secret, the plaintiff must be willing to present evidence regarding the trade secret in an open court. Moreover, the defendant can request the production of documents to the court, which are relevant for defence. When the defendant requests documents in relation to the trade secret, the plaintiff is not authorized to ask for a protective order, which would require the document to be sealed and restrain the defendant lawyers from revealing them. As a result, the plaintiff is naturally prevented from suing for infringement of a trade secret. In order to facilitate the infringement suit, the *Unfair Competition Prevention Act, Law No. 47/1993* was amended in 2004 to allow the court to close its trial during examination of the parties and witnesses regarding infringement of a trade secret (art. 13). The Court is also allowed to examine the document in chambers to see whether the party has a legitimate reason for refusing to submit the document to the Court (art. 7[2]) and to issue a protective order against the parties and their lawyers restraining them from using the trade secret information obtained through production to the Court other than for the purpose of litigation (art. 10[1]). See Makiko Takabe, "Titekizaisansoshou niokeru Himitsuhogotetsuduki no Genjou to Kadai," (Current Situation and Tasks for Protection of Trade Secret in Intellectual Property Litigations) *Jurist* 1317 (2006): 187.

12. Junichirou Koizumi, "Prime Minister Junichirou Koizumi's Opening Address to the 154th Diet," http://www.kantei.go.jp/jp/koizumispeech/2002/02/04sisei.html
13. Conference on Intellectual Property Strategy, "On Establishment of Strategic Council for Promotion of Intellectual Property," http://www.kantei.go.jp/jp/singi/titeki/konkyo.html
14. Strategic Council for Promotion of Intellectual Property, "Outline for Promotion of Intellectual Property (3 July 2002)," http://www.kantei.go.jp/jp/singi/titeki/kettei/020703taikou.html
15. *Law No. 122/*2002 (promulgated on 4 December 2002). For English translation, see http://www.cas.go.jp/jp/seisaku/hourei/data/ipba.pdf
16. Strategic Headquarters for Protection of Intellectual Property, "Order on Strategic Headquarters for Protection of Intellectual Property (*Cabinet Order No. 45/2003*)," http://www.kantei.go.jp/jp/singi/titeki2/hourei/honburei.html
17. Strategic Headquarters for Protection of Intellectual Property, "Strategic Program for the Creation, Protection and Exploitation of Intellectual Property," http://www.kantei.go.jp/jp/singi/titeki2/kettei/030708f.html
18. See also Expert Committee on the Strengthening of Basic Structure for Protection of Intellectual Property Rights of the Strategic Headquarters for Protection of Intellectual Property, "On Establishment of the Intellectual Property High Court," http://www.kantei.go.jp/jp/singi/titeki2/houkoku/151211kousai.pdf
19. *Act to Facilitate Judicial Reform, Law No. 119/2001*, art. 8.
20. Headquarters for Promotion of Judicial Reform, "On Establishment of Study Group on Intellectual Property Litigation," http://www.kantei.go.jp/jp/singi/sihou/kentoukai/kaisai2.html
21. *Law No. 119/2004* (promulgated on 18 June 2004). For English translation, see http://www.cas.go.jp/jp/seisaku/hourei/data/IPHC.pdf
22. Nobuhiro Nakayama, "Titekizaisankoutousaibansho eno Mitinori," (The Path to the Establishment of the Intellectual Property High Court) *Jurist* 1293 (2005): 6; Nobuhiro Nakayama, "Titekizaisanseidokaikaku no Keii to Kadai," (History and Agenda of Intellectual Property System Reform) *Jurist* 1326 (2007): 2, 5. Some countries of the world have courts dealing exclusively with patent suits. But since the Japanese government wanted to establish a court which has jurisdiction on all intellectual property issues, it was difficult to define its jurisdiction precisely. Former Chief Judge Katsumi Shinohara points out the following four reasons for the rejection: 'First, it might invite incidental disputes over subject matter jurisdiction. Second, relevant cases that should be resolved in the same court may go to different appeal courts. Third, it might hamper the interest of local residents especially with respect to cases related to the Copyright Act and Unfair Competition Prevention Act since those cases tend to have community-oriented and local nature. Fourth, creation of a specialized court seems to be heterogeneous in the Japanese judicial system which have traditionally addressed new challenges by reinforcing existing courts.' See Katsumi Shinohara, "A Retrospective and a Prospective Look at the First Year of the Intellectual Property High Court," *AIPPI Journal* 50 (2006): 197.
23. During the course of the debate, some have also argued for the appointment of judges who have a background in technology and not in law. However, this proposal was similarly rejected because such judges do not have a wide knowledge of law, which is necessary to resolve legal issues involving intellectual property. Nakayama, "History and Agenda of Intellectual Property System Reform," 5–6.
24. Shinohara, "Outline of the Intellectual Property High Court of Japan," 136–40.
25. The IPHC is located on the 17th floor of the Tokyo Court Complex in Kasumigaseki, Tokyo. IPHC, "Organization," http://www.ip.courts.go.jp/eng/aboutus/organization.html

26. There are six branches of the High Court, but they have limited territorial jurisdiction and do not have any independent judicial conference or authority to manage their administrative matters.
27. IPHC, "List of Divisions and Judges," http://www.ip.courts.go.jp/eng/info/list.html
28. *Code of Civil Procedure, Law No. 109/1996* art. 310–2; *Patent Act, Law No. 121/1959* art. 182–2.
29. *Code of Civil Procedure, Law No. 109/1996* art. 92–8.
30. Tomokatsu Tsukahara, "Tizaikousai niokeru Soshouunei no Joukyou to Tizaisoshou niokeru Senmonka no Katsuyou no Jissai," (Suit Management in the Intellectual Property High Court and the Practice of Utilizing Experts in Intellectual Property Litigation) *Jurist* 1326 (2007): 9, 16. Judicial research officials are appointed after resignation from the JPO but usually return to the JPO after several years of service. See Yukihide Umeda, "Tizaikousaichousakan no Chousahoukokusho," (Investigation Report of the Judicial Research Officials of the Intellectual Property High Court) *Tokugikon* 244 (2007): 127, 134.
31. The number of technical advisors appointed is currently over 200. IPHC, "Technical Advisors in Intellectual Property Lawsuits," http://www.ip.courts.go.jp/eng/documents/expert.html
32. *Code of Civil Procedure, Law No. 109/1996* art. 92–2.
33. The IPHC usually appoints three technical advisors to one case with the consent of the parties.
34. Shinohara, "Outline of the Intellectual Property High Court of Japan," 140–44; IPHC, "Jurisdiction," http://www.ip.courts.go.jp/eng/aboutus/jurisdiction.html
35. *Patent Act, Law No. 121/1959* art. 178(1); *IPHC Act Law, No. 119/2004* art. 2(2).
36. *Patent Act, Law No. 121/1959* art. 47.
37. *Patent Act, Law No. 121/1959* art. 51.
38. *Patent Act, Law No. 121/1959* art. 66.
39. *Patent Act, Law No. 121/1959* arts 100, 102.
40. *Patent Act, Law No. 121/1959* art. 121(1)
41. *Patent Act, Law No. 121/1959* art. 123(1), (2).
42. *Patent Act, Law No. 121/1959* art. 136(1).
43. *Patent Act, Law No. 121/1959* art. 178(1).
44. Supreme Court (3rd Petty Bench), 11 April 2000, *Minshu* 54 (2000): 1368. In this case, the appellant claimed patent infringement by the appellee, and the appellee sought declaration of the non-infringement. The appellant had a patent on semiconductor equipment and applied for another patent based on the original patent. Yet, the Tokyo High Court held that the original patent was invalid since everyone could have easily invented the product based on pre-existing public knowledge, and therefore the second patent should also be clearly invalid, since the second product was basically the same as the original product. The appellant appealed to the Supreme Court arguing that the patent should be treated as valid unless the patent decision was overturned by administrative litigation and that court should not thus invalidate the patent in the infringement suit. Yet, the Supreme Court rejected the appellant's argument and held that the court should not uphold the infringement when the underlying patent is clearly invalid.
45. *Patent Act, Law No. 121/1959* art. 104–3.
46. Tetsuya Obuchi, "Tokkyososhou oyobi Shinpanseido no Genjou to Kongo no Kadai (Current Situation and Future Agenda of Patent Litigation and Adjudication)," *Jurist* 1326 (2007): 34–7.
47. *Code of Civil Procedure, Law No. 109/1996* art. 6(3); *IPHC Act, Law No. 119/2004* art. 2(1).
48. The civil cases involving patents, utility model rights, the rights of the layout design of the integrated circuit, and copyrights on program work are assigned to the Tokyo

District Court or the Osaka District Court. *Code of Civil Procedure, Law No. 109/1996* art. 6(1).

49. *IPHC Act , Law No. 119/2004* art. 2(1).
50. *IPHC Act , Law No. 119/2004* art. 2(3).
51. The number of new cases seeking revocation of adjudication of the JPO filed in the IPHC in 2005 was 598, while the number of new civil appellate cases filed in 2005 was 87. See Tsukahara, "Suit Management in the Intellectual Property High Court and the Practice of Utilizing Experts in Intellectual Property Litigation," 9–10. An overwhelming number of cases filed in the IPHC are thus those seeking revocation of adjudication on patents made by the JPO.
52. Shinohara, "Outline of the Intellectual Property High Court of Japan," 144–45; IPHC, "Shinketsutorikeshisoshou no Shinkou ni tsuite," (On Procedure for Administrative Suit against Decision of the Panel) http://www.ip.courts.go.jp/documents/form_youkou.html
53. IPHC, 30 September 2005, *Hanreijihou* 1904 (2005): 47, http://www.ip.courts.go.jp/documents/pdf/g_panel/10040.pdf
54. IPHC, 31 January 2006, *Hanreijihou* 1922 (2006): 30, http://www.ip.courts.go.jp/documents/pdf/g_panel/10021.pdf
55. The Supreme Court ultimately upheld the judgment of the IPHC and dismissed an appeal from the Recycle Assist Company. See Supreme Court (1st Petty Bench), 8 November 2007, *Minshu* 61 (2007): 2989. It is noteworthy that the IPHC rejected the suit filed by Seiko-Epson Corporation against Ecorica Inc., maker and distributor of the refilled ink cartridge, because the patent Epson claimed was void for lack of novelty. See IPHC, 30 May 2007, http://www.courts.go.jp/hanrei/pdf/20070607095821.pdf, and the Supreme Court decided not to accept appeal. See Supreme Court (2nd Petty Bench), 10 November 2007, http://www.yomiuri.co.jp/net/news/20071112nt0b.htm. See also the judgment of IPHC, 11 November 2005, *Hanreijihou* 1911 (2005): 48, http://www.ip.courts.go.jp/documents/pdf/g_panel/10042.pdf, which upheld the decision of the JPO to cancel the patent of the plaintiff, Nippon Synthetic Chemical Industry Co. Ltd, on the manufacturing method of polarizing film because the invention was not sufficiently supported by the specifications.
56. IPHC, 30 May 2008, *Hanreijihou* 2000 (2008): 47, http://www.ip.courts.go.jp/documents/pdf/g_panel/10563.pdf
57. The grand panel of the IPHC was also reviewing the patent infringement suit filed by Toshiba Corporation against Hynix Semiconductor Japan, Inc., a subsidiary of Korean Hynix Semiconductor, regarding NAND type flash memory. Toshiba claimed that the memory the defendant was importing infringed its patent and sought stopping of import or distribution, destruction of infringing goods, and damages, while the defendant claimed that the patent was invalid since it lacked novelty. The Tokyo District Court upheld the Toshiba's claim. Yet, the suit was settled and the IPHC did not have a chance to render its judgment. IPHC, "Disposed Cases," http://www.ip.courts.go.jp/eng/documents/g_panel.html
58. IPHC, 29 November 2006, *Hanreijihou* 1950 (2006): 3, http://www.courts.go.jp/hanrei/pdf/20061129162739.pdf. The Supreme Court of Japan dismissed an appeal on 12 April 2007. Supreme Court (1st Petty Bench), 12 April 2007, unreported.
59. IPHC, 29 May 2008, *Hanreijihou* 2006 (2008): 36, http://www.ip.courts.go.jp/hanrei/pdf/20080529172621.pdf
60. IPHC, 22 December 2006, http://www.courts.go.jp/hanrei/pdf/20061222160510.pdf
61. IPHC, 29 March 2007, *Hanreijihou* 1990 (2007): 122, http://www.courts.go.jp/hanrei/pdf/20070330151920.pdf. The Supreme Court affirmed this judgment. Supreme Court (Grand Bench), 18 December 2007, *Minshu* 61 (2007): 3460.
62. IPHC, 6 October 2005, http://www.ip.courts.go.jp/hanrei/pdf/0C642A4A124DC13D492570970018104B.pdf

63. Unlike the *en banc* decision of the Court of Appeals for the Federal Circuit, in which all the members of the court participate, the grand panel of the IPHC consists of merely five members of the Court. However, the head judges of each of the four divisions are all included as members, and it is assumed that the head judge of each division seeks the opinions of other judges on the division. The decision of the grand panel can be thus said as representing the opinion of the whole IPHC. See Tsukahara, "Suit Management in the Intellectual Property High Court and the Practice of Utilizing Experts in Intellectual Property Litigation," 13.
64. However, unlike the decision of the Court of Appeals for the Federal Circuit, in which a dissenting opinion can be added, the decision of the IPHC carries no dissenting opinion.
65. The average trial length of civil appellate cases was 9.0 months in 2004 but was reduced to 8.5 months in 2006, IPHC, "Average Trial Length of Intellectual Property Civil Appellate Cases," http://www.ip.courts.go.jp/aboutus/stat_01.html, and the average trial length of administrative cases on patent was 12.8 months in 2004 but was reduced to 8.6 months in 2006, IPHC, "Average Trial Length of Administrative Cases on Patent," http://www.ip.courts.go.jp/aboutus/stat_02.html
66. Nakayama, "History and Agenda of Intellectual Property System Reform," 6–7.
67. Eiji Katayama, "Tizaikousai nitaisuru Jitsumukai karano Komento," (A Practitioners' Comment on the Intellectual Property High Court) *Jurist* 1326 (2007): 18. While the reversal rate of decisions supporting the rejection of patent application fell below 10 per cent, the reversal rate of decisions which affirmed the validity of patent was more than 50 per cent in 2004. See Shinohara, "A Retrospective and a Prospective Look at the First Year of the Intellectual Property High Court," 205.
68. Oda, *Japanese Law*, 339–40.
69. *Patent Act, Law No. 121/1959* art. 29.
70. Katayama, "A Practitioners' Comment on the Intellectual Property High Court," 20–1. It is not uncommon for the patent applicant to claim the patent for invention based on a combination of several public documents. In such a case, it was assumed that the onus is upon the defendant to prove that one can easily combine these public documents to create the invention. Yet, it has been speculated that the Japanese courts tend to assume that the combination was easy and the plaintiff should be required to show that the combination was difficult in order to argue for the protection of patent. Moreover, it is generally assumed that the courts should judge the novelty of invention based on the information at the time of application. But it has been speculated that the Japanese courts tend to bring the information which had been published after the invention to judge the novelty, thus making them likely to deny novelty.
71. Ibid.
72. Ibid., 19.
73. Asked about 'how a court can ensure fairness if judges are supported by staff who comes from an office which appear as a party,' Former Chief Judge Shinohara replied that '[i]t is our tradition ... that research officials faithfully accomplish their duty as a court official by strictly reviewing the Board decisions and submitting a fair and precise report to judges'. See Shinohara, "A Retrospective and a Prospective Look at the First Year of the Intellectual Property High Court," 201.
74. Katayama, "A Practitioners' Comment on the Intellectual Property High Court," 23–4.
75. Das Deutschland-Portal, "Federal Patent Court," http://www.bundesrepublikdeutschland.us/link.php?lang = 2&category1 = 5&category2 = 203&link_id = 763&page_view_start = 10
76. Her Majesty's Courts Service, "The Patents Court and Patents County Court Guide," http://www.hmcourts-service.gov.uk/cms/files/Patents_Court_Guide_7_July_2008_final.pdf

77. European Patent Office, "EPLA – European Patent Litigation Agreement," http://www.epo.org/patents/law/legislative-initiatives/epla.html. See also European Patent Office, "Draft Statute of the European Patent Court," http://www.european-patent-office.org/epo/epla/pdf/statute_draft.pdf
78. Vichai Ariyanuntaka, "Intellectual Property and International Trade Court: A New Dimension For IP Rights Enforcement In Thailand," http://asialaw.tripod.com/articles/ipvichai.html

5 Specialized intellectual property courts in the People's Republic of China

Myth or reality?

Connie Carter

Introduction

During the first years of the twenty-first century, the People's Republic of China (PRC or China) has emerged as the undisputed factory of the world. China's strength as an economic powerhouse is based primarily on its success as this all-embracing production facility, and secondarily as a potentially huge market for the consumption of commercial products. However, the recognition of China's new status and the growth of fake, pirated or counterfeited products in world markets have developed hand in hand. Many owners of intellectual property rights (IPRs) – especially those in the West – fight a losing battle to protect their interests, such as patents, copyrights, trademarks, brands, logos and domain names, both within China and outside.

This chapter discusses some of the steps that are being taken in the Chinese legal system to alleviate the problem.[1] Specifically, it considers the media announcement in early 2006 that China was establishing special intellectual property (IP) courts nationwide in order to ensure legal enforcement of IPRs in compliance with domestic and international laws.[2] This 2006 announcement follows on from China's enactment of IP laws in the 1980s and 1990s,[3] which were designed to comply with the *Agreement on Trade-Related Aspects of Intellectual Property Rights* (*TRIPs Agreement*),[4] and thus assist China in joining the World Trade Organization (WTO). However, it is one thing to have comprehensive domestic laws on the books and quite another to enforce them. A long-standing objective of China's government has been to establish special IP courts and tribunals throughout the country. The questions are: Are special IP courts in China now a myth or reality? And what difference would special IP courts make to the protection of IPRs in China?

This chapter is divided into five main parts, of which this introduction is part one. Part two briefly considers the basis for, and nature of, China's obligation to protect and enforce the IPRs of all companies and individuals within and at its national borders. Part three examines the current legal structure for protecting and enforcing those rights. Part four explores and speculates on the difference that the existence of specialized IP courts might have made, or might make, in China in the next years. Part five concludes that although pressure from the United States and the European Union, particularly the former, obviously causes some embarrassment to China and therefore might elicit some short-term response, a significant improvement in the legal enforcement of IPRs in China will not happen until Chinese companies have a significant number of their own IPRs to protect, and the Chinese people become more aware of the importance of IPRs.

The basis for legal protection of intellectual property rights in China

Others may argue differently,[5] but this chapter holds that for all practical purposes, the basis of China's commitment to protect IPRs in China is to be found in China's membership of the WTO. China joined the WTO in 2001. Through its WTO membership, China committed to comply fully with the *TRIPs Agreement*, and thereby to protect and enforce the IPRs of all companies and individuals in China. China had sought membership of the WTO (or, more correctly, of the WTO's predecessor, the General Agreement on Trade and Tariffs [GATT]) since the early 1980s, a quest which became more pronounced from about 1985.[6] Therefore, China had been improving its legal system – especially its system for protecting IPRs – long before 2001. Indeed, China promulgated a new 'Western-friendly' trademark law as early as 1982.[7] Consequently, because of China's long march towards inclusion in this global trading club, with obviously ample time for preparation, China was not granted a transition period regarding compliance with the *TRIPs Agreement*. It should be noted that China gained concessions in many other areas,[8] but as the pervasiveness of its production outputs was recognized as troubling by the United States and the members of the European Union, China was not categorized as a 'developing country' for the purposes of the *TRIPs Agreement*.[9]

The *TRIPs Agreement* establishes minimum standards for the protection of, *inter alia*, trademarks, copyright and patents.[10] It also sets out minimum standards for the enforcement of those rights in civil, criminal and administrative actions, including customs actions at national borders.[11] WTO members may confer more extensive protection as long as such provisions do not contravene the provisions of the *TRIPs Agreement*.[12] Article 1 also allows members to determine the appropriate means by which the provisions of the *TRIPs Agreement* are implemented in their own domestic legal system and practice.

Following general WTO principles, the *TRIPs Agreement* also requires that China provide national treatment to the nationals of all other WTO members with regard to the protection and enforcement of IPRs.[13] In its definition of the term 'nationals', the *TRIPs Agreement* follows the approach taken in existing intellectual property conventions under the World Intellectual Property Organization (WIPO) treaties.[14] 'Nationals' are 'persons, natural or legal, who are domiciled or who have a real and effective industrial or commercial establishment in that customs territory'.[15]

The *TRIPs Agreement* specifically incorporates the 'most favoured nation' principle and compels members to adhere to it. Article 4 provides that '[w]ith regard to the protection of intellectual property, any advantage, favour, privilege or immunity granted by a Member to the nationals of any other country shall be accorded immediately and unconditionally to the nationals of all other members'.[16] Several exceptions to this obligation are listed in Articles 4(a–d). They include policies regarding the exhaustion of intellectual property rights, technology transfer and public interest issues, for example those relating to health and safety.

The *TRIPs Agreement* compels members to adhere to certain procedural and substantive standards regarding the enforcement of IPRs, their acquisition and maintenance, including the opposition and revocation of those rights. Furthermore, Article 41(1) requires members to integrate the enforcement procedures listed in Part III into 'their national laws so as to permit effective action against any act of infringement of intellectual property rights covered by this Agreement'. It stipulates that the procedures shall be 'fair and equitable' and shall 'not be unnecessarily complicated or costly, or entail unreasonable time-limits or unwarranted delays'.[17] According to Article 41(3), decisions on the merits of a case shall be reasoned, and made available (at least) to the parties, preferably in writing and without undue delay.

On 1 November 2003, the Beijing Higher People's Court (Beijing Court) decided to better the publication aspect of this requirement by announcing that henceforth all IP judgments, including judicial review of Patent Review Board decisions made by the Beijing courts, would be posted on their website.[18] This unprecedented move surprised many legal scholars, especially as the Court promised to publish every IP judgment 'regardless of its nature, possible impact, and quality' within a month after the decision was handed down.[19] The Beijing Court was unable to deliver on its promise. For instance, according to the State Intellectual Property Office (SIPO), a total of just over 1,000 patent cases were adjudicated in 2004 and 2005. However, only 536 cases were posted on the court website for the period 1 November 2003 up to June 2006.[20]

Nevertheless, China seems to be striving to meet most of the *TRIPs Agreement* requirements. One of the most important procedural standards required for the enforcement of IPRs, which is new to Chinese legal practice, is the availability of interlocutory or pre-trial injunctions. Thus, for example, the *Trademark Law 1993* (*TML*) was amended to enable cease-and-desist orders as well as evidence preservation orders. Article 57 of the Chinese *TML* stipulates that:

> Where a trademark registrant or interested party who has evidence to show that another person is committing or will commit an infringement of the right to use its or his registered trademark, and that failure to promptly stop the infringement will cause irreparable damages to its or his legitimate rights and interest, it or he may file an application with the People's Court to order cessation of the relevant act and to take measures for property preservation before instituting legal proceedings in the People's Court.

And Article 58 of the Chinese *TML* allows that:

> In order to stop an infringing act, any trademark registrant or interested party may file an application with the People's Court for preservation of the evidence before instituting legal proceedings in the People's Court where the evidence will possibly be destroyed or lost or difficult to be obtained again in the future. The People's Court must make adjudication within forty-eight hours after receipt of the application; where it is decided to take the preservative measures, the measures shall be executed immediately. The People's Court may order the applicant to place [a] guaranty; where the applicant fails to place the guaranty, the application shall be rejected.

Those provisions of the *TRIPs Agreement*, in broad outline, are China's main obligations; the rules with which China must comply and in the main, the rules with which China is complying – at least in so far as the enacting of laws is concerned. For it is a fact that there are now modern Chinese laws to regulate all major areas of IPRs[21] as required by the *TRIPs Agreement.*

At this juncture, however, I hasten to add that there is no provision in the *TRIPs Agreement* that requires the establishment of specialized IP courts. For instance, Article 41(5) of the *TRIPs Agreement* clearly states:

> It is understood that this Part does not create any obligation to put in place a judicial system for the enforcement of intellectual property rights distinct from that for the enforcement of law in general, nor does it affect the capacity of members to enforce their law in general. Nothing in this Part creates any obligation with respect to the distribution of resources as between enforcement of intellectual property rights and the enforcement of law in general.

In effect, the *TRIPs Agreement* would seem to accept that IPRs will be enforced and protected within the legal framework that existed in China at the time of its accession in 2001.

The current legal framework for protecting and enforcing IPRs in China

When China acceded to the WTO in December 2001, the structure of the existing domestic legal regime for handling infringements[22] of IPRs was simple and straightforward – at least on paper. The regime, which had been under development in spirit since the 'open-door' policy announcement in 1978 and in reality since 1982, when China's first Western-friendly *TML* was promulgated, allows actions to be brought in four ways:

1 administrative or extra-judicial channels (e.g. the State Administration for Industry and Commerce (SAIC), Customs Authorities);

2 judicial channels in the Civil Chambers;
3 judicial channels in the Criminal Chambers; and
4 judicial channels (judicial review in Administrative Chambers).[23]

China also has a system of procuracy and public security organs, which also assists in the criminal prosecution of IPR infringements. To bring a criminal action, one must persuade the People's Procuracy that a serious offence has been committed. The Procuracy's structures are parallel to the courts and public security organs, comprising four hierarchical levels that are similar to the court system.

The administrative system

Needless to say, the most popular and most well-developed machinery for resolving disputes involves the extra-judicial channels, that is, the administrative authorities. This is a legacy from traditional law in China, in which most civil or commercial disputes would be settled by non-judicial bodies of the clan or *tsu*. There is a host of these administrative bodies in China and all have a three- or four-tier structure encompassing the national, provincial and local levels. In some cases, the fourth tier is either a so-called 'big city' that is usually one in addition to the provincial capital;[24] or a 'coastal open city', that is, usually a Special Economic Zone (SEZ), like Xiamen.

The administrative authority involved will depend on the area of intellectual property that is being dealt with. In relevant areas the authority is involved in the examination, registration and validation of the IPRs as well as actions regarding redress in cases of infringement of those rights. Thus, for trademarks, this means the State Administration for Industry and Commerce (SAIC) and the various levels of the Administration for Industry and Commerce (AIC). For instance, Articles 54 and 55 of the *TML* provide that the AIC

> has the power to investigate and handle any act of infringement of the exclusive right to use a registered trademark according to law; [and] where the case is so serious as to constitute a crime, it shall be transferred to the judicial authority for handling.

Article 42 of the *Implementing Regulations under the Trademark Law* 1993 clarifies that this means the AIC has the power to investigate and handle the matter at the '*infringer's location or the place where the infringing act was committed*'. Article 55 of the *TML* lists the powers which the AIC 'at or above the county level' may exercise. These are surprisingly wide. For instance, the AIC can investigate infringements and decide punishments; it can order the infringer to stop the infringing act immediately but has no power to assess and order damages. However, upon the parties' request, the AIC can mediate an agreement on damages.[25] Either party can lodge an infringement civil lawsuit with the

Intermediate People's Court under the *Civil Procedure Law* 2007 if the mediation fails.[26] The administrative case and the civil lawsuit can proceed simultaneously. However, since most plaintiffs choose the administrative route only, there are few incidents of administrative and civil lawsuits proceeding simultaneously. For instance, in 2003, some 26,000 trademark cases were dealt with by the AICs across China, whereas only 900 trademark infringement cases were handled by the courts.

For copyrights, the administrative authority means the National Copyright Administration and local Copyright Administrations at the provincial level and in 'big cities'. Again, cases brought to the administrative route far outnumber those filed as civil lawsuits.[27]

The State Intellectual Property Office (SIPO) deals with the examination, validation, registration, cancellation and infringement of patents and integrated circuit rights (ICRs) at the national level and IP (Patent) Administrations deal with patents and ICRs in provincial capitals and coastal open cities. Anecdotal evidence and the few reported cases point to the importance of SIPO. For instance, it was at SIPO's Patent Re-examination Board that Pfizer's Viagra patent was invalidated.[28] It took an appeal to the Beijing Intermediate People's Court to revoke that decision.[29] However, the final outcome remains uncertain since the decision of an appeal to the Higher People's Court is pending and (theoretically) an appeal to the Supreme People's Court could also be made.

For cases involving new varieties of plants, there are the Agricultural Administrations under the Ministry of Agriculture and the National Administration of Forests with its Provincial Administrations. For cases involving the entry or exit of counterfeit or pirated goods or any other infringement of IPRs leaving or entering China, there are the Customs General Administration and its local Customs offices. Other relevant administrative authorities include: the Ministry of Public Security and local Public Security Bureaus; the General Administration of Quality Supervision, Inspection and Quarantine of the State and local Technical Supervision Bureaus; and the Ministry of Culture and Culture Bureaus.

Obviously, it is in the areas of trademarks, patents and copyright that most damage is caused to the holders of IP rights and it is on cases in these areas that we will focus when considering the work of IP courts in China.

The court system

The court system for pursuing judicial review of the decisions of administrative bodies and adjudicating cases about IPR infringements in China is far less developed than the administrative system. Nevertheless, a straightforward judicial system is in place, which has been praised by many observers from the West, mainly because the system was almost non-existent just three decades ago. Indeed, China's legal system was all but abolished during the Cultural Revolution from 1966 to 1976,[30] but it rose from the ashes like a phoenix from 1978 onwards.

The court hierarchy

Since 1978 China has developed and rejuvenated its four-tier judicial system:

1 Supreme People's Court
2 Higher People's Court
3 Intermediate People's Court
4 Basic People's Court (county, town or district levels).[31]

The Supreme People's Court in Beijing is the final court of appeal, at least in theory. I say 'at least in theory' because this court, China's highest judicial organ, reports to and is responsible to the Standing Committee and the National People's Congress (NPC). The NPC meets for several weeks but it meets only once per year (or as requested by its Standing Committee). Therefore, the NPC's Standing Committee, comprising 150 people, is regarded as the permanent body of the NPC. According to Articles 57 and 67 of the 1982 *Constitution of the People's Republic of China* (*Constitution*), the Standing Committee has extensive judicial powers, including interpretation of the *Constitution*, the making and revision of national laws, the interpretation of those laws, supervision of the work of the State Council (China's cabinet), the Supreme People's Court, the Central Military Commission, the Supreme People's Procuracy, and the approval and appointment of senior government and judicial officials. Thus, frequent reports of NPC interference with judicial decisions are not anecdotal but part of the functioning of China's legal system. There is no judicial independence or separation of powers, although some scholars argue that in recent years, China has attempted to curb the most blatant flaws and that the communist leadership is embracing judicial independence as a principle.[32]

Below the Supreme People's Court is the Higher People's Court at the provincial level (usually domiciled in the provincial capital), then the Intermediate People's Court at the municipal and 'big city' level, followed by the Basic People's Court at the county, town or district levels. Since about 1985, the judicial channels for IP actions have included special divisions, chambers or tribunals at a few directly specified intermediate level courts and at the Higher People's Courts in Beijing, Shanghai and Tianjin.

It seems as if that overall situation has not changed markedly since the mid-1980s and 1990s. For as Jie Liu confirmed to WIPO at a session in Geneva in June 2004:

> Intellectual Property Tribunals [divisions] have been set up since 1982 in the Higher People's courts in a number of provinces and municipalities, such as the municipalities of Beijing, Shanghai and Tianjin, and the provinces of Jiangsu, Guangdong, Fujian and Hainan, so as to meet the actual demands. Intellectual Property Tribunals have also been set up in the Intermediate People's Courts in the Special Economic Zones as well as in Beijing and Shanghai. In other

> provinces, autonomous regions and municipalities, a specialized collegiate bench for intellectual property cases is set up in the Intermediate People's Courts of the cities where the people's governments are located.[33]

Actions involving foreigners could also only be commenced in intermediate-level courts. The intermediate-level courts were chosen as the starting points, because they are considered more sophisticated than the Basic People's Courts, both with regard to the court personnel, their legal knowledge and their appreciation of business transactions[34] – especially when there might be an element of foreign investment involved. By 1995, there were IP divisions or IP tribunals at 11 Intermediate People's Courts, and at six Higher People's Courts.[35] During the next decade IP divisions were added at five Intermediate People's Courts.[36]

Finally, the Intellectual Property Appellate Division in the Beijing Higher People's Court was vested with the exclusive appellate jurisdiction for the entire country. Since about 2003, specialist IP judges, notably people like Jiang Zhipei and Yongjian Zhang, leading Supreme People's Court judges, have been available at China's final court of appeal. However, as Justice Jiang Zhipei noted, foreign companies tend to complain to the media and their own politicians rather than taking their complaints to the Chinese courts.[37] Between 2003 and 2005 fewer than 4 per cent of IP cases filed in China were brought by foreign companies or foreign holders of IPRs.[38]

Specialized IP Court or specialized IP Division

At this point, it might be beneficial to define two key concepts: 'specialized IP Court' and 'specialized IP Division'. For the purposes of this chapter,[39] 'specialized IP Court' means a permanently organized body with independent judicial powers defined by law, consisting of one or more judges who sit to adjudicate disputes and administer justice solely in the IP field.[40] Specialized IP Courts are separate and distinct from a country's courts of general jurisdiction. A 'specialized IP Division' is a 'chamber' or 'division' within an existing court of general jurisdiction which deals solely with IP issues and ancillary matters. A specialized IP Division will only have judges or specialists assisting judges who have in-depth knowledge and expertise in IP matters.

In China, the four-tier court system also has chambers or divisions within each tier. Thus, for example, at the Intermediate People's Courts, there are chambers or divisions for adjudicating criminal, civil, economic, administrative, and in many instances, also IP cases. This system of chambers has been under development since the early to mid-1980s. In recent years, the legal profession has become more and more specialized. However, the specialization of the court system has lagged behind the profession. What is clear is China's commitment to 'educate' the judiciary, so that not only lawyers and judges but also other court personnel become familiar with, and even gain a degree of competence in, IP matters.

The media announcement in early 2006 that China was establishing an IP court system was met with cautious optimism by all holders of IP rights who do business in China – both Chinese and foreign holders. However, at the time, some commentators were of the opinion that 'a Chinese IP court ... may never come to fruition' because

> some courts (sic) [divisions] in the [Higher] People's Courts in major cities do not necessarily want IP appeal cases centralized in one specialized court in Beijing or Shanghai. Thus, the promising news being reported concerning the implementation of a specialized IP court system may prove to be somewhat premature.[41]

The sceptics were probably right. Over two years later, there still seems to be no evidence of the establishment of a separate IP court system in China. My contact with lawyers and academics in Beijing, Shanghai, Xiamen, Suzhou, Guangzhou, and in other cities, has revealed no evidence of a new IP court system. The most recent official international survey conducted by the International Bar Association reveals no new IP court system.[42] It is feared that a misunderstanding of an expansion in the number of 'divisions' or 'chambers' within the Higher People's Courts and Intermediate People's Courts were mistakenly or inappropriately named 'courts'. Indeed, most Intermediate People's Courts have always had specialized 'divisions' or 'chambers' for criminal, civil, economic and administrative cases, and more recently also IP cases.

What is more likely and also a welcome development is that the Chinese government in 2006 was putting focus on its efforts to move forward in making the IP institutions more efficient – mainly by developing the IP expertise of certain judges within the court system. Thus, it is now clear that the widely reported Chinese IP court is not a new court at all, but merely a firmer implementation of China's ongoing policy to have specific judges rule on IP cases and thereby develop greater knowledge and expertise in IP issues. As David Washington rightly points out:

> The expertise developed by these 'IP Judges' could be somewhat analogous to expertise in patent and trademark litigation developed by the judges of the US Court of Appeals for Federal Circuit in Washington, DC, which hears appeals of patent and trademark litigation.[43]

Therefore, this is also somewhat analogous to the court system in the United Kingdom, where the High Court of England and Wales has three divisions: the Chancery, the Queen's Bench and the Family Divisions. The Chancery Division hears all IP cases, and the Queen's Bench Division also has jurisdiction to hear copyright and confidential information actions. Within the Chancery Division, the Patents Court has exclusive jurisdiction to hear patent and registered design infringement actions. The judges who are assigned to the Patents Court are full-time professionals, dealing only with patent and registered design actions. They also have a technical background, and their work allows them to develop extensive experience in patent law and the ability to deal with more complex technological issues. In addition to the Patents Court of the Chancery Division of the High Court of England and Wales, there is a Patents County Court, which is relatively new as it was established only in 1990. Its purpose is to provide a faster, less expensive, less complex access to justice for small and medium-sized enterprises and private individuals, who would otherwise find the High Court route in the Chancery Division expensive, slow and procedurally complex, and perhaps also somewhat overwhelming.

In any event, the situation in China, although not yet as far-reaching as the England and Wales' model or the United States' model, still provides an opportunity for some reasonable knowledge and competency-building of IP law among legal practitioners and special IP judges.

Specialized IP judges

The creation of specialized IP divisions or chambers within Intermediate People's Courts and Higher People's Courts encourages the development of a network of IP specialists, at least in the major cities, coastal areas and in the SEZs, where foreign IPRs are notoriously most exposed to infringement. However, the notion and characteristic of judges in China differ greatly from their counterparts in, say, England or the United States.

Until about 10–15 years ago, most Chinese judges lacked legal training of any kind, since they were mainly military veterans who were appointed to positions of honour. However, in recent years, the level of competency and quality of China's judges and other legal practitioners have improved significantly. Of China's total of reportedly 210,000 judges, about 43 per cent or 90,000 have gained at least a bachelor's degree in law; while 2 per cent or 4,000 have gained a master's degree or a doctorate.[44] The level of competency and improvement of judges' education varies according to whether they preside in courts in a big prominent city like Shanghai or Beijing, or whether they are in a smaller city or province. For instance, in Shanghai, some 87 per cent of all judges have gained at least a bachelor's degree, though not necessarily a law degree.[45] However, the issue of the independence of judges is still a major obstacle since, as two scholars from Eastern China University of Legal and Political Studies – who wish to remain anonymous – put it, 'those who manage the money bags manage those who manage the law'. This leads to a court system with, among other ills: (1) unpredictability, since judges often abuse their discretion; (2) local protectionism; (3) bribery and corruption among judicial personnel; (4) inefficiency and lack of respect for court personnel.

In addition, in Chinese courts it is customary, and indeed is required by the *Organic Law of the People's Courts*, that a panel of judges preside, except in very simple cases.[46] The panel is often referred to as an adjudication or trial committee and comprises young trained legal experts or older lay persons, depending on the level and location of the court. Each panel is led by a presiding judge or president, who has a very powerful voice. In fact, in some lower courts it is almost wrong to speak of a presiding panel of judges, since the 'juniors' and lay persons rarely, if ever, get the opportunity to adjudicate and make independent decisions. They are obliged to follow the leader. In some cases, the panel members execute functions, which in a court in England and Wales or in the United States would be carried out by the court's clerks. The inefficiency of this system is obvious, but of even greater importance is whether the functioning of this structure undermines due process throughout the system. In the highest court, the Supreme People's Court, the panel comprises one president (chief justice), eight vice-presidents, 80 judges, and 120 assistant judges.[47] There are indications that changes are being made and fortunately IP divisions seem to have been selected for the experiment of introducing a single-judge system.

What difference might the existence of specialized IP courts have made?

There are both advantages and disadvantages to having specialized IP Courts. In any country, but arguably this is even more applicable in an emerging market economy like China's, the key advantages of having specialized IP Courts[48] relate to four distinct areas: (1) building greater expertise, (2) gaining greater efficiency, (3) consistency, and (4) effectiveness.[49] For instance, it is thought that judges working in specialized IP Courts may deliver more well-reasoned and practical judgments on complex technical cases owing to the acquired understanding and the experience they build up in IP issues over time.

Since intellectual property cases usually contain technological issues, judges will experience a need for increased understanding of complex scientific information. While the basic concepts of IP law are not that difficult to understand, their application can be intricate and perplexing for those who are not familiar with the subject. Moreover, judges need to appreciate the economic consequences of judicial decisions that involve IP issues. This can be a challenge for judges in China who have little or no experience of commerce, trade or general business transactions, because of the way in which China's previous command economy functioned.

One Chinese judge, who is thought to be a good example of demonstrating this knowledge and expertise building, is Justice Jiang Zhipei, the leading IP judge in the Supreme People's Court in Beijing. His judgment in the trademark infringement and unfair competition case of *Fuzhou Wan Da Pencil Stationery Ltd and Fuzhou Pencil Factory v. Fuzhou Ren Yu Stationery Ltd and Fujian Light Industrial Products Import & Export Group*[50] is reasonable and well argued and therefore encouraging for foreign investors. His reasoning demonstrates a professional grasp of the concepts, content and context of IPRs. Faced with the low percentage of cases filed by foreign holders of IPRs, he is also constantly urging foreigners to make use of China's legal courts. This will directly and indirectly help the courts grow and become more professional.

Another advantage is that specialized IP Courts may increase consistency of legal doctrine in the IP field. Thus, the more comprehensive understanding of, and familiarity with, cases that a judge possesses, the more consistency we may expect him or her to provide when deciding cases. This should allow for greater predictability of the outcome of proceedings and therefore benefit litigants and society as a whole, since predictability supports confidence in the legal system. Inconsistency in decision-making can result in a lack of confidence in the system, and can erode the courts' authority and integrity as well as undermine the viability of the business environment.

Furthermore, specialized IP Courts allow quicker and more effective decision-making processes. This is because the time usually needed to 'educate' the non-specialist judges when they deal with aspects of IP cases will be reduced, and thereby the overall time needed for hearing a case will be reduced. The result will be greater savings for litigants, as well as the court and administrative staff.

Finally, specialized IP Courts are more likely to manage the challenges of complex IP cases more efficiently and more precisely than courts of general jurisdiction. Appeals may be made directly to the highest court, bypassing ordinary appeal courts and thereby saving on costs and obtaining faster final adjudication of cases.

The major disadvantages of specialized IP Courts relate to the costs of their maintenance. For instance, the cost of initially training and later maintaining knowledgeable judges, court personnel and public prosecutors may be high – especially if the case-load is low. However, in China, evidence suggests that the case-load is substantial, so this cost-factor disadvantage would be minimized. Far worse is the 'intimacy' that might develop between repeat litigators and full-time judges; or the advantages that repeat litigators might gain from their special knowledge of the procedural quirks in these specialized courts. Conversely, lack of such intimacy or special knowledge might put one-time litigators at a substantial disadvantage. Lastly, specialized IP Courts with their specialized IP judges may lead to a closing of the open mind that a 'generalist' might otherwise bring to IP cases. Again, in the case of China, this is considered less detrimental, since the advantages of having judges with specific knowledge of an area of law that is considered 'alien' and cumbersome far outweigh the disadvantages.

However, as discussed elsewhere,[51] the entire issue of local protectionism is still rampant in China, and until the fundamental flaws inherent in the payment of judges are solved, the pervasiveness of protectionism might be another major disadvantage of having specialized IP Courts.

Conclusion

One is tempted to conclude by saying it is 'back to reality'. In April 2007, the United States filed two consultations against the PRC with the WTO's Dispute Settlement Body (DSB). United States' Trade Representative, Susan Schwab announced:

> we are requesting formal WTO consultations over China's inadequate protection of copyrights and trademarks – these key intellectual property rights are critical to products, brands and technologies in businesses large and small, ranging from machine tools to consumer goods. Second, we are asking for separate WTO consultations over serious Chinese market barriers

> to products that are prime targets for pirates – movies, home entertainment DVDs, music and publications. Impeding trade in legitimate versions of these products exacerbates the problems we face with the pirates in China's marketplace. We need to open China's markets to legitimate commerce and eradicate this IPR theft and profiteering.[52]

While the United States recognizes that China has made progress in some important areas, such as amending and updating IP laws, and in stepping up actions, such as raids on factories and stores producing and selling pirated and counterfeit goods, the Trade Representative said that China still had

> significant WTO related problems that bilateral dialogue has not been able to resolve: current Chinese laws impede effective attacks on piracy and counterfeiting, and legitimate audiovisual products and publications continue to face serious problems with market access. We hope the initiation of these two WTO actions will, first, encourage changes to laws and other measures that have stood in the way of effective protection of IPR in China for a wide range of products, and, second, tear down the legal barriers that keep legitimate copyrighted products from competing effectively in the Chinese marketplace.[53]

Thus, far from being satisfied that China might be moving quickly to improve its protection of IPRs through an improved IP court system, the United States is of the opinion that even the Chinese laws are still inadequate. The government in China seems to agree in part, since on 6 April 2007 officials revealed yet another national action plan on IPR protection. In their 2007 plan, the PRC government promised to accelerate the revision of the *TML* and to 'study on the Copyright Law', and to 'harness criminalization tools to achieve better punitive and deterrent effects'.[54] So, apart from amendments to the *TML* and the *Copyright Law*, we can also look forward to amendments to the *Criminal Law*.

However, like the early 2006 announcement regarding a new IP court system, this 2007 announcement might also turn out to entail more myth than reality. Having studied the vagaries of the legal protection of IP in China for well over a decade, I am still of the opinion that the key to China's more robust enforcement of the comprehensive set of IP laws, which are on the books, is the development of Chinese companies which have intellectual property rights to protect. Only when Chinese companies become more credible and more numerous stakeholders in the equation will China's leadership strongly support the many aspects of legal reform that are necessary to secure satisfactory enforcement of IP laws. Indeed, help may be on the way: the PRC's leadership has called on Chinese companies to show more creativity and focus on technological innovation.[55] So, if the world's factory becomes the world's innovator or at least one of its main innovators, the conundrum will be on its way to a solution. President Hu Jintao promised to turn China into an innovative country by 2020.[56] The question is, can this promise be kept? Or is China as an innovative country another myth – a pipe dream to scare or pacify, depending on one's outlook?[57]

Notes

1. For discussion of developments in Japan see Shigenori Matsui's chapter in this publication. For discussion of intellectual property cases in the Indonesian Commercial Court see David Linnan's chapter in this publication.
2. See address of Wu Yi, "Address of Vice Premier Wu Yi at the Conference of Enterprise IPR Protection and Self-initiated Innovation, Friday, February 24, 2006," http://english.mofcom.gov.cn/article/newsrelease/significantnews/200602/20060201583273.html. See press release (in Chinese) issued during the annual meeting of the National People's Congress, which is available at www.chinacourt.org/public/detail.php?id = 197947. Discussed at "IPR in China: Management, Protection and Enforcement" (paper presented at IP Conference, London, March 20, 2006), http://www.iplawportal.com/china. See Joshua Pantesco, "China Creates Special Intellectual Property Courts," http://jurist.law.pitt.edu/paperchase/2006/03/China-creates-special-intellectual.php See State Intellectual Property Office, "Annual Report 2006," http://www.sipo.gov.cn/sipo_English/laws/annualreports/ndbg2006/
3. For instance: the *Trademark Law* was enacted in 1982, with amendments in 1993 and 2001; the *Patent Law* was enacted in 1984 and amended in 1993 and 2001; and the *Copyright Law* was enacted in 1990 and amended in 2001.
4. Opened for signature 15 April 1994, 1869 UNTS 299 (entered into force 1 January 1995).
5. For a comprehensive discussion of China's motivation for legal reform, see Chris X. Lin, "A Quiet Revolution: An Overview of China's Judicial Reform," *Asian-Pacific Law and Policy Journal* 4 (2003): 255. See also Mei Ying Gechlik, "Judicial Reform in China: Lessons from Shanghai," *Columbia Journal of Asian Law* 19 (2006): 97.
6. China applied to (re)-join the GATT in 1986, claiming that its membership had merely lapsed in 1950 and that China was technically still a contracting party, and indeed a founding member of the GATT. China asserted that the *Kuomintang* (China's national government in exile) on Taiwan was in no position to withdraw China from the GATT in 1950, as it was not the authorized government of China. For a discussion, see Ya Qin, "China and GATT: Accession Instead of Resumption," *Journal of World Trade* 27 (1993): 77.
7. Connie Carter, *Fighting Fakes in China: The Legal Protection of Trade Marks and Brands in the PRC* (London: Intellectual Property Institute, 1996), 42.
8. For instance, China was allowed to institute various limitations on market access in areas such as professional services (lawyers, accountants, auditors, and so on) and in financial services and insurance. Thus, initially foreign lawyers would only be allowed to establish one representative office in 19 specified cities in China – the remainder would be out of bounds until one year after accession. Professionals offering taxation services would be required to wait up to six years after accession to be permitted to establish wholly foreign-owned enterprises. See Article 18 of China's WTO Accession Protocol which established a Transitional Review Mechanism (TRM) for reviewing China's compliance with its WTO commitments. The TRM is conducted annually for eight years following accession. A final review will be conducted in the tenth year or earlier as agreed by the General Council. See *Accession of the People's Republic of China*, WTO Doc WT/L/432 (23 November 2001). According to United States, China is still not complying with market access commitments in myriad areas, see for example the United States Trade Representative, "2007 Report to Congress on China's WTO Compliance," http://www.ustr.gov/assets/Document_Library/Reports_Publications/2007/asset_upload_file625_13692.pdf
9. Developing countries were granted a five-year transition period and 'least developed nations' were given 10 years in which to comply with the *TRIPs Agreement*.
10. Part II of the *TRIPs Agreement* sets out seven areas to which the term intellectual property applies (Article 1[2]) and for which protection is required: (1) copyright and

related rights; (2) trademarks, including service marks; (3) geographical indications, including appellations of origin; (4) industrial designs; (5) patents, including the protection of new varieties of plants; (6) layout designs (topographies) of integrated circuits; and (7) undisclosed information including trade secrets.

11. *Agreement on Trade-Related Aspects of Intellectual Property Rights*, opened for signature 15 April 1994, 1869 UNTS 299, Section 4 of Part II (entered into force 1 January 1995).
12. *Agreement on Trade-Related Aspects of Intellectual Property Rights*, opened for signature 15 April 1994, 1869 UNTS 299, art. 1(1) (entered into force 1 January 1995).
13. *Agreement on Trade-Related Aspects of Intellectual Property Rights*, opened for signature 15 April 1994, 1869 UNTS 299, arts 1(3), 3 (entered into force 1 January 1995).
14. *Agreement on Trade-Related Aspects of Intellectual Property Rights*, opened for signature 15 April 1994, 1869 UNTS 299, art. 1(3) (entered into force 1 January 1995). This article specifically co-opts into the *TRIPs Agreement*, the *Paris Convention for the Protection of Industrial Property*, opened for signature 14 July 1967, 828 UNTS 305 (entered into force 27 April 1970), the *Berne Copyright Convention*, opened for signature 14 July 1967, 828 UNTS 222 (entered into force 29 January 1970), the *Rome Convention for the Protection of Performers, Producers of Phonograms and Broadcasting*, 496 UNTS 72 (signed and entered into force 26 October 1961), and the *Treaty on Intellectual Property in Respect of Integrated Circuits*, opened for signature 26 May 1989, 28 ILM 1484 (not yet in force).
15. *Agreement on Trade-Related Aspects of Intellectual Property Rights*, opened for signature 15 April 1994, 1869 UNTS 299, note 1 (entered into force 1 January 1995).
16. *Agreement on Trade-Related Aspects of Intellectual Property Rights*, opened for signature 15 April 1994, 1869 UNTS 299, art. 4 (entered into force 1 January 1995).
17. *Agreement on Trade-Related Aspects of Intellectual Property Rights*, opened for signature 15 April 1994, 1869 UNTS 299, art. 41(2) (entered into force 1 January 1995).
18. See Zhang Xuecong, "Intellectual Property Judgments Can Be Searched on the Net," http://www.chinacourt.org.
19. M. Y. Gechlik, *Protecting Intellectual Property Rights in Chinese Courts: An Analysis of Recent Patent Judgments* (Washington, DC: Carnegie Endowment for International Peace, 2007), 4.
20. Ibid., 8.
21. For a list of Chinese IP laws, many of which were amended in 2001, see Supreme People's Court of the PRC, http://www.chinacourt.org. In fact, during the Transitional Review Mechanism of the TRIPs Council, on 26 October, 2006, the Chinese representative boasted that five years after China joined the WTO, its intellectual property rights laws complied fully with the *TRIPs Agreement*: International Centre for Trade and Development, "WTO Scrutinizes China's Trade Policies," *Bridges Weekly Trade New Digest* 10 (2006): http://www.ictsd.org/weekly/06 11 01/story4.htm. However, while acknowledging that China's legal system has improved immensely in the years since 1979, scholars such as Stanley Lubman argued that law reform is a work in progress, as it still exhibits what Lubman called 'rolling uncertainty'. See Stanley Lubman, "Looking for Law in China," *Columbia Journal of Asian Law* 20 (2006–7): 1.
22. In general, disputes regarding the *validity* of IPRs are addressed administratively by a re-examination board for the appropriate property right, for example, the State Intellectual Property Office (SIPO) for patents and the Trademark Review and Adjudication Board (TRAB) for trademarks. Their decisions were final but following amendments in the laws in 2001, they can now be appealed to the Administrative Division of the No. 1 or No. 2 Intermediate Court in Beijing or to the IP Division of Intermediate Courts where these are available. These court decisions may themselves be appealed to the Higher People's Court in Beijing acting in its capacity as final appeal court for these Intermediate Courts.

23. *Trademark Law* arts 2, 6, 17, 20, 22.
24. Beijing, Shanghai and Tianjin are usually referred to as 'big cities'. They are the three biggest in China.
25. *Implementing Regulations under the Trademark Law* 1993 art. 43.
26. *Trademark Law* 1993 art. 39.
27. See, for instance, State Intellectual Property Office, "Annual Report 2005," http://www.sipo.gov.cn/sipo_English/laws/annualreports/ndbg2005/; State Intellectual Property Office, "Annual Report 2006," http://www.sipo.gov.cn/sipo_English/laws/annualreports/ndbg2006/
28. For a discussion of the Viagra case, see Samson Yu and Ying Zhang, "Lessons from the Viagra Case," *Managing Intellectual Property* 2 (2005): 1.
29. See BBC, "China Court in Viagra Crackdown," http://news.bbc.co.uk/1/hi/business/6213835.stm; BBC, "Pfizer Wins Chinese Viagra Ruling," http://news.bbc.co.uk/1/hi/business/5047640.stm
30. For a discussion, see Walter Gellhorn, "China's Quest for Legal Modernity," *Journal of Chinese Law* 1 (1987): 1; Stanley Lubman, *Bird in a Cage: Legal Reform in China after Mao* (Stanford, CA: Stanford University Press, 1999).
31. For an analysis of the People's Courts in Xinjiang, see discussion in Pitman Potter's chapter in this publication. For an analysis of the administrative chambers of the People's Courts see Michael Palmer's chapter in this publication.
32. Lin, "A Quiet Revolution: An Overview of China's Judicial Reform," 293.
33. Jie Liu, "Judicial and Administrative Protection of Intellectual Property in China" (paper presented to Advisory Committee on Enforcement Second Session, Geneva, June 28–30, 2004), *www.wipo.int/edocs/mdocs/enforcement/en/wipo_ace_2/wipo_ace_2_8.doc*
34. Remember that it is only in recent years that Chinese citizens became involved in commercial transactions without the interference of the state or organs that administered China's command economy.
35. See State Intellectual Property Office, "Annual Report 2005," http://www.sipo.gov.cn/sipo_English/laws/annualreports/ndbg2005/
36. Ibid.
37. Justice Jiang Zhipei quoted in Chris Buckley, "Chinese Antipiracy Laws Take Root Slowly," *International Herald Tribune*, October 5, 2005, 5. See also Justice Jiang Zhipei's website: Jiang Zhipei, "Judicial Protection of IPR in China," http://www.chinaiprlaw.com/english/forum/forum76.htm
38. See State Intellectual Property Office, "Annual Report 2006," http://www.sipo.gov.cn/sipo_English/laws/annualreports/ndbg2006/
39. These definitions were adopted from the International Bar Association's definition in "International Survey of Specialized Intellectual Property Courts and Tribunals," http://www.ibanet.org/images/downloads/International_IP_Survey_February_2005.pdf
40. The IP field includes, at a minimum, trademarks, patents and copyright. However, other IP areas as specified in the *TRIPs Agreement* may be included. See note 10.
41. David Washington, "No Focussed Intellectual Property Court in China," http://www.internationaliplawforum.com/subjects.php?subject_id = 1
42. International Bar Association, "International Survey of Specialized Intellectual Property Courts and Tribunals," http://www.ibanet.org/images/downloads/International_IP_Survey_February_2005.pdf.Specialized
43. Washington, "No Focussed Intellectual Property Court in China".
44. Gechlik, *Protecting Intellectual Property Rights in Chinese Courts: An Analysis of Recent Patent Judgments*, 7.
45. Ibid.
46. *Organic Law of the People's Courts*, revised 2006, art 22.
47. Lin, "A Quiet Revolution: An Overview of China's Judicial Reform," 313.

48. For a summary of key advantages of specialized IP courts, see Vichai Ariyanuntaka, "Intellectual Property and International Trade Court: A New Dimension for IP Rights Enforcement in Thailand," http://www.thailawforum.com/articles/ipvichai.html.
49. The discussion in this section is adopted from Section 4.2 of the International Bar Association, "International Survey of Specialized Intellectual Property Courts and Tribunals," http://www.ibanet.org/images/downloads/International_IP_Survey_February_2005.pdf.
50. (2001), http://www.chinaiprlaw.com/english/judgemts/jmgao4.htm
51. Carter, *Fighting Fakes in China: The Legal Protection of Trade Marks and Brands in the PRC*; Donald Clarke, "The Execution of Civil Judgments in China," *China Quarterly* 65 (1995): 65.
52. Susan Schwab, "Announcement of Requests for Consultations with China on IPR and on Certain Market Access Issues for Copyright Intensive Industries," http://www.ustr.gov/assets/Document_Library/Transcripts/2007/April/asset_upload_file755_11065.pdf?ht =
53. Ibid.
54. State Intellectual Property Office, "Annual Report 2007," http://www.sipo.gov.cn/sipo_English/laws/annualreports/ndbg2007/
55. See State Council of the People's Republic of China, "Outline of the National Intellectual Property Strategy," http://www.sipo.gov.cn/sipo_English/news/iprspecial/20080621_407693.htm. It should be noted that during the past couple of years, several leadership announcements have been made regarding China's need to transition to focus on innovation and creation rather than on labour intensive, low-wage production. However, it was only in July 2008, when the *Scientific and Technological Progress Law* came into force that a degree of support was given to the promises and declarations.
56. China Daily, "Hu Jintao's Report at 17th Party Congress," http://www.chinadaily.com.cn/china/2007–10/25/content_6226673_4.htm
57. To further compound the issue, the 'National Intellectual Property Strategy' whose outline was released in June 2008 also states at section 4, paragraph 45 that: 'Studies need to be carried out on establishing special tribunals to handle civil, administrative or criminal cases involving intellectual property. Studies also need to be done to reasonably centralize jurisdiction over cases involving patents or other cases of a highly technical nature. Explore issues on setting up courts of appeal for cases involving intellectual property'.

Part III

Constructing constitutional courts

6 The Constitutional Court of Thailand, 1998–2006

A turbulent innovation

Andrew Harding

> A forward retention of custom is as turbulent a thing as an innovation; and they that reverence too much old times are but a scorn to the new. It were good therefore that men in their innovations would follow the example of time itself, which indeed innovateth greatly, but quietly and by degrees scarce to be perceived.[1]
>
> (Francis Bacon)

Introduction

On 19 September 2006, a bloodless military coup, which followed a period of intense political division and protest in Thailand during 2005–6, removed the Prime Minister Thaksin Shinawatra and his Thai Rak Thai Party government from office, abolished the National Assembly and the Constitutional Court, and overturned the 1997 *Constitution*. Thaksin was the first elected Prime Minister in Thailand to survive a full parliamentary term and be elected to office in two successive elections; his period in office was, however, as controversial as the method of his overthrow. Critical in the turn of opinion against Thaksin was the 2005 sale of one of Thailand's leading companies, Shin Corporation, to Temasek Holdings, a Singapore government-linked company, which provoked a public outcry. Not only were provisions rushed through Parliament to nullify the capital gains tax implications for Thaksin and his family, but also the sale of a large telecommunications company raised questions relating to foreign ownership of key assets and the security of Thailand's defence communications.[2] The deal led to street demonstrations and prompted a snap election called by the Prime Minister but boycotted by the opposition parties. After an appeal by King Bhumipol to the judiciary to resolve the resulting constitutional crisis, the election was declared invalid on technical grounds by the Constitutional Court in May 2006.[3]

Thaksin then promised to step down after new elections that were to be held in October 2006. On 19 September 2006, while Thaksin was attending a summit meeting in New York, the tanks rolled into central Bangkok and ended an episode of acute constitutional crisis. By this time Thaksin and his government had showed blatant disregard for both the letter and the spirit of the constitution and the law. As well as widely reported human rights abuses, particularly in the Muslim southern provinces of Thailand, the freedom of the press and broadcasting media had been called into question, and the independence of many constitutional bodies and the military had been undermined. Thaksin had also committed the cardinal error of slighting the King on more than one occasion.

The constitutional crisis of 2005–6, culminating in the military coup of 19 September 2006, also brought to an end, at least temporarily, a process of constitutional reform in Thailand that had begun with the enactment of the 1997 *Constitution of Thailand*.[4] The experience of the last decade, since the Constitutional Court opened its doors in 1998, will be highly instructive in considering the next steps in developing constitutionalism in Thailand, as it will also be instructive to other countries in the region[5] and elsewhere that may be contemplating or implementing their own constitutional reforms. The Constitutional Court was essential to those reforms, just as its replacement (under the 2007 *Constitution of Thailand*, for which see below) will be essential to their continuance.[6]

Like many constitution-makers interested in democratic, rule-of-law reforms during the 1990s, the Thai constitution-makers of 1997 decided to create a range of 'watch-dog' bodies[7] constituting a complex series of checks and balances to ensure that power would be exercised in the public interest; these were the Election Commission, the National Counter-Corruption Commission, the National Audit Commission, the Administrative Courts,[8] the National Human Rights Commission,[9] the Ombudsman,[10] the Special Division of the Supreme Court for Criminal Cases Against Persons Holding Political Office and the Anti-Money-Laundering Office.[11] They also decided to create a Constitutional Court as a capstone that would ensure that the entire constitutional architecture would withstand external forces. Concerning the importance of this institution, James Klein observed as follows in 2001:

> Thai politicians, the military and senior civilian bureaucrats have always reserved for themselves the power to interpret the meaning of law and the intent of the constitution. The 1997 Constitution seeks to remedy these problems by reversing the course of Thai constitutional law. It establishes the Constitution as the basis for all law, thereby reducing the power of politicians and bureaucrats to subvert constitutional intent. Second, it establishes a judicial review process independent of the executive, legislative, and judicial branches, thereby enhancing government accountability and the protection of civil liberties. The central mechanism for these reforms is the Constitutional Court.[12]

This statement is significant, because it is becoming increasingly true in other parts of Asia,[13] and because interpretation is indeed the essence of constitutionalism. Interestingly enough, it seems that, contrary to Klein's assertion and what was thought by many to be a fundamental shift in the Thai polity in which military coups would be a thing of the past, the military still, it now appears, reserves for itself the power to dismiss governments and make constitutional dispensation. For this reason, many who were deeply opposed to Thaksin's authoritarian government were also doubtful about the coup as an appropriate method of removing him. The coup also leaves the question as to whether the device of the military coup will ever be effectively abolished as a means of bringing governments to an end. Be that as it may, in Asia as elsewhere, constitutional courts have in general become the new guardians of constitutional reform, democratic process and the rule of law.[14] Thailand is therefore by no means alone in East Asia in putting its faith in a specialist court of this kind. Taiwan, South Korea, Mongolia, Cambodia, Indonesia and four of the Central Asian former Soviet states also have constitutional courts,[15] and no doubt the constitution-makers had in mind also the then recent example of the Constitutional Court of South Africa.[16] Around the world some 58 states, almost exclusively those with a general system of law based on civil law, have a constitutional court.[17] Considering that no constitutional court is more than 100 years old, this is a remarkable example of the diffusion referred to by Tom Ginsburg:

> The incorporation of Western norms of liberal constitutionalism should not be viewed only as an imposition of ideas from the First World to Third. Instead, it is part of a two-century process of institutional diffusion and transformation ... The emergence of constitutional review ... may involve not only Westernization but also localization of a Western institutional form.[18]

A constitutional court creates what has been called a 'centralized' as opposed to 'decentralized' system,[19] or a 'European' as opposed to an 'American' system,[20] of judicial review. The essential feature of the constitutional court-based system of judicial review, whatever name one attaches to it – and however the meaning of 'constitutional' may differ from one state to another – is that only one court, the constitutional court, has authority to adjudicate questions of constitutional interpretation or to review legislation, and this court is separate from the ordinary judicial system as such, forming in effect a fourth branch of government. It is also clear that many of the countries that have a constitutional court also have a civilian legal system based on that of France or Germany, which offers two strikingly different models of constitutional review, and no doubt the apparent compatibility of a constitutional court and a civilian legal system, as opposed to a common-law system (in which constitutional courts, with the possible exception of the 'hybrid' South African system, have not featured) has been a factor in favour of the creation of a constitutional court in some countries.[21] It is, of course, an interesting avenue of inquiry to discover the genealogy of the institutions that are indispensable to the new Asian constitutionalism.[22] In this case, as with the Indonesian Constitutional Court, the South Korean Court was iconic and that in turn is based on the German model.[23]

The reasons that usually motivate constitution-makers in creating a constitutional court are: first, to ensure adherence to a new constitution and its protection against legislative majorities; second, to ensure unity and finality in interpretation, avoiding the possibility of different courts adopting different interpretations of the constitution; third, to provide a visible symbol of constitutional progress; and fourth, to ensure that judicial deferentialism, which may have characterized previous regimes of judicial review, does not undermine the constitution.[24]

One of the many paradoxes about constitutional courts is that, while their creation is usually the result of a perception that they have succeeded in other jurisdictions, they are peculiarly subject to the political tensions of the jurisdiction in which they were introduced, which are also, of course, highly relevant to the initial decision to create a constitutional court.[25] Not all experiments introducing such a body have been successful, and usually it is politicization, or mishandling by the court of its admittedly difficult role, that is the culprit.[26] Nowhere is this truer than in Thailand.

The two factors indicated above may, however, come together where the prevailing political trend works *in favour* of a process of constitutionalization and democratization; however, this is a trend that may be apparent rather than real, or may be relatively short-lived. The experience of the interplay of these two factors of politics and legal transplantation is quite varied. The creation of a constitutional court[27] may be the result of an axial moment such as the catastrophic defeat of a regime, as occurred with the fall of fascism in Germany and Italy; or political revolution as with the fall of communism in the states that had formed the Soviet Union in Eastern Europe, or the fall of apartheid in South Africa. In East Asia, by contrast, it has generally resulted from a gradual rather than revolutionary emergence of constitutional government, in place of authoritarian or military government. This seems to be true in South Korea, Taiwan, and Indonesia, and also in Thailand. As Victor Ferreres Comella indicates, in such a situation a constitutional court may be 'fragile'; this does not mean, however, that it is more likely to be deferential in its approach compared with 'ordinary' courts. On the contrary, he argues, fragility will more likely lead to judicial activism as a means of asserting the relevance and legitimacy of the court.[28] Such activism may compound the complexity of its legitimation and in turn render the court even more fragile.

There are several typical or possible adjudicatory functions of a constitutional court, so that 'constitutional jurisdiction' may cover a number of different aspects. It may concern any of the following (those applicable to the Thai Constitutional Court of 1998–2006 are indicated in italics):

- the constitutionality of constitutional amendments;[29]
- *the constitutionality of laws in advance of legislation (*ante factum*)*;
- *the constitutionality of laws after legislation (*ex post facto*)*;
- *the constitutionality of decisions by the legislature*;
- the constitutionality of executive actions and decisions;[30]
- petitions from individuals alleging a violation of the constitution;[31]
- *ruling on references from the courts as to constitutionality*;
- *impeachment proceedings against holders of public office*;

- consideration of criminal cases in respect of official corruption;[32]
- *consideration of the qualifications of individuals to hold public office*;
- *disputes as to the competence of organs of state*;
- *the dissolution or merger of political parties and control over the constitutionality of their actions*;
- *the legality of elections and election results*; and
- *control over the constitutionality of regulations made by bodies established under the constitution.*

It may be seen here that the Thai Constitutional Court of 1998–2006 enjoyed a comparatively broadly defined jurisdiction. Most constitutional courts exercise only some of these functions, and some functions may overlap. Clearly, although review of legislation or proposed legislation is a major function, the roles of protecting human rights and checking executive actions as such are not necessarily the most important functions of a constitutional court, which may indeed be carried out by other agencies such as ordinary courts, administrative courts and human rights commissions. In the Thai context, for example, the Constitutional Court of 1998–2006 was not empowered to rule on the constitutionality of executive rules and regulations, except for emergency decrees, review of which was specially mandated to it under the 1997 *Constitution*.[33] The reason for this restriction was that the Administrative Courts were given jurisdiction over these matters, and to give them to the Constitutional Court would have undermined the Administrative Courts, which were also a new institution.[34] Given that, as Klein points out,[35] it is often in relation to executive rules and regulations that real issues arise regarding fundamental rights, the role of the Administrative Courts is possibly at least as important as that of the Constitutional Court.[36] Interestingly enough, the 2007 *Constitution* gives an individual right of petition to the Constitutional Court, which will tend to make fundamental rights much more central to the role of the new Court.[37]

This chapter discusses the role of the Thai Constitutional Court during the reform period of 1998–2006.[38] With the political crisis resulting in the ousting of Prime Minister Thaksin Shinawatra by the military coup of 19 September 2006, the constitutional history of Thailand appeared to move into another of its many phases since 1932.[39] Following the coup, a new constitution, the 2007 *Constitution*, which is the 18th in Thailand's constitutional history (i.e. since the end of the absolute monarchy in 1932), was drafted under the provisions of the 2006 *Constitution of the Kingdom of Thailand (Interim)* (2006 *Interim Constitution*), and was approved by a majority in a referendum in August 2007.[40] The 2007 *Constitution* also makes provision for a Constitutional Court, which differs in composition, and to some extent in powers, compared with its 1998 predecessor.

The 1997 *Constitution* was drafted by a Constitution Drafting Assembly (CDA) consisting of 99 members. Electoral process was used in the choice of members representing the provinces, numbering 76 (one for each province); the balance of 23 members consisted of lawyers, political scientists, civil servants and politicians.

Its remit, expressed in the Preamble to the resulting *Constitution*, embraced everything except the constitutional nature of the monarchy and the system of democracy.[41] The *Constitution* was drafted and brought into effect during the first 10 months of 1997, in the middle of which period the Asian currency crisis – commencing with the floating of the *baht* in June 1997 – convulsed the country and then the entire East Asian region.

The CDA debates and their outcome were an education in constitutional law to the entire political class and the public. Many innovations were adopted, and many existing institutions were reformed. Naturally, not everyone was happy with the result, as in some respects compromises had to be made, not least in respect of the Constitutional Court. But on the whole it has to be said that in terms of fulfilling its objectives, the CDA adopted a strict approach towards corruption and the abuse of power. Considering that the country passed through a cataclysmic economic crisis during precisely the period of enactment and implementation of the 1997 *Constitution* (1997–99), one might be forgiven for asking if this was indeed the right time for such endeavours, and whether the gargantuan efforts involved would not have been better directed to more immediate, that is economic, problems. Thai public opinion, on the contrary, generally regarded the economic and constitutional issues as inextricably linked, and viewed both as coming down to the problem of good governance. Critical therefore to the reforms, to governmental stability and economic recovery, and to human rights, was the Constitutional Court.

The implementation of the 1997 *Constitution* revealed many problems with Thai constitutionalism. The text itself could hardly have been clearer in its unequivocal adherence to constitutional values: it made extensive provision for human rights,[42] the rule of law, accountability for abuse of power, and for stable, elected, civilian government.[43] The result in practice was, as is indicated above, much more ambiguous, especially during 2001–6, the period in which Thaksin and the Thai Rak Thai Party were in power. Abuses of power and of human rights, and widespread corruption,[44] were stated reasons for the 19 September coup. Constitutional devices to ensure the independence of watchdog agencies were manipulated by the party in power, whose critics were harassed by the government-controlled media and some of the subverted watchdog agencies. The members of the National Counter-Corruption Commission (NCCC) resigned in June 2005 after making an unlawful decision in their own interest, and were all replaced. Other difficulties gave rise to Constitutional Court decisions, which are discussed below.

Most critically, a decision of the Election Commission of Thailand (ECT) to allow the election, which was held on 2 April 2006, was challenged in the courts.[45] During the election itself, there were many allegations of widespread vote-buying.[46] The ECT failed to uphold objections to the results, and the Constitutional Court initially confirmed individual results that had been called into question.[47] Although Thaksin's Thai Rak Thai Party won the election, following street demonstrations he announced that he would only serve as a caretaker Prime Minister until a new government was formed; but after taking a short vacation he showed no signs of going. In an unprecedented move the King intervened on 26 April 2006 by addressing the judges of the Constitutional and Administrative Courts directly. He suggested in typically oblique royal language that they should assert their authority under the constitution to invalidate the election, which had been boycotted by opposition parties.[48] Further investigation of the conduct of the political parties (Thai Rak Thai and the Democrat Parties) in the elections of 2 April 2006 was expedited by the military government after the September 2006 coup (see below), resulting in the dissolution of Thai Rak Thai, but not the Democrat Party, as a result of a decision by the Constitutional Tribunal under the 2006 *Interim Constitution*.[49] There was also considerable criticism following the failure of the ECT to disqualify candidates for the senatorial elections with suspected party affiliations[50] and the ECT's failure to prevent vote-buying in those elections.[51] In July 2006, three Election Commissioners were sentenced to four years' imprisonment for mishandling the April 2006 elections.[52]

Inauguration of the Constitutional Court of Thailand

In assessing the Constitutional Court it is, of course, pertinent first to inquire why the Court was set up, especially in the light of Ferreres' correct observation that, 'after all, Constitutional Courts are not strictly necessary';[53] and why it took the form it did.

The Constitutional Court of Thailand derives from the concept of a Constitutional Tribunal, which appears in some of the 1997 *Constitution*'s forerunners since 1945 and again in the 2006 *Interim Constitution*;[54] the constitution-makers were also influenced by the French *Conseil Constitutionnel* (which would be a natural model given that Thailand's private law system, as well as its public law system, is partly at least based on French law), and also by the German Federal Constitutional Court and the Austrian Constitutional Court, with which, like the Indonesian Constitutional Court, it has more in common.[55] The creation of the Constitutional Court was strongly opposed by the Supreme Court judges on the ground that constitutional jurisdiction should be vested in the Supreme Court rather than a separate, specialist court; and that the Constitutional Court should in any event not include political scientists, as had been proposed by the CDA. The constitution-makers were, however, of the view that a Constitutional Court would be more likely to take a broad, as opposed to a narrow, view of its function based on legal interpretative techniques, and that there was merit in having a flagship institution with responsibilities only in respect of the constitution. Even so, the CDA conceded something to the judges in that seven of the fifteen judges of the Constitutional Court were drawn from the ranks of the ordinary judiciary (five from the Supreme Court and two from the Supreme Administrative Court); and the proportion of political scientists on the Court was reduced to three out of fifteen, as opposed to three out of nine as originally proposed.

The Constitutional Court in its final form thus consisted of a President and fourteen judges, appointed by the King on the advice of the Senate, and comprising five judges elected by the Supreme Court Justices from among their own number, two judges elected by the Supreme Administrative Court from among their own numbe, five persons qualified in law, and three persons qualified in political science. The judges held office for one, nine-year term, or until the age of 70 years, if earlier.[56]

The process for electing the members of the Court in the last two categories was complex, and in fact several appointments, especially some of the initial ones, gave rise to sharp differences between the Senate and the Supreme Court over the Senate's investigation of the backgrounds and qualifications of proposed justices, in particular the then Vice-President of the Supreme Court, Amphorn Thongprayoon, Supreme Court Justice Jumphol na Songkhla, and former President of the Parliament, Ukrit Mongkolnavin. These differences resulted in several rulings by the Constitutional Tribunal, which exercised jurisdiction during 1997–8 while the Constitutional Court was being established; these rulings alone indicate the necessity of having a body empowered to adjudicate divisive issues arising between organs of state, even where one of those is the higher judiciary.

In fulfilment of the complex and in fact unique constitutional provisions relating to the appointment of the Constitutional Court, first of all a Selection Committee was chosen, consisting of the President of the Supreme Court; four Deans of law and four Deans of political science chosen from among their own number; and four members of parliament representing parliamentary political parties, each party having one representative, and such representatives electing four from their own number. The Committee, by a resolution supported by three-fourths of its members, nominated ten persons qualified in law and six qualified in political science; the final choice was made by the Senate, the first five lawyers and three political scientists on the list receiving at least one-half of the votes. The Constitutional Court, under Section 268 of the 1997 *Constitution*, had final authority over all matters of constitutional interpretation. This jurisdiction arose principally:

- by reference to the Court from an ordinary civil or criminal court, where a constitutional question arose;[57]
- by a reference from members of the National Assembly or the Prime Minister before an impugned bill became law, on grounds of unconstitutionality;[58]
- by reference from the Ombudsman on grounds of the unconstitutionality of a law;[59]
- by reference under various provisions relating to control of the constitutionality of political parties and their operation;[60]
- by reference from one-fifth of the members of each House of the National Assembly on grounds of the unconstitutionality of an emergency decree;[61]
- in the case of a dispute as powers and duties of state organs by reference of such organs or the President of the National Assembly;[62]
- in respect of legislative procedure and membership of the legislature;[63]
- in respect of the unconstitutionality of regulations made by the NCCC and the ECT;[64]
- in respect of qualifications of members of independent agencies;[65] and

- by reference from the NCCC for further decision as to disqualification from office for failure to declare assets.[66]

One-tenth of the total membership of the National Assembly (or the Prime Minister acting alone) had the power, if of the opinion that a bill which had been passed by the Assembly was inconsistent with the constitution or was enacted contrary to the provisions of the constitution, to have the bill referred to the Constitutional Court for its opinion. In the case of a bill for enactment of an organic law, this power of reference could be exercised by 20 members of the Assembly. If the Constitutional Court ruled that provisions of the bill were unconstitutional, then if the unconstitutional provisions formed the 'essential element' of the bill, the bill would lapse; otherwise only the unconstitutional provisions would lapse and the bill would go for the royal assent.[67]

It is interesting to note that individual citizens adversely affected did not have any right to petition the Court, except indirectly through the Ombudsman or by reference by the court in a civil or criminal case.[68] This perceived defect was corrected in the 2007 *Constitution.*

The procedure in Constitutional Court cases was laid down by unanimous decision of the Court itself, and had to conform to the basic principles of natural justice.[69] The quorum for a decision of the Court was nine, and decisions were taken by a majority, each Judge being required to give a decision and make an oral statement. The Court was required to give a decision setting out the allegations, facts, reasons of law and fact, and the legal provisions relied upon;[70] and the decisions of the Court and of each Judge were required to be published in the gazette. Dissenting opinions were therefore published and were actually quite frequent, an interesting innovation in a civilian jurisdiction, where dissenting judgments are not usual.[71] Recent work on the constitutional courts in Asia indicates that the interpretive techniques and the style of the rendering of judgments in the court are critical to establishing its legitimacy.[72] In the case of the Thai Court, as with the Indonesian *Mahkamah Konstitusi*, formalistic, French-style judgments were given which avoided elaboration as to the reasoning processes, creating the impression that the decisions were arbitrary and unrelated to each other. This impression needs to be moderated, however, by certain other considerations. First, all justices were obliged to render judgment. Second, dissents were allowed and became a regular feature of the decisions, which were often split ones in important cases. Third, the Court made some reference to its own previous decisions in an attempt to provide a consistent and rational jurisprudence; it also consistently consolidated the sometimes large numbers of cases raising similar issues.[73] Since jurisdiction was exercised in cases arising from the ordinary civil and criminal courts only by way of reference to the Constitutional Court,[74] the latter had no power to overrule the Supreme Court, where the latter had given final judgment on a question before the Constitutional Court; its decisions on constitutional issues were simply binding on the court considering the case in question, as indeed they were on all state organs.[75] The Court was not empowered to accept for review a specific provision of law on which it had previously issued a decision.

The Constitutional Court was set up under Chapter VIII of the 1997 *Constitution* with effect from April 1998. The Court was terminated with the revocation of that *Constitution* by royal decree in September 2006 following the military coup. Cases pending in the Court were transferred under Section 35 of the 2006 *Interim Constitution* to the (interim) Constitutional Tribunal, which comprised nine judges: the President of the Supreme Court as President; the President of the Supreme Administrative Court as Vice-President; five other Supreme Court Justices; and two other Supreme Administrative Court Justices. On this point, it should be noted that the 2006 *Interim Constitution* was careful to replace the Constitutional Court with a Constitutional Tribunal in order to prevent challenges concerning the legitimacy of the coup, and any possible criminal or other implications for those responsible for engineering the coup under the 1997 *Constitution*.[76]

Cases in the Constitutional Court

We now proceed to look at the performance of the Constitutional Court during its period of operation, 1998–2006, under headings reflecting main areas of constitutional litigation that arose in practice.

Human rights cases

As a preliminary point, any analysis of the contribution of the Constitutional Court to the enforcement of human rights should take account not only the decisions of the Court itself, but also the larger human rights milieu and the enforcement role of other institutions, such as the National Human Rights Commission (NHRC).[77] In light of this, it is apparent that the role of the Constitutional Court was not as significant as a reading of the 1997 *Constitution* would suggest it ought to have been. A large number of important human rights issues have arisen in Thailand in recent years,[78] and the Constitutional Court has made virtually no contribution to their resolution. There have, for example, been many human rights violations in the south of Thailand in connection with the Muslim separatist movement there.[79] Despite a damning report by the NHRC, those responsible have not been brought to justice.[80] In a few cases, discussed below, the Court gave rather negative and unimpressive judgments. Part of the explanation for this is the absence of a right of individual petition. When the Constitutional Court did consider directly a matter of alleged unconstitutionality of legislation, it was slow to enforce the fundamental rights set out in the *Constitution*.

Disappointing examples of what appears to be an unduly deferential approach that exalted existing legislation over the 1997 *Constitution* (despite the clear provisions of the *Constitution* indicating otherwise) were two cases where the Court considered the rights of the disabled.[81] In 2002, the Ombudsman, who was empowered to submit petitions on behalf of citizens, petitioned on behalf of two lawyers, disabled as a result of childhood poliomyetlitis, who had applied to become an assistant judge in one case and a prosecutor in the other, but were rejected on grounds of their disability. The *Justice Personnel Law*, Section 26(10), prohibits persons with physical disabilities from taking the examination to become a judicial official; it was argued that this section was unconstitutional in that it contravened Section 30 of the *Constitution*, which prohibited discrimination 'on the basis of physical or health conditions'. The Court, in a highly controversial 8–3 decision, ruled Section 26(10) was constitutionally valid, basing its decision on prevailing cultural norms and public policies rather than a progressive ideal of inclusiveness. This decision sent a signal that, despite the constitution-makers' intention that the Constitutional Court should exercise its jurisdiction in a transformative manner, the Court on the contrary saw its position as maintaining the status quo. Interestingly enough, this decision is quite specifically countermanded by provisions of the 2007 *Constitution*, so all is not lost on this issue.[82]

A further example may be seen in the area of freedom of religion. The overtly secular nature of the state in Thailand was modified under the 1997 *Constitution* by the fact that Buddhist monks, novices, and clergy were prohibited under the *Constitution* from voting or standing as a candidate for (or from continuing to sit as a member of) the House of Representatives or the Senate.[83] Muslim *imam*, *ulama*, Catholic monks, nuns and clergy, and so forth, were not subjected to the same restrictions. The Court refused to hold unconstitutional a statutory provision disqualifying a man who became a Buddhist priest from continuing as a member of a local authority, despite the fact that the *Constitution* at Section 38 guaranteed the liberty of a person:

> to profess a religion, a religious sect or creed, and observe religious precepts or exercise a form of worship in accordance with his or her belief, provided it is not contrary to his or her civic duties, public order or good morals.

In exercising this liberty, the section continued, a person was:

> protected from any act of the state, which was derogatory to his or her rights or detrimental to his or her due benefits on the grounds of professing a religion, a religious sect or creed or observing religious precepts or exercising a form of worship in accordance with his or her different belief from that of others.

Also, Section 29 laid down the principle that the restriction of rights and liberties as recognized by the *Constitution* should not be imposed on a person, except by virtue of provisions of the law specifically enacted for the purpose determined by the 1997 *Constitution*, and only to the extent of necessity, and provided that it should not affect the essential substances of such rights and liberties (this section did not apparently suffice to give any priority to the rights of the disabled in the cases mentioned in the examples above). The Constitutional Court held[84] that the law was not unconstitutional as it was saved by the fact of its predating the *Constitution*. Part of the argument, however, was that the prohibition did not actually cause the local authority member to lose his right of freedom of religion, as that right still existed despite the prohibition. This part of the decision seemed to fly in the face of Section 29 and Section 38, as clearly his right had been abridged at the very least, and it could be argued that, in terms of Section 38, it was in fact his civic duty, if anything, to continue to serve as a member of the local authority. The Court, however, considered the other sections of the 1997 *Constitution* that had the effect of prohibiting Buddhist priests, novices, monks or clergy from voting or standing as a candidate as stated above. Thus in approximating the position of a member of a local authority to that of an elected member of the National Assembly, the Court privileged the principle of religious disqualification over that of religious freedom, and in a sense implicitly downgraded constitutional human rights as well as civic duty.

Sometimes, however, the Court asserted fundamental rights. In a 1998 case the Court struck down a regulation of the ECT that purported to deprive of state assistance those who had failed to cast a vote in an election. The ECT had powers to prescribe punishments for failure to vote, but the Court held that the punishment was in effect prescribed by the 1997 *Constitution* itself, which at Section 68(2) stated that citizens who fail to vote lose only their right to vote, but can suffer no other penalties; further sanctions could only be imposed by an Act of Parliament.[85] In another case the Court ruled as unconstitutional a law requiring a married woman to assume her husband's surname, on the grounds that such law was gender-discriminatory.[86] The same principle, however, was not applied to a law which allowed the wives of Thai men to acquire Thai nationality automatically but did not accord the same status to husbands of Thai wives, who were told by the Court that they could acquire Thai nationality by other means.[87] It also upheld the principle of judicial independence and restricted the powers of military courts, when it held that a military judge can only deliver judgment if he or she presided over the case; and that where the military court sought to impose a sentence heavier than that prescribed in the ordinary law, the case should be referred to the local civil court.[88] Other cases failed to assert the rights of traditional communities to have their interests taken into account with regard to development projects.[89]

The performance of the Court in this area has been at best patchy, the road to vigorous enforcement of the 1997 *Constitution* remaining one on which the Court apparently feared to tread.

Cases concerning corruption

The other main group of cases concerns issues of direct political interest relating to official corruption. The case of Sanan Kachornprasart in 2000 was an indication that the anti-corruption function of the Court was producing results. Sanan was the second most important politician in Thailand, Deputy Prime Minister, Minister of the Interior, and Secretary-General of the (then ruling) Democrat Party, when he was investigated on corruption charges in 1999. He resigned from his ministerial offices immediately after being indicted in March 2000 for falsification of his declaration of assets and liabilities. In August 2000 he was found guilty by the Constitutional Court, was barred from political office for five years, and resigned his party political office.[90]

However, in another of its major early cases, concerning the then Prime Minister Thaksin Shinawatra in 2001, the Court damaged its standing irrevocably.[91] The case involved an investigation of claims that Thaksin in his declaration of assets, before being elected Prime Minister in early 2001, had concealed vast sums, most of his fortune, in fact, as part of a dishonest scheme to conceal conflicts of interest, which were unlawful under the 1997 *Constitution*. It was found that the assets had been registered in the names of his housekeeper, chauffeur, driver, security guard and business colleagues.[92] Thaksin was charged not long before the general election. NCCC had been granted wide ranging powers not only to investigate, but where it found that a person had failed to disclose assets and liabilities, or had attempted to supply false information, it could order that person from office with immediate effect for five years. However, as a safeguard, this power to issue what has been termed a 'red card' had first to be approved by the Constitutional Court.[93] The NCCC duly conducted its investigation and passed judgment by an 8–1 margin against Thaksin. If the decision of the NCCC had been allowed to stand unchallenged, the result would have been an automatic suspension from politics for five years operating with immediate effect, thus depriving Thaksin of the premiership. Instead of accepting the findings as part of a process, Thaksin was able to subvert the 1997 *Constitution*. He countered the accusations openly on the political stage by suggesting that the findings were merely part of a political smear campaign.[94] The NCCC's decision was appealed to the Constitutional Court, where it was argued that the failure to declare these assets was no more than an honest mistake. Although the argument was not accepted, the Constitutional Court voted narrowly in Thaksin's favour. The 8–7 outcome was reached after two votes: the first rejected by a margin of 11–4 (Thaksin's argument that he was not required to make an asset declaration); the second rejected by a margin of 7–4 (Thaksin's assertion that the concealment of assets had been an honest mistake). Overall, according to the conventions of the Court's unusual voting system, the two votes of four were added together to make eight which is set against the seven who had voted him guilty on the second ballot. This result raised serious questions about the impartiality of the Court, the role of the political scientists on the Court whose votes were crucial in turning the result in Thaksin's favour, and a voting system which seemed to defy logic.

This decision was indeed a surprising outcome on the facts, given that in 17 other similar cases[95] decided previously, the Constitutional Court had always endorsed the decision of the NCCC. The failure to act decisively and punish the Prime Minister for this manifest breach of the rules severely undermined the Court's credibility in the face of political interference and a challenge at the highest level. It should be recognized that quite apart from any illegitimate pressures that may have been placed on them, the judges on the Constitutional Court had an unenviable choice in making their decision. A vote confirming Thaksin's disqualification by the NCCC, if it had been carried through, would have in effect invalidated the result of the election with the prospect of political turmoil, and the ensuing crisis would have placed further strain on the constitutional arrangements with what the experience of 2005–6 would indicate to be unpredictable effects.

In a later case in 2006, 28 senators submitted an impeachment petition to the Court against the Prime Minister for conflicts of interest and improprieties in the sell-off of Shin Corporation (referred to earlier), citing Section 209 which limits the power of ministers to hold shares and partnerships. The Court rejected the petition, a majority of the judges deciding that the petition failed to present sufficient grounds to support the Prime Minister's alleged misconduct.

The election case

Another controversial case concerning Thaksin related to the 2 April 2006 elections, called as a snap election, three years ahead of schedule, to counter widespread public opposition to his premiership. Thaksin's Thai Rak Thai Party obtained 57 per cent of the votes, but the elections were boycotted by opposition parties, which meant that many seats were not filled. Two rounds of by-elections failed to fill the vacant seats. In a widely reported speech to the judges of the Constitutional Court and the Administrative Court on 25 April 2006 the King urged them to intervene under the 1997 *Constitution* to resolve the crisis following the contested election on 2 April 2006. The judges of the Supreme Court, the Supreme Administrative Court and the Constitutional Court met to discuss the situation, and predictably the Constitutional Court on 5 May 2006, in a suit brought by a group of academics, held by an 8–6 majority that the election was invalid. Their grounds were that the Thai Rak Thai Party had manipulated the attainment of a quorum of votes cast in certain constituencies order to 'validate' the election, and that voter privacy had been invaded by the placement of polling booths and ballot boxes.

Cases concerning powers of economic regulation

Given the economic situation obtaining as the 1997 *Constitution* moved into its implementation phase, it is not surprising that economic regulation featured in many of the Court's early cases. In its very first decision in 1998, the Court ruled on the constitutionality of four emergency executive decrees issued by the previous Democrat government of Chuan Leekpai in response to the economic crisis.[96] The government had issued the decrees in May 1998, expanding the role of the Financial Restructuring Authority and the Assets Management Corporation, to settle the debts of the Financial Institutions Development Fund through the issue of 500 billion *baht* (about US$14.2 million) in bonds, and to authorize the Ministry of Finance to seek 200 billion *baht* (about US$5.7 million) in overseas loans. On the last day of parliamentary debate on these decrees when it was clear they would be passed and in order to postpone a vote, a minor political party invoked Section 219 of the 1997 *Constitution* relating to emergency powers to question their constitutionality. It was argued that, since there was no emergency or necessary urgency as required by Section 218(2) of the 1997 *Constitution*, the Government could not make any emergency decrees. Section 218(1) allows emergency decrees to be passed on the basis of national economic security, and the Court ruled that it was obvious that the nation was in an economic crisis, and that the decrees were in fact designed to deal with national economic security.[97] A similar suit by the same party impeaching Prime Minister Chuan for signing Letters of Intent with the International Monetary Fund to secure an emergency loan without parliamentary approval under Section 224 of the 1997 *Constitution* was also rejected on the grounds that the Letters of Intent were not in the nature of treaties falling under Section 224, nor were they contractual agreements, as they lacked any enforcement provisions.

Cases concerning appointment processes

One of the most important functions of the Court was to rule on the validity of sometimes extremely complex processes of appointment of state officials and independent agencies, and the qualifications of particular persons to hold office. Many of these cases were politically contentious. As we have seen, this phenomenon commenced during the transitional phase, even before the Court assumed jurisdiction. A notable example was the case of Auditor-General Jaruvan Maintaka. Jaruvan was one of three nominees for the position of Auditor-General in 2001, but had received fewer votes than one other nominee when the State Audit Commission (SAC) voted on the nominations under the provisions of the *State Audit Act* 1979. However, all three nominees were forwarded to the Senate, which was constitutionally empowered to advise the King whom to appoint, and the Senate had voted in her favour. It was argued before the Court that the SAC should, under Section 135 of the 1997 *Constitution*, have forwarded only the name of a single nominee, that is, the one with the most votes. In July 2004 the Court ruled this selection process unconstitutional, but failed, apparently inconsistently with another similar case concerning the Chairman of the EC, to hold that Jaruvan should accordingly leave office, thus causing some uncertainty about her status.[98] Jaruvan, who had considerable public support for her vigorous approach to her task, refused to resign without an instruction from the King. The SAC then made another nomination, which was approved by the Senate. Yet again, the crisis was resolved by royal intervention. The King refused his assent to the appointment; the Senate rejected a motion to reaffirm Jaruvan's appointment, and referred the matter back to the SAC who voted unanimously in favour of Jaruvan after receiving a memorandum from the King's Principal Private Secretary advising that the situation should be resolved. This episode, although it represented a significant defeat for the Thaksin government, was hardly a victory for the rule of law. A proper course following the Court's decision, which should have clarified its own consequences, should have resulted in Jaruvan's resignation and new appointment process following the constitutional provisions.

Conclusions

What should appear then on the Constitutional Court's tombstone? That it represented a failed experiment, or an incomplete but promising step forward? In the broadest context, the Thai Constitutional Court should be seen as a part of the development of Thai constitutionalism since 1932. At one level it was indeed a failed experiment in that in the final analysis it was able to survive neither the September 2006 coup,[99] nor the scrutiny of public or expert opinion, nor indeed the critical appraisal of the process of constitution-drafting during 2007. In its defence, the real reason for the abolition of the Court was not the indifference of its performance, but the danger that the Court would rule the coup itself an unconstitutional action, with adverse criminal and political consequences for the generals: the fact that this danger was clearly perceived by them is probably indeed, somewhat backhandedly, to the Court's credit. The Court certainly failed however to call to account in any meaningful way the authoritarian and manipulative government of 2001–6, save for the ruling on the April 2006 election, which was in any case a ruling prompted by the King and the judiciary as an entity, rather than one irresistibly demanded by the situation and the Court's jurisdiction in the ordinary course. It failed also to correct serious human rights abuses. In reply to these charges one could say that it was the responsibility not just of the Constitutional Court but of *all of* the constitutionally-established organs to resist and correct executive excesses, so that the Court was no more guilty than many of the other watch-dog agencies that, unlike the Court, survived the coup. Having said that, the Court's treatment of the emergency decrees indicates a potentially large area of executive immunity untrammelled by anything the Court has said.[100]

In his book on constitutional courts in East Asia, Tom Ginsburg[101] establishes a theory under which the powers of a constitutional court will depend on the extent to which it is seen as an insurance mechanism at the time it was created. In other words, in a dominant party system, the court will have weak powers, as the constitution-makers will not conceive the court as having an extensive role which could undercut the dominant party's control of the political system; whereas under a more balanced or fragmented political system where the party in power may lose control, the court will be given broad powers to enable the party to pursue its agenda through the court and successfully control the more divergent policies of its opponents. The Thai case provides an interesting example to test this theory. It was created under a balanced political system in which there had been invariably coalition governments, and there were several changes of government during the drafting process; in fact the constitution-making process had to a significant extent fallen out of the hands of the political parties during the mid-1990s. On Ginsburg's theory the Court should have been designed as an institution with broad powers, as indeed was the case. However, in practice the Court did not exercise its jurisdiction vigorously during 1998–2001, and was in effect, during 2001–5 at least, converted into a weak institution carrying no really significant threat to Thaksin's party which appeared, given the election results of 2000 and 2004, to be emerging as the dominant party in a dominant party system. Ironically, it was one of the objectives of the 1997 *Constitution* to create conditions for strong governments, which could not be easily dismissed as in the past. Thus, Ginsburg's theory in the Thai context could be seen as not simply applying to the Constitutional Court's creation, but also (or rather) as extending beyond that to its actual performance over time, subject perhaps to the objection that this view does not explain the Court's behaviour during 1998–2001.

The task of interpreting a constitution is given in the final analysis to those with the power of constitutional review. In general it is felt that this important power should be given to the judicial branch. Indeed, it is a reasonable indication of the existence of constitutionalism in a given society that there is an independent agency that not only has jurisdiction to review legislative and executive actions, but in practice performs that task in a consistent and concerted manner. Without this kind of judicial review it is highly doubtful if constitutionalism, or the rule of law as properly defined, actually exists. What the Thai experiment does *not* prove is that judicial review will not work, or will *only* work under a decentralized judicial-review system. The constitution-makers of 1997 were right to create the Court. Their successors of 2007 paid some attention to the mistakes that were undoubtedly made and have created a new court designed according to better principles, which is to say that the new Court is appointed under a process that is simpler and perhaps less open to manipulation by the executive, and has a somewhat broader jurisdiction. Arguably, it should also have had only judges who are legally qualified, and who are able and clearly mandated to give judgment in an accountable, rational and if necessary vigorous way that also recognizes the logical and practical limits of a constitutional court's jurisdiction and responds to demonstrated needs reflected in the text of the *Constitution*. To this end the judges should be qualified lawyers of considerable standing; the selection process should be thorough and transparent; the reasoning and interpretive process should be open, explanatory, and represent a continuous and logically structured discourse; the Court's jurisdiction should be accessible to any citizen; and the Court should be given adequate resources for legal research.

Although it is not the burden of this chapter to examine the Constitutional Court in its second manifestation under the 2007 *Constitution*, it is worth noting a few points of difference, which may help to understand the way in which the new Court has been conceived in light of the 1998–2006 experience. As things rest following the 2007 reforms, the following points seem pertinent.

The Court consists of nine judges, that is a President and eight other judges, comprising three Supreme Court judges elected from amongst their own number (they also elect the President); two Supreme Administrative Court judges elected from amongst their own number; four others, being two lawyers and two persons qualified in political science, public administration, or social sciences (these four must have held high office under the constitution or be a lawyer of 30 years standing or a professor, and must not have been a member of any political party during the previous three years).[102] The Selection Committee consists of the President of the Supreme Court, the President of the Supreme Administrative Court, the President of the House of Representatives, the Leader of the Opposition and the President of one of the watch-dog bodies.[103] The Senate has power to approve or send back names of candidates, but unlike under the 1997 *Constitution* the

Selection Committee can *confirm rejected nominees*. As previously mentioned, the Court has the extra power to entertain petitions directly from individuals, and thus the range of issues potentially before it is greater.[104]

The question remains, does the Thai experience indicate that it was a mistake to set up a separate constitutional jurisdiction? The Thai view, based on express and implied responses to the experience of 1998–2006 is that setting up a separate constitutional jurisdiction was not in itself a mistake; rather, the weak performance of the Court is attributed to the overweening nature of executive power during that period, and the solution is to link constitutional jurisdiction more firmly to judicial independence as such by giving the Supreme Court a large role in the appointment process. In this sense, the settlement of 2007 seems to accede partly to the objections raised by the Supreme Court with regard to the 1997 version of the Court. Whether this means that the Court has or will behave more or less vigorously is a matter for further inquiry.

If the Constitutional Court of 1998–2006 has an important legacy, it would be that it has been demonstrated that an institution of this kind is needed and potentially can function effectively, provided it is properly set up and provided it performs its task with care and wisdom. It is of cardinal importance that the new Court be insulated as far as possible from political pressures, so that it becomes a careful moderator of the political process rather than a mere barometer of it.

Notes

1. F. Bacon, *Francis Bacon's Essays* (London: Dent, 1966), 74.
2. "Singapore's Troubled Shin Corp Deal," *Asian Times*, December 13, 2006; Peter Leyland, "Constitutional Problems and Constitutional Reform: The UK, Thailand and the Case of Preservation as well as Change," in *Constitution Reform: Comparative Perspectives*, ed. Andrew Harding and Thawilwadee Bureekul (Bangkok: King Prajadhipok's Institute, 2009), 69–88.
3. See Note 48.
4. For discussion of the reforms, see generally D. McCargo, ed., *Reforming Thai Politics* (Copenhagen: NIAS, 2002); M. H. Nelson, ed., *Thailand's New Politics: KPI Yearbook 2001* (Nonthaburi: King Prajadhipok's Institute and White Lotus Press, 2001); William A. Callahan and Institute of Southeast Asian Studies, *Imagining Democracy: Reading 'the Events of May' in Thailand* (Singapore: Institute of Southeast Asian Studies, 1998); Andrew Harding, "May There be Virtue: 'New Asian Constitutionalism' in Thailand," *Australian Journal of Asian Law* 3 (2001): 24–48. The account in the text is broadly based on Leyland, "Constitutional Problems and Constitutional Reform: The UK, Thailand and the Case of Preservation as well as Change".
5. The ASEAN Charter of November 2007, an initiative commenced with the Kuala Lumpur Declaration on the Establishment of the ASEAN Charter, December 2005, is another significant context in which this experience would be valid. The Charter affirms Association of Southeast Asian Nations (ASEAN) commitment to strengthening democracy, good governance and the rule of law, and promoting and protecting human rights and fundamental freedoms. See further, R. C. Severino, *Framing the ASEAN Charter: An ISEAS Perspective* (Singapore: Institute of Southeast Asian Studies, 2005).
6. See further, S. Imaizumi, "Political Reform and the Constitutional Court of Thailand," in *Law, Development and Socio-Economic Changes in Asia*, ed. N. Sakumoto, M. Kobayashi and S. Imaizumi (Chiba: Institute for Developing Economies, Japan

External Trade Organisation, 2003), 227–56; A. Harding and P. Leyland, "The Constitutional Courts of Thailand and Indonesia: Two Case Studies from South East Asia," *Journal of Comparative Law* 3:2 (2008): 118. T. Ginsburg, "Constitutional Courts in East Asia: Understanding Variation," *Journal of Comparative Law* 3:2 (2008): 80. T. Ginsburg, "Constitutional Afterlife: The Continuing Impact of Thailand's Postpolitical Constitution," *International Journal of Constitutional Law* 7 (2009): 83–105.

7. P. Leyland, "Courts and Watchdog Bodies: Appointment Processes Reviewed and Compared," in *Constitution Reform: Comparative Perspectives*, ed. Andrew Harding and Thawilwadee Bureekul (Bangkok: King Prajadhipok's Institute, 2009), 357–79; Uwanno Bowornsak and W. D. Burns, "The Thai Constitution of 1997: Sources and Process," *University of British Columbia Law Review* 32 (1998): 227.
8. P. Leyland, "Droit Administratif Thai Style: A Comparative Analysis of the Administrative Courts in Thailand," *Australian Journal of Asian Law* 8 (2006): 121–54; King Prajadhipok's Institute, *Monitoring and Evaluating of Performance of the Administrative Court* (Bangkok: King Prajadhipok's Institute, 2003).
9. A. J. Harding, "Thailand's Reforms: Human Rights and the National Commission," *Journal of Comparative Law* 1 (2006): 88–100; King Prajadhipok's Institute, *Monitoring and Evaluating of Performance of Independent Organisations: The National Human Rights Commission of Thailand* (Bangkok: King Prajadhipok's Institute, 2004).
10. P. Leyland, "The Ombudsman Principle in Thailand," *Journal of Comparative Law* 2 (2007): 137–50.
11. The Anti-Money-Laundering Office was set up under statutory provisions, but may be seen as a significant part of the reform process.
12. J. R. Klein, "The Battle for the Rule of Law in Thailand: The Constitutional Court of Thailand," in *Constitutional Court of Thailand: The Provisions and the Working of the Court*, ed. A. Raksasataya and J. R. Klein (Bangkok: Constitution for the People Society, 2001), 3.
13. Tom Ginsburg, *Judicial Review in New Democracies: Constitutional Courts in Asian Cases* (New York: Cambridge University Press, 2003).
14. Colin Durkop and Yap Hui Bin, eds, *Present Status and Future Development of Constitutional Jurisdiction in Asia* (Singapore: Konrad Adenauer Stiftung, 2003). See further, the chapters by Tom Ginsburg and Hendrianto in this book; and the special issue of the *Journal of Comparative Law* 3 (2008).
15. All created since 1988, except that of Taiwan's Constitutional Court which dates from 1947 but was reformed during the mid-1980s. See, further, Ginsburg, *Judicial Review in New Democracies: Constitutional Courts in Asian Cases*, 13. See also, Lee Epstein, Olga Shvetsova and Jack Knight, "The Role of Constitutional Courts in the Establishment and Maintenance of Democratic Systems," *Law and Society Review* 35 (2001): 117.
16. Set up under the interim *Constitution of the Republic of South Africa* in 1993 and retaining a key position in the 1996 *Constitution of the Republic of South Africa*. For comparative discussion of a number of constitutional courts, see the forthcoming special issue of the *Journal of Comparative Law* 3:2 (2008). See also the chapters by Tom Ginsburg and Hendrianto in this book.
17. Ramos states that of those states having at some point contemplated constitutional review, 46 per cent have set up a constitutional court: Francisco Ramos, "The Establishment of Constitutional Courts: A Review of 128 Democracies," *Review of Law and Economics* 2 (2006): 103.
18. Tom Ginsburg, "Confucian Constitutionalism? The Emergence of Constitutional Review in Korea and Taiwan," *Law and Social Inquiry* 27 (2002): 763. The present author has called this phenomenon 'new Asian constitutionalism': Andrew Harding, "New Asian Constitutionalism: Myth or Reality?," in *Constitution Reform: Comparative*

Perspectives, ed. Andrew Harding and Thawilwadee Bureekul (Bangkok: King Prajadhipok's Institute, 2009), 25–49. For constitutional courts in general, see the forthcoming special issue of the *Journal of Comparative Law* 3:2 (2008): 1.

19. That is, one in which only one court, as opposed to any court of law, is empowered to interpret the constitution. See further, A. Harding, P. Leyland and T. Groppi, "Constitutional Courts: Forms, Functions and Practice in Comparative Perspective," *Journal of Comparative Law* 3 (2008): 1.
20. Reflecting that fact that it was created initially in Austria and then in continental European systems, whereas many states are also influenced by the United States' system and the constitutional role of the United States Supreme Court. For a review of constitutional courts globally, see Arne Mavcic, *The Constitutional Review* (Den Bosch: Bookworld Publications, 2001); R. Machacek, *Austrian Contributions to the Rule of Law: The Constitutional Court, the Administrative Court, European Perspectives* (Kehl, Arlington, VA: N. P. Engel, 1994).
21. Mark Tushnet, "Alternative Forms of Judicial Review," *Michigan Law Review* 101 (2002–3): 2781. Some civil law countries such as Japan and Philippines have adopted the 'American' model of review by the Supreme Court.
22. Andrew Harding, "New Asian Constitutionalism: Myth or Reality?," *International Islamic University Law Journal* 14 (2006):153–75.
23. See Hendrianto's and Tom Ginsburg's chapters in this book.
24. Victor Ferreres Comella, "The Consequences of Centralizing Constitutional Review in a Special Court: Some Thoughts on Judicial Activism," *Texas Law Review* 82 (2004): 1705–36.
25. Harding, Leyland and Groppi, "Constitutional Courts: Forms, Functions and Practice in Comparative Perspective."
26. T. Ginsburg and G. Ganzorig, "When Courts and Politics Collide: Mongolia's Constitutional Crisis," *Columbia Journal of Asian Law* 14 (2001): 309.
27. Or, for that matter, its resuscitation from a condition of comparative irrelevance, as in the case of the Council of Grand Justices in Taiwan, for which see Ginsburg, "Confucian Constitutionalism? The Emergence of Constitutional Review in Korea and Taiwan."
28. Ferreres, "The Consequences of Centralizing Constitutional Review in a Special Court: Some Thoughts on Judicial Activism."
29. Although it could propose constitutional amendments: *Constitution of the Kingdom of Thailand* 1997 s. 336.
30. These are, however, scrutinized by the Administrative Courts: see Leyland, "Droit Administratif Thai Style: A Comparative Analysis of the Administrative Courts in Thailand."
31. Named officials such as the Ombudsman could challenge constitutionality in the Constitutional Court, but not citizens as such. This has been changed by *Constitution of the Kingdom of Thailand* 2007 (see Notes 68 and 104).
32. This was reserved for the ordinary courts.
33. *Constitution of the Kingdom of Thailand* 1997 s. 219. They were considered in several cases: see below.
34. Leyland, "Droit Administratif Thai Style: A Comparative Analysis of the Administrative Courts in Thailand"; Peter Leyland, "The Emergence of Administrative Justice in Thailand under the 1997 Constitution," in *Administrative Law and Governance in Asia*, ed. T. Ginsburg and A. Chan (Oxford: Routledge, 2009), 230–56. See also, Peter Leyland's chapter in this book.
35. Klein, "The Battle for the Rule of Law in Thailand: The Constitutional Court of Thailand," 3.
36. Leyland, "Constitutional Problems and Constitutional Reform: The UK, Thailand and the Case of Preservation as well as Change," xx.

37. See below for discussion of the new Constitutional Court.
38. During 1998–2002 the Court decided 237 cases, 56 per cent of which concerned the constitutionality of laws, and 27 per cent concerned political parties and removals from office. Statistics are not available for the later period due to the abolition of the Court.
39. Pinai Nanakorn, "The Remaking of the Constitution in Thailand," *Singapore Journal of International and Comparative Law* 6 (2002): 50; Andrew Harding, "South East Asia 1997–2006: Two Case Studies on the Politics of Law and Development," in *Globalisation and Resistance: Law Reform in Asia after the Financial Crisis*, ed. Christoph Antons and Volkmar Gessmer (Oxford: Hart Publishing, 2007), 133–55.
40. Andrew Harding, "Dynamics and Problems of Constitution-making in Asia and Beyond" (paper presented at the King Prajadhipok's Institute Congress VIII, Bangkok, Thailand, November, 2006).
41. The phrase used in Thailand is 'the democratic regime with the King as head of state'.
42. Harding, "Thailand's Reforms: Human Rights and the National Commission," 88.
43. Bowornsak and Burns, "The Thai Constitution of 1997: Sources and Process."
44. For discussion of corruption in Thai politics, see P. Phongaichit and S. Piriyarangsan, *Corruption and Democracy in Thailand* (Chiang Mai: Silkworm Books, 1996).
45. An early election was called by the Prime Minister to head off the controversy which had arisen from the Shin Corporation (a telecommunications company) deal. The Shinawatra family sold their 49.6 per cent stake in the corporation of US$1.88 billion without any payment of capital gains tax following a change in the law to make this exemption legal.
46. These led to the Constitutional Tribunal's decisions of 30 May 2007 dissolving the Thai Rak Thai Party: see Note 49.
47. See "*End of the Beginning in Thailand's Crisis," Bangkok Post, May 19, 2006.*
48. See "April 2 Election: Charter Court to Examine the Legality of Poll," *The Nation*, May 1, 2006.
49. See The Constitutional Court, "Summary of the Decision of the Constitutional Tribunal Case Group 1," http://www.concourt.or.th/download/news/Party1.pdf; The Constitutional Court, "Summary of the Decision of the Constitutional Tribunal Case Group 2," http://www.concourt.or.th/download/news/Party2.pdf. Thai Rak Thai was unanimously found guilty on all charges, together with three minor parties which were also dissolved. In particular, the verdict was based on the fact that a few high-ranking party members were directly involved in bribing several small parties into competing in constituencies that were bases of the former opposition parties, in order to ensure that the minimum 20 per cent turnout requirement was met; the Court dissolved Thai Rak Thai and banned 111 members of its executive committee, including Thaksin himself, from politics for a period of five years. It was also ruled that there was inadequate evidence supporting the charge that the Democrats bribed small parties into exposing some high-profile Thai Rak Thai party members' involvement in election fraud in a series of by-elections in April 2006; and that the Democrat Party did not defame Thaksin or urge voters to cast a 'no' vote in the election. Accordingly, this party avoided dissolution.
50. "Democrats Mull Suit against EC," *The Nation*, 7 April, 2006.
51. "EC's Conduct Panned as Inefficient, Incompetent," *The Nation*, April 20, 2006; "Major Party is Buying' Likely Vote Winner," *The Nation*, April 9, 2006.
52. "Thai Court Convicts 3 for Election Missteps," *International Herald Tribune*, July 26, 2006.
53. Ferreres, "The Consequences of Centralizing Constitutional Review in a Special Court: Some Thoughts on Judicial Activism," 1736.

54. The text of the 2006 *Interim Constitution* can be found at http://www.senate.go.th/pdf/const.pdf. The text of the 2007 *Constitution* can be found at http://www.asianlii.org/th/legis/const/2007/1.html
55. King Chulalongkorn set up a 'Council of State' in 1892, with himself as President, but this was short-lived. The idea was partially revived in the creation of the present Council of State (*Krisdika*), which is not an independent body but part of the executive responsible mainly for drafting laws and training public lawyers.
56. See *Constitution of the Kingdom of Thailand* 1997 ss. 255–68 for provisions on the composition and procedure of the Constitutional Court.
57. *Constitution of the Kingdom of Thailand* 1997 s. 264.
58. *Constitution of the Kingdom of Thailand* 1997 s. 262.
59. *Constitution of the Kingdom of Thailand* 1997 s. 198.
60. *Constitution of the Kingdom of Thailand* 1997 ss. 47, 63, 96–97, 118.
61. *Constitution of the Kingdom of Thailand* 1997 s. 219.
62. *Constitution of the Kingdom of Thailand* 1997 s. 266.
63. *Constitution of the Kingdom of Thailand* 1997 ss. 133, 177, 180.
64. *Constitution of the Kingdom of Thailand* 1997 ss. 319, 320, 324.
65. See, for example, *Constitution of the Kingdom of Thailand* 1997 s. 142.
66. *Constitution of the Kingdom of Thailand* 1997 s. 295. In addition the Constitutional Court, like other independent agencies, had power to make proposals for constitutional amendment: *Constitution of the Kingdom of Thailand* 1997 s. 336.
67. *Constitution of the Kingdom of Thailand* 1997 s. 262.
68. For examples of instances where the lack of an individual right of petition has worked detrimentally on fundamental rights, see Asian Human Rights Commission, "Thailand: What Can be Done When a Constitution Cannot be Enforced," http://www.ahrchk.net/statements/mainfile.php/2006statements/427/; Asian Human Rights Commission, "Thailand: Somchai Case Reveals Flaws in Thai Constitution," http://www.ahrchk.net/statements/mainfile.php/2006statements/418/
69. *Constitution of the Kingdom of Thailand* 1997 s. 269.
70. *Constitution of the Kingdom of Thailand* 1997 s. 267.
71. Interestingly, the same applies in the Indonesian Court, another recent creation. See the chapter by Hendrianto in this book.
72. S. A. Butt, "Judicial Review in Indonesia: Between Civil Law and Accountability? A Study of Constitutional Court Decisions" (PhD diss., University of Melbourne, 2006), 81ff.
73. For example, a large number of cases involving changes in bank interest, brought in 1998–9.
74. Under the *Constitution of the Kingdom of Thailand* 1997 s. 264.
75. *Constitution of the Kingdom of Thailand* 1997 s. 268.
76. See 2006 *Interim Constitution* Section 35, which introduced a Constitutional Tribunal in place of the Constitutional Court, and Section 37, which specifies the extent of the immunity for the coup. But for these provisions, the coup-leaders would have been liable to prosecution under Section 63 of the 1997 *Constitution* and the ordinary criminal law.
77. Harding, "Thailand's Reforms: Human Rights and the National Commission," 83.
78. There have been many allegations of extra-judicial killing in pursuance of the government's anti-drug policy. None of these has given rise to any proceedings in the Constitutional Court. Concern along similar lines relates to the disappearance of a human rights lawyer, Somchai Neelaphaijit, while in police custody. While it has been accepted in general terms that the police were responsible for his death, no one has been punished even three years after the disappearance. For further discussion of humans rights abuses in the Muslim Southern provinces, see Harding, "Thailand's Reforms: Human Rights and the National Commission."
79. Ibid., 88.

80. Ibid.
81. Cases 16 and 44/2002. See also Case 3/2001, where the Court failed to enforce fundamental rights provisions in favour of an accused who had been subjected to an ankle restraint for 28 months; and Case 11/2001 on presumptions in drug-trafficking cases.
82. The *Constitution of the Kingdom of Thailand* 2008 extensively recognizes the rights of disabled persons in Sections 30, 40, 49, 54, 80, 152.
83. *Constitution of the Kingdom of Thailand* 1997 ss. 106(2), 118(5), 109(3), 126(4), 133(5).
84. Case 44/1999.
85. Case 15/1998.
86. Case 21/2003.
87. Case 37/2003. Cf. Case 48/2002 and Case 45/2003.
88. Case 24/2003.
89. Case 59 and Case 62/2002.
90. See "Thai Minister in Corruption Scandal," *BBC News*, August 10, 2000, http://news.bbc.co.uk/2/hi/asia-pacific/874086.stm
91. This passage is based on Leyland, "Constitutional Problems and Constitutional Reform: The UK, Thailand and the Case of Preservation as well as Change."
92. Thaksin's staff were recorded as among the top 10 holders of shares on the Thai stock exchange.
93. *Organic Act on Counter Corruption* 1999. Section 34 was drafted to suggest that where there was such evidence the confirmation would be a formality: 'when the Constitutional Court gives a final decision that it is the case of an intentional submission of the account showing particulars of assets and liabilities and supporting documents with false statements being included therein or failure to disclose facts which should have been disclosed'. Most decisions have been confirmed, but Thaksin was very much an exception.
94. See P. Phongpaichit and C. Baker, *Thaksin: The Business of Politics in Thailand* (Chiang Mai: Silkworm Books, 2005), 3.
95. P. Leyland, "Thailand's Constitutional Watchdogs: Dobermans, Bloodhounds, or Lapdogs?," *Journal of Comparative Law* 2 (2007): 151.
96. Case 1/1998.
97. Case 1/1998. In a similar case, 12/1998, the Court held that statutory immunity of public officials from negligence suits in respect of administrative decisions was not unconstitutional. And in cases 3–5, 9–35, 38–43 and 50/1999 the Court repeatedly ruled in favour of the validity of economic legislation, including agreements with the International Monetary Fund designed to deal with the economic crisis. Clear limits appeared to be drawn in these cases on the Court's willingness to fetter executive action in economic and banking matters: cases 9–10, 14–15/2001; 33, 35–49/2001; 9, 13, 19 34, 40, 45–47, 49, 57, 61/2002; 4, 8–11, 14, 30, 34–36/2003.
98. For a chronology of facts and decisions in the Jaruvan case, see "Chronology of Events in the Auditor-General's Deadlock," *The Nation*, August 30, 2005.
99. Military coups invariably obliterate the executive and the legislature, but leave the judiciary intact: J. Hatchard and T. Ogowewo, *Tackling the Unconstitutional Overthrow of Democracies: Emerging Trends in the Commonwealth* (London: Commonwealth Secretariat, 2003), 14ff. A Constitutional Court is exposed to being neutralized without damage to the judiciary as a whole, an occupational hazard of being a fourth branch of government.
100. For further discussion of emergency powers cases, see Andrew Harding, "Emergency Powers with a Moustache: Special Powers and Evolving Constitutionalism in Thailand" (paper presented at International Symposium on Emergency Powers in Asia: Exploring the Limits of Legality, Singapore, May 2008).

101. Ginsburg, *Judicial Review in New Democracies: Constitutional Courts in Asian Cases.*
102. *Constitution of the Kingdom of Thailand* 2007 s. 205(6).
103. *Constitution of the Kingdom of Thailand* 2007 s. 206(1).
104. *Constitution of the Kingdom of Thailand* 2007 s. 212.

7 The Constitutional Court and judicialization of Korean politics

Tom Ginsburg

The Constitutional Court of Korea has just celebrated its 20th anniversary, a significant milestone. Of the five designated constitutional courts in East and Southeast Asia (the others being found in Indonesia, Taiwan, Thailand and Mongolia), it is arguably the most important and influential, and therefore deserves close scrutiny as a case-study in judicialization of constitutional politics in Asia. This chapter examines some of the leading decisions of the Constitutional Court in light of the issues raised in this book.

The Court was established in late 1988 as part of the 1987 constitutional establishment of Korea's Sixth Republic. Though expected by the constitutional drafters to be a relatively quiescent institution, the Court has become the embodiment of the new democratic constitutional order of Korea. The Court is routinely called on to resolve major political conflicts and issues of social policy. Since its establishment in late 1988, the Constitutional Court has rendered over 7,000 decisions.[1] It is consistently rated as one of the most effective institutions in Korea by the public. In a recent poll, for example, it received the highest ratings of any government body – and just behind several large corporations – in terms of public influence and trust.[2] For an institution expected to be rather peripheral, this is a remarkable achievement.

How did the Court get to this position? No doubt a major factor was the decision-making prudence of the justices, who when faced with major cases were able to resolve them in a manner that was perceived as neutral and legitimate. But there are also some structural factors that gave the justices these opportunities, notably the paralysis of, and occasional open conflict among, other more partisan government institutions. This led to a gradual judicialization of Korean politics, in which major social and political questions are increasingly determined in the court-room rather than the more conventional political institutions.[3] This chapter will review some of the leading case-law of the Constitutional Court and offer some thoughts on what lessons it might hold for other courts being established in new democracies.

Structure and jurisdiction

An initial point to note is that the Court was established as a distinct constitutional court of the Kelsenian type, in which the power of constitutional review is reserved to a designated court rather than shared with other courts. This decision was a natural one, given the history of borrowing from civil law legal systems, though the model adopted differed from that adopted in the former colonial power of Japan. In general, concentrating the power of review in a single court can provide an incentive for a degree of activism, to the extent that the justices have some sense of needing to play the role they were assigned.[4]

The Court consists of nine justices who serve six-year renewable terms, now staggered so that justices are appointed in sets. Six votes are required to declare a law unconstitutional, to dissolve a political party, to accept a constitutional complaint or to overrule a previous precedent of the Constitutional Court. Three justices each are appointed by the Supreme Court, the National Assembly and the President. Some 25 persons have now served as justices, from a variety of backgrounds, including judges, prosecutors and politicians.

Modelled closely on the Federal Constitutional Court in Germany, the Court's jurisdiction includes: providing interpretations of the *Constitution of the Republic of Korea* (*Constitution*) at the request of ordinary courts (as in the German system of concrete norm-control); hearing public petitions relating to the *Constitution* as prescribed by law; deciding issues of impeachment; the constitutionality of political parties; and deciding jurisdictional conflicts between local and central governments or central government branches. There are, however, a couple of jurisdictional differences between the Korean and German courts. Unlike the German Court, the Korean Court cannot be requested by designated government agencies to perform 'abstract' review outside the context of a real dispute, nor can it review ordinary court decisions.

In rendering decisions, the Court in its early years adopted from the German system the notion of levels of constitutionality. The Court can hold the act constitutional or unconstitutional in whole or part, but also can find challenged acts to be limitedly conforming (constitutional if interpreted in a particular way), constitutional but applied in an unconstitutional fashion, or 'nonconforming,' in which case the National Assembly may be required to amend the act in the near future. These various gradations of declarations of constitutionality and unconstitutionality place the Court in dialogue with the legislative branches and executive agencies, and give it some flexibility in terms of how to handle politically sensitive issues. It need not render a binary decision of constitutionality. This feature of its institutional structure has proved useful at certain points in the Court's history.

Petitions from the public are governed by Article 68 of the *Constitutional Court Act*. As in the German system, any person who asserts that his or her constitutional rights have been infringed by government action or inaction may directly petition the Court for relief. There are two separate grounds for such petitions. Article 68(1) of the *Constitutional Court Act* allows petitions, after all available legal remedies have been exhausted, by citizens whose rights have been infringed by unconstitutional state action. Most of these cases have involved allegations of abuse of prosecutorial discretion when prosecutors do not indict.[5] Article 68(1) cases dominate the docket, in part because decisions of ordinary courts (to whom plaintiffs must turn to exhaust legal remedies) are excluded from the jurisdiction of the Constitutional Court. Article 68(2) allows filings after a party has unsuccessfully sought referral by an ordinary court under Article 41 of the *Constitutional Court Act*, and leads to a stay in ongoing litigation pending the Constitutional Court judgment.

The Court's case-law

Space only permits discussion of a few of the cases the Court has decided. I focus especially on those involving the political process, in which the Court has become a final arbiter of major political conflicts. It bears mentioning, however, that the Court has been heavily involved in transforming Korea's military–bureaucratic regime into a constitutional democracy, in large part by striking down individual statutes left over from the previous regime.[6] At the same time, new political forces in a democracy often seek to entrench their position through rigging the rules of the game. The Court has done some important work in balancing between new political forces, while also serving as an instrument of transformation marking a break from the past.

The Court and the political process

The Korean Court has been frequently called on to adjudicate issues related to elections and political conflict. Many of these disputes involve schemes designed to restrict involvement in the political process, and the Court has consistently sided with political minorities in this regard. For example, a minority party challenged the *Local Election Law* of 1990, which required large registration fees from candidates. This provision served as a strong disincentive for minority parties to field candidates. The Court found that the provision in question violated the constitutional guarantee of equality, as it prevented sincere but resource-poor candidates from participating.[7]

Similarly, in 1989, the Court struck Article 33 of the *National Assembly Members Election Act*, which required a higher deposit from independent candidates than from those affiliated with a party. In its decision, the Court identified the right to vote and to run for office as core democratic freedoms that could not be granted unequally.[8] In 1992, the Court struck provisions in the same law that provided party-based candidates advantages over independent candidates in campaign appearances and leafletings.[9] The Court found that these provisions limited the *Constitution*'s guarantees of equality of opportunity and of the right to hold public office.[10] The Court thus rejected a party-based view of democratic governance, facilitating independent participation.

The Court in 1995 found several provisions of the *National Assembly Elections Law* to be 'non-conforming' because of excessively disproportional representation for rural districts compared with urban ones.[11] As in Japan, Korean districting has been designed to maximize the influence of rural areas at the expense of urban voters. Relying in part on Japanese, German and American cases, the Court set an explicit limit of 1: 4 disproportionality between urban and rural districts.

In an instructive contrast with similar cases before the Japanese Supreme Court, the National Assembly amended the election law to conform with the Court's decision.[12]

The Court's most prominent intervention in the political process no doubt involved the attempted impeachment of President Roh Moo-Hyun in 2004.[13] Roh, an activist labour lawyer who took office in 2003 with a reformist agenda, governed with an opposition-controlled National Assembly. His position became even less tenable when his own party split as a result of generational tensions in September 2003, and a corruption scandal related to campaign contributions erupted that October. Roh staked his future on a mid-term legislative election, but – in violation of South Korean law – appeared to campaign for his own party by urging voters to support it. The majority in the National Assembly responded with a motion for impeachment, which passed by the necessary two-thirds vote.

Under Korean law, Roh was suspended from office and the Prime Minister assumed the duties of the President. The case was then sent to the Constitutional Court for confirmation, as required under the *Constitution*.[14] During the deliberations of the case, however, the mid-term election was held and Roh's party received overwhelming support, winning an absolute majority in the Assembly.

It is pure speculation to suggest that this indicator of the public's preferences influenced the Court in its decision. However, the Court did reject the impeachment motion one month later.[15] The *Constitution* requires six out of nine justices to uphold the impeachment. In addressing the issue, the Court bifurcated the issue into the question of whether there was a 'violation of the *Constitution* or other Acts,' the predicate for impeachment, and whether those violations were severe enough to warrant removal. Although the Court found that Roh had violated the election law provisions that public officials remain neutral, along with other provisions of law, they decided that it would not be proportional to remove the President for the violation. Instead, they asserted that removal is only appropriate when the 'free and democratic basic order' is threatened. Roh's violations were not a premeditated attempt to undermine constitutional democracy. The court further rejected some of the charges, namely those concerned with campaign contributions that took place before he took office.

The incident illustrates two themes in the study of judicial politics. First is the great sensitivity of constitutional courts to delicate political questions. By splitting the difference in a manner that responded to recent signals from the electorate, the Court gave both sides what they wanted while avoiding a constitutional crisis. Second, and more importantly, is the subtle way in which the Court aggrandized its own power in making the decision. By failing to simply confirm to the National Assembly's factual findings, the Court placed itself in the position of reviewing the *political* assessment of the impact that the removal of the President would have on Korean democracy. The Court established itself, and not the Assembly, as the final arbiter of whether removal was actually warranted. In this sense, the Court ended up enhancing its ability to say what the law is, and did so in a manner that ensured it would be accepted by the majority of the public.

The Court was able to return to some of the issues in impeachment proceedings in 2007 and 2008. Incumbent President Roh Moo-Hyun had made some remarks concerning the presidential election; even though he was not running for re-election, the National Election Commission considered this to be a violation of his duty, and Roh petitioned the Constitutional Court in his personal capacity, claiming that his right to political expression was infringed by the electoral law. The Court rejected Roh's petition in early 2008, but did acknowledge that he had a right to file it in his personal capacity.

Roh's party lost the 2008 presidential election to Grand National Party leader Lee Myung-bak, a former chief executive officer who had been accused in the campaign of financial improprieties. After prosecutors cleared Lee of all charges in December 2007, the legislature passed a law calling for an independent prosecutor to investigate the allegations. The law was challenged by Lee's allies, and the Court upheld most of the law, though it found unconstitutional a provision allowing the special prosecutor to subpoena witnesses without a warrant. Lee took office in February 2008, and was thus immune from further investigation, but the case again illustrates the theme of political conflict ending up before the Court.

The Court and issues of retroactive justice

The Court has also been heavily involved in sensitive political and historical issues. For example, it was called upon to consider whether the legislature committed an unconstitutional omission for failing to launch an inquiry into a massacre conducted in the Korean War. The Court found that the *Constitution* did not create an individually justiciable right to legislative consideration.[16]

In one notable series of cases in the mid-1990s, the Court was drawn into questions of retroactive justice for the famous 1980 'Kwangju incident,' in which military personnel slaughtered hundreds of non-violent protesters.[17] Two of the generals implicated in the incident (and the preceding military coup of 1979) were later Presidents, Chun Doo-Hwan and Roh Tae-Woo. When President Kim Young-Sam took power in 1992 as the first civilian, prosecutors investigated the two generals and found that no charges could be pursued. This failure to prosecute was challenged in the Constitutional Court through a petition under Article 68(1), and the Court was asked to toll the statute of limitations, whose 15-year period for prosecution would soon expire. In January 1995, the Constitutional Court upheld the tolling of the 15-year statute of limitations against the two men during their presidencies, on the grounds that the *Constitution* expressly provides that sitting presidents may not be prosecuted for any crimes other than insurrection or treason.

For rule of law reasons, however, the Court would not allow retroactive application of the tolling so as to include offences for which the statutory period had already expired. On its face, this decision would have rendered the 1979 *coup d'état* unprosecutable. Other crimes, however, including those related to the Kwangju incident, would remain prosecutable for several more years. This decision served notice that efforts to bring the two men to justice would have to conform to the dictates of the rule of law. However, the Court did not force the prosecution to prosecute Chun and Roh by declaring their exercise of discretion unconstitutional.

The National Assembly, under the solid control of Kim Young-Sam's party, then passed special legislation to facilitate the prosecutions. These laws were challenged in trial court proceedings, and the issue of constitutionality become before the Constitutional Court. The Court eventually upheld the controversial Acts in 1996, although a majority of justices dissented.[18] The Court's decision allowed the prosecutors to proceed with the case in a local court, and both men were found guilty. Chun was sentenced to death and Roh to 22 years in prison. Both sentences were reduced on appeal, and the men were subsequently pardoned through the initiative of President-elect Kim Dae-Jung in December 1997.

The performance of the Constitutional Court through this series of decisions is ambiguous, but on balance reflects the Court's independence as well as its institutional sophistication. On the one hand, the Court ultimately allowed the prosecution to go forward, and in this sense can be seen as bending to the dictates of a popular political movement. Apparently, the Court was prepared to prevent the prosecution in December 1995, before the plaintiffs withdrew their case. Its mooting of that case after the withdrawal allowed the political process to continue. However, the dissenting opinion issued by a majority of the justices questioned the dubious legislation of the ruling party by calling attention to the rule of law values of consistency and predictability in criminal justice. Special legislation would be acceptable, but not if applied to those for whom the statute of limitations had already expired, a category that by 1996 included everyone involved in both the 1979 coup and the 1980 Kwangju incident. The Court thus avoided a direct challenge to the dominant political interests, but at the same time managed to focus on issues of legality, and caused maximum embarrassment to President Kim through dissent.

Economic rights

Although not the most spectacular line of decisions, perhaps the Court's greatest contribution to liberalization has been undermining the legacy of government controls over the economic system. In the Kukje case in 1993, the Court considered the Chun regime's dissolution of one of Korea's *chaebol* industrial conglomerates, allegedly because of its failure to make donations to the ruling party. The Court held that the government's action toward the private firms was an unconstitutional taking of private property, and that the former owner could retake control of the firms through the ordinary judicial process.[19] In a country where the state has always had tremendous power over the economy, this decision struck a blow at state interference, and marked a qualitative difference in the new era. The Court has also invalidated tax legislation and provisions of property law that provided special privileges for state-owned firms.[20] Such mechanisms previously allowed Korean state capitalism to blur the distinction between the state and private economic activity.[21] In striking down these rules, the Court has bolstered the private–public distinction, a core principle of modern liberalism as well as of German legal theory.

Confucian constitutionalism?

A crucial issue implicit in the organization of this publication is whether or not there is anything particularly Asian about the activities of the new courts. In another article, I have articulated a model of 'Confucian Constitutionalism,' which suggests that judicial review can be understood in terms compatible with Confucian political tradition.[22] Government by judges is akin to the Confucian ideal of government by a generalist meritocracy, in which notions of 'remonstrance' may be revitalized in the language of constitutional law. Whatever the compatibilities, it is useful to examine the Court's behaviour in cases that confront Confucian or traditional norms. As in other areas, the Court seems to have walked a line between transforming the highly traditional Korean social order, in particular by striking at features of the law that reflect Confucian paternalism, while upholding certain principles.

In July 1997, the Court struck out an Article in the *Civil Code* that prohibited intermarriage of Koreans with the same family name and regional origin.[23] This provision reflected a law originally written in 1308, when clan-based social structure prevailed. The decision had immediate effects on an estimated 60,000 couples who lived together but whose clan names had prevented them from legally marrying. The decision prompted protests from Confucian groups but was celebrated by women's groups.

In another case, these two social forces found themselves on the same side. Adultery in Korea is considered a criminal act, reflecting Confucian values and the broader tendency of utilizing the criminal law to regulate what might otherwise be considered private behaviour. The relevant provision of the *Criminal Code* was challenged as a violation of the constitutional right to pursue happiness, but an odd alliance of traditionalists, women's groups and the bar association supported the law. The Court refused to strike down the law, but the Ministry of Justice, responding to dissenting opinions in the Court decision, announced that it would initiate amending legislation to eliminate the controversial provisions. However, it ultimately failed to do so in the wake of protests by social activists. This decision illustrates the myriad ways a constitutional decision can shape social change: although the Court appears to speak for traditional values, it also reflects active interest-group politics. The interest of advocacy groups in the constitutional litigation process shows that the Court is an increasingly important political arena; furthermore, the role of these groups reflects the strengthening of civil society vis-à-vis the formerly dominant state apparatus.

Another case demonstrating the Court's willingness to uphold traditional norms involved criminal law. Like Japan and other Confucian societies, Korea has traditionally punished those who kill a spouse or lineal ascendant more severely than ordinary murder. The party who brought review of the case argued that the statute violated his constitutional right of equality. The Court highlighted that the constitutional guarantee of equality prohibits only differential treatment without a reasonable basis in legislative purpose. The Court noted the importance of love and respect in the Korean familial situation, and said that the statute is not unconstitutional because protection of such relationships is a valid legislative purpose. The Court upheld the statute.[24]

The National Security Act cases and military secrets

The Court has been especially visible in dealing with the legacies of the authoritarian regime, particularly the *National Security Act* (*NSA*) and the *Anti-Communist Act*. These laws were used to suppress independent political organizations by providing draconian sanctions against dissenters and loosely-defined illegal associations. The laws were therefore a target of human rights activists and regime opponents. The two laws operated by carving out exceptions to normal requirements of criminal procedure. For example, Article 19 of the *NSA* of 1980 allowed longer pre-trial detention for those accused of particular crimes, and this article was struck down by the Constitutional Court in 1992.[25] The provisions in question extended pre-trial detention for up to 50 days, an exception from the normal period of 48 hours allowed under the *Code of Criminal Procedure*.[26] The Court held that the extended period constituted an excessive limitation on the basic right to a speedy trial.

Even more important was the Court's limitation of offences defined under the Act. Article 7(1) of the *NSA* penalized any person who 'praises, encourages, or sympathizes with the activities of an anti-state organization or its members, or any person who receives orders therefrom; and any person who by any means whatever benefits an anti-state organization'.[27] This provision was held to be vague and overbroad, and to threaten constitutional guarantees of freedom of the press and speech,[28] freedom of academic study[29] and freedom of conscience.[30] Noting the continuing confrontation with North Korea, the Court did not actually strike down the law, but ruled that the provisions only be applied in the case of danger of actual security risks. The Court restricted interpretations of the law and asked lower courts to balance the proximity of danger with the constitutional position of freedom of expression. In particular, the Court held that the law could only be used to punish activities posing a substantive danger, so merely 'encouraging' or 'sympathizing' without a showing of substantive danger could not be prosecuted. However, a dissenting opinion called for the Court to require a higher standard of 'clear and present danger' before a prosecution could be upheld in an *NSA* case.[31] The next year, the National Assembly amended the law so as to apply only where the person charged had *knowledge* that his or her actions might endanger the existence or security of the state or the 'fundamental order of liberal democracy'.[32] Once again, a Court decision led the legislature to substantially narrow its definition of an offence, introducing the element of specific knowledge to limit the application of a law that had been subject to serious abuse.

In 1994, the Court struck out a provision of the *Private School Act* requiring that any teacher prosecuted in a criminal case would lose her or his job.[33] In the case at issue, a teacher was prosecuted under the *NSA* and immediately fired. The Court found that this rule violated the presumption of innocence. This group of decisions had the effect of domesticating the administration of the *NSA*, the single most egregious law associated with military rule, by bringing it into conformity with the dictates of ordinary procedural law.

The *Military Secrets Protection Act* of 1972, which prohibited the collection or dissemination of military secrets, led to another politically charged case for the Court. The Act had been interpreted quite broadly, and was used to prevent any media coverage of military matters whatsoever. The Court found that the constitutional freedom of expression encompassed a public right to information, and that this could not be infringed by a broad application of the law.[34] The Assembly subsequently revised the bill, narrowing the interpretation of military secrets, so the decision had a direct impact on broadening freedom of expression.

Relations with the Supreme Court

In all systems with designated constitutional courts, relations between the constitutional review body and the top ordinary tribunals can be complex. This is particularly true in Korea, where the Supreme Court has been assigned the explicit power to adjudicate the constitutionality of administrative regulations, in accordance with post-war Korean tradition.[35] Indeed, the past few years have witnessed a battle over jurisdiction between the two top courts, not unusual for courts in the early years of a new democracy.[36]

The two courts are clearly separate but equal bodies in formal terms, each described in a separate constitutional article as an organ of state power. Ideally, the two courts have mutually independent jurisdictions, while retaining equally high status. In fact, of course, cases do not neatly fit into one or the other's purview, and each court seeks to assert its predominance. The distinction between administrative and legislative interpretation is not as clear or straightforward as might be imagined. The question of the constitutionality of an administrative regulation frequently requires interpretation of the relevant statutory text. A restrictive interpretation of a statute will tend to void on constitutional grounds any administrative actions taken under it, where those actions rely on a broad reading of the statute. So, the Constitutional Court is able to shape Supreme Court constitutional interpretations where the Constitutional Court is able to issue a prior decision on the statute underlying administrative action.

In 1990, the Constitutional Court unilaterally decided that it had implied jurisdiction over administrative regulations issued pursuant to statutes, and that the assignment of administrative review in Article 107(2) to the ordinary courts was not exclusive.[37] The case was especially controversial, because it concerned the administrative action of the Supreme Court itself in its role as the licensing authority for lower level judicial officials known as judicial scriveners. The petitioner had charged that scriveners' licences were given disproportionately to those with experience in courts' and prosecutors' offices, without justification. The Constitutional Court found that, by failing to administer examinations, the Supreme Court had not followed its own administrative regulations under the *Judicial Scriveners Act*. In response to the decision, the Supreme Court issued a statement to all ordinary judges condemning the Constitutional Court decision, and stating that it had 'gone beyond its domain'.[38]

The problem is caused in part by the design flaw that ordinary court decisions are not explicitly included within the jurisdiction of the Constitutional Court.[39] At the same time, the law provides that rulings of the Court on unconstitutionality are to be respected by ordinary courts, other state agencies and local government bodies.[40] This means that while ordinary courts must abide by Constitutional Court decisions, they are themselves the sole determiners of what those decisions require. Ordinary courts cannot be corrected by the Constitutional Court for failure to apply its decision correctly. Rather the Supreme Court is the sole body able to overrule lower court decisions. Therefore, much is at stake on the question of whether Supreme Court decisions can be appealed to the Constitutional Court. On the one hand, the maintenance of the *Constitution* as the highest normative level of the legal system would seem to require reviewability of Supreme Court decisions. On the other hand, if Supreme Court decisions can be appealed, that means they are not final.

In keeping with its efforts to expand access to constitutional justice, the Constitutional Court has sought to extend its jurisdiction to cover ordinary court decisions. In 1995, the Court declared a tax law partially unconstitutional, and dictated that it could only be applied if given a particular, narrow interpretation by ordinary courts.[41] The Supreme Court responded in April 1996 saying that since the Constitutional Court had no authority over ordinary court judgments; its decision could only be taken as an expression of opinion regarding constitutionality, and had no binding force over ordinary courts. The ordinary courts then proceeded to apply the controversial tax law in the manner that the Constitutional Court had criticized. In December 1997, the original petitioner again sought relief from the Constitutional Court, and the Court obliged by annulling the Supreme Court judgment, even though it had no explicit power to do so in the *Constitutional Court Act*. The Court also voided that portion of the *Constitutional Court Act* that excluded ordinary court decisions from constitutional review, saying that Constitutional Court decisions must be binding on all. The Supreme Court responded by holding a press conference, asserting that it would reply through a judgment.[42] Subsequently, the Constitutional Court continued to consider ordinary court judgments in certain cases and it now appears that the theory of the Constitutional Court has been accepted.

Ultimately, the conflict may be about competing ideas of the role of courts and the meaning of judicial independence. The Constitutional Court sees itself as the embodiment of a new constitutional order, a vehicle for making a bold break from the past. The Supreme Court sees itself as the inheritor of Korean legal tradition, a tradition that sought to preserve professional autonomy under difficult conditions of authoritarian rule. As such, the Supreme Court has always sought to insulate itself from other institutions intent on interfering with its position at the apex of the legal hierarchy.

Conclusion

The Korean Constitutional Court has managed to become a major institution in Korean governance. The Court is a forum for groups seeking to advance social change as well as for individual disputes. The Court frequently strikes down legislative action and also regularly overturns prosecutorial decisions. The Court has demonstrated its independence in politically charged cases, such as in the retroactive justice case where it embarrassed the ruling party, while remaining responsive to the broad trends of public opinion. The Court has participated in the subjugation of both state and military to civilian political control, transforming the character of state–society relations. At the same time, the Court has avoided decisions that might provoke hostile reactions from prominent political forces. The Court has thereby contributed to the consolidation of Korean democracy.

What explains this early and unexpected success?[43] One important factor has been the Court's formation as a new and distinct body with the express mission of protecting the 1987 *Constitution*. The Court's position as designated protector of the constitutional bargain has given it a sense of institutional mission, identified closely with a broad notion of democratic values.

A second important factor is the extent to which the design reflected what I have called elsewhere the needs for political 'insurance'.[44] The 1987 constitutional design reflected the deep political uncertainty faced by three political forces of roughly equal strength. No party could confidently predict it would win power, and the institutions of the 1987 *Constitution* reflected this, both in the single-term presidency and the Constitutional Court. A system of constitutional review served the interests of all parties under such uncertain conditions, and the design of the court provided it with institutional power to expand its power. This has been assisted by the fragmented and dysfunctional nature of Korean politics since the Court was established. Korean parties remain weak and unstable, and each President has failed to maintain high ratings throughout their term. Calls for constitutional amendment are picking up.

Finally, one must credit the justices of the Court themselves for the success of the institution. The ability to remain a relevant body, responsive to Korean political and social forces, requires a certain degree of prudence and skill on the part of the members of the Court. This is a variable that one cannot always anticipate, and reminds us of the contingency of effective judicialization.

Notes

1. Constitutional Court of Korea, http://english.ccourt.go.kr/
2. Shin Chang-un JoongAng Ilbo, "Poll: Giant Firms Most Influential," *JoongAng Daily*, July 3, 2007, http://joongangdaily.joins.com/article/view.asp?aid = 2877553
3. On judicialization, see J. Ferejohn, "Judicializing Politics, Politicizing Law," *Law and Contemporary Problems* 65 (2002): 41. C. Neal Tate and Thorsten Vallinder, *The Global Judicialization of Politics* (New York: NYU Press, 1995), 1–13.

4. V. F. Comella, "The European Model of Constitutional Review of Legislation: Toward Decentralization?," *International Journal of Constitutional Law* 4 (2004): 461.
5. K. W. Ahn, "The Influence of American Constitutionalism on South Korea," *Southern Illinois Law Journal* 27 (1997): 114; J. West and D. K. Yoon, "The Constitutional Court of the Republic of Korea: Transforming the Jurisprudence of the Vortex," *American Journal of Comparative Law* 40 (1992): 101–2.
6. T. Ginsburg, *Judicial Review in New Democracies* (New York: Cambridge University Press, 2003), 226–46.
7. One-Person One-Vote Case, 13–2 KCCR 77; 2000Hun-Ma91; 2000Hun-Ma112; 2000Hun-Ma134 (Consolidated) July 19, 2001.
8. National Assembly Members Act Case, 89 HonKa 6, 1 KCCR 199, 249 September 8, 1989.
9. National Assembly Members Act Case, 92 HonMa 37, 39, 4 KCCR 137 March 13, 1992.
10. *Constitution of the Republic of Korea* arts 11, 25.
11. Electoral District Disproportionality Case, 95 HonMa 224, 7–2 KCCR 760 December 17, 1995.
12. Cf. Supreme Court, Grand Bench, 14 April 1976, 30 *Minshu* (1976): 223, where the Court declared that the Diet had failed to correct unconstitutional levels of malapportionment, and declared the system illegal, but refused to invalidate it or the election held under it.
13. Y. Lee, "Law, Politics and Impeachment: The Impeachment of Roh Moo-Hyun from a Comparative Constitutional Perspective," *American Journal of Comparative Law* 53 (2005): 403.
14. *Constitution of the Republic of Korea* art. 112.
15. Impeachment of the President Case, 16–1 KCCR 609, 2004Hun-Na1 May 14, 2004.
16. Legislative Omissions with respect to Civilian Massacre during The Korean War Case, 15–1 KCCR 551; 2000Hum-Ma192, etc. (Consolidated) May 15, 2003.
17. J. M. West, "Martial Lawlessness: the Legal Aftermath of Kwangju," *Pacific Rim Law and Policy Journal* 6 (1997): 85.
18. Six votes are required to find a law unconstitutional.
19. Kukje Case, 89 HunMa 31, 5–2 KCCR 87 July 29, 1993.
20. Ahn, "The Influence of American Constitutionalism on South Korea," 104–5.
21. P. Evans, *Embedded Autonomy: States and Industrial Transformation* (Princeton, NJ: Princeton University Press, 1995), 45.
22. T. Ginsburg, "Confucian Constitutionalism? Globalization and Judicial Review in Korea and Taiwan," *Law and Social Inquiry* 27 (2002): 763.
23. J. Lim, "The Korean Constitutional Court, Judicial Activism and Social Change," in *Korean Legal Reform*, ed. T. Ginsburg (London: Routledge Curzon, 2004), 19; 95 Hun-Ga 6–13 Byung-Hap, 1995.
24. Legislative Omissions with respect to Civilian Massacre during The Korean War Case, 15–1 KCCR 551; 2000Hum-Ma192, etc. (Consolidated) May 15, 2003.
25. National Security Act Case, 90 HonMa 82, 4 KCCR 194 April 14, 1992.
26. K. Cho, "Tension Between the National Security Law and Constitutionalism in South Korea: Security for What?," *Boston University International Law Journal* 25 (1997): 125.
27. *National Security Act* art. 7(1).
28. *Constitution of the Republic of Korea* art. 21(1).
29. *Constitution of the Republic of Korea* art. 22(1).
30. *Constitution of the Republic of Korea* art. 19.
31. In characterizing the majority test as one of 'bad tendency' Justice Byon Chong-soo self-consciously modeled his decision on the opinion of United States Supreme Court

Justice Holmes in *Schenk v. US*, 249 US 47 (1919). His phrasing subsequently influenced a Supreme Court *NSA* case, on May 31, 1992, where the minority argued that the threat must be a 'concrete and possible danger' for prosecution, under Korea's 'liberal democratic basic order': Cho, "Tension Between the National Security Law and Constitutionalism in South Korea: Security for What?," 169.

32. Cho, "Tension Between the National Security Law and Constitutionalism in South Korea: Security for What?," 161.
33. *NSA* Case, 93 HonKa 3, 7, 6–2 KCCR 1 July 29, 1994.
34. K. H. Youm, "Press Freedom and Judicial Review in South Korea," *Stanford Journal of International Law* 30 (1994): 12–14; 89 Hon-Ka 104 February 25, 1992.
35. *Constitution of the Republic of Korea* art. 107(2).
36. L. Garlicki, "Constitutional Courts vs. Supreme Courts," *International Journal of Constitutional Law* 5 (2007): 44–68.
37. Rules implementing the Certified Judicial Scriveners Act Case, 2 KCCR 365, 89Hun-Ma178 October 15, 1990. Article 107(2) reads '[t]he Supreme Court shall have the power to make a final review of the constitutionality or legality of administrative decrees, regulations or dispositions, when their constitutionality or legality is a prerequisite to a trial'.
38. West, "The Constitutional Court of the Republic of Korea," 103.
39. *Constitution of the Republic of Korea* art. 111(1).
40. *Constitutional Court Act* art. 47(1).
41. See discussion in Ginsburg, *Judicial Review in New Democracies*, 232.
42. This high-profile conflict led the *Korea Herald* to call for legislative resolution of the problem: 'This complicated and subtle conflict between the two supreme juridical bodies calls for an intervention of the President and the National Assembly which can exercise their legislative prerogatives toward illuminating the balance of power and division of labour between the two highest courts'. "Editorial," *Korea Herald*, December 30, 1997, 14.
43. T. Ginsburg, "Constitutional Courts in East Asia: Understanding Variation," *Journal of Comparative Law* 3 (2008): 80–100.
44. Ginsburg, *Judicial Review in New Democracies*, 21–33.

8 Institutional choice and the new Indonesian Constitutional Court

Hendrianto

Introduction

In 2000, a number of Indonesian parliamentarians travelled to the Northern Hemisphere for so-called international study missions. They visited 21 countries with an ambitious plan to conduct comparative research on a wide range of issues, from civil–military relations to judicial systems.[1] Despite many criticisms of the study missions,[2] they became one factor that fuelled fresh debate in the parliament on the creation of the new Constitutional Court in Indonesia.[3]

Upon their return from the study missions, various political blocs in the People's Consultative Assembly (*Majelis Permusyawaratan Rakyat*) came out with a proposal for a constitutional court that could review Acts of Parliament.[4] The politicians who went on the study missions, however, insisted that their proposal was purely of their own invention and not a carbon copy of any overseas institutional model. That statement is not totally correct because the structure of the new Indonesian Constitutional Court is roughly modelled on the South Korean Constitutional Court. Why did Indonesian politicians choose the Korean Constitutional Court as their role model? I commence the analysis of the institutional character of the Indonesian Constitutional Court with this question.

The historical origins of the Indonesian Constitutional Court

Political dynamics

In studying the emergence of constitutional courts in new democracies, some scholars have concluded that the political dynamics in a country in democratic transition are one of the main driving forces behind the creation of constitutional courts. Tom Ginsburg, in his study on constitutional courts in East Asian countries, argues that as political outcomes are uncertain during periods of democratic transition in many countries, politicians often decide to set up independent courts to protect themselves in the future.[5] Therefore, judicial review provides insurance for the past against the future.[6] Ran Hirschl argues that the adoption of judicial review is best understood as the product of a strategic interplay among three key groups: threatened political elites who seek to preserve their political hegemony; economic elites who may view constitutional reform as a means of promoting a new economic agenda; and judicial elites who seek to enhance their political influence.[7]

In the context of the establishment of the Korean Constitutional Court, the decision to adopt a designated court was the result of a compromise between the ruling party and the opposition parties. In the lead up to the constitutional amendment in 1987, the political parties in South Korea differed on which entity should have the power of constitutional adjudication. Early in July 1987, the parties agreed on placing the power of constitutional review with the Supreme Court, but they disagreed on which body would have the power to review disputes relating to party dissolution, impeachment and intra-branch matters.[8] The ruling party argued that it was inappropriate for the Supreme Court to intervene in political matters, and it proposed an independent constitutional committee.[9] On the other hand, the opposition parties argued in favour of granting all constitutional powers to the Supreme Court.[10] After significant debate, the opposition party proposed a compromise: if a system of constitutional complaint were introduced, it would agree to the proposal of the ruling party.[11] It was the Headquarters of the People's Movement for Democracy that recommended to the opposition parties that the ruling party's proposal should be accepted, but only in the form of a German style of constitutional court.[12] Their reasoning was that under such a system, constitutional complaint could be introduced and this system would improve the protection of basic rights.[13] The ruling party accepted the proposal, and as a result of this compromise, the Constitutional Court was established and a system of constitutional complaint introduced. Ginsburg argues that the ruling party in South Korea preferred a centralized body to exercise judicial review, because it would be more responsive and easier to influence, and perhaps produce more predictable judgments.[14] On the other hand, the opposition believed that a constitutional court with a German style of constitutional complaint would ensure open access to the courts for those who might lose in the elections.[15]

It was the similarities in the historical and political contexts of South Korea and Indonesia that ultimately influenced Indonesian politicians to look to the Korean Constitutional Court as their model. As in South Korea, the creation of the Indonesian Constitutional Court entailed long negotiations and a compromise among political elites. After the constitutional reform process started in 1999, there were at least three different political stances on the Constitutional Court. The first group explicitly proposed an independent constitutional court.[16] The second group proposed that the power of judicial review should be vested in the Supreme Court and a 'constitutional court' should be established as a chamber within the Supreme Court.[17] The last group proposed that the constitutional court should be neither part of the Supreme Court nor a specialized court because statutes should not be reviewed by the judiciary, which has an equal position with the law-making institution, the parliament and the President. Therefore, they argued that statutes should only be reviewed by the People's Consultative Assembly, the highest institution of the state.[18] By the end of the 2000 annual session, the Assembly could not reach any consensus on the structure of the Constitutional Court, and therefore they did not produce any resolution with regard to judicial review.

The different stances on the proposed Constitutional Court need to be understood in the context of political transition in Indonesia. The Indonesian Constitutional Court was mooted during a period of democratic transition, in which significant sections of the old regime continued to exist.[19] The primary actors in the constitutional reform process were the political blocs in the Assembly. The political blocs included the five largest party-based blocs – PDI-P (Indonesian Democratic Party of Struggle), *Golkar*, PPP (United Development Party), PKB (National Awakening Party) and Reform (a coalition between National Mandate Party and Justice Party) – and the military/police bloc. However, none of those political blocs shared the view that judicial review was important for reconstructing the new Indonesian state.

For the two pillars of the New Order military regime, *Golkar* and the military, their interests were served by a weak judicial branch, as weak judicial oversight would enhance their ability to avoid accountability for their past abuses.[20] Therefore, *Golkar* and the military preferred not to have a new judicial institution, but rather to vest the power of judicial review with the old Supreme Court, which had a bad track-record in exercising its judicial authority. The biggest bloc in the Assembly, the PDI-P, also did not regard judicial review as their top priority. PDI-P leaders were aware that under a structure with a strong judicial institution, the presidency would become a weaker institution.[21] The primary interest of the PDI-P was in the power of the presidency, with the expectation that the Chairwoman, Megawati Soekarnoputri, would someday become President. As a result, they did not wish to circumscribe the broad powers granted to the President by the old *Constitution of the Republic of Indonesia*.[22] Thus, the PDI-P was not in favour of the idea of a constitutional amendment that included judicial review and a constitutional court.

It was only a fraction of the political groups in the Assembly that had an interest in adopting judicial review and a constitutional court.[23] As discussed previously, the idea of adopting a constitutional court was primarily driven by the 2000 international study missions and the majority of politicians did not propose a solid concept for the model and scope of the new proposed court.[24] When they announced a proposal to establish a constitutional court they immediately faced strong resistance from the major political blocs in the Assembly. When the political blocs in the Assembly could not reach any consensus over the proposal for a new court – whether it would be an independent court or part of the Supreme Court – they made a compromise: the Constitutional Court would be an independent court with limited authority to review only Acts of Parliament.[25] In the meantime, the Supreme Court would have the authority to review regulations and ordinances inferior to Acts of Parliament.[26]

Some political actors involved in the constitutional amendment stated that the compromise came out of the Korean constitutional model.[27] As a matter of fact, the 1987 *Constitution of the Republic of Korea* (*Korean Constitution*) provides two high courts, like the Indonesian system: the Constitutional Court and the Supreme Court, with each having separate jurisdiction. The *Korean Constitution* provides that the constitutionality of statutes shall be adjudicated upon the request of the ordinary courts,[28] which means that whenever the constitutionality of a statute is at issue in a case, the courts of ordinary jurisdiction can request a decision of the Constitutional Court.[29] In addition, the Supreme Court has the power to make a final review of the constitutionality or legality of administrative decrees, regulations or actions when there is constitutionality at issue in the trial.[30]

Judicial appointment: personnel

Apart from the debate over the structure of judicial review, the appointment of judges was the other issue upon which Indonesian politicians looked to the Korean model for guidance.[31] Judicial appointments became an important issue, primarily because of the character of political transition in Indonesia. Andrew MacIntyre argues that the constitutional reform process increased the number of supposed veto players in Indonesia, from one (General Soeharto) prior to *Reformasi* to three or four after *Reformasi*: the President and the two or three political blocs necessary to achieve a majority in the House of Representatives.[32] Indonesian politics in the *Reformasi* era moved from a centralized institutional configuration to a heavily fragmented configuration. Under this fragmented configuration, it was difficult to reach consensus among the political blocs, especially on the selection of the Constitutional Court judges.

The Constitutional Court was created just after Megawati Soekarnoputri's rise to the position of President. She and her party, the PDI-P, were fully aware that the selection process might lead to political conflict among the veto players in the parliament. President Megawati, who became President in 2001, still needed to maintain political support from different political blocs in the parliament. Therefore, the PDI-P tried to avoid political conflicts by proposing a selection method that distributed the power to appoint judges equally among the different political blocs. In addition, the PDI-P may have also believed that if the President were perceived as controlling the power of appointment, it would be likely that the PDI-P would face strong resistance from inside and outside parliament. For many years under military rule, the President monopolized the selection process for the Supreme Court in order to secure a compliant judiciary. Hence, there was great distrust of the presidential power to nominate judicial candidates.

Having realized that judicial selection might create conflict in the Assembly, the PDI-P proposed that the Constitutional Court be composed of nine justices: three nominated by the President; three nominated by the People's Representative Council; and three nominated by the Supreme Court.[33] Later this proposal was accepted as the judicial appointment clause in the *Constitution of the Republic of Indonesia*.[34] The inspiration for this selection method, not surprisingly, came from the Korean Constitutional Court.[35] One of the leading politicians in the constitutional reform process described the situation as follows:

> We did not want to have any conflict in the selection process. When we looked at the Korean Constitutional Court, each political branch has the power to nominate three justices. Why then should we go through hardship by debating the selection method, when we can just follow the Korean model and everything will go easily because we will not have any debate.[36]

Impeachment as a catalyst for the Indonesian Constitution Court

Finally, the Constitutional Court's jurisdiction over the impeachment process was one of the most important factors in the establishment of the Indonesian Constitutional Court.[37] With regard to this feature, the Korean Constitutional Court again became a model for the Indonesian Constitutional Court. The importance of the Court's jurisdiction over the impeachment process should be understood in the context of the political upheaval in Indonesia prior to establishment of the Constitutional Court. In July 2001, the Assembly decided to impeach President Abdurrahman Wahid, based on the allegation that his aid used his name to illegally secure US$4,000,000 worth of funds from the State Logistic Agency. Following the impeachment, the Assembly pushed the Vice President, Megawati Soekarnoputri, to be Wahid's successor.

When the Assembly decided to impeach President Wahid, they were in the midst of the debate about whether judicial review should be vested in a constitutional court or the Supreme Court.[38] However, in September 2001, two months after the impeachment, the PDI-P bloc suddenly came out with a proposal to establish a constitutional court with the authority to adjudicate the presidential impeachment process.[39] It was obvious that the proposal was driven by the experience of Wahid's impeachment. President Megawati and the PDI-P feared that what had happened to Wahid could also happen to her.[40] Therefore, the PDI-P tried to propose a mechanism that might prevent, or at least decrease, the likelihood of impeachment through the involvement of the Constitutional Court. In mid-October 2001, a majority of the political blocs in the Assembly agreed to adopt the PDI-P's proposal that the Constitutional Court should have the jurisdiction to adjudicate the impeachment process.[41]

The establishment of the Indonesian Constitutional Court evidences a form of political insurance that Ginsburg does not discuss. Ginsburg's insurance theory suggests that judicial review and a constitutional court may serve as insurance for those who lose elections. However, in Indonesia, the Constitutional Court served as insurance in a different way. It was the winning party, the PDI-P, who proposed a constitutional court as an insurance mechanism to safeguard its power. With the fragmented division of power in the post-authoritarian regime and multiple veto players,[42] the President found it difficult to establish a firm base of support in the House of Representatives, either through coalition or majority control.[43] Therefore, the President also needed additional insurance in the form of the Constitutional Court's jurisdiction over impeachment proceedings.

How different or similar? A Korean–Indonesian comparison (Table 8.1)

Martin Shapiro, a leading academic in the study of judicial institutions, argues that a division of powers can drive the establishment of judicial review.[44] Indeed, both South Korean and Indonesian politics shared a similar experience of divided

Table 8.1 Comparison between the Korean Constitutional Court and the Indonesian Constitutional Court

	The Korean Constitutional Court	*The Indonesian Constitutional Court*
Number of judges	9	9
Appointing authorities	The President (3); the National Assembly (3); and the Supreme Court (3)	The President (3); the House of Representatives (3); and the Supreme Court (3)
Length of term	6 years (renewable). Retirement at the age of 65 years	5 years (renewable). Retirement at the age of 65 years
Jurisdictional cohabitation with the Supreme Court	Yes	Yes
Abstract review initiated by public officials	No	No
Constitutionality of a statute:		
(a) Upon request of ordinary courts	Yes	No
(b) By direct challenge by the claimant	No	Yes
Constitutional complaint:		
(a) Against governmental power	Yes	No
(b) Against a statute	Yes	No
Impeachment	Yes	Yes
Dissolution of political parties	Yes	Yes
Competence disputes between state agencies	Yes	Yes
General election disputes	No	Yes

political configuration. Korean politics from 1987–8 was divided between the opposition parties, who controlled the majority in the National Assembly, and the ruling party, who controlled the Presidency. Indonesian politics from 1999–2003 was divided between five major political parties in the House of Representatives and a weak President. It is the similarity of a fragmented political configuration that ultimately influenced the Indonesian politicians to look to the Korean Constitutional Court as their model.

Access to the Court makes a difference

At the time of its constitutional amendment in 1987, not many people anticipated that the Korean Constitutional Court would play an important role in the Korean political scene.[45] The ruling party at the time believed that the new Constitutional Court could be easily managed.[46] The Court, however, has performed well beyond expectations in curbing governmental authority.[47] A recent scholarly work on the Korean Constitutional Court hailed the Court for its contribution to democratic transition and consolidation in Korea.[48] During the early democratization period, the Court was very active in liberalizing political and economic rights and made strategic moves in redistributing political and economic resources based on equality.[49] In the recent impeachment case against President Roh Moo-Hyun, the Court also issued a striking statement on the doctrine of judicial supremacy: that the Court has the final say on the meaning of the *Korean Constitution*.[50] However, how about the Indonesian Constitutional Court? Will the Court move in the same direction as its Korean counterpart or will it move in a different direction? This question now becomes the focus of discussion in this chapter.

Case-load

One of the parameters by which to judge how the Court exercises its authority is the number of cases that arrive before the Court. The Court's case-load is important, because even judges armed with unlimited powers of judicial review cannot exercise that authority unless there is a case to decide. For this reason, the Court's case-load will be examined in order to assist in analysing the development of the Indonesian Constitutional Court.

After the Constitutional Court was established on 9 November 2001, the *Constitution of the Republic of Indonesia* mandated the Supreme Court to take over judicial review authority temporarily, before the Constitutional Court technically opened.[51] Within a three-month period, the Supreme Court received 14 judicial review cases, none of which did the Supreme Court resolve until the Constitutional Court opened in August 2003. On 15 October 2003, the Supreme Court handed over the 14 judicial review cases from its docket to the Constitutional Court. Later, when the Constitutional Court finished its fifth calendar year in August 2008, it had decided 147 statutory review cases—with an average of 25 cases per year (Table 8.2). With such a small number of cases, the Court did not have a significant workload in its early years, except for the year of 2004, when the Court was inundated with election dispute cases after the 2004 general election.

The docket of the Indonesian Constitutional Court is quite small for a country with a population of more than 200 million people (Table 8.2). For instance, we could compare it with Hungary – a country with a population of approximately 10 million people – whose Constitutional Court received around 1,625 cases in its first year of operation, and by the sixth year of its operation that Court had received 11,092 cases in total.[52] If we compare the Indonesian Constitutional Court docket with the Korean Constitutional Court docket, there is a huge difference as well. When the Korean Constitutional Court finished its first three years of operation in 1992, the Court had received 246 cases concerning the constitutionality of laws and 1,195 cases of constitutional complaint.[53]

What accounts for the differences between the court docket of the Constitutional Court in Indonesia and constitutional courts in other countries? Is the Indonesian Constitutional Court less attractive than its counterparts in other nations are?

Table 8.2 Cases handled by the Indonesian Constitutional Court as of 31 August 2008[54]

	Type of case		
Decision	*Constitutionality of statute*	*Dispute between state institution*	*Election dispute*
Granted	39		41
Denied	50	2	135
Dismissed	44	5	89
Miscellaneous			
–Administrative requirement Incomplete			23
–Not a constitutional court case			152
Case withdrawn by the claimant	14	3	9
Total	147	10	449

Or does the legal culture in Indonesia not support the existence of the new Constitutional Court?

Role of human rights protection

This chapter notes that both the Korean and Indonesian Constitution Courts were created in politically fragmented environments. However, in Korea, the Constitutional Court partly grew from a concern for the protection of human rights in a post-authoritarian regime. Since the beginning, the opposition parties and representatives of civil society had advocated for a constitutional court as a way of improving the protection of basic rights.[55] The adoption of a constitutional complaint mechanism is a reflection of a strong commitment for the protection of basic rights in Korea.

The constitutional complaint (*verfassungsbeschwerde*) mechanism itself originated from the German Constitutional Court, under which any person who asserts that her or his constitutional rights have been infringed upon by the government may directly petition the Court for relief. In South Korea, the constitutional complaint mechanism provides standing to any persons who claim that a basic right of theirs, as guaranteed by the *Korean Constitution*, has been violated by an exercise or non-exercise of governmental power, provided that any other available relief process has been exhausted.[56] In addition, the Court may also grant standing to an ordinary citizen to challenge the failure of an ordinary court to refer a constitutional case to the Court.[57] Thus, the constitutional complaint mechanism provides citizens with reasonably easy access to the Court to bring a case.[58] Indeed, petitions under constitutional complaint have been the largest source of cases for the Korean Constitutional Court since its establishment in 1988.[59]

In Indonesia, the division of powers is the sole basis for flourishing judicial review. The issue of individual rights never featured during the debate on the formation of the Constitutional Court. In 2000, the Assembly adopted a long catalogue of rights in the *Constitution of the Republic of Indonesia*; however, there was no extensive discussion on how those rights could be defended in the Constitutional Court. As a matter of fact, the amendment to the 1945 *Constitution of the Republic of Indonesia* did not provide for a constitutional complaint mechanism that enabled individual citizens to ask the Court to review any act as to its conformity with constitutionally protected rights. None of the political groups in the Assembly mentioned the constitutional complaint mechanism in Assembly sessions.[60] The same situation occurred during the discussion of the Bill on the Indonesian Constitutional Court in 2003; none of political blocs proposed a constitutional complaint mechanism. The Bill on the Indonesian Constitutional Court did not provide a mechanism for individual citizens to challenge the constitutionality of Acts of Parliament.[61]

Standing of the Court

Currently, the Constitutional Court has authority to review the constitutionality of a law upon the request of an individual, customary community, public or private entity or state agency.[62] However, this mechanism does not mean that the Court has authority to hear a constitutional complaint. Essentially, a constitutional complaint is not a specific action to obtain judicial review of a statute. For instance, a constitutional complaint or *amparo* under the Spanish Constitutional Court cannot be exercised against statutes which violate fundamental rights in a direct way. It can only be exercised against administrative or judicial decisions.[63] In Germany, as a general rule, a question on the constitutionality of a statute can only be submitted to the Court via the referral of a lower court, or via a constitutional complaint against an administrative action enforcing the statute.[64] However, there is a narrow exception in the Federal Constitutional Court of Germany: a constitutional complaint against a statute is possible if the challenged statute personally affects the complainant's fundamental rights in a direct way, without the need for any further administrative application of the challenged statute.[65] The constitutional complaint against a statute will not be heard if the challenged statute requires further administrative action, and thus the claimant must first challenge the administrative action before the statute can be challenged through a constitutional complaint.[66]

In short, under the current mechanism, the Indonesian Constitutional Court has the authority to review the constitutionality of a statute but not ordinances, regulations, administrative actions or the application of the law.[67] The chapter will demonstrate how this mechanism operates through the following case analyses.

The West Papua case[68]

One of the finest illustrations of the unique feature of judicial review in Indonesia is the *West Papua* case, in which the claimant challenged the government decision to establish three new provinces in the Papuan island. Papua, the most eastern province of Indonesia, is home to a secessionist movement that has been struggling for independence for 40 years.[69] In an attempt to weaken the independence movement, the central government divided the region into three provinces: Papua, West Papua and Central Papua. On 27 January 2003, President Megawati Soekarnoputri issued an instruction, which ordered the Minister of Home Affairs, the Minister of Finance and the Governor of Papua to take immediate action to establish the west Papuan province and central Papuan province.[70] The West Papua province was officially established in February 2003. However, after violent clashes, which left several people dead, the central government put on-hold plans to divide off the province of Central Papua.[71] John Ibo, the Speaker of the Papuan Provincial Parliament, brought a complaint to the Constitutional Court and claimed that the division of the Papua province was based on an unconstitutional law. The trigger for this case was actually *Presidential Instruction No. 1/ 2003* (*Presidential Instruction*), which led to the establishment of the new province. However, the Constitutional Court had no authority to review the constitutionality of the *Presidential Instruction*, and therefore the claimants had to challenge the statute that became the basis for the *Presidential Instruction*. In the end, the Court decided to accept the claimant's petition and ruled that *Law No. 45/1999* on the division of Papua was unconstitutional.[72]

The Bali bombing case[73]

The second case that helps to explain how the Indonesian judicial review mechanism operates is the *Bali bombing* case. On 12 October 2002, a suicide bomber detonated a bomb in his backpack inside a nightclub in the tourist district of Kuta, Bali. A year later, charges were laid against some key participants in the bombing. The lawyers for two main defendants, Amrozi bin Nurhasyim and Imam Samudra, argued that the trials were unconstitutional on the grounds of retroactivity.[74] They argued that the *Emergency Law No. 1/2002* under which the two had been charged was invalid because it breached the constitutional provision that prohibits retrospective prosecution.[75] The judges rejected the argument and the trial was ordered to proceed. By the end of 2003, the four important participants in the Bali bombing were found guilty and sentenced to death or life imprisonment.

At the same time, Masykur Abdul Kadir was also tried for his participation: helping the bombers rent lodging, driving them around the southern part of Bali to survey targets and meeting with the bombers several hours after the blast.[76] Masykur Abdul Kadir was found guilty under *Law No. 15/2003* on anti-terrorism for assisting the bombers and received 15 years imprisonment. Like his fellow accused, Masykur Abdul Kadir may have had a reason to challenge the constitutionality of his conviction; however, under the current system Masykur Abdul Kadir could not challenge the constitutionality of the Court decision. Masykur's lawyers then focused their challenge on *Law No. 16/2003* that allowed retroactive application of *Law No. 15/2003*, and not on *Law No. 15/2003* itself. On 23 July 2004, the Indonesian Constitutional Court with a 5–4 decision ruled that *Law No. 16/2003*, which allowed retroactive application of *Law No. 15/2003*, was unconstitutional.[77]

The Human Rights Court Law case[78]

The *Human Rights Court Law* case involved the question of the constitutionality of *Law No. 26/2000* on the Human Rights Court, which was closely connected with the trials of human rights' violators in East Timor.[79] In response to international condemnation of alleged, gross human rights' violations in its former colony, East Timor, the Indonesian government and the House of Representatives enacted *Law No. 26/2000.*[80] The House of Representatives and the government decided to allow *Law No. 26/2000* to operate retrospectively, but made it subject to a special procedure, in which the President could only establish an *ad hoc* court on the explicit recommendation from the House of Representatives.[81]

Soon after the trials of military and police officers began, the issue of the constitutionality of the Human Rights Court was raised. The lawyers for the defendants argued that *Law No. 26/2000* was unconstitutional and therefore the court had no right to hear the case.[82] However, the judge dismissed the arguments and ordered the trials to proceed.[83] In August 2003, the East Timor trials came to an end. In total, 6 out of 18 defendants were convicted including the former Governor of East Timor, Abilio Soares. As in the *Bali bombing* case, Soares could not challenge the constitutionality of his conviction before the Constitutional Court and only had the option to challenge the constitutionality of *Law No. 26/2000* that allowed the Human Rights Court to operate retrospectively.[84] The Constitutional Court with a 6–3 decision decided to reject Soares' complaint.

The Abdurrahman Wahid case[85]

Another important case that relates to the issue of judicial review is the *Abdurrahman Wahid* case. Abdurrahman Wahid, or Gus Dur as he was also known, was the fourth President of Indonesia. He was removed from office in 2001 after his aide allegedly used Wahid's name to illegally secure US$4,000,000 worth of funds from the State Logistic Agency, *Bulog*. In 2004, Wahid wanted to run for President again. However, his candidacy was rejected by the Election Commission (EC) because he did not pass the physical examination. In fact, Wahid was nearly blind as the result of diabetes and two strokes. In 1999, when he was nominated as President and then elected, there was no constitutional requirement that the presidential candidate should be physically capable of performing his duties.[86] It was later in 2001 that the People's Consultative Assembly passed the third amendment to the *Constitution of the Republic of Indonesia*, which required that the Presidential candidate be physically capable.[87]

The Constitutional Court has no authority to review the constitutionality of the decision of the EC, and therefore Wahid could not challenge the EC decision before the Court. The only option left for Wahid was to challenge the constitutionality of the law that became the basis of the decision: *Law No. 23/2003* on the Presidential Election. Wahid then challenged the constitutionality of the provision in *Law No. 23/2003*, which states that any candidate for President and

Vice President shall be mentally and physically capable of performing the tasks and duties of President and Vice President.[88] Wahid argued that *Law No. 23/2003* violated his constitutional rights to be treated equally before the law.[89]

The Court simply ruled that *Law No. 23/2003* was constitutional, because the *Constitution of the Republic of Indonesia* clearly states that any candidate for President and Vice President shall be mentally and physically capable of performing the tasks and duties of President and Vice President.[90] Furthermore, the Court ruled that the *Constitution of the Republic of Indonesia* also mandated that the legislature must enact a statute that provides detail on the mechanism for presidential election and thus the legislature was fulfilling its obligation.[91] Therefore, the Court rejected Wahid's petition.

These selected cases show that the Court had to deal with certain problems caused by restrictions on the ability of individuals to make constitutional complaints. There are significant limitations that leave the claimant only able to challenge the constitutionality of a law and unable to challenge either the application of the statute or the implementing regulation. In general, the statute itself never directly infringes upon the claimants' constitutional rights, but the application of the law either through ordinary court decisions or administrative decisions do infringe on the claimants' constitutional rights. However, the claimant cannot challenge the constitutionality of these administrative decisions or applications of the law.

In many ways, Indonesian politicians looked to the Korean Constitutional Court as a model, except in one important respect: access to the Court. Indonesian politicians did not adopt a constitutional complaint mechanism that enabled individual citizens to defend their constitutional rights before the Court. Since the beginning, Indonesian politicians tried to limit the scope of the Court's authority in many ways. First, they imposed the limitation that the Court may only review the constitutionality of a law that was enacted after the 1999 amendment to the *Constitution of the Republic of Indonesia*.[92] Then, during the discussion of the Bill on the Indonesian Constitutional Court, they started to think about how to create a certain mechanism that could prevent access to the Court.

When parliament prepared the Bill on the Indonesian Constitutional Court in late November 2002, it was obvious that the politicians in the parliament tried to limit the access of individuals to the Court. The Bill on the Indonesian Constitutional Court stated that, 'the Constitutional Court shall receive petitions from the National Ombudsman Commission who will act on behalf of individual citizens, classes or institutions that request for judicial review'.[93] Furthermore, the Bill on the Indonesian Constitutional Court stated that the National Ombudsman Commission would scrutinize requests for judicial review before filing petitions to the Constitutional Court.[94] In other words, it was the National Ombudsman Commission that had the right to file judicial review before the Constitutional Court. The proposal immediately faced strong resistance from inside and outside the parliament. The first and most obvious critics were the non-governmental organizations and a large section of civil society who strongly criticized the Bill on the Indonesian Constitutional Court for the reason that it diminished individual access to the Court.[95]

The parliament then dropped the proposal for Ombudsman approval and came out with a new proposal that aimed to create a higher threshold for the claimant to bring a case before the Court. The proposal was then accepted as the standing provision in the *Constitutional Court Act*, with the expectation that it might become an effective device to prevent a flood of litigation.[96] In other words, the politicians in the parliament did not want to create a constitutional court with wide access to individual citizens.

In sum, the Indonesian politicians adopted a unique mechanism that looks like a constitutional complaint, but essentially, it is not a constitutional complaint. Under this unique mechanism, a state institution, private or public institution or individual citizen can challenge the constitutionality of a statute. Indonesian politicians did not exclusively design the mechanism for individual citizens to challenge the constitutionality of a statute. Instead, they give many different groups a right to challenge the constitutionality of statute.

Since its establishment in 2003, the Indonesian Constitutional Court has tried to expand its influence through handing down many important decisions that uphold constitutionally protected rights. The Indonesian Constitutional Court has issued some important decisions in the area of civil and political rights. The Court restored the voting rights of former Communists,[97] and the Court upheld the principle of the non-retroactive effect of a law.[98] In the economic area, the Court issued an interpretation on the meaning of a state-controlled economy.[99] In the social policy area, the Court ruled that the government should fulfil the constitutional mandate of allocating a minimum of 20 per cent of the state budget to education.[100]

The Court managed to review many important issues, because it imposed a lenient standing test. The leadership of Chief Justice Jimly Asshiddiqie was a significant factor in shaping the Court's treatment on standing. Chief Justice Asshiddiqie had a vision that the Court should play an important role in the transitional period, and in order to accomplish its mission, the Chief Justice managed to convince his brethren to apply lenient standing rules that gave the Court a chance to review many important issues.

The performance of the Indonesian Constitutional Court, however, is still far from that of its Korean counterpart. In its first five years, the Korean Constitutional Court was very active in addressing the errors of the authoritarian regimes by striking down old laws and practices.[101] In the first several years following its establishment, the Korean Constitutional Court struck down many laws that neglected the normative role of the *Korean Constitution* and people's basic rights.[102]

Despite the Court's best efforts, a structural limitation makes it difficult for the Indonesian Constitutional Court to protect constitutionally protected rights. In the first five years of its operations the Court had a limited opportunity to issue judgments, because the Court only had limited authority to adjudicate on the constitutional matters. The Court has authority to review the constitutionality of a statute upon the request of designated subject, but it has no authority to review the application of statutes, to interpret statutes by administrative apparatuses, or to review administrative decisions or actions. From the standpoint of civil society, access to the Court is very limited. It is not easy for individual citizens, interest groups and non-governmental organizations to file judicial review because there is no constitutional complaint mechanism that enables them to challenge the constitutionality of administrative actions or decisions. In sum, the Indonesian Constitutional Court took a different path from its Korean counterpart, primarily because of the institutional choice made by the creators of the Court to limit access to the Court.

Conclusion

The Korean Constitutional Court has become a model for the Indonesian Constitutional Court, except in one respect: access to the Court. The Korean Constitutional Court partly grew from a concern for the protection of human rights in a post-authoritarian regime, and therefore the judicial system provides citizens with reasonably easy access to bring a case before the Court. Unlike their Korean counterparts, the creators of the Indonesian Constitutional Court never had any intention of creating a court with easy access. They created a legislative framework that only allows the Court to conduct statutory review, but excludes review of administrative actions, administrative decisions and government regulations from the Court's jurisdiction. The government and legislature expected that such a mechanism would be an effective device in preventing a flood of litigation in the Constitutional Court and that consequently it would minimize Court business. Indeed, they were successful in preventing such a flood of litigation. In the early years of its operation, the Constitutional Court only received a small number of cases.

The small number of cases in the Court docket, however, has implications for the Court's operation. The current mechanism successfully helps the Court manage its docket and performance. With less workload, the Court manages to issue decisions in a timely manner and avoid backlogs. The new Constitutional Court has successfully created an image of an efficient and disciplined court, an image in contrast to that of the old Supreme Court, which was known as inefficient and slow. On the other hand, the small number of cases creates a new challenge for the Court. Essentially, a constitutional court is a specialized court whose main business is to conduct constitutional review. If there are not enough cases to review, then what is the efficacy of establishing a special court? Indeed, how can the Court gain respect from other branches of government and from the public, and thus cement its place in Indonesian society, if it does not have the opportunity to receive important constitutional complaints?

The Indonesian Constitutional Court is still in its early stages of development and there are many years to go for the Court to build itself as an institution that safeguards the rights enshrined in the *Constitution of the Republic of Indonesia*. Although the Court has not emerged with a perfect image yet, at least it has been trying to establish itself as a strong and respectable institution.

Notes

1. The members of the Ad Hoc Committee of the People's Consultative Assembly (*Majelis Permusyawaratan Rakyat* or MPR) were divided into nine groups, in which each group visited at least two countries. Group one (Iran and Russia); group two (Malaysia, Philippines and South Africa); group three (People's Republic of China, Japan and South Korea); group four (United States and Canada); group five (Egypt and United Kingdom); group six (Greece and Germany); group seven (Italy and Netherlands); group nine (Spain and France); group 10 (Denmark, Hungary and Sweden). See minutes of sixth meeting, BP MPR, May 23, 2000.
2. Denny Indrayana, "Indonesian Constitutional Reform 1999–2002: An Evaluation of Constitutional-Making in Transition" (PhD diss., University of Melbourne, 2005), 157.
3. Hamdan Zoelva, "Hubungan Mahkamah Konstitusi dengan Lembaga Negara Lainnya," (The Relationship between the Constitutional Court and the Other State Agencies) *Jentera Jurnal Hukum*, January–March (2006): 44.
4. Minutes of 41st meeting, BP MPR, June 8, 2000.
5. Tom Ginsburg, *Judicial Review in New Democracies: Constitutional Courts in Asian Cases* (Cambridge: Cambridge University Press, 2003), 25.
6. Ibid.
7. Ran Hirschl, *Towards Juristocracy: The Origins and Consequences of the New Constitutionalism* (Cambridge, MA: Harvard University Press, 2004), 43.
8. The Constitutional Court of Korea, *The First Ten Years of the Korean Constitutional Court 1988–1998* (Seoul: The Constitutional Court of Korea, 2001), 16.
9. Ibid.
10. Ibid.
11. Ibid., 17.
12. Ibid.
13. Ibid.
14. Ibid., 216–17.
15. Ibid.
16. *Utusan golongan* (functional representatives) and small factions of the PDI-P (Indonesian Democratic Party of Struggle) and Indonesian National Unity blocs (*Kesatuan Kebangsaan Indonesia* or KKI) were in this group.
17. The military bloc, United Development Party bloc (PPP), reform bloc, Association of Moslim Sovereignty bloc (*Perserikatan Daulat Ummat* or PDU), National Love Democratic Party bloc (*Partai Demokrasi Kasih Bangsa* or PDKB) and PDI-P were in this group.
18. The former ruling party *Golkar*, National Awakening Party (*Partai Kebangkitan Bangsa* or PKB) and a faction of the PDI-P were in this group.
19. Richard Robison and Vedi R. Hadiz, *Reorganising Power in Indonesia: The Politics of Oligarchy in an Age of Markets* (London: Routledge Curzon, 2004), 224–5
20. Blair King, "Empowering the Presidency: Interest and Perceptions in Indonesia's Constitutional Reforms, 1999–2002" (PhD diss., Ohio State University, 2004), 109.
21. Ibid.
22. Ibid., 94.

23. The political groups that explicitly proposed a specialized constitutional court were *Utusan Golongan* (Functional Representatives), KKI blocs, and a small faction of PDI-P blocs (Indonesian Democratic Party of Struggle). See Benny Harman, "Perkembangan Pemikiran Mengenai Perlunya Pengujian UU Terhadap UUD Dalam Sejarah Ketatanegaraan Indonesia (1945–2004)" (The Development of Legal Thought on the Judicial Review of Acts of Parliament against the Constitution in the Indonesian Constitutional History) (PhD diss., University of Indonesia, 2006), 304.
24. Minutes of 51st meeting, BP MPR (Working Committee of the People Consultative Assembly), July 29, 2000.
25. Harman, "Perkembangan Pemikiran Mengenai Perlunya Pengujian UU Terhadap UUD Dalam Sejarah Ketatanegaraan Indonesia (1945–2004)" (The Development of Legal Thought on the Judicial Review of Acts of Parliament against the Constitution in the Indonesian Constitutional History), 337–9. Both of the ruling parties and opposition parties reached the compromise without much thought. The ruling party believed that the new Constitutional Court could be managed easily and, on the other hand, the opposition parties believed that the Constitutional Court would improve the protection of basic rights.
26. Ibid.
27. A senior politician in the Assembly, in discussion with the author, July 24, 2006; Adviser to the Ad Hoc Committee of the Assembly, in discussion with the author, August 23, 2006.
28. 1987 *Constitution of the Republic of Korea* art. 111.
29. 1987 *Constitution of the Republic of Korea* art.107 § 1.
30. 1987 *Constitution of the Republic of Korea* art. 107 § 2.
31. A former parliamentarian described this situation as follows: 'We did not want to have any conflict in the selection process. When we looked at the Korean Constitutional Court, each political branch has the power to nominate three justices. Why then should we go through hardship by debating the selection method, when we can just follow the Korean model and everything will go easily because we will not have any debate.'
32. Andrew MacIntyre, *The Power of Institutions: Political Architecture and Governance* (Ithaca: Cornell University Press, 2003), 153.
33. Minutes of plenary meeting, PAH I BP MPR, September 25, 2001.
34. *Constitution of the Republic of Indonesia* art. 24C(3).
35. The minutes of the plenary meeting also clearly recorded that the proposed selection method was modelled on the selection method for the Korean Constitutional Court. See minutes of plenary meeting, PAH I BP MPR, September 25, 2001.
36. A former member of the Assembly, in discussion with the author, July 26, 2006.
37. Scholars who study the Indonesian Constitutional Court do not argue that the issue of impeachment was the primary driving force behind the establishment of the Constitutional Court. For example, the Australian legal scholar, Tim Lindsey, noted that the creation of the Constitutional Court was a response to the political crisis provoked by Wahid's impeachment; however, he argued that the creation of the Court was primarily a response to the long absence of judicial review in Indonesia. Tim Lindsey, "Indonesian Constitutional Reform: Muddling Towards Democracy," *Singapore Journal of International and Comparative Law* 6 (2002): 244.
38. Harman, "Perkembangan Pemikiran Mengenai Perlunya Pengujian UU Terhadap UUD Dalam Sejarah Ketatanegaraan Indonesia (1945–2004)" (The Development of Legal Thought on the Judicial Review of Acts of Parliament against the Constitution in the Indonesian Constitutional History), 327. The debate is now divided into two after those proposing that the Constitutional Court should be under the power of the Assembly, dropped their proposal. The groups of PDI-P, PDU, UG and PPP were in

favour of a specialized and independent court. The Reform bloc, *Golkar*, Military bloc, and PBB were in favour of the establishment of a constitutional court as part of the Supreme Court.

39. Minutes of lobby meeting, PAH I BP MPR, September 18, 2001, 36.
40. King, "Empowering the Presidency: Interest and Perceptions in Indonesia's Constitutional Reforms, 1999–2002," 116. PDI-P mistrusted to a certain degree the political blocs in the Assembly as a result of the 1999 presidential election, in which the political blocs in the Assembly united against Megawati.
41. Minutes of plenary meeting, PAH I BP MPR, October 16–19, 2001.
42. MacIntyre, *The Power of Institutions: Political Architecture and Governance*, 153.
43. In 2004, President Susilo Bambang Yudhyono and Vice President Jusuf Kalla, who were elected through the first direct election, had to cope with a fragmented political configuration in which seven political parties were significant players in the parliament. In the weeks following their inauguration, the so-called National Coalition that was hostile to Yudhoyono's presidency seriously threatened his government's stability by issuing "interpellation." Therefore, Yudhoyono had to make his Vice President take control of the leadership of *Golkar* (which controlled the largest number of seats in the parliament) in order to establish a solid political base in the parliament. See R. William Liddle, "Year One of the Yudhoyono–Kalla Duumvirate," *Bulletin of Indonesian Economic Studies* 41 (2005): 325–40.
44. Martin Shapiro, "The Success of Judicial Review," in *Constitutional Dialogues in Comparative Perspective*, ed. Sally J. Kenney, William M. Reisinger and John C. Reitz (Princeton, NJ: Princeton University Press, 1988), 197.
45. James M. West and Dae-Kyu Yoon, "The Constitutional Court of the Republic of Korea: Transforming the Jurisprudence of the Vortex?," *American Journal of Comparative Law* 40 (1992): 73.
46. The Constitutional Court of Korea, *The First Ten Years of the Korean Constitutional Court 1988–1998*, 18.
47. Ginsburg, *Judicial Review in New Democracies: Constitutional Courts in Asian Cases*, 221.
48. Dongwook Cha, "The Role of the Korean Constitutional Court in the Democratization of South Korea" (PhD diss., University of Southern California, 2005), 176.
49. Ibid.
50. Youngjae Lee, "Law Politics and Impeachment: The Impeachment of Roh Moo-Hyun from a Comparative Constitutional Perspective," *American Journal of Comparative Law* 53 (2005): 403.
51. Transitional Provision of the Fourth Amendment to the 1945 *Constitution of the Republic of Indonesia* art. III.
52. Laszlo Solyom and Georg Brunner, *Constitutional Judiciary in a New Democracy: The Hungarian Constitutional Court* (Ann Arbor, MI: University of Michigan Press, 2000), 71.
53. The Constitutional Court of Korea, *The First Ten Years of the Korean Constitutional Court 1988–1998*, 18.
54. Constitutional Court of the Republic of Indonesia, *Annual Report of the Constitutional Court of the Republic of Indonesia 2003* (Jakarta: Constitutional Court of the Republic of Indonesia, 2003); Constitutional Court of the Republic of Indonesia, *Annual Report of the Constitutional Court of the Republic of Indonesia 2004* (Jakarta: Constitutional Court of the Republic of Indonesia, 2004); Constitutional Court of Republic of Indonesia, *Guarding the Constitutional Rights: Annual Report Year 2005* (Jakarta: Constitutional Court of the Republic of Indonesia, 2005); Constitutional Court of Republic of Indonesia, *To Build A Democratic State based on Rule of*

Law: Three Years of the Indonesian Constitutional Court: 2003–2006 (Jakarta: Constitutional Court of the Republic of Indonesia, 2006); Constitutional Court of the Republic of Indonesia, *Annual Report 2006*, (Jakarta: Constitutional Court of the Republic of Indonesia, 2007).

55. The Constitutional Court of Korea, *The First Ten Years of the Korean Constitutional Court 1988–1998*, 18.
56. *Constitutional Court Act* art. 68(1).
57. *Constitutional Court Act* art. 68(2).
58. Peter Kwon, "Reassessing Korean Legal Culture and the Rule of Law: Legal History, Constitutional Review and Negotiations in Cross-Border Finance" (PhD diss., the University of Sydney, 2006), 206.
59. Ginsburg, *Judicial Review in New Democracies: Constitutional Courts in Asian Cases*, 223.
60. A former member of the Assembly, in discussion with the author, August 9, 2006.
61. Minutes of the parliamentary hearing, PANJA, July 15, 2003. These are unofficial minutes of the parliamentary hearing that I obtained through informal sources.
62. *Constitutional Court Act* art. 51.
63. Allan R. Brewer-Carias, *Judicial Review in Comparative Law* (Cambridge: Cambridge University Press, 1989), 228.
64. Alfred Rinken, "The Federal Constitutional Court and the German Political System," in *Constitutional Courts in Comparison. The US Supreme Court and the German Federal Constitutional Court*, ed. Ralf Rogowski and Thomas Gawron (New York: Berghahn Books, 2002), 67.
65. Brewer-Carias, *Judicial Review in Comparative Law*, 211.
66. Ibid.
67. Articles 24 (1) and (2) of the 1945 *Constitution of the Republic of Indonesia* provide that the Indonesian Constitutional Court shall have jurisdiction over these issues: (1) constitutionality of a statute; (2) disputes over the authorities of state institutions; (3) dissolution of a political party; (4) disputes on the results of general elections; and (5) motions for impeachment against the President or Vice President.
68. Case No. 018/PUU-I/2003 (the *West Papua* case).
69. See Adam Schwarz, *A Nation in Waiting: Indonesia's Search for Stability* (Boulder, Colorado: Westview Press, 2000), 62–4.
70. *Presidential Instruction No. 1/2003*.
71. See Jaap Timmer, "West Papua," *Contemporary Pacific* 16 (2004): 409–19.
72. Case No. 018/PUU-I/2003, 131.
73. Case No. 013/PUU-I/2003 (the *Bali bombing* case).
74. Ross Clarke, "Retrospectivity and the Constitutional Validity of the Bali Bombing and East Timor Trials," *Australian Journal of Asian Law* 5 (2003): 20. Six days after the bombing took place the government passed the *Emergency Law No. 1/2002* on ant-terrorism (*Emergency Law No. 1*) that created easier procedures to investigate, prosecute and convict terrorists plus substantial penalties for terrorists and those who assist terrorists. *Emergency Law No. 1* was issued by the President under the emergency legislative powers and was ratified by the House of Representatives at its following session. On the same day, the government also passed the *Emergency Law No. 2/2002* (*Emergency Law No. 2*) that provided that *Emergency Law No. 1* could be used with respect to the Bali bombings. *Emergency Law No. 2* authorized the police, prosecutors and judges to apply *Emergency Law No. 1*, because *Emergency Law No. 1* was not in force at the time the bomber prepared and detonated the bomb. Later on, the House of Representatives adopted *Emergency Law No. 1* as *Law No. 15/2003* on anti-terrorism and *Emergency Law No. 2* was adopted as *Law No. 16/2003*.

75. Article 28 § 1 of the 1945 *Constitution of the Republic of Indonesia* states that the right not to be prosecuted under retrospective laws is a basic human right that must not be diminished in any circumstances.
76. Simon Butt and David Hansell, "The Masykur Abdul Kadir Case: Indonesian Constitutional Court Decision No. 013/PUU-I/2003," *Australian Journal of Asian Law* 6 (2004): 177.
77. Case No. 013/PUU-I/2003.
78. Case No. 065 /PUU-II/2004 (the *Human Rights Court Law* case).
79. See discussion by Mark Cammack in his chapter in this publication.
80. Clarke, "Retrospectivity and the Constitutional Validity of the Bali Bombing and East Timor Trials," 15–16.
81. *Law No. 26/2000* art. 43. Some human rights' campaigners have suggested *Law No. 26/2000* was only made retrospective due to the Indonesian government's desire to avoid an international criminal tribunal being established, which would usurp their national jurisdiction.
82. Clarke, "Retrospectivity and the Constitutional Validity of the Bali Bombing and East Timor Trials," 17.
83. Ibid.
84. Soares specifically challenged arts 43 § 1 and 2 of the *Law No. 26/2000.*
85. Case No. 008/PUU-II/2004 (the *Abdurrahman Wahid* case).
86. In the 1999 presidential election, Wahid's health was not a major problem, partly because Wahid was the only candidate who could possibly challenge the favourite presidential candidate, Megawati Soekarnoputri. Wahid was put forward as a presidential candidate by the coalition of Moslim forces, who attempted to block Megawati's candidacy. See Yang Razali Kassim, *Transition Politics in Southeast Asia: Dynamics of Leadership Change and Succession in Indonesia and Malaysia* (Singapore: Marshall Cavendish Academic, 2005): 146–7.
87. Third Amendment to 1945 *Constitution of the Republic of Indonesia* art. 6.
88. *Law No. 23/2003* art. 6(d).
89. 1945 *Constitution of the Republic of Indonesia* art. 27 § 1
90. Case No. 008/PUU-II/2004; 1945 *Constitution of the Republic of Indonesia* art. 6 § 1.
91. Case No. 008/PUU-II/2004; 1945 *Constitution of the Republic of Indonesia* art. 6 § 2.
92. *Constitutional Court Act* art. 50.
93. Bill on the Indonesian Constitutional Court art. 55 § 1.
94. Bill on the Indonesian Constitutional Court art. 55 § 2.
95. "Antara Keinginan Memonopoli dan Membuka Partisipasi," (Between a Desire to Monopolize and to Open the Participation), *Kompas*, June 9, 2003; "Pembahasan RUU Mahkamah Konstitusi Berlarut: Bingungkan Posisi MA," (The Discussion on the Bill Continued: Confusion over the Position of the Supreme Court) *Kompas*, June 21, 2003.
96. Minutes of the house meeting, PANSUS Mahkamah Konstitusi (the Special Committee on the Constitutional Court), August 2, 2003, 14–15.
97. Case No. 011–17/PUU-I/2003 (the *Communist Party* case).
98. Case No. 013/PUU-I/2003; Case No. 065 /PUU-II/2004.
99. Case No. 001-021-022/PUU-I/2003 (the *Electricity Law* case); Case No. 002/PUU-I/2003 (the *Oil and Gas Law* case); Case No. 058-059-060-063/PUU-II/2004 (the *Water Resources Law* case).
100. Case No. 011/PUU-III/2005 (the *National Education System Law* case); Case No. 012/PUU-III/2005 (the *State Budget Law I* case); Case No. 026/PUU-III/2005 (the *State Budget Law II* case).
101. Cha, "The Role of the Korean Constitutional Court in the Democratization of South Korea," 93–4.

102. Ibid. The percentage of the decisions where unconstitutionality was found remained high and relatively stable during five years of the first term of the Korean Constitutional Court (1988–93). However, from 1994 to 1996, the percentage of unconstitutional decisions declined dramatically. The most frequently filed areas of cases were criminal procedure and due process, economic liberties and political rights.

9 The Indonesian human rights court

Mark Cammack

Introduction

In March 2002, prosecutors read out charges in the first trial to be conducted before Indonesia's newly established Human Rights Court (HRC). The accused in the case, Abilio Soares, was the former Provincial Governor of Indonesian East Timor. The indictment accused Soares of commission of crimes against humanity during the period leading up to and after the independence referendum held in East Timor in September 1999. Over the next year and a half, a total of 18 Indonesian military and civilian authorities would be tried for crimes against humanity committed in East Timor. The East Timor prosecutions were followed by trials of military officials for an incident in 1984, in which the military fired into a group of protestors outside a mosque in the Tanjung Priok district of Jakarta, and the trial of police officers for an incident in 2000, in which police in Papua killed three people and arrested and assaulted scores more in retaliation for an attack on a police station.

The East Timor prosecutions make up the majority of the cases tried before the HRC. However, the idea for the creation of a specialized human rights court in Indonesia pre-dated the East Timor violence, and while the HRC is most closely identified with the East Timor and Tanjung Priok prosecutions, the jurisdiction of the HRC is not limited to a predefined set of incidents. The proposal for the creation of the HRC was first put forward as part of the broader political restructuring in Indonesia following the forced resignation of President Suharto in 1998. The most significant post-Suharto reforms were to the political branches of government, including direct election of the President, limitation of presidential tenure to two, five-year terms, transfer of primary legislative functions from the executive to the legislature (*Dewan Perwakilan Rakyat*, People's Representative Council, or DPR) and a major devolution of power from the central government to the regions. Reforms to the legal system, which 30 years of New Order rule had rendered utterly corrupt and dysfunctional, were less far-reaching.[1] One change, which was over-sold at the time as offering a complete solution to the problems of the legal system, was an administrative reorganization that transferred control over the judiciary from the executive branch to the Supreme Court. The other major post-Suharto initiative with respect to the legal system was the creation of a number of new specialized courts. The most significant addition to the legal system is a new Constitutional Court with the power to review the constitutionality of legislation.[2] Other new courts with a specialized jurisdiction that were created as part of the post-Suharto reforms include a Commercial Court, Anti-Corruption Court, Tax Court, Labour Court and the HRC.[3]

The proposal for a human rights court was put forth as part of the post-1998 reforms, but the immediate impetus for the creation of the Court came from outside the country. As will be shown below, the establishment of the HRC and the first set of trials before the Court were in direct response to demands by the international community for trial of Indonesians suspected of human rights crimes in East Timor in 1999.

The East Timor prosecutions before the HRC have been the subject of extensive comment. Observers both in and out of Indonesia have condemned the trials for failing to expose the truth and impose accountability for the violence.[4] I approach the trials from a different perspective. My aim is not to evaluate the success or failure of the prosecutions, but to use the record of the trials to undertake an assessment of the HRC. While the prosecutions as a whole must be judged a failure, the HRC was not the cause of that failure, but was virtually the only actor in the process that exerted any influence to prevent it. In so far as the aim of creating a new tribunal was to establish an independent judicial body by making an end-run around the corruption-plagued courts, the effort was at least partially successful. Ultimately, however, the actions of the HRC proved essentially irrelevant, as other more powerful actors intervened in the process to overturn what the HRC had accomplished.

The creation of the human rights court

The idea for the creation of a human rights court first appeared in the 1999 Indonesian *Law No. 39/1999* (*Human Rights Act*). This statute, which was part of a flood of legislation passed as a part of the *Reformasi* following Suharto's resignation,[5] consists primarily of a catalogue of basic rights protected against infringement by the state. One brief article of the Act mandates the creation of a human rights court with jurisdiction to try serious human rights crimes.[6] The Act sets a four-year deadline after enactment for creation of the Court.

Although the concept of a human rights court was first formally endorsed in the *Human Rights Act*, the creation of the Court is a direct consequence of events in East Timor in 1999. East Timor, now officially Timor-Leste, comprises the eastern half of the island of Timor, a 'crocodile-shaped' island 440 kilometres in length located at the eastern end of the Malay archipelago.[7] The western half of the island was colonized by the Dutch and became part of Indonesia after World War II. The eastern half of the island was ruled by Portugal. The Portuguese remained in East Timor until 1974, when a leftist military revolt in Lisbon ousted the country's authoritarian right-wing government and declared its intention to offer the East Timorese self-determination. After some 20 months of often-violent debates about the territory's future, the left-leaning Revolutionary Front for an Independent East Timor (*Fretelin*)[8] declared East Timor's independence on 28 November 1975. A massive Indonesian military invasion followed on 7 December 1975.[9]

The Indonesian military remained in East Timor until 1999. The East Timorese people never accepted Indonesian rule, however, and East Timorese separatists fought a guerrilla war against the Indonesian military throughout the quarter century of Indonesian rule. An estimated 200,000 East Timorese died during the period of Indonesian occupation.[10] The Indonesian military suffered 1,400 deaths fighting the insurgency.

In January 1999, Indonesian President Habibie, who took over the presidency following Suharto's resignation, precipitously announced that the people of East Timor would be permitted to choose whether to remain a part of Indonesia or become independent. The abrupt change of policy, which was apparently motivated by the need to cultivate international support as Indonesia struggled to recover economically,[11] surprised virtually everyone. Included among those caught unawares was the Indonesian military. More to the point, many within the military strongly opposed East Timorese independence. The military paid a high price to acquire and hold East Timor; in the view of many that sacrifice would have been for nothing if the Indonesian claims to the territory were surrendered. There were also fears that if East Timor were offered the opportunity for independence, other regions with separatist aspirations might demand the same privilege.

Preparations for the referendum proceeded notwithstanding military opposition. In May an agreement was signed by the United Nations, Indonesia and Portugal regarding the conduct of the vote.[12] Under the terms of the so-called 'New York Agreement' the United Nations was to organize and carry out the balloting and Indonesia undertook responsibility for security. By the time the New York Agreement was signed in May the importance of security should have been apparent. Election-related violence began to occur almost as soon as the independence referendum was announced, and a number of particularly deadly incidents occurred in April.[13] It should have been apparent as well that assigning responsibility for maintaining security during the election to the Indonesian military was like assigning the proverbial fox to guard the hen house, since the Indonesian military not only recruited, armed and trained pro-integration militias but sometimes joined with the militiamen in the attacks.

The vote was held on 30 August 1999 and 95 per cent of more than 400,000 registered voters cast ballots; they voted overwhelmingly in favour of independence.[14] The results of the vote were announced on 4 September 1999. There followed an orchestrated rampage of killing, terror, arson and forced dislocation that left more than 1,000 dead, 250,000 forcibly removed to West Timor and the destruction of an estimated 70 per cent of the territory's infrastructure.[15] The violence finally ended and order was restored, only after a United Nations authorized peace-keeping force led by Australian troops entered East Timor on 20 September.

As the organizer of the vote, the United Nations could not easily ignore its violent aftermath. Even as the violence in East Timor was ongoing, preparations were begun for possible prosecutions of those responsible. A special session of the United Nations Commission on Human Rights meeting 23–27 September in Geneva adopted a resolution calling on the Secretary General to appoint an international commission of inquiry to investigate human rights crimes committed in East Timor (United Nations Commission on Human Rights 1999).[16] Pursuant to that resolution, the Office of the United Nations High Commissioner for Human Rights announced the appointment of a five-member International Commission of Inquiry on East Timor (ICOIET) on 15 October.

ICOIET completed its work on 31 January 2000.[17] In its report to the Secretary General, ICOIET found evidence of a pattern of serious violations of fundamental human rights and humanitarian law. These violations took the form of systematic and widespread intimidation, humiliation and terror, destruction of property, violence against women and displacement of people. ICOIET also found evidence of a systematic attempt to destroy and conceal evidence of the violations. With respect to responsibility for the violations, ICOIET found that militia groups were responsible for the intimidation and terror, and that the Indonesian military and civilian authorities in East Timor, as well as some officials in Jakarta, had pursued a policy of engaging the militias to influence the outcome of the vote. This policy, which was designed to give the impression that the East Timorese were fighting among themselves, manifested itself in the form of active recruitment, funding and arming of the militias and in the provision of logistical support to the militias in carrying out acts of intimidation and terror. ICOIET placed ultimate responsibility for the violence against civilians in East Timor on the Indonesian army. Finally, ICOIET recommended the creation of an international tribunal charged with prosecuting persons guilty of serious human rights violations as well as ensuring reparations for the victims and considering issues of truth and reconciliation.

The Indonesian government responded to ICOIET's report in a letter signed by the Minister of Foreign Affairs and addressed to the Secretary General.[18] While not conceding to the report's findings, the letter asserted that any violations committed while East Timor was part of Indonesia were subject to the exclusive jurisdiction of Indonesian law. It was further insisted that the Indonesian legal system was fully capable of dispensing justice, that the international community should respect the principle of exhaustion of national remedies and that the degree and extent of alleged human rights violations did not justify the establishment of an international tribunal. The letter also argued that convening an international tribunal would complicate efforts to achieve reconciliation between Indonesia and East Timor.

In a February 2000 letter to the Secretary General, the President of the Security Council wrote that the Council welcomed the commitment by the Indonesian government to bring to justice those responsible for human rights violations in East Timor.[19] The Council's letter to the Secretary General also encouraged Indonesia to institute a swift, comprehensive, effective and transparent legal process, noting that early and effective action by the government of Indonesia would contribute to improved relations between the peoples of Indonesia and East Timor.

Meanwhile, Indonesian authorities had launched their own investigation into the crimes committed in East Timor. Indonesia had initially attempted to prevent the United Nations Human Rights Commission from meeting on the situation in East Timor. When it became clear that a special session was inevitable, the government urged the National Human Rights Commission (*Komisi Nasional Hak Asasi Manusia* or *Komnas HAM*) to undertake an investigation. At first *Komnas HAM* resisted the idea because of concern that the results would never be acted upon.[20] The government gave its assurance that the investigation would be followed with appropriate legal action, and on 22 September 1999 *Komnas HAM* appointed a special investigative team (*KPP-HAM*) to carry out an inquiry into events in East Timor.[21] *KPP-HAM* was charged with investigating the commission of genocide, extrajudicial executions, rape, torture and arson for possible trial before a proposed national human rights tribunal.[22]

KPP-HAM completed its work and submitted its final report on 31 January 2000, the same day the United Nations-appointed ICOIET submitted its report.[23] The report documents gross human rights violations that were committed in all of East Timor's 13 administrative districts.[24] The abuses cited in the report were committed over a 10-month period, from January 1999 when the plan for an independence vote was announced, through to October 1999 when international troops finally restored order. The violations included mass murder, persecution, forced disappearances, gender-based violence and forced movement of civilian populations. *KPP-HAM* concluded that the massive and widespread attacks against civilians were not simply the result of the inability of the security forces to protect the population, but resulted from a conscious and planned effort. *KPP-HAM* found evidence that the military, the police, and the civil administration had close ties to the militia groups that committed much of the violence, and that the military and the civil administration were involved in the creation, support, arming and training of the militias.[25]

The report lists a total of 106 suspected perpetrators divided into three groups.[26] The first group includes persons suspected of direct, personal commission of crimes against humanity in the field. This group includes militia leaders and members, members of the Indonesian military and police, and officials in the East Timor civil bureaucracy. The second group consists of 18 named individuals who were suspected of gross human rights violations because of their positions and actions in controlling or coordinating operations in the field. The third group of four suspects consists of high-level military personnel in Jakarta who held responsibility for national security. Among those named in this final section is General Wiranto, former Minister of Defence and Supreme Commander of Armed Forces.

The human rights court statute

Upon completion of the investigations, attention turned to the establishment of institutions to carry out prosecutions. It was assumed that the trial of human rights crimes would require the creation of a specialized court. In order to expedite the process and preclude international intervention, the Ministry of Justice prepared an executive decree providing for the establishment of a human rights court. President Habibie signed the decree – a Government Regulation in Lieu of Legislation – on 8 October 1999 (*Perpu No. 1/1999*). The Regulation inexplicably failed to provide for retroactive application, and the legislature declined to approve it.[27] The government then drafted a legislative proposal containing express provision for retroactive application. This proposal was submitted to the legislature in June 2000 and approved the following November.[28]

The *Human Rights Court Act* both creates a new court and establishes new criminal offences and new principles of criminal liability. The crimes defined by the law are genocide and crimes against humanity.[29] The law also includes rules imposing vicarious liability on commanders, both military and civilian, for crimes committed by persons under the commander's effective command and control.[30] In addition to liability for affirmative acts, the Act's command responsibility provisions also impose liability for acts of omission based on the commander's failure to prevent or punish crimes committed by subordinates.[31] Both the substantive definitions of crimes and the command responsibility provisions are closely patterned after the *Rome Statute for the International Criminal Court*.[32]

The Act grants *Komnas HAM* the exclusive power to conduct preliminary investigations into the commission of serious human rights crimes.[33] If *Komnas HAM* finds 'sufficient preliminary proof' of crimes defined in the Act, the results of its investigation are to be delivered to the Attorney-General.[34] The Attorney-General is charged with conducting a further investigation and is responsible for charging and prosecuting crimes within the jurisdiction of the Act.[35]

The HRC is designated as a branch of the courts of general jurisdiction, the *Pengadilan Negeri* (State Court).[36] Unlike the general courts, which are made up of three career judges, the HRC is comprised of five judges – two career judges and three '*ad hoc*' judges.[37] The *ad hoc* judges are appointed by the President on the recommendation of the Supreme Court, and serve for a renewable five-year term.[38] The Act authorizes the initial establishment of courts in four cities, each with a defined territorial jurisdiction.[39]

The Act also provides for appeal of HRC judgments to both the High Court (*Pengadilan Tinggi*) and the Supreme Court (*Mahkamah Agung*), and prescribes the same combination of career and *ad hoc* judges used at the trial level: an appeal to the High Court is heard by a panel of two High Court judges and three *ad hoc* judges,[40] and an appeal to the Supreme Court is heard by a panel of two Supreme Court judges and three *ad hoc* judges.[41] As with *ad hoc* judges at the first instance, *ad hoc* judges on the High Court are nominated by the Supreme Court and appointed by the President.[42] The power to nominate *ad hoc* judges to hear cases in the Supreme Court is assigned to the legislature.[43]

The permanent jurisdiction of the HRC is prospective only. In addition to its permanent jurisdiction, however, the Act also authorizes the establishment of *ad hoc* tribunals to prosecute gross human rights crimes committed before the Act took effect.[44] Creation of an *ad hoc* court with retroactive jurisdiction requires a presidential decision, which may only be issued on the recommendation of the legislature.[45] The Act also requires that the *ad hoc* court's retrospective jurisdiction be specified and limited.[46] In a clear reference to the East Timor investigations, it is expressly provided that investigations begun or completed pursuant to the earlier regulation are valid.[47]

The trials

Law No. 8/1981 (*Code of Criminal Procedure*) establishes a two-stage process for the investigation of ordinary crimes. The first stage – the *penyelidikan* (inquiry) – is under the authority of the police. If this initial inquiry finds sufficient preliminary proof that a crime has been committed the case is turned over to the Office of Public Prosecutor for a second investigation. This second investigation, referred to as the *penyidikan* (investigation), involves the preparation of the dossier (*berita acara*) that serves as the basis for the trial. The *Human Rights Court Act* specifies the same two-step procedure that is used with ordinary crimes.[48] However, the initial inquiry is assigned to *Komnas HAM*.[49]

The *penyelidikan* phase of the East Timor case was completed in early 2000 when *Komnas HAM* delivered its report on East Timor to the Office of the Attorney-General.[50] In April 2000, Attorney-General Marzuki Darusman appointed a task force of investigators.[51] At the time he appointed the task force, Darusman also announced that his office would give priority to five out of the many incidents investigated by *KPP-HAM*.[52] The five priority cases were the 6 April 1999 massacre of civilians in a church compound in the town of Liquisa; the attack on the home of pro-independence leader Manuel Carrascalao in Dili on 17 April; the massacre of civilians inside a church compound in Suai on 6 September; a 6 September attack on the home of Bishop Belo; and the murder of Dutch journalist Sander Thoenes on 23 September.

In retrospect, the decision to limit the investigation to five priority cases had important lasting consequences. First, focusing on five incidents, rather than examining the violence in all of East Timor as the *KPP-HAM* inquiry had done, shaped the way the charges were framed and the cases tried. The prosecutors tended to view the incidents as discrete crimes rather than as parts of a systematic plan. Second, this early decision to give priority to five cases effectively limited who would be prosecuted, since the investigation was never expanded beyond those five incidents.

On 21 March 2001, the Indonesian legislature paved the way for the creation of a court to try crimes committed in East Timor by authorizing the establishment of an *ad hoc* court with the power to try crimes committed prior to the passage of the *Human Rights Court Act*.[53] In his speech to the legislature, Deputy Speaker Soetardjo Soerjogoeritno urged quick action on East Timor 'in order to prevent outside interference'.[54] Not coincidentally, perhaps, the timing of the legislation coincided with the annual meeting of the Human Rights Commission in Geneva.[55] In April the President of the Human Rights Commission warned once again that an international tribunal could be created if Indonesia failed to act.[56]

Shortly thereafter, on 24 April, Indonesian President Abdurrahman Wahid issued a decision establishing the *ad hoc* Court.[57]

The April Presidential Decision authorized the establishment of an *ad hoc* court for East Timor, but inexplicably restricted the jurisdiction of the Court to crimes committed after 30 August 1999, the date of the independence referendum. In July 2001 Wahid was forced from office and replaced by his Vice President, Megawati Sukarnoputri. On 1 August 2001, in her first official act, Megawati issued an amended decision redefining the jurisdiction of the *ad hoc* Court.[58] Although broader than the previous decision, the August 2001 decision also contained seemingly arbitrary restrictions on the Court's jurisdiction; the jurisdiction of the *ad hoc* Court would be limited to crimes committed in three districts – Dili, Liquisia and Suai – and limited to crimes committed in two months – April or September 1999. The limitations contained in the Wahid government's decree are totally inexplicable and may have been a result of an honest mistake; the Megawati decree appears to have been intended to confine the Court to the five priority cases identified by the Attorney-General.

With the issuance of the presidential decree in August 2001, the legal structure was in place for trial of crimes committed in East Timor. It was another seven months before the first trials began. On 14 March 2002, prosecutors read out charges against Abilio Soares who was Governor of the province of East Timor in 1999.[59] Soares was the first of a total of 18 individuals who would be charged before the Court. None of the four senior military officers named in the *KPP-HAM* report were among those charged. The highest-ranking individuals charged were Soares, Timbul Silaen, Chief of Police, and Adam Damiri, regional military commander for the area that included East Timor. The defendants also included two regional military commanders with a province-wide command, two district heads (*bupati*), three district level military commanders, three district level police commanders, a special forces task force commander and three lower level officials. The only person charged before the Court who was not part of either the civilian administration or the armed forces was Eurico Guterres. In 1999, Guterres was commander of the *Aitarak* militia and the deputy commander of a province-wide umbrella group for the militias, the Forces for Integration Struggle (*Pasukan Pro-Integrasi* or PPI).

The primary charge against all of the defendants alleged a violation of Article 9(a) of the *Human Rights Court Act*.[60] That article, which is taken essentially verbatim from Article 7(1)(a) of the *Rome Statute for the International Criminal Court*, defines a sub-species of 'crimes against humanity' based on commission of 'murder' 'as part of a widespread or systematic attack that is directed against any civilian population, with knowledge of the attack'.[61] Many of the indictments also included a subsidiary charge alleging a violation of Article 9(h) of the Act. That Article defines as a crime against humanity (provided other requirements are satisfied) an act of 'persecution against any specific group or collectivity based on political beliefs, race, nationality, ethnicity, culture, religion, gender, or other grounds universally recognized as prohibited under international law'.[62] This provision tracks Article 7(1)(h) of the *Rome Statute for the International Criminal Court*.

None of the indictments alleges guilt based on the defendant's personal commission of crimes against humanity. All of the indictments charge the accused with criminal responsibility for acts committed by others under either a command responsibility theory of criminal liability or as an accomplice.

The majority of prosecution witnesses were past or present members of the Indonesian military, police or civilian administration.[63] Many of the witnesses called to prove the prosecution's case either were or could have been charged with the commission of crimes within the jurisdiction of the Court. Despite pressure from the judges to call East Timorese victims of the crimes,[64] the prosecution presented only seven victim witnesses in the 12 trials, though some of these witnesses testified in more than one trial. A total of four witnesses testified from East Timor via video link, and the pre-trial statements of several witnesses who did not appear for trial were read into the record. The prosecution's case included little documentary or tangible evidence, and the documentary evidence that was presented provided only minimal proof of guilt.

Most of the testimony presented by Indonesian witnesses called by the prosecution was favourable to the defence. Although the emphasis and details varied, the Indonesians called to testify by the prosecution presented a narrative of events in East Timor in 1999 that was consistent in its broad outline. According to this account, the problems in East Timor began in January 1999 when President Habibie announced what came to be known as the 'second option', the opportunity for East Timorese to choose independence instead of autonomous status within Indonesia. Emboldened by this announcement, 'anti-integration' groups who had been operating underground came out into the open and began advocating independence and, according to some witnesses, terrorizing their political opponents.

As a result of the political tumult and general deterioration of security resulting from the announcement of the 'second option', the civil authorities, through the Governor and the District Heads or Regents, reactivated the *Pam Swakarsa*,[65] a civilian security force or watch group, which had been authorized by national legislation in 1982 and used in various parts of Indonesia to provide support to the state security forces. The membership of the *Pam Swakarsa* were paid a small monthly stipend or honorarium, often described as cigarette money, to compensate them for performing night-watch duties.[66]

The *KPP-HAM* report found that the *Pam Swakarsa* were essentially a front for the militia groups that committed much of the violence.[67] The prosecution witnesses generally dismissed this, however. Many prosecution witnesses denied that the militias even existed. Several witnesses testified that the word 'militia' and its application to East Timor in 1999 was invented by elements of the international community or the United Nations to discredit Indonesia. The names used by the local militia groups – *Aitarak* (thorn), *Besi Merah Putih* (iron red and white), *Sakunar* (scorpion) – were obviously not invented by outsiders, and the prosecution's witnesses offered differing explanations for these groups. Some witnesses testified that these labels were simply the names adopted by local *Pam Swakarsa* units. Although these witnesses also generally denied that *Aitarak*, etc. were anything other than civilian watch groups, the identification of these groups with the *Pam Swakarsa* could, of course, be used as the basis for inferring Indonesian government support for the actions of those groups. Other prosecution witnesses insisted that there was a fundamental difference between the *Pam Swakarsa*, which was acknowledged to have ties to the Indonesian government, and the more colourfully named local units, which were described as voluntary and spontaneous political groupings committed to the integrationist cause.

A central element of the defence story was that the implementation of the 5 May New York Agreement that designated the United Nations as the party responsible for conducting the vote effectively crippled the Indonesian government's ability to rule the province. The establishment of the United Nations Mission in East Timor and the arrival of non-Indonesian – usually referred to by witnesses simply as 'white' – United Nations officials, completely undermined the authority of the Indonesians. This occurred in part because the presence of United Nations personnel, who were regarded as supporting the independence cause, had the effect of giving independence supporters licence to do as they pleased, and in part because the terms of the New York Agreement took control over the Indonesian security apparatus away from the exclusive control of Indonesian authorities. More generally, however, it was intimated that the presence of an alternative quasi-governmental authority within Indonesian territory inevitably undermined the authority of the duly established Indonesian government to the point that power could no longer be exercised effectively to maintain order.

Thus, the announcement of the independence vote and the arrival of what amounted to a foreign power in Indonesian territory resulted in a general breakdown of governmental authority and control. As some witnesses put it, it cut the legs off from under the Indonesian government. This had the effect of liberating what were perceived to be the naturally violent tendencies of the East Timorese. Freed from the constraints of external controls, the East Timorese armed themselves with a combination of sharp implements, home-made guns, and conventional firearms left behind after the end of the Portuguese occupation and fought among themselves. In addition, the terms of the New York Agreement imposed restrictions on the Indonesian security apparatus, especially on the army, that hamstrung efforts to maintain order. Try as they might, the Indonesian authorities were simply unable to prevent bloodshed.

The pre-vote violence was explained in general terms as resulting from the combined effects of a severely weakened security apparatus and the introduction of outside influences that politicized the population and unleashed its inherent violent proclivities. The causes of the post-referendum violence were identified with more specificity. The Indonesian witnesses explained the violence and destruction that occurred after the vote as a spontaneous reaction to fraud perpetrated by the United Nations. The integrationist camp felt aggrieved not because they had lost the vote but because the process itself was biased, if not rigged. As one witness put it, the independence side did not win the vote, it was won for them by the United Nations.[68] These feelings of victimization were aggravated by the decision to accelerate the announcement of the vote which, according to some witnesses, was cynically designed to cut short inquiries into irregularities that were then under investigation.

Anger and frustration that outsiders had manipulated, and thereby effectively stolen, the vote (and with it the country) was given as the underlying cause of the violence. But each of the three September incidents being tried before the tribunal was explained as the direct consequence of a more specific provocation. A common explanation for the attacks on both Bishop Belo's residence and the Offices of the Diocese of Dili was that ballot boxes had been concealed at those locations, presumably to avoid being counted. The explanation for the attack on the church in the town of Suai was that the pro-independence supporters inside the church provoked the attack by taunting the losers with their victory.

The defence story also included an explanation for the widespread destruction of property and mass exodus to West Timor that occurred after the announcement of the results of the voting. By this time, after the eventual independence of the province was assured, law and order had broken down completely. The supporters of integration, including large numbers of non-Timorese Indonesians who had relocated to East Timor, left the territory and burned their houses and businesses as they left to prevent them from falling into the hands of their political opponents. Indonesian government buildings and property on the other hand were destroyed by supporters of Timorese independence as an act of revenge. The existence of the so-called contingency plan providing for the movement of large numbers of East Timorese out of the province after the vote proved nothing, since the military drafters of the plan simply anticipated that the losers in the vote, whoever that might be, would choose to leave.

As noted, what is referred to here as the defence story was presented in the testimony of witnesses called by the prosecution. It should be mentioned, moreover, that the questions through which this pro-defence testimony was elicited were posed by prosecutors as well as defence attorneys and sometimes judges.

Explaining the verdicts

Perhaps the most surprising fact about the process before the *ad hoc* Court is that any of the defendants were convicted; one-third, six of the 18 defendants charged before the Court were found guilty, including Adam Damiri, the highest ranking military official charged, who held a region-wide command in 1999.

One possible explanation for the guilty verdicts is that the return of several token convictions was a calculated component of an orchestrated plan to give a modicum of plausibility to the prosecution, and thereby forestall international action that would deprive Indonesia of control over the process. While this interpretation would be consistent with the actions of the government as a whole, it does not coincide with the conduct of individual actors or the dynamics of the process as it unfolded. A close examination of the trials reveals significant differences among the judges in the performance of their function. In addition to the differences among the judges, the process itself evolved over the course of the trials as some of the judges became increasingly frustrated with the performance of the prosecutors. Because the commencement of the trials was staggered, the completion of the 12 cases took more than a year. In the later cases some of the judges began to assert considerable control over the process, demanding that the prosecution take steps to produce Timorese witnesses, arranging for the taking of testimony from Dili via video link, and tolling the time limits for completion of the trial.

The key to explaining the guilty verdicts lies in the pattern of convictions and acquittals in the various cases. Although the trials have been criticized on the ground that the majority of those prosecuted were exonerated, the voting record of the judges is not as lopsided as these criticisms suggest. The 18 defendants were tried in 12 separate proceedings. Ten of the 12 trials involved a single defendant. The two multi-party trials – one involving six defendants and the other three defendants – both ended with the acquittal of all of the accused. Among the ten trials with a single defendant, four resulted in acquittals and six in convictions. Thus, if one measures the results in terms of *trials* rather than *defendants*, the judges actually returned an equal number of convictions and acquittals; six of the 12 trials resulted in acquittals, and six of the trials resulted in convictions.

An analysis of the voting record of the judges demonstrates that the outcome of the trials is largely a result of the composition of the panels. The Court is comprised of five judges – two career judges and three '*ad hoc*' judges. The 12 panels that tried the East Timor defendants were assembled from a pool of 23 judges, 12 of whom were from the country's career judiciary, and 11 of whom were non-career *ad hoc* judges selected for service as HRC judges for a five-year term. By Supreme Court regulation, the *ad hoc* judges must hold positions on Indonesian law faculties.[69] Individual judges were assigned to a minimum of one case (three judges) to a maximum of six cases (one judge). The process by which judges were assigned has never been made public.

An examination of the voting records of the judges across all of the cases shows that the prior performance of the judges is highly predictive of the outcome in a particular case (Tables 9.1 to 9.12). Each of the 12 tables corresponds to one of the 12 trials. Each table identifies the defendant or defendants in the case, states whether the Court returned a judgment of conviction or acquittal, and lists, in the left column, the judges (identified by number only) who served on that case. In the right column, I report the voting record of the judges in the other trials in which they served. Since all of the decisions were reported as unanimous, I am assuming that the decision of the panel reflects the decision of the individual judges who served on that panel. I then tabulate the voting record in other cases for the panel as a whole. For example, the judges who decided the Abilio Soares case – the first case to be decided by the Court – had a combined voting record in other cases of nine votes for conviction and zero votes for acquittal. In other words, the five judges who served on that panel cast a total of nine votes in trials of defendants other than Abilio Soares, and all nine of those votes were guilty verdicts (Table 9.1).

In all but one of the trials, the outcome in the case was consistent with the voting record of the judges in other cases. The one case in which the verdict went against the voting record of the judges was the trial of Soedjarwo (see Table 9.5). The judges on the Soedjarwo panel had a combined voting record in other

Table 9.1 Abilio Soares (convicted)

Judge (Number)	*Voting record other cases convictions–acquittals*
2	1–0
8	2–0
14	2–0
23	4–0
20	0–0
Panel total	9–0

Table 9.2 Timbul Silaen (acquitted)

Judge (Number)	*Voting record other cases convictions–acquittals*
1	1–1
7	0–0
13	1–2
19	1–1
16	1–4
Panel total	4–8

Table 9.3 Herman Sedyono *et al* (acquitted)

Judge (Number)	*Voting record other cases convictions–acquittals*
3	0–2
5	2–0
15	0–1
18	0–2
21	0–1
Panel total	2–6

Table 9.4 Endar Priyanto (acquitted)

Judge (Number)	*Voting record other cases convictions–acquittals*
4	0–0
9	0–0
16	1–4
13	1–2
22	3–0
Panel total	5–6

Table 9.5 Soedjarwo (convicted)

Judge (Number)	*Voting record other cases convictions-acquittals*
1	0–2
10	0–1
13	0–3
19	0–2
16	0–5
Panel total	0–13

Table 9.6 Hulman Gultom (convicted)

Judge (Number)	*Voting record other cases convictions–acquittals*
5	1–1
11	1–0
17	2–0
23	4–0
22	2–1
Panel total	10–2

Table 9.7 Asep Kuswani *et al.* (acquitted)

Judge (Number)	*Voting record other cases convictions–acquittals*
3	0–2
12	0–1
18	0–2
15	0–1
16	1–4
Panel total	1–10

Table 9.8 Yayat Sudrajat (acquitted)

Judge (Number)	*Voting record other cases convictions–acquittals*
3	0–2
12	0–1
18	0–2
16	1–4
21	0–1
Panel total	1–10

Table 9.9 Tono Suratman (acquitted)

Judge (Number)	*Voting record other cases convictions–acquittals*
1	1–1
10	1–0
13	1–2
19	1–1
16	1–4
Panel total	5–8

Table 9.10 Noer Muis (convicted)

Judge (Number)	*Voting record other cases convictions–acquittals*
5	1–1
11	1–0
23	4–0
17	2–0
22	2–1
Panel total	10–2

Table 9.11 Eurico Guterres (convicted)

Judge (Number)	*Voting record other cases convictions–acquittals*
6	0–0
8	2–0
14	2–0
23	4–0
17	2–0
Panel total	10–0

Table 9.12 Adam Damiri (convicted)

Judge (Number)	*Voting record other cases convictions–acquittals*
2	1–0
8	2–0
14	2–0
23	5–0
22	2–1
Panel total	12–1

cases of 13 votes for acquittal and no votes for conviction, but found Soedjarwo guilty. My unsubstantiated explanation for the outcome in that case is that the chair of the panel, who had returned two prior acquittals and, as spokesperson for the Court was the most visible of all of the judges, concluded after having observed his more courageous colleagues return convictions that he preferred a more ambiguous record. In another case – the Endar Priyanto trial – the voting record of the judges was nearly evenly divided between convictions and acquittals; the judges on the panel cast a total of six votes for acquittal and five votes for conviction (see Table 9.4). The judges returned a verdict of guilty. Significantly, however, the two career judges on the Endar Priyanto panel had no voting record, since the Priyanto case was the only trial to which they were assigned.

In nine of the 12 trials the voting record of the judges was clearly consistent with the outcome of the case. Among those nine cases, the panels that returned judgments of guilty had conviction–acquittal records of 9–0, 10–2, 10–2, 10–0, and 12–1, and the panels that returned not guilty verdicts had conviction-acquittal records of 4–8, 2–6, 1–10, and 1–10. In a tenth case a panel with a 5–8 record acquitted.

Thus, the voting patterns of the judges indicate that the outcomes in individual cases are a result of the composition of the panels. Panels comprised of judges inclined to convict rendered verdicts of guilty, whereas panels of acquittal-prone judges found the prosecution's evidence insufficient. As is true of criminal trials generally, these inclinations were mediated through the interpretive framework employed by the judges in evaluating the evidence. While most of the testimony presented at the trials was exculpatory rather than inculpatory, the task of judicial decision-making is everywhere more complicated than simply totalling up the witnesses for and against. Judges must make determinations concerning the credibility of the evidence, and because most evidence in all trials is circumstantial, judges must make decisions about reasonable inferences from the evidence. This process of sorting and organizing the evidence is guided by an array of non-evidentiary assumptions and beliefs, some of them individual and some cultural.

In the East Timor trials, the panels that convicted discounted the testimony of military and police witnesses as self-serving and incredible. They were also more willing to draw inferences consistent with guilt, even when the prosecution did not vigorously argue those inferences or argued against them. The panels that acquitted credited the exculpatory accounts of military and other government witnesses, and accepted the official Indonesian version of the violence in East Timor as the spontaneous expression of long-standing political divisions and outrage at the United Nations and other international actors over the perceived partiality of the conduct of the vote.

In focusing exclusively on the composition of the panels deciding the case, this analysis does not consider the influence of other factors, such as the quality of the evidence, the effectiveness of counsel, or the identity of the defendant. Although the possible effect of these factors cannot be measured quantitatively, available evidence suggests that none of them had a significant bearing on the results.

Observers of the trials have not noted significant differences in the evidence presented at the various trials. Nor do the judgments, which contain a thorough summary of the evidence, disclose any notable difference in the evidence presented at the various trials. There is considerable overlap in the witnesses called at the various trials. As mentioned above, during the latter phases of the trials, the judges on some of the panels pressured prosecutors to increase their efforts to secure the testimony of Timorese victims, and while the possibility of taking testimony through video link with East Timor began to be discussed relatively early in the process, it was only towards the very end that this occurred. But the same judges, who in the later stages of the trials pressured judges to present inculpatory testimony, returned guilty verdicts on the basis of less substantial records in cases decided earlier in the process.

The Adam Damiri trial

The judges assigned to the *ad hoc* HRC for East Timor can hardly be faulted for not convicting guilty defendants if not presented with evidence of their guilt. On the other hand, some judges, especially in the later phases of the process as the prosecution's complete capitulation became apparent, refused to allow themselves to be party to a sham and exerted their authority to assume control of the process. These judges refused to permit themselves the easy option of relying on the lack of evidence, but attempted to compel prosecutors to do their jobs or, in some circumstances, did it for them.

Both the determination of the prosecutors to surrender and the refusal of some judges to accept are clearly apparent in the trial of Adam Damiri, the last of the trials to be completed. Although the prosecution's utter lack of commitment to its cause was most clearly evident in the Damiri trial, the same basic attitude was manifest, albeit more subtly, in all of the trials. Moreover, not all of the judges displayed dissatisfaction with the presumptive script for the trials, a variation on the often repeated official Indonesian line on East Timor, which casts Indonesia as the generous bearer of 'development', and East Timor as ungrateful and both uncivilized and uncivilizable. At some points the judges were not only neutral observers of trials in which prosecutor and defence were on the same side, but sided with the prosecutor and defence in these one-sided affairs. The scene became positively ugly during the testimony of some of the Timorese witnesses, in which judges joined with prosecutors, defence attorneys and jeering trial spectators in a courtroom orgy of humiliation.[70] But while some judges were willing, if not eager, to take advantage of an opportunity for easy escape from disapproval by the most powerful elements in Indonesian society, other judges went out of their way to redeem the process despite the risks. And while the Damiri trial is atypical in the extent to which the judges attempted to compensate for the failings of the prosecution, the action of the judges in the Damiri case reflect the maturation of tendencies present from the very beginning.

Adam Damiri headed the Udayana territorial command which was headquartered in Bali and included East Timor. He was charged with crimes against humanity on a theory of command responsibility for failing to prevent, repress or punish actions committed in the districts of Liquisa and Covalima and the city of Dili in April and August 1999. The charges included incidents on 6 April and 6 September of that year in which Indonesian military and police joined with militiamen to attack civilians who had taken refuge inside local church compounds. The charges also included attacks on the house of independence leader, Manuel Carrascalao, the house of the Catholic Bishop of East Timor, Carlos Xemenes Belo, and the Offices of the Diocese of Dili.

In most respects the Damiri trial was little different from the other 11 trials before the *ad hoc* HRC. One significant difference, however, is that the Damiri trial took much longer to complete than any of the other cases, and more than twice as long as is permitted by applicable law. The statute governing the HRC requires that trials before the Court be completed within six months after commencement. The prosecution read out the charges against Damiri on 10 July 2002 and the Court announced its verdict 13 months later.

One of the reasons the trial was not completed within the prescribed time period is because the Court was intent on obtaining the testimony of two witnesses who were at the centre of incidents charged against Damiri. The first of the two witnesses, Bishop Carlos Xemenes Belo, was inside his residence in Dili on the morning of 6 September when armed men stormed the house and burned it to the ground. The second witness was Pastor Rafael dos Santos, Pastor of the Catholic congregation in the town of Liquisa located on the north coast, west of Dili. Liquisa was the scene of an especially horrifying incident that occurred on 6 April 1999, when militiamen backed by military and police attacked several thousand refugees inside the church compound. Pastor Rafael was inside the compound at the time of the attack. He narrowly escaped death when a home-made gun failed to discharge, and members of the local military command rescued him from a machete attack by militiamen and led him out of the compound to safety.

Although the testimony of Bishop Belo and Pastor dos Santos would seem to be indispensable in any trial that involved the attacks against them, several cases involving the Dili and Liquisa incidents were tried without ever receiving their testimony. In mid-November the judges in the Damiri case and judges presiding over two other trials[71] demanded that prosecutors present the testimony of Bishop Belo via video link.[72] The prosecutors objected on the ground that the taking of testimony from a remote location was not recognized in the Indonesian *Code of Criminal Procedure* and that the expense was prohibitive. Four months earlier, in mid-July, the Attorney-Generals for East Timor and Indonesia had announced an agreement to receive testimony via video link, but prosecutors in the courtroom continued to cite excuses for failing to make the necessary arrangements.[73] Belo and dos Santos were both finally scheduled to testify in mid-December.[74]

Belo never testified, though through no fault of the prosecutors or the Court. In lieu of live testimony, Belo's pre-trial statement was read into the record.[75] On 23 January 2003 Rafael dos Santos testified via video link from East Timor.[76] Though the 180-day deadline for completion of the trial had already expired, the Court nevertheless scheduled additional testimony from witnesses from East Timor to be heard at the end of the following month.[77] The anticipated testimony was never introduced, however, because the Indonesian government failed to provide funds for the satellite link.

Another even more significant initiative by the judges on the Damiri panel related to the presentation of documentary evidence. In many of the earlier trials the prosecution introduced virtually no significant documentary evidence. The judgment in the Damiri case, by contrast, cites a substantial number of secret internal military communications and other inculpatory documents. Though it is uncertain from public pronouncements precisely who was responsible for introducing these documents, it is certain that the judges played a significant role, either in producing the material themselves or forcing the prosecutors to do so. For example, during the testimony of General Kiki Syaknari in September 2002, one of the judges confronted the witness with a telegram bearing his signature and addressed to the Commander in Chief of the armed forces. The telegram appeared to indicate that the military was responsible for the 'scorched earth' destruction of East Timor after the announcement of the vote.[78] At the time the telegram was written in September 1999, Syaknari was assigned as commander of the military emergency in East Timor. Damiri's defence team, which included some of the most aggressive and successful litigators in the country, voiced immediate verbal objection to the introduction of evidence from outside of the dossier, and later filed a formal protest with the Court. The chair of the panel later defended the use of the document, stating that its use fell within the 'corridors of the law'.[79]

The evidentiary phase of the Damiri trial was finally completed in April 2003. On 22 April the prosecution was scheduled to present its final statement and sentence recommendation, but the hearing was postponed when the prosecution stated it was not prepared. The Court then granted four more postponements, each time because the accused did not appear. The reason for his failure to appear was because, instead of arresting or at least suspending Damiri from the armed forces, he had been promoted and assigned a leading role in a new offensive against the separatist insurgency in the north Sumatran region of Aceh. Finally, on 5 June, the prosecution presented its final statement. In a move that astonished even cynics, the prosecutor asked the Court to acquit Damiri of the charges on the ground that his guilt had not been proven.

The prosecution's final plea in the Damiri case captured the essence of the process as a whole, a process described by a leading observer as 'intended to fail'.[80] The prosecutor's recommendation that Damiri be acquitted, delivered after the defendant's repeated failure to appear, at a trial in which the accused human rights abuser had received a military promotion and a new command, expressed to perfection the attitude of dismissive disdain exhibited throughout the trial.

It was generally assumed that any inclination to convict Damiri that might have existed previously was completely deflated by the prosecutors' recommendation that the accused be acquitted. On the date scheduled for delivery of the judgment the defendant's family and supporters were present in the court-room in large numbers anticipating an acquittal. Indonesian court judgments are lengthy, tedious, legalistic documents, and the Indonesian *Code of Criminal Procedure* requires that the court's final judgment be delivered in its entirety in open court. The delivery of the judgment, read out in relays by the judges, typically takes an entire court day. The reading of the Damiri judgment continued for several hours with no indication of the final verdict. Some of the Court's findings of fact seemed to go against the accused, but most of those in the courtroom were not sufficiently attentive to notice. Indonesian legal culture regards the abstract question of guilt or innocence as secondary to the matter of punishment, and the Court's announcement that it had found the defendant guilty of all charges caused barely a stir among the spectators. But pandemonium erupted when the judges announced the Court's sentence of five years' imprisonment. Damiri, seated facing the judges in the middle of the courtroom, emitted an angry, inarticulate roar. The spectators were on their feet screaming protests and threats against the judges. Visibly shaken by the atmosphere of incipient violence, the five judges left the courtroom as quickly as possible after one of the defence attorneys exerted his authority to quiet the crowd.

Adam Damiri ultimately escaped punishment for his crimes. He was never detained or even removed from active military duty during or after the trial, and in August of 2004 the judgment of conviction entered by the trial court was reversed by the High Court on appeal.[81] On the date the reversal of Damiri's conviction was announced it was also announced that the High Court had overturned the convictions of M. Noer Muis, Hulman Goeltom and Soedjarwo.[82] The conviction of Abilio Soares was initially upheld by both the High Court and the Supreme Court but finally overturned when the Supreme Court reviewed the case a second time.[83] The sixth defendant found guilty at trial, Eurico Guterres, was also ultimately exonerated on appeal. Guterres, the only defendant tried before the *ad hoc* Court for East Timor who was not a member of the military or the civilian administration, was unsuccessful in his initial appeals, but the Supreme Court invalidated the conviction in March 2008, citing newly discovered evidence presented by Guterres' lawyers.[84]

The appellate process in Indonesian courts has, until recently, been extremely opaque, and publicly available information about the East Timor appeals includes little beyond an announcement of the result. Although I have no information on the details of the East Timor appeals, the record of appellate reversals comes as no surprise. The appeals courts and the Supreme Court in particular were often in the position of correcting trial courts that acted contrary to the wishes of the executive during the Suharto era, and it stands to reason that the military and other powerful elements that disapproved of the East Timor prosecutions would be more effective once the process moved out of public view.

Further trials

That the East Timor trials would ultimately end in failure was never really in doubt. It is simply inconceivable that Indonesian officials responsible for the violence in East Timor would be punished for their crimes or that the true story of the military's role in the violence would be presented in an Indonesian court. While the eventual exoneration of the East Timor defendants was all but certain, it could not have been anticipated that a sizable minority of the accused would be convicted at trial. The proceedings before the HRC for East Timor have been properly criticized for having failed in their essential purpose, but the efforts of the HRC to redeem the process have been largely overlooked. As has been shown, the performance of the judges on the HRC was decidedly mixed, but some of the judges displayed an unexpected determination to act independently. Ultimately, however, the Court was incapable of countering the forces intent on a whitewash and preventing the inevitable.

As of December 2008, there have been two further sets of trials before the HRC. These subsequent trials have followed much the same pattern as the East Timor prosecutions. The Tanjung Priok trials involved the prosecution of 14 military defendants accused of firing on demonstrators who had gathered to protest an incident in which members of the military allegedly defiled a Muslim prayer house while removing posters regarded as inflammatory.[85] As with the East Timor trials, the prosecutors declined to bring charges against the most high-level officials implicated in the incident,[86] though the accused included three individuals who had achieved the rank of major-general, including Major General Sriyanto Muntrasan who, at the time of trial, held the position of Chief of the Army's Special Forces (*Komando Pasukan Khusus* or *Kopassus*). At the trial, the prosecutors displayed the same combination of incompetence, indifference, and active subversion that characterized the presentation of evidence in the East Timor prosecutions. Nevertheless, 12 of the 14 defendants were convicted at trial, including retired Major General Rudolf Butar Butar.[87] All of the convictions were later overturned on appeal.[88]

The third set of trials related to an incident that occurred in late 2000 in the town of Abepura about 20 kilometres south of Jayapura, the capital of Papua. The incident began when a group of about 30 local residents attacked a police station, killing one policeman and injuring several others. In retaliation for the attack, Abepura police and members of the Jayapura mobile police brigade scoured nearby neighbourhoods in search of the attackers. In the course of the sweep police arrested, assaulted and tortured nearly 100 residents suspected of having been involved in the attack. Three persons died, allegedly tortured to death.

Prosecutors eventually filed charges of crimes against humanity against two individuals in connection with the Abepura attack – Brig. General Johny Wainal Usman, who was the Deputy Chief of the Police Mobile Brigade (Brimob), and Daud Sihombing who was Chief of Police for Jayapura. Both were charged under the command responsibility provisions of the statute for having failed to prevent attacks committed by persons under their control.

The Abepura case is the first and so far only case to be tried before the permanent HRC. Separate trials for the two defendants began in May 2004 in the south Sulawesi city of Makassar. In September 2005 the Court issued decisions acquitting both defendants of all the charges.[89]

Conclusion

From the outset, expectations for the East Timor trials were extremely low. It is perhaps only against this backdrop of pessimism that the performance of the HRC appears at all hopeful. The process as played out departed from expectations only in the fact that the judges proved less compliant than originally anticipated.

As of 2008 *Komnas HAM* has recommended further investigation and possible prosecution in at least six additional cases. The cases recommended for further action include incidents in Jakarta in May and November 1998 and in September 1999 and incidents in the Papuan districts of Wasior and Wamena in June 2001 and April 2003.[90] Although the Office of Attorney-General has held some of the files for more than six years, none of the cases has proceeded beyond the initial investigation by *Komnas HAM*. Progress on the Jakarta cases has been blocked by the People's Representative Council (DPR), which has refused to give the approval required for prosecutions of crimes pre-dating the passage of the *Human Rights Act*.[91]

Komnas HAM and a range of civil society groups continue to press for prosecutions, and trial of some or all of the pending cases is still a possibility. However, there is little reason to believe that future trials will be anything other than a replay of the trials held so far. Any meaningful study of judicial institutions must consider that courts are more than simply judges. In order to function effectively courts depend on the performance of a range of other institutions including police, prosecutors, the private bar, executive branch agencies and other elements of the judicial branch. The *Human Rights Court Act* of 2000 provided for the appointment of judges with a specialized jurisdiction to try serious human rights crimes, but left the institutional environment in which the Court operates largely unchanged. As the trials before the HRC demonstrate, creating new courts is likely to prove an empty gesture, so long as the forces within the larger system in which the courts operate are aligned against them.

Notes

1. Sebastiaan Pompe, *The Indonesian Supreme Court: A Study of Institutional Collapse* (Ithaca, NY: Cornell Southeast Asia Program, 2005), 77–133.
2. See the chapter by Hendrianto in this publication.
3. See the chapters in this publication by David Linnan and Benjamin H. Tahyar.
4. Institute for Policy Research and Advocacy (ELSAM), "Monitoring Report on Ad Hoc Human Rights Court Against Gross Human Rights Violations in East Timor, Report No. 9," http://socrates.berkeley.edu/~warcrime/ET-ELSAM-Reports/ELSAM09.pdf; David Cohen, "Intended to Fail: The Trials Before the Ad Hoc Human Rights Court in Jakarta" (paper presented for International Committee for Transitional Justice, New York, August, 2003); Suzannah Linton, "Unravelling the First Three Trials at Indonesia's Ad Hoc Court for Human Rights Violations in East Timor," *Leiden Journal of International Law* 17 (2004): 303–61; Open Society Justice Initiative, Coalition for International Justice, "Unfulfilled Promises: Achieving Justice for Crimes Against Humanity in East Timor," http://www.justiceinitiative.org/db/resource2?res_id = 102368
5. On the collapse of the Suharto government see Donald Emmerson, "Exit and Aftermath: The Crisis of 1997–98," in *Indonesia Beyond Suharto: Polity, Economy, Society, Transition*, ed. Donald Emmerson (London: M. E. Sharpe, 1999).

6. *Law No. 39/1999* art. 104.
7. For a brief history of East Timor, see Geoffrey Gunn, "The Five-Hundred-Year Timorese Funu," in *Bitter Flowers Sweet, Flowers: East Timor, Indonesia, and the World Community*, ed. Richard Tanter, Mark Sheldon and Stephen R. Shalom (Boston: Rowan & Littlefield, 2001), 3–14.
8. *Fretelin* was created out of an earlier party, the Timorese Social Democratic Association (ASDT), which had roots in a clandestine anti-colonial movement. See generally, Sarah Niner, "A Long Journey of Resistance: The Origins and Struggle of CNRT," in *Bitter Flowers Sweet, Flowers: East Timor, Indonesia, and the World Community*, ed. Richard Tanter, Mark Sheldon and Stephen R. Shalom (Boston: Rowan & Littlefield, 2001), 15–30.
9. Indonesia had been engaged in clandestine efforts to undermine *Fretelin* since late 1974. In October 1975, claiming to act on the invitation of the UDT, Indonesian forces captured the western town of Batugade. Six weeks later, on 28 November, the town of Atabe was also taken. On that same date *Fretelin* made a formal declaration of independence of the Democratic Republic of East Timor in a ceremony in Dili.
10. Joseph Nevins, "The Making of 'Ground Zero' in East Timor in 1999: An Analysis of International Complicity in Indonesia's Crimes," *Asian Survey* 42 (2002): 626.
11. On the circumstances leading to the abrupt change in policy regarding Indonesia see Don Greenlees and Robert Garran, *Deliverance: The Inside Story of East Timor's Fight for Freedom* (Crows Nest, NSW: Allen & Unwin, 2002).
12. Nevins, "The Making of 'Ground Zero' in East Timor in 1999," 626.
13. On 6 April, a month before the agreement was signed, pro-integration militias, which had been organized and armed by the Indonesian military, attacked a group of several thousand independence supporters who had taken refuge inside a church compound in the town of Liquisa: Greenlees, *Deliverance: The Inside Story of East Timor's Fight for Freedom*, 120–6. Indonesian military and police not only failed to prevent the bloodshed, but fired tear gas into the compound as the attack began and joined with the militia members in the assault: Greenlees, *Deliverance: The Inside Story of East Timor's Fight for Freedom*, 120–6. Later that same month pro-integration militia in Dili attacked refugees inside the house of a leading independence supporter, Manuel Carrascalao: Greenlees, *Deliverance: The Inside Story of East Timor's Fight for Freedom*, 133–4.
14. The ballot offered a choice between independence and special autonomy status as a part of Indonesia. Nearly 78 per cent of those voting chose independence: Greenlees, *Deliverance: The Inside Story of East Timor's Fight for Freedom*, 196.
15. Nevins, "The Making of 'Ground Zero' in East Timor in 1999," 626.
16. United Nations Commission on Human Rights, "Report on the Fourth Special Session (23–27 September 1999)," http://www.un.org/esa/documents/ecosoc/docs/1999/e1999–23a.pdf
17. International Commission of Inquiry on East Timor (ICOIET), *Report of the International Commission of Inquiry on East Timor to the Secretary General* UN SCOR, 54th Sess., UN Document A/54/726, S/2000/59 (31 January 2000).
18. Minister of Foreign Affairs of Indonesia, *Letter Dated 26 January 2000 from the Minister of Foreign Affairs of Indonesia to the Secretary-General*, UN SCOR, 54th Sess., UN Document A/54/726, S2000/65 (26 January 2000).
19. President of the Security Council, *Letter Dated 18 February 2000 from the President of the Security Council to the Secretary General*, UN SCOR, 54th Sess., UN Document A/54/726, S/2000/137 (18 February 2000); Asmara Nababan, "Commission of Inquiry for Human Rights Violations in East Timor (KPP-HAM)" (paper presented for International Committee for Transitional Justice, New York, August, 2003).
20. Nababan, "Commission of Inquiry for Human Rights Violations in East Timor (KPP-HAM)," 2–3.

21. KPP-HAM Komnas HAM, "Ringkasan Eksekutif Laporan Penyelidikan Pelanggaran Hak Asasi Manusia di Timor Timur," (Executive Summary of the Report on the Investigation of Human Rights Violations in East Timur) January 31, 2000, para. 5. The report of the *KPP-HAM* was never made public, but the Executive Summary was circulated widely both in the original Indonesian and in English. The Executive Summary (Indonesian), still marked "confidential," is available at http://www.elsam.or.id/pdf/monham/timtim/EXECUTIVE%20SUMMARY%20KPP%20HAM%20Tim-tim%20oleh%20Komnas%20HAM.pdf. The investigative team had eight members – four from *Komnas HAM* and four individuals from civil society to assure objectivity: KPP-HAM Komnas HAM, "Ringkasan Eksekutif Laporan Penyelidikan Pelanggaran Hak Asasi Manusia di Timor Timur," (Executive Summary of the Report on the Investigation of Human Rights Violations in East Timor), para. 9. The team was initially nine persons, but Marzuki Darusman resigned from the team shortly after its formation upon being appointed Attorney-General of Indonesia.
22. Nababan, "Commission of Inquiry for Human Rights Violations in East Timor (KPP-HAM)," 13–14.
23. The simultaneous release of the two reports was not a coincidence; the two committees had informally arranged for the release of their reports on the same day in order to avoid accusations that the *KPP-HAM* had simply copied the work of the UN body: Nababan, "Commission of Inquiry for Human Rights Violations in East Timor (KPP-HAM)," 6.
24. In addition to the Executive Summary of the *KPP-HAM* report, reliable information on the Commission's investigations and conclusions is also contained in David Cohen, "Intended to Fail: The Trials Before the Ad Hoc Human Rights Court in Jakarta," a report prepared for the International Committee for Transitional Justice (ICTJ). Asmara Nababan, who served as the Secretary of the *KPP-HAM*, assisted in the preparation of the ICTJ report and prepared a summary of the work of the *KPP-HAM* included as an annex to the ICTJ report: Nababan, "Commission of Inquiry for Human Rights Violations in East Timor (KPP-HAM)".
25. Commentators have expressed surprise at the high quality and hard-hitting character of the *KPP-HAM* investigation. But the members of the Committee were not individuals inclined to whitewash the commission of human rights crimes. *Komnas HAM*, which was initially created as a palliative for criticisms of Indonesia following a massacre committed by Indonesian troops in East Timor in 1991, had demonstrated an unexpected independence and willingness to criticize the human rights record of the government and security services. The eight members of the *KPP-HAM* included several of the Commission's most committed and courageous members, and four of Indonesia's most prominent human rights advocates.
26. Nababan, "Commission of Inquiry for Human Rights Violations in East Timor (KPP-HAM)," 13–14.
27. Although an early draft of the regulation would have made the regulation retroactive for 15 years, the final version stated that crimes committed before the effective date of the regulation would be submitted to a truth and reconciliation commission: "Draft Law on Rights Court Attacked for not being Retroactive," *Kompas*, January 24, 2000, http://www.blythe.org/nytransfer-subs/2000pac/Indon:_Draft_law_on_rights_court_attacked_for_not_being_retroactive
28. *Law No. 26/2000.*
29. *Law No. 39/1999* arts 8, 9.
30. *Law No. 39/1999* art. 42.
31. *Law No. 26/1999* art. 42.
32. Opened for signature 17 July 1998, 2817 UNTS 90 (entered into force 1 July 2002).
33. *Law No. 39/1999* art. 18.
34. *Law No. 39/1999* art. 20.

35. *Law No. 39/1999* arts 21, 23.
36. *Law No. 39/1999* art. 2.
37. *Law No. 39/1999* art. 27.
38. *Law No. 39/1999* art. 28.
39. *Law No. 39/1999* art. 45.
40. *Law No. 39/1999* art. 32(2).
41. *Law No. 39/1999* art. 33(2).
42. *Law No. 39/1999* art. 32(4).
43. *Law No. 39/1999* art. 33(4).
44. *Law No. 39/1999* art. 43(1).
45. *Law No. 39/1999* art. 43(2).
46. *Law No. 39/1999* art. 43(2).
47. *Law No. 39/1999* art. 48.
48. *Law No. 39/1999* arts 17–22.
49. *Law No. 39/1999* art. 17.
50. Human Rights Watch, "Unfinished Business: Justice for East Timor," http://www.hrw.org/backgrounder/asia/timor/etimor-back0829.htm
51. The 64-member task force included officials from the Office of the Attorney-General, military police, members of the national police, and officials from the office of home affairs: Human Rights Watch, "Unfinished Business: Justice for East Timor," http://www.hrw.org/backgrounder/asia/timor/etimor-back0829.htm
52. Human Rights Watch, "Unfinished Business: Justice for East Timor," http://www.hrw.org/backgrounder/asia/timor/etimor-back0829.htm
53. "House Approves Ad Hoc Human Rights Court," *Jakarta Post*, 22 March 2001.
54. Ibid.
55. Linton, "Unravelling the First Three Trials at Indonesia's Ad Hoc Court for Human Rights Violations in East Timor," 308–9.
56. Ibid.
57. *Presidential Decision No. 53/2001.*
58. *Presidential Decision No. 96/2001.*
59. "Rights Trial Begins Amid Strong Public Skepticism," *Jakarta Post*, March 14, 2002.
60. English translations of 10 of the 12 indictments are available at UC Berkeley War Crimes Study Center, "The Indonesian Ad Hoc Court Tribunal for East Timor: Indictments and Judgments," htpp://socrates.berkeley.edu/~warcrime/East_Timor_and_Indonesia/Indictments_and_judgments/Indictments_and_judgments.html
61. The official elucidation to Article 9 defines an attack that is 'directed against a civilian population' as 'a course of conduct carried out against a civilian population in furtherance of policy of the authorities or some organization.' This language is similar to the definition of the same term contained in Article 7(2) of the *Rome Statute for the International Criminal Court*, opened for signature 17 July 1998, 2817 UNTS 90 (entered into force 1 July 2002).
62. *Law No. 39/1999* art. 9(h).
63. This summary of the proceedings is based on my first-hand observation of the trials. Information on the evidence presented at the trials is also available in Linton, "Unravelling the First Three Trials at Indonesia's Ad Hoc Court for Human Rights Violations in East Timor," 303–61; Cohen, "Intended to Fail: The Trials Before the Ad Hoc Human Rights Court in Jakarta." The Court's judgments also contain extensive reviews of the evidence presented at trial.
64. The Indonesian *Code of Criminal Procedure* (*Law No. 8*/1981) requires that the victim of the crime be the first witness to be called by the prosecution in a criminal case.
65. *Pam Swakarsa* is an acronym for *Pengamanan Swa Kars*a, which means 'voluntary security forces.'
66. Some witnesses testified that the emergence of the *Pam Swakarsa* was entirely spontaneous; that the authorities had no part in their creation or support.

67. KPP-HAM Komnas HAM, "Ringkasan Eksekutif Laporan Penyelidikan Pelanggaran Hak Asasi Manusia di Timor Timur," (Executive Summary of the Report on the Investigation of Human Rights Violations in East Timor), para. 64.
68. Testimony of prosecution witness Mateus Maya, Mayor of the city of Dili from December 1996 to September 1999, at trial of Soedjarwo, August 6, 2002.
69. Open Society Justice Initiative, Coalition for International Justice, "Unfulfilled Promises: Achieving Justice for Crimes against Humanity in East Timor," http://www.justiceinitiative.org/db/resource2?res_id = 102368
70. See Linton, "Unravelling the First Three Trials at Indonesia's Ad Hoc Court for Human Rights Violations in East Timor," for a description of the testimony of Timorese witness Dominggas dos Santos Mouzinho.
71. The other two trials were trials of Soedjarwo, District Military Commander for Dili, and Tono Suratman.
72. Wahyu Dhyatmika, "Majelis Hakim Kasus Timor Timur Minta Jaksa Hadirkan Uskup Belo," (Panel of Judges in the East Timor Case Ask the Prosecutor to Summon Bishop Belo) *Tempo Interaktif*, November 12, 2002, http://www.tempointeraktif.com/news/2002//11/12/1,1,18,id.html; Tutut Herlina, "Kasus Pelanggaran HAM di TimTim: 'Terseok-seoknya' Pembuktian dan Rendahnya Tuntutan Jaksa," (The East Timor Human Rights Cases: Prosecutors' Half-Hearted Efforts at Proof and Lenient Sentence Requests) *Sinar Harapan*, November 19, 2002, http://www.sinarharapan.co.id/berita/0211/19/nas04.html
73. Tertianin Simanjuntak, "TNI Formed East Timor Militias: Eyewitness," *Jakarta Post*, July 18, 2002, http://www.thejakartapost.com/news/2002/07/17/tni-formed-east-timor-militias-eyewitness.html. It had become apparent early on in the process that many potential Timorese were unwilling to travel to Jakarta because of concerns for their security.
74. Wahyu, "Uskup Belo Batal Berikan Kesaksian," (Bishop Belo Cancels [Scheduled] Testimony) *Koran Tempo*, December 18, 2002, http://www.mirifica.net/printPage.php?aid = 341. In early December the judges presiding in another case, the trial of the Dili District Military Commander, announced that the decision in that case was postponed, and that instead of announcing its judgment the court would reopen the case to hear from Bishop Belo via video link: "Vonis Soedjarwo Ditunda Tunggu Teleconference Uskup Belo," (Soedjarwo's Verdict is Postponed Awaiting Teleconference of Bishop Belo) *Kompas*, December 4, 2002.
75. Bishop Belo's explanation for not appearing was that on the date scheduled for his testimony he was travelling in East Timor in order to explain his recent retirement. He later issued a statement that he would only agree to give evidence before an international court: "Bishop Belo Vows Never to Appear in Indonesian Rights Court," *Agence France-Presse*, December 20, 2002.
76. "Pengadilan ad hoc HAM TimTim: Anggota TNI/Polri Ikut Menyerbu," (Ad-Hoc Human Rights Court on East Timor: Members of the Indonesian Military/Police Join in Attacks) *Kompas*, January 24, 2003, http://www2.kompas.com/kompas-cetak/0301/24/nasional/95573.htm
77. "Pengadilan HAM Timtim: Teleconference Terancam Tidak Dilanjutkan," (Ad-Hoc Human Rights Court on East Timor: Planned Teleconference Threatened) *Suara Pembaruan*, February 19, 2003, *www.suarapembaruan.com/News/2003/02/19/*.
78. Syahnan Rangkuti, "Pengadilan HAM Kasus TimTim: Ketika Hakim Melakukan Lankah Terobosan," (Ad-Hoc Human Rights Court on East Timor: When the Judges Take Breakthrough Steps) *Kompas*, September 21, 2002, http://www2.kompas.com/kompas-cetak/0209/21/nasional/keti08.htm. Although the report credited both a judge and the prosecutor with this 'improvisation,' the attitude manifest toward the prosecution by the prosecutor's other actions clearly contradicts that report. Considering the criticism levelled at the judges for introducing the new evidence, it is not surprising that they would be willing to cultivate the false perception that the prosecutor was at least partly responsible.

79. "Pengacara Adam Damiri Sesalkan Sikap Majelis Hakim," (Lawyers for Adam Damiri Deplore Attitude of the Panel of Judges) *Kompas*, 25 September 2002.
80. Cohen, "Intended to Fail: The Trials Before the Ad Hoc Human Rights Court in Jakarta".
81. Sukma Loppies, "High Court Releases Adam Damiri from Human Rights Violations Charges," *Tempo Interactive*, August 8, 2004, http://www.tempointeractive.com/hg/nasional/2004/08/06/brk,20040806–06,uk.html
82. Ibid.
83. Indriani Dyah Setiowati, "Mahkamah Agung Kabulkan PK Abilio," (Supreme Court Grants Abilio's Reconsideration [Petition]) *Tempo Interaktif*, November 4, 2004, http://www.tempo.co.id/hg/nasional/2004/11/04/brk,20041104–62,id.html
84. Sukma Loppies, "Eurico Guterres Bebas," (Eurico Guterres Freed) *Tempo Interaktif*, April4,2008 http://www.tempointeraktif.com/hg/nasional/2008/04/04/brk,20080404–120491,id.html
85. For a discussion of the trials, including the tortuous process that preceded them, see Priyambudi Sulistiyanto, "Politics of Justice and Reconciliation in Post-Suharto Indonesia," *Journal of Contemporary Asia* 37 (2007): 73–94.
86. The most conspicuous omissions from the list of accused were L. B. Moerdani, who was Supreme Commander of the Armed Forces in 1984, and Try Sutrisno, who was the military commander in Jakarta in 1984 and later served as Commander of the Armed Forces and Vice President.
87. M. Taufiqurrahman, "Ex-general Jailed for Priok Killing," *Jakarta Post* May 1, 2004; Sari P. Setiogi and Abdul Khalik, "Sriyanto Not Guilty in Priok Massacre," *Jakarta Post*, August 13, 2004; "Indonesian Rights Tribunal Acquits General Accused in 1984 Massacre," *Asian Political News*, August 16, 2004; Sari P. Setiogi, "Tanjung Priok's Last Defendants Get up to Three Years," *Jakarta Post*, August 21, 2004.
88. Sulistiyanto, "Politics of Justice and Reconciliation in Post-Suharto Indonesia," 73–94.
89. "Acquittal of Senior Officers Condemned," *Jakarta Post*, September 10, 2005. Based on their voting record from the East Timor trials, the judges who served on the Abepura case were a group disposed to acquit. The five judges on the Abepura panel had a combined voting record of 13 votes for acquittal and three votes for conviction. The selection of judges who will serve in a particular case is the responsibility of the Supreme Court. I have no information on the criteria used to select judges. But considering the Supreme Court's 100 per cent acquittal rate of human rights defendants on appeal, it is perhaps not too cynical to suggest that in choosing the judges for the Abepura trial the Supreme Court was mindful of the judges' performance in earlier cases.
90. The cases recommended for further action include incidents in Jakarta in May and November 1998 and September 1999 (see KPP HAM Komnas HAM, "Ringkasan Eksekutif Komisi Penyelidikan Pelanggaran Hak Asasi Manusia Trisakti, Semanggi I dan Semanggi II," (Executive Summary of the Commission for the Investigation of Human Rights Violations [in the Cases of] Trisakti, Semanggi I and Semanggi II) www.komnasham.go.id/home/index.php?/43; KPP HAM Komnas HAM, "Penyelidikan Pelanggaran HAM yang Berat dalam Peristiwa Kerusuhan 13–15 Mei 1998," (Investigation into Gross Human Rights Violations during the Riots of 13–15 May 1998) www.komnasham.go.id/home/index.php?/43) and incidents in the Papuan districts of Wasior and Wamena in June 2001 and April 2003 (KPP HAM Komnas HAM, "Rinkasan Eksekutif Hasil Penyelidikan Tim Ad Hoc Penyelidikan Pelanggaran HAM Berat di Papua," (Executive Summary of the Results of the Investigation by the Ad Hoc Team into the Investigation of Gross Human Rights in Papua) www.komnasham.go.id/home/index.php?/43)
91. The DPR has refused to provide the authorization required by the *Human Rights Court Act* for prosecutions of crimes that occurred before the effective date of the Act

(Heru Margianto, "Kasus Trisakti dan Semanggi: Komnas HAM Desak DPR Ubah Putusannya," (The Trisakti and Semanggi Cases: Komnas HAM Presses the DPR to Change its Decision) *Kompas*, March 5, 2003, http://www2.kompas.com/utama/news/0303/05/043037.htm. The matter was addressed most recently in March 2007 when a legislative consultation group (*Badan Musyawarah/Bamus*) comprised of representatives of the ten legislative factions blocked consideration of the issue by the full body: Sugandi, "Kasus Trisakti-Semanggi: Bamus DPR Tolak Pengadilan HAM Ad Hoc," (The Trisakti and Semanggi Cases: DPR's Consultation Group Rejects Ad Hoc Human Rights Court) *Suarakarya-Online*, March 14, 2007, http://www.suarakarya-online.com/news.html?id = 168615

Part IV

Assembling administrative courts

10 'Shopping forums'

Indonesia's administrative courts

Adriaan Bedner

Introduction

If one of Indonesia's state branches has been in constant flux before and after independence, it is the judiciary. The struggle of the colonial administration to ensure 'peace and order' and to respond to the demands for an administration of justice on the basis of the rule of law required an ongoing expansion of the state court system. The condition of the colonial coffers and the lack of qualified personnel available, however, slowed down this process and indigenous, customary courts continued to play an important role.

This situation changed after Indonesia gained independence. Between 1950 and 1980 successive Indonesian governments established dozens of new courts to replace the indigenous ones, which had been abolished during and after the revolution. Unfortunately, this led to the 'near-total devastation of the judicial machine' owing to lack of funds and properly trained personnel.[1] The combination of this 'overstretch' with the purposive destruction of judicial independence under Presidents Soekarno and Soeharto, ultimately gave rise to a situation where it would be extremely hard to restore the independence of the general courts, particularly in matters involving government interests.[2]

As a result, during the 1970s, reformers started to think about alternatives. One of the ideas that quickly gained prominence was to establish new courts, separate from the general court system, dealing with only a special field of law. Isolation and specialization should thus become the key to a better administration of justice. The first tangible result of this strategy was the Administrative Courts, which were established by law in 1986 to become operative in 1991. They were followed by the reform of the Islamic Courts (1989), the Commercial Courts (1998),[3] the Tax Courts (1999), the Human Rights Courts (2000),[4] the Constitutional Court (2004),[5] the Corruption Courts (2005),[6] the Labour Courts (2006) and the Fisheries Courts (2007). In the near future, special courts for land affairs and environmental matters may be established as well.

This chapter evaluates to what extent the first branch of specialized courts in Indonesia – the Administrative Courts – have indeed improved the administration of justice in their field. It will first provide a short overview of the history of the establishment of the Administrative Courts, followed by an analysis of their performance. Its focus will not only be on issues of law, but also on the actual remedies these courts offer to plaintiffs.

On the basis of this analysis, I will argue that if specialized courts are not well designed regarding the scope of their jurisdiction, the negative effects of this may overshadow all of their achievements. This may seem obvious, but it is doubtful whether those concerned with designing new specialized courts sufficiently consider this issue.

Reasons for establishing the Administrative Courts[7]

The reasons for establishing the Administrative Courts cannot be reduced to a straightforward attempt at creating a new, specialized and independent institution. Establishing new courts is a matter of politics and while, in this case, some of the reformers explicitly subscribed to the objective foreshadowed in the Introduction, other actors pursued quite different interests, as will be outlined here.

Nonetheless, the main 'ideological' idea underlying the establishment of the Administrative Courts was that the general courts were considered ineffective in redressing unlawful acts by the government. The jurisdiction of the general courts in administrative matters was considered as limited, and the opinion prevailed that they had failed to exercise to the full the powers assigned to them. Administrative Courts with specialized judges were thought of as the most logical answer to resolve this problem. Such an idea was rooted in civil law history, where administrative courts have been developed as the most appropriate institution to deal with claims against the government. This approach to judicial reform reached Indonesia through the ideas of colonial jurists.[8]

In fact, it was questionable from the start whether legal change was the most appropriate way to address the problems associated with litigation against the government. An action before the general courts on account of government tort potentially allowed for non-monetary damages; for instance, the order to refrain from a certain action or to provide a speedy remedy in the form of an injunction based on a provisional claim. However, in practice these powers were seldom or never exercised and therefore created the impression that the system was inadequate.[9]

Such reasoning squared well with the legal blueprint for the organization of the judiciary in Indonesia, laid down in *Law No. 14/1970*. This statute refused all of the demands made by the coalition of advocates and judges seeking to reintroduce the rule of law during the first years of the New Order.[10] However, it did establish a specialized branch of Administrative Courts on paper, even if only intended as a rhetorical device.[11]

During the 16 years preceding the promulgation of the *Administrative Courts Act* (*ACA*) in 1986, Administrative Courts increasingly became the main target of reformers. With the rising authoritarianism of the New Order ruling out the possibility of introducing other meaningful reforms, the fact that Administrative Courts were mentioned in *Law No. 14/1970* as a separate branch gave this reform some legitimacy and made it hard for the government to distance itself from the idea. Moreover, not all the Ministers of Justice serving under Soeharto were against the Administrative Courts, although their support for them was for various reasons. Thus, Mochtar Kusumaatmadja, serving from 1973 until 1978, took several steps in order to prepare a draft law, in the genuine belief that judicial control of the government was something basically good.

Ismail Saleh, the Minister of Justice who finally established the Administrative Courts, may have been partly motivated by similar sentiments, but his main objective was probably different. Saleh was convinced that administrative courts would not constitute a serious threat for executive dominance under the New Order, but that they would be an effective means to boost its legitimacy.

There is little doubt that this was the main political reason for the establishment of the Administrative Courts.[12] Both internally and externally, visible judicial control of the executive would reinforce the image of the New Order as a basically benevolent regime, allowing for ordered and lawful redress of some of its actions.

This design obviously had consequences for the way in which the Administrative Courts were introduced. First, the jurisdiction of the Courts and their powers of review had to be limited. Control that could effectively hamper projects held dear by the New Order could not be tampered with, as had been made very clear in those cases where general courts had attempted something of the sort. Never again was there to be a *Kedung Ombo*, the court case against the government alleging insufficient compensation for land clearance, which turned into a publicity nightmare for the Soeharto regime.[13]

Second, a separate administrative court would serve better to establish the New Order's legitimacy, and this explains why the government championed separate courts, instead of adding a specialized chamber to the general courts. While Minister of Justice Saleh liked to point out that *Law No. 14/1970* demanded a separate court system, this was in fact not altogether obvious.[14] Separate courts are expensive and entail a host of organizational problems, such as staffing and housing. The real reason for wanting separate courts was that they are far more visible than specialized chambers. In order to attain the legitimizing effect that Saleh aimed for, he needed a separate institution.[15]

Finally, the form of the specialized Administrative Courts made it possible for the government to control their number. In fact, for many citizens the new Courts were a substantial step backwards in protection. Since the general courts lost their jurisdiction over cases involving administrative decisions, plaintiffs now had to bring cases to Administrative Courts of first instance, which in theory could be thousands of miles away from their domicile, as initially only five of them were set up.[16]

This aligned the government with those supporters of the Administrative Courts who argued that a separate courts' system would help create an independent pool of judges, better educated than those in the general courts and less susceptible to corruption. While they would have liked a broader jurisdiction for the new Courts, they were prepared to compromise on this issue, without fully acknowledging the consequences this would eventually have for the effectiveness of the system.

The same logic underlined the decision, generally resisted by judges, to allow for so-called 'ad hoc judges'. These were outsiders who could be appointed to serve as judges on the benches of the new Courts. In this manner, the 'closed shop' nature of the Indonesian judiciary would be opened up, by introducing other perspectives and skills to the councils of judges than those commonly held by career judges.

Finally, a decisive factor in the process leading to the establishment of the Courts was the programme of legal cooperation with the Netherlands, and the fact that the Netherlands presented a system so limited in jurisdiction that it was acceptable to the New Order. The cooperation programme was instrumental in drafting the *ACA*, using the Dutch AROB (*Administratieve Rechtspraak Overheidsbeschikkingen*) procedure as a model. This system only allowed review of individual, concrete and final government decisions. How important the limits on the powers of the courts were to the lawmakers was demonstrated by the persuasion it took to allow proper principles of administration as a ground for review.[17]

Not surprisingly, the result of this process was a mixed bag of limitations and opportunities. There were high expectations, but the courts also enjoyed much goodwill. Newspaper comments showed awareness of the political constraints they had to face and emphasized the judicial intrepidness required for serving on them.[18]

The Administrative Courts in law and practice: legal issues

Jurisdiction

As indicated above, the jurisdiction assigned to the Administrative Courts was quite limited. They were only allowed to review administrative decisions of an individual, concrete and final nature, which left out all factual acts and their consequences, as well as all regulations of a general nature. This is not to say that these latter two were not subject to any form of judicial review, as both could still be dealt with by the general courts in the framework of an action based on government tort.[19] Officially, the reason not to give this jurisdiction to the Administrative Courts was that they lacked the expertise required to deal with damages, which would be often involved in such suits. However, this is not very convincing as basically everything was new to them. More likely, it was the uncertainty of the government as to what they could expect of the new Courts that motivated this choice and to attempt to seriously restrict the latter's case-load.

Indeed, after they opened their gates, it soon became clear that the Administrative Courts were not going to receive a flood of cases. Rather, from inception the Administrative Courts' dockets have remained relatively empty, even in such large cities as Jakarta and Surabaya. In response the lower courts tried to broaden their jurisdiction, albeit, in a rather erratic and tentative manner and unsupported by the Supreme Court, which in almost all cases has struck down these judgments.

The first target of judicial expansion was the definition of administrative decisions, meaning decisions taken by an administrative official.[20] Literally any decision-maker who could be considered an administrative official has been so defined, at least once. Thus, the Courts have allowed claims against decisions by state-owned limited liability companies, private universities, local government coordination boards without decision-making powers, secret service agencies, political parties, notaries and political parties.[21]

It was not clear from the outset that the Supreme Court was going to strike down such interpretations, and neither have all judges gone with the flow. However, in a number of instances, for example state-owned limited liability companies, the judges involved must have known that their decisions were not going to last, because Supreme Court Junior Chairman of Administrative Litigation, Indroharto, had published a book in which he clearly stated that the managers of these companies were not administrative officials.[22]

Similar interpretations aimed at widening jurisdiction have been proposed for the other elements of the definition of administrative decisions. Thus, the Administrative Courts have also accepted claims against decisions of a general nature. For example, in Medan the Administrative Court considered the appointment of a private agency as the administrator of requests for land certificates as an individual decision, in spite of the fact that the legal consequences of the litigated decision clearly affect an indefinite number of individuals.[23]

Likewise, Administrative Courts have attempted to assume jurisdiction over decisions by the state auction office, which forms perhaps the most remarkable inroad on general court jurisdiction. The auction office acts under the authority of the chairman of the general court of first instance in executing general court judgments, and thus clearly falls within the realm of general court supervision. Nonetheless, on several occasions Administrative Courts accepted cases against these offices and even suspended their decisions – which were later always overturned by the Supreme Court.[24]

A similar story can be told about term of limitation. Although the term of limitation in the Indonesian Administrative Court procedure is relatively long (90 days), it is obviously intended to act as a barrier to prevent uncertainty of government. As many government decisions constitute the basis for subsequent action, governing would become highly problematic if claims against them were allowed at any time.

Neither this argument nor the article concerned have prevented judges in some cases from attempting to develop new doctrines that would give them virtually unlimited powers in circumventing terms of limitation. The most extreme example is *Dahniar and others v. Head of the National Land Agency*,[25] where the judges were asked to give effect to a 1967 sales contract concerning a plot of land in Central Jakarta. This contract involved a whole series of administrative decisions, the first one being a 1972 certificate of ownership, with only the last one – a land use permit – falling inside the 90 days' term. The Court accepted the case nonetheless, arguing that if the government issued a decision bearing a connection to earlier decisions, the entire 'chain' of decisions would fall within its jurisdiction. Just as in the other cases, this judgment was later overturned by the Supreme Court.[26]

The only field where the Supreme Court has allowed the Administrative Courts to assume jurisdiction over objects that in most jurisdictions would not qualify as administrative decisions is that concerning land law. This idea has certainly not come from the Dutch AROB example. It usually concerns land certificates and related acts, which are only corollary to civil law relations. Consequently, the Administrative Courts in fact have little to decide. However, instead of referring cases back to the general courts for the civil law questions, the Administrative Courts have tended to answer these questions themselves – and in this case, decisions have not been reversed by the Supreme Court.[27]

The Administrative Courts' jurisdiction has also been gradually limited in some fields, notably concerning litigation against decisions taken on administrative appeal. Such decisions are open to Administrative Court review on the basis of Article 48. They constituted the bulk of cases in the Administrative High Court in Jakarta, where both the Tax Tribunal and the Central Tribunal for Labour Disputes resided. However, both tax and labour disputes have now been brought under the powers of special courts, the former in 1994 on the basis of *Law No. 9/1994* (later replaced by *Law No. 14/2002*) and the latter in 2007 by *Law No. 2/2004*. In both cases this led to critique by administrative court supporters, the first one being a mere complaint about the violation of the formally prescribed structure of Indonesia's court system,[28] but in the more recent case of the Labour Court, even with an explicit reference to the consequences of the drop in caseload for the Jakarta Administrative High Court.[29]

Altogether, the lower courts' tendency to expand jurisdiction has been unsuccessful. The Supreme Court has consistently struck down all decisions transgressing jurisdictional boundaries, except in the case of land law. This has created serious jurisdictional problems between administrative and general courts, with uncertainty for litigants as a result.

The consequence of these developments is that the Administrative Courts receive few cases, and most of them concern land law. According to the estimate of an administrative court judge, today about 95 per cent of all the cases in the Administrative Courts concern land,[30] and actually most of them should be dealt with by the general courts. While Courts in the cities of Jakarta, Bandung, Semarang, Surabaya, Makassar and Medan still receive sufficient cases to keep their judges at work, this is certainly not true of those in more outlying areas such as Denpasar, Kupang and Jayapura, where the Courts have consistently confronted sparsely filled dockets.[31] This may have far-reaching consequences for all aspects of judicial performance and psychology. As one judge remarked during an interview in 2000: 'I like to go fishing ... But if you don't have any hobbies, like fishing, tennis, sports, etc., well, you get stressed. You just wait in your office every day.'[32]

One can therefore see that the Administrative Courts remain tempted to continue their search for new cases – and to ignore the Supreme Court judgments. And indeed, this is apparent from the records. Thus, more recently, Administrative Courts have again assumed jurisdiction over administrative decisions clearly outside their powers, such as Environmental Impact Assessments,[33] a decision to repeat a tendering procedure, a decision to build a road, a decision to use money from the district budget for new cars for members of the District Parliament, or a decision to raise parking tariffs.[34]

This problem has been exacerbated by the equivocal status of precedent in Indonesia. Although in every civil law country Supreme Court precedents are effectively binding or at least highly persuasive on lower courts, some Indonesian judges have developed an alternative theory, claiming that Indonesia is not a common law country and, therefore, judges are not bound by precedent.[35] Nonetheless, most judges probably still accept case law from the Supreme Court as binding, at least informally, but only if the Court has twice used the same interpretation. Therefore, they feel unbound for future cases by a cassation judgment overturning their own decision. This explains why in 2005 the Supreme Court published a volume containing several judgments on one interpretational subject – all of them concerning jurisdiction. This volume has probably closed the door for some of the more peculiar deviations of jurisdictional doctrine, but it is unlikely that anything other than a substantial extension of administrative court jurisdiction can really solve this problem.

In fact, an increase to jurisdiction was recently promised by the Supreme Court Junior Chairman in the field of Administrative Litigation, Paulus Lotulung. Asked about the consequences of the allocation of labour cases to the Courts for Industrial Relations, Lotulung said that the Administrative Courts should not worry, because it is envisaged that they will acquire jurisdiction over all cases involving unlawful acts by the government. This plan, which would indeed strongly boost administrative court jurisdiction, should be realized through the enactment of a new act on state administration.[36] However, the problems concerning the basic design of this bill seem to prevent it from being adopted in the near future. As a result the Administrative Courts will probably continue being creative in inventing jurisdiction.[37]

Powers of review

Article 53 of *ACA* lists three grounds for review: first, contravention of laws and regulations; second, misuse of power; and third, arbitrariness. If we compare this list to the Dutch AROB-law, there is one remarkable difference: the AROB-law also included general principles of proper administration. The minutes of the parliamentary debates on the *ACA* show that the government agreed that the Administrative Courts would effectively apply such principles as well, but that for political reasons it did not want to include them explicitly as a ground for review in the Act itself. This would have antagonized certain powerful segments of the political establishment, and would have reduced the chances of the bill being passed.[38]

In effect, from the start, the Administrative Courts have invoked this ground for review, using the list of principles expounded by Indroharto in his influential book on administrative litigation as a guide.[39] Of these, the Supreme Court has explicitly upheld carefulness and equality,[40] and in interviews which I conducted in 1994, all the judges concerned agreed that the Courts held the power to apply the full list of Indroharto.

A problem with the application of principles of proper administration has been that there is little uniformity in their interpretation. The Supreme Court has failed to guide in this matter, as it has neither published judgments in which it applied any other principles than the two mentioned above, nor has it provided any guidelines in the form of circular letters.[41] It is therefore not surprising that the novelty of this subject has spawned various readings, but in some cases these make one wonder whether the judges concerned really understand the objective of the principle they apply. In a case at the Bandung Administrative Court, for instance, the judges quashed a decision on the basis of 'fair play'.[42] According to Indroharto, this means that 'the official who issues the decision will not attempt to frustrate the opportunity for someone holding an interest (in this decision) to acquire a favourable decision'.[43] In their ruling the judges instead argued that the fair principle meant that 'all possibilities which are open to a citizen to defend his interest should never be frustrated by formal acts according to laws formulated by the authorities'. Taken seriously, this interpretation would mean that the government can hardly act at all, even if it followed the rules conscientiously. Similar problems in interpretation have been recorded regarding the principle of trust and the hearing principle.[44]

Nonetheless, despite the troublesome communication between higher and lower courts, one would expect this problem to be resolved in the longer run – by means of courses and published judgments. Judges do not hold a clear interest in maintaining such interpretations, as they do not significantly widen their scope of discretion. Unfortunately, however, this opportunity has now been thwarted by the legislature.

In a move that in itself should be lauded, the 2004 amendments to the 1986 *ACA* (*Law No. 32/2004*) have introduced principles of proper administration as a separate ground for judicial review, thus justifying the development of judicial practice since the start of the Administrative Courts. These grounds remain undefined in the law itself, but their interpretation is not left to the discretion of the judiciary. Instead, the Elucidation refers to *Law No. 28/1999* (*Anti Corruption Act*), and lists six principles largely unknown in the Administrative Courts' practice. Only two of them overlap with those of Indroharto: the principles of legal certainty and proportionality. The others – disciplined state management, openness, professionalism and accountability – are entirely new.[45]

Except for the fact that in this manner most of what has been developed as common interpretation has been undone, these principles also seem hard to apply in the context of the Administrative Courts. They simply serve another purpose in the *Anti-Corruption Act*, where they apply to *internal* management of the state rather than *external* relations with citizens. This is apparent, for instance, when we compare the principle of proportionality's definition in administrative court practice with its definition in the *Anti-Corruption Act*. Whereas the former refers to the proportionality between the effects of the disputed decision with the purpose it serves, the Elucidation to the *Anti-Corruption Act* states that 'proportionality is the principle that puts first the balance between the rights and the duties of the State Authorities (*Penyelenggara Negara*)' – not a very lucid definition, and definitely a different issue.

How these changes have worked out in practice is unclear, because of lack of published data. If taken seriously, it would mean that the development of a consistent interpretation of these principles has to start anew and under much less favourable conditions than in 1991, when at least information had been available regarding the application of these principles as it had developed in the Netherlands.

Remedial powers

Suspension

One of the main improvements to the *ACA* for those seeking justice in cases against the government was the introduction of a form of injunction. Although civil procedure knew the possibility of a provisional claim in government tort cases which could potentially achieve the same result, this opportunity was never, or seldom, used and the explicit possibility to demand suspension of the litigated decision on the basis of Article 67 seems to considerably strengthen the position of many plaintiffs.

Suspension finds its basis in the fact that a litigated decision in principle maintains its validity. This is obviously a serious problem in those cases where the said decision allows the government to perform actions that cannot be undone, or only at great cost or difficulty. A good example is demolition or eviction orders, which indeed have been frequently addressed in court for this purpose.[46]

But it has not only been these kinds of orders that have been suspended. During the first years, the Administrative Courts developed a suspension practice that was rather similar to its expansive jurisdictional policy, with the Supreme Court attempting to constrain this tendency of granting suspensions. A particular problem underlying this practice was that Article 67 of the *ACA* had not been drafted very well. It basically argued that the suspension of the litigated decision remained in place until the judgment in the case was entered. With such cases often going through at least appeal and cassation, and therefore usually taking more than two years, suspension had in fact become a formidable weapon – a situation judges used to their own and some plaintiffs' advantage.

Nevertheless, the Supreme Court has been able to put limitations on its use. By Circular Letter No. 2/1991 at VI-2 a., the Court authorized the Chairman of the Court concerned to rescind a suspension order. In *Tanumihardja v. National*

Electricity Company the Supreme Court argued that if the Court denies the claim, the Chairman was even under an obligation to do this.[47]

However, other Supreme Court limitations on suspension have not been consistently followed. Thus, the stipulation in Supreme Court Guideline No. 51/Td./TUN/III/1992 that a request for suspension can at the latest be submitted together with the rejoinder has at times been disregarded.[48] It is hard for the Supreme Court to control this matter, as few or no such cases come up for cassation. The same goes for the reasoning underlying suspension orders. In many cases judges have simply granted suspension without giving any reasons at all, or providing statements such as 'the case is not entirely clear yet'[49] or 'because it has not been clearly proven during the preparatory investigation where the faults of both parties lie'.[50]

The main explanation for the unruliness of lower court judges in this matter is that in some cases suspension itself is the main objective of the plaintiff. The simplest reason is that it can reinforce a party's bargaining position. In a case in Bandung, for instance, a developer had in the view of the municipal authorities transgressed the limits of the building plan, by extending its basement under the sidewalk. After the fear of immediate demolition had been removed by a suspension order, the plaintiff could work out an agreement with the municipality.[51]

In other cases suspension allows the plaintiff to perform certain actions on time before the litigated decision takes effect. This mainly applies to eviction, where the leeway provided by a suspension order may grant the plaintiff sufficient time to save his or her belongings, knowing how slim the chances are of winning the case. In the early days of the Administrative Courts, when they still assumed jurisdiction over state auction orders (see above), the owners of property that was to be auctioned went to court for similar reasons. For example, the owner of a beauty parlour (who had gone bankrupt) advised that she had been able to sell her parlour by herself and thus received a much higher price as a result of securing a suspension order to auction her property.[52]

In any case, suspension is an interesting remedy for many litigants in the Administrative Courts and judges are fully aware of this. Hierarchical control on the use of suspension is indirect or even absent, and as a consequence the practice is neither consistent nor well-argued. It is therefore no wonder that, as I will discuss further below, many defendants have little respect for suspension orders, and violations occur with some frequency.

Judgments

Whereas suspension has a clear added-value for plaintiffs, the other remedies the Administrative Courts can offer are rather limited. As stated earlier in this chapter, the main difference with the situation as it existed before the Administrative Courts were established is that they can actually order the defendant to revoke the contested decision, whereas an action based on government tort could lead to compensation only. However, because the general courts gave a very extensive interpretation to the concept of damages, in fact their powers equalled those of the Administrative Courts.[53]

A superficial reading of Article 116, in its original form, gives the impression that the Administrative Courts are even less powerful, in the sense that their powers are limited to ordering revocation of the decision only. If the defendant fails to fulfil this obligation the Court can address his or her superior. However, the Courts do not depend on this superior *legally*, because if the defendant still has not complied with this court order after four months, the decision 'shall have no legal force anymore'.[54]

An important development has been the interpretation by the Administrative Courts of Article 116's para. 9, which allows the Administrative Court to order the defendant to issue a new decision. In his textbook, Indroharto has argued that the judge could give the defendant some guidance on this matter, by stipulating that the new decision should be in line with the considerations in the judgment.[55] Given the general tendency of the Administrative Courts to widen their powers, it will come as no surprise that the Courts have interpreted this liberal reading of the *ACA* in an even more liberal manner. Judges have not themselves issued an administrative decision *in lieu of* the original one, but in some cases they have actually prescribed for the defendant what should be the contents of the new administrative decision.[56]

Sometimes Administrative Court judges themselves seem not to fully understand the legal consequences of their judgment annulling the litigated decision. Thus, in the widely applauded *Tempo v. Minister of Information*, the Jakarta Administrative Court not only ordered the defendant to rescind his revocation of *Tempo*'s publication permit, but also to issue a new one. Apparently, the judges were not aware that rescission of the revocation would automatically bring back to life the original publication permit. In itself, this is not such a serious matter, but it becomes an issue if we take into account how many problems occur in implementing administrative court judgments, a matter discussed below.

Damages and rehabilitation

By the shrewd resistance of Minister Ismail Saleh, who managed to get away with misinforming parliament on this matter, the article on damages in the 1986 *Law on Administrative Courts* had a very limited scope only.[57] Damages have been provided for by Article 97(10), which says nothing more than that this matter is to be further set out in a government regulation. The required regulation was enacted with remarkable speed in 1991 but turned out to be an empty shell: damages are limited to Rp 5 million, at that time the equivalent of US$2,000, today reduced to a mere US$530. For additional compensation the plaintiff has to start a separate suit in the general court. In short, the inability of the Administrative Courts to award damages is another example of the effective reduction of citizens' protection against the government, this time by introducing complex procedures.[58]

Upon reading Articles 117 and 121(2) on rehabilitation of civil servants who have successfully litigated against their removal from office one gets the impression that here the legislator has provided the protection absent in the case of damages. The said articles contain a detailed procedure for restoring unlawfully dismissed civil servants to their former position, and clear rules on full damages if this is practically possible. One can imagine that this procedure was not to the liking of the government at the time, and indeed Saleh strongly opposed its introduction. However, in this case parliament proved immune to his arguments.[59] Finding himself unable to defend his bill on this point, Saleh tried to introduce limitations on rehabilitation through the backdoor of *Government Regulation No. 32/1991*. Going flatly against the *ACA*, which speaks of full compensation, this piece of subordinate legislation sets a limit of Rp 2 million on the amount to be paid to the litigant if the latter cannot effectively be rehabilitated. It thus removes any monetary incentive for the government to seriously consider rehabilitation.

Remedial powers in practice: claims upheld

In summary, the Administrative Courts have provided an extension for citizens' protection against the government regarding the grounds for compensation, but apart from this they have little more to offer to plaintiffs than the general courts. By complicating jurisdiction and effectively limiting access, it seems that they have reduced rather than improved the position of those seeking justice against the government.

This is not to say that the Administrative Courts have nothing to offer at all. First, their sheer existence and visibility are likely to have promoted preventative measures to government officials in order to avoid their being summoned to court. In some cases this has led to procedural changes, for instance, by imposing the obligation on administrative bureaux to first submit their decisions to the legal department before issuing them. Likewise, several officials told me – in the framework of research on other matters – that after the introduction of the Administrative Courts they had become more cautious in issuing decisions. The question remains, however, to what extent do the Administrative Courts offer justice in individual cases? Have they upheld claims of litigants in a consistent manner, and has this led in practice to the realization of the plaintiff's entitlement?

The first question is how often Courts have upheld claims by litigants. Unfortunately, such data are not easily available. The Supreme Court website now features a search engine for case-law, but offers insufficient data for this purpose. Therefore, I have to rely on my own data of the early 1990s and data about the Bandung Administrative Court contained in a study by Fachruddin.[60] These indicate that filing an administrative court procedure is a rather unpredictable, but by no means vain, effort to redress unfavourable government actions.

The data referred to show that plaintiffs have a considerable chance of winning their cases in first instance. Even though during the New Order the political odds were very much against the courts, for their survival they had to show that they dared to defy officials. Rejecting all claims would have amounted to a bid for doing nothing. This is reflected in the numbers of cases won by plaintiffs in the Administrative Courts of Jakarta, Bandung and Semarang between 1991 and 1995. Table 10.1 shows the results of the cases taken to these Administrative Courts, in so far as they had been completed by 1995.

Table 10.1 Results of cases in Administrative Court completed by 1995

Court	*No. of cases*	*Withdrawn by the plaintiff*	*Settled*	*Declared inadmissible or fallen due*	*Rejected*	*Upheld*
Jakarta	73	7	15	21	14	16
Bandung	45	23	7	4	6	5
Semarang	64	15	7	27	10	5
Total	182	45	29	52	30	26

If we look at the number of claims upheld compared to the overall case-load, the chances of success are not strikingly high, standing at about 15 per cent. However, if we subtract the number of cases withdrawn by the plaintiff or settled, we get a much higher percentage, of almost 25 per cent. If we then take into account that most of the claims declared inadmissible or having fallen due were really outside the jurisdiction of the Court, the conclusion is that if plaintiffs bring a case clearly falling within the jurisdiction of the Administrative Court they stand a chance of almost one in two of being successful in first instance.

However, the outcome of cases in first instance has turned out not to be a very reliable indicator of the outcome on appeal. Neither plaintiffs nor defendants easily accept a judgment of the first instance court, appealing against almost half the cases where an appeal is legally possible. Table 10.2 gives an overview of all cases appealed (i.e. both those appealed by plaintiffs and those appealed by defendants).

If, however, we take as our point of departure the cases that were really adjudicated in first instance on the substance of the matter (the total number of claims upheld or rejected from Table 10.1), the picture changes further: out of 56 cases, 44 were appealed against, which is almost 80 per cent.

That appeal is so popular is no wonder, when we see that almost half of the claims for appeal are upheld; if – again – we only look at the cases decided on substance, we see that this even turns into a majority of cases.

Cassation is not as popular as appeal, but between 1991 and 1995 more than half of the appellate judgments were submitted to the Supreme Court.[61] The number of judgments overturned stands at about 20 per cent and has tended

Table 10.2 Cases appealed from the Administrative Court

Court	*No. of cases eligible for appeal*	*No. of cases appealed*	*Appeals rejected*	*Appeals upheld*
Jakarta	51	26	16	10
Bandung	15	3	2	1
Semarang	52	26	3	6
Total	118	55	21	17

to decrease to below 15 per cent in 2000. This seems to indicate a rise in legal certainty, or at least predictability.[62]

One problem of appeals for cassation is that they can take a long time; in fact, appealing for cassation can be used as a strategy to delay a case by officials who have lost on appeal in cases where no suspension order applies. Although backlogs are not as serious as those of the general courts, 831 cases were waiting to be judged by the end of 2000.

However, a judgment in cassation in Indonesia is not as final as one might assume. Originally intended as a remedy for extraordinary cases, review of cassation judgments has matured into a sort of fourth instance in Indonesia. Between 1991 and 1999 more than 20 per cent of cassation judgments in administrative litigation were submitted for revision and one in ten cases were overturned. To me, this inconsistency within the Supreme Court is more worrisome than the number of appellate judgments overturned upon cassation, and provides a clear incentive to parties to exhaust all avenues for appeal.

In any case, these figures do offer an indication that the interpretation of administrative law in individual cases considerably diverges in each instance. The Supreme Court record indicates that this even holds for one court itself. It seems therefore that there is not yet much consistency in judging, which could be an indicator of judicial professionalism.

While these figures provide some indication of the state of administrative litigation, they do not indicate how much chance of success a plaintiff has, let alone to what extent the Administrative Courts provide an effective remedy, based on a proper application of the law. Legal assessments of administrative court judgments have not been very favourable,[63] while allegations of corruption have continued to be voiced.

Remedial powers in practice: the problem of non-execution

Administrative Court judges themselves usually refer to non-execution of their judgments as the most serious problem they have to confront. This is quite understandable given the damage non-execution does to their effectiveness in providing remedies. Given the dearth of cases that Administrative Courts have to face, such a challenge to their authority is, in fact, a direct threat to their existence.

Research undertaken in Indonesia on the Administrative Courts in the early 1990s established that few judgments were yet implementable. Press reports indicated that in three cases – two concerning certificates of land ownership and one concerning the license to harvest birds' nests – the defendant did not implement the judgment. At that time, many judges complained about execution problems, but this did not concern final judgments but suspension orders (of which I recorded 26 cases of non-implementation at the time).[64]

A more recent doctoral study by Administrative Court judge Irfan Fachruddin provides more insight into this matter.[65] The author, who conducted his research at the Bandung Administrative Court, found that from 1994 – when the Court became operative – until 1999, 25 judgments were liable for execution; a meagre 5 per cent of all claims only.

Fachruddin further shows that of these 25 judgments only eight were actually implemented. In four cases the execution was suspended, and in 13 cases the defendant refused to implement the judgment. If cast in the terms of a 'black and white' success rate, we find that one out of every 33 plaintiffs gets the result desired *ab initio*.[66]

To put this gloomy image into proper perspective, however, it is important to look at the reasons for non-implementation. The most valuable part of Fachruddin's evaluation is the interviews he conducted with the officials involved in the cases concerned. These show that the problem of non-execution is not a simple one of corrupt or arrogant officials scorning the rule of law, but that in most cases problems with the Courts' jurisdiction underlie the decisions not to implement. It seems actually as if the faults in the design of the Administrative Courts haunt all aspects of its functioning.

The first reason officials put forward for non-compliance concerned three cases where the object of the claim was a land certificate. According to the interviewees, the factual situation in these cases had changed to the extent that the contested certificates could no longer be revoked. In the absence of a reliable system of land registration, they argued that third parties who had acquired the land concerned were entitled to legal protection.[67] This problem was exacerbated when the Administrative Court acted outside its jurisdiction by deciding questions of civil law.

Two other cases were not executed because of conflicting judgments from the administrative and the general courts. One of them concerned the annulment of a location permit (a permit for land acquisition) by the Administrative Court, followed by a successful attempt to get an objection against execution of this judgment from the general court.[68] In the other case, the defendant followed the same avenue, with the difference that the object of the original claim – a mortgage certificate – had been clearly outside the jurisdiction of the Administrative Court.[69] Nonetheless, in these cases it was the general courts that transgressed their jurisdictional boundaries, by interfering in the implementation of administrative court judgments. However, from a defendant's viewpoint it is understandable to follow the line of least resistance in such cases by not implementing the judgment.[70] This also applies to a case where the Administrative Court had ordered the annulment of a use right to land (*hak pakai*), but where litigation about this matter was still ongoing in the general court.[71]

The reverse has also happened, in a case about land ownership when the Administrative Court ordered suspension of the execution of a general court order until the case had been entered.[72] However, as the defendant correctly decided that the Administrative Court held no jurisdiction, he did not follow this order.

Less extreme, but not dissimilar, was the case where the Administrative Court ordered the defendant to issue a demolition order because the plaintiff claimed the wall concerned had been built on his land.[73] Of course, this is a matter of civil law which the plaintiff had attempted to turn into administrative law, and therefore the defendant refused to implement this judgment.

The third reason for non-compliance also concerned problems with jurisdiction between the administrative and the general court. In two cases the Administrative Courts ordered the defendant to quash a notarial deed: in one case, because it had been drafted on a national holiday; in the other, because the general court had ordered its annulment. The notary in the first case argued that since notaries fall outside the jurisdiction of the Administrative Courts – in which he was correct – he could not take any action.[74] In the second one, the notary refused to implement the judgment since the deed was void anyway, because of the general court judgment, so it made no sense to do anything more about it.[75] Likewise, the Islamic registry refused to annul a divorce certificate because it considered this a matter of civil law.[76]

The fourth reason given for non-implementation is of a less fundamental nature and concerns ambiguities of the facts. Thus, in one case the numbers of the certificates in the register and the certificates that had been the object of the litigation did not match.[77] Confronted by a similar case, the defendant in another instance started a re-examination of the data and in the end did provide the plaintiff with a new certificate,[78] while in a third case the judgment had not been implemented yet because such an examination (*rehabilitasi administrasi*) had not been completed.[79]

The fifth reason is less forgivable. The head of the Cianjur branch office of the National Land Agency (NLA) refused to revoke a certificate of ownership, because the 'facts on which the judgment had been based had been incorrect'.[80] Worse still was the 'fake' reason provided by his colleague from the Land Agency in Bandung. This official argued that he had not implemented because the Chairman of the Court concerned had failed to provide an execution order (which he only gives in case of non-compliance).[81]

In summary, with the exception of two cases, the defendants interviewed had reasonable grounds to refuse the implementation of these court judgments. In most of them issues of jurisdiction played a major role. The tendency of the Administrative Courts to deal with civil law issues concerning land therefore overshadows all its achievements in other fields – in the end frequently leaving plaintiffs empty-handed and the courts vulnerable to attack. For the sake of clarity: almost all of the cases which were properly implemented concerned matters clearly outside the realm of general court jurisdiction.[82]

As already indicated above, the perception of non-compliance has not been concerned much with such underlying problems, but rather portrayed officials as arrogant or corrupt 'spoilsports'. This has led to an amendment in the *ACA*, which now allows for a daily fine in case of non-compliance to be incorporated in the judgment,[83] and a bailiff to collect that money.[84] As the powers of the bailiff have not been elucidated in any manner, it is uncertain what he should do if an unruly official refuses to pay. Of course, there are also clear cases of a truly administrative nature where officials do refuse to implement court judgments.[85] For such cases this measure seems to be quite proper. However, if we take the data of Fachruddin as representative, the large majority of non-implementation cases are equivocal at best.

Conclusion

After 15 years of Administrative Court practice, the inevitable conclusion is that these Courts have not provided the improvements commonly associated with specialization and isolation. On the contrary, by designing a system whose jurisdiction was neither broad enough nor well-attuned to the jurisdiction of the general courts, the lawmakers seem to have created rather than resolved problems of administration of justice. The political rationale of the New Order regime's decision to introduce Administrative Courts explains why the Administrative Courts were designed in this way, but probably no one would have expected that for 'common' cases the Administrative Courts would complicate matters to this extent.

The dearth of cases has incited judges to constantly look for expansion of their jurisdiction and become 'shopping forums' to the detriment of legal certainty. This is not only visible in the large number of judgments overturned by the Supreme Court on account of inadmissibility of claims, but also in the high rates of cases overturned on appeal, in cassation and finally on review. There has been some improvement in this matter more recently, but lack of communication within the court system has reduced the speed of this process considerably. Legislative interventions such as introducing new principles of proper administration rather than codifying those evolved in administrative court practice have further hindered this process.

Perhaps most remarkable is that jurisdictional problems even extend to the phase of execution of the Administrative Courts' decisions. While complaints about non-execution are frequently voiced in Indonesian newspapers and usually blamed on the 'arrogance of power' (*arogansi kekuasaan*), examination of such cases has demonstrated that more often than not the officials responsible for execution have proper reasons to hesitate. As shown almost all these cases of non-implementation concerned land disputes where the Administrative Courts glossed over the civil law issues contained in them – sometimes even going flatly against general court judgments. In any case, it is unlikely that the new system of daily fines and bailiffs to collect them will improve the situation.

This overview indicates that the first task of those designing new courts administering justice in special fields of the law is to pay serious attention to harmonizing jurisdictions between the new and already existing institutions. In this process they should also be aware of the practical conditions judges have to face. Delimiting jurisdictions too narrowly (including lack of review powers), with too few cases to keep judges busy, will inevitably render judges susceptible to forum shoppers. Inadequate judicial salaries, the spread of corruption, and a lack of hierarchical control will reinforce this process and ultimately lead to a situation where courts complicate matters rather than resolve them.

This raises the question as to whether it would be better to simply abolish the Administrative Courts and return to a unified system of jurisdiction. However, despite all these unfavourable observations the Administrative Courts also have had notable achievements. Their function as a symbol against government power should not be underestimated, while their existence has propelled many government officials and institutions to operate in a more careful manner. But apart from that, their record in cases for which they had originally been invented may not be bad at all. Before abolition, a study of these cases where jurisdiction exists is required.

The most proper way forward, therefore, would seem to be to take away the jurisdiction from the Administrative Courts in cases concerning land, while at the same time extending their jurisdiction to include decisions of a general nature and the power to compensate. If that reform were to see no improvements, then perhaps the Administrative Courts should better be reintegrated with their general counterparts. That, however, is very unlikely to happen in the near future. My prediction is that we will see a new court emerge first: land courts, which will deal with both civil and administrative law aspects of disputes concerning land. Perhaps this institution would then finally be merged with the Administrative Courts.

Notes

1. S. Pompe, *The Indonesian Supreme Court: A Study of Institutional Collapse* (Ithaca: Cornell Southeast Asia Program, 2005), 188.
2. S. Pompe, *The Indonesian Supreme Court: A Study of Institutional Collapse* (Ithaca: Cornell Southeast Asia Program, 2005), 136–41.
3. For further information see David Linnan's chapter in this book.
4. For further information see Mark Cammack's chapter in this book.
5. For further information see Hendrianto's chapter in this book.
6. For further information see Benjamin H. Tahyar's chapter in this book.
7. For a detailed account, see Ch. 2 of A. W. Bedner, *Administrative Courts in Indonesia: A Socio-Legal Study* (The Hague: Kluwer Law International, 2001).
8. Bedner, *Administrative Courts in Indonesia*, 11–15.
9. A survey of reported general court cases on government tort shows that the general court record was in fact not as bad as often assumed. However, with the appointment in 1974 of Oemar Seno Adji as Supreme Court Chairman, the judiciary did lose many of its teeth in this respect: Pompe, *The Indonesian Supreme Court*, 120. It shows, however, that this was a matter of policy rather than limits to the jurisdiction of the general courts.
10. D. S. Lev, "Judicial Authority and the Struggle for an Indonesian Rechtsstaat," *Law and Society Review* 13 (1978): 37–71.
11. Bedner, *Administrative Courts in Indonesia*, 26–8.
12. D. Bourchier, "Magic Memos, Collusion and Judges with Attitudes: Notes on the Politics of Law in Contemporary Indonesia," in *Law, Capitalism and Power in Asia: The Rule of Law and Legal Institutions*, ed. K. Jayasurya (London: Routledge, 1999), 233–52; Bedner, *Administrative Courts in Indonesia*, 30, 50.
13. Pompe, *The Indonesia Supreme Court*, 148–53.
14. Article 10(1) of *Law No. 14/1970* only determines that justice is administered by courts in the areas of general, religious, military and administrative justice.
15. Just as the National Human Rights Commission, established a few years later.

16. Two courts were established on Sumatra (Medan and Palembang), two on Java (Jakarta and Surabaya) and one on Sulawesi (Ujung Pandang, now Makassar).
17. In the end they were smuggled in through the backdoor. They were not listed in the relevant Article 53, but only hinted at. See Indroharto, *Usaha Memahami Undang-Undang Tentang Peradilan Tata Usaha Negara. Buku II: Beracara di Pengadilan Tata Usaha Negara* (An Attempt at Understanding the Act on Administrative Courts. Book II: Conducting a Procedure at the Administrative Court) (Jakarta: Pustaka Sinar Harapan, 1993), 311. For a comparison in detail between the Dutch form of administrative litigation and the Indonesian, see A. W. Bedner, "De Indonesische bestuursrechtspraak: een windmolen tussen de sawah's?," (Indonesian Administrative Litigation: A Wind Mill in between Paddy Fields?) *Nederlands Tijdschrift voor Bestuursrecht* (Dutch Journal for Administrative Law) 6 (2001): 149–56.
18. A survey of newspaper comments in 1991, when the courts became operative, showed that expectations were not extreme.
19. In 1993 the Supreme Court moreover issued a Circular Letter (No. 1/1993) which allowed a direct action against provisions of a general nature, below the level of acts of parliament, to the Supreme Court.
20. *Administrative Courts Act* art. 1(3).
21. Bedner, *Administrative Courts in Indonesia*, 54–60.
22. Indroharto, *Usaha Memahami Undang-Undang Tentang Peradilan Tata Usaha Negara. Buku I: Beberapa Pengertian Dasar Hukum Tata Usaha Negara* (An Attempt at Understanding the Act on Administrative Courts. Book I: Some Understandings of the Legal Basis of Administrative Litigation), 68.
23. Case No. 16/G/1991/PTUN-Mdn.
24. Bedner, *Administrative Courts in Indonesia*, 72–4.
25. Case No. 10/G/1991/PTUN-Jkt.
26. Case No. 5K/TUN/1992. The Administrative Courts of appeal have not always sided with the courts of first instance in these cases, but they have mostly left their judgments in place: see Bedner, *Administrative Courts in Indonesia,* 53–92.
27. An explanation would be that the Supreme Court prefers to get the case resolved rather than refer it back for some legal questions to the general courts and for another legal question to the administrative. This would also be hard to explain to plaintiffs, however, from a jurisdictional perspective it is not a very wise policy: Bedner, *Administrative Courts in Indonesia,* 169–70.
28. P. Lotulung, "Development of the Administrative Jurisdiction on Tax Cases in Indonesia," *Indonesian Law and Administration Review* 1 (1996): 28–31.
29. "Perkara Perburuhan masih mendominasi Peradilan TUN," *Hukumonline*, January 24, 2005, http://www.hukumonline.com/detail.asp?id=12073&cl=Berita. According to the registrar of the Jakarta Administrative High Court, about 80 per cent of the court's case-load concerned labour disputes.
30. Interview with Administrative High Court judge, June 2007.
31. The official figures for Denpasar for 2006–8 are 18, 16 and 11 cases, for Kupang 17, 14 and 21, and for Jayapura 6, 10 and 13. Courtesy of Administrative Court judges Maftuh Effendi and Irfan Fachruddin. The figures of Denbpasar can also be accessed through the Internet, at http://ptundenpasar.net/Direktori%20Putusan.html
32. Interview with Bandung Administrative Court judge, July 1999.
33. Suparto Wijoyo, "AMDAL Dalam Gugatan Hukum: Studi Kasus Gugatan Terhadap AMDAL Reklamasi Pantura Jakarta" (EIA in Legal Claims: A Case Study of the Claim Against the EIA on the Reclamation of Jakarta's North Coast) (paper presented at a seminar organized by LP3ES, Jakarta, 27 January 2004).
34. "PTUN Jakarta Perintahkan PLN Tunda Tender Ulang," *Kompas*, August 1, 2000; "Kalangan DPR tak Setuju Dana APBN untuk OPIC," *Kompas*, August 8, 2000; "Sidang Lapangan Perambahan TNGL Hakim Dihadang Massa," *Kompas*, March 6,

2000; "Soal Dana Yatim Piatu: 43 Pengacara PTUN-kan Gubernur dan DPRD Massa," *Kompas*, October 12, 2000; "Pemda-PDRD akan Naikkan Tarif Parkir," *Kompas*, May 16, 2002.

35. As I have argued elsewhere, the Supreme Court has to blame itself to a large extent for the present situation by its own inconsistency in judging: Bedner, *Administrative Courts in Indonesia,* 216–17. See also Pompe, *The Indonesia Supreme Court*, 428–38.
36. "Wawancara: Paulus E. Lotulung: Hakim PTUN Tak Usah Takut Kehilangan Perkara," *Hukumonline*, January 17, 2006, http://www.hukumonline.com/detail.asp?id = 14224&cl = Wawancara
37. According to the Director of Harmonization of Law from the Department of Justice, Wicipto Setiadi, the draft has been developed in cooperation with the German Development Agency, GTZ, and because of its having been oriented on German administrative law it contains a number of mismatches with the Law on Administrative Courts. These need to be resolved first before the draft can proceed to the next stage: Wicipto Setiadi, (Director of Harmonization of Law, Department of Justice), in discussion with the author, September 2006.
38. Bedner, *Administrative Courts in Indonesia*, 42.
39. These included formal carefulness, fair play, justification, formal legal certainty, substantive legal certainty, trust, equality, substantive carefulness and proportionality.
40. Case No. 10/K/TUN/1992.
41. See also Pompe, *The Indonesia Supreme Court*, 252–5.
42. Case No. 54/G/BPTUN-Bdg./1993.
43. Indroharto, *Usaha Memahami Undang-Undang Tentang Peradilan Tata Usaha Negara. Buku II: Beracara di Pengadilan Tata Usaha Negara* (An Attempt at Understanding the Act on Administrative Courts. Book II: Conducting a Procedure at the Administrative Court), 179.
44. The hearing principle means that the government official concerned must provide an interested party the opportunity to be heard before he or she may take a decision which may be harmful to this party's interests. The principle of trust refers to the situation that a citizen may trust on the expectations raised by an official regarding the legality of certain behaviour or the outcome of a procedure to take a certain decision. This principle may be even applied *contra legem*. Bedner, *Administrative Courts in Indonesia*, 99–100; J. Hamidi, *Penerapan Asas-asas Umum Penyelenggaraan Pemerintahan Yang Layak (AAUPPL) Di Lingkungan Peradilan Administrasi Indonesia* (The Application of General Principles of Proper Administration (GPPR) within the Scope of Indonesian Administrative Litigation) (Bandung: Citra Aditya Bakti, 1999), 146–56.
45. The principle of 'public interest', also listed in the Elucidation of the *Anti-Corruption Act*, has been left out of the list. The reason probably is that if the administrative court could apply this as a ground for review, it would become a 'full' review of the efficiency of the administrative decision at stake instead of only a 'marginal appreciation'. The drafters of the administrative court amendment have apparently not considered the practice of the Administrative Courts developed thus far, but they have certainly made sure that such wide powers were not given to the Administrative Courts.
46. Bedner, *Administrative Courts in Indonesia*, 112.
47. Case No. 15K/TUN/1992. It seems that this court ruling is generally followed. This is not surprising if we take into account that an important reason for judges to disregard jurisdiction or remedial limitations is improper – meaning that they have received a bribe from one of the parties. In cases where they have granted suspension for such reasons, common sense dictates that they will make sure that this party will also win the case.
48. See for instance, Case No. 140/G/1992/PTUN-Jkt.
49. Case No. 140/G/1991 /PTUN-Jkt.

50. Case No. 45/G/1993/PTUN-Jkt.
51. Interview with an employee of the plaintiff, October 1994.
52. A fact she attributed to the unfairness of the auction procedure, where according to her usually secret deals had been concluded by the participants: Interview with the plaintiff, October 1994.
53. This is a rather technical issue, as in principle the general court could allow compensation of a non-monetary nature. In fact, there are several precedents where the general courts quashed government decisions on the basis of government tort, for instance a housing permit (Case No. 278/1953 in *Yurisprudensi Indonesia Tentang Perbuatan Melanggar Hukum Oleh Penguasa (Onrechtmatige Overheidsdaad): Tahun 1950 s\d Tahun 1977* (Indonesian Case Law on Government Tort: 1950–77), ed. C. Ali (Bandung: Binacipta, 1978) or an eviction order (Case No. 95/K/Sip/1962 in *Yurisprudensi Indonesia Tentang Perbuatan Melanggar Hukum Oleh Penguasa (Onrechtmatige Overheidsdaad): Tahun 1950 s\d Tahun 1977* (Indonesian Case Law on Government Tort: 1950–77), ed. C. Ali (Bandung: Binacipta, 1978). Other examples can be found in the same collection of cases.
54. *Administrative Courts Act* art. 116–2. This issue raises all kinds of problems concerning the consequences of the annulment. It is unclear whether a decision must have been assumed to have never existed, or that it must be supposed to have been legal *until* it lost its legal force. This has important consequences for determining damages in particular, but as yet no legal doctrine on this matter has been developed.
55. Indroharto, *Usaha Memahami Undang-Undang Tentang Peradilan Tata Usaha Negara. Buku I: Beberapa Pengertian Dasar Hukum Tata Usaha Negara* (An Attempt at Understanding the Act on Administrative Courts. Book I: Some Understandings of the Legal Basis of Administrative Litigation), 245–6.
56. See Case No. 04/G/TUN/1994/PTUN-Smg.; Case No. 25/G/PTUN-Bdg./1993; Case No. 06/G/TUN/1994/PTUN-Smg.
57. Bedner, *Administrative Courts in Indonesia*, 47.
58. It is, moreover, exceedingly difficult to calculate the amount of damage incurred because of the above-mentioned problems in determining the day from which the litigated decision must be deemed to have lost its legal consequences.
59. Bedner, *Administrative Courts in Indonesia*, 47.
60. I. Fachruddin, *Pengawasan Peradilan Administrasi Terhadap Tindakan Pemerintah* (Supervision of Government Actions by Administrative Litigation) (Bandung: P. T.Alumni, 2004).
61. There were 167 appeals from 321 cases from 1991–5.
62. These data derive from the Steering Committee on the Commercial Court and Preparations for the Establishment of the Anticorruption Court, *Blueprint and Action Plan for the Establishment of the Anticorruption Court* (Jakarta: National Development Planning Agency of the Republic of Indonesia, 2004).
63. Bedner, *Administrative Courts in Indonesia*, 191 Hamidi, *Penerapan Asas-asas Umum Penyelenggaraan Pemerintahan Yang Layak (AAUPPL) Di Lingkungan Peradilan Administrasi Indonesia* (The Application of General Principles of Proper Administration (GPPR) within the Scope of Indonesian Administrative Litigation), 171–3.
64. Bedner, *Administrative Courts in Indonesia*, 230–2.
65. Fachruddin, *Pengawasan Peradilan Administrasi Terhadap Tindakan Pemerintah* (Supervision of Government Actions by Administrative Litigation).
66. Unfortunately, no research is available to provide any insight into how plaintiffs evaluate their experiences in the Administrative Courts, or why they made their decision to go to court in the first place.
67. Case No. 8/G/PTUN-Bdg./1995 jo. no. 68/B/1995/PT.TUN.Jkt. jo. no. 285K/TUN/1995; Case No. 12/G/PTUN-Bdg./1995 jo. no. 02/B/1996/PT.TUN.Jkt. jo. no. 310/K/TUN/1999; Case No. 27/G/PTUN-Bdg./1994 jo. no. 41/B/1994/PT.TUN.Jkt.

jo. no. 108K/TUN/1994 jo. no. 14PK/TUN/1996); Case No. 60/G/PTUN-Bdg./1997 jo. no. 60/B/1998/PT.TUN.Jkt. jo. no. 277K/TUN/1998.

68. Case No. 59/G/PTUN-Bdg./1995 jo. no. 145/B/1996/PT.TUN.Jkt. jo. no. 240K/TUN/1997.
69. Case No. 42/G/PTUN-Bdg./1999.
70. In both cases the defendant was no party to the original dispute.
71. Case No. 68/G/PTUN-Bdg./1999 jo. no. 109/B/2000/PT.TUN.Jkt. jo. no. 152K/TUN/2001.
72. Case No. 100/G/PEN/2000/PTUN-Bdg. jo. no. 100/G/PTUN-Bdg./2000.
73. Case No. 10/G/PTUN-Bdg./1995 jo. no. 88/B/1995/PT.TUN.Jkt. jo. no. 91K/TUN/1996.
74. Case No. 18/G/2001/PTUN-Bdg.
75. Case No. 62/G/PTUN-Bdg./1995.
76. Case No. 74/G/PTUN-Bdg/1996 jo. no. 38/B/1998/PT.TUN.Jkt. jo. no. 210 K/TUN/1998. The reason the plaintiffs sought the annulment of the certificate was that they wanted to stay married after all, so now they had to marry again.
77. Case No. 52/G/PTUN-Bdg./1995 jo. no. 132/B/1996/PT.TUN-Jkt. jo. no. 340 K/TUN/1998.
78. Case No. 18/G/PTUN-Bdg./1998 jo. no. 178/B/1998/PT.TUN-Jkt.jo. no. 359 K/TUN/1999.
79. Case No. 161/G.TUN/1999/PTUN-Jkt. jo. no. 103/B/2000/PT.TUN.Jkt. jo. no. 66K/TUN/2001.
80. Case No. 17/G/PTUN-Bdg./1998 jo. no. 06/B/PT.TUN.Jkt. jo. no. 358K/TUN/1999.
81. Case No. 46/G/PTUN-Bdg./1999 jo. no. 66/B/2000/PT.TUN.Jkt. jo. no. 289 K/TUN/2001.
82. Fachruddin provides data on this matter for most, though not all of them. Three concerned the appointment of plaintiffs as members of the Provincial Parliament of West Java (Case no. 64/G/1999/PTUN-Bdg. jo. no. 69/B/2000/PT.TUN-Jkt. jo. no. 207K/TUN/2001; Case no. 64/ PEN/G/1999/PTUN-Bdg.; no. 80/G/2000/PTUN-Bdg.), one a document providing data on a piece of land (Case no. 18/G/PTUN-Bdg./1994), one concerning the revocation of a nuisance license (Case no. 58/G/PEN/1998/PTUN-Bdg. and Case no. 58/G/PTUN-Bdg./1998),
83. *Administrative Court Act* art. 116–4.
84. *Administrative Court Act* art. 39A-E.
85. F. H. Winarta, "Pelaksanann Putusan PTUN dan Perwujudan 'Civil Society'," (The Execution of Administrative Court Judgments and the Formation of 'Civil Society') *Sinar Harapan*, May 26, 2004, http://www.sinarharapan.co.id/berita/0407/26/opi01.html

11 Genealogy of the administrative courts and consolidation of administrative justice in Thailand*

Peter Leyland

Introduction

Thailand's constitutional narrative over the past 80 years has been extremely turbulent, but viewed from a different perspective it is possible to identify the antecedents of the contemporary Thai state originating from the reign of King Chulalongkorn (Rama V) (1868–1910). In particular, the foundations of the modern bureaucracy were laid down during a pre-constitutional era at national and local level and the Council of State from which the modern Administrative Courts originated was introduced in 1874. During the course of the twentieth century, Thailand acquired a substantial permanent civil service,[1] and with it an effective functional administrative mechanism for implementing policy, but only a limited range of administrative remedies were open to its citizens.[2] It is against this background that a national system of administrative courts was launched as one of the important innovations of the 1997 *Constitution of the Kingdom of Thailand* (*Constitution*). However, it was because there was already an existing Thai Council of State, closely modelled on the French example, that it was possible to have a system of courts up and running within four years. Indeed, this reform as it has been drafted might be regarded as part of a continuing modernization which replicates the institutional characteristics and principles of established Western European models. Put another way, there are few, if any, features of the new system of administrative justice which display obvious autochthonous Thai characteristics relating to Thailand's traditional law.[3]

The discussion in this chapter begins with locating administrative justice in Thailand's historical context by assessing the relevance of the reforms of Rama V as well as considering the impact of the transition to a form of constitutional rule in 1932. In particular, we will see that administrative courts were eventually established under Thailand's 1997 *Constitution* as part of an ambitious attempt to provide the institutional basis for democracy and good governance. The next section explores the concept of a grievance chain in Thailand. This reveals that the Administrative Courts have been located as part of a hierarchical system of justice, which includes the Constitutional Court, the ordinary courts, the Office of the Thai Ombudsman as well as other less formal methods of grievance resolution, such as an arbitration service. In the following section the issue of the independence of these courts is assessed, with reference to salaries and the arrangements for the appointment and dismissal of judges, before turning to consider their judicial character which is defined in terms of the extent of the court's jurisdiction, some basic procedures, the grounds of review and the nature of the remedies at their disposal. Finally, the contribution of the Administrative Courts is assessed with reference to available data indicating the throughput of cases.

The Thai historical context

The historical antecedents of a modern Thai administrative state have been traced back to King Rama V. As David Wyatt has explained it was in his reign that:

> the entire structure of modern Thailand was brought into being – almost literally from scratch – and a traditional Southeast Asian kingdom, ringed by dependent tributary states, was transformed into a modern nation. Provincial administration was brought under centralized direction and control and serviced by specialized functional ministries staffed by competent specialists. Modern law codes were drafted and put into force by administrators, judges, and lawyers.[4]

The Council of State in its embryonic form was introduced early in the reign of King Rama V as an advisory council modelled on the French *Conseil d'Etat* to assist in exercising control over the King's most prominent ministries.[5] This initiative was taken against the background of a factional struggle within the royal palace, which saw the King, shortly after his accession, having to deal with opposition from the old guard within the royal court.[6] The Council was staffed with a carefully selected group of loyal and progressive senior officials of *Phraya* rank.[7] Under King Rama V the Council of State worked alongside the Privy Council, which was also formed in 1874, and which had overlapping personnel and functions. At the same time, the functional reorganization of ministries and departments based in Bangkok was part of reforming the Thai bureaucracy.[8]

The Council of State was conceived as a powerful tool to be placed in the King's hands, which could be used as a mechanism for the consolidation of centralized power and as an advisory body to help implement royal policy. At the same time the Council of State accepted petitions from citizens who had a grievance against any administrative organ of the state. It thereby assumed a role in improving the administrative process, and it was this adjudicative function in relation to grievances which was recently given to Thailand's Administrative Courts. In addition, the Council of State has made a pivotal contribution to the Thai system of law and administration; after it emerged as the agency responsible for drafting legislation. The law drafting department that was established under King Rama VI to revise Thailand's legal codes was transferred from the Ministry of Justice to the Council of State following the abolition of absolute monarchy in 1932. In coordinating the drafting of laws the Council of State assisted in the consolidation of centralized power, but it also maintained its petitioning function, which meant that it played a major part in containing the abuse of official power. Following the abdication of King Rama VII and the introduction of the first Thai *Constitution*, the Council of State was officially recognized under the *Council of State Act* 1933 as falling under the Office of Prime Minister.[9] Further, the Act outlined the structure and competence of the Council of State as being equivalent to that of the French *Conseil d'Etat*.[10]

In the second quarter of the twentieth century, the path towards the Administrative Courts was strongly influenced by the politician and scholar, Pridi Banomyong, who was, in part at least, responsible for drafting Thailand's first *Constitution*. In his writings Pridi displayed knowledge of European and the Japanese constitutional systems. In addition, he explained the distinction between constitutional law and administrative law. For him, the former lays down general principles and supreme powers in the country, while the latter codifies the regulations and procedures of the executive or administrative powers in detail, and deals with the use of those powers. Pridi pointed out that there were already many laws which regulated the practices of the administration, particularly in the areas of policing, social welfare and the economy.[11] In a wider sense, administrative law was thus understood in terms of the law relating to the administration or the government (*kan pokkhrong*).[12] French legal theory had already taught Pridi that the 'legislative power and the judicial power should be separate from the executive power, because if they were combined it may lead to injustice. In other words, those adjudicating are adjudicating on laws which they themselves legislated'.[13]

After the implementation of the Pridi reforms, an aggrieved citizen had a number of options available. A case could be taken against an administrative official in the ordinary courts. A right of appeal to a court against the administrative act or order might be available. A petition could be issued against the superior of an administrative official if wrongdoing was suspected. Finally, it was possible to petition to the King directly.[14] The introduction of administrative law meant that if an administrative order was wrong, a process of petitioning to the Council of State would have become available. In order to perform these dual functions the staff of the Council of State were divided into two categories: law councillors whose primary function was statutory drafting; and petition councillors who were entrusted to adjudicate administrative cases as prescribed by law.[15] From the 1930s when this upheaval was taking place until relatively recently, it was much too costly to introduce an administrative court, and therefore, the existing system of administrative appeals was expanded into the Petition Council of the Office of State to deal with the administrative cases that arose.

Thailand's constitutions

Since the end of absolute monarchy in 1932,[16] Thailand has been very unstable politically. Not only has there been an extraordinary number of constitutions (18 to date), but periods of civilian government have alternated with phases of military rule. It is significant that the Administrative Courts were set up under the 1997 *Constitution*. Many commentators considered that this reform might be an important turning point in the direction of liberal democratic rule.[17] The influence of the generals appeared to be in decline by the end of the 1980s but yet another military coup in 1991 failed to deliver an immediate transition to civilian rule. Street demonstrations for democracy were brutally suppressed. By this time the Bangkok business and urban class demanded a restoration of civilian rule and there were wider calls for political reform.[18] The abrupt onset of a severe economic crisis in the mid-1990s[19] made it very difficult for the established element to resist proposals for constitutional reform, which had resulted from a much more broad-based drafting process based on popular consultation.[20] At this point 'Bangkok's businessmen and middle class began to blame the crisis on mismanagement by politicians, and seized on the Constitution as the way to bring politics into line with the needs of the globalized economy'.[21]

The onset of this sudden economic crisis prompted the introduction of the 1997 *Constitution*.[22] At the time it was adopted, optimism about its effectiveness arose from the fact that as a radically improved constitutional text,[23] it contained many provisions which genuinely seemed to offer a new way forward.[24] For example, the 1997 *Constitution* introduced measures designed to guarantee democracy and human rights, exclude military influence in the political process and eliminate corruption in public life. To achieve these goals a new set of watchdog organizations was set up under the *Constitution*, which have been the subject of much discussion.[25] The Election Commission, the National Counter-Corruption Commission, the Anti-Money-Laundering Office and the State Audit Commission were each designed to tackle particular aspects of malfeasance and corruption associated with politics. Meanwhile, the Human Rights Commission was intended to deal with abuses of group rights and individual human rights. In the domain of law and administration, a system of administrative courts and an ombudsman were introduced for the first time, to further protect citizens' rights by extending the range of remedies available. Finally, the entire constitutional scheme was patrolled by a constitutional court.

A bloodless military coup on 19 September 2006 resulted in the abrogation of the 1997 *Constitution* and the imposition of martial law. A temporary constitution was set in place during this period of military rule, but the generals kept their promise to hand back power to a civilian government under a newly drafted constitution. The 2007 *Constitution* was approved by referendum in August 2007 and it came into force at the beginning of 2008, following a general election held in December 2007. The institutional reforms, including the watchdog bodies mentioned above and the Administrative Courts, which were established under the 1997 *Constitution*, continued to operate during the interim period, and all these bodies were included as part of the 2007 *Constitution*.

Administrative justice and the Thai legal process

In assessing the position of the Administrative Courts it is important to be aware of their jurisdictional scope in relation to other courts and the Office of the

Ombudsman. In regard to constitutional issues, the 2007 *Constitution* establishes a Constitutional Court,[26] which consists of a President and eight judges appointed for a nine-year term.[27] A quorum of five judges can preside over cases that come before it.[28] As the judicial body with jurisdiction over many constitutional issues, this Court is vested with formidable powers,[29] some of which are comparable to those exercised by the United States Supreme Court. In this capacity the Thai Constitutional Court under the 1997 *Constitution* was often exposed to political criticism and censure.[30]

The present Constitutional Court is responsible for hearing challenges to draft legislation, statutes and regulations on the grounds of unconstitutionality.[31] The Court also determines matters of overlapping authority between official bodies, including the National Assembly, the Council of Ministers and other non-judicial organs of the state.[32] The Constitutional Court has been designed to operate as a constitutional safeguard, particularly in relation to the protection of civil liberties and human rights.[33] A contentious issue under the 1997 *Constitution* was the resort to emergency decrees in order to circumvent the safeguards under the *Constitution*. The 2007 *Constitution* gives the Constitutional Court the final say in ruling upon the legality of emergency decrees.[34] In addition, the 2007 *Constitution* reinforces the role of the Thai Human Rights Commission by enhancing its legal powers. However, if violations are identified, the Commission has several different options, which bring into play different parts of the legal hierarchy. For example, where the Commission agrees with a complainant that a law (statutory provision) conflicts with a citizen's rights, the matter can be referred to the Constitutional Court. However, where it is a regulation, order, or administrative act that conflicts with a person's right, the determination of legality lies with the Administrative Courts. Finally, the Human Rights Commission must resort to the ordinary courts to secure legal correction of any rights violation against an individual.[35] In principle, under the 2007 *Constitution* any citizen who considers that his or her rights have been violated by any 'State organ or State agency' is able to make a challenge on grounds of constitutionality before the Constitutional Court. This constitutional provision potentially opens up the system to widespread challenges, but this has been made a remedy of last resort, to the extent that the claimant must first exhaust all other existing remedies, which might include the right to take a case to the Administrative Courts.[36]

The 2007 *Constitution* has recalibrated authority between the Constitutional Court, the Administrative Courts and the ordinary courts by placing the Constitutional Court above all other jurisdictions on nearly all constitutional issues.[37] Should controversial political disputes arise, attention will be focused on the even smaller cohort of nine constitutional court judges.

Thailand has a system of criminal and civil courts. Further, the Administrative Courts have no jurisdiction over matters triable by other specialist courts,[38] matters of military discipline and matters falling under the remit of the Judicial Commission.[39] Where there is a dispute as to the jurisdictional limits of the Administrative Court, the outcome is determined by a special committee comprising of the President of the Supreme Court of Justice, the President of the Supreme Administrative Court and the President of the other court involved.[40]

In addition to the ordinary courts, Thailand has a well-developed system of informal justice / alternative dispute resolution, and particularly of arbitration, which is available through the Thai Arbitration Institute (TAI),[41] or under a scheme run by the Board of Trade. The recent *Arbitration Act* 2002 in the main recognizes United Nations Commission on International Trade Law (UNCITRAL) model law.[42] The arbitration approach offers a less formal process by diverting cases from the ordinary courts.[43] This model (usually binding) arbitration clause forms part of an agreement. Additionally, arbitration also offers greatly reduced costs should there be a dispute. Normally, fees and expenses will be paid by the parties as specified in the award. Otherwise, the parties may request a court order to determine fees, expenses and remuneration of the arbitrator.[44] TAI and the Board of Trade have a specified rate which may be charged for their schemes.[45]

Finally, the Office of the Ombudsman[46] (referred to hereafter as the Ombudsman, although there are, in fact, three Thai Ombudsmen in post) was conceived as *one* of several watchdog bodies that were custom-designed under the 1997 *Constitution* to exercise a specialized oversight function.[47] In this regard the Ombudsman was intended to work alongside the watchdog bodies listed above. Additionally, the Ombudsman was granted a special role, in relation to the referral of matters to the Constitutional Court and the Administrative Courts for formal legal resolution, acting as a special guardian of the *Constitution* itself.[48] In addition to dealing with routine administrative shortcomings, the pressing reason for introducing an ombudsman in Thailand has been to combat the endemic corruption, which has had the effect of undermining not only the efficient running of government, but also public confidence in the entire system of administration.[49] It was envisaged that the introduction of an independent ombudsman with formidable investigatory powers would extend beyond complaint handling and amount to another weapon in the armoury for tackling the particular forms of corruption associated with central and local government in Thailand.

The Thai Ombudsman is empowered to consider and investigate complaints when an official at any level of government violates the law or exceeds the jurisdiction of his or her authority.[50] The Ombudsman is also empowered to investigate when the action or inaction of a public body or official causes harm, damage or injustice to an individual or to the general public, whether or not this action or inaction by the public body or official is within his or her jurisdiction, and regardless of whether the action is in breach of the law. In addition, the Ombudsman is competent to look into the 'performance of or omission to perform duties ... which unjustly causes injuries to the complainant or the public' notwithstanding whether or not the action has been lawful.[51] In other words, a wide jurisdiction has been granted to the Thai Ombudsman. It encompasses routine complaints associated in other nations with the concept of maladministration,[52] it extends also to questions of legality,[53] and goes beyond legal questions to allow investigation of injustice and unfairness. As a result, there is considerable potential for overlap with the role of the Administrative Courts. The essential difference lies in the types of role the respective bodies perform; with the Ombudsman able to undertake investigations, recommend remedial action and refer matters on to other bodies to pursue further. The Administrative Courts lack an investigatory role, but they have at their disposal a wide range of legal remedies. As with the Administrative Courts, the Office of the Ombudsman has continued to operate following the military coup in 2006. This constitutional apparatus was introduced in recognition of the need to introduce far-reaching controls over the exercise of public power, and it appears that these institutions have been established as permanent fixtures under whatever constitution is in force.

The character of Thailand's administrative courts

In the face of opposition from elements in the existing judiciary, the 1997 *Constitution* fulfilled the aspirations of a previous generation[54] with the introduction of a specialized system of administrative courts in addition to the ordinary courts.[55] The Administrative Courts were designed to fill a particular gap in the grievance chain by offering full legal redress against official bodies. They were set up by statute in 1999[56] and began operating in 2001, replacing the Petition Council of the Council of State. Prior to their introduction citizens sometimes had a right of appeal to a court against an administrative act or order. Also, a petition could be issued against the superior of an administrative official if wrongdoing was suspected. Finally, it was possible to petition the King directly.[57]

A two-tier Administrative Court system was introduced: the Supreme Administrative Court and Administrative Courts of first instance (comprising the Central Administrative Court for Bangkok and provinces local to Bangkok, and the Regional Administrative Courts).[58] The characteristics of the Administrative Courts and the limits of their jurisdiction can be distinguished from the ordinary courts and from other means of redress that are available under the *Constitution*. The Supreme Administrative Court, apart from acting as an appellate court, hearing appeals from judgments of the Administrative Court of first instance, exercises a jurisdiction which is directed at issues relating to the operation of central government. For example, it has competence to try cases concerning the legality of royal decrees or by-laws issued by the Council of Ministers. It also tries cases involving disputes in relation to decisions of a quasi-judicial council (as prescribed by the general assembly of judges of the Supreme Court).[59]

Issues of independence and separation of powers

An effective separation of powers between the executive and judicial branches is central to providing judicial independence. However, what is meant by judicial independence in the context of the Thai legal system? The originators of modern conceptualizations of the separation of powers sought to conceive a system of checks which would ensure that power vested in governors cannot be turned to personal advantage and that the personalized rule by men is replaced by the impersonal rule of rules. It was further recognized that this required 'an independent judiciary acting as a bulwark against executive power. It is this aspect of the rule of law which is critical in distinguishing between liberal and despotic regimes.'[60] In practical terms the result is that the judiciary requires first 'a set of relatively clear and general rules which can establish an impartial system and, secondly, independence to apply the law without fear or favour'.[61]

There are a number of ways in which judicial independence is relevant. In a macro-constitutional sense this independence is most apparent when the judicial branch is seen to be separated from, and thus independent of, the executive branch. Since under most constitutional and legal provisions in most nations, judicial appointments ultimately have to be approved by the executive branch and the judicial personnel are remunerated from public funds, it is obvious that isolating the judicial branch from political and economic considerations is never entirely straightforward.[62]

The *Constitution* coupled with the legislation introducing the Administrative Courts include elaborate provisions to establish the independence of the court's judges.[63] The court administration is clearly separated from the executive and made independent from any government department.[64] A Judicial Commission of the Administrative Courts is responsible for disciplinary matters and promotion.[65] Any resolutions for dismissal, for malfeasance in office, gross disciplinary breach or imprisonment for a serious offence can only go ahead after an investigation by a specially formed committee comprising, among others, of four judges of the Supreme Administrative Court who have reported on the matter.[66]

Important safeguards have been set in place in a number of ways to guarantee that the Administrative Courts are staffed by a cohort of professional judges. Judges are appointed to the Administrative Court by the Judicial Commission of the Administrative Courts until their retirement. The salaries of judges are protected.[67] To prevent interference once a case has commenced, judges cannot be taken off a case once they have been assigned to it.[68] The application requirements to the court are rigorous. In order to be nominated as an Administrative Court judge, candidates must be Thai nationals over 35 years old with appropriate academic qualifications. In addition, they must have relevant experience.[69] There are complex procedures for the dismissal of judges, which are placed in the hands of a judicial commission.[70] For the Supreme Administrative Court the age limit is 45 years and candidates must have served as a law councillor, petition councillor or councillor of state.[71] Conflicts of interest are prohibited under Section 14.[72] Such stringent requirements limit the pool of possible appointees to suitably qualified candidates. Courts must not only meet certain age requirements and qualifications, but they also need to demonstrate relevant experience. Furthermore, administrative judges are specialists who only hear cases in the Administrative Courts. The system thus differs from the situation in England and Wales where the panel of High Court judges who staff the Administrative Court have legal training and experience but are not specialists in public administration, and these judges for part of the year will also hear a range of cases with entirely different subject matter as part of their assigned workload.

In order to form a professional cadre of judges who are unlikely to be tempted into corrupt practices, and at the same time attract candidates of sufficiently high calibre, it is essential that the incumbents are adequately remunerated. The salary levels for Administrative Court judges at 550,200 *baht* per annum (approximately £8500) and supreme court judges at 709,080 *baht* per annum (approximately £11,000) may appear relatively modest by European standards, but these figures represent a substantial salary in terms of the cost of living and the pay levels in the public domain granted to high-ranking Thai officials.[73] Nevertheless, public sector salaries are a sensitive subject in Thailand, and it should be stressed that the alleged 'self-award' of pay increases by independent watchdog bodies without obtaining parliamentary approval (including the Constitutional Court and the Administrative Courts) has been subject to far-reaching and continuing controversy, which has encouraged an emerging scepticism over the constitutional reform programme.[74]

Susceptibility to political interference crops up at a later stage in the appointments' process, because the appointment of the President of the Supreme Administrative Court requires that a candidate is first nominated by the Commission, after which approval by the Senate is required before the name is submitted to the King for final approval.[75] At this stage interference is possible in the form of opposition to particular candidates from private individuals or business interests exerting an influence. For example, a nominated candidate with a reputation for protecting the natural environment could find resistance from businesses that consider their interests might be affected by environmentally friendly judgments. Cases in the Administrative Courts of first instance are heard by a panel of three judges and in the Supreme Administrative Court by five judges.[76]

The public/private law distinction

It is commonly assumed that administrative courts are fundamentally concerned with the accountability of public bodies and the containment of public power (as well as having other responsibilities, e.g. over administrative contracts and tort claims against public bodies) and, given this assumption, the reach of any public law jurisdiction becomes a question of crucial importance.[77] A separate public law jurisdiction has been justified on the basis that the state should have a monopoly over the exercise of certain types of coercive power: in particular, the creation and enforcement of laws relating to the capacity of the state to act as an instrument of social regulation.[78] Thailand's French connection[79] has contributed to the local conceptualization of a distinct public law which is associated with: designing state organizations; ascribing varying degrees of importance to state agencies and state officials in regard to members of the public; and formulating criteria and measures for controlling the discharge of state organs and officials.[80] In many European nations it has been increasingly recognized that any public/private distinction has been made more problematic by the emergence of a 'contracting state' in which there is expanding private sector involvement; for example, in the delivery of public services which were formerly provided by government and local government,[81] as well as the privatization of formerly state-run industries, and the reliance on private companies to construct and manage many publicly financed enterprises.[82] Thailand is a nation which has also seen trends towards privatization and a contracting state and the Thai Administrative Courts have been introduced as the most potent constitutional mechanism designed to regulate the exercise of these aspects of public power. As a result, a restricted definition of what constitutes public law matters falling under the ambit of the Administrative Court would have limited the application of public law remedies and would have excluded judicial supervision over functions formerly exercised by the state which now are manifested in a private form.[83]

How then do the courts approach the task of determining their jurisdictional boundaries? In assessing a claim the court must decide whether the contested matter has a sufficient public law dimension to fall under its jurisdiction.[84] In cases where this issue is contestable the judge will consider: (1) whether the body/enterprise/individual is providing a public service; and (2) whether a public power is being exercised – the test employed asks whether a power has been granted that would not be granted or exercised in the private sector; (3) whether the body/enterprise or individual is exercising a public service function.[85]

From the reported case law it appears that the courts have defined ‘public’ broadly. For example, the court has heard cases involving privatized state enterprises which provide a universal service and it has ruled that the Telephone Organisation of Thailand (TOT) remained an administrative agency subject to the jurisdiction of the Administrative Courts.[86] The role of the *Tribunal des Conflits* in deciding contested matters of jurisdiction is closely replicated by the Thai Jurisdictional Conflict Tribunal which adjudicates when such disputes arise in the Thai legal context.[87] By way of comparison it is worth remembering that the major justification for the exclusivity principle as part of the modern law of judicial review in England and Wales was the introduction of both a special procedure and specially designed remedies.[88]

Powers, procedure and remedies

It is significant that wide-ranging grounds of intervention have been granted to the Administrative Courts which include: the power to grant a remedy if a public body is acting without or beyond the scope of its powers and duties; if it is behaving inconsistently with the law; or there has been conduct amounting to undue exercise of discretion.[89] An application can be made to the Court over an alleged neglect of duty or unreasonable delay.[90] Equally, the Court can be required to adjudicate over a ‘wrongful act or other liability’[91] associated with the administration or state official in the discharge of legal duties.[92] In this sense the Administrative Court has a jurisdiction which potentially overlaps with that of the Ombudsman. Indeed, the Ombudsman is specifically empowered to refer matters to the court if, in the course of an investigation, he or she believes that any by-law or act of an administrative agency is unlawful.[93] Additionally, a matter can be referred to the Court by an administrative agency or state official to force a person or body to do a particular act prescribed by law or to prevent either from acting contrary to the law.[94] Finally, the Thai Administrative Courts took over the jurisdiction previously exercised by the Court of Justice and the Petition Council for disputes relating to administrative contracts.[95] Contracts concerned with the management of public services, or to do with public construction projects, are usually considered administrative in character.[96]

Given the strong influence of the French *droit administratif*, it is not surprising that in Thailand there is an inquisitorial style of court procedure and a continental system of law based on legal codes.[97] This means that case law has a different status in comparison with common law systems whereby important decisions are reported in detail and the higher courts bind the lower courts on decided questions of law, so that the doctrine of *stare decisis* operates.

The Thai Administrative Court is in possession of formidable powers when it comes to granting remedies,[98] and many of the remedies it is able to award are tailored to an administrative law context. The court can issue a decree revoking a by-law or an order.[99] It can also revoke an act in whole or part where it is alleged that an administrative agency or state official has done an unlawful act under Section 9(1) of the *Act on Establishment of Administrative Court and Administrative Procedure* 1999. Furthermore, the court can direct whether any such decree is going to be retrospective or non-retrospective. In addition, the Administrative Courts have powers which roughly correspond to the mandatory orders and injunctive relief available under English or common law systems. They are granted powers to order the performance of a duty or order a person to act or to refrain from an act in compliance with the law. Moreover, the Court has powers to order the payment of money or the delivery of property.[100]

The Thai system departs from the French system most obviously in the way these far-reaching powers are set out. The decisions of the French Administrative Courts were normally obeyed without any need for enforcement, but reforms were introduced to allow a follow-up to judgments where a decision has not been implemented, for example, *astreinte*.[101] The lack of enforceable remedies in France used to be viewed by some commentators as an obvious weakness.[102]

In Thailand, recourse to the Administrative Court is considered as a remedy of last resort that will only be available if other available avenues of redress have been exhausted.[103] Following an application to the Court there is judicial discretion which determines whether a case will proceed.[104] Another feature of the Thai system allows an official of the Office of the Ombudsman to take up a case on a claimant's behalf in the Administrative Courts.[105] In this sense the Administrative Court can be regarded as a body that lines up alongside the other organs of the state, which have been designed to act as watchdog bodies at a number of different levels. Causing unnecessary process or excessive burden to the public is recognized as a ground of review in its own right.[106] Additionally, a matter can be referred to the Court by an administrative agency or state official to force a person or body to do a particular act prescribed by law or to prevent either from acting contrary to the law.[107]

In sum, it will be apparent from the discussion in this section that the Thai Administrative Court has a wide jurisdiction that allows it to oversee the administration at central and local government levels.[108]

The performance of the administrative courts

Since its inception in 2001, the impact of the Court can be assessed in two ways. First, there are some statistics available relating to its workload. Second, it is possible to highlight particular cases with political, constitutional or legal significance, which have tested the independence of the Court. Turning first to raw statistics of referrals, the figures reveal a significant case-load.[109] Between March 2001 and 31 December 2006 a total of 26,689 cases have been referred to the Courts of first instance concerning the ministries set out in Table 11.1, which also

Table 11.1 Ministries subject to litigation before the Administrative Court since its formation to 31 December 2006

No.	*Administrative Court* / *Ministerial departments attacked*	*Central Administrative Court*	*Chiang Mai Administrative Court*	*Songkhla Administrative Court*	*Nakhon Ratchasima Administrative Court*	*Khon Kaen Administrative Court*	*Phitsanulok Administrative Court*	*Rayong Administrative Court*	*Nakhon Si Thammarat Administrative Court*	*Total*
1	Ministry of Interior	4,852	1,106	1,090	1,130	599	736	33	404	9,950
2	Ministry of Education	2,298	341	181	292	328	153	0	65	3,658
3	Ministry of Transport	2,350	188	262	87	96	125	38	144	3,290
4	Ministry of Agriculture	1,631	166	387	86	236	373	6	54	2,939
5	Office of Prime Minister and ministerial departments directly reported to the Prime Minister	2,561	44	8	47	131	24	13	72	2,900
6	Ministry of Finance	1,636	59	50	36	50	35	1	16	1,883
7	Ministry of Public Health	541	63	38	36	44	35	6	35	798
8	Ministry of Justice	404	15	23	34	25	19	83	6	609
9	Ministry of Labour	275	23	8	14	10	10	0	7	347
10	Ministry of Defence	250	14	6	28	2	10	0	5	315
	Total	16,798	2,019	2,053	1,790	1,521	1,520	180	808	26,689

shows the distribution of cases taken against the various government departments and public bodies.

The figures reveal that the highest proportion of cases, nearly 10,000, have concerned the Ministry of the Interior; this ministry includes the Land Department, the Department of Local Administration, the Office of the Permanent Secretary of the Interior, and the Department of Town and Country Planning. A total of 2,900 cases have been initiated against the Office of the Prime Minister; this Ministry includes the National Police Bureau, and a fuller breakdown would reveal that actions concerning the police account for the largest share of cases. Finally, it may appear surprising that only 798 cases have been filed against the Office of Public Health. However, these statistics do not reveal the subject matter of these actions. So, for example, it is not possible to discover what proportion of the case-load concerns issues relating to administrative contracts of public employees, as against issues to do with legality, or cases seeking damages against governmental bodies. Furthermore, in some fields there may be overlapping jurisdictions and alternative remedies available. Nevertheless, from these statistics it is apparent that the Administrative Courts have assumed an important role in hearing a substantial number of cases that fall within their jurisdiction. Additional statistical information concerning the throughput of cases of these courts is available in English from the Court's website.[110]

Conclusion

This chapter has concentrated on providing a critical account of the introduction of a formalized system of administrative justice in Thailand. The Thai model has been strongly influenced by the French *droit administratif* and the *Conseil d'Etat*. At one level, the Administrative Courts and the Office of the Ombudsman fill an important gap in the grievance chain, by providing an impressive range of remedies for the aggrieved citizen against public bodies. Moreover, under the 1997 *Constitution* there was a genuine attempt to underline the separation of powers and functions between the executive and judicial branches in order to ensure the independence and the effectiveness of the Administrative Courts. For example, the funding for the Court's administration was ring-fenced and a rigorous system of appointments limited the selection of judges to qualified candidates. Once raised to the bench, these judges have been adequately remunerated.[111]

However, in an unequal society like Thailand, which lacks a comprehensive system of legal aid, access to justice is a crucial issue. Perhaps the ability to pursue matters in the courts may be all the more important to promoting good governance and defending of public institutions against the abuse of power. As noted above, the Thai Ombudsman was granted the right – under the 1997 *Constitution* and related legislation – not only to refer matters to the Constitutional or Administrative Courts, but also to provide formal representation in court. Another possible way forward in the future might be to allow an expanded role for other watchdogs and non-governmental organizations in championing cases where issues of legality and good governance are at stake.[112]

The introduction of the Administrative Courts has resulted in the strengthening of the judicial branch as part of a constitutional order embodying checks and balances. This conference of powers on the courts raises basic questions which are familiar to constitutional commentators.[113] Should the potency of the courts be limited? Do non-elected and non-politically accountable judges lack the legitimacy to frustrate the will of elected politicians?

However, Thailand is a nation where the entire political process has frequently been subverted by the systematic abuse of power, as was widely evident under Prime Minister Thaksin Shaniwatra (2001–6). Indeed, given the record of abuse in Thailand and the problems in embedding democratic government, it is difficult to give credence to claims to political legitimacy that elected politicians rely upon in resisting judicial intervention. On the other hand, the judicial resolution of disputes seldom provides a way for any society to focus clearly on the real issues at stake when there are disagreements about politics and about rights.[114] In the modern, part-privatized contracting state, administrative law relies fundamentally on designing effective schemes of statutory regulation, setting out the respective rights and duties of government, commercial interests and citizens, and enabling judicial oversight. The fact that the Administrative Courts have continued to function as an accepted part of the Thai legal system despite the collapse of their constitutional foundations provides evidence of incremental progress in the creation of institutions capable of defending the rights of Thai citizens.[115] Undoubtedly, the challenge for these Courts under the 2007 *Constitution* will be to consolidate and develop this crucial role.

Acknowledgements

I am very grateful to his honour Judge Dr Vishnu Varunyou of the Administrative Court for supplying me with invaluable information and clarifying many matters during my work on this subject. Also many thanks to Professor Andrew Harding, Professor Tom Ginsburg, Pip Nicholson, Philippa Duffy and Sonja Zivak for their helpful comments on earlier drafts. I would also like to tahnk Anna Razeen for her help with my research. See also P. Leyland, "Droit Administratif Thai Style: A Comparative Analysis of the Administrative Courts in Thailand," *The Australian Journal of Asian Law* 8 (2006): 121–55.

Notes

1. What Girling has described as: 'a colonial-style, centralized, functionally differentiated bureaucratic state'. See J. Girling, *Thailand: Society and Politics* (London: Cornell University Press, 1981), 46.
2. See F. Riggs, *The Modernization of a Bureaucratic Polity* (Honolulu, HI: East West Center Press, 1966).
3. A. Huxley, "Introduction," in *Thai Law: Buddhist Law*, ed. A. Huxley (Bangkok: Orchid Press, 1996), 1–29.
4. D. Wyatt, *Studies in Thai History* (Chiang Mai: Silkworm Books, 1994), 281–2.
5. L. Brown and J. Bell, *French Administrative Law*, 5th edn (Oxford: Oxford University Press, 1998), 6.

6. B. Terwiel, *Thailand's Political History: From the Fall of Ayuthhaya to Recent Times* (River Books: Bangkok, 2005), 178ff.
7. High ranking civil servants were given ranks and title of conferred nobility, 'Phraya' was the next to highest rank.
8. Girling, *Thailand: Society and Politics*, 52.
9. *Council of State Act* 1933 s. 7.
10. *Council of State Act* 1933 ss. 5, 6.
11. C. Baker and P. Phongpaichit, *Pridi by Pridi: Selected Writings on Life, Politics and Economy* (Chiang Mai: Silkworm Press, 2000), 31ff.
12. Ibid, 43ff.
13. Ibid.
14. B. Bhalakula, *Pridi and the Administrative Court* (Bangkok: Office of the Administrative Courts, 2001), 9.
15. Bhalakula, *Pridi and the Administrative Court*, 13
16. C. Baker and P. Phongpaichit, *A History of Thailand* (Cambridge: Cambridge University Press, 2005), 166ff.
17. P. Chambers, *Good Governance, Political Stability and Constitutionalism in Thailand 2002* (Bangkok: King Prajadhipok's Institute, 2002), 16.
18. Baker and Pongpaichit, *A History of Thailand*, 243ff.
19. For further economic and political analysis see Priyambudi Sulistiyanto, *Thailand, Indonesia and Burma in Comparative Perspective* (Aldershot, UK: Ashgate, 2003). In particular see chapter three, "Thailand's Boom," and chapter four "Thailand's Crisis," especially at 103ff.
20. M. Connors, "Framing the 'People's Constitution'," in *Reforming Thai Politics*, ed. D. McCargo (Copenhagen: Nordic Institute of Asian Studies, 2002), 52.
21. Baker and Pongpaichit, *A History of Thailand*, 255.
22. Ibid., 256. See also M. Connors, "From the Abstract Citizen to Concrete Struggle," in *Democracy and National Identity in Thailand*, ed. M. Connors (Copenhagen: Nordic Institute of Asian Studies, 2007), 248–65.
23. Thailand remained a constitutional monarchy, with the King as head of state at the apogee of power (mainly symbolically but also with limited capacity to intervene in certain circumstances), but the 1997 *Constitution* modified the electoral system, changed the composition of both the House of Parliament, and reformed the structure of the courts.
24. A. Harding, "May There be Virtue: 'New Asian Constitutionalism in Thailand'," *Australian Journal of Asian Law* 3 (2001): 24–48.
25. P. Leyland, "Thailand's Constitutional Watchdogs: Dobermans, Bloodhounds, or Lapdogs?," *Journal of Comparative Law* 2 (2007): 151–77.
26. *Constitution of the Kingdom of Thailand* 2007 s. 204.
27. *Constitution of the Kingdom of Thailand* 2007 s. 208.
28. *Act on Establishment of Administrative Court and Administrative Procedure* 1999 s. 54.
29. Under Section 268 of the *Constitution of the Kingdom of Thailand* 1997: 'The decision of the Constitutional Court shall be deemed final and binding on the National Assembly, Council of Ministers, Courts and other State organs'.
30. For example, following a case brought against him alleging corruption, which was decided on 3 August 2001, former Prime Minister, Thaksin Shinawatra, criticized the Constitutional Court and declared that the independent bodies should have their powers curtailed. Moreover, a petition was later filed demanding the removal of four Constitutional Court judges. See Chambers, *Good Governance, Political Stability and Constitutionalism in Thailand 2002*, 28ff.
31. *Constitution of the Kingdom of Thailand* 2007 ss. 154, 212.
32. *Constitution of the Kingdom of Thailand* 2007 s. 214.
33. Under the 1997 *Constitution* the Constitutional Court exercised a very important role in determining controversial constitutional question ranging from the validity of

legislation to the validity of general elections. For an evaluation of this role see A. Harding, "The Constitution Court of Thailand 1998–2006: Turbulent Innovation," in this book.

34. *Constitution of the Kingdom of Thailand* 2007 s. 185.
35. *Constitution of the Kingdom of Thailand* 2007 ss. 257(2), (3), (4).
36. *Constitution of the Kingdom of Thailand* 2007 s. 212.
37. Since the limits of its authority were not defined in the 1997 *Constitution* it was unclear whether the Constitutional Court was placed at the pinnacle of a hierarchy of jurisdictions or merely one jurisdiction among others.
38. *Act on Establishment of Administrative Court and Administrative Procedure* 1999 s. 9(6) sets out the matters falling outside the jurisdiction of the Administrative Courts.
39. The Judicial Commission is an organization established by the Law of Judicial Organisation which deals with administration relating to the judges of the civil and criminal courts.
40. *Constitution of the Kingdom of Thailand* 2007 s. 199.
41. Office of the Judiciary, "Thai Arbitration Institute: Administering Excellence and Due Process," http://www.judiciary.go.th/adro/sub/tai/en/
42. *United Nations Commission on International Trade Law Arbitration Rules*, GA Res 31/98, UN GAOR, 31st Sess., Supp 17, UN Doc A/31/17 (15 December 1976).
43. *Arbitration Act* 2002 s. 6: 'where the provisions of this Act empower the parties to determine any issue, the parties may authorize a third party or institution to make that determination on their behalves'.
44. *Arbitration Act* 2002 s. 46.
45. *Arbitration Act* 2002 s. 47 provides that bodies set up under the act are empowered to prescribe 'fees, expenses and remunerations'.
46. See P. Leyland, "The Ombudsman Principle in Thailand," *Journal of Comparative Law* 2 (2007): 137–51. There had been much earlier proposals to introduce an ombudsman notably as part of the 1975 *Constitution*.
47. The first Thai Ombudsman was appointed in 1999 and there are currently three in post. The *Ombudsman Act* 1999 s. 18 provides 'each shall allocate duties among themselves in order that each may work independently, within agreed parameters'.
48. The *Constitution of Spain* provides an example of an ombudsman (*Defensor del Pueblo*) who is granted standing to bring actions of unconstitutionality. See Article 162 of the *Constitution of Spain* and Article 32 of the *Organic Law No. 2/1979* on the Constitutional Court.
49. See P. Phongpaichit and C. Baker, *Thaksin: The Business of Politics in Thailand* (Chiang Mai: Silkworm Books, 2004), particularly chapters 5, 6 and 7; Pasuk Phongpaichit and Chris Baker, "Thailand's Rotten Politics," *New York Times*, April 14, 2006, 21.
50. *Ombudsman Act* 1999 s. 16.
51. *Ombudsman Act* 1999 s. 16.
52. The term was explained in the United Kingdom Parliament during the debate on the 1967 bill as including: 'bias, neglect, inattention, delay, incompetence, ineptitude, perversity, turpitude, arbitrariness and so on' 734 HC Deb. (5th Series), col. 51.
53. Under Section 197 of the 1997 *Constitution* the Ombudsman is able to inquire into questions of legality coinciding with the review functions of administrative court, namely, a failure of public bodies to perform in compliance with the law or performance beyond their powers and duties as provided by the law.
54. In particular, see Baker and Phongpaichit, *Pridi by Pridi: Selected Writings on Life, Politics and Economy*; Leyland, "Droit Administratif Thai Style: A Comparative Analysis of the Administrative Courts in Thailand," 128.
55. *Constitution of the Kingdom of Thailand* 1997 Part 4, s. 276. It should be noted that Jean-Michel Galabert, former *Président de la section du Rapport et des Études au Conseil d'Etat*, played a part in the introduction of the Thai Administrative Courts.

See Jean-Michel Galabert "The Influence of the Conseil d'Etat Outside France," *International and Comparative Law Quarterly* 49 (2000): 700.

56. *The Act on the Establishment of Administrative Courts and Administrative Courts Procedure* 1999.
57. Bhalakula, *Pridi and the Administrative Court*, 9.
58. *The Act on the Establishment of Administrative Courts and Administrative Courts Procedure* 1999 s. 7.
59. *The Act on the Establishment of Administrative Courts and Administrative Courts Procedure* 1999 s. 11.
60. M. Loughlin, *Sword and Scales: An Examination of the Relationship Between Law and Politics* (Oxford: Hart Publishing, 2000), 183.
61. Ibid., 185.
62. See the British *Constitutional Reform Act* 2005 which set up a Judicial Appointments Commission for England and Wales whose recommendations must then be ratified by the Lord Chancellor / Minister of Justice; and see Article 64, 65 and 66 of the *Constitution of France* in regard to judges but the *Conseil d'Etat* consists of what are really special civil servants schooled in administration and recruited by examination or experience.
63. *Constitution of the Kingdom of Thailand* 2007 ss. 224, 225 and generally *The Act on the Establishment of Administrative Courts and Administrative Courts Procedure* 1999 ss. 12–30.
64. *Constitution of the Kingdom of Thailand* 2007 s 227.
65. *The Act on the Establishment of Administrative Courts and Administrative Courts Procedure* 1999 ss 15, 23.
66. *The Act on the Establishment of Administrative Courts and Administrative Courts Procedure* 1999 s 23.
67. *Constitution of the Kingdom of Thailand* 2007 s 202 and *The Act on the Establishment of Administrative Courts and Administrative Courts Procedure* 1999 s 30.
68. *The Act on the Establishment of Administrative Courts and Administrative Courts Procedure* 1999 s 56.
69. To qualify a candidate must show service for at least three years as: petition commissioner or secretary to law councillors in the Office of the Council of State; administrative court official; judge of the civil court, criminal court or central military court; provincial public prosecutor; level-eight government official; associate professor in higher education in law, political science, public administration or social science. Also masters' graduates with 10 years public service and doctoral graduates with six years public service and attorneys with 12 years experience are eligible as candidates.
70. *The Act on the Establishment of Administrative Courts and Administrative Courts Procedure* 1999 s 24.
71. In France judges of the Administrative Courts are recruited in two ways, the predominant method is from the National School of Administration which has acted as a training ground but they are also recruited from *le tour exterieure*. These are judges that have distinguished themselves as administrators and latterly by competitive examination.
72. Judges cannot be: permanent government officials; employees of a state agency; holders of political positions, directors of a state enterprise or state agency; director, manager or consultant with a partnership or company; acting as attorney or other professional capacity.
73. Salary levels for judges are openly published, *The Act on the Establishment of Administrative Courts and Administrative Courts Procedure* 1999 s 103.
74. See for example, Sucheera Pinijparakarn and Weerayut Chokchaimadon, "Constitutional Court Pay Rise: Give it Back," *The Nation*, October 25, 2004, http://www.nationmultimedia.com/search/read.php?newsid = 107920&keyword = Constitutional+Court+Pay+Rise

75. *Constitution of the Kingdom of Thailand* 2007 s. 225.
76. *The Act on the Establishment of Administrative Courts and Administrative Courts Procedure* 1999 s. 54.
77. M. Hunt, "Constitutionalism and the Contractualisation of Government," in *The Province of Administrative Law*, ed. M. Taggart (Oxford: Hart Publishing, 1997), 38.
78. N. Bamforth, "Public Law-Private Law Distinction: A Comparative and Philosophical Approach," in *Administrative Law Facing the Future: Old Constraints and New Horizons*, ed. P. Leyland and T. Woods (London: Blackstone Press, 1997), 151.
79. The acceptance of a separate public jurisdiction based on the recognition of the distinct objectives of public law has been integral to the French system. See for example, J. M. Auby and R. Ducos-Ader quoted in B. Rudden, *A Sourcebook on French Law*, 3rd edn (Oxford: Oxford University Press, 1991), 14.
80. B. Bhalakula, *Administrative Contract in the Thai Legal Context* (Bangkok: Office of the Administrative Courts, 2003), 19.
81. P. Cane, "Accountability and the Public/Private Distinction," in *Public Law in a Multi-Layered Constitution*, ed. N. Bamforth and P. Leyland (Oxford: Hart Publishing, 2003), 248 and generally I. Harden *The Contracting State*, (Buckingham, UK: Open University Press, 1992).
82. C. Harlow and R. Rawlings, *Law and Administration*, (London: Butterworths, 1987), 128ff.
83. Hunt, "Constitutionalism and the Contractualisation of Government," 23.
84. It has been pointed out that in France, 'The key decision of the French *Tribunal des Conflits* in *Blanco* (1873) established the function criterion of *service publique* to define the boundary between the administrative jurisdiction and regular jurisdiction'. See Cane, "Accountability and the Public/Private Distinction," 253.
85. The judicial guidelines regarding the determination of this issue were explained in an interview with His Honour, Judge Dr Vishnu Varunyou, Vice President of the Court, January 5, 2005.
86. Usanee Mongkolporn, "Ruling Will Help NTC Take Power over Concession Deals," *The Nation*, May 13, 2005, http://www.nationmultimedia.com/search/read.php?newsid = 115634&keyword = Ruling+Will+Help+NTC+Take+Power+over+Concession+Deals
87. Red Case Nos. 1733–34/2002.
88. See Lord Diplock's discussion of these issues in *O'Reilly v. Mackman* [1983] 2 AC 237.
89. *The Act on the Establishment of Administrative Courts and Administrative Courts Procedure* 1999 s. 9(1). See also Leyland, "Droit Administratif Thai Style: A Comparative Analysis of the Administrative Courts in Thailand," 135, where the grounds of intervention are discussed from a comparative perspective.
90. *The Act on the Establishment of Administrative Courts and Administrative Courts Procedure* 1999 s. 9(2): 'involving a dispute in relation to an administrative agency or State official neglecting official duties required by the law to be performed or performing such duties with unreasonable delay'.
91. For example, The Office of Atomic Energy for Peace was found negligent in the storage of spent isotopes around the country and was ordered by the Central Administrative Court in 2002 to pay 5.2 million *baht* to 12 survivors of the radiation leak. Original judgment referred to in Anan Paengnoy, "COURT RULING: Long battle ends in Bt20 refund," *The Nation*, August 10, 2004, http://www.nationmultimedia.com/search/read.php?newsid = 103906&keyword = %5C%5C%5C%22court+ruling%5C%5C%5C%22
92. *The Act on the Establishment of Administrative Courts and Administrative Courts Procedure* 1999 s. 9(3): 'involving a dispute in relation to a wrongful act or other

liability of an administrative agency or State official arising from the exercise of power under the law or from a by-law, administrative order or other order, or from neglect of official duties required by the law to be performed or the performance of such duties with unreasonable delay'.

93. *Rule of the General Assembly of Judges of the Supreme Administrative Court on Administrative Court Procedure* 2000 cl. 28: 'The referral by an Ombudsman of a matter, together with the opinions thereon, to the Court in the case where the Ombudsman is of the opinion that any by-law or act of an administrative agency or State official is unlawful'.
94. *The Act on the Establishment of Administrative Courts and Administrative Courts Procedure* 1999 s. 9(5) provides: 'The case prescribed by law to be submitted to the Court by an administrative agency or State official for mandating a person to do a particular act or refraining therefrom'.
95. *The Act on the Establishment of Administrative Courts and Administrative Courts Procedure* 1999 s. 9(4). It should also be noted that under s. 9(3) the Administrative Court is granted jurisdiction over 'wrongful acts' which can be understood in common law terms as for cases concerning public bodies which concern tort liability. See generally, Bhalakula, *Administrative Contract in the Thai Legal Context.*
96. In Thailand there are five principal procedures of government procurement: price agreement; price inquiry; invitation for bidding; special procedure; and special case procedure. See *Rule of the Office of the Prime Minister on Procurement* 1992 and *Act on Private Participation in State Undertakings* 1992. See also Leyland, "Droit Administratif Thai Style: A Comparative Analysis of the Administrative Courts in Thailand," 138ff.
97. Leyland, "Droit Administratif Thai Style: A Comparative Analysis of the Administrative Courts in Thailand," 134ff.
98. *The Act on the Establishment of Administrative Courts and Administrative Courts Procedure* 1999 s. 72.
99. For example, in March 2003 the Office of Consumer Protection Board issued regulations banning the sale of high pressure water guns which, following commercial pressure, were considered to be unlawful by the Administrative Court but remained in operation pending an appeal. See Sucheera Pinijparakarn and Piyanuch Thamnukasetchai, "Big Water Guns Still Banned," *The Nation*, April 13, 2004, http://www.nationmultimedia.com/search/read.php?newsid=97074&keyword=Office+of+Consumer+Protection+Board
100. *The Act on the Establishment of Administrative Courts and Administrative Courts Procedure* 1999 s. 72.
101. Enforcement through *astreinte* is a comparatively recent development, first introduced by the law of the 16 July 1980 and it became available to the *Cours Administatives d'Appel* and the *Tribunaux Administratifs* from 1995.
102. Brown and Bell, *French Administrative Law*, 114.
103. For example, it is provided in respect of administrative contracts that where arbitration is part of the contract this option has to be exhausted before recourse to the Administrative Court.
104. *Rule of the General Assembly of Judges of the Supreme Administrative Court on Administrative Procedure* 2000 Clause 37. See Leyland, "Droit Administratif Thai Style: A Comparative Analysis of the Administrative Courts in Thailand," 135.
105. *The Act on the Establishment of Administrative Courts and Administrative Courts Procedure* 1999 s. 43.
106. *The Act on the Establishment of Administrative Courts and Administrative Courts Procedure* 1999 s. 9(1).
107. *The Act on the Establishment of Administrative Courts and Administrative Courts Procedure* 1999 s. 9(5) see n 94 also.

108. Brown and Bell, *French Administrative Law*, 56, 82. The *Conseil d'Etat* exercises an advisory function for the administration as well as acting in a separate capacity in a role where it adjudicates over the administration. This aspect is referred to as the *section contentieux*. It is worth remembering the Diceyan critique of the *droit administratif* which concentrated on the fact that the fact that the administrative court was part of the administration.
109. This chart and the figures therein were supplied by the Office of the Thai Administrative Court in May 2007and translated especially for this publication.
110. The Administrative Court, "Case Statistics," http://www.admincourt.go.th/amc_eng/02-KADEE/stat.htm
111. See Leyland, "Droit Administratif Thai Style: A Comparative Analysis of the Administrative Courts in Thailand," 129–32.
112. The role of public interest litigation in India might be regarded as an obvious parallel here. See for example, S. Jain, *Public Interest Litigation* (New Delhi: Deep & Deep, 2002); M. Rao, *Public Interest Litigation in India: Legal Aid and Loks Adalat*, 2nd ed. (Lucknow: Eastern Book Company 2004).
113. See J. Griffith, "The Political Constitution," *Modern Law Review* 1 (1979): 14ff.
114. J. Waldron, "The Core of the Case Against Judicial Review," *Yale Law Review* 115 (2006): 1353.
115. See for example, rulings by the Constitutional Tribunal under the 2006 *Constitution of the Kingdom of Thailand (Interim)* which disbanded Thai Rak Thai and banned 111 officials from politics for five years. "Joy, Relief, Sadness and Anger for Most; for Others it is Poetic Justice," *The Nation*, June 1, 2007, http://www.nationmultimedia.com/search/read.php?newsid = 30035719&keyword = Joy%2C+Relief%2C+Sadness++Anger+f+Most%3B+f+Others+it+is+Poetic+Justice

12 Compromising courts and harmonizing ideologies

Mediation in the administrative chambers of the people's courts in the People's Republic of China

Michael Palmer

Introduction

This chapter looks at certain aspects of the position and work of the administrative chambers of the people's courts in the People's Republic of China (PRC). These chambers were established in various areas of China on an experimental basis in the 1980s, in order to give greater effect to provisions in Article 41 of the 1982 *Constitution of the People's Republic of China* (*Constitution*) empowering aggrieved citizens to seek compensation from the state when their civil rights have been infringed by a state organ or functionary. The administrative chambers became nation-wide with the introduction of a special administrative litigation process provided for in the 1989 *Administrative Litigation Law* (in force, 1990). Particular attention is given in this chapter to the question: what is the nature and significance of the robust provision in Article 50 of the *Administrative Litigation Law* 1989 prohibiting a people's court from using mediation in its decision-making in administrative suits? In answering this question, the chapter considers both judicial practice in the administrative chambers of the people's courts and the jurisprudence of administrative litigation in the PRC, and contextualizes the changes that have been taking place in the system of administrative suits in the shifting institutional and ideological environment of the PRC post-Deng. This chapter chronicles the use of mediation by the administrative courts and the somewhat reluctant acceptance by the central authorities of this practice, arguing *inter alia* that the party–state commitment to a 'socialist harmonious society' appears to encourage mediatory practices.

The advent of administrative chambers in the PRC

This essay considers the nature and role of the administrative chambers (*xíngzhèng shěnpàn tíng*: 行政审判庭, literally 'administrative adjudication chambers,' but often also referred to in the abbreviated form as: *xíngzhèng tíng*: 行政庭, or administrative chambers) of the people's courts (*rénmín fǎyuàn*: 人民法院) in the PRC. The constitutional basis for the work of these chambers is Article 41 of the 1982 *Constitution*, which declares:

> Citizens of the People's Republic of China have the right to criticize and make suggestions to any state organ or functionary. Citizens have the right

> to make to relevant state organs complaints and charges against, or exposures of, violation of the law or dereliction of duty by any state organ or functionary; but fabrication or distortion of facts with the intention of libel or frame-up is prohibited. Where complaints, charges or exposures are made by citizens, the state organ concerned must deal with them in a responsible manner after ascertaining the facts. Nobody may suppress such complaints, charges and exposures, or retaliate against the citizens making them. Citizens who have suffered losses through infringement of their civil rights by any state organ or functionary have the right to compensation in accordance with the law.

The administrative chambers were established on an experimental basis in a number of areas of the PRC in the 1980s, becoming nation-wide after the 1989 *Administrative Litigation Law* (*ALL*) (*Xíngzhèng Sùsòng Fǎ*: 行政诉讼法)[1] was promulgated, in order to provide a special procedural track for citizen cases against the state. In that Law, Article 50 strictly forbids a people's court from using mediation in its decision-making in administrative suits (*xíngzhèng sùsòng* 行政诉讼). In examining the emergence and operations of these courts in this chapter, particular attention will be given, firstly, to the relationship between this provision and the changing decision-making practices of judges in the administrative chambers of the people's courts; and secondly, to the shifting ideological environment within which the PRC legal system operates and; thirdly, to recent jurisprudential thinking and legislative reforms proposal regarding administrative litigation in the PRC.

The PRC's 'new courts' for administrative justice

In the PRC, administrative courts are most obviously 'new' institutions in the sense that they were only established in the 1980s, at a point when the party–state decided that a specific procedural mechanism was needed in order to deal with citizen suits against the government. In the early 1980s, during the initial stages of the post-Mao era of reform, such suits were handled by the civil chambers of the people's courts, applying the rules of the provisional code of civil procedure.[2]

The administrative courts (or, more specifically, the administrative chambers in the people's courts) were also 'new' in another *processual* sense, in that the legislative intention underlying this development was that the new chambers would handle administrative cases by the process of *adjudication* only, thereby eschewing the traditional Chinese legal value that social conflict is best dealt with by the process of mediation (*tiáojiě*: 调解) and yielding (*ràng*: 让).[3]

This development was, however, also processually innovative in a third sense. In the PRC, it was believed traditionally that '*mín bù kěyǐ gào guǎn*' (民不可以告官) – that is, an ordinary person – may not sue an official. In a powerful moment in Zhang Yimou's insightful and delightful 1992 film '*Qiu Jiu Da Guansi*' (秋菊打官司) or 'Qiu Jiu Goes to Court,' which concerns a brave peasant woman's suit against the administrative head of her village, our heroine is distressed to learn that redress for her grievance will have to be secured by a process of suing – under the then new *ALL* 1989 – a superior level chief of police for his subordinates' inability to handle her complaint properly. Local-level police had not handled the case correctly when they were mediating the complaint in its early stages and in particular, she alleges, they showed bias in their treatment of the parties. This saddens her, because – so the film tells us – the police chief was a really good guy, politely taking the complainant heroine for a bowl of steaming noodles, kindly sending her safely back to her hotel in his official car, and diplomatically declining to accept the gift of a tasteless painting that the female protagonist, played by Gong Li, wished to heap on him in gratitude for lending a listening ear. Sue him? How *could* she?[4] In addition, the 1989 *ALL*'s prohibition on mediation reflected in part an innovative concern with procedural as well as substantive justice: in suing the state, the citizen could be assured that there was an official concern not just with outcomes, but also with appropriate decision-making processes.

In considering the 'newness' of the administrative chambers in people's courts, then, it is apparent that the chambers were new in several different ways. Additionally, it should not be forgotten that in a very real sense, *all* courts in contemporary China are fairly new – that is, they are only a little more than two decades old. As Stanley Lubman points out succinctly, 'for the first 30 years of the People's Republic, Chinese courts essentially existed in form but not in substance, and they all but disappeared during the Cultural Revolution'.[5] It is only since the PRC's post-Mao change of developmental direction, pursuing a somewhat more orthodox model of 'socialist legality', that the construction and reform of a meaningful court system has been attempted. So, in introducing new administrative chambers in the mid- and late 1980s – initially on only an experimental basis – the PRC's leadership was hanging new wallpaper on a very recently plastered wall. And that foundational edifice owed rather more to the inspiration of China's symbol of Legalist authoritarian rule, the 'Great Wall,'[6] than it did to the 'Democracy Wall' that Deng Xiaoping had only briefly tolerated at the beginning of the reform process. Put another way, the Legalist-style spirit of court reconstruction was, in the initial phase, to provide a legitimate and regular forum in which the might of the people's democratic dictatorship would be applied sternly to political dissidents and serious criminals. Thus, much of the work of the people's courts in the PRC during the first decade of the reform era – in the 1980s – focused on the application of criminal law, and was guided by a code of criminal procedure. Some sense of the novelty of this approach may be gleaned from the fact that both the *Criminal Law* and the *Criminal Procedure Law* which the revived criminal chambers were applying had only been promulgated and put into force for the first time in 1979. During the first 30 years of a socialist PRC, the formal criminal justice system lacked full codes of both criminal procedure and substantive criminal law.

As the era of reform began to unfold, Deng Xiaoping also increasingly promoted the view that both state and party might function better if they were not as fused as they had been during the much-despised Cultural Revolution (1966–76). In 1980, Deng Xiaoping gave a speech on 'Reform of the Party and State Leadership System'.[7] This was an important talk, but one which was politically sensitive. In it he suggested 'political reform' in a number of areas, of which perhaps the most important was that the PRC needed a much clearer distinction between state organs and party committees:

> [I]t is time for us to distinguish between the responsibilities of the Party and those of the government and to stop substituting the former for the latter. Those principal leading comrades of the Central Committee who are to be relieved of their concurrent government posts can concentrate their energies on our Party work, on matters concerning the Party's line, guiding principles and policies. This will help strengthen and improve the unified leadership of the Central Committee, facilitate the establishment of an effective work system at the various levels of government from top to bottom, and promote a better exercise of government functions and powers.[8]

This thinking was adopted and developed in Zhao Ziyang's late-1980s proposals for reform. These suggestions occupied an important place in his official report to the 13th National Congress of the Party in October 1987.[9] In that report, Zhao asserted that economic reform required a degree of political change, and advocated the development of new types of organization that would serve better the development of a market economy and also strengthen the PRC's socialist legal system.[10] The move towards separated party and state (*dǎng-zhèng fēnjiā*: 党政分家) was therefore an important factor in the development within the people's courts of a special forum – the administrative chamber – and a special procedural track, provided by the *ALL* 1989 – for dealing with citizen actions against the state and its functionaries. A more autonomous state, no longer entirely dominated by the party, would need to be kept in check by other means, and these included the idea that a special administrative procedure law would be a useful mechanism for constraining the arbitrary use of state power.

The processual starting point for this new approach is found at the beginning of the 1980s. From 1982 onwards, administrative decisions could be challenged under the *Civil Procedure Law (for Trial Implementation)* 1982.[11] In 1982, a new *Constitution* was promulgated and put into force with the important provision that citizens had the right to sue for compensation against any state organ or functionary if their civil rights had been infringed and they had, as a result, suffered loss (Article 41). This right was subsequently confirmed in the *General Principles of the Civil Law* 1986, at Article 121.[12] Then, in 1989, the *ALL* was promulgated, providing for citizen suits against state organs and functionaries – although Article 12 defined the courts' jurisdiction in such a way as to protect the Communist Party from such intrusive judicial conduct.[13] The *ALL* 1989 represented 'both in an effort to build legitimacy for the new law and [was meant to be seen] as a reflection of the increased openness of the Chinese government'.[14] In more recent times – in particular after the amendment to the

1982 *Constitution* in 1999 declaring the PRC to be a rule-of-law state, and also following the PRC's accession to the World Trade Organization in 2001 – the nature, effectiveness and, above all, the independence of the PRC's system of judicial review are characterized as critically important for future legal and political development in the PRC.[15]

The politically sensitive nature of citizen suits against governmental organs and functionaries in a jurisdiction that adheres to a 'people's democratic dictatorship' meant that the *ALL* 1989 was not put into force until some 18 months later on 1 October 1990.[16] In the meantime, trials would be conducted in carefully chosen areas, reflecting also a distinctively socialist Chinese approach to legal development, in which practice is allowed to run ahead of the law. The *ALL* 1989 was thus implemented in selected locations on a preliminary basis, and the views were then sought of local officials involved in judicial administration on the likely overall impact of the *ALL* 1989. Accordingly, judges would be able to shape their decision-making in administrative cases with the experience gained from this preparatory work. The new system of administrative litigation offered tangible benefits to the Communist Party, providing an apparatus by means of which ordinary citizens could challenge the conduct of the state. The *ALL* 1989 could thereby assist continued, albeit indirect, party dominance of the state. Consistent with this approach, while the *ALL* 1989 provides for citizen suits against state organs and functionaries, it also characterizes the courts' jurisdiction in such a way as to protect the Communist Party itself from such invasive judicial meddling.[17]

The court system of the PRC

In the PRC, the administrative chambers have, since the late 1980s, been an integral element in the court system. This system primarily consists of a four-level structure of courts with general jurisdiction, with an additional layering of local tribunals where these are considered necessary.[18] At the national level, the Supreme People's Court (*Zuìgāo Rénmín Fǎyuàn*: 最高人民法院) is located in Beijing. Below, at the provincial level, Higher People's Courts (*Gāojí Rénmín Fǎyuàn*: 高级人民法院) sit in the provinces, autonomous regions and special municipalities. At the prefecture level and also in certain areas of provinces, autonomous regions, and special municipalities, are found the Intermediate People's Courts (*Zhōngjí Rénmín Fǎyuàn*: 中级人民法院).[19] Below these come the Basic People's Courts (*Jīcéng Rénmín Fǎyuàn*: 基层人民法院) located in counties, towns, and municipal districts, and which may themselves contain branches or People's Tribunals (*Rénmín Fǎtíng*: 人民法庭) which do not, however, have jurisdiction over administrative cases.[20] In addition, special courts – again operating within a hierarchically organized system – deal with cases involving issues relating to the military, railways, maritime and inland water transportation and forestry. PRC courts operate a two-trial system, in which there is one trial at the court of first instance, followed by an appeal if allowed. (Although it should be pointed out that there is the possibility, especially in criminal cases, of a review of the case by a superior level court if it is felt that an erroneous decision has been made.) Jurisdiction is determined by a combination of place and the seriousness and complexity of the case. The people's courts at all levels are divided into a number of chambers (*tíng*: 庭), and the majority of courts now have separate chambers each for administrative, criminal and civil matters (indeed, often there are now two civil chambers, one dealing with more commercially orientated cases, and previously called economic chambers (*jīngjì tíng*: 经济庭) and the other handling more general types of civil case). Moreover, especially in large urban areas, there may be additional chambers, such as those for intellectual property disputes,[21] foreign (and Hong Kong, Macao and Taiwan) related cases, and for bankruptcy suits.

It is a very important feature of the PRC court system that the courts are subject to both vertical and horizontal control. Thus, a court is accountable not only to its immediately superior court, but also to the Standing Committee of the People's Congress – a key unit in the PRC's parliamentary system – at the same level. As a result, the Supreme People's Court is obliged each year to submit its annual work report to the National People's Congress (NPC) and to seek the approval of the NPC for that report. In addition, it is the NPC – in the PRC system, the supreme organ of state power – that elects the President of the Supreme People's Court.[22] The Supreme People's Court bears the obligation to supervise the manner in which justice is administered by both the local and special people's courts according to Article 30 of the revised *Organic Law of the People's Courts* 2006 and the *Constitution* 1982 (Article 127). Under a system of delegated legislative authority, the Supreme People's Court also bears the responsibility for issuing interpretations and opinions on specific issues of law that arise in the course of litigation, although in practice the Court tends to exceed its lawful authority and sometimes has in effect introduced new legislation through these normative statements.[23] Nevertheless, the Court is clearly subordinate to the NPC, and this subordination is experienced at all levels of the system, right down to the basic level courts. This leaves the courts exposed to environing forces that may well undermine their independence.

Other elements in the political environment within which the courts operate also work against judicial independence. Thus, the system of court financing is decentralized, with the courts at all levels being funded by the equivalent level of government, rendering the courts vulnerable to financial pressure, especially in the sense that there is often an expectation that the court will do the 'right thing' in many cases and protect local interests rather than apply the law fairly and without fear or favour. In addition, there is the key institution within the court of the adjudication committee (*shěnpàn wěiyuánhuì*: 审判委员会). This body, it is sometimes claimed within the PRC, counteracts the lack of legal professionalism found in many lower level courts, combats outside influences and corrupt practices, coordinates and unifies practice, and integrates practice and policy within the court as a whole. But it also serves as an important mechanism for the application of the principle of democratic centralism in adjudicative decision-making:

> People's courts at all levels set up judicial committees which practice democratic centralism. The task of the judicial committees is to sum up judicial

experience and to discuss important or difficult cases and other issues relating to the judicial work.[24]

As a result, it is the court rather than an individual judge that enjoys the judicial independence guaranteed by Article 126 of the *Constitution* 1982, and the adjudication committee has wide-ranging powers in theory and practice to decide cases (as well as practical issues within cases) on the basis of the dossier of the case, thereby effectively undermining the principle of the right to a fair trial. The trial court is obliged to carry out the decision of the adjudication committee.

Since 1999, the Supreme People's Court has been pursuing a major programme of judicial reform. Efforts have been made to improve the workings of the courts and the professional standards of the judges, and to make the courts more open to the public gaze. Legal aid has been actively promoted since the mid-1990s as a way of enhancing access to justice through the courts.[25] In addition, trials are progressively more open to the public and the scrutiny of the media, and selected judgments are published, although there is still a long way to go before judicial transparency is properly established[26] – as we shall see when we examine the growing phenomenon of mediation in administrative suits. In general, it should be noted here that the judicial reform programme has yet to promote significant changes in the work of the administrative chambers of the people's courts.

Administrative adjudication and other forms of decision-making

Since the end of the 1970s, as indicated above, an increasingly pragmatic Chinese leadership has attempted to rebuild the legal system. It has moved away from some of Mao's more radical ideas (in particular, that the PRC should be governed in accordance with the messianic principle of 'continuous revolution' [*jìxù gémìng*: 继续革命]) to signing the *International Covenant on Political and Cultural Rights*[27] in 1998, declaring governance in accordance with the rule of law (*yīfǎ zhìguó*: 依法治国) as a constitutional norm in 1999, and amending Article 33 of the current *Constitution* in 2004, so that the state now confirms that it protects the human rights of PRC citizens. An important step on this road to greater formal legality and better human rights' protection was the introduction in 1989 of the *ALL*.[28]

The *ALL* 1989 introduced novel procedures by means of which new administrative chambers in the people's courts were empowered to cancel administrative orders deemed illegal, compel administrative actions, or adjust administrative punishments considered to be unfair. A plaintiff – an individual citizen, or a group of citizens, or a legal person such as a business – may bring a suit under the *ALL* 1989 against an administrative organ in order to challenge an administrative decision. The burden of proof is placed on the defendant agency – the agency must show that the conduct about which the plaintiff has complained was indeed lawful. However, the courts have a broad authority to refuse to hear cases, and in particular it should be noted that no challenge may be made against what is often the real decision maker namely, the Communist Party, as the party is not a state agency. Nor may the validity of administrative rules (referred to as 'abstract administrative acts') be challenged. Moreover, if the relevant regulations within which the administrative decision was taken to contain a requirement of lodging a complaint with a superior level of the organ against whom redress is sought, then this requirement must be met before any court proceedings may be contemplated. Only if there is no response after two months may the case then be taken directly to court. In addition, the courts are primarily empowered to consider the legality of administrative decisions and conduct,[29] not their reasonableness within the scope of the defendant organ's discretionary authority. A further problem is that under the PRC's system of legislative power of interpretation, it is often the defendant administrative organ itself that has the power to interpret and ascertain the validity of the relevant rules. Another limitation is that according to Article 54 of the *ALL* 1989, a court may only modify an imposed administrative penalty if the sanction is obviously unfair. And although the court may strike out a decision that is *ultra vires*, it is often reluctant to do so, as many PRC regulations are drafted in such broad language that ascertaining the correct position may be quite difficult.

Perhaps not surprisingly, the growth in administrative litigation has lagged significantly behind criminal and especially civil case-loads. There has been a notable growth in administrative suits – in 1989, there were only 9,934 cases, and by 2006, the number had grown to 95,052 – but this latter figure is still only something like 2 per cent of the overall annual case-load of the people's courts. Initially, suits were predominantly brought against the police by urban residents, but this has gradually changed to a predominance of property disputes, and disagreements over business activity (especially licences and permits). And while state-owned enterprises and private companies are now the principal types of plaintiff, 'peasants' (*nóngmín*: 农民) are increasingly challenging decisions made in the context of the government's rural development programmes. Sometimes such challenges are made by means of collective suits (*gòngtóng sùsòng*: 共同诉讼) in which large numbers of plaintiffs may be grouped together in accordance with Article 26 of the *ALL* 1989. A collective suit may have good publicity value, whatever the legal outcome of the action itself.

As noted above, before the *ALL* came into force on 1 October 1990 administrative cases were handled by the courts under the provisional *Code for Civil Procedure* that had been introduced in 1982.[30] This permitted judicial mediation of administrative cases and some courts, such as the Wuhan Intermediate People's Court, considered that the system of judicial mediation should continue, despite the fact that the Chinese party–state felt it necessary to introduce a special track of litigation for administrative cases. Traditional Chinese legal culture, as well as the emphasis placed on mediation in the handling of civil and economic cases under the provisional *Civil Procedure Law* 1981, encouraged courts such as those in Wuhan to use judicial mediation in experiments with administrative cases that increasingly took place from 1987 onwards, following a Supreme People's Court instruction to local courts in January of that year to set up administrative chambers in order to hear administrative cases on a tentative basis.

In Wuhan, the courts took the view that mediation was an important process, which would bring considerable benefits if its use was continued in the handling of administrative cases. Among the many other virtues that the Wuhan judiciary claimed such a policy would bring were, first, that in many judicial review cases there would be significant overlap between the administrative and civil aspects of the case and it would not be easy to keep these elements distinct. A ban on mediation for the administrative dimensions in such cases might make decision-making overly complicated. In addition, judicial mediation of administrative cases would provide a simple mode of proceeding which could be understood by, and be beneficial for, the masses, enabling disputes to be resolved quickly and amicably. It would also provide a didactic and consensual opportunity for the courts to make administrators realize the errors of their administrative decision-making, correct their unlawful rules, and thereby promote sound administrative standards. In this way, not only would aggrieved citizens be encouraged to bring a suit against state agencies and their functionaries, but also good relations between citizens and the state would be promoted. Thus, this would be a very effective way of bridging the gap between the government and the citizen. The courts in Wuhan also asserted that to prohibit the use of mediation in administrative cases would represent a rejection of the principal of equality of procedural rights and duties between the parties, undermine the authority of the court, and be inconsistent with the use of mediation in private prosecutions under the then *Criminal Procedure Law* 1979.

However, a number of objections to the use of mediation in administrative cases were raised. These were similar to, but apparently put forward quite independently of, critical points of view expressed in alternative dispute resolution discourses in the Anglo-American common law world in the late 1980s.[31] In the PRC, reservations were expressed in especially forceful language at the time of the drafting of the *ALL* 1989. The Wuhan Court found itself up against powerful local judiciaries elsewhere in China who argued strongly against employing mediation in administrative cases that came before the courts. In particular, in Shenzhen and Shanghai – two parts of China with growing exposure to the outside world – the courts stressed the inappropriateness of a mediatory approach to decision-making in administrative cases. They emphasized several specific problems in particular. First, in their view, either the administrative behaviour about which the citizen felt aggrieved was lawful or it was not. Accordingly, the new administrative chambers need only consider the legality of the administrative conduct about which a complaint had been brought. Moreover, it should not be open to an individual administrator to surrender state power by making to a plaintiff the concessions that are often necessary in order to achieve a settlement. Furthermore, it is argued that many administrative cases are not amenable to mediatory intervention, because of the power imbalances between the parties that often exist when the citizen sues the state. This was especially important at the time, as it was anticipated that many complaints would be based on accusations of police misconduct, including excessive use of force.

The opinion that prevailed among legislators and judges was that in administrative cases there should not be any reliance by the people's courts on mediation as a means of dealing with the substance of a dispute.[32] This was the position finally taken in the law on administrative suits when it was promulgated in 1989. Although earlier drafts permitted judicial mediation as a decision-making process in administrative litigation, in the final stages of drafting this proposal was abandoned. The pro-mediation judges had lost the argument, and the *ALL* 1989 provides at Article 50[33] that mediation may not be used to determine the outcome of the substance of a claim brought against the state body under the law – mediation may only be used to determine the level of compensation to be awarded to a successful plaintiff under the *State Compensation Law* 1994.

This did not mean that mediation could not be used in decision-making in administrative cases – other forms of administrative dispute resolution allow, and even encourage, its use. Two particularly important processes for resolving citizen complaints are 'Letters and Visits' (*Xìnfǎng*: 信访), and 'Administrative Reconsideration' (*Xíngzhèng Fùyì*: 行政复议).[34] These are administrative grievance systems by which the state attempts to deal 'in-house' with complaints lodged by PRC citizens.[35] They are seen as alternatives to administrative litigation, and as more consensual avenues to administrative justice than judicial review and similar types of litigation.[36] Thus, the Letters and Visits system enables citizens who disagree with administrative decisions to lodge a complaint with a special office established to handle such matters within the relevant administrative body. This mode of complaining is low-cost, non-confrontational and growing in importance. Its popularity reflects in part the continued belief that, as in imperial China, officials bear a quasi-parental moral duty to correct bureaucratic wrongdoing and errors. The system has also been utilized by country folk who, in the past 10 years or so, have become increasingly restless, largely as a result of what they often see as unlawful confiscation of their land for construction and other developmental projects. Inadequate compensation and subsequent environmental degradation often present significant additional complications. As a result, rural protests have proliferated.[37]

The response from the authorities to this development has been vigorous. In particular, the regulations governing Letters and Visits have been revised in an effort to enhance their effectiveness.[38] Additionally, new police units have been established in order to crack down on more serious cases of unrest.[39] There are also indications that local government is prepared to go further, and use agent provocateurs and criminal gangs in order to suppress local complaints about administrative misconduct at the local level.[40] But in addition to these developments, which I describe in greater detail elsewhere,[41] a new policy has been introduced specifically intended to draw together the citizen and the state by the creation of special 'Letters and Visits Mediation Sub-Centres' (*Xìnfǎng Tiáojiě Fēn Zhōngxīn*: 信访调解分中心).[42] The personnel of the Sub-Centres will draw on the experienced mediators serving in the PRC's ubiquitous, semi-official community mediation system in order to have a better chance of ensuring that the increasingly difficult state–citizen 'contradictions [are] resolved' (*máodùn huàjiě*: 矛盾化解).[43]

In addition, there is the important process of administrative review (also sometimes referred to in English as administrative reconsideration). This is a system that permits an aggrieved citizen to challenge an unsatisfactory decision by filing an application for review at the next superior level within the same branch of government. In theory, this process encourages informed decision-making in respect of difficult issues, and enables the administration to understand better the workings and problems of subordinates. For the complainant, the system is relatively quick and usually does not bring with it the opprobrium of 'challenging the state'. The scope of reconsideration is also very broad. The superior level may review both the legality and the propriety of particular administrative conduct, including an abstract act that may underpin such conduct.

In apparent contrast to the system of administrative litigation, administrative reconsideration allows for the use of mediation as a decision-making process. Although the complainant may be represented by a lawyer in the process, this is unusual. Indeed, most hearings are conducted on the basis of the complaint file, as the *Administrative Review Law* 1999 stipulates at Article 22 that 'in principle, administrative reconsideration shall take the form of written examination'.[44] Other than this, the law provides very little detail on the decision-making process in review cases. This leaves much room for negotiating and mediating a compromise between the complaint and the administrative body that made the relevant decision. If a party disagrees with an attempted mediation, then she or he may bring a suit in a people's court.[45] As in the system of Letters and Visits, increasing attention is now being given to the possibility of a greater and more firmly institutionalized role for mediation in administrative review cases, as part of the party–state's efforts to make the system more effective. And, as is the case also for Letters and Visits, the argument is put forward that this renewed emphasis on mediation will help the PRC to promote a more stable and harmonious society.[46]

Overall, the administrative review regime for responding to complaints from citizens is limited in effectiveness by the political environment in which it has to operate, as well as other difficulties. Among the most important of these additional weaknesses is a failure on the part of some governmental organs to set up administrative reconsideration offices, and to resource adequately such offices where they have been set up. In addition, following a revision to the earlier regulations on administrative review in 1994, there has been a growing perception that superior levels are inclined to defend what they see as the interests of the agency whose conduct is the focus of complaint.[47] Thus, there is an apparent lack of independence in the process of reconsideration. Furthermore, a complainant has a relatively short period to lodge an application for review.[48] Moreover, the system may not be used to challenge administrative decisions that are made by a Communist Party Committee but then carried out by a governmental agency.

Thus, in the PRC – as in many other jurisdictions around the world – there are well-established alternatives to the courts for seeking administrative justice. It is clear, however, that such alternatives contain inherent limitations, and that for the ordinary PRC citizen this means that the courts and their powers of adjudication may sometimes seem to be the most effective way forward.

Administrative adjudication and its re-incorporation of mediatory decision-making

It has become clear that the administrative chambers in the people's courts no longer offer such a clear-cut option. Although untransformed in law, the firm prohibition on mediation in the *ALL* 1989 has for several years been increasingly relaxed by judicial practice. In addition, we can now sense in the PRC a strong move formally to incorporate mediatory processes more firmly into administrative litigation. Early in 2008, the Supreme People's Court, in all but name, gave the practice formal recognition, introducing new rules of court, which acknowledge that one of the outcomes in administrative cases is often a mediated settlement.[49] In these new rules, the term 'mediation' (*tiáojiě*: 调解) is not used: instead, the Court's enormously important normative document contents itself with the expression 'settlement' (*héjiě*: 和解) and silently assumes that in many instances this outcome will have been achieved by mediatory intervention by a judge.

Thus, Article 1 declares that if a people's court takes the view that the 'specific administrative conduct' about which the suit has been brought is illegal or improper (*bùdàng*: 不当), then the Court may 'propose' (*jiànyì*: 建议) to the defendant that the administrative conduct which is in dispute be modified. Subject to certain conditions, if the suggested change is made and the plaintiff then applies for withdrawal of suit, the court may formally approve the withdrawal. These conditions are, first, that the proposed withdrawal is the plaintiff's 'true intention' (*zhēnshí yìsi*: 真实意思); secondly, that the changes in administrative conduct proposed by the defendant are lawful, compatible with administrative regulations, consistent with the defendant administrative organs' functions, and do not infringe either the public interest or the lawful rights and interests of other persons; thirdly, that the people's court is notified in writing of the changes in administrative conduct to be made by the defendant; and finally, that no objection is raised by a third party (Article 2). According to Article 5 of the 'Withdrawal Rules', the 'change in specific administrative conduct' by the defendant includes delayed or on-going performance. Article 6 of the Rules allows the wording of the court ruling which approves the withdrawal of suit to include the relevant details of the agreed changes in administrative conduct. Article 8 provides for settlement and withdrawal of suit in appellate and retrial hearings.

Some procedural safeguards for the plaintiff in addition to those noted above in Article 2 are made available in Article 7. These give the plaintiff the right to refuse to withdraw an administrative suit, and to expect a prompt ruling or judgment in such circumstances. Furthermore, another set of Rules, introduced at the same time as the 'Withdrawal of Suit Rules', but dealing specifically with jurisdictional issues,[50] are relevant here. The 'Rules of the Supreme People's Court on Some Issues Concerning Jurisdiction in Administrative Cases' 2008 provides that in a case in which an organ of the *local* people's government is the defendant, the plaintiff may bring suit directly in the relevant *Intermediate* People's Court if the case is considered by the plaintiff (or indeed any of the parties) to be very significant or complicated, or unsuitable (*bùyí*: 不宜) for the Basic Level People's Court with jurisdiction (Article 2). My understanding is that the exercise of jurisdiction by the *Basic* Level People's Court is primarily considered inappropriate in circumstances in which it is feared that 'local protectionism' (*dìfang bǎohù zhǔyi*: 地方保护主义) will intrude – that is, there is a perceived danger that the local government will interfere in the case in order to defend its own interests. It should be added that Article 1 provides for a number of other important situations in which jurisdiction is assumed not by the Basic People's Court, which would otherwise exercise jurisdiction, but rather by the Intermediate People's Court: certain types of real-estate registration case; a collective suit (*gòngtóng sùsòng*: 共同诉讼; *jítuán sùsòng*: 集团诉讼);[51] a foreign (or 'Greater China')[52] related case; or 'other significant or complicated cases'. Here, the thinking is that these are technically more complicated cases, and therefore require the greater legal expertise found in the intermediate level courts. But another consideration is that in these cases the local government may put a great deal of pressure on the plaintiff and the court, and the plaintiff in particular therefore needs greater formal protection. This danger may well be greater in cases which are mediated – or, as the Rules characterize the situation, 'settled' and then 'withdrawn' – rather than adjudicated.

The semantic fig leaf of '*héjiě*' or 'settlement' protects the Court against assertions that the 'Withdrawal Rules' contravene the provisions in the *ALL* 1989 prohibiting the use of mediation for dealing with the substantive issues in an administrative suit. Certainly, judges in the administrative chambers of the PRC's people's courts, acknowledge that the new rules are in reality an endorsement of pre-trial judicial mediation.[53] Indeed, an earlier draft of the new rules apparently *did* explicitly employ the term *tiáojiě*. However, this use was apparently not accepted by the Standing Committee of the NPC on the ground that it would explicitly contradict national legislation: Article 50 of the *ALL* 1989. It was therefore abandoned in favour of more ambiguous, less challenging language. But the Supreme People's Court legislative intention is clear. The 'Withdrawal Rules' 2008 are to provide a legitimating framework for the practice of the pre-trial judicial mediation of administrative suits in all but name.

The pressure for the adoption of a more mediatory approach to decision-making in administrative suits has been growing for several years. In 2005, an important news report in the *People's Court Daily* (*Rénmín Fǎyuàn Bào*: 人民法院报) pointed to a high rate of withdrawal in administrative suits in many localities in China – as much as 60 per cent in some localities – and emphasized that this phenomenon needed appropriate analysis. Careful examination revealed that one very important cause of the high rate of withdrawal is that on the doorstep of the administrative trial there has often been encouragement of settlement through an 'informal' process of judicial mediation. However, because of the strict prohibition in the *ALL* 1989 on mediation of the substantive issues in an administrative case, the various pressures that have encouraged mediation in administrative cases have resulted in a practice of 'mediation without the mediation [written] agreement' (*méiyǒu tiáojiěshū dì tiáojiě*: 没有调解书的调解).[54] The court mediates pre-trial, but does not formally endorse the settlement achieved by its mediatory intervention.

This mediation has typically been conducted by one of the judges who will hear the case if it goes to trial. Here we should note that the approach taken in the PRC to judicial mediation in general is that the judge who adjudicates a case in which mediation has failed should be the same judge who attempted the unsuccessful mediation. One important reason for this distinctive approach is that procedural rules – especially those for civil cases – encourage a reversion to mediation at any stage of the proceedings short of judgement, and it is helpful therefore to retain the flexibility that comes with use of the same judge throughout. In the case of administrative disputes, the mediating judge is usually the 'lead judge' (*zhǔshěn fǎguān*: 主审法官) in the three-person collegial panel (*héyì tíng*: 合议庭) that ordinarily hears an administrative suit. The other two judges will not normally involve themselves in the mediation, as they have their own cases to deal with, and are inclined simply to approve whatever outcome is reached as a result of the lead judge's efforts. In appellate cases, the situation is a little different, as the superior level judges may have more time to deal with cases, and the cases themselves tend to raise more significant legal issues. As a result, where there is the possibility of a mediated compromise, the other judges on the panel may intervene – in particular, a draft outcome is likely to be discussed with, and agreed by, all members of the collegial panel before it is proposed to the parties as a settlement.

However, the judicial practice of mediation in public law suits is, as I have noted, still not explicitly provided for in the *ALL* 1989, nor indeed in any other relevant codes. Somewhat paradoxically, such judicial mediation has been made possible by a lack of any detailed provision for active judicial case management prior to the commencement of the trial itself. The relevant section in the *ALL* 1989 (Chapter VII: Trial and Judgment) contains very few rules on pre-trial issues. This, in part, reflects the fact that the notion of a distinctive pre-trial stage is actually not one that has been clearly conceptualized in PRC procedure law. As a result, the judge in many cases is expected to have very little to do with the parties prior to the trial and, instead, ordinarily only meets with them when the trial actually begins. In essence, her or his pre-trial duties are to liaise with the parties, receive from the parties the written evidence they seek to use in support of their case, and make sure the parties know the details of the hearing. Neither the judge nor the parties themselves may compel a party to provide documents relevant to the case, as there is no system of discovery. In some courts, such as those in Shenzhen and Shanghai, the policy – at least until very recently – has been that judicial mediation prior to the trial is not permissible, as the law makes no formal provision for such a process.[55] Indeed, in these and other economically well-developed areas, there are experiments with a system – authorized by the Supreme People's Court – of 'Judge's Assistants' (*Fǎguān Zhùlǐ*: 法官助理) in which it is the Assistant who handles all the pre-trial formalities in administrative suits.

Therefore, the important question arises: how has a policy and practice supportive of judicial mediation in administrative cases been allowed to re-emerge in a legal system which still places a strict legal prohibition on its deployment in the trial itself? In substantial part the immediate answer, for a variety of reasons, is that judges (and by extension, the courts in which they serve) have been prepared to take advantage of the lack of detailed provisions on pre-trial issues in the *ALL* 1989 to intervene in the dispute and in effect to manage the case through mediation, or at the very least by active encouragement of settlement. In many cases, the intervention of the judge is tacitly or even implicitly welcomed by the defendant state agency or functionary. It is reported that an outcome of 'compromise' (*xiétiáo*: 协调) is one that is 'silently approved' (*mòxǔ*: 默许) or even 'actively encouraged' (*dòngyuán*: 动员) by the courts. In the informal compromise agreement that is reached, the defendant may agree to change its position, performing the administrative conduct that the plaintiff seeks, or withdraw the administrative act that is the cause of the suit. Alternatively, the defendant confers on the plaintiff certain benefits outside the litigation process, but without necessarily changing the administrative decision that is the ostensible cause of the plaintiff's grievance. The plaintiff then applies for withdrawal, as the objective in bringing suit has in effect been achieved: the court approves the plaintiff's application, and the case is thus concluded. According to the analysis of reported materials on the subject by Dai, noted above, plaintiff withdrawal of cases occupies more than one-third of the total number of administrative suits, and has sometimes reached 60 per cent of the total, as we have observed.[56] In the many cases in which there is an application for withdrawal, only rarely is the request rejected by the court. There has been a mediatory intervention by the judge, who is therefore unlikely to reject the subsequent application for withdrawal.[57]

Thus, the 'Rules on Withdrawal' 2008 are a somewhat belated response to the development over the past decade or so of an informal and 'underground' practice of judicial mediation of administrative suits. Until the introduction of the new Rules on 1 February 2008, the terms of the mediated settlements were sometimes drawn up in written form – often referred to as a 'mediation agreement' (*tiáojiěshū*: 调解书), but the anti-mediation provision in the *ALL* 1989 prevented such agreements from being made an order of the court. Instead, the written agreement would be notarized, thereby giving the defendant some protection against subsequent attempts by the claimant to achieve an improved result. Notaries who I have asked about this phenomenon confirm that ordinarily it was the defendant who most wanted the notarization, driven by worries that the plaintiff might later renege on the settlement in a search for improved terms.

Although various reports indicate that often the plaintiff is in fact satisfied with the outcome achieved by judicial mediation,[58] the growth in the practice of pre-trial mediatory intervention by the judge has sometimes been the subject of fiercely critical comments within PRC legal circles. Perhaps the most serious condemnations have focused on the uncertain legal status of the conduct of the judge in attempting mediation. Although the judge who mediates is likely also to be the judge who will conduct the trial if the parties are unable to achieve a settlement, since mediation in administrative cases is prohibited in the 1989 *ALL*, so the process should be described as one of 'settlement outside the case' (*ànwài héjiě*: 案外和解). Withdrawal of suit is, in actuality, something of a legal fiction, which covers up the reality of judicial mediatory intervention. It is a process in which all the players – the defendant, the plaintiff and the court – are often satisfied with the outcome, and this helps explain why the practice has become so widespread. But it is at the very least inconsistent with the spirit of Article 50 of the *ALL* 1989, and this line of criticism is, in effect, saying that the mediatory intervention by the judge should not be given legal recognition.

In addition, the absence of procedural safeguards in the *ALL* 1989 has encouraged some commentators to emphasize the danger that a mediated case can degenerate into an arbitrary process. The judge may exercise over-forcefully her or his informal authority, perhaps thereby compelling mediation, so that it is experienced by the plaintiff in particular as a mandatory phase.[59] As already stressed, it is important to keep in mind the fact that judicial mediation in the PRC takes a somewhat distinctive form. The judge who mediates a case is also likely to adjudicate that case should mediation be unsuccessful. The judge is thus in a strong position to put pressure on the parties to make concessions during the mediation process.

The informal 'mediatory' techniques that have been used to put pressure on the parties consist of, *inter alia*: 'mixing everything up' (*hè xīnì*: 和稀泥) in order to distract the plaintiff's attention from the essential points in the dispute (particularly effective in the Basic Level People's Court where the parties are less likely to be legally represented); 'encouraging mediation by applying pressure' (*yǐ yà cù tiáo*: 以压促调); 'threatening [the parties with] adjudication in order to press mediation on the parties' (*yǐpàn yàtiáo*: 以判压调); 'using inducements in order to promote mediation' (*yǐyōu cùtiáo*: 以优促调); and 'procrastination in order to compel mediation' (*yǐ tuō yà tiáo*: 以托压调). In one or more of these ways, the court may, for example, secure a concession that satisfies the court but not the plaintiff, such as the demotion of an official involved in the decision about which the suit has been brought. Pressure on the plaintiff in the mediation to settle on unfavourable terms may also, of course, come in the form of local intimidation by the defendant state organ, which the court is unable to counter.

Thus, the system of judicial mediation in administrative cases which has developed in the PRC is one in which the plaintiff may well be subject to significant coercion and find mediation in practice to be a mandatory rather than a consensual process. Indeed, in one analysis of a sample of nearly 200 cases, the investigators found that only in one out of every five cases did the plaintiff *consensually* withdraw her or his case, and that in all the remaining cases there was an element of coercion in the withdrawal.[60] Therefore, while in substantive terms, many plaintiffs have come away from a withdrawn suit with important gains, they may have done so only after going through a mediatory phase that was in effect compulsory and sometimes coercive. As we have seen, the

'Rules on Withdrawal' and the 'Rules on Jurisdiction' attempt to deal with some aspects of this problem, but there is an obvious need for a much more detailed set of procedural guarantees and related reforms. In the absence of provisions in the *ALL* 1989, PRC judges look to the rather elementary rules in the *Civil Procedure Law* (1991, revised 2007), Chapter 8,[61] for guidance – a practice which, in effect, defeats one of the main purposes of the *ALL* 1989, which was to provide a procedural track in administrative cases quite different from that for civil justice, especially in respect of the role of mediation.

The worries about the wisdom of mediation for the judicial management of administrative cases expressed above have not, however, been sufficient to prevent a significant rethinking of the approach to be taken by the courts in dealing with claims against the state brought by aggrieved citizens under the *ALL* 1989. There has been a major shift in the theorizing of the place of administrative suits in contemporary China. It is now asserted, *inter alia*, that the increased complexity and scope of administrative law and regulation in the PRC mean that the merits of a plaintiff's case are often not as clear cut as they once were, and that the public and rule of law dimensions in much administrative conduct are not any longer as obvious as they once were, such conduct often consisting of everyday, small-scale decision-making. In addition, we are reminded that state–citizen conflicts are, for the most part, 'contradictions among the people' (*rénmín nèibù máodùn*: 人民内部矛盾) for which the largely binary decision-making process of adjudication is often an oversimplification that fails to capture the complexities of many 'administrative activities' (*xíngzhèng huódòng*: 行政活动). In such circumstances, relations between the state and its citizens are not inherently confrontational and antagonistic, and settlement is therefore often the most appropriate outcome in an administrative suit. Indeed, if litigation and adjudication are solely relied on in order to deal with administrative disputes, then there is a real danger that the contradictions will not be resolved but, rather, intensify.[62]

This reminder of the importance of mediation in resolving 'contradictions among the people' not only harks back to the class analysis of Mao Zedong in his more conservative political–legal thinking;[63] it is also consistent with the Hu Jintao leadership's new goal of creating within the PRC a 'harmonious society' (*héxié shèhuì*: 和谐社会). Mediation of administrative cases will, it is argued, help to maintain social harmony by keeping state and citizen close together. These efforts to infuse administrative litigation with mediation match similar developments in the dispute resolution processes of 'Letters and Visits' and 'Administrative Reconsideration'. They are in part a response to the growing sense of social injustice that has come to haunt the PRC in the wake of the economic reforms. Rapid economic growth in socialist China should be under firm political leadership; namely, that of a Chinese Communist Party which manages to balance the interests of different social groups, avoids (or at least contains) social conflict, and maintains political stability.[64] An important part of the construction of a system of 'rule of law government' (*fǎzhì zhèngfǔ*: 法治政府) and, in particular, the creation of a much improved administrative or governance system is the resolution of social contradictions and the creation of a harmonious socialist society. Therefore, while the importance of the rule of law continues to be stressed by the Chinese leadership, there is now also a strong emphasis on the need for the people and the state to enjoy a close and harmonious relationship. The construction of this 'harmonious society' is the responsibility of both the Communist Party and the Chinese state – whose interests are now seen as fused rather than in need of separation.[65] Indeed, reports in the PRC legal press of 'heroic judges' who have pressed ahead with experimental approaches that seek settlement as an outcome in administrative suits explain that one of the virtuous techniques used to achieve settlement is seeking and securing support from the local Communist Party Committee and the relevant government departments.[66] And the concept of harmonious society, in placing emphasis on peace and harmony (*hé wéi guì*: 和为贵), draws on the Confucian inspired 'Eastern Experience' (*dōngfāng jīngyàn*: 东方经验). The extension of the official preference for mediation in civil justice to administrative cases is an important aspect of the attempt to adjust judicial reform in the PRC, so that such reform is more consistent with the values of traditional Chinese society, especially those of Confucianism (*Rújiā*: 儒家).[67]

In addition, efforts are now being made to change the legal position of mediation in administrative cases. The Supreme People's Court 'Withdrawal Rules' 2008 are not an isolated development. The introduction of the Rules follows various officially-sanctioned experiments in provincial court practice with 'administrative litigation compromise' (*xíngzhèng sùsòng xiétiáo*: 行政诉讼协调).[68] In addition, draft revisions of the *ALL* 1989, and a planned Administrative Litigation Procedures Law (*Xíngzhèng Sùsòng Chéngxù Fǎ*: 行政诉讼程序法) both make provision for judicial mediation.[69] The President of the Supreme People's Court, speaking at a national conference on the work of judges, argues not only that administrative suits are amenable to judicial mediation, but also that for this and other reasons PRC administrative chamber judges now need training both in adjudication *and* in mediation.[70] So, it seems clear that when the *ALL* 1989 is finally revised, the ban on the use of mediation for dealing with substantive issues in administrative suits will be lifted. In the meantime, what is needed in the pre-trial, judicially-mediated settlement of administrative cases is the creation of a more open and accountable system, and the 'Withdrawal Rules' 2008 are a small but highly significant step in that direction. Another key requirement is better procedural safeguards for the plaintiff, and the 'Withdrawal Rules' and the 'Jurisdiction Rules' 2008 take some tentative steps in that direction too.

Conclusions

As noted, the covert but steadily intensifying embrace in the PRC over the past decade or so of judicial mediation in administrative proceedings reflects a number of factors, some practical, some ideological and cultural, and some institutional. The impact of these factors has given mediation in administrative suits a new – albeit not yet fully legal – status, despite serious worries within PRC legal circles about the advisability of this processual practice. Many of the objections raised in the late 1980s to the incorporation of judicial mediation remain important today: in particular, the need for the administrative chambers in the people's courts to focus on the lawfulness of administrative conduct; the uncertain authority of the administrator to agree to compromise elements in settlements; and the problem of the sometimes gross disparities of power between the plaintiff and the defendant in administrative suits. To these criticisms have now been added others derived from the practical experience of judicial mediation: the uncertain legal status of the judge's conduct and of the outcome of the mediation; and the excessive use of judicial authority to compel participation in mediation and acceptance of proposed outcomes.

In considering the practical dimensions of the transformation of the relationship between administrative litigation and judicial mediation, it is worth considering the PRC case in a comparative context. For the PRC is not alone in the drift towards greater use of mediation in administrative suits. In both the Anglo-American common law world and in a number of continental jurisdictions, notably France and Germany, we may discern an increased reliance on mediation as a mode of decision-making in public law cases.[71] Although, as in the PRC, doubts have sometimes been raised about this development,[72] increased case-loads, the search for more flexible resolutions, a more relaxed view of the nature of administrative disputes, and a more proactive role for the judge have encouraged an expanded use of mediation – sometimes by the judge, sometimes by the processes of court-annexed or court-referred mediation. Elsewhere, too, there have been difficulties with the incorporation of mediation into the handling of administrative cases. In France, for example, 'the lack of formal implantation meant that many procedural and organisational issues were never solved', and even today this problem has not been fully overcome, and in Germany 'in practice, a few committed individuals are the driving force behind the mediation movement in the German administrative courts [so that] future evolution is likely still to be conditioned by the effort and conviction of administrative law judges'.[73] In the PRC, too, the move towards judicial mediation of administrative cases has proceeded inductively, and indeed on an even less secure legal basis than in Europe, and apparently with less careful official consideration of the wider implications of the growth of the judicial practice of mediatory intervention.

In the PRC, it is clear that the new developmental goal of creating a 'socialist harmonious society' has *also* been a very important factor in the transformed attitude to mediation. With party and state much more closely aligned, compromise and ostensibly consensual decision-making are now considered especially appropriate for resolving unfortunate contradictions between the state and its citizens. This 'harmony ideology', drawing on both Confucian and socialist communitarian values, also carries within itself an impulse of social control and rights suppression, as well as serving as something of an expression of the Chinese collective self-pitted against the external world.[74] In this era of rapid economic change in the PRC, the imperatives of social stability and political control make adjudicative decision-making in administrative disputes distinctly unattractive from the point of view of the Chinese leadership. As a result, the *ALL* 1989 may be seen now not as primarily an attempt by the Communist Party to scrutinize and control the conduct of state actors[75] (and even less a reflection of the leadership's respect for citizens' rights and the rule of law), but rather as an arena for containment and suppression of citizen grievance. There are significant parallels here too with the Chinese leadership's continuing unwillingness to recognize the 'right to strike', despite growing conflicts in employment relations and considerable episodes of labour unrest. Here, too, significant efforts are being made to encourage the use of mediation as the primary mode of decision-making.[76]

It is, however, in the area of institutional factors that the transformation in the judicial approach to administrative suits is most important. A most remarkable change in party–state relations underpins the shift, with the party turning its back on the Dengist ideal of separating party and state after Tiananmen in the summer of 1989 and, instead, recreating a close knit and unified relationship between the two key elements of the Chinese leadership. That relationship now seeks to create and maintain, in the face of rapid economic change and resulting social inequality and unrest, a socialist harmonious society in which there is only limited, incremental political change. In this system, too, there is only restricted room for the autonomy of the courts, especially on politically sensitive issues. From this point of view, judicial mediation of administrative cases has the very important advantage of restricting the independence of the judge, for the mediating judge is much less able than in a full trial to make and justify a decision in terms of application of the law. Mediation, far from giving the judge a great deal of discretion, leaves the judge directly accountable to court and local Communist Party leaders for the mediated outcome of an administrative suit.

Notes

1. Adopted at the Second Session of the Seventh National People's Congress on 4 April 1989, promulgated by Order No. 16 of the President of the People's Republic of China on 4 April 1989, and effective as of 1 October 1990.
2. *Law of Civil Procedure (for Trial Implementation)* 1982.
3. An important Confucian value that continues to finds its way from time to time is contemporary PRC legislation. For example, in the *Law of Inheritance* 1985 at Article 15, the parties to an inheritance dispute are advised to settle any differences between them, *inter alia*, in a spirit of 'yielding'.
4. For a very interesting account of this film from a lawerly point of view see Jerome A. Cohen and Joan Lebold Cohen, "Did Qiu Ju Get Good Legal Advice?," in *Cinema, Law and the State in Asia*, ed. Cory K. Creekmur and Mark Sidel (New York: Palgrave Macmillan, 2007), 161–73.
5. Stanley B. Lubman, *Bird in a Cage: Legal Reform in China after Mao* (Stanford, CA: Stanford University Press, 1999), 251.
6. On the Great Wall as a monument to Qin authoritarianism, as inspired by Legalism, see for example, Edgar Kiser and Yong Cai, "War and Bureaucratization in Qin China: Exploring an Anomalous Case," *American Sociological Review* 68 (2003): 511–39. William Jenner concludes that the Wall and other grand architectural and infrastructure projects completed by the Qin 'would have constituted a formidable list of undertakings by a modern state that had plenty of earth-moving machinery, could wield massive repression and did not care about economic rationality or the rights and well being of its citizens. I wonder whether even Ceausescu's Romania could have done it, and I am

sure Trajan's Rome could not'. W. J. F. Jenner, *The Tyranny of History: The Roots of China's Crisis* (London: Allen Lane, Penguin Books, 1992), 21. A somewhat revisionist view of Legalism is provided by Kenneth I. Winston, the noted interpreter of the work of Lon Fuller, in his essay on "The Internal Morality of Chinese Legalism," *Singapore Journal of Legal Studies* December (2005): 313–47.

7. For an English-language version of the speech, see Editorial Committee for Party Literature and Central Committee of the Communist Party of China, eds, *Selected Works of Deng Xiaoping (1975–1982)* (Beijing: Foreign Languages Press, 1983), 302–25.
8. Ibid., 303.
9. Zhao Ziyang, "Advance Along the Road of Socialism with Chinese Characteristics, Report Delivered at the Thirteenth National Congress of the Communist Party of China on October 25, 1987," in *Documents of the Thirteenth National Congress of the Communist Party of China* (Beijing: Foreign Languages Press, 1987), 3–77.
10. Ibid., 3, 47, 50.
11. Article 3 of the *Law of Civil Procedure (for Trial Implementation)* 1982 stated, 'the provisions of this Law are applicable to administrative cases that by law are to be tried by the people's courts'.
12. This provides, 'if a state organ or its personnel, in the course of executing its duties, encroach upon the lawful rights and interests of a citizen or legal person and causes damage, it shall bear civil liability'. *General Principles of the Civil Law* 1986 art. 121.
13. Article 12 stipulates that, 'the people's courts shall not accept suits brought by citizens, legal persons or other organizations against any of the following matters: (1) acts of the state in areas like national defence and foreign affairs; (2) administrative rules and regulations, and regulations, or decisions and orders with general binding force formulated and announced by administrative organs; (3) decisions of an administrative organ on awards or punishments for its personnel or on the appointment or relief of duties of its personnel; (4) specific administrative acts that shall, as provided for by law, be finally decided by an administrative organ'. In addition, Article 14 ensures that more complex cases are handled by a superior tribunal: the Intermediate People's Court, who 'shall have jurisdiction as courts of first instance over the following administrative cases: (1) cases of confirming patent rights of invention and cases handled by the Customs; (2) suits against specific administrative acts undertaken by departments under the State Council or by the people's governments of provinces, autonomous regions or municipalities directly under the Central Government; and (3) grave and complicated cases in areas under their jurisdiction'.
14. Pitman B. Potter, "The Administrative Litigation Law of the PRC: Judicial Review and Bureaucratic Reform," in *Domestic Law Reforms in Post-Mao China*, ed. Pitman B. Potter (Armonk, NY: M. E. Sharpe, 1994), 276.
15. See, for example, Ulric M. Killion, "China's Amended Constitution: Quest for Liberty and Independent Judicial Review," *Washington University Global Studies Law Review* 4 (2005): 43–80; Veron Mei-ying Hung, "China's WTO Commitment on Independent Judicial Review: Impact on Legal and Political Reform," *American Journal of Comparative Law* 52 (2002): 77–132; Hon S. Chan, "Judicial Review and Control Over Administrative Discretion in the People's Republic of China," *Review of Central and East European Law* 18 (1992): 135–63.
16. See, for example, Potter, "The Administrative Litigation Law of the PRC: Judicial Review and Bureaucratic Reform," 270–304; Susan Finder, "Like Throwing a Stone Against an Egg: Administrative Litigation in the People's Republic of China," *Journal of Chinese Law* 3 (1989): 9–10.
17. See *Administrative Litigation Law* 1989 arts 12, 14. With the advent of Deng Xiaoping's leadership, there was a significant shift in socialist ideology. Class struggle was dropped as the 'key link', mass campaigns were banned, and 'equality before the law' was emphasized in Deng's criticisms of corrupt cadres who presumed that

they were above the law. See Ronald C. Keith, "Chinese Politics and the New Theory of 'Rule of Law'," *The China Quarterly* 125 (1991): 112.

18. Necessary that is, for dealing with minor cases. It should also be noted that for criminal matters and trial supervision, the court system is paralleled by a bureaucratic ladder of prosecuting organs – the People's Procuracies – at the apex of which is found the Supreme People's Procuracy.
19. See Pitman Potter's chapter in this publication.
20. Interview with judges serving in a local people's tribunal, Wuyi Shan, Fujian Province, July 19, 2008.
21. See Connie Carter's chapter in this publication.
22. In addition, following proposals from the President of the Supreme People's Court, the Standing Committee of the National People's Congress assigns judges to specific positions within the Court – it appoints the Vice Presidents of the Court, the Chief Judge and Deputy Chief Judge in each Chamber, individual judges and – very importantly – the members of the adjudicative committee.
23. See, for example, William C. Jones, "The Significance of the *Opinion* of the Supreme People's Court for Civil Law in Post-Mao China," in *Domestic Law Reforms in Post-Mao China*, ed. Pitman B. Potter (Armonk, NY: M. E. Sharpe, 1994): 97–108.
24. *Organic Law of the People's Courts*, as revised 2006 art. 11.
25. See Michael Dowdle, "Completing Teubner: Foreign Irritants in China's Clinical Legal Education System and the 'Convergence' of Imaginations," in *Examining Practice, Interrogating Theory: Comparative Legal Studies in Asia*, ed. Sarah Biddulph and Pip Nicholson (Leiden, The Netherlands: Martin Nijhoff, 2008), 169–94.
26. See Colin Hawes, "Seeds of Dissent: The Evolution of Published Commercial Law Court Judgments in Contemporary China," *Australian Journal of Asian Law* 5 (2003): 1–41.
27. Opened for signature 19 December 1966, 999 UNTS 171 (entered into force 23 March 1976).
28. For a concise and insightful account of the workings of the *ALL*, see Lubman, *Bird in a Cage: Legal Reform in China after Mao*, 206–10. A preliminary analysis of some of the issues considered here is contained in Michael Palmer, "Controlling the State?: Mediation in Administrative Litigation in the People's Republic of China," *Transnational Law and Contemporary Problems* 16 (2007): 165–87.
29. Article 11 of the *ALL* enumerates the kinds of administrative case that a People's Court may accept: nearly all categories concern the lawfulness of administrative conduct, although there is also provision for accepting cases in which, for example, a manager's decision-making powers have allegedly been infringed.
30. The *Civil Procedure Law (for Trial Implementation)* 1982 provided for review by the people's courts of administrative decisions at Article 3 and, as noted above, the revised *Constitution* of the following year declared at Article 41 that 'citizens who have suffered losses through infringement of their civil rights by any state organ or functionary have the right to compensation in accordance with the law'. Subsequently, this right was also incorporated into other legislation including, in particular, the *General Principles of the Civil Law* 1986, at Article 121, which provides 'if a state organ or its personnel, in the course of executing its duties, encroach upon the lawful rights and interests of a citizen or legal person and causes damage, it shall bear civil liability'.
31. Simon Roberts and Michael Palmer, *Dispute Processes: ADR and the Primary Forms of Decision-Making*, 2nd edn (Cambridge: Cambridge University Press, 2005), 44–77.
32. For a review of the debates about this issue in the period preceding the promulgation of the *Administrative Litigation Law* in 1999, see Michael Palmer, "The Revival of Mediation in the People's Republic of China: (2) Judicial Mediation," in *Yearbook on Socialist Legal Systems 1988*, ed. W. E. Butler (New York: Transnational Books, 1989), 143–71.

33. Specifically, Article 50 of the *ALL* stipulates firmly that: 'the people's courts in hearing administrative cases may not use mediation'.
34. For a succinct account of these two systems see: Randall Peerenboom, *China's Long March toward Rule of Law* (Cambridge: Cambridge University Press, 2002), 417–21.
35. Ibid.
36. Ibid.
37. See, Jonathan Watts, "Groundswell of Protest Feared by Party Officials," *The Guardian*, October 10, 2005, http://www.guardian.co.uk/world/2005/oct/10/china.jonathanwatts; Li Lianjiang and Kevin J. O'Brien, "Villagers and Popular Resistance in Contemporary China," *Modern China* 22 (1996): 28–61.
38. See, Michael Palmer, "Towards a Greener China? Accessing Environmental Justice in the People's Republic of China," in *Access to Environmental Justice: Comparative Perspectives*, ed. A. J. Harding (Leiden, The Netherlands: Martin Nijhoff, 2007): 205–35.
39. Jane MaCartney, "China Establishes Crack Unit to Crush Poverty Protests," *The Times*, August 20, 2005, 43.
40. See, for example, Watts, "Groundswell of Protest Feared by Party Officials".
41. Palmer, "Controlling the State?: Mediation in Administrative Litigation in the People's Republic of China."
42. "Zuohao Xinfang Gongzuo ba Maodun Huajie zai Shequ," (Try to Resolve the Contradiction within the Community by Doing Well the Work of Letters and Visits) 2005–6, http://xw.bjcs.gov.cn/sqjs/sqjsAction.go?operate = viewand lm = SQJS_SQFWand jbshj_id = 449166
43. Ibid.
44. *Administrative Review Law* 1999 translated into English at the website of China's State Environmental Protection Administration (SEPA), http://english.sepa.gov.cn/zffg/fl/199904/t19990429_49746.htm
45. The precise wording of the relevant article – that is Article 8 – in the *Administrative Review Law* 1999 indicates that mediation is extensively relied upon where there is a 'civil dispute' between the Parties. In practice, however, negotiation and mediation are extensively relied upon.
46. Chu Shenjing, "You yiqi Xingzheng Fuyi Anjian Chenggong Tiaojie Dedao de Qishi," (The Revelation Obtained by a Successfully Mediated Administrative Review Case) http://www.chinalaw.gov.cn/jsp/contentpub/browser/contentpro.jsp?contentid = co700194811
47. Peerenboom, *China's Long March toward Rule of Law*, 418.
48. According to Article 9 of the *Administrative Review Law* 1999, the time limit in most instances is a mere 60 days.
49. Zuigao Renmin Fayuan Guanyu Xingzheng Susong Chesu Ruogan Wenti de Guiding (Supreme People's Court Rules Concerning Several Problems in the Withdrawal of Administrative Suits), promulgated on 1 January 2008, and in force 1 February 2008, http://news.xinhuanet.com/legal/2008–01/16/content_7432440.htm. See also, "Guanyu renzhen guanche zhixing 'Zuigao Renmin Fayuan Xingzheng Susong Chesu Ruogan Wenti de Guiding' de Tongzhi," (Notice on Seriously Carrying Out the 'Supreme People's Court Rules Concerning Several Problems in the Withdrawal of Administrative Suits') *Zuigao Renmin Fayuan Gongbao (Gazette of the Supreme People's Court)* 1 (2008): 19–20.
50. Zuigao Renmin Fayuan Guan yu Xingzheng Anjian Guanxia Ruogan Wenti de Guiding (Rules of the Supreme People's Court on Some Issues Concerning Jurisdiction in Administrative Cases), promulgated 14 January 2008, and in force on 1 February 2008, http://www.legalinfo.gov.cn/misc/2008–01/17/content_783022.htm. See also "Guanyu renzhen guanche zhixing 'Zuigao Renmin Fayuan Xingzheng Anjian Guanxia Ruogan Wenti de Guiding' de Tongzhi," (Notice on Seriously

Carrying Out the 'Supreme People's Court Rules on Some Issues Concerning Jurisdiction in Administrative Cases'), 17–18.

51. The term '*jítuán sùsòng*,' referring to a form of collective action, is not found in the *Administrative Litigation Law* 1989 itself, but is conceptualized as a type of '*gòngtóng sùsòng*' in an important judicial explanation approved in the late 1990s by the Supreme People's Court, at Article 8: Zuigao Renmin Fayuan Guanyu Zhixing, "Zhonghua Renmin Gongheguo Xingzheng Susong Fa Ruogan Wenti de Jieshi," (Supreme People's Court Explanation on Several Problems in Carrying Out the Administrative Litigation Law of the PRC), promulgated and in force 10 March 2000. For an account of the varying forms of collective suits in PRC civil and administrative procedure law see, for example, Michael Palmer and Xi Chao, "China," *The ANNALS of the American Academy of Political and Social Science* 622 (2009) (Special Issue entitled 'The Globalisation of Class Actions'): 270–9.
52. That is, a case involving a Hong Kong, Macao or Taiwan element.
53. Xing Hui and Yuan Dingbo, "Zuigao Renmin Fayuan Xingzhengting Tingzhang Zhao Daguang shuo – woguo xingzheng susong anjian shenli jidai chuangxin," (Head of the Administrative Chamber of the Supreme People's Court, Zhao Dawen, speaks: there is an urgent need for new ideas in handling administrative litigation cases in China) http://www.legaldaily.com.cn/misc/2007–03/11/content_555917.htm
54. Dai Weizhong, "Xingzheng Susong Tiaojie Zhidu Yinggai Gaige," (The System of Mediation in Administrative Litigation should be Reformed) *Renmin Fayuanbao* (People's Court Daily), August 28, 2005, 4.
55. The position in Shanghai changed in 2007, when the Shanghai Higher People's Court authorized in administrative suits mediatory intervention by judges on an experimental basis in order to deal with the 'contradictions between officials and citizens' (*guān-min máodùn*: 官民矛盾). See Chen Qingke, "Shanghai Gaoyuan Chutai Xin Guiding 'Min Gao Guan' Anjian Keyi Hejie," (The Shanghai Higher People's Court Makes Public New Rules in which 'People Sue Officials' Cases May Settle) http://www.zpzs.gov.cn/info/20070408085008.htm
56. Dai Weizhong, "Xingzheng Susong Tiaojie Zhidu Yinggai Gaige," (The System of Mediation in Administrative Litigation should be Reformed) *Renmin Fayuanbao* (People's Court Daily), August 28, 2005, 4.
57. Wang Weiyun and Wang Jianbing, "Guanyu Jianli Xingzheng Susong Tiaojie Zhidu de Tantao," (An Inquiry Concerning the Establishment of the System of Mediation in Administrative Litigation) http://www.chinacourt.org/public/detail.php?id = 180843
58. Minxin Pei, "Citizens v. Mandarins: Administrative Litigation in China," *The China Quarterly* 152 (1997): 843–4; Wang Weiyun and Wang Jianbing, "Guanyu Jianli Xingzheng Susong Tiaojie Zhidu de Tantao," (An Inquiry Concerning the Establishment of the System of Mediation in Administrative Litigation) http://www.chinacourt.org/public/detail.php?id = 180843
59. Wang Weiyun and Wang Jianbing, "Guanyu Jianli Xingzheng Susong Tiaojie Zhidu de Tantao," (An Inquiry Concerning the Establishment of the System of Mediation in Administrative Litigation) http://www.chinacourt.org/public/detail.php?id = 180843
60. Ibid.
61. Especially Article 85, which provides that 'in the trial of civil cases, the people's court shall distinguish between right and wrong on the basis of the facts being clear and conduct mediation between the parties on a voluntary basis'.
62. See L. I. Guangyu, "'Guanyou xingzheng susong chesu ruogan wenti de guiding', de lijie yu shiyong," (Explanation and Applicability of 'The Supreme People's Court Rules Concerning Several Problems in the Withdrawal of Suit in Administrative Litigation') http://rmfyb.chinacourt.org/public/detail.php?id = 116585; Wang Weiyun and Wang Jianbing, "Guanyu Jianli Xingzheng Susong Tiaojie Zhidu de Tantao," (An Inquiry Concerning the Establishment of the System of Mediation in Administrative Litigation) http://www.chinacourt.org/public/detail.php?id = 180843

63. See Michael Palmer, "The Revival of Mediation in the People's Republic of China: (1) Extra-Judicial Mediation," in *Yearbook on Socialist Legal Systems 1987*, ed. W. E. Butler (New York: Transnational Books, 1988), 219–77.
64. See, for example, Willy Lam, "Socialism with a Harmonious Face: HU Jintao's Plans for Reform," *China Brief* 4 (2004): 5–7.
65. Cao Kangtai, "Renzhen Guanche 'Quanmian tuijin yifa xingzheng shishi gangyao' jianshe fazhi zhengfu, goujian hexie shehui," (Strive to Implement the 'Program for Administration According to the Law' to Build a Government under Rule of Law and to Create a Harmonious Society) in *Zhongguo Falü Nianjian* (Law Year Book of China 2005) (Beijing: Zhongguo Falü Nianjian She, 2006), 44–51.
66. Li Jinggeng, "Ta zhao dao guan-min hexie de jidian – ji dang de shiqi daibiao, quanguo youxiu faguan Wang Hongwei," (She found the fulcrum for harmony between officials and the people – chronicling Seventeenth Party Congress Representative and exemplary judge, Wang Hongwei) http://rmfyb.chinacourt.org/public/detail.php?id = 110922
67. Wu Jing, "Xiao Yang: Neng Tiao Ze Tiao, Dang Pan Ze Pan: Buneng gei Tiaojie Ding Zhibiao," (Xiao Yang [says] Mediate a Case if it can be Mediated, Adjudicate a Case when Adjudication is Appropriate: But a Target for Mediation Need Not be Set) http://www.china.com.cn/policy/txt/2007–01/17content_7668085.htm
68. See, for example, Higher People's Court of Jiangsu Province, *Xingzheng Susong Xietiao Wenti Yanjiu* (Research into the Problem of Conciliation in Administrative Litigation), unpublished manuscript, on file with author.
69. Interviews with legislators working on the revised law, May 2005.
70. Wu Jing, "Xiao Yang: Neng Tiao Ze Tiao, Dang Pan Ze Pan: Buneng gei Tiaojie Ding Zhibiao," (Xiao Yang [says] Mediate a Case if it can be Mediated, Adjudicate a Case when Adjudication is Appropriate: But a Target for Mediation Need Not be Set) http://www.china.com.cn/policy/txt/2007–01/17content_7668085.htm
71. In the United States, the *Administrative Dispute Resolution Act* of 1996 (Pub. Law 104–320) specifically encourages the use of alternatives, especially mediation, and has been an important stimulus to the use of mediation in administrative cases (see http://www.adr.gov/pdf/adra.pdf). In England and Wales, in several leading judgments, one of the most senior judges, Lord Woolf, has himself declared in robust language that the emphasis on mediation and other reforms introduced by the 1998 *Civil Procedure Rules* (which he inspired) should also govern administrative cases. Indeed, in the *Cowl* case (*R (Cowl)* v. *Plymouth City Council* [2001] EWCA Civ 1935), he also indicated the manner in which mediation might be best incorporated into judicial review. In France and Germany the judge has long been permitted to attempt mediatory intervention. Here, there is a well-established view that the involvement of the judge as a kind of mediator in administrative cases should be possible so that important principles or values in administrative law can be given some consideration or protection in the mediation process, but in recent years, the judicial propensity to use this authority has significantly increased. Thus, in France, there has been a series of initiatives designed to incorporate pre-trial mediation into the processes of the administrative courts. A revision in 1986 to the *Administrative Code* encouraged the use of mediation in first instance administrative courts and subsequently, in 1989, a case decision in effect gave the courts wide-ranging discretion in deciding whether or not to employ a mediatory approach. In Germany, although there is no new special legislation encouraging mediation, the provisions in Article 87 of the *Administrative Code* have been relied on in order to expand the role of mediation. These authorize the judge to seek a settlement between the parties, and is deemed to be a justification for mediation. For examinations of these developments see: Varda Bondy, "Who Needs ADR," *Legal Action* September (2004): www.publiclawproject.org.uk/downloads/WhoNeedsADR.pdf; Sophie Boyron, "The Rise of Mediation in Administrative Law Disputes: Experiences from England, France and

Germany," *Public Law* (2006): 320–43; Michael Supperstone, Daniel Stilitz and Clive Sheldon, "ADR and Public Law," *Public Law* (2006): 299–319.

72. Lord Irvine, "Paper given by Rt Hon Lord Irvine of Lairg at the Inaugural Lecture of The Faculty of Mediation and ADR" (paper presented at the inaugural lecture of the Faculty of Mediation and ADR, London, UK, 27 January 1999), www.academy-experts.org/docs/fmadr270199.pdf; Martin Partington, "ADR: Prospects and Challenges," www.academy-experts.org/docs/fmadr221003.pdf
73. Boyron, "The Rise of Mediation in Administrative Law Disputes," 329–31.
74. Laura Nader, *Harmony Ideology: Justice and Control in a Mexican Zapotec Village* (Stanford, CA: Stanford University Press, 1990), 1–11.
75. See also Tom Ginsburg's insightful and extended analysis of the principal–agent relationship and administrative law elsewhere in "Administrative Law and the Judicial Control of Agents in Authoritarian Regimes," in *Rule by Law: The Politics of Courts in Authoritarian Regimes,* ed. Tom Ginsburg and Tamir Moustafa (Cambridge: Cambridge University Press, 2008), 58–72.
76. *Law on Labour Dispute Mediation and Arbitration*, adopted at the 31st Session of the Standing Committee of the 10th National People's Congress on 29 December 2007, and in force 1 May 2008, http://tradeinservices.mofcom.gov.cn/en/b/2007-12-29/27880.shtml. The new law seeks, *inter alia*, to promote 'harmonious and stable labour relations' (*laódonġ guānxi héxíe weǹdinġ*: 劳动关系和谐稳定), prioritizes the use of negotiation (*xíeshāng*: 协商) and mediation for resolving labour disputes (Article 5), and in arbitration encourages not only settlement and withdrawal of suit (Article 41) but also mediatory intervention by the arbitral tribunal (Article 42).

Part V

Analysing anti-graft courts

13 The politics of Indonesia's anti-corruption court

Benjamin H. Tahyar

Introduction

On 11 April 2005, Indonesia's Anti-Corruption Court (*Pengadilan Tindak Pidana Korupsi, Tipikor*) found Abdullah Puteh, the former provincial governor of Nanggroe Aceh Darussalam, guilty of corruption and sentenced him to 10 years in prison. In addition, the *Tipikor* fined Puteh Rp. 500 million (about US$55,400)[1] and sought restitution for some Rp. 3.6 billion (about US$399,600) in alleged losses to the state. Puteh had been found guilty of overcharging the state in the purchase of an official helicopter and pocketing the difference. He was the first defendant to be tried before the *Tipikor*. Since his conviction, more than 30 people accused of corruption have been tried before the *Tipikor* and found guilty. One can quibble about the severity of some of the sentences handed down by the Court but, on the whole, the *Tipikor* has been very positively received in the mass media. There is a widespread perception that justice has been done in the way the Court has handled itself. This widespread perception has helped the *Tipikor* to achieve a large measure of legitimacy.

To date, no corruption suspect brought before the Court has escaped conviction. This 100 per cent conviction rate has raised eyebrows among critics and even among a number of supporters of the *Tipikor*, and has led to allegations that perhaps the Court is less than impartial. Most supporters have countered, however, that none of the *Tipikor's* judgments has been reversed on appeal. Indeed, the appellate courts have on occasions seen fit to augment the sentences handed down by the *Tipikor*. Whatever the merits of the positions of both critics and supporters of the Court, the perception popularized in the press and by non-governmental organizations (NGOs) involved in governance reform is that the *Tipikor* has been a success, if only because it has done what it was designed to do: try people accused of corruption and, if found guilty, put them behind bars. To the extent that the *Tipikor* has so far fulfilled its mandate, it can be considered a success.

But on 19 December 2006, Indonesia's new Constitutional Court declared the *Tipikor* unconstitutional.[2] The *Tipikor* was established on the basis of *Law No. 30/2002*, the enabling law of the Corruption Eradication Commission (*Komisi Pemberantasan Korupsi*, KPK). As such, it has no independent legal basis. To the Constitutional Court, this was a fatal flaw. Moreover, the Constitutional Court held that the existence of the *Tipikor* caused a 'duality' in Indonesia's judicial system.

Corruption suspects are tried before the *Tipikor* only if they have been prosecuted by the KPK.

Corruption suspects prosecuted by the Attorney-General's Office and other public prosecutors continue to be tried before the District Courts. Since the *Tipikor* had different procedural rules from the District Courts, two different persons accused of violating the same laws – *Law No. 31/1999* as amended by *Law No. 20/2001* – would be given different protections under the law. This would violate Article 28D(1) of the 1945 *Constitution of the Republic of Indonesia*, which guarantees citizens equal protection of the law. However, in a move highly atypical for a court of law, the Constitutional Court gave the government three years in which to cure the constitutional defect of the *Tipikor*.[3] Absent positive action on the part of the government and the People's Representative Council (*Dewan Perwakilan Rakyat*, DPR), the country's legislature, the *Tipikor* will cease to exist on 19 December 2009.

What is the likely fate of the *Tipikor* and of Indonesia's anti-corruption drive in general? Corruption is widely considered as a significant obstacle to economic development in third world countries. International financial institutions (IFIs) like the World Bank have consistently advocated the eradication of corruption as a necessary step to economic development.[4] Indonesia clearly needs an effective anti-corruption strategy that includes a strong judicial component. The government has set up a drafting committee, headed up by Teuku Nasrullah, a law professor at the University of Indonesia, to rewrite *Law No. 30/2002*, but nothing much has been heard about it. One would have thought that the government would take swift measures to insure the continued constitutional viability of the *Tipikor*. Yet, nothing concrete has been heard from the government on this issue. How are we to explain this inaction?

Institution-building – especially of legal institutions – does not take place in a vacuum. The political economic context is all-important. Institutions are built by individuals not only as a way to solve collective action problems, but also to consolidate their positions in the political economy.[5] Thus, institutions are not always efficiency-enhancing.[6] But they are always built to secure a particular system of power.[7] Those who are in power, therefore, have every incentive to maintain the institutional matrix that supports their particular political economy.[8] In Indonesia, corruption is not simply deeply ingrained culturally; it is an important institution in the country's political economy. Corruption or rent-seeking is the key element in the 'political capitalism' that remains the essential feature of Indonesia's political economy, where often firms succeed not because they are more efficient than their competitors, but because they received preferential treatment from the government. This chapter argues that any informed speculation as to the likely fate of the *Tipikor* must be made against this backdrop.

Why a special anti-corruption court?

Why was it necessary to create a special anti-corruption court? Corruption suspects prosecuted by the Attorney-General's Office and other public prosecutors working under the authority of the Attorney-General are tried today before the District Courts. Indeed, more corruption suspects are tried before the District Courts than before the *Tipikor*. The simple answer is that the career judiciary could not be trusted to do the job. Indonesia's career judges are typically perceived as being corrupt and neither independent nor impartial. Although judges currently on the bench had to pass an exam and be subjected to psychological testing to assess their suitability for the job, the selection process is typically not transparent. Getting into the judiciary depends more on bribery and/or political connections rather than merits.[9] Consequently, those selected are not necessarily the most qualified or the most suitable.

The career pattern of Indonesian judges typically involves promotions and transfers. Judges are very often promoted or transferred based on how long they have been in their current position and not necessarily for good performance. How many times their decisions have been reversed by a higher court, for example, is not really taken into consideration in promotions and transfers. The process is often used both to reward and punish individual judges. At least one judge has publicly claimed that he was being punished for having spoken out about the 'judicial mafia'.[10] Sahlan Said, a Yogyakarta District Court judge, saw his move as a punishment, although he was technically being promoted to an appellate court. Said claimed that promotions and transfers in the judiciary are typically made on the basis of nepotism and corruption.[11] In this way, the system actually compromises the independence of individual judges. Judges may decide cases in a way that advances their careers rather than render a judgment based on an objective interpretation of the law. The possibility that judges may be transferred to remote locations away from family and social circles and be left there for a good number of years, obviously has a significant impact on how they do their job.

The Indonesian judiciary is also perceived to be susceptible to outside interference, particularly by the government. Indeed, political interference in judicial matters has had a long history in Indonesia. Through *Law No. 19/1964*, President Sukarno asserted his right to intervene in judicial matters 'for the sake of the ongoing revolution' or when 'national interests' warranted interference.[12] This law was subsequently superseded by *Law No. 14/1970*, but the new law, enacted under former President Soeharto's New Order regime, provided no better guarantee for a judiciary independent from political interference. Although less common since the downfall of the New Order, political interference has probably continued to occur. For example, political interference was suspected in the acquittal of four former leaders of the Bandung City Council of corruption charges (about US$1.08 million) by the local District Court.[13] Indeed, there are many examples of acquittals and inappropriately light sentences in corruption cases brought before District Courts.[14] According to Indonesia Corruption Watch, of 71 corruption cases involving 243 suspects tried before the District Courts in 2005,[15] 27 cases (38 per cent) resulted in 'not guilty' verdicts. Of the 44 cases in which 'guilty' verdicts were reached, sentences of two years or less were meted out in 25 cases (nearly 57 per cent), whereas only in five cases (just over 11 per cent) were sentences higher than five years handed down.[16]

The impartiality of judges has also been questioned because the career judiciary has been notoriously corrupt. Transparency International recently conducted a survey in which more than half of Indonesians surveyed thought that the country's legal system was corrupt.[17] The chairman of the Indonesian Bar Association would put the figure at closer to 90 per cent.[18] This is consistent with the estimates of Januari Siregar, an advocate practising before the Medan District Court, who estimated that about 75 per cent of criminal and civil cases brought before the court 'were turned into commodities by judges and prosecutors'.[19] At least in part, corruption among judges can be attributed to the career system. To obtain a transfer or a promotion, judges have to bribe the relevant authority. In this way, transfers and promotions are 'investments' that have to be recouped. Considering also the extremely low salaries that judges earn, corruption becomes practically inevitable. For example, a district judge with over 20 years experience on the bench makes salary of about Rp. 5 million (about US$554) per month.[20] By contrast, the *Needs Assessment* for the Commercial Court in Jakarta stated that a reasonable minimum monthly salary for a judge serving on the Commercial Court is Rp. 17,549,000 (about US$1,944) per month.[21]

But very few judges – perhaps not surprisingly – have been sent to jail for corruption. In the past 30 years, only two have been convicted and sent to prison.[22] Yet, there is ample circumstantial evidence to suggest that public perception of rampant corruption among judges in Indonesia is probably correct. Frans Winarta, a lawyer in private practice and a member of the National Law Commission, remarked that some lawyers 'openly boast that they can guarantee a judicial outcome, and taunt their opponents with the inevitability that they will lose, not because of legal arguments, but because of the inadequacy of judicial salaries'.[23] Todung Mulya Lubis, another private practitioner and chairman of Transparency International Indonesia, stated that he has encountered two judgments that are word-for-word identical to each other issued by two courts in different parts of Indonesia. The connection? The plaintiffs in the two cases had the same counsel.[24]

If the unreliability of the career judiciary were a big concern, then why not create an anti-corruption court designed to hear all corruption cases and not just those brought by the KPK? Moreover, such an arrangement would have passed muster at the Constitutional Court, as we now know. A draft law contemplating exactly such a court was, in fact, published as an appendix to a book by a consortium of NGOs active in governance reform.[25] The book – published in early 2002 well before *Law No. 30/2002* was enacted at the end of that year – advocated a completely independent court that would hear all corruption cases.[26] Under Indonesian law, however, only four types of courts are allowed: (1) courts of general jurisdiction, (2) military courts, (3) religious courts and (4) administrative courts. Special courts like the *Tipikor* had to be constituted as chambers of District Courts.[27] Establishing a fifth type of court was considered to be very difficult to achieve.[28] Reformers eventually accepted that a completely independent anti-corruption court was not politically feasible.[29] In the end, the effort ended up as a compromise. Reformers got a special anti-corruption court but one that could only to hear cases brought by the KPK.

Stepchild of the judiciary

From the very beginning, the *Tipikor* has always been a stepchild of the Indonesian judiciary. The story is one of wilful neglect. The Supreme Court, whose responsibility it was to insure the viability and independence of the *Tipikor*, failed to live up to that responsibility. On 19 March 2003, Kwik Kian Gie, the then Minister for National Development Planning, issued a ministerial decree[30] authorizing the formation of a Steering Committee[31] whose task would be to lay the groundwork for the establishment of the *Tipikor*. Pursuant to the ministerial decree, two justices of the Supreme Court were appointed chairperson and vice chairperson, respectively, of the Committee. Members of the Committee came from the government, the judiciary, academia, NGOs active in governance reform and lawyers from private practice. A member of *Bappenas*, the National Development Planning Agency, served as secretary to the Committee. Thus a broad spectrum of stakeholders and other interested parties were represented in the Committee.

The Committee's mission was to publish a 'blueprint' containing specific recommendations as to how the *Tipikor* was to be established with regards to its 'recruitment system, development of human resources, organization, procedural law, supervision and equipment and infrastructure support for judges of the Tipikor'.[32] The Blueprint was published on 15 March 2004. According to the Blueprint's 'Action Plan',[33] it was the Supreme Court that bore most of the responsibilities for implementing the Blueprint's recommendations. But many, if not most, of these recommendations were never implemented. Indeed, the Supreme Court never bothered to set up a special committee in-house to implement the Blueprint's recommendations, but left it instead to six existing committees responsible for judicial reform within the Supreme Court.[34]

Many of these recommendations were designed to insulate the *Tipikor* from the Central Jakarta District Court. Many lessons had been learned from the disastrous experience of the Commercial Court.[35] Its decisions in the *Manulife* and *Prudential* cases were the most notorious.[36] But many cases during the early life of the Court also added to its reputation as the premier example of what *not* to do when establishing a new court. For example, reformers recalled that the Chief Judge of the Central Jakarta District Court was able to determine the distribution of cases as well as the composition of panels of judges that heard them in such a way as to affect the outcome.[37] Thus, the Blueprint had recommended that a special deputy responsible exclusively for the *Tipikor* be appointed to assist the Chief Judge of the Central Jakarta District Court administer and oversee the operations of the new court. However, pursuant to Article 11(1) of *Law No. 2/1986*, each District Court is only allowed one deputy chief judge. The Blueprint recommendation therefore required a change in the existing law. The task of making sure that this law was amended was delegated to the Supreme Court.[38] This recommendation was never implemented.[39]

Similarly, the Supreme Court never implemented the Blueprint recommendation that a deputy registrar exclusively responsible for anti-corruption cases be appointed. Judicial corruption in Indonesia often involved the participation of registry personnel. The Supreme Court also failed to carry out its responsibility to insure that the *Tipikor*'s budget be kept strictly separate from the budget of the Central Jakarta District Court.[40] The purpose here was to prevent the District Court from using funds intended for the *Tipikor* and, in the process, perhaps deprive the *Tipikor* of the funds it needs to carry out its mandate.[41]

A visit to the *Tipikor* on Jalan H. R. Rasuna Said in Jakarta shows that the Court is making do with the bare necessities. The judges have no access to any secretarial support and, judging from the state of the facilities, probably only the minimum of janitorial support. In the judges' 'chambers', which all the judges have to share, there was only one photocopier in evidence. There were no computers, no laser printers and no library. In the beginning, the judges had to buy their own printer paper and ink. It was not until May 2006, about 10 months after the Court was officially established, that these basic stationery supplies began to be provided.[42] The judges also had to resort to their own pockets to buy the books necessary for legal research. A court stenographer was provided but the judges had little faith in the fidelity of the records thus provided.[43] A closed-circuit television camera to record court proceedings has now been installed, but the money needed to pay for the system was provided by the KPK and not the Supreme Court.[44]

Perhaps most controversial was the Supreme Court's failure to make sure that sufficient funds were available to pay the salaries of the ad hoc judges appointed to the *Tipikor*.[45] Article 58(2) of *Law No. 30/2002* provided that persons accused of corruption be tried by a panel consisting of two career judges and three *ad hoc* judges. The *ad hoc* judges were appointed by *Presidential Decree (Keppres) No. 111/M/2004*, signed by President Megawati Soekarnoputri on 26 July 2004. But their investiture as judges of the *Tipikor* did not take place until 7 October 2004. It is unclear which of these two dates marked the beginning of their appointment as *ad hoc* judges of the *Tipikor*. Dudu Duswara, one of the *ad hoc* judges, believed that his appointment began on 26 July 2004, since this was the date on which he was required to relinquish his post as associate law professor at Langlangbuana University.[46] If we take this date as the beginning of the *ad hoc* judges' appointment, then it was to take over 13 months before they received their official salary. President Susilo Bambang Yudhoyono signed *Presidential Regulation (Perpres) No. 49/2005* on 27 July 2005 – a year and one day after his predecessor signed the decree appointing the *ad hoc* judges – authorizing payment of a monthly salary of Rp. 10 million (about US$1,108). However, *Presidential Regulation No. 49/2005* was to take over a month to travel the short distance from the Cabinet Secretary's office to the Supreme Court. It did not get there until 30 August 2005.[47]

It should be noted that the judges had been given loans – initially from *Bappenas* and subsequently from the Supreme Court – to tide them over. The first of these loans was given to the *ad hoc* judges on 5 February 2005, four months after their investiture or six months after their appointment as *ad hoc* judges.[48] One can only speculate as to whether loans would have been advanced had there not been a public outcry in the press.[49] The *ad hoc* judges had complained that they had gone through their savings and were living on their credit cards.[50] There was concern that given this situation, the three *ad hoc* judges too would fall prey to the temptation that has clearly overtaken most of the career judiciary. Achmad Linoh, an *ad hoc* judge at the *Tipikor*, believes that the Supreme Court's failure to make timely arrangements for the *ad hoc* judges' salaries was done on purpose to tempt them into receiving bribes.[51] Judge Duswara also believes that the oversight was on purpose but that it was intended to intimidate them into resigning.[52]

How serious was the Indonesian government in its declared intention to combat corruption? The government and the Supreme Court had about 16 months in which to prepare the budget of the *Tipikor*: from 19 March 2003, when the establishment of the Steering Committee was authorized, to the date that the *ad hoc* judges were appointed on 26 July 2003; more than ample time, one would have thought, for a concerted effort to prepare the groundwork for what was ostensibly an important national objective. Indeed, a pro-forma budget, which included judicial salaries, had in fact been published in mid-January 2004 along with the Blueprint.[53]

It is the practice of the Ministry of Finance to ask each government department every April whether their respective budgets for the current fiscal year are adequate to meet their expenditure.[54] Thus, ostensibly, there was time, even counting from the time that the Blueprint was published, for the Supreme Court to ask for supplementary funding. In fact, an alert Supreme Court had the chance to take the budgetary needs of the *Tipikor* into account in April 2003. April is the month when the Supreme Court normally begins to calculate its budgetary needs for the following fiscal year.[55] It is unclear whether the issue of the *Tipikor*'s budget was raised at that time, but in any event the funding needs of the *Tipikor* were not included in the Supreme Court's budget for 2004.

The Supreme Court was not only well represented in the Steering Committee, it also enjoyed a leadership position, since the chair and vice-chair were both occupied by Supreme Court justices. But the perception within the Supreme Court was that the *Tipikor* was an artifice imposed from the outside. The Supreme Court thus had no sense of ownership over the project.[56] Worse, the very existence of the *Tipikor* could be construed as an indictment of the career judiciary's competence and integrity. With hindsight, therefore, one could argue that the Supreme Court should have been the last institution to be trusted to ensure the welfare of the *Tipikor*.

To be fair to the current incumbent of Merdeka Palace, all of the planning for the *Tipikor* had been more or less completed by the time he was sworn into office on 20 October 2004. But perhaps President Yudhoyono could have done more to insure that the Blueprint was fully implemented given his strong anti-corruption campaign pledges. It still remains a mystery, for example, why *Presidential Regulation No. 49/2005*, the presidential regulation authorizing the payment of the *ad hoc* judges' salaries, took over a month to get from the Cabinet Secretary's office to the Supreme Court, just a few buildings away. Given his campaign pledges, it is also strange that President Yudhoyono did not react to the very public outcry in the media about the non-payment of the *ad hoc* judges' salaries.[57]

Ad hoc judges and the KPK

Despite the wilful neglect by the Supreme Court, the *Tipikor* did succeed. Thus far, it has tried 33 corruption suspects and found them all guilty as charged. Sentences meted out ranged from a low of 18 months to a high of 11 years imprisonment. Substantial fines have been levied and demands for restitution have been made. The *Tipikor*'s success has been attributed to two reasons: *ad hoc* judges and the KPK itself.

The *ad hoc* judges have made a crucial difference.[58] Precisely because they are not part of the career judiciary, they are far less timid in their attitudes towards the authority of the Supreme Court. This is perhaps best illustrated by the controversy that raged during the Harini Wijoso trial. A former career judge turned advocate, Wijoso was the lawyer representing Probosutedjo, former President Soeharto's half-brother, who had been tried and found guilty of corruption. Wijoso was caught attempting to bribe the Supreme Court justices, allegedly including Chief Justice Bagir Manan, who were reviewing the cassation petition of Probosutedjo's case. Probosutedjo claimed that he had given Wijoso Rp. 6 billion (about US$665,000) with which to bribe the Supreme Court justices.[59]

Wijoso was subsequently tried for corruption before the *Tipikor*. During her trial, the prosecutor demanded that Chief Justice Bagir Manan appear before the Court as a witness. Kresna Menon and Sutiyono, the two career judges on the panel, refused to summon the Chief Justice to appear before the Court. Pursuant to Article 160(1)(c) of Indonesia's *Code of Criminal Procedure* (*Law No. 8/1981*), all witnesses called by either the prosecution or the defence must appear before the Court to give testimony. There are no exceptions.[60] After repeated but unsuccessful entreaties by the three *ad hoc* judges for the Court to summon Bagir Manan, they decided to 'walk out' in protest. They were subsequently replaced by three other *ad hoc* judges.[61] Judge Sutiyono reportedly admitted to the Judicial Commission that he thought calling Chief Justice Bagir Manan to the stand would have been the correct thing to do legally but that concern for his own career prospects made him decide otherwise.[62]

The *ad hoc* judges, who are drawn from outside the career judiciary – mostly from private practice and academia – therefore provide a much-needed counterweight in terms of integrity and independence. In the case of the *Tipikor*, the initial three *ad hoc* trial judges were selected from an original pool of over 800 candidates.[63] Applications were solicited through an advertisement in the mass media. The candidates were examined on their knowledge of the law. Those who successfully passed the legal knowledge test were subjected to extensive psychological testing administered by an independent firm to see whether they had the character and personality suitable for the job, including honesty and independence. At this stage, the names of successful candidates were published in the media and public comments were invited. Throughout this process, various NGOs that were active in legal and judicial reforms and anti-corruption conducted background checks on more than 20 leading candidates. The final phase was the 'fit-and-proper' test, during which the final few candidates were once again questioned to ascertain their fitness for the job and to address any public comments that had been received.[64] The selection process was objective, thorough and transparent. Interestingly, the task of recruiting the *ad hoc* judges was not left to the Supreme Court but to a selection committee comprised of Supreme Court justices as well as individuals outside the judiciary and outside the government (e.g. NGOs). Committee members from outside the judiciary plus some reform-minded judges helped to set higher standards in terms of both competence and integrity as well as independence than would otherwise have been achieved.

The panels of judges in the *Tipikor* always comprise three *ad hoc* judges and two career judges. Thus, the *ad hoc* judges are always in the majority. Advocates pleading a client's case have to convince at least one *ad hoc* judge of their client's innocence. In practice, this structure has proved formidable for defendants and where a unanimous verdict has not been reached, the split has typically been three *ad hoc* judges, against two career judges, voting to convict. This has been the pattern since the Abdullah Puteh case. This pattern has not held at the sentencing phase and has resulted in more lenient sentences than demanded by the prosecution.[65] This rule of having three *ad hoc* judges and two career judges serving in one panel is replicated at both the appellate level and at cassation in the Supreme Court and probably explains why, to date, no *Tipikor* verdict has been reversed. Given that corruption permeates all levels of the judiciary, including the Supreme Court,[66] reversals of *Tipikor* decisions would probably have been more common had it not been for the presence of *ad hoc* judges sitting at the appellate level and in the Supreme Court.

Ironically, the harsh treatment they received probably contributed to an enhanced *esprit de corps* among the *ad hoc* judges, which was particularly strong among the first three *ad hoc* judges appointed.[67] When first appointed, *ad hoc* Judges Dudu Duswara, Achmad Linoh and I Made Hendra Kusuma had to share an apartment for about 18 months.[68] In addition to not having their salaries regularized in a timely manner, the three judges also experienced other humiliations in common. For example, the *ad hoc* judges had been promised the use of two official cars but saw only one old car, which was subsequently commandeered for use by the Chief Judge of the Central Jakarta District Court.[69] The unreliable nature of Jakarta's public transportation made it an unacceptable option for the *ad hoc* judges. In any case, it would not have been in keeping with their status as judges for them to resort to buses; so, they at first resorted to taxis and subsequently purchased their own vehicles.

Because so much of their personal and professional needs had not been properly met by the Supreme Court, the *ad hoc* judges eventually turned to the KPK for help. For example, when the Court needed a more reliable form of record-keeping, it was the KPK that came to the rescue with a closed-circuit television system. As a result of this relationship, the *Tipikor* has sometimes been seen simply as an arm of the KPK and not really independent. Reformers who should have been sympathetic to the *Tipikor* and hailed it as a success began to question whether a person accused of corruption could really get a fair trial before the *Tipikor*.[70] Lawyers who have represented clients before the *Tipikor* have been especially critical. These lawyers believe that *ad hoc* judges are not impartial but instead identify themselves with the prosecution. They claim that *Tipikor* decisions tend to incorporate all of the points made by the KPK, while de-emphasizing those made by the defence. Their bias is also allegedly apparent in the questions the *ad hoc* judges ask, which tend to help the prosecution.[71]

Supporters of the *Tipikor*, however, argue that the KPK has contributed to the Court's success by bringing only well-prepared, solid cases before the Court. Pursuant to Article 40 of *Law No. 30/2002*, the KPK is not allowed to terminate a case once it has named a suspect. Corruption among the public prosecutors has meant that investigations and prosecutions are often terminated early upon the issuance of a SP3 (*Surat Perintah Perhentian Perkara*, Order to Close the Case). A SP3 is often 'purchased' by a suspect from the prosecutors. Article 40 of *Law No. 30/2002* was intended to stop this practice from taking hold in the KPK. In this way, the KPK chooses its cases very carefully and only prosecutes those where the evidence is compelling. Teten Masduki, of Indonesia Corruption Watch, believes that Article 40 has been key to the KPK bringing strong and solid cases before the *Tipikor*.[72]

Corruption, collusion and nepotism in Indonesia's political economy

It has become conventional wisdom that corruption exacts a heavy price on a country's economic development. Studies have shown a correlation between high levels of corruption and low levels of economic growth and per capita income.[73] Moreover, corruption is seen as a causal factor contributing to the Asian Financial Crisis; perhaps more importantly, however, corruption is widely perceived as preventing a quicker and more robust recovery from taking place. Corruption is believed to deter foreign direct investment,[74] which is needed for a speedier recovery. There should be every incentive, therefore, for the Indonesian government to put the eradication of corruption at the top of its policy agenda. Yet, the establishment of the *Tipikor* shows that with respect to a very important aspect of its anti-corruption strategy, the government was lackadaisical in its implementation. Its failure to insure that the *ad hoc* judges' salaries were paid on time or to give the *Tipikor* all the support it needed to function properly could be taken to mean that the government was not really serious about eradicating corruption.

Why didn't the government take a more active role in helping the Supreme Court to implement the Blueprint?

Corruption in Indonesia is a well-entrenched social phenomenon that cannot be seen simply as a governance problem,[75] or the results of authoritarian rule.[76] Under the New Order's patrimonialistic politics, KKN (*korupsi, kolusi dan nepotism*, corruption, collusion and nepotism) lay at the heart of power relations. Soeharto 'bought' political loyalty by dispensing patronage to his clients. The survival of his regime depended upon the loyalty of the armed forces. As John Bresnan pointed out, '[w]hen the youth of the capital were in the streets, the armed forces were the ultimate political resource'.[77] Soeharto insured their loyalty by rewarding supporters within the armed forces as well as 'dissident or potentially dissident officers with appointments to civilian posts that offered prospects of material gain'.[78] Civilian cronies also benefitted from Soeharto's largesse. Favours bestowed upon crony businessmen included tax breaks, subsidized government loans, access to import and trading licenses and outright monopolies. In return, these crony businessmen helped to generate the economic growth that Soeharto needed to maintain his legitimacy among Indonesia's ordinary citizens, and which helped insure their political quiescence.[79] This benefice-for-loyalty arrangement was what kept Soeharto in power for 32 years.

But the arrangement did not stop there. The politico-bureaucrats who controlled gate-keeping institutions – like General Ibnu Sutowo, the one-time chief of Pertamina (the state-owned oil company), and Soeharto himself, as well as their respective families – actually entered the business world as capitalists, instead of simply remaining rent-collecting bureaucrats. From politico-bureaucratic families, they had turned into politico-business families.[80] But because their beginnings as capitalists depended so much on sweetheart deals from the government, the type of capitalism that has evolved in Indonesia is, as a result, qualitatively different from what we would recognize today as 'rule-based free-market' capitalism. Corruption is at the heart of this political capitalism. It is the 'institution' – in Douglass North's sense of the word – that furthered the interests of business empires and consolidated political power.[81] That this political economic order survived the downfall of the New Order and the demand for *Reformasi* is perhaps most vividly illustrated by the inability of the present and two preceding governments to bring Soeharto to justice. To be sure, immense political changes have come to Indonesia since 1998 and many of the prominent characters of the New Order have quietly gone by the wayside, but others have survived and, as Richard Robison and Vedi Hadiz argued, have 'reorganized' themselves into the country's new democratic politics.[82] For example, *Golkar*, the vehicle through which Soeharto wielded power, is still the dominant political party in the DPR, the country's legislature. Moreover, the Indonesian Democratic Party of Struggle, PDI-P,[83] also has members tied to Soeharto's New Order. A number of *Golkar* members have jumped over to join the PDI-P, the other dominant political party in the DPR. Thus, in democratic Indonesia many of the elements of the old regime are still politically active and remain powerful.

How did this form of political capitalism survive the downfall of the New Order? Crises are supposed to be an opportune time to impose reforms upon a weakened regime. Why weren't IFIs like the International Monetary Fund and the World Bank able to do more to impose neoliberal reforms on the Indonesian government in the aftermath of the Asian Financial Crisis? The hope had been for foreign companies to buy the assets of financially-distressed cronies and for them to manage these assets according to the principles of good corporate governance. Were this to take place, then a demand for a rule-based, free-market political economy might begin to materialize in Indonesia. But this hope was frustrated by the unwillingness of foreigners to buy Indonesian assets, and the resistance of economic nationalists who wanted to see Indonesian assets remain in Indonesian hands.[84]

Cronies and politico-business families were also to benefit from another government hand-out that helped save their conglomerate empires: the Bank Indonesia Liquidity Support (*Bantuan Liquiditas Bank Indonesia*, BLBI). The BLBI was ostensibly a facility to help ailing Indonesian banks meet their financial commitments to other banks as well as to their own depositors. But recipients of BLBI credits instead used the facility to pay off their conglomerates' corporate debts and to invest within their groups in Indonesia as well as abroad. As a sign of the continued vitality of their political influence, the politico-business families and conglomerates were to make it extremely difficult for the Indonesian government to recover these hand-outs. As security for the BLBI credits, the conglomerates were required to pledge their assets to IBRA (Indonesian Bank Restructuring Agency). But conglomerates were often allowed to hand over complicated portfolios consisting of bits and pieces of assets that made verification of their true value exceedingly difficult. For example, the Salim group – once headed by Liem Sioe Liong, whom Schwarz called 'the most visible beneficiary of Suharto's patronage'[85] – was allowed to 'hand over a complex package of assets from 105 companies [that] made due diligence appraisals a nightmare', when pledging just three companies – Indofood, Bogasari and Indasair – would have been more than adequate to cover all of the group's debts.[86] As it turned out, the assets pledged by the Salim group to cover a debt of Rp. 47.7 trillion (said to be worth Rp. 53 trillion) were later valued at merely Rp. 24 trillion.[87] The BLBI scandal continues to bedevil successive Indonesian governments, with many promises of action being made but no clear resolve being shown to bring those involved to justice.[88]

The BLBI scandal illustrated the impotence of the Indonesian government to root out political capitalism.[89] Many of the conglomerates involved were controlled by the Chinese business families. After the Asian Financial Crisis, Chinese businesses were the only ones that could be relied upon to return to Indonesia. Foreign businesses were not interested in coming to Indonesia because of the rampant corruption and the lack legal certainty. But the Chinese business families were reluctant to come back if they were going to be prosecuted for corruption. For this reason, Robison and Hadiz suggest, corruption could not be prosecuted with vigour.[90] In addition, the Chinese businesses thrive in an environment where there is a clientilistic relationship between officialdom and business.

While his new Attorney-General was preparing to bring BLBI suspects to justice, President Yudhoyono himself pleaded just a year ago for these very same persons to come back to Indonesia to invest their money in the country.[91] To what extent can the Indonesian government effectively prosecute the very people the country needs to regenerate its flagging economy?

In certain cases, foreign interests protested against the confiscation of cronies' assets. For example, foreign partners of producers of electricity complained vigorously and brought action in foreign courts to stop PLN (the state-owned electricity company) reneging on contracts that were disadvantageous to the state and that were clearly entered into without the benefit of a public tender conducted in a transparent manner. Foreign governments backed up these companies' complaints because, very often, foreign taxpayers' money was used to finance the foreign partners' investments through such entities as the Exim Bank in the United States. Thus, foreign pressure often prevented the confiscation of cronies' assets.[92]

For the reasons discussed above, it may be argued that if Indonesia's political economy, forged during the New Order, did not survive the downfall of the regime totally intact, then it survived substantially so. Some of the more high-profile cronies have disappeared but others have remained. For example, the Liem family still controls Indofood and Bogasari, while Prajogo Pangestu is still at the helm of his Barito Pacific group. The Bakrie group is another conglomerate that survived the Asian Financial Crisis intact. It is controlled by the family of Aburizal Bakrie, the current Coordinating Minister for the People's Welfare. The group is currently embroiled in a high-profile controversy, involving the Sidoarjo mudflow – an ecological disaster – due to Lapindo Brantas, a natural-gas drilling company controlled by the group. A mishap at a drilling site in Sidoarjo, East Java, allegedly caused hot mud to flow and submerge the surrounding locality. The homes and businesses of about 15,000 people in Sidoarjo were destroyed, resulting in damages that were calculated by Bappenas to be in the region of Rp. 27.4 trillion (over US$3 billion).[93] But responsibility for the disaster, including compensation for the victims, seems to have been shifted away from the Bakrie group to the public. By *Presidential Regulation No. 14/2007,* the government has agreed to bear most of the cost, leaving Lapindo Brantas responsible for only a small percentage of the damages. The case clearly presented a conflict of interests for Aburizal Bakrie, the senior minister ostensibly responsible for the welfare of the 15,000 victims of the mudflow.

Despite this conflict of interests, Aburizal Bakrie's position in President Yudhoyono's cabinet seems fairly secure for the moment.[94] Indeed, some would argue that the Bakrie group has recently received another government largesse. The group won the contract to build a 35-km long toll road in Central Java, from Cirebon to Brebes, and received loans from two state-owned banks. Economist Faisal Basri has questioned why the Bakrie group, which has no experience in toll-road construction, should have been awarded the contract. In addition, it appeared that one of the state-owned banks financing the toll-road, Bank Rakyat Indonesia, which normally lends exclusively to small and medium-sized enterprises as well as to farmers, has no experience in financing infrastructure projects and therefore would not have the expertise to judge, at arm's length, the financial viability of such projects.[95]

In newly democratic Indonesia, the DPR also plays an important part in the country's politics. The impeachment of former President Abdurrahman Wahid is an eloquent testimony to how much power the legislative branch of government in Indonesia has garnered for itself. Wahid developed sterling reformist credentials as an opponent of the New Order. Yet, as President, he could not implement a reform agenda that included the effective prosecution of corruption cases.[96] Wahid was elected president by the People's Consultative Assembly (*Majelis Permusyawaratan Rakyat*, MPR), the super legislature that is comprised mainly of the DPR. In the 1999 general elections, his party, the PKB (National Awakening Party) garnered only 10.2 per cent of the seats in the DPR. To stay in power, Wahid needed the cooperation of the PDI-P, with its 30.8 per cent share of the seats in the DPR. Together they controlled 41 per cent of the seats, which was still short of the majority of the DPR. Wahid thus also needed the support of the seats controlled by the military and the national police (TNI/*Polri*). Because of this, Wahid could not afford to prosecute the cases of alleged corruption related to the military's commercial interests.[97] These interests were a primary source for the armed forces extra-budgetary funding.

But even with the TNI/*Polri*'s 7.6 per cent of the seats, Wahid was still short of an absolute majority in the DPR. Wahid thus had to court select members of *Golkar* – the people whose support helped to catapult him to presidency – to support him. Thus, Wahid could not afford to alienate his *Golkar* supporters by investigating their members for alleged cases of corruption. Irwan argued that this is one of the main reasons for Wahid's reluctance to replace Marzuki Darusman, a member of *Golkar*, whose foot-dragging in pursuing corruption cases made him very unpopular with reformist NGOs and the general public, and with Baharuddin Lopa, a well-known uncompromising warrior against KKN.[98]

One cannot draw a direct comparison between Wahid's presidency and that of Yudhoyono. The latter was popularly elected in 2004 and so does not need the support of other parties in the DPR to stay in power. But with his *Partai Demokrat* controlling only 10.4 per cent of the seats in the DPR, Yudhoyono is similarly handicapped, if only in terms of governing and not in terms of staying in office. He cannot afford to alienate too many of the other parties in the DPR on whose goodwill his ability to govern depends. This is particularly true of *Golkar*, which is chaired by his Vice President, Jusuf Kalla. Todung Mulya Lubis, a prominent human rights advocate, remarked that the position is not that Yudhoyono's government does not have the political will to bring about reforms to the judiciary, but that it is politically very weak and does not have the political capital to push for the necessary reforms.[99]

The increasing prevalence of money politics in Indonesia has also made it very difficult for any government to pursue an active campaign against KKN. Of course, money politics had also been a feature of the New Order. But with the demise of authoritarian rule, money politics has taken on even greater importance in Indonesia. During the 1999 general elections, *Golkar* was alleged to have 'bought' votes in a number of ways.[100] For example, a *Golkar* advisor who is an important local political figure in South Sulawesi was reported to have travelled throughout his region giving away money to important constituents, such as village chiefs.[101] In Wonogiri Regency, Central Java, a *Golkar* functionary was caught trying to distribute money to each resident in the regency in a direct attempt at vote-buying.[102] The money for these attempts to buy or influence votes does not only come from party coffers: it also comes from wealthy individuals and corporations, often in violation of laws limiting campaign contributions; in addition, as the recent Rokhmin Dahuri case before the *Tipikor* shows, the money comes from off-budget accounts in government ministries. Revelations in the case recently embroiled President Yudhoyono in the scandal when Dahuri testified that he had given the Yudhoyono/Kalla 2004 presidential campaign Rp. 200 million (about US$22,000). Another prominent politician, Amien Rais of PAN (National Mandate Party), has publicly admitted receiving a similar amount from Dahuri through his presidential campaign organization. The list of contributions was long and touched practically every serious presidential contender in 2004.[103]

KKN has a long history in Indonesia. It was central to the way Soeharto wielded and maintained power. Although much political change has taken place in Indonesia within the last nine years, the practice of KKN seems to have remained central to power relations in Indonesia today. An analysis of the *Tipikor* would be incomplete without a thorough regard for the hostile environment into which it was born.

Conclusion

The experience of the *Tipikor* shows that reformers must take heed of the political economic terrain in which new courts are to be established. Depending on the type of court to be established, a hostile reception could await. Implementation of reform plans must pay attention to details, because at this level the best of intentions may go awry. In the case of the *Tipikor*, there was insufficient supervision on the part of reformist elements in Indonesia. Leaving the implementation of the Blueprint mostly in the hands of the Supreme Court predictably resulted in poor implementation. With hindsight, it should have been obvious that the very existence of the *Tipikor* impugned the collective self-worth of the career judiciary. The project of implementing the Blueprint was therefore bound to be taken on with the greatest of reluctance.

Without proper funding, any new enterprise is bound to founder. Therefore, one of the most important tasks for reformers is to make sure that the money will be available to insure success. In the case of the *Tipikor*, reformist elements failed to make sure that the Supreme Court made the proper effort to seek funding for the new court. There was certainly sufficient time for the Supreme Court to submit a supplementary budget request to the Ministry of Finance. It is unclear why salaries for the *ad hoc* judges could not have been processed in a timely manner. A best-case explanation was sheer inertia on the part of the Supreme Court brought on, perhaps, by its distaste for the project. A darker explanation, forwarded by the *ad hoc* judges themselves, may be that the delay was meant to encourage them to abandon the project or, worse still, to leave them vulnerable to the temptation to emulate the venal disposition of many of their career brethren. Perhaps a more vigilant attitude on the part of reformists with the financial aspects of the project could have avoided the controversies that eventually ensued.

But the most telling lesson of the *Tipikor* is that new courts are unlikely to succeed without new blood. The most important contribution that reformists made to the project was to ensure that *ad hoc* judges would always be in the majority in any decision of whether or not to convict. They also provided invaluable service in making sure that the recruitment process was objective and transparent. Without the *ad hoc* judges, it is unlikely that the *Tipikor* would have enjoyed the success that it did. But clearly, not everyone would consider the contributions of the *ad hoc* judges in such a positive light. This is true even among reformers who want to see the re-establishment of an honest and functional judiciary. These criticisms of the *ad hoc* judges have certainly qualified any statements made about the success of the *Tipikor*.

At this stage, the future of the *Tipikor* is uncertain. Reformers are drafting an alternative bill to replace *Law No. 30/2002*, in opposition to the bill being drafted by Professor Teuku Nasrullah. Whether reformers have the votes to pass their bills in the DPR is, of course, another matter entirely. Anti-corruption legislation creating a court that would be honest and independent, with jurisdiction to hear all corruption cases – not just those brought by the KPK – may not be all that popular among politicians whose livelihoods and hold on power depend to a significant extent on KKN.

Notes

1. Currency conversions were done at the rate posted in the *International Herald Tribune* on 19 June 2007 at Rp. 9,025 to US$1.
2. Case No. 012-016-019/PUU-IV/2006.
3. In the interim, the *Tipikor* is functioning normally.
4. World Bank, *Building Institutions for Markets, World Development Report 2002* (Oxford: Oxford University Press, 2002).
5. Terry M. Moe, “Power and Political Institutions,” *Perspectives on Politics* 3 (2005): 215–33.
6. Douglass C. North, *Institutions, Institutional Change and Economic Performance* (Cambridge: Cambridge University Press, 1990).
7. Richard Robison and Vedi R. Hadiz, *Reorganizing Power in Indonesia: The Politics of Oligarchy in an Age of Markets* (London: Routledge Curzon, 2004).
8. Moe, “Power and Political Institutions”.
9. Mardjono Reksodiputro, “Corruption in the Indonesian Legal System,” in *The Big Feast: Soldier, Judge, Banker, Civil Servant*, ed. Richard Holloway (Jakarta: Aksara Foundation, 2002), 36–7; Ali Budiardjo, Nugroho, Reksodiputro, *Law Reform in Indonesia: Results of a Research Study Undertaken for the World Bank* (Jakarta: Cyberconsult, 1997), 147.
10. “Menolak Dimutasi, Hakim Laporkan Mafia Peradilan kepada Ketua MA,” (Refusing Transfer: Judge Reports the Judicial Mafia to the Chief Justice of the Supreme Court) *Koran Tempo*, June 15, 2003.
11. “Sahlan Fights Against ‘Court Mafia’,” *Jakarta Post*, October 21, 2003.
12. Daniel S. Lev, “Judicial Authority and the Quest for an Indonesian Rechtstaat,” *Law and Society Review* 13 (1978): 50.

13. "Recent Acquittals a 'Blow' for Anti-graft Movement," *Jakarta Post*, June 7, 2007.
14. Indonesian Institute for an Independent Judiciary, *Pengadilan Khusus Korupsi: Naskah Akademis dan Rancangan Undang-Undang Pengadilan Khusus Korupsi* (Special Corruption Court: Academic Draft and Bill of the Special Corruption Court) (Jakarta: Touchprint, 2002), 5.
15. The cases cited included cases brought on cassation and civil review (*peninjauan kembali*) before the Supreme Court (five cases).
16. Pengadilan Masih Milik Koruptor (Courts Still Controlled by Corruptors), *Laporan Kasus Korupsi yang Diperiksa dan Divonis Pengadilan Selama Tahun 2005* (Report on Trials and Sentencing in Corruption Cases in 2005) (Jakarta: Indonesia Corruption Watch, 2005).
17. "Graft Still Reigns in Judicial System: TI," *Jakarta Post*, June 2, 2007.
18. Michael Backman, *Asian Eclipse: Exposing the Dark Side of Business in Indonesia* (New York: John Wiley & Sons, 1999), 33.
19. "Corruption Rampant in Medan Courts: Lawyers," *Jakarta Post*, February 9, 2004, http://old.thejakartapost.com/Archives/ArchivesDet2.asp?FileID = 20040209.D04
20. "Law: 'Three Against the World'," *Tempo*, 2003.
21. Steering Committee for the Commercial Court and Preparations for the Establishment of the Anticorruption Court, *Needs Assessment* (Jakarta: PT Nagadi Ekasakti, 2005), 41–56.
22. "Crooked Judges Key Obstacle to Corruption Fight: Indonesian Panel," *Business Times Singapore*, June 15, 2007.
23. Frans Winarta, "Judicial Corruption not only Rampant but also Shameful," *Jakarta Post*, October 31, 2005.
24. Todung Mulya Lubis, "Judicial corruption: Where to go?" *Jakarta Post*, December 8, 2005.
25. Indonesian Institute for an Independent Judiciary, *Pengadilan Khusus Korupsi* (Special Corruption Court).
26. Ibid., 13–14.
27. Ali Budiardjo, Nugroho, Reksodiputro, *Law Reform in Indonesia*, 125–6.
28. Ibid.
29. Rifqi Assegaf (member of the Secretariat of the Steering Committee on the Commercial Court and Preparations for the Establishment of the Anticorruption Court), in discussion with author, 9 May 2007.
30. *Ministerial Decree No. 025/M.PPN/03/2003.*
31. The Steering Committee actually had dual responsibility for both the Commercial Court and the *Tipikor*.
32. *Ministerial Decree No. 025/M.PPN/03/2003*, 2(4).
33. Steering Committee on the Commercial Court and Preparations for the Establishment of the Anticorruption Court, *Blueprint and Action Plan for the Establishment of the Anticorruption Court* (Jakarta: National Development Planning Agency of the Republic of Indonesia, 2004), 61–80.
34. The six committees are responsible for (1) case management, (2) information technology, (3) supervision, (4) finance, (5) human resources, and (6) training. The committee on human resources is responsible for recruitment, promotions and transfers, whereas the one on supervision is responsible for supervising judges and the bureaucrats within the judiciary. The day-to-day coordination of these six committees was the responsibility of Justice Paulus Lotulung: Wiwiek Awiati (Consultant to the Judicial Reform Committee in the Supreme Court of Indonesia), in discussion with author, 3 May 2007.
35. For discussion of the Commercial Court, see David Linnan's chapter in this publication.
36. In these two cases, the Commercial Court declared two financially healthy companies bankrupt. See John Roberts, "Indonesian Supreme Court Bows to International Pressure in Key Bankruptcy Case," World Socialist Website, http://www.wsws.org/articles/2002/jul2002/indo-j17.shtml

37. Indonesian Institute for an Independent Judiciary, *Pengadilan Khusus Korupsi* (Special Corruption Court), 13.
38. Steering Committee on the Commercial Court and Preparations for the Establishment of the Anticorruption Court, *Blueprint and Action Plan for the Establishment of the Anticorruption Court*, 61–2.
39. Rifqi Assegaf (member of the Secretariat of the Steering Committee on the Commercial Court and Preparations for the Establishment of the Anticorruption Court), in discussion with author, 10 April 2007.
40. Steering Committee on the Commercial Court and Preparations for the Establishment of the Anticorruption Court, *Blueprint and Action Plan for the Establishment of the Anticorruption Court*, 63–4.
41. Ibid., 9.
42. I Made Hendra Kusuma (Ad Hoc Judge at the *Tipikor*), in discussion with author, 18 April 2007.
43. Dudu Duswara Machmudin (Ad Hoc Judge at the *Tipikor*), in discussion with author, 10 May 2007.
44. I Made Hendra Kusuma (Ad Hoc Judge at the *Tipikor*), in discussion with author, 18 April 2007; Dudu Duswara Machmudin (Ad Hoc Judge at the *Tipikor*), in discussion with author, 10 May 2007.
45. "Puasa Gaji Sang Hakim," (Judges on a Salary Fast) *Tempo*, December 12, 2004; "Insya Allah, Bulan Depan Gajian," (God Willing Next Month We'll Get Paid) *Pilars*, March 13, 2005; "Lebih Baik Menuntut Hak Dari Pada Bermain Mata," (Better to Insist on Your Rights than to Flirt) *Forum Keadilan*, March 22, 2005.
46. Dudu Duswara Machmudin (Ad Hoc Judge at the *Tipikor*), in discussion with author, 10 May 2007. Ad hoc judges serving on the *Tipikor* are required by statute to resign from any and all prior employment (Article 57(2)(i) of *Law No. 30/2002*).
47. "Perpres Gaji Hakim Tipikor Turun, Realisasinya Ditunggu," (Presidential Instruction on Salaries of Tipikor Judges Handed Down, Still Awaiting Actual Implementation) *Kompas*, September 1, 2005.
48. "Hakim Digaji dari Utang," (Judges Paid on Credit) *Indonesia Pos*, February 2, 2005.
49. "Puasa Gaji Sang Hakim," (Judges on a Salary Fast) *Tempo*, December 12, 2004.
50. "Malangnya Hakim Antikorupsi," (Bad Luck for Anti-Corruption Judges) *Tempo*, February 20, 2005.
51. Achmad Linoh (Ad Hoc Judge at the *Tipikor*), in discussion with author, 10 May 2007.
52. Dudu Duswara Machmudin (Ad Hoc Judge at the *Tipikor*), in discussion with author, 10 May 2007.
53. Steering Committee on the Commercial Court and Preparations for the Establishment of the Anticorruption Court, *Blueprint and Action Plan for the Establishment of the Anticorruption Court*, Appendix 2.
54. Pande Silalahi (Senior Economist at the Centre for Strategic and International Studies [CSIS]), in discussion with author, 3 May 2007. Dr Silalahi's research interests include government finances.
55. Wiwiek Awiati (Consultant to the Judicial Reform Team in the Supreme Court of Indonesia), in discussion with author, 3 May 2007.
56. Diani Sadiawati (Director of Law and Human Rights, Bappenas), in discussion with author, 25 April 2007; Rifqi Assegaf (member of the Secretariat of the Steering Committee on the Commercial Court and Preparations for the Establishment of the Anticorruption Court), in discussion with author, 9 May 2007; Wiwiek Awiati (Consultant to the Judicial Reform Team in the Supreme Court of Indonesia), in discussion with author, 3 May 2007.
57. Of course, the failure to pay the *ad hoc* judges' salaries on time could also have been due to bureaucratic inertia. Often, government initiatives go unfinanced in Indonesia. I am grateful to Professor Erman Rajagukguk for pointing this out to me.
58. Teten Masduki (Coordinator, Indonesia Corruption Watch), in discussion with author, 9 April 2007.

59. "Probo's Case Highlights Corrupt System: Experts," *Jakarta Post*, October 17, 2005, http://old.thejakartapost.com/Archives/ArchivesDet2.asp?FileID = 20051017.A04
60. In defence of his position, Judge Menon argued that pursuant to a 1985 Supreme Court Circular (*Surat Edaran No. 2/1985*), it was up to his discretion, as Chairman of the Panel, to limit the number of witnesses each side is able to present. Therefore, the issue was whether a 1985 Supreme Court Circular should trump an article of the *Code of Criminal Procedure* (*Law No. 8/1981*).
61. "Malang Nian Nasib Tiga Hakim 'ad Hoc'," (Bad Luck for Three 'ad Hoc' Judges) *Media Indonesia*, June 13, 2006; "Replacement of Antigraft Court Judges Unfair: Todung," *Jakarta Post*, June 15, 2006, http://old.thejakartapost.com/Archives/ArchivesDet2.asp?FileID = 20060615.H03
62. "Independensi Hakim Versus Loyalitas Bawahan," (Judge's Independence Versus a Subordinate's Loyalty) *Kompas*, June 14, 2006. See also, "Tiga Hakim Lakukan Perlawanan Moral," (Three Judges Take a Moral Stand) *Kompas*, May 4, 2006.
63. I Made Hendra Kusuma (Ad Hoc Judge at the *Tipikor*), in discussion with author, 18 April 2007.
64. Ibid.
65. Dudu Duswara Machmudin (Ad Hoc Judge at the *Tipikor*), in discussion with author, 10 May 2007.
66. Reksodiputro, "Corruption in the Indonesian Legal System," 42.
67. Dudu Duswara Machmudin (Ad Hoc Judge at the *Tipikor*), in discussion with author, 10 May 2007; Achmad Linoh (Ad Hoc Judge at the *Tipikor*), in discussion with author, 10 May 2007.
68. Dudu Duswara Machmudin (Ad Hoc Judge at the *Tipikor*), in discussion with author, 10 May 2007.
69. Dudu Duswara Machmudin (Ad Hoc Judge at the *Tipikor*), in discussion with author, 10 May 2007; I Made Hendra Kusuma (Ad Hoc Judge at the *Tipikor*), in discussion with author, 18 April 2007.
70. Frans Winarta (Private Practitioner and Member of the National Law Commission), in discussion with author, 4 May 2007.
71. Mohammad Assegaf (Member of the Indonesian Criminal Defense Bar), in discussion with author, 15 November 2007.
72. Teten Masduki (Coordinator, Indonesia Corruption Watch), in discussion with author, 9 April 2007.
73. World Bank, *Building Institutions for Markets, World Development Report 2002*, 105; Paulo Mauro, "Corruption and Growth," *The Quarterly Journal of Economics* 110 (1995): 681–712.
74. Shang-Jin Wei, "How Taxing Is Corruption on International Investors?," *The Review of Economics and Statistics* 82 (2000): 1–11.
75. Gary Goodpaster, "Reflections on Corruption in Indonesia," in *Corruption in Asia: Rethinking the Governance Paradigm*, ed. Tim Lindsey and Howard Dick (Sydney: Federation Press, 2002), 105.
76. Howard Dick, "Corruption and Good Governance: The New Frontier of Social Engineering," in *Corruption in Asia: Rethinking the Governance Paradigm*, ed. Tim Lindsey and Howard Dick (Sydney: Federation Press, 2002), 82.
77. John Bresnan, *Managing Indonesia: The Modern Political Economy* (New York: Columbia University Press, 1993), 111.
78. Harold Crouch, "Patrimonialism and Military Rule in Indonesia," *World Politics* 31 (1979): 577.
79. Benedict R. O'G. Anderson, "Old State, New Society: Indonesia's New Order in Comparative Historical Perspective," in *Language and Power – Exploring Political Cultures in Indonesia*, ed. Benedict R. O'G. Anderson (New York: Cornell University Press, 1990), Ch. 3.
80. Robison and Hadiz, *Reorganizing Power in Indonesia*, 71–102 and *passim*. Much of the discussion in this section draws heavily upon Robison and Hadiz's book.

81. North, *Institutions, Institutional Change and Economic Performance.*
82. Robison and Hadiz, *Reorganizing Power in Indonesia.*
83. *Partai Demokrasi Indonesia-Perjuangan* (the Indonesian Democratic Party for Struggle).
84. Robison and Hadiz, *Reorganizing Power in Indonesia*, 197–9.
85. Adam Schwarz, *A Nation in Waiting: Indonesia's Search for Stability* (St Leonards: Talisman Publishing, 2004), 109.
86. Robison and Hadiz, *Reorganizing Power in Indonesia*, 194.
87. Ibid., 194–5.
88. Hendarman Supanji, President Yudhoyono's new Attorney-General, recently announced the formation of two special teams to investigate these cases: "AGO to Form Special Teams to Investigate BLBI cases," *Jakarta Post*, June 6, 2007, http://old.thejakartapost.com/Archives/ArchivesDet2.asp?FileID = 20070606.H05
89. The Attorney-General's Office (AGO) has recently closed the case against Liem Sioe Liong and Sjamsul Nursalim relating to the BLBI scandal. The AGO claimed that its investigations failed to uncover evidence of corruption: "AGO Drops Two Major BLBI Cases," *Jakarta Post*, March 1, 2008, http://old.thejakartapost.com/Archives/ArchivesDet2.asp?FileID = 20080301.@03. But the KPK has recently caught the lead prosecutor in these two cases accepting a bribe of US$660,000, allegedly from Sjamsul Nursalim: "KPK Seeks Link in Bribery Case," *Jakarta Post*, March 5, 2008, http://old.thejakartapost.com/Archives/ArchivesDet2.asp?FileID = 20080305.@01. The prosecutor is now under investigation and the Attorney-General has promised to re-open the cases if evidence shows that Nursalim has indeed bribed the prosecutor: "AGO Set to Reopen Probe into BLBI Funds,' *Jakarta Post*, March 6, 2008, http://old.thejakartapost.com/Archives/ArchivesDet2.asp?FileID = 20080306.@01
90. Robison and Hadiz, *Reorganizing Power in Indonesia*, 213.
91. "SBY Urges Troubled Tycoons to Return Home," *Jakarta Post*, April 19, 2006, http://old.thejakartapost.com/Archives/ArchivesDet2.asp?FileID = 20060419.L01
92. Robison and Hadiz, *Reorganizing Power in Indonesia*, 202.
93. "Fresh Wind for Bakrie," *Tempo*, April 17–23, 2007.
94. The *Jakarta Post* has commented: 'The fact that Yudhoyono has kept Aburizal in the Cabinet, despite the blatant conflict of interest, even protecting him by not exposing him to the handling of mudflow problems, has led many to believe that Yudhoyono cannot afford to lose the support of this former businessman. There is much suspicion that Yudhoyono badly needs Aburizal's financial support for his re-election bid in 2009.' "Resolving the Muddy Conflict of Interest in Sidoarjo," *Jakarta Post*, June 29, 2007, http://old.thejakartapost.com/Archives/ArchivesDet2.asp?FileID = 20070629.A07
95. "Precious Gifts for Bakrie," *Tempo*, March 20–6, 2007.
96. Alexander Irwan, "KKN as a Political Commodity in the Struggle for Power," in *Corruption – From Top to Bottom*, ed. Richard Holloway (Jakarta: Aksara Foundation, 2002), 72.
97. Ibid.
98. Ibid., 72–3. Lopa was eventually appointed Attorney-General at Wahid's second cabinet reshuffle on 1 June 2001. A little over a month later, after announcing his intention to pursue alleged human rights violations in East Timor and corruption in the banking sector, Lopa died under what many people have since alleged to be mysterious circumstances. See "Mulya: Kematian Munir Mirip dengan Baharuddin Lopa," (Mulya: Munir's Death Reminiscent of Bacharuddin Lopa's) *Tempo*, November 12, 2004.
99. Todung Mulya Lubis (Human Rights Advocate), in discussion with author, 30 April 2007.
100. Irwan, "KKN as a Political Commodity in the Struggle for Power," 92–5.
101. Ibid., 92–3.
102. Ibid., 94–5.
103. "Build Case on Amien Admission," *Jakarta Post*, May 19, 2007, http://old.thejakartapost.com/Archives/ArchivesDet2.asp?FileID = 20070519.@02

14 The Philippines' *Sandiganbayan*

Anti-graft courts and the illusion of self-contained anti-corruption regimes

Raul C. Pangalangan

Introduction

The *Sandiganbayan*, the Philippines' specialized anti-corruption court, is best seen as part of an entire governmental structure designed deliberately to vindicate the constitutional norm of 'public accountability'. Its dismal record attests not just to its institutional weakness as a court, but also the frailty of the political and normative commitment to stop corruption itself.

Corruption is widely conceded to be one of the country's most serious problems, one that has drained its meagre coffers and sapped its capacity to carry out desperately needed social programmes. Through almost every President since independence in 1946, the Philippine government has strived to contain corruption. These efforts have gone through several stages, some of which have overlapped historically.

The first stage involved the codification of norms in statutes that target corruption – this scourge in the nation's life. These statutes are both substantive and procedural. They punish the various crimes through which public officers use their office for private aggrandizement, and also streamline the procedure by which the culpable are prosecuted and convicted.

The second stage was the creation of the institutional mechanisms to implement these norms, and it is here that the *Sandiganbayan*[1] fits into the picture, together with the Ombudsman[2] which has now evolved into a chief prosecuting agency; both of them constitutional bodies designed to be independent from the executive and legislative branches of government.

The third stage is the current experiment with extra-legal measures through citizens' watchdog groups, investigative journalists, and the re-orientation of public officers to attack the 'culture of corruption'. These efforts are enhanced by the proliferation of redundant government agencies whose work, it is hoped, will lead to transparency and fuel the political processes that supplement the formal structures of government.

The subsequent discussion of the codification of these norms into statute will actually demonstrate the dominant thinking in the country, namely, that the problem lies in the concentration of powers in the executive and in the weak or non-existent checks and balances by the other branches; the poor transparency surrounding executive decisions combined with restricted access to information; excessive discretion in decision-making due to elaborate regulatory systems; and 'soft social control systems/high tolerance for corrupt activities'.[3]

The 'politically correct' solution, therefore, is to minimize discretion held by public officers, and insulate institutions like the *Sandiganbayan* and Ombudsman from politics. This solution assumes that the evil is 'politics' (loosely understood as undue influence by outsiders on an institution), which rears its ugly head through 'discretion'. In that formalist imagination, the good is represented by a highly formalistic rule of law, so that government decisions are reduced to the most ministerial. It will remove all discretionary power from the public officer, who is thus called upon to act mechanically 'in accordance with law'.

This chapter acknowledges the power and limits of this approach. It begins with the classic legal realist critique that discretion cannot be avoided altogether; that to reduce it significantly, the rules will have to be codified into such minutiae that either it is impossible to govern; and/or, at worst, the technicalities will inevitably contain so many loopholes and unforeseen gaps that we are back to square one, namely, law becoming the source of corruption itself.

Rather, I see the wisdom of the more recent approaches built on transparency and popular power, namely, to decentralize anti-corruption duties, proliferate duties to many persons and institutions, and shift the anti-corruption initiative away from formal institutions and towards the democratic political process, namely, citizens' watchdog organizations and a free press.

Recognition of corruption as a national problem

The Philippines has been ranked as one of the most corrupt nations in the world. In the last four years, Transparency International's annual Corruption Perception Index has shown its steadily deteriorating position, as indicated in Table 14.1.

Out of 32 countries in the Asia–Pacific region, the Philippines ranked eighth from the bottom in 2008, beating the likes of Bangladesh, Afghanistan, Cambodia and Myanmar for the dishonour of being the most corrupt country.[4] The Global Corruption Survey 2007 found that 32 per cent of Philippine respondents said they had paid a bribe in the past year to obtain a service.[5]

Locally, the leading public opinion polling group, Social Weather Stations, has surveyed business people, who confirm that they in varying degrees have given bribes to win government contracts.[6] Corruption has also impaired the delivery of public services. For instance, the decentralization of health services from the national government to local governments has also opened the door to the widespread pilferage of health funds devolved to lower levels of government where accountability controls were even weaker.[7]

The following areas of government activities have been identified as the most vulnerable to corruption: public procurement, the re-zoning of land (to exempt it from agrarian reform) and tax collection. Corruption has been carried out through cronyism via family members and support for politicians' electoral campaigns.[8]

Table 14.1 Transparency International's corruption perception index rankings 2005–8

Year	*Rank in relation to total*
2005	117th from the top (the first being the least corrupt) out of 158[1]
2006	121st out of 163 countries[2]
2007	131st out of 179 countries[3]
2008	141st out of 180 countries[4]

Source: 1,2,3,4

1 Transparency International, "Corruption Perception Index," http://www.transparency.org/policy_research/surveys_indices/cpi/2005
2 Transparency International, "Corruption Perception Index," http://www.transparency.org/policy_research/surveys_indices/cpi/2006
3 Transparency International, "Corruption Perception Index," http://www.transparency.org/policy_research/surveys_indices/cpi/2007
4 Transparency International, "Corruption Perception Index," http://www.transparency.org/policy_research/surveys_indices/cpi/2008

Internationally, the Philippine government under incumbent President Gloria Macapagal-Arroyo has been rather active in international campaigns against corruption, and has ratified the *United Nations Convention against Corruption*[9] and the *United Nations Convention against Transnational Organized Crime.*[10]

Codification of the norm of public accountability

The grand normative declaration that is the cornerstone of the entire anti-corruption campaign is set forth in the Constitution of the Republic of the Philippines (Constitution). Article XI provides that:

> Public office is a public trust. Public officers and employees must at all times be accountable to the people, serve them with utmost responsibility, integrity, loyalty, and efficiency, act with patriotism and justice, and lead modest lives.[11]

Those norms are carried out through anti-graft statutes that have been adopted over the past decades, starting with the Revised Penal Code. The anti-graft laws were further strengthened with jurisdictional and procedural reforms, broadening their reach to enable prosecutors to charge private-party cohorts, or enlist them as witnesses, shifting the evidentiary burden in cases of unexplained wealth, and requiring public officers periodically to disclose their wealth.

The very first codification was through the Revised Penal Code, which contains a separate title specifically for 'Crimes Committed by Public Officers', and punishes bribery (both the bribe taker as well as giver),[12] frauds against the public treasury,[13] and malversation of public funds.[14] The title also covers other non-corruption related abuses of governmental power, including dereliction of duty,[15] maltreatment of prisoners[16] and open disobedience to authority.[17]

The first attempt at specific anti-graft rules was in 1960 through the Anti-Graft and Corrupt Practices Act (AGCPA).[18] The AGCPA covered measures to stem influence-peddling and hidden bribery through gifts, 'behest loans' and crony contracts, and made more explicit the range of threats that a public officer may use against private persons. If the Revised Penal Code extended its reach to the private party cohorts of corrupt officials, the AGCPA covered transactions with family members of the public officer. It adapted itself further to the local culture and significantly defined 'close personal relation' to include 'personal ..., social and fraternal connections, and professional employment ... which assures free access' to the official.[19]

In addition to this statutory attempt to spell out every prohibited act, the AGCPA contains the catch-all clause that punishes any act that 'caus[es] any undue injury to any party, including the Government'.[20] This expands the scope of prosecutorial discretion, but opens the door to the danger of selective and politically-motivated prosecution using the subjectivity of the term 'undue advantage'.

Finally, the AGCPA required the disclosure by public officials of their financial assets,[21] a requirement that is now fully constitutionalized[22] and its violations statutorily criminalized.[23]

The next legislative reform was to shift the evidentiary burden for unexplained wealth and to provide for forfeiture of ill-gotten wealth. The Act Declaring Forfeiture of Ill-gotten Wealth of Public Officers and Employees provides that:

> Whenever any public officer... has acquired... property which is manifestly out of proportion to his salary and the income from legitimately acquired property, said property shall be presumed to be prima facie to have been unlawfully acquired.[24]

After President Marcos was ousted in 1986, the first post-Marcos Congress passed a new Code of Conduct and Ethical Standards for Public Officials.[25] The code began with an express normative statement, and contained an even more specific list of prohibited acts. For example, it prohibited having a financial interest in matters regulated by one's office, outside employment or professional practice, or solicitation of gifts.

The crowning glory of the Philippines' anti-graft campaign is the Plunder Law.[26] The law encompasses acts already punishable under other laws: bribery, malversation, and taking undue advantage of one's official position for private enrichment. What the law sought to solve was the prosecutorial burden of filing indictments for each separate act, when the true crime is the 'combination or series of the [such] means or similar schemes'.[27]

The most recent piece of legislation significantly streamlines bureaucratic processes and promotes transparency in government procurement and biddings. An Act to Improve the Efficiency in the Delivery of Government Service to the Public by Reducing Bureaucratic Red Tape, Preventing Graft and Corruption and Providing Penalties Therefore[28] fixes a five to ten-year period for the processing of government permits, minimizes the number of signatures required for each transaction, requires public officers to reply to citizen requests, makes public these guidelines in serving the public, and creates public complaints desks.[29]

Institutionalization of the anti-corruption campaign

The formal institutions of public accountability

Sandiganbayan

The Philippines created a specialized anti-corruption court under its 1973 Constitution; the Constitution that Marcos foisted on the nation, soon after assuming martial law powers. It is the newest court in the country's judicial system, which was established in 1901.

Despite the restoration of democracy in 1986, the *Sandiganbayan's* performance has not been stellar either, despite the further fine-tuning of anti-graft laws in response to the wanton depredation during the Marcos years. The Court has been like a web that traps small insects but lets larger birds fly through, its few proud moments tarnished by reversals before the Supreme Court or by the in famous presidential pardon for its most famous respondent, the former President, Joseph Estrada.

This chapter proposes that the *Sandiganbayan's* performance depends on the strength of another constitutional body, the Ombudsman, which has been transformed in the Philippines into a mainly prosecutorial body, unlike in other jurisdictions. It is institutionally designed to be a standing 'independent prosecutor', detached from the Department of Justice which belongs to the political arm of government.[30]

The *Sandiganbayan* is a special court created 'in an effort to maintain honesty and efficiency in the bureaucracy, weed out misfits and undesirables in the government and eventually stamp out graft and corruption'.[31] It consists of five justices sitting in divisions, with exclusive jurisdiction over both elective and appointive public officers, as well as officers of state corporations, high ranking military officers and members of the judiciary. As recognized by the Supreme Court, the *Sandiganbayan* is unique in that it is a collegial court performing trial functions. Whereas trials are typically conducted by a solitary judge, the *Sandiganbayan* is a collegial court that helps insulate the judge from having to face alone the political fall-out of contested verdicts.

The prosecutorial processes

The prosecutorial process for public accountability may be divided into the explicitly political process for impeachable offices, and the decidedly non-political process for everyone else.

Only the highest officers of the land are subject to impeachment, namely: the President and Vice-President, the Supreme Court justices, the Ombudsman and the independent constitutional commissions (for Audit, for the Civil Service, and for Elections).[32]

The impeachment power is reposed in the bicameral Congress, a virtual copy of the American model. The power to prosecute (and to indict, i.e. to file the 'articles of impeachment') is reposed in the House of Representatives, whose members are elected from electoral districts and with 20 per cent of the seats reserved for party-list representatives.[33] The Senate has the 'sole power to try and decide', consisting of 24 senators elected nationally.[34] The high bar against the removal of these officers demonstrates the constitutional intent to insulate these offices from harassment before the usual judicial processes. On the other hand, the explicit political nature of these accountability mechanisms is also a candid recognition that whether an officer's transgression rises to the level of an impeachable offence is a political call assigned to electorally responsible legislators.

Contrast this to the highly judicialized and deliberately non-political process for every other public officer. The Philippine Ombudsman has evolved into a mainly prosecutorial rather than investigative body,[35] and is constitutionally insulated from the political branches. It is a constitutional body designed theoretically to stand above the three branches of government.

The Ombudsman and his or her deputies are appointed by the President, but are vetted by a supposedly non-political Judicial and Bar Council, the same Council that shortlists all judicial appointees, including the Supreme Court justices. The Ombudsman enjoys a fixed, non-renewal appointment, and is insulated in a budgetary sense through 'fiscal autonomy' from the political branches of government.

Apart from the Ombudsman, the power to prosecute is exercised by the Department of Justice, an agency directly under the power of the President and headed by a cabinet officer.[36] The Philippine Ombudsman therefore has become a standing and permanent 'Independent Special Prosecutor'.

In 2001, President Macapagal-Arroyo created yet another anti-corruption agency, this time squarely under her wing – and therefore a clearly political agency. The Presidential Anti-Graft Commission is an investigative body empowered to file anti-corruption charges against all presidential appointees.[37]

Problems with the formal institutions of public accountability

Excessive delay

The problem of docket congestion and delay at the *Sandiganbayan* is, mercifully, fully documented by the Supreme Court, in a decision appropriately titled *Problem Of Delays In Cases Before The Sandiganbayan*.[38] The Integrated Bar of the Philippines, the national association to which all lawyers mandatorily belong, filed a petition before the Supreme Court complaining about the snail's pace of work by the *Sandiganbayan*, and the Court chastised the presiding judge and placed him under strict supervision. He was fined and relieved of administrative duties to devote himself solely to decision-writing.[39]

Low conviction rate by the Ombudsman

The *Sandiganbayan*'s actual record of performance shows yet another problem that is more properly laid at the foot of the Ombudsman. From 2001 to 2006, a total of 7,324 cases were filed with the Court, of which approximately 20 per cent were 'archived' (no action has been taken, but the case remains in the Court's docket), and only 1.3 per cent were decided. Of these, acquittals accounted for 0.7 per cent and only 0.6 per cent resulted in convictions.[40]

This means that the conviction rate of 0.6 per cent is actually the 'success rate' of the prosecuting agency, the Ombudsman. All its other indictments were either thrown out without trial, dismissed upon demurrer to the evidence (meaning, after presentation of prosecution evidence and without the need of defence evidence), withdrawn by the prosecutor himself/herself, or dismissed after trial on the merits.

Conviction of 'small fry'

From 1979 to 2006, or during a 27-year period, the highest elective officials convicted were provincial governors, one for malversation of a total of P 13 million (approximately US$260,000), another for violations of the anti-graft law.[41] There were 20 cases filed against incumbent and sitting provincial governors from 2001 to 2006.[42] The next highest level was city and town mayors. A total of 168 mayors were indicted, but only 5 were eventually convicted.[43]

In contrast, the 'biggest fish' ever convicted by the *Sandiganbayan* was no less than Imelda Marcos, former First Lady and former member of the Marcos cabinet and of the Marcos-era parliament, for self-dealing and conflict of interest,[44] and former President Joseph Estrada, for plunder and perjury.[45]

In the case of Imelda Marcos, three things stand out. First, Imelda's conviction arose from a conflict of interest over the lease of shopping stalls, a petty case comparatively speaking, vis-à-vis more sophisticated frauds involving larger amounts, for example: malversation of P 97 million (or approximately US$2 million) in public funds;[46] the use of a dummy to facilitate a US$25-million loan;[47] transfer of shares of stock attributed to Marcos as beneficial owner,[48] including shares in the largest telecommunications company.[49]

This confirms the logic of the legislative finessing of anti-graft standards, in order to aid the prosecutor with the codification of specific standards and detailed regulations.

Second, the *Sandiganbayan*'s judgment of conviction in the Imelda Marcos case was actually affirmed by the Supreme Court. Despite the historical pattern of judicial aversion to stepping on the toes of the politically powerful, the conviction was upheld by a division of the Court.[50] The 15-person Supreme Court works either in plenary or, at its discretion, in divisions typically of five justices each; a decision of a 'division' is considered a decision of the entire Court.[51] Yet, in a dramatic departure from established practice, the Court allowed Marcos' counsel to appeal from the division to the plenary, which then reversed the conviction.

Third, Marcos was eventually acquitted because her co-accused had earlier been acquitted.[52] Since they were all Marcos' co-conspirators, without her cohorts, the Court *en banc* held that there was no one she could have conspired with and

Marcos could be held liable only for her own acts. The Court, in reversing the conviction, also glossed over the earlier finding of a conflict of interest. Finally, the Court in plenary even questioned the division's finding of acts 'manifestly and grossly disadvantageous to the government,' despite evidence that the actual rental rate was way below market rates. The verdict shows a court going out of its way to find a ground upon which to acquit a prominent political figure.

The case of President Joseph Estrada was, despite the institutional independence of the *Sandiganbayan*, seen as the litmus test for the government's commitment to end corruption. Considering that Estrada remained popular with the mass of Filipinos, the guilty verdict was expected to provoke political outrage whichever way it went. After six-and-a-half years of imprisonment, Estrada was convicted of plunder but acquitted of perjury and sentenced to life imprisonment.[53]

The indictment itself had earlier been challenged before the Supreme Court, in which the Court upheld the validity of the Plunder Law.[54] Next, the Court denied a petition by anti-Estrada lawyers for full media coverage of the trial, since apparently wide coverage of the aborted impeachment trial was instrumental in generating public outrage against Estrada.[55] This decision by the Supreme Court recognized the political context of the *Sandiganbayan* trial, and the undue influence of the media on judicial processes.

Within barely a month of the verdict, Estrada received a presidential pardon from Arroyo in an order which claimed a general policy to pardon inmates above the age of 70 years.[56] Strangely enough, the pardon contained the cryptic language, noting that Estrada 'ha[d] publicly committed to no longer seek any elective position or office'. This was widely interpreted as part of a 'conditional' pardon to ensure that Estrada stayed out of electoral politics upon his release.[57]

Virtual impunity for big corruption scandals

If there is any single factor that undermines public confidence in the anti-corruption campaign, it is that the biggest scandals in the Philippines today remain unpunished, due to either inaction or manipulation by the Ombudsman and the *Sandiganbayan*. The most prominent of these are described in detail below, in order to demonstrate the factual circumstances:

1 In 2001, two days after Arroyo assumed office, one of the very first acts by her newly appointed Secretary of Justice (equivalent to the Attorney-General) was to approve a US$470 million (approximately P 23 billion) hydroelectric contract that was frozen under the past administration due to concerns that it was disadvantageous to the government.[58] It was alleged that the Secretary of Justice took a US$2-million (approximately P 104-million) bribe from a former congressman who brokered the deal and who was being

extradited by the United States for making unlawful campaign donations. Full documentation was offered by Swiss and Hong Kong authorities.[59]

The Ombudsman, after dragging her feet between 2002 and 2007, finally filed robbery, graft, extortion and falsification of public documents charges against the Secretary,[60] but significantly refrained from filing the heavier charges for plunder.

The *Sandiganbayan*, for its part, dismissed the graft charges against the Secretary, citing the Ombudsman's delay as a violation of the constitutional right to the 'speedy disposition of their cases'.[61] In addition, the *Sandiganbayan* cited defects in the indictment filed by the Ombudsman, in that it failed to make the essential allegation that the harassment committed by the Secretary was made for a monetary consideration.[62]

2 The new Ninoy Aquino International Airport (Terminal 3) was mired in complex arbitration in which the newly installed Arroyo government kicked out the German contractors who built the airport, claiming they had given bribes to win the contract. Interestingly, the Ombudsman rejected several complaints arising from the contract,[63] even after the Supreme Court had struck down the contracts as tainted with fraud.[64] The Ombudsman has thus failed to indict a single person for that fraud. Worse, two legal officers involved in the expropriation proceedings over the airport have been assassinated, namely, the trial judge (in the case for the eminent domain taking of the airport)[65] and the most senior Assistant Solicitor-General.[66] The Supreme Court later ordered the *Sandiganbayan* to dismiss the criminal charges against the private co-conspirators.[67]

3 In 2003, the Supreme Court struck down a P1.3 billion (approximately US$2 million) poll computerization project of the Commission on Elections (COMELEC) for fraud.[68] No less than the former COMELEC chief and at the time of the investigation, the Solicitor-General, said that the contract was overpriced by P 500 million (approximately US$10 million). Also, the bidding rules were revised and tailored to favour one bidder. Having invalided the contract, the Court directed the Ombudsman to file criminal charges against all those involved, but despite this, the Ombudsman cleared the entire Commission. Indeed, a private citizens' watchdog had to ask the Supreme Court to reiterate its order and tried to make the Ombudsman comply with the order.[69] This episode demonstrates that despite the Supreme Court's findings and order to prosecute, this case did not reach the *Sandiganbayan* owing to a failure by the Ombudsman.

4 In 2003, United States customs officials seized US$100,000 (approximately P 5 million) in undeclared cash from the wife and the son of the Armed Forces Comptroller upon their entry to the United States. However, only in September 2004 did the Philippine government begin to act, and this was only after United States Customs and the Federal Bureau of Investigation transmitted a list of the amounts that the comptroller and his family had brought into the United States: approximately P 71 million (approximately US$14.2 million) from 1993 to 2003.

The comptroller was charged by the Judge Advocate General's Office for violating the Articles of War on 'conduct unbecoming' for failing to declare all his assets in the statutorily-required Statement of Assets and Liabilities. In 2006, the Military Court sentenced him to a two-year confinement without pay and allowance and dishonourable discharge. In February 2009, he was sentenced by the *Sandiganbayan* to two years' imprisonment for perjury in failing to declare some US$2 million worth of real estate in the United States as well as cash.[70]

5 In 2005, the rehabilitation of the northern arm of the national railway was investigated by the Senate (not by the Ombudsman) for being grossly overpriced, despite the fact the other costs for clearing, relocation and resettlement of informal dwellers occupying the railroad right-of-way were borne by the Philippine government. The President invoked her executive privilege to prevent the Senate from investigating the scam, but it was in large part struck down by the Supreme Court. The Court upheld the confidentiality of executive secrets, but required that the President – and not subordinate officers – invoke the privilege. The Court also recognized the power of the Senate to override that privilege under its power of 'legislative inquiry'.[71] This episode affirms likewise that there is a blockage in the process such that fraud cases, the *Sandiganbayan*'s raison d'être, do not reach it. In addition, it demonstrates that in default of a functioning Ombudsman, the political branches have stepped into the gap and performed the fact-finding that should have been done by both the Ombudsman and the *Sandiganbayan*.

To compound these problems, impunity has actually been abetted by no less than the Supreme Court. Soon after the ousting of Marcos, the allies of newly-installed President Corazon Aquino made midnight transfers of Marcos-related assets to Shell Company right before Aquino enabled a Presidential Commission on Good Government to seize and 'sequester' ill-gotten wealth.[72] An independent Senate investigation was blocked by the Supreme Court, in deference to the *Sandiganbayan* which, in turn, cleared the accused.[73]

Failure of impeachment process

Due to the steady flow of corruption scandals directly implicating the President, the incumbent President, Gloria Arroyo, was threatened with impeachment in 2005, 2006 and 2007.[74] The *Constitution* allows only one impeachment proceeding against a public official each year, and Arroyo has exploited that technicality to the hilt.

In 2005, a weak impeachment complaint was filed some ten minutes ahead of the bona fide complaint for corruption and violation of the public trust. Arroyo's congressional majority ruled that the bogus complaint pre-empted the genuine, and then proceeded to throw out the bogus complaint for being defective.[75]

Shifting from formal institutions to the informal processes of democracy

Given this record, the recent anti-corruption efforts have shifted towards transparency as the processes by which citizens' groups can compel formal institutions to function. This chapter identifies three distinct modes of mobilizing the democratic process to enhance weak institutions.

First, citizens' groups have filed test cases to compel the Ombudsman to investigate and to charge persons implicated in corruption scandals. The *Kilosbayan* (Community Action) and *Bantay Katarungan* (Justice Watch),[76] for instance, have petitioned the Supreme Court to compel the Ombudsman to prosecute those involved in the computerization scam of 2003,[77] and also asked the Ombudsman to investigate the telecommunications scandal of 2007.[78] Moreover, Transparency International's Philippine branch has monitored actively the anti-corruption campaign.[79]

Second, public polling groups enable ordinary citizens to document their experiences with government corruption without the risk of harassment as a whistle-blower, or without the usual legal requirement of testifying under oath. A prime example is the Social Weather Stations, a private opinion pollster, which has been monitoring corruption in the judiciary for the past decade.[80]

Third, investigative journalists and activist academics gather and systematize the facts that would otherwise not be investigated by the prosecutorial agencies. The Philippine Center for Investigative Journalism has exposed corruption scandals and, in fact, provided the leads in the prosecution against President Estrada.[81] The Probe Team exposed the fertilizer scam that diverted farmers' subsidies to Arroyo's presidential campaign.[82] The Center for People Empowerment in Governance is a university-based, non-governmental organization (NGO) that has done a systematic study of the annual performance of the Ombudsman and *Sandiganbayan*.[83]

Conclusion

The Philippine Constitution has created several layers of formal institutions for public accountability, yet the record over the past two decades shows that each fail-safe device has failed, merely shifting the checking function to the next default mechanism. The locus of the anti-corruption campaign has shifted away from the Ombudsman, *Sandiganbayan* (both supposedly non-political by design) and the Congress (explicitly political), towards the Senate (likewise political), the last government agency that has remained independent of the President – but which in turn is frustrated by the mantle of secrecy provided by executive privilege.

The dominant approach aims to perfect the institutions of public accountability. It seeks to insulate the *Sandiganbayan* and Ombudsman from politics, and to cabin discretion with strict codified standards. This approach embraces the underlying philosophy of the nation's liberal Constitution, wherein public norms are generally enforced through non-political institutions that respect the rights of the accused and protect him/her through several layers of review. The Philippine experience, however, shows the excessive 'juridification' of public norms, a shift away from substance to process and misconstruing or recasting 'due process' merely as endless process.

The more recent approaches have begun to appreciate the cultural and political context of the anti-corruption campaign. In that sense, the shift unwittingly represents the opposite of the dominant approach. It accepts the fact that norms and institutions do not operate above the political fray, and that the weak communal commitment to anti-corruption is in fact the real problem faced by the Ombudsman and *Sandiganbayan*. It openly attempts to pressurize the formal institutions from the outside – from media, activist NGOs, citizens' groups, and opinion polling organizations.

At the same time, these campaigns cannot succeed unless they work hand-in-hand with the formal institutions. In other words, a concerted media campaign and massive public protests – ideally – merely aim to prod and push, say, the Ombudsman and *Sandiganbayan* to do their work.

The informal processes are not seen as a substitute for the institutional enforcement of public norms. This most recent shift towards the democratic enforcement of norms is just about the last remaining mechanism to make the post-Marcos *Constitution* work. It is merely part of a continuing constitutional experiment that rejects revolution but seeks to mobilize popular power within the confines of a liberal constitution.

Notes

1. *Constitution of the Republic of the Philippines* art. XI §4.
2. *Constitution of the Republic of the Philippines* art. XI §5.
3. Philippine Institute for Development Studies, "Enemy Within (Report 2006/ASCC/014)," http://www.apec.org.au/docs/06ASCC_HCMC/06_9_1_Balboa.pdf), 2
4. Transparency International, "Regional Highlights," http://www.transparency.org/policy_research/surveys_indices/cpi/2008/regional_highlights_factsheets
5. Transparency International, "Transparency International Global Corruption Barometer 2007," http://www.transparencyintl.org/archives-12-2007-2008/news-11-7-07.htm
6. Social Weather Stations, "2007 SWS Business Survey on Corruption," http://www.sws.org.ph/TAG7%20for%20Cabinet%20Aug21-final.pdf
7. Omar Azfar and Tugrul Gurgur, "Local-level Corruption Hits Health Service Delivery in the Philippines," in *Transparency International – Global Corruption Report – 2006*, ed. Transparency International, http://www.transparencyintl.org/archives/gcr-2006-PH.htm
8. Philippine Institute for Development Studies, "Enemy Within (Report 2006/ASCC/014)," http://www.apec.org.au/docs/06ASCC_HCMC/06_9_1_Balboa.pdf), 2
9. GA Res 58/4, UN Doc A/Res/58/4 (2005).
10. GA Res 55/25, UN Doc A/Res/55/25 (2000).
11. *Constitution of the Republic of the Philippines* art. XI ('Accountability of Public Officers') §1.

12. *Republic Act No. 3815(1930)* ('The Revised Penal Code of the Philippines') arts 210–12.
13. *Republic Act No. 3815(1930)* ('The Revised Penal Code of the Philippines') arts 213–16.
14. *Republic Act No. 3815(1930)* ('The Revised Penal Code of the Philippines') arts 217–22. 'Malversation' is committed by any public officer 'who, by reason of the duties of his office, is accountable for public funds or property, shall appropriate the same, or shall take of misappropriate or shall consent, or through abandonment or negligence, shall permit any other person to take such public funds or property, wholly or partially'. (*Republic Act No. 3815(1930)* ('The Revised Penal Code of the Philippines') art 217).
15. *Republic Act No. 3815(1930)* ('The Revised Penal Code of the Philippines') Ch. 2 §1 arts 204–9.
16. *Republic Act No. 3815(1930)* ('The Revised Penal Code of the Philippines') art 235.
17. *Republic Act No. 3815(1930)* ('The Revised Penal Code of the Philippines') art 231.
18. *Republic Act No. 3019 (1960)* ('Anti-Graft and Corrupt Practices Act').
19. *Republic Act No. 3019 (1960)* ('Anti-Graft and Corrupt Practices Act') §4 ('Prohibition on Private Individuals') and §5 ('Prohibition on Certain Relatives').
20. *Republic Act No. 3019 (1960)* ('Anti-Graft and Corrupt Practices Act') §3.e.
21. *Republic Act No. 3019 (1960)* ('Anti-Graft and Corrupt Practices Act') §7 ('Statement of Assets and Liabilities').
22. *Constitution of the Republic of the Philippines* art. XI §17.
23. *Republic Act No. 6713 (1989)* ('Code of Conduct and Ethical Standards for Public Officials and Employees') §8 ('Statements and Disclosure').
24. *Republic Act No. 1379 (1955)* ('Act Declaring Forfeiture of Ill-gotten Wealth of Public Officers and Employees').
25. *Republic Act No. 6713 (1989)* ('Code of Conduct and Ethical Standards for Public Officials').
26. *Republic Act No. 7080 (1991)* ('An Act Defining and Penalizing the Crime of Plunder').
27. *Republic Act No. 7080 (1991)* ('An Act Defining and Penalizing the Crime of Plunder') §1.d., upheld by the Supreme Court in *Joseph Ejercito Estrada v. Sandiganbayan and People of the Philippines*, G.R. No. 148560 (2001).
28. *Republic Act No. 9485 (2007)* ('An Act to Improve the Efficiency in the Delivery of Government Service to the Public by Reducing Bureaucratic Red Tape, Preventing Graft and Corruption and Providing Penalties Therefore').
29. Minerva B. C. Newman, "President Arroyo signs Anti-Red Tape Act," http://www.gov.ph/news/default.asp?i = 17919
30. Executive Order No. 292, The Administrative Code of 1987, Book IV, Title III, Ch. 1 (1987).
31. Re: *Problem Of Delays In Cases Before The Sandiganbayan*, A.M. No. 00-8-05-SC (2001).
32. *Constitution of the Republic of the Philippines* art. XI §3.
33. *Constitution of the Republic of the Philippines* art. VI §5.(2); *Republic Act No. 7941 (1995)* ('An Act Providing for the Election of Party List Representatives Through the Party List System and Appropriating Funds Therefore'). The party-list representatives come from groups representing 'marginalized and under-represented sectors, organizations and parties, and who lack well-defined political constituencies but who could contribute to the formulation and enactment of appropriate legislation'. (*Republic Act No. 7941*). A party gets one seat if it garners at least 2 per cent of all votes cast for all party-list groups altogether, and another seat for each additional

2 per cent it garners, to a maximum of three seats per party, and subject to a formula for 'proportional representation among the winning political party-list groups: *Veterans Federation Party v. Commission on Elections*, G.R. No. 136781 (2000).
34. *Constitution of the Republic of the Philippines* arts XI §3, VI §2.
35. *Constitution of the Republic of the Philippines* art. XI §§5–14; *Republic Act No. 6770 (1989)* ('An Act Providing for the Functional and Structural Organization of the Office of the Ombudsman and for Other Purposes).
36. Executive Order No. 292, The Administrative Code of 1987, Book IV, Title III, Ch. 1 (1987).
37. Executive Order No. 12, Creating the Presidential Anti-Graft Commission and Providing For Its Powers, Duties and Functions and For Other Purposes (2001); Executive Order No. 531, Strengthening the Presidential Anti-Graft Commission by Amending Executive Order No. 12 Series of 2001 (2006).
38. Re: *Problem Of Delays In Cases Before The Sandiganbayan*, A.M. No. 00-8-05-SC (2001).
39. Ibid.
40. Center for People Empowerment in Governance, *Is the Philippine Judicial System Effective in Fighting Corruption?* (Quezon City: Center for People Empowerment in Governance, 2006).
41. Ibid.
42. Ibid., ii.
43. Ibid.
44. *Dans v. Sandiganbayan*, G.R. No. 127073 (1998).
45. *People v. Joseph Ejercito Estrada*, Sandiganbayan Crim. Case No. 26558 (Plunder) (2007); *People v. Joseph Ejercito Estrada*, Sandiganbayan Crim. Case No. 26905 (Perjury) (2007).
46. *Marcos v. Sandiganbayan*, G.R. Nos. 124680–81 (2000).
47. *Chiudian v. Sandiganbayan*, G.R. No. 139941 (2001).
48. *Republic v. Sandiganbayan*, G.R. No. 112710 (2001).
49. *Yuchengco v. Sandiganbayan*, G.R. No. 106244 (1997).
50. *Dans v. Sandiganbayan,* G.R. No. 127073 (1998).
51. *Constitution of the Republic of the Philippines* art. VIII §4.1.
52. *Marcos v. Sandiganbayan*, G.R. No. 126995 (1998).
53. *People v. Joseph Ejercito Estrada*, Sandiganbayan Criminal Case No. 26558 (Plunder) (2007); *People v. Joseph Ejercito Estrada*, Sandiganbayan Criminal Case No. 26905 (Perjury) (2007).
54. *Estrada v. Sandiganbayan*, G.R. No. 148560 (2001) (upholding *Republic Act No. 7080 [1991]*).
55. Re: *Request for Radio-TV Coverage of the Trial in the Sandiganbayan of the Plunder Cases against the Former President Joseph E. Estrada and Integrated Bar of the Philippines*, A.M. 01-4-03 SC (2001).
56. The Official Website of the Republic of the Philippines, "President Gloria Macapagal-Arroyo's Order Granting Pardon to Former President Joseph Estrada," http://www.gov.ph/news/?i = 19158
57. Lira Dalangin-Fernandez, "(UPDATE 3) Arroyo Grants Pardon to Estrada," *Philippine Daily Inquirer*, October 25, 2007, http://newsinfo.inquirer.net/breakingnews/nation/view_article.php?article_id = 96730
58. College of Social Work and Community Development, University of the Philippines, *National Study Conference on Corruption* (Manila: College of Social Work and Community Development, University of Philippines, 2005), 44, 58.
59. Jomar Canlas and Angelo S. Samonte, "Nani Perez Faces Graft Case," *Manila Times*, April 17, 2008, http://www.manilatimes.net/national/2008/apr/17/yehey/top_stories/20080417top1.html

60. Alecks P. Pabico, "Perez Isn't Only One Responsible for Controversial IMPSA Deal," http://www.pcij.org/blog/?p = 1396
61. *Constitution of the Republic of the Philippines* art. III §16.
62. Tetch Torres, "Robbery, Graft vs Perez, et al. Junked," *Philippine Daily Inquirer*, November 24, 2008, http://newsinfo.inquirer.net/breakingnews/nation/view/20081124–174041/Robbery-graft-vs-Perez-et-al-junked
63. *Rogelio Estrella v. Vicente Rivera* (2000); *Leto Raul Descallar v. Primitivo Cal* (2002); *Aileen Sanchez v. Pantaleon Alvarez* (2003). See College of Social Work and Community Development, *National Study Conference on Corruption*, 44.
64. *Agan v. Piatco*, G.R. No. 155001 (2003).
65. Purple Romero, "Rights Lawyers Want Supreme Court to Act on Killing of Judges," *Newsbreak*, November 13, 2008, http://newsbreak.com.ph/index.php?option = com_content&task = view&id = 5580&Itemid = 88889
66. "Nestor Ballacillo: Champion of Consumer Causes," Newsbreak, February 12, 2007, http://newsbreak.com.ph/index.php?option = com_content&task = view&id = 2407&Itemid = 88889
67. *Go v. Fifth Division*, G.R. No. 172602 (2007).
68. *Information Technology Foundation of the Philippines v. COMELEC, Kilosbayan and Bantay Katarungan, Intervenors*, G.R. No. 159139 (2004).
69. *Information Technology Foundation of the Philippines v. COMELEC, Kilosbayan and Bantay Katarungan, Intervenors*, G.R. No. 159139 (2006).
70. "Ex AFP Comptroller Convicted of Perjury," *Philippine Daily Inquirer*, February 18, 2009, http://161.58.192.236/2009/02/18/ex-afp-comptroller-convicted-of-perjury/
71. *Senate of the Philippines v. Ermita*, G.R. No. 169777 (2006); see also, Aries Rufo and Gemma B. Bagayaua, "Gloria's Mark: Big Corruption Cases Involving Her Family and Associates Remain Unresolved," *Newsbreak*, February 11, 2007, http://www.newsbreak.com.ph/index.php?option = com_content&task = view&id = 2398&Itemid = 88889066
72. *Bengzon v. Senate Blue Ribbon Committee*, G.R. No. 89914 (1991).
73. *Republic v. Romualdez*, Sandiganbayan Civil Case No. 0035 (1987).
74. De Jesus, "The Death of Public Accountability: An Analysis of Presidential Impeachment Proceedings" (L.L.B. thesis, University of the Philippines, 2007).
75. "Impeachment Complaints Filed Against President Arroyo in 2005," *GMA News*, May 11, 2007, http://www.gmanews.tv/story/67288/Impeachment-complaints-filed-against-President-Arroyo-in-2005.
76. *Kilosbayan* and *Bantay Katarungan* were established by the nation's senior statesman, Jovito R. Salonga, who was Senate President before Marcos declared martial law, was jailed by Marcos, and became Senate President again after Marcos fell. The author chairs *Bantay Katarungan*.
77. *Information Technology Foundation of the Phils. v. COMELEC, Kilosbayan and Bantay Katarungan, Intervenors*, G.R. No. 159139 (2006).
78. *Kilosbayan and Bantay Katarungan v. President Gloria Macapagal-Arroyo*; see also Tetch Torres, "Ombudsman Panel: Probe Salonga rap vs Arroyo Further," *Philippine Daily Inquirer*, September 26, 2008, http://www.inquirer.net/specialreports/nbndeal/view.php?db = 1&article = 20080926–163087
79. Transparency International, "Global Corruption Report 2008," http://www.transparency.org/publications/gcr/download_gcr#7.3
80. Social Weather Stations, "Summary of the 2007 SWS Survey Review," http://www.sws.org.ph
81. Yvonne Chua, Sheila Coronel and Vinia Datinguinoo, "Can Estrada Explain His Wealth," http://www.pcij.org./stories/2000/erapwealth.html

82. "Joc-Joc Bolante and the Fertilizer Fund Scam," *ABS-CBN News*, October 7, 2008, http://www.abs-cbnnews.com/nation/07/10/08/timeline-joc-joc-bolante-and-fertilizer-scam
83. Gabriella Quimson, "National Integrity Systems Transparency International Country Study Report," www.cenpeg.org/image/PDF_download/NIS_philippines_2006.pdf

Part VI

Setting up special courts

15 Malaysian royalty and the Special Court

H. P. Lee

Introduction

The Federation of Malaysia consists of 13 states, nine of which have a hereditary ruler. The states with hereditary rulers are commonly referred to as the Malay States and they are Johore, Kedah, Kelantan, Negeri Sembilan, Pahang, Perak, Perlis, Selangor and Terengganu.[1] These Malay Rulers choose from among themselves one who would hold office as the *Yang di-Pertuan Agong* or King for a term of five years.[2] This rotational form of kingship is an autochthonous element of the *Federal Constitution of Malaysia* (*Constitution*).

The constitutional dimensions of the sovereignty and immunity of the Rulers prior to 30 March 1993 were aptly described in an essay by Tun Haji Mohd Salleh bin Abas as follows:

> The Constitution provides that the Yang di-Pertuan Agong shall not be liable to any proceedings whatsoever in any Court. As regards other Rulers, their sovereignty, prerogatives, powers and jurisdiction remain unaffected and no proceedings whatsoever shall be brought in any Court against the Ruler of any State in his personal capacity. The Constitution also makes provisions preserving the prerogatives, powers and jurisdiction of the ruling Chiefs of Negeri Sembilan in their respective territories and they too are immune from court proceedings in their personal capacity.[3]

The absolute immunity of the *Yang di-Pertuan Agong* was entrenched in Article 32(1) of the *Constitution* which provided: 'There shall be a Supreme Head of the Federation, to be called the *Yang di-Pertuan Agong*, who shall take precedence over all persons in the Federation and shall not be liable to any proceedings whatsoever in any court.' In *Stephen Kalong Ningkan v. Tun Abang Haji Openg and Tawi Sli (No 2)*,[4] Pike CJ (Borneo) said that Article 32(1) could not be construed to protect the federal government from action in the courts in respect of acts committed in the name of the *Yang di-Pertuan Agong*. He added that 'when the Yang di-Pertuan Agong acts on the advice of the cabinet his act must be deemed to be the act of the Federal Government'.[5] Article 181(2) of the *Constitution* stated that 'no proceedings whatsoever shall be brought in any court against the Ruler of a State in his personal capacity'.

The absolute immunity of the Malay Rulers as guaranteed by the *Constitution* generated disquiet over the course of time. This disquiet was fuelled by a growing number of incidents involving the Malay Rulers. Dr Khoo Boo Teong recited a few of these instances:

> In 1986 Daeng Baha Ismail alleged in a suit that he was beaten by the Yang di-Pertuan Agong but the High Court in an unreported judgment of Justice Harun held that the court had no jurisdiction to hear the case because of legal immunity. In 1987, the Yang di-Pertuan Agong Sultan Mahmood Iskander at a golf course hit a caddy on the head leading to his death. The Prime Minster Dr Mahathir took no action at that time.[6]

The domestic press and general public were too intimidated to publicize these incidents. However, the disquiet over absolute immunity led Tunku Abdul Rahman, the first Prime Minister of Malaysia, to question the absolute immunity of the Malay Rulers:

> [A] Ruler who commits a breach of any Federal law is not subject to the jurisdiction of the courts. At Federal level, therefore, nothing can be done in relation to, for example (taking an extreme case), a Ruler maliciously killing a citizen – although subsequent public outcry may well give rise to a need to amend the law.[7]

Tunku Abdul Rahman added that it was undesirable in this democratic, egalitarian age that anyone should be above the law.[8] Three years later he voiced these sentiments again and suggested for the first time the establishment of a special court to deal with offences committed by the Malay Rulers. Tunku Abdul Rahman envisaged a court comprising their fellow Malay Rulers.[9]

A constitutional crisis erupted in 1993, which resulted in the enactment of the *Constitution (Amendment) Act 1993* which effected the establishment of 'The Special Court' whereby proceedings could be brought against a Ruler 'in his personal capacity'. The impetus for the titanic struggle between the Rulers and the Mahathir administration was the reported assault by the Ruler of the State of Johore (Sultan Mahmood Iskandar) of a school hockey coach (Douglas Gomez).[10]

As a result of the constitutional amendments, the amended Articles 32(1) and 181(2) provide:

> There shall be a Supreme Head of the Federation, to be called the Yang di-Pertuan Agong, who shall take precedence over all persons in the Federation and shall not be liable in any proceedings whatsoever in any court except in the Special Court established under Part XV.[11]

No proceedings whatsoever shall be brought in any Court against the Ruler of a State in his personal capacity except in the Special Court established under Part IV.[12]

Composition, role and functions of the Special Court

The composition of the Special Court is unusual. It consists of the Chief Justice of the Federal Court, the Chief Judges of the High Courts and two other persons who hold or have held office as judge of the Federal Court or a High Court 'appointed by the Conference of Rulers'.[13] Under the *Constitution* there are two High Courts: the High Court in Malaya and the High Court in Sabah and Sarawak. The unusual feature lies in the fact that two out of the five members of the Special Court are appointed by the Conference of Rulers. As the Special Court is designed to adjudicate on cases involving members of the Conference of Rulers who are the hereditary Rulers it amounts to a situation where a party to a matter before the Special Court has a say in determining the composition of the Special Court. It can be asserted that in an indirect fashion this amounts to a case of judging one's own cause and therefore in violation of the rule against bias. As the composition is dictated by an amendment to the *Constitution*, its validity, however, cannot be impugned on this ground.

A second interesting feature of the Special Court is that the person presiding over it – the Chief Justice of the Federal Court – is called the Chairman. This is perhaps a pragmatic recognition that the Special Court functions on an *ad hoc* basis and on very rare occasions.

The Special Court is given exclusive jurisdiction to try all offences committed in the Federation by the King or a State Ruler, and all civil cases by or against the King or a State Ruler notwithstanding where the cause of action arose. In the 1996 case of *Faridah Begum bte Abdullah v. Sultan Haji Ahmad Shah Al Mustain Billah Ibni Almarhum Sultan Abu Bakar Ri'Ayatuddin Al Mu' Adzam Shah*[14] it was pointed out that Article 182(3) 'confers exclusive jurisdiction on the Special Court to try all offences committed by a Ruler and all civil cases brought by, or against, a Ruler'.[15] The proposition that proceedings 'whether by or against a Ruler in his personal capacity must be brought in the Special Court' was reaffirmed by Dennis Ong JCA delivering judgment of the Federal Court in *DYTM Tengku Idris Shah Ibni Sultan Salahuddin Abdul Aziz Shah* v. *Dikim Holdings Sdn Bhd & Anor.*[16] A Ruler may be able to institute a suit in the ordinary courts provided it is brought by a person to whom he has given a power of attorney.[17] The rationale was stated by Low Hop Bing J of the High Court (Seremban) explaining:

> In my judgment, art. 181(1) would include the Rulers' prerogative in granting a power of attorney to any person of legal capacity in order to authorize the donor of the power of attorney to act as his lawful attorney to do all things in accordance with the law e.g. in the instant case to commence legal proceedings for and on behalf of the principal. Had this action been commenced by the principal in this court in his personal capacity, there can be no doubt this court would have no jurisdiction at all and the suit ought to be struck out.[18]

The Special Court is expressly declared to have the same jurisdiction and powers as are invested in the inferior courts, the High Court and the Federal Court by the *Constitution* or any federal law. The registry of the Special Court is located in the federal capital, Kuala Lumpur.[19]

Proceedings in the Special Court are governed by the practice and procedure applicable in any proceedings in the inferior courts, any High Court and the Federal Court. However, Parliament is empowered to make special provision to the contrary in respect of procedure (including the hearing of proceedings *in camera*) in civil or criminal cases and the law regulating evidence and proof in civil and criminal proceedings.[20]

The proceedings in the Special Court are decided in accordance with the opinion of the majority of the members. The decision of the Special Court is 'final and conclusive' and cannot be challenged or called into question in any court on any ground.[21]

Given that the introduction of a special court is an unprecedented development, it is not possible to envisage future imbroglios arising from the operation of this Court. When defects become apparent the King is empowered to act to cure such defects. Thus, Article 182(7) of the *Constitution* sets out a 'saving' provision:

> The [King] may, on the advice of the Chief Justice, make such rules as he may deem necessary or expedient to provide for the removal of any difficulty or anomaly whatsoever in any written law or in the carrying out of any function; the exercise of any power, the discharge of any duty, or the doing of any act, under any written law, that may be occasioned by [Article 182]; and for that purpose such rules may make any modification, adaptation, alteration, change or amendment whatsoever to any written law.[22]

Article 183 of the *Constitution* provides that no action can be instituted against the King or a Ruler except with the consent of the Attorney-General personally.

In *DYTM Tengku Idris Shah Ibni Sultan Salahuddin Abdul Aziz Shah v. Dikim Holdings Sdn. Bhd & Anor,*[23] the plaintiff was appointed the Regent of Selangor, about a year after he had filed a writ of summons and statement of claim against the defendants at the High Court in Kuala Lumpur. In a special case stated to the Federal Court – pursuant to s. 84 of the *Courts of Judicature Act 1964* – the Federal Court answered in the negative the question whether the plaintiff, who was appointed to exercise the functions as 'Sultan', was a 'Ruler' for the purposes of Articles 181, 182 and 183 of the *Constitution*.

On 21 November 2001, Sultan Salahuddin Abdul Aziz Shah Al Haj passed away and on 22 November 2001, the plaintiff was proclaimed the Sultan of Selangor. In a special case, again referred to the Federal Court, the Court held that with the plaintiff's accession as a Ruler, the High Court ceased to have jurisdiction over the plaintiff and also lacked the power to transfer the suit to the Special Court. The plaintiff would have to commence the action afresh in the Special Court and that the defendant's counterclaim would require the prior consent of the Attorney-General.

The Special Court in action

Faridah Begum bte Abdullah v. Sultan Haji Ahmad Shah Al Mustain Billah Ibni Almarhum Sultan Abu Bakar Ri'Ayatuddin Al Mu'Adzam Shah[24] (the *Faridah* case) is the first reported case in which the Special Court was called into operation. In the case, an action for alleged libel and for damages was brought by Faridah, a Singapore citizen, against the Sultan of Pahang in his personal capacity. In accordance with Article 183, consent was given by the Attorney-General for the action to be instituted.

The issue posed to the Supreme Court was whether the plaintiff, not being a Malaysian citizen, had the right to sue the Sultan of Pahang in his personal capacity in the Special Court. The action of the plaintiff was defeated on the preliminary legal issue as the Special Court, by a 4–1 majority, held that the plaintiff, being a Singaporean citizen, had no entitlement to sue the Ruler of Pahang in his personal capacity.

The decision of three of the majority members of the Special Court was based on the invocation of Article 155(1) of the *Constitution* which provides:

> Where the law in force in any other part of the Commonwealth confers upon citizens of the Federation any right or privilege it shall be lawful, notwithstanding anything in their Constitution, for Parliament to confer a similar right or privilege upon citizens of that part of the Commonwealth who are not citizens of the Federation.[25]

According to Eusoff Chin CJ and Mohd Suffian, Article 155(1) of the *Constitution* was decisive of the matter. Mohd Suffian said:

> [A]rt. 155 renders art. 182(3) void to the extent that it purports to allow a non-citizen to sue a Ruler in the Special Court. ... In Singapore, its Head of State the President enjoys total immunity and may not be sued by anybody. If, and only if, Singapore amends its Constitution to allow a Malaysian citizen to sue the President in Singapore – in other words, only if there is reciprocity only then may the Malaysian Parliament confer on a Singapore citizen a similar right or privilege to sue a Ruler in our country. The Singapore Constitution has not been amended. Giving effect to the very clear language of art. 155, I am of the opinion that the plaintiff, a Singapore citizen, has no right or privilege of suing HRH in the Special Court.[26]

Chong Siew Fai CJ (Sabah and Sarawak) also acknowledged the doctrine of reciprocity stipulated by Article 155. He was also of the view that the wording of Article 182(2) itself was 'ambiguous or imprecise', and that in order for a foreigner to be allowed to sue the Rulers, 'clear and unequivocal words' were required.[27] Mohd Azmi FCJ simply stated that a foreigner could not effect a suit against the Rulers and the King in the Special Court given the 'absence of clear and express provision'.[28] To hold otherwise, he added, would admit 'the absurdity that Malaysia and the states comprising the Federation have no sovereignty in international law, and would open the floodgate of litigation by foreigners against His Majesty the King himself'.[29]

On 15 October 2008 the Special Court, in an unanimous decision, held that the Ruler of Negeri Sembilan (Tuanku Ja'afar Abdul Rahman) was required to honour the terms of a letter of credit and ordered the Ruler to pay US$1 million to Standard Chartered Bank Malaysia Berhad.[30]

Criminal prosecutions and the pardoning power

The *Faridah* case involved a civil suit. So far, no criminal action has been instituted in the Special Court. If a criminal prosecution is successfully brought against the King or a State Ruler, can the conviction be negated by the King or a State Ruler invoking the royal power of pardon? The *Constitution (Amendment) Act 1993* sought to eliminate this possibility.

Article 42(1) of the *Constitution* expressly empowers the King to grant 'pardons, reprieves and respites' in respect of all offences which have been tried by court martial and all offences committed in the federal territories of Kuala Lumpur, Labuan and Putrajaya. It similarly empowers the Ruler or a Governor of a State to grant 'pardons, reprieves and respites' in respect of all other offences committed in his State.

In the exercise of the pardoning power, the King is assisted by a Pardons Board constituted for the Federal Territories of Kuala Lumpur, Labuan and Putrajaya and the State Rulers and Governors by a Pardons Board constituted for each of the States. Although it is provided that the Ruler or a Governor of a State is required to exercise the power of pardon on the 'advice' of a Pardons Board constituted for that State, a majority of the members of a Pardons Board for a State are appointed by the State Ruler or Governor. This in reality could mean that a Ruler or Governor could influence the outcome of the Pardons Board's deliberations.

Y. A. M. Raja Azlan Shah (as he then was) narrated an incident which illustrates the influence of the Malay Rulers in the exercise of the pardoning power. He wrote:

> The then Crown Prince of Johore was convicted of a number of offences. The feelings of the public were strongly against him. The public did not expect him to be pardoned. The Sultan, however, pardoned him. Even though the Crown Prince and heir to the throne was demoted because of the incident, just before his death the Sultan reinstated him to his former position. He became the Sultan after the death of his father.[31]

Y. A. M. Raja Azlan Shah concluded that in the exercise of the power of pardon, 'the Ruler may be influenced by other factors, personal or political'.[32]

It was recognized by the government that the effective removal of the personal immunity of the Rulers could not be achieved by just amending Article 181(2).

New clauses 12 and 13 were inserted into Article 42 to preclude a Ruler from hearing an appeal on his own behalf and pardoning himself.

If the pardoning power is to be exercised in respect of the King, a State Ruler, or his Consort, it is the Conference of Rulers which shall exercise the power.[33] A prerequisite for the making of a decision is that the Conference of Rulers must consider any opinion delivered by the Attorney-General.[34] In the case of an exercise of the pardoning power by the King or a State Ruler in respect of his son or daughter, it is to be exercised by a Ruler of a State nominated by the Conference of Rulers 'who shall act in accordance with the advice of the relevant Pardons Board' constituted under Article 42.[35] Where the power is to be exercised in respect of a State Governor or his wife, son or daughter, it shall be exercised by the King 'acting on the advice of the Pardons Board constituted for that State' under Article 42.[36]

Concluding observations

Dr Khoo Boo Teong queried the rationale for creating a Special Court:

> In relation to the establishment of a Special Court, it needs to be asked why there must exist a Special Court for the Malay Rulers. The very concept of a Special Court, in itself creates problems with the doctrine of equality under the substantive justice theory of the Rule of Law. A Special Court implies being set apart, being separate, being privileged. Such notions are inimical to substantive equality. It would have been better to have the Malay rulers being subject to the jurisdiction of the Federal Court, which is the highest court in the land, as part of the Federal Court's original jurisdiction. Such an approach would be consonant even with Dicey's second meaning of the Rule of Law, that is, 'equality before the law or the equal subjection of all classes to the ordinary laws of the land administered by the ordinary law courts'.[37]

This criticism seeks to provide for a meaningful application of the equality doctrine. However, this criticism fails to take into account the historical and political dimensions of the matter. Denis Ong JCA, delivering judgment of the Federal Court in *DYTM Tengku Idris Shah Ibni Sultan Salahuddin Abdul Aziz Shah v. Dikim Holdings Sdn Bhd* said:

> The Special Court is a court created for the ruling class over which it has exclusive jurisdiction whereas the ordinary courts which constitute the judiciary is for the ordinary litigants. Further, ... waiver aside, the ordinary courts never had jurisdiction over the Rulers.[38]

Considered against the backdrop of Malaysian constitutional traditions and understandings, the creation of the Special Court accorded recognition to the practical realities of Malaysian politics. The Malay Rulers were not without support from among the grassroots of the Malay community. They were also supported by members of the elite of Malay society. The move reflected the desire to achieve a compromise which would give some 'face-saving' comfort to the Malay Rulers. At the 11th hour the Malay Rulers baulked at this concession by the government. The Conference of Rulers, in a statement issued by the Keeper of the Rulers' Seal, said:

> The Conference of Rulers is of the view that such a court is not the most suitable forum for such a purpose. The Conference of Rulers recommends that an Advisory Board be established whose function would be to make recommendations to the appropriate State authority for the removal of the Ruler before he is charged or sued.[39]

The Conference of Rulers called for further consideration and discussion of 'the mechanics and the details relating to the Advisory Board and of the said State authority, together with its powers and composition'.[40] The Mahathir government refused to budge on its proposed Special Court. In the end the Bill was passed by the Malaysian Parliament and was assented to by the *Yang di-Pertuan Agong*.

Dr Khoo Boo Teong also criticized the requirement for the Attorney-General to give his personal consent before a suit or prosecution can be instituted. He argued that it would have been better 'if an office of an independent Ombudsman was created and the power to give consent for a civil suit or prosecution was given to the Ombudsman, if there was a necessity for a vetting provision'.[41] The concern underlying this criticism is understandable. As the Attorney-General is the legal advisor to the government, the Malay Rulers are unlikely to have confidence that he will exercise full independence of judgment in deciding whether to give his consent. This is particularly so, given that it is the government that had been in conflict with the Malay Rulers. The suggestion for an Ombudsman is not necessarily a sound one. Suits or prosecutions against the Malay Rulers are rare occurrences and, accordingly, would not justify the outlay of public funds to establish a position which would have little or no work to perform. Even if such an office is created, it cannot be guaranteed that the independence of the Ombudsman would not be interfered with, especially when viewed again the backdrop of the 'Tun Salleh' affair.[42] Given the rare instances of possible invocation of the jurisdiction of the Special Court, it would be better to delete the requirement for the consent of the Attorney-General for the institution of a suit or prosecution against a Malay Ruler. The Special Court should be able to deal with a vexatious litigant or should be expressly empowered to deal with it.

Finally, the constitutional amendments provided that the removal of the Malay Rulers' personal immunity was to operate prospectively. Thus, the Malay Ruler who was alleged to have assaulted the school hockey coach could not be prosecuted in respect of the alleged assault.

Notes

1. In every Malay State, except for Negeri Sambilan and Perlis, the Ruler is referred to as Sultan. In Negeri Sambilan, Article 160(2) defines 'Ruler' as meaning the 'Yang

di-Pertuan Besar' acting on behalf of himself and the ruling chiefs in accordance with the Constitution of that State. In Perlis the hereditary ruler is known as the Raja. See Y. A. M. Raja Tun Azlan Shah, "The Role of Constitutional Rulers," in *The Constitution of Malaysia – Further Perspectives and Developments*, ed. F. A. Trindade and H. P. Lee (Singapore: Oxford University Press, 1986), 76; and Tun Haji Mohd Salleh bin Abas, "Traditional Elements of the Malaysian Constitution," in *The Constitution of Malaysia – Further Perspectives and Developments*, ed. F. A. Trindade and H. P. Lee (Singapore: Oxford University Press, 1986), 3. See also *Dato Menteri Othman bin Baginda & Anor v. Dato' Ombi Syed Alwi bin Syed Idrus* [1981] 1 Malayan Law Journal 29.

2. The mode provided by the *Federal Constitution of Malaysia* for the election of the King is described by F. A. Trindade, "The Constitutional Position of the Yang di-Pertuan Agong," in *The Constitution of Malaysia – Its Development: 1957–1977*, ed. Tun Mohammed Suffian, H. P. Lee and F. A. Trindade (Kuala Lumpur: Oxford University Press, 1978), 103–6.
3. Tun Haji Mohd, "Traditional Elements of the Malaysian Constitution," 3. Prior to the 1993 constitutional amendments, Article 32(1) provided as follows: 'There shall be a Supreme Head of the Federation, to be called the Yang di-Pertnan Agong, who shall take precedence over all persons in the Federation and shall not be liable to any proceedings whatsoever in any court.'
4. [1967] 1 Malayan Law Journal 46.
5. Ibid., 47. See also Trindade, "The Constitutional Position of the Yang di-Pertuan Agong," in *The Constitution of Malaysia – Its Development: 1957–1977*, ed. Tun Mohammed Suffian, H. P. Lee and F. A. Trindade (Kuala Lumpur: Oxford University Press, 1978), 107–8.
6. Khoo Boo Teong, "Rule of Law and Fundamental Liberties in Malaysia" (PhD diss., University of Sydney, 1999), 327.
7. Tunku Abdul Rahman, *Challenging Times* (Petaling Jaya: Pelanduk Publications, 1986), 35–6.
8. Ibid., 36.
9. "Opening Speech of YTM Tunku Abdul Rahman Putra," in *Reflections on the Malaysian Constitution*, ed. Aliran (Penang: Persatuan Aliran Kesedaran Negara, 1987), 20.
10. The move to strip the Rulers of immunity was not one which developed overnight. A number of incidents between some Rulers and their state chief ministers had led to tensions between the ruling *Barisan Nasional* party and these Rulers. The tension culminated in a first confrontation which led to the removal of the power of the Rulers and the King to refuse royal assent to state and federal legislation, respectively. See H. P. Lee, *Constitutional Conflicts in Contemporary Malaysia* (Kuala Lumpur: Oxford University Press, 1995), 22–42. In the early years after the attainment of independence in 1957, the hereditary Rulers had not fully adjusted to a new constitutional order based on a Westminster system of government. A number of them behaved in such a way that their state governments were rather intimidated, with Chief Ministers who commanded majority support in the State legislatures having to step down as they had incurred the displeasure of their State Ruler. See Raja Tun Azlan Shah, "The Role of Constitutional Rulers," 80–2. See also Roger Kershaw, "Shattered Symbiosis: The Road to Conflict between Malay Nationalism and Monarchy," *Internationales Asienforum* 24 (1993): 283.
11. *Federal Constitution of Malaysia* art. 32(1).
12. *Federal Constitution of Malaysia* art. 181(2).
13. *Federal Constitution of Malaysia* art. 182(1).
14. [1996] 1 Malayan Law Journal 617.
15. Ibid., 622 (Eusoff Chin CJ).
16. [2003] 2 Malayan Law Journal 1, 16.

17. *Dato' Hari Menon @ Dato' T Puraharan a/l CP Ramakrishnan (suing as legal representative of DYMM Tuanku Ja'afar Ibni Almarhum Tuanku Abdul Rahman, Yang Di Pertuan Besar Negeri Sembilan Darul Khusus) v. Texas Encore LLC & Ors* [2005] 4 Malayan Law Journal 506.
18. Ibid., 524.
19. *Federal Constitution of Malaysia* art. 182(4).
20. *Federal Constitution of Malaysia* art. 182(5).
21. *Federal Constitution of Malaysia* art.182(6).
22. *Federal Constitution of Malaysia* art. 182(7).
23. [2003] 2 Malayan Law Journal 1.
24. The discussion of the case here draws largely from my article, "Constitutional Heads and Judicial Intervention," in *Public Law in Contemporary Malaysia*, ed. Wu Min Ann (Petaling Jaya: Longman, 1999), 9–11.
25. *Federal Constitution of Malaysia* art. 155(1).
26. [1996] 1 Malayan Law Journal 617, 636.
27. Ibid., 627–8.
28. Ibid., 631.
29. Ibid., 631–32.
30. Malaysian National News Agency, http://www.bernama.com/bernama/v5/newsindex.php?id = 36452. The members of the Special Court were Chief Justice Tun Abdul Hamid Mohamad, Chief Judge of Malaya Tan Sri Alaudin Mohd Sheriff, Chief Judge of Sabah and Sarawak Tan Sri Richard Malanjum, and Federal Court judges Datuk Arifin Zakaria and Datuk Zulkefli Ahmad Makinudin.
31. Raja Tun Azlan Shah, "The Role of Constitutional Rulers," 86–7.
32. Ibid., 87.
33. *Federal Constitution of Malaysia* art. 42(12)(b).
34. *Federal Constitution of Malaysia* art. 42(12)(b)(ii).
35. *Federal Constitution of Malaysia* art. 42(12)(c).
36. *Federal Constitution of Malaysia* art. 42(12)(a).
37. Khoo, "Rule of Law and Fundamental Liberties in Malaysia," 327.
38. [2003] 2 Malayan Law Journal 1, 15.
39. "Decision of the Special Meeting of the Conference of Rulers on Jan. 18," *New Straits Times*, January 19, 1993, 2.
40. Ibid.
41. Khoo, "Rule of Law and Fundamental Liberties in Malaysia," 327–8.
42. The 'Tun Salleh' affair was a constitutional crisis which resulted in the removal of the Lord President (now renamed Chief Justice) Tun Salleh bin Abas and two senior justices of the Supreme Court (now renamed the Federal Court). For an account of this crisis, see H. P. Lee, "The Judiciary under Siege" in *Constitutional Conflicts in Contemporary Malaysia*, ed. H. P. Lee (Kuala Lumpur: Oxford University Press, 1995).

16 Informed by ideology

A review of the court reforms in Brunei Darussalam

Ann Black

Introduction

For over a century, two parallel legal orders have operated in Brunei Darussalam, with each employing distinctive bodies of law in separate systems of courts, one religious and one secular. The secular system imposed under years of British colonial rule embodies very different principles and procedures from those of the religious system, yet jointly they provide the official and formally sanctioned means of dispute resolution. Neither legal order is indigenous to Brunei. Both were received from foreign lands and cultures. The means of reception was different in each case, but both were premised on liberating the people from the perceived deficits in the existing social ordering. Islamic law was to enlighten the animistic tribal people of Borneo with knowledge of the ways brought by Allah to his Prophet in Arabia, while secular Western law was introduced to civilize and modernize the stagnating practices of people perceived as backward.[1] Distain for Brunei methods of dispute resolution and governance is well set-out in the early documents and writings of Colonial Office officials in Brunei: Peter Leys, British Consul General, in 1885 wrote that the existing system in Brunei 'should be replaced by the clearer and stronger rule of the more enlightened European in whose justice and integrity they have perfect confidence'.[2]

Islamic law was received gradually, voluntarily and partially into Brunei from the fourteenth century onwards, while English law was received rapidly, involuntarily and extensively during the colonial period from 1905 to 1959. Although both now form the official law of Brunei Darussalam, the Western model has, to date, continued to be dominant, in that it is applied to all persons in Brunei, whereas the religious courts have jurisdiction over Muslims only and for a limited range of matters. Muslims, who are mainly Brunei Malays, are almost 70 per cent of the population,[3] with Buddhists, Christians, Hindus and indigenous animists comprising the remaining non-Muslim population.[4] The wider jurisdiction of the secular courts has cemented their designation as the definitive or dominant dispute resolution institution for the country. The *Laws of Brunei,* as revised in 1984 at independence, establish that:

> Subject to the provisions of this Act and save in so far as other provision has been and may hereafter be made by any written law in force in Brunei,

> the common law of England and the doctrines of equity, together with any statutes of general application, as administered or in force in England at the commencement of this Act shall be in force in Brunei.[5]

The dominance of the transplanted common law model, a legacy and reminder of colonial control and Western culture, creates tension in a nation proclaimed to be a Malay Sultanate. The incongruence lies at the heart of the changes introduced into the courts of Brunei over the last decade. It brought about an impetus for the Islamic courts to be reformed, restructured, revitalized and, importantly, renamed. The reforms were not mere window-dressing, though there is an aspect of that inherent in the agenda, but were designed to bring about substantive change. In addition, the reforms may have laid the foundation for greater Islamization. In this Malay Sultanate, the reforms undertaken in its courts are important to Bruneian identity and to Brunei's credentials in the Islamic world community.

Brunei's identity and Islamic credentials were always going to be important in a nation delineating itself as a Sultanate, as the term imports rule by a sovereign with Islamic authority. The present Sultan, Haji Hassanal Bolkiah Muizzaddin Waddaulah, who claims direct descent from the Prophet Mohammad, is both head of the Islamic faith and head of state. As well, Brunei is a tiny nation with a small population (less than 400,000); it is geographically small (boundary length is less than 400 km); and it shares the region with two large Muslim nations, Malaysia and Indonesia, the latter being the world's most populous Muslim society. Moreover, Brunei has to share the island of Borneo, which in centuries past was under its control, with the two Malaysian States of Sabah and Sarawak and the Indonesian province of Kalimantan. Furthermore, Brunei is a newcomer to the international stage. Although Brunei became a Sultanate in the fourteenth century when Islam came to the region and the then Raja of Brunei converted to Islam, the nation only shed its colonial heritage to become a fully independent country 24 years ago. These reasons go part of the way to explaining why asserting a distinctive identity and promoting the country's Islamic credentials post-independence have been so important. Central to this identity, has been the adoption and promotion of the national ideology – *Melayu Islam Beraja* or MIB (Malay Islamic Monarchy). MIB impacts on all aspects of life in the Sultanate and consequentially underpins the revamping of the religious courts.

The ideology of *Melayu Islam Beraja*

At the proclamation of independence in 1984 the Sultan announced that MIB would be the nation's national ideology, and it 'must be honoured and practised by all people of Brunei'.[6] The Sultan explained it was:

> a concept which upholds Islamic principles and values based on the Quran and Hadith as the basis of all activities concerning the racial necessity, language, Malay culture and the monarchy institution as the governing system and administration of Brunei Darussalam.[7]

Although national ideologies are not uncommon in Asia, MIB assumed particular importance in this nation where executive, religious and legislative power reside in the Sultan and his chosen power elite. This consolidation of power, along with the rejection of elections and representative democracy, is justified internally and externally, by the MIB ideology.

The 'B' component in MIB – *beraja* or 'monarchy' – is employed to legitimize the Sultan's absolute authority over all matters pertaining to governance of the county. This includes his unfettered legislative power. The basis of the legitimation has two premises. The first is that *beraja* is a time-honoured and indigenous, integral part of Bruneian culture. In the Sultan's justification, Brunei 'has practiced the monarchical system of government for six hundred years'[8] and is a means, with the other two MIB pillars, to prevent infiltration of 'unwanted elements which are not suitable to the nation's very own identity'.[9] Representative democracy is in the category of an unwanted foreign element, as the retention of the monarchy in Brunei has shown that a 'just and benevolent government is more excellent and universal compared to Western concepts of governance which are only meant to benefit their proponents'.[10] Although opposing views are not countenanced within Brunei,[11] scholars from outside Brunei such as G. Braighlinn[12] and R. Kershaw,[13] argue that the architects of MIB have artificially recreated Brunei's past and projected a 'false consciousness' on the citizens in order to rationalize Brunei's medieval political structure. As the structure operates for the benefit of the royal family, the process has been described as 'self-legitimation'.[14] The Sultan stresses that MIB is 'God's will' and thus has divine legitimation.

The second basis for legitimation of Brunei's absolute monarchy comes from Islam. There is a view in Islamic jurisprudence which finds Western democracy incompatible with Islam. In preference, the Islamic (and now Malay) concept of *shura* (consultation) from which consensus can be achieved is relied on to justify the validity of autocratic and monarchical forms of governance, with the proviso that the Ruler's decisions are made in a consultative and caring manner. This *shura*-based alternative to Western democracy is said to be manifest in Brunei by the Sultan's oft-cited special symbiotic relationship with his people, the *rakyat*, who are able to directly consult with him when he visits the villages, mosques and workplaces – a process described as 'living democracy'. As well, Brunei points to its 'grassroots democracy' whereby village headmen fulfil a role of mediating agents between the government and the people, being accountable through a network of Consultative Councils and the occasional *Mukim* (sub-district led by a *penghulu*) and Village Assembly. The first such assembly was held in 1996 and the second, with 3,500 representatives drawn from 37 *mukims* and 168 villages, was in August 2007.

Section 39 of the *Constitution of Brunei Darussalam* (*Constitution*) enables the Sultan to enact laws for the 'peace, order, security and good government' of Brunei with advice from the Legislative Council. This too is a further embodiment of the *shura* concept, as the Council is 'to provide opportunities to his people to contribute constructively... through a formal structure of consultation'.[15]

During the reign of Sultan Bolkiah, this Council has not been intended to be a representative institution nor one that actively or critically informs or participates in the legislative process. This was guaranteed when the Legislative Council was reconstituted five years ago in 2004, with all its members directly appointed by the Sultan. Each holds his seat at the Sultan's pleasure.[16] When the number of members (all male) was increased the next year to 29 the process continued to be by royal appointment, with members of the royal family, including Sultan Bolkiah's two brothers and his son the Crown Prince Al-Muhtadee Billah, in the contingent.

A hand-picked and appointed Legislative Council was never meant to be a forum for vigorous debate and for scrutiny of legislation, but it did achieve the Sultan's hope, as stated in his *titah* marking the occasion, that 'the new Legislative Council would be a strong and loyal institution'.[17] Loyalty had been assured. In addition, further safeguards on loyalty were enacted. A member of the Council would lose his seat if 'disloyal' or 'disaffected' or if he employed language or exhibited behaviour deemed 'irresponsible, derogatory, scandalous, or injurious'.[18] At the MIB Forum in 2006 the Sultan explained that views and opinions expressed by members of the Council should be in a 'constructive manner to achieve consensus'.[19] As well, the *Sedition Act* (Cap 24) Section 4 was amended in 2005 to make it an offence to 'directly or indirectly lower or adversely affect the rights, status, position, powers, privileges, sovereignty or prerogatives of the sultan, his spouses, successors or members of the royal family'. MIB was similarly protected from negative or derogatory commentary.[20] The Sultan is not convinced that his people are ready yet for elections, though on several occasions he has reassured them it may happen. He stated,

> A system of the people's representation should be implemented with more caution, for the sake of the people and the future of the nation ... [requiring] closer study as well as an infrastructure for electing the representatives so that the system is organized and trustworthy.[21]

In addition, it needs to be noted that in Brunei legislation is enacted as emergency orders. Brunei has been in a proclaimed 'State of Emergency' for the last 47 years. This emergency status has been renewed every two years since the brief 1962 uprising against the government.[22] This ignores the fact that the rebellion was quickly quashed over four decades ago, and since that time Brunei has been a very peaceful country with no civil unrest and minimal dissent. Even its title of Darussalam – the Abode of Peace – belies the continuance of a state of emergency. That it is continued in perpetuity serves to consolidate power, limit dissent and ensures no opposition to the Ruler's agenda.

While MIB has effectively maintained cohesion against inroads from Western, democratic ideals and processes, it also rejects secularism. The 'I' tenet of MIB requires Islamic[23] principles to be the basis of all activities. Given the centrality of law in Islam, this provides a direct challenge to the dominance of the transplanted secular courts and laws.

To address this, Brunei has in the last decade rejuvenated and restructured its Islamic courts to increase their standing and to accord them greater parity with the secular courts. This is in keeping with the goal of placing 'Islamic laws as the principal legal system in the country and not the colonial system as widely practised today'.[24] Also there has been some minor tinkering with the secular courts to reflect, symbolically, a more Bruneian (Malay) heritage. Each will be considered here. An outline of the changes is provided followed by analysis of the rationale for the change and its significance.

Transforming the Islamic Courts: Kadis Courts to Syariah Courts

Since the *Courts Enactment* (1908),[25] Brunei has had separate religious courts to provide forums for adjudication of particular disputes between Muslims, ones that are excluded from the jurisdiction of the secular courts. The format of these courts and their jurisdiction is outlined below, but essentially the religious courts deal with inter-personal matters relating to the Islamic faith, family and inheritance laws. From 2000, the religious courts in Brunei Darussalam have undergone significant reform witnessed by a change in designation, from *Kadis* Courts to *Syariah* Courts, and by the repeal of major sections of the *Religious Council and Kadis Courts Act* (Cap 77), which were replaced by the new *Syariah Courts Order* (Cap 184) (the *Order*). The *Order* was given royal assent in 2001.

What's in a name?

The morphing of *Kadis* Courts into *Syariah* Courts and the removal of the term *kadi* for *Syar'ie* judge, in Malay *Hakim Syar'ie,* has considerable symbolic significance. If changes were to occur in the religious courts, whereby their standing and jurisdiction were to be increased, it could best be encapsulated and promoted by a new nomenclature. The reforms were not simply a reversion to an Islamic model of the past, nor to a pre-colonial Bruneian model. Although the Minister of Law stated that the reforms would 're-enact' the *Syariah* judicial system to its 'pre-colonial status', the operative word is 'status' not 're-enact'.[26] It was not a return to pre-colonial form. History shows that prior to the English residency (1905 –59) Brunei had neither Islamic courts nor used *kadis* or *hakim* as judges. Administration of law and the settlement of disputes devolved from the Sultan. He played a significant role as mediator and adjudicator, especially for disputes involving land or members of the nobility, a trend A. C. Milner notes was 'echoed time and time again for Muslims in South-East Asia'.[27] Tenets of Islamic law were employed through the application of the *Hukum Qanun Brunei* which was a mixture of Islamic and indigenous rules. Disputes at the local level were dealt with by an *imam* (leader in prayer for a mosque community), the *ulama* (religious scholars and teachers),[28] or for day-to-day matters by village (*kampong)* headman.[29]

Nor was the new nomenclature a response to traditional Islam. Traditionally, authority to judge cases between Muslims in accordance with the *Syariah* was vested in the *kadi* in Malay (*qadi* in Arabic), as a single judge of the court, *mahkamah*.[30] Although some criminal offences could be tried in *Kadis* Courts, serious criminal offences more often came under the jurisdiction of the political ruler.[31] Hence the term *kadi* was used for the adjudicator in disputes of an inter-personal nature including marriage, succession, divorce, maintenance, custody, trusts and for offences against Islam. *Hakim*, also derived from Arabic, referred to one who can make a decision imposing a criminal punishment.[32] However, except for minor offences against Islam, criminal law in Brunei currently remains common law and is determined by the secular courts.

A further outcome of the name change which also goes to increasing status is that the descriptor *Syariah* distances the new court from its *kadi* predecessor. The term '*hakim*' places the Islamic judge on equal footing with the secular judge, as in Malay, the terms 'judge' or 'justice' in the common law courts translate as *hakim*. This is because the common law judge lacks jurisdiction over Muslims for family and personal status law, and re-enforces the common law judge's jurisdiction over criminal law and sentencing.

Underlying the name change is symbolic removal of any comparative subordination of the Islamic courts and their personnel vis-à-vis the common law courts. It also negates Western perceptions of '*kadi* justice'. The terms '*kadi*,' and '*kadi* justice,' have been used negatively by Western scholars and judges to import a lesser standard of objectivity and professionalism. According to United States Supreme Court Justice Frankfurter in *Terminello v. Chicago*, 'We do not sit around like a *kadi* under a tree dispensing justice according to consideration of individual expediency'.[33] Similarly in *Clark v. Harleysville Mutual Casualty Co.*, 'We sit after all as an appellate court, administering justice under the law, not as an ancient cadi dispensing a rough and ready equity according to the dictates of his own unfettered discretion'.[34] *Kadi* justice became a euphemism for arbitrary, personalized, judicial decision-making, particularly when based on religious precepts.[35] Max Weber promoted the descriptor of '*Kadijustiz*' as a typology of what he called 'irrational law', that is, law based on ethical, patriarchal, religious postulates rather than the fixed rules of formally rational law. M. Peletz notes that although Weber's assessment was a reflection and elaboration of the Orientalist biases of his time, its impact has shaped Western discourses on Islamic legal systems and Islamic societies in general.[36]

As a consequence, a prejudicial image of the *kadi* and the decision-making in *Kadis* Courts developed in the West.[37] While such conclusions on '*kadi* justice' have been criticized,[38] particularly for failing to take into account the cultural context in which judicial decision-making occurs, the perception of a different or lesser standard of adjudication has been equated with the term *kadi*. Hence the re-designation of the reformed courts as *Syariah* Courts removes this link, as does the substitution of *Hakim Syar'ie* for the former *kadi*. Parity with the secular courts becomes readily apparent to all.

The structural changes

The Sultan's position remains unchanged, as he remains at the apex of the new Islamic court system. Article 3 of the *Constitution* states 'the head of the religion of Brunei Darussalam shall be His Majesty the Sultan and Yang Di-Pertuan' (head of state). The *Religious Council and Kadis Courts Act* also acknowledged the Sultan as 'Head of the Religion of Brunei'[39] and that the *Majlis Ugama Islam* or Council of the Islamic Religion shall 'aid and advise His Majesty on all matters relating to the religion of Brunei, and shall in all such matters be the chief authority in Brunei'.[40] These sections have not been repealed by the new legislation. The Sultan also retains the right to exercise his prerogative of mercy[41] and can commute, suspend or remit any sentence,[42] but the former avenue of appeal to the Sultan in Religious Council[43] has been repealed.

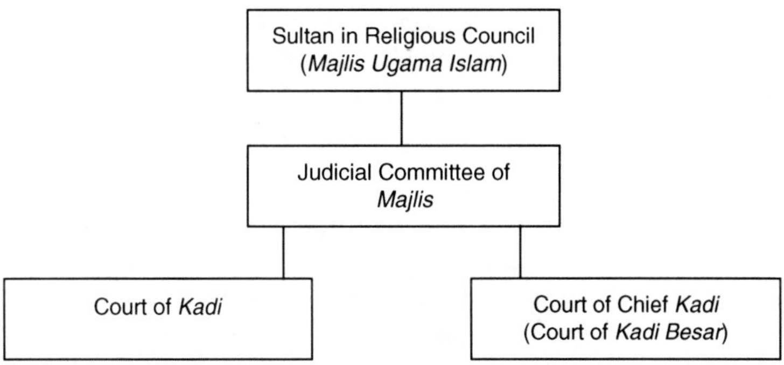

Figure 16.1 Pre-March 2001 Islamic Court structure under Religious Council and Kadis Courts Act (1984).

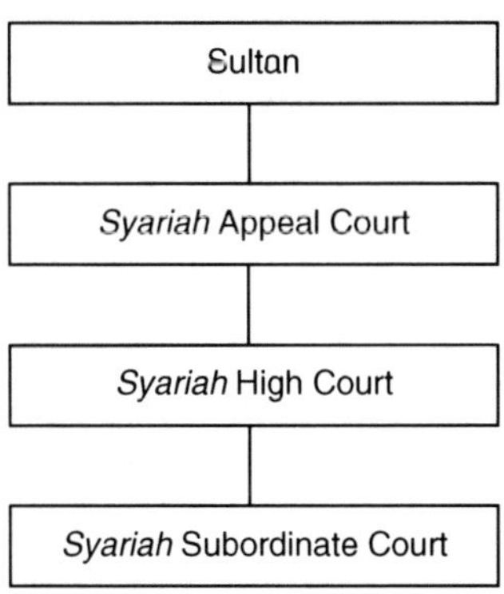

Figure 16.2 Post-2001 court structure under the Syariah Courts Order (1998).

Prior to the new *Order*, one role of the Judicial Committee of *Majlis* (which consisted of the state *Mufti*[44] and two other members appointed by the Sultan) had been to give opinions on questions of Muslim law or doctrine for the purposes of the courts other than religious courts.[45] Hence the *Religious Council and Kadis Courts Act* distinguished the process for giving opinions on Islamic law for Muslims from opinions given to the secular common law courts. This latter function appears to have been retained for the Committee.

The second role for the Judicial Committee had been to determine appeals arising from the civil or criminal cases in the *Kadis* Courts. The Sultan in Religious Council could direct appeals to the Judicial Committee, which in turn would advise the Sultan as to the manner in which they considered the appeal should be determined.[46] The final decision rested with the Sultan. The new *Order* has removed the appellate function from the Judicial Committee[47] and transferred it to the *Syariah* Appeal Court, which retains all powers of the former Committee.[48] The changes are initially symbolic, as the person who was Chairman of the Judicial Committee before the commencement of the *Order* was deemed to be the Chief *Syar'ie* Judge.[49] Similarly, existing members of the Judicial Committee were deemed to form the panel of judges for the new *Syariah* Appeal Court.[50] The new appellate court is constituted by a Chairman (either the Chief *Syar'ie* judge or the most senior judge on the panel) and two *Syariah* Appeal Court judges, who are specified by the Chief *Syar'ie* judge. Any *Syariah* High Court judge can be appointed to the Appeal Court, providing he was not the judge who made the original decision being appealed against.[51] An appeal is determined by the decision of the majority of members, and there are provisions for cases where an appeal judge is sick or is unable, for other reasons, to conclude his function in the proceedings.[52]

The *Syariah* Appeal Court can hear and determine any appeal from the *Syariah* High Court exercising its original jurisdiction. A decision from the Subordinate *Syariah* Court that has already been determined on appeal to the *Syariah* High Court requires an application for leave from the *Syariah* Appeal Court. Leave will be granted where it is a question of law and in the public interest.[53] The *Syariah* Appeal Court can make any order that the *Syariah* High Court might have made. This Appeal Court also has been given supervisory and revisionary jurisdiction over the *Syariah* High Court. Where the interests of justice make it necessary, either on its own motion or on application by any party or interested person, the *Syariah* Appeal Court may call for and examine the record of the *Syariah* High Court, thereby suspending those proceedings. The *Syariah* Appeal Court can give the High Court any direction as is needed for a just outcome.[54] This supervisory and revisionary power given to the higher *Syariah* Courts over the lower ones was not present in the *Kadis* Courts, and is a substantial increase in jurisdiction.

Lastly, in the new appellate hierarchy, the *Syariah* High Court can hear appeals from the *Syariah* Subordinate Court in civil cases where 'any person is aggrieved by or dissatisfied with any decision'.[55] In criminal cases where a person has been convicted and sentenced to imprisonment or fined, there can be an appeal.

In addition, a *Syar'ie* prosecutor can appeal against an acquittal,[56] which differs from the position at common law where there is no appeal from an acquittal.

As outlined above, the introduction of a system of appeals into the Islamic court structure in Brunei is a major practical and ideologically significant reform. Having an hierarchical judicial structure in which higher courts review the decisions made by lower courts to ensure consistent application of law is not traditionally inherent in Islamic systems.[57] Accordingly, under the earlier *Religious Council and Kadis Courts Act, kadis* did not hear or determine appeals.[58] All avenues of appeal from a decision by a *kadi* or chief *kadi* were directed to 'His Majesty in Religious Council'[59] for determination by the Judicial Committee of the *Majlis*. No *kadi* could be a member of this committee.[60] This provision reflected the traditional view in Islamic law that there is no authority for judicial review of another judge's/*kadi*'s decision,[61] although unsuccessful litigants could complain to the authority, political or religious, responsible for the judge's appointment.[62] In Brunei, this authority rested with the Sultan. Islamic courts elsewhere in the Muslim world rarely developed formal hierarchical structures until there was contact with Western judicial systems.

Powers argues that the prevailing wisdom among Islamists is that without appellate structures the decision of the *kadi* should be final and irrevocable.[63] Support for this view is derived from historical evidence that there were no appeal courts established by the Prophet, nor under the pious Caliphs from Abu Bakr to Ali, who were his political and religious successors. Adjudication of disputes was rendered in a single decision that was valid and conclusive of the matter. So 'when the *qadi* has pronounced his decree it is effective upon pronouncement and not liable to reversal by the decree of another *qadi* whatsoever'.[64] This is in keeping with the position that judicial decisions are declaratory in character, applying the existing rules (God's rules) contained in the *Syariah*, to cases that come before them. Law-making was not a function of the *kadi*, and so the law-making role inherent in appellate review was obviated. Because Islamic law was held to be sacred, the head of state was also head of the religion, and the *kadi* exercised authority as the representative of the Sultan in his dual capacity. Under this model, only those with religious authority in Brunei – the Sultan and the *Majlis* – could review a *kadi*'s decision. This had been the endorsed position until the new *Order*.

However, there had been ongoing debate within Islamic jurisprudence on the place for appellate review in Islamic law, with many modernist scholars rejecting the traditional view on theoretical and practical grounds. It was argued that to remove an 'error that leads to injustice is a fundamental teaching' of Islam[65] and a practical necessity in any court system. It has been long accepted that a *kadi* could review his own decision prior to enforcement. This comes from a *hadith*[66] of the Prophet in which he admitted no one, including himself, was immune from error.[67] Hence the alternate view developed that decisions based on sound reasoning (*ijtihad*), are not reviewable merely because another judge may come to a different conclusion; but where there is an error based on a clear departure from the *Syariah*, or where an injustice may result, then the decision is reviewable and can be reversed. Muslim nations such as Pakistan have established appeal courts[68] on the basis, that

> the views of earlier imams and jurists are entitled to the highest respect and no court would differ from them except for very compelling and sound reasons ... this difference in interpretation does not and can not mean a departure from a clear injunction of law as contained in the Quran or Sunnah or even ijma.[69]

The emergent view that judicial review through an appellate process is valid where there is a clear error and where an injustice could result if a decision of a lower *Syariah* Court were not reversed, gives legitimation to the recent court reforms in Brunei.

The introduction of a three-tiered hierarchy of courts with appellate jurisdiction also enables the Islamic courts to mirror the secular courts. It also parallels changes that occurred earlier in the Malaysian States when Islamic courts were given appellate jurisdiction, described as restoring 'their self-confidence and self-respect' and facilitating their role as 'protectors of the rule of the Shariah'.[70] It is felt likely that the direction and guidance that appellate review would provide for the subordinate court judges would give both the practitioners and the public greater confidence in the court system.[71]

In the past, appeals that went to the Sultan in Religious Council were not reported. The establishment of appellate jurisdiction necessitates the reporting of appellate decisions. This should enable the development of a body of law in which decisions from jurisdictions outside and also within Brunei would inform the process, as in common law. In the former *Kadis* Courts, reports of cases from other Islamic courts or centres of jurisprudence (other than Malaysia) were not readily available nor cited. This contrasted markedly from the common law court where English decisions predominantly, but also Singaporean, Australian and Malaysian decisions, were regularly cited. Achieving a similar body of *Syariah* jurisprudence for Brunei has been recommended to enable 'Islamic solutions as they must be applied in an integrated form in the Muslim society'.[72] The reporting of cases, rather than legal opinions in the *fatawa* of legal scholars, would also bring the adjudication process in the *Syariah* courts into closer alignment with the common law.

Jurisdiction

Under the *Order*, the *Kadis* Courts, which had operated in each of the four districts of Brunei, have been remodelled as *Syariah* Subordinate Courts. Previously, the former civil jurisdiction of the *Kadi*s Courts extended to the same matters as the Chief *Kadi,* but the amount or value of the subject matter could not exceed B$5,000 and had to be to be capable of estimation in monetary terms.[73] In the new *Order* for the equivalent Subordinate Courts the amount has significantly increased to B$500,000.[74] Similarly with the criminal jurisdiction, where the limitations of maximum punishment for the *Kadi* Court had been punishment not exceeding imprisonment for one month or a fine not exceeding B$1,000, or both,[75] these limits have been increased to imprisonment not exceeding seven years, and a fine not exceeding B$10,000, or both.[76]

Under the *Order* all proceedings that would have been instituted in the Court of the Chief *Kadi* come under the jurisdiction of the *Syariah* High Court. In its civil jurisdiction this includes: actions and proceedings arising out of betrothal, marriage, divorce,[77] nullity of marriage or judicial separation;[78] disposition of property arising from those proceedings; maintenance of dependents, legitimacy, guardianship or custody; division of or claims to *sapencharian*[79] property; the validity and entitlement from deceased estates of Muslims; wills or death-bed gifts of a Muslim deceased; gifts *inter vivos*; *wakaf*[80]and *nazr*;[81] and other matters where jurisdiction is conferred by written law.

The criminal jurisdiction under the *Order* includes any offence 'punishable under any written law providing for *Syariah* criminal offences, or Islamic family law or any written law that confers jurisdiction to try an offence and impose punishment in the *Syariah* High Court'.[82] This section does not contain the limitation present in the *Religious Council and Kadis Courts Act* that the criminal jurisdiction of the Court of the Chief *Kadi*, applies only to 'an offence committed by a Muslim'.[83] This may not be significant, as currently the Islamic criminal offences contained in the *Religious Council and Kadis Courts Act*, Chapter X[84] remain in force and the Chapter specifies that its application is 'only to persons professing the Islamic religion'.[85] The two offences in the Act that apply to non-Muslims[86] are to be heard in the Magistrates' Court and punishable under the provisions of the *Penal Code*. The thrust of offences contained in Chapter X is breach of Islamic conduct and morality, the most prevalent of which is Section 177 – *khalwat* (inappropriate proximity with a person of the opposite sex), usually an unmarried couple alone together in a compromising situation. It is an offence which the Ministry of Religious Affairs states is increasing, as there were 659 *khalwat* offences reported in the first seven months of 2007, which was double the number (330) for all of 2006.[87] Other offences under Chapter X include non-attendance at the mosque without lawful excuse (Section 171); the sale, purchase and consumption of alcoholic beverages (Section 172); and Ramadan violations (Section 173). Also there are offences in the *Islamic Family Law Order* (1999) for breaches of marriage and divorce requirements and for *nusyuz* (disobedience or not fulfilling marital duties).[88]

Given that the scope of Islamic criminal offences has not changed since the court reforms, it is surprising that the *Syariah Courts Evidence Order* (2001) was enacted to complement the court transitions in Brunei. As outlined above, classic *Syariah* criminal law was not introduced with the recent court reforms and at present has no application in Brunei. However, the *Syariah Courts Evidence Order* did introduce classic *Syariah* evidentiary principles, including those which would only have application for *Syariah* criminal law. These include detailed evidentiary provisions stipulating the number and gender requirements of witnesses in particular *hudud* offences.[89] For example, a conviction for *zina* (sexual intercourse outside a lawful marriage) requires evidence of four male *syahid*.[90] Conviction for the other *hudud* offences requires the eye-witness testimony of two male *syahid*. The *Syariah Courts Evidence Order* also makes the distinction between *bayyinah* and *syahadah*[91] evidence, with women (and non-Muslims) excluded from giving *syahadah* evidence, except in matters pertaining to designated women's issues: 'matters relating to menstruation, birth, breastfeeding and of embarrassment to a female'.[92] Additionally, the principle that the evidence of a woman is weighted at half that of a man prevails through the *Order*.

That these provisions have been enacted is in keeping with pronouncements by the Sultan and others of a desire for Islamic criminal laws to apply in Brunei. In the Sultan's birthday *titah* in 1996, he proclaimed that the proposed new *Syariah* Courts were not just for the implementation of family laws, but were to apply the '*Qunun Jina'I Islam* (an Islamic Criminal Law Act) in its entirety as required by Allah, the Almighty'.[93] He justified this on grounds of erosion of moral values and the proliferation of social ailments such as drug addition and HIV/AIDS, and lamented that the current secular laws and penalties were not curbing these social diseases. 'We are confident that this good intention (to enact Islamic criminal law) will become a source of blessing to the country and to the people'.[94] There have been several subsequent public announcements in this vein, with the deputy Minister of Religious Affairs in June 2003 advising that 'a new Islamic Criminal Law Order is in the process of enactment. The law will provide for certain offences such as murder, causing hurt, adultery, rape, theft, robbery and drinking intoxicating liquor'.[95] To date, there has been no such enactment but it does indicate that greater engagement with Islamic law may be under consideration and that the restructuring of the courts was a pre-condition for any future expansion. This is echoed from time to time in the local newspapers, which refer to unnamed 'informed sources' stating that the recent changes 'would pave the way for the Syariah courts to expand their scope in enforcing criminal proceedings involving Muslim followers in the country'.[96]

Judicial training and appointment

One of the more significant aspects of the court reforms, and one which goes right to the heart of increasing the status of Islamic courts, is the new judicial appointment process. The requirements for appointment of a *Syar'ie* judge now equate quite closely with those pertaining to judges in the common law courts. Specified in the new *Order* is that the appointment of a judge at any level of *Syariah* Court (other than the Subordinate Court) requires him to be 'learned in the *Hukum Syara*'.[97] Tertiary qualifications are relevant to that determination. Previously, for appointments to the *Kadis* Courts the Act prescribed simply that His Majesty could appoint 'any suitable person' to be a *kadi*.[98] To be a suitable person was generally taken to mean the appointee should meet the Islamic adjudicative requirements, specifically those of the Shafi sect, which were derived from the practices of the Prophet.[99] By examining whom he appointed from his companions to be judges, and also the qualities the Prophet displayed when performing a judicial role, the Shafi school considers the requirements for judicial appointment to be: 'Muslim, free, male adult, just, able to speak, hear and speak, have knowledge of the *Hukum Syarak*, and know the contents of the holy Quran and matters connected with it'.[100] This was a lesser test than being learned in *Hukum Syara*. Meeting the 'suitable person' test for a *kadi* appointment in Brunei did not require technical or tertiary qualifications in Islamic law and procedure. The necessary knowledge of the Quran, the *Sunnah*[101] and *Fiqh*[102] could best be obtained by religious studies in *madrassahs*, Islamic religious schools. But a shift in thinking occurred in the 1990s. Concerns about the adequacy of training at *madrassahs* surfaced, being expressed publicly on occasions by officials within the Department of Religious Affairs. Respected Islamic scholars, including Professor Dr Saedon bin Awang Othman, of the Department and later Vice-Chancellor at the University of Brunei Darussalam (1991 –2002) expressed concern that Brunei's *kadis* had not been specifically trained in all aspects of Islamic law and procedure.[103] It added to the perception that the graduates of *madrassahs* were less qualified than the graduates in law from Western universities, contributing to the view that the Islamic judges and courts were inferior to their secular counterparts.

Remedying these perceived insufficiencies was a MIB priority. In addition to recurring government-sponsored workshops and courses[104] for the judges of the Islamic courts, formal legal training at a tertiary institution was seen as the key to increased professionalism and expertise. This would provide recognized academic qualifications in law and judicial administration, and would more closely align the *Syariah* judges' qualifications with those of their secular counterparts.[105] From the mid-1990s, formal qualifications from outside Brunei, particularly from the Islamic universities in Malaysia, Pakistan or the Al Azhar University[106] in Cairo, had become important for appointment. But from 2000, to correspond with the *Kadis* Courts transition to *Syariah* Courts, a Diploma in Islamic Law and Practice commenced at the University of Brunei Darussalam. This local diploma became the formal requirement for appointment of *Syari'e* judges as well as for practitioners engaged to represent parties as *Syari'e* lawyers in the *Syariah* Courts. At the end of 2007, this training was transferred to the new Sultan Sharif Ali Islamic University (UNISSA), offering bachelor degrees in *Syariah* (*Fiqh wa Qada*)[107] and *Syariah* (*Fiqh wa Usul*)[108] plus masters degrees. The Sultan pronounced the new Islamic University to 'be a symbol of Islamic glory in the country' producing 'Muslim scholars and intellectuals needed by the nation'.[109]

Another feature of the new *Order*, which also mirrors judicial appointments in the common law courts, is the requirement for prescribed years of experience. Appointments to the *Syariah* Appeal and *Syariah* High Courts require, in addition to Bruneian citizenship, a cumulative period of not less than seven years either as judge of a *Syariah* Court, or as a *kadi*, or both for the Appeal Court, or seven years as a judge, *kadi*, Registrar or *Syar'ie* prosecutor, or a mix of these for the High Court.[110] The qualifications for appointment in the common law courts are also on the basis of seven years of judicial or legal experience.[111] Essentially the religious courts now mirror the secular courts requirements.

Melayu Islam Beraja as catalyst for court reforms

The overview just provided demonstrates the extent of change occurring in the restructuring and redesignation of the Islamic courts in Brunei. Although the reform to the courts has been mandated under MIB to increase the status and standing of the Islamic court system, it has also resulted in greater convergence between the processes in the common law and those in the religious courts. This judicious borrowing is not unique to Brunei. D. L. Horowitz's analysis of contemporary reform in Islamic countries is that it is 'produced by a system that is simultaneously more Islamic *and* more Western than the system it is displacing'.[112] Peletz also notes this trend when other nations of the region have embarked on a strengthening or reform of their Islamic legal system. He postulates that two models operate for guiding the reform process. One is the Islamic law and administration which operates in former British colonies such as India, Pakistan and Singapore, while the other is the country's own secular courts.[113] In Brunei, the language used in *titahs* and in press releases, notably with references drawing comparisons with the secular common law courts, indicates the latter as more significant, although there have been influential individuals within the Ministry of Religious Affairs from outside Brunei including Dr Anwarallah, a scholar from Pakistan, who advised the Ministry on Islamization of the legal system. There are also frequent conferences, meetings and workshops with Malaysian *Syariah* judges and legal counterparts.[114]

As discussed, the main catalyst propelling the reforms has been MIB. In striving to reassert Brunei's Islamic identity greater importance had to be given to Islamic laws, values and institutions, notably its courts. Although the transformation to *Syariah* Courts has been the focus of this chapter, it has not been in isolation, as the inculcation of Islamic values and the enactment of legislation embodying Islamic tenets has been given similar priority. Legislation prohibiting the sale and importation of alcohol (1991); prohibiting the production of pork (1992); facilitating Islamic banking, finance and insurance (from 1993); revising family law for Brunei Muslims (1999) and Islamic adoption (2001) are some examples. The direction taken gives effect to the policy that the Islamic judicial system must be reconstituted as the 'cardinal system in the law and order of the country'.[115] The reforms are also given external validation as they are in keeping with the Islamic revival or resurgence occurring throughout Asia and the Islamic world. They bear marked similarity to many of the reforms implemented in the Malaysian States.[116]

Unlike the Malaysian reforms which would have been passed through the relevant state and federal Parliaments, in Brunei this occurred without the scrutiny of parliamentary sittings, public debate, input from stakeholders or a free uncensored media. The changes may well reflect the will of the majority of Bruneians, but the Sultan's complete legislative authority means that legitimation comes from him alone, endorsed through the *Beraja* pillar of MIB. The operation of the *Beraja* was discussed earlier but it is relevant to determining whether the reforms achieved to date have sufficiently addressed the imbalance between religious and secular courts in Brunei, or whether there is further to go. In a closed society where policy shifts and new directions are announced through the Sultan's *titahs*, it can be difficult to know. As *titahs* are speeches given at special occasions, which set out themes or broad goals for the nation, they lack detail on form or implementation. Several years later an emergency order may emerge embodying the policy. There is no opportunity for questioning or briefing and the media essentially repeats the content of the *titah* without analysis.

In this context, predicting whether Islamization will continue can only be speculative. Earlier, the possibility of the *Syariah* Courts assuming full or greater criminal law jurisdiction was outlined. This was based on his Majesty's *titah* of 1996 and supported by the similar pronouncements made by government ministers and given additional credence by the provisions contained in the *Syariah Court Evidence Order*, which incorporates most of the classic Islamic rules of evidence including those pertaining to both *hudud* and *qisas* (offences against the person where retaliation for death or injury is open). Another possible reform development recently mooted in the local papers is for a merger of the *Syariah* Courts and the civil law courts. This idea has been attributed as the 'brainchild of late Professor Saedon' in keeping with 'MIB as the guiding principle' for the Sultanate. This possibility gains some traction as the new Islamic University has named one of its three faculties as '*Syariah* and civil law' and from August 2008 is offering the country's first bachelor of law degree. It will be taught in English with a mix of common law subjects and a significant number of Islamic law subjects, mostly covering the areas of law applicable in the *Syariah* Courts. That the teaching of the first law degree in Brunei has been placed in the context of an Islamic university[117] to which all religious teaching has been amalgamated,[118] and not at the University of Brunei Darussalam, sends a signal that merger of the two systems may be on the horizon. A merger is in keeping with the commitment to harmonization of civil law and *Syariah* law as was advocated by the Attorney-General's department in Malaysia.[119]

Tinkering with the common law courts

The first limb of MIB is the promotion of *Melayu*: Malay culture, language, customs, conventions and institutions. Brunei is a polyethnic community. Brunei Malays are the dominant ethnic group (65 per cent) but there are substantial Chinese (15 per cent), Indian, indigenous but non-Malay ethnic and linguistic groups, and expatriates. MIB with its prioritization on the Malay culture results in a state direction towards the monocultural, that of Malay culture, over a multicultural approach. This has had little impact on the courts, but bringing Malay identity to the fore has brought about some minor adaptations to the secular courts.

This can be seen in the removal of the right of final appeal to the Privy Council of the House of Lords for all criminal appeals from 1995 and limitations from 1997 on the right of appeal in civil matters to cases where both parties agreed prior to the hearing for the retention of the appeal avenue to the Privy Council. This step was taken to reduce colonial ties and to bolster the authority of the courts in Brunei. The limited appeal avenue was retained to sooth any fears in the commercial and international investment sector that Brunei might stray from the common law or decrease legal options. In time, the decision may allow for the emergence of Bruneian jurisprudence as occurred in former colonial jurisdictions after appeals to the Privy Council were abolished.

In 1999, wigs and red criminal robes for the judges were abolished on the basis that these were not in keeping with Bruneian tradition. The same year, the appointment of a Bruneian Malay judge to the Supreme Court, Justice Hayati,[120] made judicial history and re-enforced the desire for all courts to reflect some Malay identity.[121] In an inclusive vein, Steven Chong, a non-Malay Bruneian, was also appointed to the Supreme Court. However, the Chief Justice and several members of the High Court are expatriates and on contracts, which includes the majority of judges who sit on the Court of Appeal.[122] The long standing and continued dominance of judges from common law countries outside Brunei, in particular from Hong Kong and to a lesser extent Australia, has meant that the 'desecularisation of the civil law' which Amanda Whiting observed in Malaysia[123] has not been evident in Brunei, at least in the courts of review. Still, the desire for increased local input is reflected in changes to the admission rules for legal practice, as the *Legal Profession Act* now requires either Bruneian nationality, a residency certificate or seven years practising experience prior to lodging an application.[124] It will mean that non-Bruneians (52 per cent in 2002), especially those starting their legal careers, will find it more difficult to practise in Brunei Darussalam. The practice of admitting experienced foreign lawyers on an *ad hoc* basis enables representation by English Queen's Counsel and Singapore Senior Counsel for cases in which local advocates lack the requisite level of experience in that area of law. The Act, however, does contain a provision[125] allowing the Chief Justice to make a declaration in the *Government Gazette* that he is of the opinion that the number of advocates practising in Brunei is sufficiently adequate to serve the needs of the community and that only Brunei Darussalam nationals shall be entitled to be admitted as advocates.

Conclusion

Today in Brunei, the operation of secular and religious courts raises issues about the identity of the Sultanate, its values and how it decides to manage the tension between Western secularism and Islamic tradition. The challenge for Brunei lies in achieving what is seen as an acceptable relationship between the two. The impact of colonialism was such that many Brunei Malays, particularly those making up the political and religious elite, believed the natural balance had been adversely skewed. The elevation, for almost a century, of the common law and secular courts to superior standing had been seen as detrimental in the legal culture of Brunei. Remedying the imbalance, particularly the subjugation of the religious courts, emanates directly from MIB which is foremost a nationalist agenda that came with late independence. External forces, including those of globalization, are assessed too through the prism of MIB.[126]

However, Brunei is not alone, as many other nations with a significant Muslim population have also been rethinking and revising the role for Islamic courts and Islamic laws. The global Islamic resurgence[127] has naturally prioritized law. While there are advocates for greater Islamization in Brunei, as witnessed by the *Syariah Courts Evidence Order* and sporadic calls for implementation of *Syariah* criminal law, they fall short of gaining traction for a model in which the secular is demoted to inferior status. Instead, it seems that Brunei currently seeks to achieve greater equality between the two court streams by turning to the common law courts and adapting aspects of form and process from them. Despite nascent speculation on a future merging of the two courts systems, there is no immediate threat to the operation of the secular common law courts. These courts continue to receive the support and endorsement of the Sultan and government as well as enjoying widespread confidence and approval from the legal profession, business leaders and the community generally.[128] Although the number of cases coming to the common law courts is small, particularly in comparison to that of Western nations, it is consistent with low litigation rates in Asia generally, and particularly in small nations.[129]

This is why the changes in the secular courts are relatively minor, designed mainly to imbue a more Bruneian character into proceedings. It is the increased role and status given to the *Syariah* Courts with growing structural differentiation that is the intended outcome of Islamization pursuant to MIB. Islamization has not meant a return to Brunei's pre-colonial form of dispute resolution, which could be described as a syncretism of Muslim orthodoxy infused with indigenous customary elements. Instead, it has fostered a systematic process to establish parallel hierarchical courts, Islamic and secular, each with its own exclusive jurisdiction, both equal[130] and resembling each other in style and substance. The transformation of the *Kadis* Courts into *Syariah* Courts is a practical demonstration of the ascendancy of Islamic law within the nation. This can be seen in the reorganization of the courts to accommodate an hierarchical appellate structure; and the professionalization of legal training for *Syariah* judges and lawyers to be more akin to the secular system than it is to the *madrassahs*; and for judicial appointment and tenure provisions to mirror those in the secular courts. It seems that even under MIB the acquired ideas from the West will blend with aspects of Islam to enable legal pluralism to endure in the courts of Brunei Darussalam.

Notes

1. For the features of colonialism see J. Osterhammel, *Colonialism: A Theoretical Overview* (Princeton. NJ: Markus Wiener Publishers, 1999), 15–16.
2. Malcolm McArthur and A. V. M. Horton, *Report on Brunei in 1904* (Athens: Ohio University Center for International Studies, 1987), 128.
3. Ministry of the Hajj, Kingdom of Saudi Arabia, "Muslim Population by Country A–B," http://www.hajinformation.com/main/d21a.htm
4. The ethnic composition is outlined on p. 000 in the section 'Tinkering with the common law courts'.
5. *The Laws of Brunei* (1984) Ch. 2 was a reproduction from *Application of Laws Act* (1951).

6. From the *titah* (royal speech) at the promulgation of Brunei's Independence in 1984: "Titah 1984," in *Borneo Bulletin Brunei Yearbook* (Brunei: Brunei Press, 2000), 92.
7. Ibid.
8. Radio Television Brunei, "Constitutional Amendments Reflect Nation's Monarchical System," http://www.rtb.gov.bn/NewsUpdate/2004/September/300904/main1.htm
9. Ibid.
10. National Development Party, "Press Release on the Approval of the Formation of the Parti Pembangunan Bangsa (National Development Party)," http://www.brudirect.com/DailyInfo/News/Archive/Sept05/130905/nite01_1.htm
11. See G. C. Gunn, *Language Power and Ideology in Brunei Darussalam* (Athens, OH: Centre for International Studies Ohio University, 1997), 218. Within Brunei, constraints on criticism of prevailing system are well entrenched. Members of the Al-Arqam movement, who advocated for the return of a just and equal society based on the teachings of the Prophet, thereby challenging the existing authoritarian monarchical structure, were banned and several of their leaders detained for lengthy 'rehabilitation'. Other deviant groups include Abdul Razak Mohammad, al-Ma'unah, Saihoni Taispan, Silat lintau, Qadiyaniah and the Baha'i.
12. G. Braighlinn, *Ideological Innovation under Monarchy: Aspects of Legitimation Activity in Contemporary Brunei* (Amsterdam: VU University Press, 1992).
13. R. Kershaw, "Constraints of History: the Eliciting of Modern Brunei," *Asian Affairs* 29 (1998): 315.
14. Braighlinn, *Ideological Innovation under Monarchy*, 19.
15. A. Othamn, "His Majesty Announces Big Changes for Brunei," *Borneo Bulletin*, July 16, 2006.
16. *Constitution (Amendment) Proclamation* (2005) s. 31(1).
17. Radio Television Brunei, "Constitutional Amendments Reflect Nation's Monarchical System," http://www.rtb.gov.bn/NewsUpdate/2004/September/300904/main1.htm
18. *Constitution (Amendment) Proclamation* (2005) s. 53.
19. K. Sonia and Z. Zaini, "In Knowledge Lies Truth," *Borneo Bulletin*, September 6, 2006.
20. It is an offence under the *Sedition Act* to 'directly or indirectly lower or adversely affect the standing or prominence of the national philosophy, the Malay Islamic Monarchy concept'.
21. Radio Television Brunei, "Constitutional Amendments Reflect Nation's Monarchical System," http://www.rtb.gov.bn/NewsUpdate/2004/September/300904/main1.htm
22. The first Proclamation of Emergency was issued by Sultan Omar in December 1962 and the Legislative Council was dissolved several days later in the *Emergency (Suspension of the Constitution) Order* (1962). Section 83 of the *Constitution* sets out the emergency power provisions as applying when 'public danger exists, whereby the security or economic life of Brunei Darussalam, or any part thereof, is threatened, whether by war or external aggression or internal disturbance' and requires that 'no Proclamation of Emergency shall be in force for more than two years, without prejudice, however, to the issue of another such proclamation at or before the end of that period'. The most recent Proclamation of Emergency was issued in March 2008. The event which was the catalyst for the first proclamation was a small armed rebellion which occurred after the Legislative Council elections in 1962 in which the *Partai Rakyat Brunei* (PRB) won the majority of seats. The PRB considered they had a sweeping mandate for their policies and became incensed by the continued rejection of their demands for democratic participation. In response, the PRB's armed wing launched an armed rebellion, proclaiming independence. Invoking the *Treaty of Protection*, British military forces were called in and the rebellion was crushed within a week. The Sultan declared a state of Emergency and outlawed the *Partai Rakyat Brunei*. Thousands of the PRB men were arrested, without trial and imprisoned. As far as is known most detainees have been released after lengthy rehabilitation.

23. Islam according to the Shafeite school.
24. Radio Television Brunei, "Constitutional Amendments Reflect Nation's Monarchical System," http://www.rtb.gov.bn/NewsUpdate/2004/September/300904/main1.htm
25. Under the legislation, five courts were set up to administer civil and criminal matters in Brunei. One was the Courts of *Kathis* for personal matters or religious customs of Brunei's Muslims; another was the Courts of Native Magistrates for non-Muslim indigenous people.
26. "Syariah Law for Brunei: A Need to Return to Islamic law," *Borneo Bulletin*, June 16, 1995.
27. A. C. Milner, "Islam and the Muslim State," in *Islam in South-east Asia*, ed. M. B. Hooker (Leiden: E J Brill, 1988), 29.
28. I. A. Mansurnoor, "Islamic Reform in Brunei 1912–59: Introductory Remarks," in *Essays on Modern Brunei History*, ed. T. P. Lang, G. C. Gunn, B. A. Hussainmiya and I. A. Mansurnoor (Brunei: University Brunei Darussalam, 1992), 66.
29. This is consistent with the position in the Malay Peninsula where J. M. Gullick notes that the codes of law (copies of which were rare) were rarely referred to for guidance in settling disputes, remaining in the control of the scribes at the courts of the sultans. See J. M. Gullick, *Indigenous Political Systems of Western Malaya* (London: Athole Press, 1965), 114.
30. J. L. Esposito, ed., *The Oxford Encyclopedia of the Modern Islamic World* (New York: Oxford University Press, 1995), 3: 374.
31. This was because the ruler assumed supreme judicial authority, making the courts subject to the limits he prescribed. Reasons for restricting the *kadi*'s administration of criminal law included the limited number of crimes and punishments in the *Syariah*, leaving many ill-defined as *tazir* (a 'discretionary sentence' imposed by a judge or magistrate for offences not covered by *hudud* or *qisas* and *diyat* penalties); the laws of evidence in *Syariah* were restrictive; and rulers needed to control mechanisms for law and order rather than state security being in the hands of religious scholars. See A. Sachedina, "The Ideal and Real in Islamic Law," in *Perspectives on Islamic Law, Justice, and Society*, ed. R. S. Khare (Lanham: Rowman & Littlefield Publishers, 1999), 25. See also J. N. D. Anderson, "Law as a Social Force in Islamic Culture and History," in *Islamic Law and Legal Theory*, ed. I. Edge (Dartmouth, UK: Aldershot, 1996), 495.
32. S. A. Barakbah, "Judges and Judicial Function," *ILUM Law Journal* 4 (1994): 49.
33. *Terminello v. Chicago* 337 US 1, 11 (1949).
34. *Clark v. Harleysville Mutual Casualty Co.* 123 F.2d 499, 502.
35. M. Rheinstien, ed., *Max Weber on Law and Economy in Society* (New York: Simon & Schuster, 1968). Weber's system for classifying legal reasoning is also discussed in J. Makdisi, "Formal Rationality in Islamic Law and the Common Law," *Cleveland State Law Review* 34 (1985–86): 97–113.
36. M. Peletz, *Islamic Modern: Religious Courts and Cultural Practices in Malaysia* (Princeton, NJ: Princeton University Press, 2002), 57.
37. M. Shapiro, "Islam and Appeal," *California Law Review* 68 (1980): 353.
38. Rosen argues that judicial decision-making is a cultural phenomenon, and *kadis*, like all judges, use the cultural categories of their society in their adjudications. The legal realm is just a small part of the wider cultural context. He criticizes Western lawyers for seeing cultural factors as irrelevant to their formal legal processes. See L. Rosen, *The Anthropology of Justice: Law as Culture in Islamic Society* (Cambridge: Cambridge University Press, 1989). See also Makdisi, "Formal Rationality in Islamic Law and the Common Law," 112, where he concludes that hasty conclusions should not be made in classifying Islamic law, as a study of legal reasoning in Islamic contract law shows it to be, in Weber's terms, logically formal rationality.
39. *Religious Council and Kadis Courts Act* (Cap 77) s. 38.
40. *Religious Council and Kadis Courts Act* (Cap 77) s. 38.
41. *Religious Council and Kadis Courts Act* (Cap 77) s. 74(2).

42. *Religious Council and Kadis Courts Act* (Cap 77) s. 74(1).
43. The term means the Sultan after consulting the 'Religious Council, but not necessarily in accordance with the Council's advice': *Religious Council and Kadis Courts Act* (Cap 77) s. 2.
44. The state *Mufti* (*Mufti Kerajaan*) is Chairman of the Legal Committee of the *Majlis* and is the state authority on *Syariah* law. The *Mufti* also issues *fatawa*, or religious rulings, which, when gazetted, are binding on all Muslims in the state.
45. *Religious Council and Kadis Courts Act* (Cap 77) s. 44(7).
46. When there was disagreement among Committee members, the Act provided for members to give their own separate opinion to His Majesty. In civil matters the committee could confirm, reverse or vary any decision of the trial court, and could exercise any powers of the trial court: s. 49(4)(b). In criminal matters, an appeal could be upheld, or a conviction quashed or varied, a variation or reduction in sentence, a retrial or other order made: s. 49(4)(a).
47. *Syariah Courts Order* (Cap 184) s. 33.
48. *Syariah Courts Order* (Cap 184) s. 31(a).
49. *Syariah Courts Order* (Cap 184) s. 31(b).
50. *Syariah Courts Order* (Cap 184) s. 31(c).
51. *Syariah Courts Order* (Cap 184) s. 22(2).
52. *Syariah Courts Order* (Cap 184) ss. 24(1), (2), (3).
53. *Syariah Courts Order* (Cap 184) s. 20(1).
54. *Syariah Courts Order* (Cap 184) ss 21(1), (2).
55. *Syariah Courts Order* (Cap 184) s 17(3)(a).
56. *Syariah Courts Order* (Cap 184) s 17(2).
57. Makdisi, "Formal Rationality in Islamic Law and the Common Law," 231; Shapiro, "Islam and Appeal," 194–222.
58. *Kadis* could hear appeals from an order, act, refusal or omission of a Registrar in relation to marriage and divorce proceedings.
59. *Religious Council and Kadis Courts Act* (Cap 77) ss. 75, 94.
60. *Religious Council and Kadis Courts Act* (Cap 77) s. 44(2).
61. Sachedina, "The Ideal and Real in Islamic Law," 27. See also A. A. A. Fyzee, *Outlines of Muhammadan Law* (London: Oxford University Press, 1974), 328.
62. D. S. Powers, "On Judicial Review in Islamic Law," *Law and Society Review* 26 (1992): 316.
63. Ibid., 315.
64. M. H. Kamali, "Appellate Review and Judicial Independence in Islamic Law," in *Islam and Public Law,* ed. C. Mallat (London: Graham & Trotman, 1993), 49–83.
65. G. M. Azad quoted in Kamali, "Appellate Review and Judicial Independence in Islamic Law," 52. Schacht writes that a judgment can only be reversed where there is a grave error in law, because it goes against the Quran, a recognized tradition or consensus, in J. Schacht, *An Introduction to Islamic Law* (Oxford: Clarendon Press, 1964), 196.
66. A statement of the Prophet, which is recognized as a source of law.
67. In this *hadith* the Prophet admitted the possibility of error in his own adjudications: 'I am but a human being. When you bring a dispute to me, some of you may be more eloquent in stating their cases than others. I may consequentially adjudicate on the basis of what I hear. If I adjudicate in favour of someone something that belongs to his brother, let him not take it, for it would be like taking a piece of fire' in G. M. Azad quoted in Kamali, "Appellate Review and Judicial Independence in Islamic Law," 62.
68. The Federal *Shariat* Court hears appeals from decisions in lower courts under Islamic laws in force concurrently with ordinary laws. Its decisions can be appealed to the *Shariat* Appellate Bench of the Supreme Court.
69. *Khurshid Jan v. Fazal Dad* PLD 1964 quoted in A. Ibrahim, "Shariah Court and its Place in the Judicial System," *Shariah Law Journal* 5 (1989): 10. See also Kamali, "Appellate Review and Judicial Independence in Islamic Law," 73– 6, which includes

decisions of a *kadi* where there is suspicion of personal bias or oppressive decisions of disreputable *kadis,* as ones that could be reviewed and reversed.

70. Ibrahim, "Shariah Court and its Place in the Judicial System," 5.
71. Ibid.
72. "Recommendation of the Conference on Islamic Education" quoted in Ibrahim, "Shariah Court and its Place in the Judicial System," 5.
73. *Religious Council and Kadis Courts Act* (Cap 77) s. 48(2)(a).
74. *Syariah Courts Order* (Cap 184) s. 16(1)(b).
75. *Religious Council and Kadis Courts Act* (Cap 77) s. 48(2)(a).
76. *Syariah Courts Order* (Cap 184) s. 16(1)(a).
77. The types of divorce – *khulu', fasakh, cerai ta'liq* – are specified in the *Order*.
78. *Syariah Courts Order* (Cap 184) s. 15(b)(i); *Religious Council and Kadis Courts* (Cap 77) s. 48(b)(i).
79. This is derived from *adat* – the customary Malay law on the division of matrimonial property on divorce. It provides that the wife should normally receive either one-third or one-half share of property acquired during the marriage.
80. This is a permanent dedication by a Muslim of property for religious or charitable purposes, or for the benefit of the founder and his descendants, whereby the owner's right is extinguished, and the property is deemed to belong to God.
81. Defined in the act as an expressed vow to do any act or dedicate any property for any purpose allowed by Muslim law.
82. *Syariah Courts Order* (Cap 184) s. 15(a).
83. *Religious Council and Kadis Courts Act* (Cap 77) s. 48(1)(a).
84. The offences include: failure to attend the mosque for Friday prayers (s. 171); purchasing, selling, consuming intoxicating liquor (s. 172); consuming food, drink or tobacco during Ramadan (s. 173); abetting offences under s. 172 and s. 173 (s 174); *Khalwat* or suspicious proximity (s. 177); *Zina* or illicit intercourse (s. 178); unlawful solemnization of marriage (s. 179); unlawful conversions (s. 181); wilful neglect of statutory duty (s. 182); breach of secrecy (s. 183); unlawful mosques (s. 184); religious teaching without permission (s. 185); false doctrine (s. 186); issuing of a *fatwa* without authority (s. 187); religious books contrary to Islamic law (s. 188); misuse of the Quran (s. 189); contempt of religious authorities (s. 190); religious contempt (s. 191); non-payment of *zakat* (obligatory alms paid by Muslims) or *fitrah* (obligatory tithe given at the end of Ramadan) (s. 192); incitement to neglect religious duties (s. 193); attempts and abetment (s. 195).
85. *Religious Council and Kadis Courts Act* (Cap 77) s. 170.
86. These are knowingly selling alcohol or food in Ramadan to a Muslim (s. 195) and abetting a Muslim to commit an offence under the Act: *Religious Council and Kadis Courts Act* (Cap 77) s. 196.
87. N. Hizam, "Concern at Rise in Immoral Activities," *The Brunei Times,* October 27, 2007, http://www.bt.com.bn/en/home_news/2007/10/27/concern_at_rise_in_immoral_activities
88. *Islamic Family Law Order* (1999) s. 61.
89. *Hudud* offences are specific crimes laid down in the Quran with the form of punishment also specified.
90. *Syahids* are persons the court finds are able to give *syahadah* evidence, *Syariah Court Evidence Order* (2001) s. 106(1). For theft, highway robbery, false accusations and consuming alcohol, evidence of two male *syahids* is required
91. *Bayyinah* and *syahadah* are two types of evidence used in Islamic law. While *bayyinah* (clear evidence) encompasses all types of evidence which can be given by a range of persons including women and non-Muslims, *syahadah* is more limited in that only particular persons (*syahids*) can give this testimony in court. When all requirements are met, *syahadah* evidence must be accepted by the judge.
92. *Syariah Courts Evidence Order* (2001) s. 106(5).

93. "Titah," *Borneo Bulletin*, July 16, 1996.
94. Ibid.
95. Pehin Dato Ustaz Awang Haji Yahya's speech quoted in "Brunei to Maintain Tranquil and Moderate Islamic Laws," www.brudirect.com/DailyInfo/News/Archive/June03/100603
96. M. H. Othman, "Syariah Law to the Fore," *Borneo Bulletin*, May 17, 2001.
97. *Syariah Courts Order* (Cap 184) ss. 8 (2)(b)(ii), 9 (2)(b)(ii), 10(2)(b)(ii).
98. *Religious Council and Kadis Court Act* (Cap 77) s. 45.
99. There are *hadith* providing guidance on this, as the Prophet accepted some and rejected others. For example, the Prophet rejected the request of Abu Zarr to be appointed *kadi* on grounds that he had a weak character.
100. A. Ibrahim, "Superiority of the Islamic System of Justice," *ILUM Law Journal* 4 (1994): 54.
101. *Sunnah* is the law derived from the traditions of the Prophet Muhammad which were verified, recorded and collated by learned jurists after the Prophet's death.
102. Islamic knowledge or jurisprudence.
103. M. Saedon, "Undang-Undang Keterangan Mahkamah Kadi: Satue Keperluan," *Seminar Sistem Kehakiman Syara,* June (1995): 20.
104. These continue. See "Syariah Court Ends Law Workshop," *Brunei Times*, May 25, 2008, http://www.bt.com.bn/en/home_news/2008/05/25/syariah_court_ends_law_workshop.
105. It should, however, be noted that in the history of the common law, university training for legal practice is a relatively recent phenomenon as law traditionally was taught in the Inns of Court, which bears many similarities to the *madrassah* training. See an article on the historical similarities between the Inns of Court and the *madrassahs* in Islam: J. Makdisi, "Legal History of Islamic Law and the English Common Law: Origins and Metamorphoses," *Cleveland State Law Review* 4 (1994): 3.
106. In 2000 it was reported that there were over 100 undergraduate students from Brunei at Al-Azhar University: *Borneo Bulletin*, September 17, 2000.
107. This is a degree programme on Islamic jurisprudence and judicial process. Its aim is to prepare students for a career as Islamic judges, legal practitioners and court administrators.
108. This programme is centred on Islamic jurisprudence and prepares students for work in *ifta* (issuing *fatawa*) religious consultancy, supervision, teaching, research and mentoring.
109. The announcement that a new University would be established was made in the Sultan's 2007 Titah for the New Year. See Lyna Mohamad, "New Islamic University," *Borneo Bulletin,* January 1, 2007, http://www.brudirect.com/DailyInfo/News/Archive/Jan07/010107/nite01.htm
110. Section 9 for Appeal Court, and s. 10 for High Court in *Syariah Courts Order* (Cap 184). Appointments to the Subordinate *Syar'ie* Courts are by the Sultan on the advice of the *Majlis* and no period or type of experience is stipulated: *Syariah Courts Order* (Cap 184) s. 10.
111. *Supreme Court Act* (Cap 5) ss. 7(1), (2) where seven years experience in a Court of unlimited jurisdiction in civil and criminal matters, in another Commonwealth jurisdiction or in a Commonwealth appellate court; or, alternatively seven years experience as an advocate or solicitor in such a court is specified.
112. D. L. Horowitz, "The Qur'an and the Common Law: Islamic Law Reform and Theory of Legal Change," *American Journal of Comparative Law* 42 (1994): 265.
113. Peletz, *Islamic Modern*, 124.
114. L. Mohammad, "Conference Boost For Syariah and Civil Laws," *Borneo Bulletin,* September 5, 2006, http://brudirect.com/DailyInfo/News/Archive/Sept05/060905/nite02.htm

115. Minister for Law and Attorney-General, Yang Amat Mulia Pg Laila Kanun Diraja Pg Hj Bahrin quoted in "Syariah Law for Brunei: A Need to Return to Islamic Law, *Borneo Bulletin,* June 16, 1995.
116. *Negeri Sembilan Administration of Islamic Laws Enactment* (1991); *Pahang Administration of Islamic Law Enactment* (1991); *Selangor Administration of Islamic Laws Enactment* (1989); *Sabah Syariah Courts Enactment* (1992); *Johore Administration of Islamic Laws Enactment* (1978); *Kelantan Administration of Syariah Court Enactment* (1982).
117. Sultan Sharif Ali Islamic University (UNISSA).
118. The faculty of Islamic Studies from University Brunei Darussalam and the Islamic Studies Institute of the Ministry of Religious Affairs are now at UNISSA.
119. A. Whiting, "Desecularising Malaysian Law? in *Examining Practice, Interrogating Theory: Comparative Legal Studies in Asia,* ed. P. Nicholson and S. Biddulph (Dordrecht, Netherlands: Martinus Nijhoff, 2008), 231.
120. Hayati binte Pehin Orang Kaya Shahbandar Dato Seri Paduka Hj Mohd Salleh.
121. This appointment was not contradictory to general Islamic principles as her judicial function was limited to secular issues. A similar appointment to the *Syariah* Courts is less likely, given the general consensus that women should not be judges in Islamic courts. However, Brunei's neighbour, Indonesia, which has the world's largest Muslim population, does appoint female judges to its *Shariah* Courts.
122. In 2008, the President of the Court of Appeal in Brunei is Sir Noel Plunkett Power who is also a non-permanent judge of the Court of Final Appeal of Hong Kong. Also serving as Commissioners on the Court are Justices John Mortimer and Henry Litton, both of whom were previously judges of the Court of Final Appeal of Hong Kong; and Justice Geoffrey Davies, previously from the Court of Appeal, Queensland, Australia.
123. Whiting, "Desecularising Malaysian Law?, 223–55.
124. *Brunei Legal Profession Act* (Cap 132) s. 18.
125. *Brunei Legal Profession Act* (Cap 132) s. 11.
126. L. Mahathir and Z. Zaini, "Sultan Calls to Meet Globalization Challenges Through Bruneian Identity, *Borneo Bulletin*, September 24, 2004.
127. Chandra Muzaffar explains the use of the term 'Islamic resurgence' as having three features: one, it shows Islam is becoming important again, regaining prestige and self-respect; two, it suggests a phenomenon which has happened before, that is, the past glory of Islam; and three, it embodies a notion of challenge to other world views. See C. Muzaffar, "Islamic Resurgence: A Global View, in *Islam and Society in Southeast Asia*, ed. T. Abdullah and S. Siddique (Singapore: Institute of Southeast Asian Studies, 1985), 5.
128. The issues of undue influence (from the Sultan and the government) on judicial function and bias of the judges in the Court of Appeal and also the Chief Justice of Brunei were central to the 2006 appeal brought by Prince Jefri (Sultan Bolkiah's brother and former Minister of Finance and Chairman of Brunei Investment Agency) to the Privy Council. The appeal was dismissed by the Privy Council. It was held that the Chief Justice was a judge of unblemished reputation and that no inference of bias in the court could be sustained. See Privy Council Office, "His Royal Highness Prince Jefri Bolkiah and Others v. The State of Brunei Darussalam and Brunei Investment Agency, Privy Council Appeal No. 69 of 2006, http://www.privy-council.org.uk/files/other/Bolkiah.Bingham.rtf
129. For a comparative table, see L. Nottage and C. Wollschlaeger, "What Do Courts Do?, *New Zealand Law Journal* (1969): 369.
130. The new Order has omitted the earlier provision contained in s. 4 of the *Religious Council and Kadis Courts Act* that 'nothing in this Act contained shall derogate from or affect the rights and powers of the Civil courts'.

17 Courts in Xinjiang

Institutional capacity in China's periphery

Pitman B. Potter

Introduction

Much has been written about the Chinese court system.[1] Chinese courts combine influences from continental systems transplanted from Germany and Japan to the People's Republic of China (PRC or China) with requirements of party control and the imperatives of the unified state drawn from Chinese adaptations of Soviet policy and legal practice (itself influenced by the French civil tradition).[2] The generally civilian character of the Chinese court system seems at odds with the pattern of seeking legal training for Chinese students, lawyers and judges in the common law systems of Canada, Britain and the United States. As well, Chinese law bookstores are heavily stocked with casebooks, which are frequently used in legal education and often prized by professors and practitioners alike, even if the courts are only recently coming to rely on case precedent to guide (albeit not control) their decisions. Much of the scholarly and policy analysis on China's court system tends to focus on textual provisions of formal law and regulation and the operations of courts in the developed cities of China's globalized coastal regions. While attention is gradually turning to courts and dispute resolution in rural areas,[3] shortages of data and difficulties of access remain significant obstacles to understanding court behaviour in remote areas.

This chapter examines the role of courts in the Xinjiang Uighur Autonomous Region of far western China. Xinjiang may be considered part of China's 'Inner Periphery,' that regional borderland that separates China and the rest of Asia.[4] To a very considerable extent, court performance in China's Inner Periphery offers a counterpoint to the impressive developments in China's major coastal cities, where influences of foreign investment, economic development and ever-closer engagement with the international political economy encourage convergence (apparent, if not fully substantive) with global institutional norms. In contrast to the developed coastal areas where China's participation in the world system invites recurring questions about institutional and normative convergence, in the Inner Periphery institutions of governance such as the courts reflect more completely the policy preferences of the Chinese party–state. This results in courts being charged with enforcing a changing array of policy priorities, which in the case of Xinjiang tend to revolve around issues of suppressing purported sentiments of separatism and religious extremism. While the substantive policy focus may change, the courts' responsibility for enforcing policy priorities remains and contributes to an ever-changing institutional context for the operation of law. The courts in Xinjiang may be appreciated as 'new,' in part because of relatively recent efforts to establish institutional forms for the legalization of Chinese rule in the region. Equally importantly, the courts in Xinjiang are also subject to ongoing processes of enforcing changing policy imperatives and hence are constantly being remade according to the preferences of the party–state. While challenges of data access have not been overcome altogether in the course of preparing this chapter, a series of field visits in 2003–6 (including observations in Artush, Kashgar, Turpan and Urumqi), combined with intensive archival research have hopefully yielded useful insights to the role of Chinese courts in Xinjiang.

Historical background: Xinjiang and the inner periphery

China's relationship with Xinjiang reflects historical factors of conflict between successive Chinese dynasties and the vigorous cultures of the Silk Road.[5] Policies in Xinjiang under the PRC reflect the importance of the region to Beijing's conception of national interest.[6] Xinjiang has multiple riches of natural resources including oil and natural gas, which are seen as essential to China's economic development. Xinjiang's strategic location in central Asia has leant particular importance to China's policies,[7] most recently the Chinese government's attempt to use the United States-led anti-terrorism campaign as justification for the suppression of Islamic separatists,[8] even to the extent of attempting to link Osama Bin Laden with Xinjiang separatist movements.[9] Yet Xinjiang remains a highly contested community whose multiple ethnic groups and largely Islamic culture are wholly distinct from Han China.[10] China faces geographic, ethnic and religious barriers to unified governance and national security:

> [t]he Northwest frontier is one of the most complicated geo-political environments along China's periphery. There are quite a number of bordering states, the political systems and levels of economic development of bordering countries vary, ethnic religious problems are extremely complex, and actual or potential hotspots are concentrated. As a result of adjustment of geopolitical structures and due to issues in various countries from ethnic, territorial and boundary conflicts, ethnic separatism and religious conflict, and water and natural resources, and other issues, the central Asia region of multiple interlocking interests is a potential hot spot of interlocking forces and interwoven contradictions. Particularly in recent years, various forces representing international terrorism, religious extremism, and ethnic separatism have developed quickly and violently in central and south Asia and nearby areas.[11]

While Jiang Zemin had noted during his first inspection tour of Xinjiang in September 1990 that economic development in the region required political stability, there appeared to be little agreement among leading cadres in Xinjiang as to what were the main obstacles to stability. The link between economic development and public order was underscored by the central role of the Xinjiang Production and Construction Corps (*bīngtuán*: 兵团) in managing the implementation of the 'Regulations on Comprehensive Social Order in Xinjiang Uygur Autonomous Region.'[12] Inspection visits by Li Ruihuan in August 1994 and Zhu Rongji in September 1995 revealed the extent of local concerns with socio-economic issues such as water treatment and health, although these did not seem to receive as much attention as political factors.[13] Party Secretary Wang Lequan's focus on ethnic separatism seemed to have support from Jiang, although religion was also seen as a factor. Document No. 7 of 1996, emerging from the Politburo Standing Committee meeting of 19 March, reflected a consensus position that the main crises of stability in Xinjiang were ethnic separatism and unlawful religious activities.[14]

The violent outbreak in February 1997 at Yining and the bus explosions the same month in Urumqi impelled the central government to move beyond study documents to concrete action. In April, the Xinjiang Party Committee and People's Government began a security campaign based on the spirit of the Politburo Document No. 7 and its '[o]pinion on the work of correcting security and seriously attacking violent crime.'[15] During 1997 and through to 1999, upwards of 30,000 cadres were assigned to security work, including rectification and establishment of basic level security organs.[16] Beijing has articulated themes of 'anti-separatism' and used the rubric of 'anti-terrorism' to crack down against local dissidents.[17]

While Chinese immigration has changed the face of the provincial capital Urumqi, local nationalities – particularly Uighurs and Kazakhs – remain dominant in the south of the Autonomous Region (*Jiāng Nán*: 疆南). The area around Kashgar remains a centre of Uighur nationalism – the Idhkah Mosque near the centre of the city stands as the symbolic centre of anti-Han sentiment. Signs throughout the interior of the mosque extolling in Chinese, Uighur and English the virtues of ethnic unity and prohibiting 'splittist' (*fēnliè*: 分裂) activities seem curiously maladroit, as the only readers seem to be Chinese and foreign tourists. This mixing of religion and national identity is also evident in privately funded mosques established in such places as Artush, despite the denial of state funding. China's policy makers seem acutely aware of the power of these local religious and nationalist sentiments,[18] although often China's policies of social control in the service of national integration seem unresponsive.

China's policies of governance in Xinjiang have been criticized, often justly, as reflecting problematic values of Han chauvinism, neo-colonialism and formalistic adherence to outdated notions of sovereignty. Analyses of China's policies have tended to focus on problems of human rights,[19] disparities of economic and social wellbeing,[20] and troubling practices in the regulation of religion.[21] These and other challenges are also linked with the development of judicial institutions.

Chinese governance in Xinjiang: implications for the courts

China's governance programmes in Xinjiang are closely affected by the process of 'legalization' for China's minority nationalities policies, to support increased investment and development in minority areas, and ensure coordination with other regulatory regimes in China.[22] This is part and parcel of the Chinese government's effort to build a socialist legal system. While it has faced multiple challenges,[23] the Chinese party–state's apparent commitment to building a 'socialist rule of law' system has meant steadily increasing (albeit qualified) support for courts and other legal institutions. The combination of 'legalizing' minority nationality policy and building a 'socialist legal system' more generally raises important opportunities for the development of courts in Xinjiang.

Governance and the courts

The courts in Xinjiang are subject to formal organizational and jurisdictional requirements set for other courts in China. Pursuant to Chapter II of the *Organic Law of the People's Courts*[24] the courts of Xinjiang Autonomous Region are organized hierarchically by locality: Basic Level People's Courts at the county level within prefectures of the Autonomous Region; Intermediate Level People's Courts at the prefecture level within the Autonomous Region; and Higher Level People's Court for the Autonomous Region itself. Personnel are appointed by the local people's congresses at corresponding levels. Judicial operations remain subject to the overall control of local party committees (often working through the 'adjudication committee' that supervises court decisions and whose chair is generally the court's party secretary).

Despite these broad similarities with counterparts in China proper, courts in Xinjiang are also subject to the statutory guidance particular to Xinjiang's status as a minority nationality autonomous region. The *Constitution of the People's Republic of China* (*Constitution*) provides overall guidance on issues of local autonomy, although subject to overarching imperatives of maintaining central control. The *Constitution* requires representation on local people's congresses for nationalities inhabiting a minority autonomous area, region, prefecture, or county other than the nationality(ies) in whose name the area is designated[25] – thus ensuring representation by transplanted Han from China proper, since they are classified as one of China's 'nationalities.'[26] While Article 134 of the *Constitution* does provide for use of local nationality languages in court proceedings, Chinese language usage continues to dominate social and political life in minority areas.[27] While the enactment in 2000 of a law on simultaneous language usage was heralded as an example of the government's commitment to protecting local minority languages, its very enactment and challenges to its full implementation suggest that minority language usage remains marginalized.[28]

Constitutional provisions are augmented by the *Law of the PRC on Autonomy of Nationality Areas* (*NRAL*).[29] *NRAL* Article 46 provides that local people's courts and public prosecutions departments (procuratorates) in minority nationality areas 'should' (*yīngdāng*: 应当) include among their leadership and staff nationalities who are implementing regional autonomy.[30] Authoritative interpretations of this provision suggest that the nationalities implementing regional autonomy, which should be included in the leadership and staff of judicial institutions, are in fact not local minorities, but rather 'are intimately familiar with the history and traditional culture of local nationalities and have close ties with local nationality masses.'[31] Thus, despite its implied meaning, the *NRAL* text does not require that local minority nationalities be included in the leadership and staff of judicial institutions, but in fact permits quite the opposite.

The constitutional provision on the use of local languages is affirmed in *NRAL* Article 47. While in contrast to the question of leadership and staffing, the specification is made for use of local minority nationality languages; the point is also made that the rights of all nationalities (including the Han) to use of their own language should be protected. The potential for interpretation of these ideals in ways that do not effectively protect participation and language needs of local minority nationalities is underscored by the lack of clear standards for interpreting and enforcing the ideals set forth in the *Constitution* and the *NRAL*.

Issues of local participation are also affected by underlying principles informing the *NRAL* that highlight the dominance of central control. Thus, the basic requirements for nationality policy, namely safeguarding national unity; preserving national interests; ensuring equality and unity of all nationality groups; and conditioning central government assistance on policy compliance,[32] all diminish the capacity for the *NRAL* to support local autonomy and diversity in legal and policy areas. The potential for state intrusion on security matters is underscored in *NRAL* Article 120, which allows local governments to organize local public security forces to respond to concrete local needs, in accordance with the state military system and subject to State Council approval. As China's courts have traditionally been focused primarily on issues of social order (particularly criminal law enforcement), the application in Xinjiang of the *NRAL*'s provisions on state direction of local security activities serves to focus judicial attention on matters of border security and perceived threats of separatism and terrorism.[33] In many ways, the very objectives of the *NRAL* are in conflict with the reasons for its enactment – namely, in the course of defining what nationality autonomy means and what its limitations are, the law works to diminish the very ideal it is intended to celebrate. This has significant potential to influence the activities of the courts, as the political imperative of unity and stability constrains efforts to build autonomy for judicial behaviour.

The courts and central policy imperatives: national unity and economic development

The courts in Xinjiang have long been active participants in centrally directed campaigns to attack alleged separatism and terrorism among Xinjiang's local populace.[34] Local models for court behaviour heralded '100% rate in apprehension sanction, hearing approval, case-closing, and legitimacy,' signalling the importance of judicial compliance with the higher level direction.[35] Even after the Central Minority Nationalities Work Conference of 1992, and its policy focus on improving local living conditions and promoting economic development,[36] the courts remained focused on cracking down on separatism and counter-revolutionary crimes.[37]

Following civil unrest in Yining in February 1997, local courts were convened in remote areas such as Aksu and Yili for trial and sentencing of separatists, with punishments ranging from execution to life imprisonment.[38]

During the years following the Yining events, local courts continued to impose severe punishments on alleged separatists. In February 1999, the court in Yili conducted a public trial and execution of two convicted terrorists and imposed sentences of 3 to 12 years on eight others,[39] while in August 1999, the local court in Nongsishi (within Yili Prefecture) imposed sentences of up to 15 years imprisonment for separatist activities, following the imposition of death sentences on ten other defendants in Yili.[40] In the Autonomous Region capital of Urumqi ten people were executed in March 1999 and another 45 given suspended death sentences for crimes of provoking unrest,[41] while in October the court oversaw a public sentencing rally followed by the execution of Uighur 'terrorists,' while suspending execution and imposing prison terms on others.[42] The Urumqi Intermediate People's Court sentenced three people to death in July 2000 for homicides linked to separatist activities.[43]

Despite the intensity and duration of judicial punishments against alleged separatism, the central government directed a renewed 'Strike Hard' campaign following a Central Public Order Work Conference, 2–3 April 2001. At this meeting, Jiang Zemin, Zhu Rongji and other state and party leaders emphasized the use of legal institutions including the courts to crack down on serious crimes, including the activities of separatists.[44] Zhu's speech set the tone:

> All localities and departments must bring their thinking into line with the central authorities' judgement and policymaking arrangements on the current public order situation, resolutely act in accordance with central demands, rapidly swing into action to unfold in depth to 'strike hard' and put things in order, severely crack down on serious economic crime, fully step up the comprehensive tackling of public order, and devote great energy to resolving current outstanding problems in public order work, making efforts to achieve practical results as soon as possible.[45]

Attendance at the Central Work Conference by government and party officials from Xinjiang, including from the Xinjiang Production and Construction Corps (*bīngtuán*: 兵团), signalled the extent to which the Strike Hard campaign would be aimed at alleged separatism in Xinjiang. Shortly thereafter, Xinjiang Party Secretary, Wang Lequan, convened a regional public order conference in Urumqi from 14–15 April, at which the Strike Hard campaign was announced for Xinjiang, to be implemented by the local party Politics and Law Commission.[46] More than 500 officials, including party secretaries at all localities as well as chief justices and prosecutors were instructed to direct the campaign against separatism and terrorism.[47] Courts in particular were called upon to

> conscientiously clean up the cases on trial and ensure promptness in handling cases and making court decisions. ... In the near future all localities must

> select a group of major cases which have influence on society, hold public trials, hand out severe punishments to a group of criminals, execute a group of criminals, and swiftly form a powerful momentum for the 'strike hard' drive throughout the region.[48]

Following this meeting, the Xinjiang Autonomous Region High Court took the lead in carrying out instructions to accelerate public trials and punishments of separatists.[49] Notices issued to local courts in Xinjiang directed specific punishment for separatist activities.[50] Yet the Strike Hard effort was not aimed only at alleged separatists, as local public security organs and the courts seemed to direct significant efforts towards non-political crimes of murder and robbery, rounding up some 6,000 criminal elements and law violators in May.[51]

In addition to carrying out directives to punish separatist activity, the courts have also supported state claims against high profile human rights defendants, such as Nobel Prize nominee Rebiya Kadeer, whose appeal against a conviction and an eight-year prison sentence for leaking state secrets China was rejected by the Urumqi High Court.[52] While the state secrets regime is intended in part to ensure protection of central government interests in minority areas,[53] the decision in the Kadeer case reflects its use for more direct political repression. Following Kadeer's release and exile to the United States, her son Ablikim Abdiriyim was sentenced by the Urumqi Intermediate Court to nine-years imprisonment for secessionist activities, and two other sons were also sentenced to imprisonment and charged millions of US dollars in fines.[54]

The courts in Xinjiang have also been directed to further the purposes of the 'Western Development Strategy,' a policy aimed at expanding infrastructure investment in China's hinterlands and also at pacifying local minority nationalities through the promise of economic development and rising living standards.[55] The Western Development Strategy reflects the continued dominance of state-directed economic development models,[56] even as its application in Xinjiang is seen as a possible solution to issues of ethnic unrest.[57] Yet programmes associated with the Western Development Strategy construct notions of development around priorities of capital-intensive investment, infrastructure and urbanization.[58] Thus, central reporting on economic development in Xinjiang tends to emphasize quantitative measurements of development,[59] in contrast to perspectives of the local people, who tend to focus on qualitative indicators of wellbeing.[60]

Institutional development efforts, including expanded recruitment and training of judges and campaigns to protect the political–legal status of courts are aimed at strengthening the capacity of courts to support the economic aims of the Western Development Strategy (including attracting foreign investment).[61] As well, judicial reform of courts in China's west (including minority nationality areas such as Xinjiang) is aimed at thwarting local obstacles to policy enforcement and legalized social control campaigns.[62] While the effort to formalize central policies on governance in the periphery is part of a broader programme of legalization,[63] it has particular significance in light of the strong cultural and social resistance to expressions of Han domination in minority areas such as Xinjiang.[64] To the extent that courts have been directed to further central policy objectives, the potential to build legitimacy among local communities is limited, as their capacity to provide judicial support for local autonomy is explicitly constrained.

Reflections on institutional capacity

While court performance in Xinjiang may be taken as evidence of a preoccupation by the PRC government with interpreting and enforcing laws for parochial policy purposes, court behaviour can also be understood in the light of institutional capacity. Institutional capacity refers to the ability of institutions to perform their assigned tasks. Tentative conclusions on institutional capacity can be derived from personal observation and comparison of Xinjiang's courts with courts elsewhere in China.

Personal observations

During field visits to Xinjiang from 2003 to 2006, I had opportunities to observe courts in Artush, Kashgar, Turpan and Urumqi. Although formal meetings with court officials were not possible at the time, personal observation yielded a number of perspectives, as follows.

Urumqi

In Urumqi the Western Development Strategy and central funding supports the construction of a large court building in Urumqi. The staff are largely Han, with some Uighurs visible.

The law section at *Xinhua shudian* (新华书店) is very well stocked. This is in contrast with local small bookstores whose law books are limited to consumer protection, labour protection (suits for compensation for injury) and taxation. Uighur bookstores do not appear to have law books. The university bookstore has some Uighur books that are law related.

Turpan

A visit to a local intermediate level court revealed a run-down building, which apparently had yet to receive funds for an upgrade and seemed deserted. Some Uighur staff were visible.

Kashgar

The Court is located next to People's Government buildings on the main square in the Chinese section of town. It is an older traditional building. It appeared quite active and the staff and visitors were nearly all Han.

The Procuracy is housed next to the anti-corruption office on the main street exiting town to the west. There were mostly Han staff and visitors and quite a few cars in the parking lot.

Kashgar Bureau of Justice civil case filing office (*shòu ànlì zhōngxīn*: 受案例中心) is located in the Chinese section, but some distance from the government office and law courts. It is joined with the 'law and medicine examination and investigation office' (*fă yīxué jiăn diáo chù*: 法医学捡调处), which seems aimed at AIDS-related cases.[65]

Artush

The Court is located adjacent to the government offices. It is a relatively new building, and the Court shares the building with other agencies. It was relatively active (more Kazakh than Uighur visible).

These conditions are comparable with courts visited in Beijing and Shanghai, in terms of numbers of staff and visitors, levels of activity (all higher in Beijing and Shanghai but not outside the expected comparison range relative to the area). Establishment of courts at the prefecture level (Turpan and Kashgar) seems indicative of a national programme of judicial development. The physical conditions of Xinjiang courts (except Turpan) seem generally comparable with Beijing and Shanghai, accounting from comparative differences in population and economic conditions. This suggests that despite limitations on local funding of courts, funding for court development is being supplied, possibly from Western Development funds.

Conceptual perspectives

While personal observation can yield useful insights about institutional capacity, conceptual perspectives are also important. Institutional capacity has been examined from relational perspectives that focus on issues of responsibility between organizations and their constituencies; efficiency in performance and the use of resources; and accountability to varying sources of authority.[66] Functional perspectives have also been applied to the question of institutional capacity, in such areas as access to information; effectiveness and methods of communication; organizational symmetry; and the ability to enforce rules and directives.[67] However useful these approaches may be in the abstract, actual institutional performance remains contingent on domestic political and socio-economic conditions.[68] In the case of China, local conditions of rapid socio-economic and political transformation pose particular challenges for institutional capacity. Accordingly, institutional capacity in China may usefully be examined by reference to issues of institutional purpose, location, orientation and cohesion.

'Institutional purpose' concerns the way in which the goals of institutions reflect material and ideological contexts, the availability and nature of financial, human and other resources, and the various limitations that attend institutional performance. Institutional purpose plays a significant role in determining the capacity of institutions to respond to socio-economic change. Just as China's political reform has been driven by policy goals of social stability and the need to preserve the Communist Party's monopoly on power, so too has legal reform been driven largely by policy imperatives centred on economic growth aimed at building party legitimacy. The capacity of China's governance institutions to implement policies on national integration in relations with the Inner Periphery depends on the extent of clarity and consensus regarding policy objectives.

The performance of courts in Xinjiang reflects important questions about institutional purpose. The emphasis on using courts to enforce central policies (primarily 'Strike Hard' campaigns against alleged separatists), suggests the dominance of a central policy purpose that might well conflict with local institutional purposes of dispute resolution and socio-economic development. These questions of institutional purpose influence the issues of the legitimacy and effectiveness of the courts. These factors will also be influenced by other institutional factors of location, orientation and cohesion.

'Institutional location' involves relationships between central government authority and local socio-economic conditions. China has a long tradition of tension between local and central authorities and among the regions, and this is particularly pronounced in peripheral areas such as Xinjiang. The practical divisions of power and authority between local and central government departments permit an interplay of power and politics between the central and sub-national governments that echoes practices of federalism.[69] Yet the *Constitution* provides that China is a unitary rather than a federal state which, while nominally encouraging local initiative, still subjects local authorities to the unified leadership of the central government. In the process of bargaining that accompanies the allocation of resources and the distribution of costs and benefits of policy initiative,[70] formalistic requirements of submission to the unified state limit the flexibility of local officials. Rigid adherence to contested ideals of unitary authority also limits the ability of legal institutions at both local and national levels to exercise even limited autonomy in support of predictability and stability in socio-economic and political relations.

Tensions between central and local perspectives on the courts emerge around understanding of local conditions in Xinjiang, which can then support local efforts to expand reliance on the socialist legal system. Concerns over central government ignorance and inattention to local conditions remain evident.[71] Case studies on underground religious, economic and political relationships in Xinjiang reveal the extent to which central policies on minority affairs, economic development and national security are often based on inadequate or incorrect information about local conditions.[72] Local civil unrest reveals the extent of local dissatisfaction with central government policies and practices in Xinjiang, and reveals serious shortcomings in the government's level of knowledge about local conditions.[73] Reporting on perceived social stability problems also suggests significant differences of perspective between Beijing and local units. From Beijing's perspective, building stronger local knowledge is linked specifically to more effective propaganda efforts that, in turn, are aimed at protecting social stability.[74] This instrumentalist approach may ultimately be counterproductive, as it may weaken institutional commitments and their ability to develop a meaningful understanding of local social concerns and aspirations upon which legitimacy can be built. The *NRAL*'s provisions on local public security also reflect the central government preoccupation with issues of ethnic separatism and anti-terrorism, even as local courts and prosecutions departments are focused on local issues of standard policing.[75]

'Institutional orientation' involves the priorities and habitual practices that inform institutional performance. For governance institutions in China, orientation involves particularly the tension between formal and informal modes of operation. This is particularly sensitive in Xinjiang, where local social norms privilege non-formal mechanisms for decision-making, dispute resolution and resource allocation. The tension between statist ethics of formal institutionalism, and the pervasive local informal arrangements that the state strives to control, tends to divert resources from institutional performance and undermines institutional capacity.

The role of the courts in supporting the Western Development Strategy reveals potential issues of institutional orientation. The role of local culture and tradition in economic decision-making is marginalized, as development priorities reflect increasingly the centralized approaches to development that characterize Han China. Yet these local factors are precisely the criteria by which the legitimacy and effectiveness of courts and their decisions will be assessed locally. Even when coordination with local conditions is acknowledged, basic policy goals still privilege formalization of economic organizations and regulatory institutions.[76] Where official reporting on the Western Development Strategy does acknowledge the importance of local social support for the programme, the failure to appreciate linkages between economic and social development results in development programmes that have little relevance or support in local non-Han communities.[77] Even in environmental policy areas, the focus on using technology and engineers to 'construct' (*jiànshè*: 建设) the natural environment[78] seems quite distanced from the experience and expectations of local people. To the extent that the orientation of local courts towards the formalistic development tenets of the Western Development Strategy run counter to local expectations about socio-economic relations, legitimacy and effectiveness are undermined.

'Institutional cohesion' involves the willingness of individuals within institutions to comply with edicts from organizational and extra-organizational leaders and enforce institutional goals. Conflicts arise when the norms of particular organizations differ from those of the individuals within these organizations – such as where norms of public policy that drive organizational priorities require subordination of parochial interests of individual officials within the organization. Much has been written on the role of informal *guanxi* (关系) networks in China as a substitute for formal institutional channels of communication and resource allocation.[79] Such informal networks can serve as vehicles for socio-economic regulation,[80] or as a response to perceived inadequacies of other existing arrangements for managing social, economic and political relations.[81] *Guanxi* is not unique to Han culture and may well pose challenges to institutional cohesion in Xinjiang, as informal networks come to supplant formal organizational responsibilities as priorities for local officials. To the extent that institutional status and legitimacy are insufficient to motivate behaviour by institutional officials, *guanxi* dynamics may affect individual compliance with institutional norms.

A key element in the development of institutional cohesion for the courts in Xinjiang involves minority cadre and language policies. The *NRAL*'s requirements on staffing and leadership for courts in minority autonomy areas are purposefully vague, due in part to the frequent conclusion by local Han officials about the 'low quality' of minority cadres.[82] In his meeting with the Xinjiang delegation to the National People's Congress in March 2002, NPC Chair, Li Peng, emphasized the need to improve the quality of people of all nationalities in Xinjiang.[83] Minority cadre recruitment and training is a key element in China's minority nationalities policy,[84] which tends to focus on improving the 'quality' of minorities generally and minority cadres in particular.[85]

The content and purpose of such training is focused largely on displacing traditional cultural norms with norms of socialism and cultural civilization associated with Han China.[86] Improving the scientific and cultural 'quality' of minority cadres involves basic education but, more importantly, focuses on instilling loyalty to notions of national unity and party supremacy.[87] Indoctrination of local cadres on 'correct' views about Xinjiang's history and society are aimed to ensure political cohesion within governance organizations – reflecting a recognition of the extent to which local cadres have often retained their ethnic and religious identities. Thus, official 'cadre readers' (*gànbù xuéxí dúběn*: 干部学习读本) on ethnicity and religion note the need to accommodate local traditions and religious practices, even while emphasizing China's sovereignty over Xinjiang:

> In order to progressively strengthen great unity among various nationalities in Xinjiang and promote Xinjiang's sustainable and healthy development of Xinjiang's economy, all our cadres and masses must correctly understand the issues of Xinjiang's history, ethnic and religious issues.[88]

Yet, local minority cadres are generally highly aware of actual conditions, which often are not as described in official government training and recruitment manuals. To the extent that judicial cadres recruited from local minority nationalities are apprehensive or passively resistant to the norms associated with recruitment and training of local cadres, their compliance behaviour regarding institutional norms will be affected.

Institutional cohesion is also potentially undermined by minority cadre training approaches focused on establishing basic level cadre corps (*jīcéng gànbù duìwǔ*: 基层干部队伍).[89] While these allow local minority cadres to work at local levels and possibly to be effective agents of governance in the decentralized context of the Inner Periphery, they may also work to insulate minority cadres from participation in government administration at higher levels. This tends to underscore a perception about the role of local minority cadres as essentially translators and implementers of governance programmes, rather than interpreters and designers of policy. Reports on minority nationality training and recruitment in Xinjiang[90] suggest that these are focused at the basic entry level, with little attention to recruitment and training for more prestigious and important positions. Despite its utility in terms of programme implementation, this has the potential to undermine institutional cohesion more broadly.

The extent to which minority cadre recruitment and training policies undermine institutional cohesion is evident in the degree to which local cadres have been identified as participating in local dissident activities. In Xinjiang, for example, local cadres are alleged to have leant support to separatist and illegal religious activities.[91] Thus, while the *NRAL* provides for expanded recruitment and training of minority nationality cadres, the ways in which these goals are conceived and implemented poses problems for institutional cohesion that may undermine the capacity of the *NRAL* to achieve its desired balance between central control and local autonomy.

The challenges of building cohesion in local political institutions are no less evident for local courts than other governance institutions. Legal educational requirements for judicial personnel are generally out of reach for local minority nationality cadres – the law school classes at Xinjiang University and Xinjiang Academy of Social Sciences, for example, are overwhelmingly populated by Han Chinese. To the extent that local judges continue to be drawn from the military and the Xinjiang Construction and Production Corps (*bīngtuán*: 兵团), minority nationality representation is also very low. As a result, recruitment of local staff in the courts tends to discriminate between Han, who have opportunities at the judicial level, and local minorities (Uighurs and Kazakhs), who are generally confined to staff positions. While selected local Uighur and Kazakh students are being sent for law training to institutions in China proper (including Peking University and China University of Political Science and Law), upon returning to Xinjiang they face continued marginalization by the Han-dominated institutional cultures of the courts, which affects their adherence to institutional norms. This has potential to undermine institutional cohesion, which has broader implications for institutional capacity.

Summary

The increased role of the courts in Xinjiang reflects central government policies on the 'legalization' of governance, both generally and more specifically with regard to minority nationalities policies in the Inner Periphery. Courts in Xinjiang have been made instruments of policy enforcement – with particular attention to changing policies on security and development. In contrast to institutional arrangements where factors of legitimacy, procedural rigor and relative independence lend a modicum of consistency to judicial behaviour, in Xinjiang the instrumentalist approach to law that informs party management of the judiciary means that courts are constantly being subjected to new policy priorities. In an important sense, the courts are constantly being made 'new' as they struggle to comply with party edicts and enforce party policy.

The performance of courts will depend on factors of institutional capacity. Factors of institutional purpose reveal tensions over central government policies on repression of minority culture and identity under the guise of attacking separatist terrorism. Factors of institutional location suggest that the knowledge and understanding of central authorities, whose policy priorities courts are called upon to enforce, are often at variance with local realities. Factors of institutional orientation suggest that formal judicial institutions and government development policies may stand apart from the informal realities of local socio-economic and cultural relations. Issues of institutional cohesion arise in the context of language and local cadre recruitment issues, where the potential for divisiveness arises within court institutions. These elements of institutional capacity affect the potential for courts to build some measure of effectiveness as relatively autonomous legal institutions in the Inner Periphery area of Xinjiang.

Notes

1. Ronald C. Brown, *Understanding Chinese Courts and Legal Process: Law with Chinese Characteristics* (The Hague: Kluwer, 1997); Albert H. Y. Chen, *An Introduction to the Legal System of the People's Republic of China*, 3rd ed. (Hong Kong: Butterworths, 2004); Renmin sifa (People's Judicature), *<<Renmin sifa>> zhuankan wushi zhounian jinian: 1957–2006* (<<People's Judicature>> 50th Anniversary special issue) (Beijing: People's Courts Electronic Video Press, 2006).
2. William C. Jones, "Trying to Understand the Current Chinese Legal System," in *Understanding China's Legal System: Essays in Honor of Jerome A. Cohen*, ed. C. Stephen Hsu (New York: New York University Press, 2003), 7–45.
3. See for example, Zhu Suli, *Song fa xia xiang: Zhongguo jiceng sifa zhidu yanjiu* (Sending law to countryside: Research on China's basic level judicial system [2000]) (Beijing: Chinese University of Politics and Law Press, 2000); Kevin J. O'Brien and Lianjiang Li, "Suing the Local State: Administrative Litigation in Rural China," in *Engaging the Law in China: State, Society, and Possibilities for Justice*, ed. Neil J. Diamant, Stanley B. Lubman and Kevin J. O'Brien (Stanford, CA: Stanford University Press, 2005), 31–53; "Enforcement of Civil Judgments: Harder Than Reaching the Sky," *China Law and Governance Review* 2 (2004): http://www.chinareview.info/PDFs/Issue%20No%202%20.pdf
4. Pitman B. Potter, "Governance of the Periphery: Balancing Local Autonomy and National Unity," *Columbia Journal of Asian Law* 19 (2006): 293–322.
5. James A. Millward and Nabijan Tursun, "Political History and Strategies of Control, 1884–1978," in *Xinjiang: China's Muslim Borderland*, ed. S. Frederick Starr (Armonk, NY: M. E. Sharpe, 2004), 63–98; Peter C. Perdue, *China Marches West: The Qing Conquest of Central Eurasia* (Cambridge, MA: Harvard University Press, 2005), 15–50.
6. Ma Dazheng, *Guojia liyi gaoyu yiqie* (National interests precede everything else) (Urumqi: Xinjiang People's Press, 2003); Dru Gladney, "Chinese Program of Development and Control, 1978–2002," in *Xinjiang: China's Muslim Borderland*, ed. S. Frederick Starr (Armonk, NY: M.E. Sharpe, 2004), 101–19.
7. Nicolas Bequelin, "Xinjiang in the Nineties," *The China Journal* 44 (2000): 65–90; Yitzhak Schichor, "The Great Wall of Steel: Military and Strategy in Xinjiang," in *Xinjiang: China's Muslim Borderland*, ed. S. Frederick Starr (Armonk, NY: M. E. Sharpe, 2004), 120–60.

8. Vivien Pik-Kwan Chan, "War on Terrorism: Local Foes in Mainland's Sights," *South China Morning Post*, September 19, 2001, 4.
9. "'Apparent Text' of PRC State Council Article on 'East Turkestan' Terrorists," *Xinhua* (HK) January 21, 2002, in *FBIS Daily Report – China* (FBIS-CHI-2002-0121) (January 22, 2002).
10. Dru Gladney, *Muslim Chinese: Ethnic Nationalism in the People's Republic* (Cambridge, MA: Harvard Council on East Asian Studies, 1991); Felix K. Chang "China's Central Asian Power and Problems," *Orbis* 47 (1997): 401–26.
11. Ding Jianwei, *Diyuan zhengzhi zhong de xibei bianjiang anquan* (Security of the northwestern China border land in geopolitics) (Beijing: Nationalities Press, 2004), 15–16.
12. "Xinjiang Issues Social Order Management Regulations," *Xinjiang Ribao* (Xinjiang Daily), February 16, 1994, in *FBIS Daily Report – China* (FBIS-CHI-94-076) (April 20, 1994), 58–61.
13. Zhu Peimin, Chen Xiong and Yang Hong, *Zhongguo gongchandang yu Xinjiang minzu wenti* (The Chinese Communist Party and nationality policy in Xinjiang) (Urumqi: Xinjiang People's Press, 2004), 263–64.
14. Ibid., 257–9.
15. Ibid., 260.
16. Ibid., 260–61.
17. You Ji, "China's Post 9/11 Terrorism Strategy," *China Brief* 4 (April 15, 2004): 7–9.
18. Ma Dazheng, *Guojia liyi gaoyu yiqie* (National interests precede everything else), 31, 126–8.
19. Amnesty International, *Secret Violence: Human Rights Violations in Xinjiang* (London: Amnesty International, 1992).
20. Colin Mackerras, *China's Ethnic Minorities and Globalisation* (London: Routledge, 2003). But see Barry Sautman, "Is Xinjiang an Internal Colony?," *Inner Asia* 2 (2000): 239–71.
21. Pitman B. Potter, "Belief in Control: Regulation of Religion in China," *The China Quarterly* 174 (2003): 317–37.
22. Dai Xiaoming, *Minzu fazhi wenti tansuo* (Inquiry on legal issues of nationalities) (Beijing: Nationalities Press, 2002), 34–42.
23. Nicolas Bequelin, "Beijing's Rule of Law Retreat," *Wall Street Journal*, July 2, 2007, http://online.wsj.com/article/SB118334159185354906.html; Pitman B. Potter, "Legal Reform in China – Institutions, Culture, and Selective Adaptation," *Law and Social Inquiry* 2 (2004): 465–95.
24. *Organic Law of the People's Courts* (1980, rev. 1983, rev. 2006), http://www.novexcn.com/organic_law.html
25. *Constitution of the People's Republic of China* art. 113.
26. Gladney, *Muslim Chinese: Ethnic Nationalism in the People's Republic*, 16.
27. Gardner Bovington, "Heteronomy and Its Discontents: 'Minzu Regional Autonomy' in Xinjiang," in *Governing China's Multiethnic Frontiers*, ed. Morris Rossabit (Seattle, WA: University of Washington Press, 2004), 133–7.
28. "Xuexiao shi guanche shishi <<Guojia tongyong yuyan wenzi fa>> de jiben zhendi," (Schools are the basic front for fully implementing the Law on Simultaneous Language and Characters Usage by the State) in *Zhonghua renmin gonghe guo guojia tongyong yuyan wenzi fa xuexi duben* (Study reader on the Simultaneous Language Law of the PRC), ed. NPC Committee on Education, Science, Culture and Health and Ministry of Education (Beijing: Language Press, 2001), 34–6.
29. "Zhonghua renmin gongheguo minzu quyu zizhi fa" (*Law of the PRC on Autonomy of Nationality Areas*) (rev. 2001).

30. Shi Hong, "Xinjiang People's Congress Hears Report on Procuratorate Reform," *Xinjiang Ribao* (Xingiang Daily), May 31, 2002, in *FBIS Daily Report – China* (FBIS-CHI-2002-0710) (July 10, 2002).
31. Wu Shimin, *Zhongguo minzu zhengce duben* (Reader on China's nationalities policy) (Beijing: Central Nationalities University Press, 1998), 51.
32. Xinjiang CPC Propaganda Department, *'Si ge rentong' duben* (Reader on 'four identities') (Urumqi: Xinjiang People's Press, 2004); Song Caifa, ed., *Minzu quyu zizhifa tonglun* (General Survey on the Law on Autonomy in Minority Areas) (Beijing: Nationalities Press, 2003), 51–7.
33. Ma Dazheng, *Guojia liyi gaoyu yiqie* (National interests precede everything else), 137–46, 191–201.
34. Robert Saiget, "Muslim Separatists Still Bubbling Under Repression in Western China," *Hong Kong Agence France Presse*, August 27, 2000, in *FBIS Daily Report–China* (FBIS-CHI-2000-0827) (August 27, 2000); Amnesty International, *Secret Violence: Human Rights Violations in Xinjiang*.
35. "Legal System Publicity Viewed in Xinjiang," *Renmin Gongan Bao* (Public Security Report), February 23, 1990, 3 in *FBIS Daily Report – China* (FBIS-CHI-90-076) (April 19, 1990), 51–2.
36. Jiang Zemin, "Gaodu zhongshi minzu gongzuo he zongjiao gongzuo," (Emphasize to a high degree nationalities work and religion work) in *Zhongguo gongchandang guanyu minzu wenti de jiben guandian he zhengce* (Basic viewpoints and policies of the Chinese Communist Party on nationalities issues), ed. State Nationalities Affairs Commission (Beijing: Nationalities Press, 2002), 295–302.
37. "Xinjiang Regional Law Court Presidents' Meeting Ends," *Xinjiang Ribao* (Xinjiang Daily), February 16, 1994, in *FBIS Daily Report – China* (FBIS-CHI-94-056) (March 23, 1994), 64–5.
38. "China Said to Arrest 21 in Koranic Schools in Xinjiang," *Hong Kong Agence France Presse*, February 18, 1997 in *FBIS Daily Report – China* (FBIS-CHI-97-033) (February 20, 1997); "Xinjiang Daily Says 11 Separatists Executed," *Hong Kong Agence France Presse*, January 27, 1998, in *FBIS Daily Report – China* (FBIS-CHI-98–027) (February 27, 1998).
39. "PRC Executes Two Moslem Separatists After Rally," *Hong Kong Agence France Presse*, February 5, 1999, in *FBIS Daily Report – China* (WNC Doc #: 0F6VIIO00FBP2Q) (February 8, 1999).
40. "PRC Sentences 18 Moslems for Separatist Activities," *Hong Kong Agence France Presse*, August 17, 1999, in *FBIS Daily Report – China* (FBIS-CHI-1999-0817) (August 18, 1997).
41. Marat Abulkhatin, "Ten Executed in Xinjiang-Uygur District," *ITAR-TASS World Service*, March 3, 1999, in *FBIS Daily Report – China* (FBIS-CHI-1999-0303) (March 3, 1999).
42. "Muslim 'Terrorists' Executed in Xinjiang," *Hong Kong Agence France Presse*, October 7, 1999, in *FBIS Daily Report – China* (FBIS-CHI-1999-1007) (October 7, 1999).
43. Dong Yang and Yan Wenlu, "Xinjiang Urumqi Intermediate Court Executes 3 Separatists, 3 Other Criminals," *Zhongguo Xinwen She* (China News Service), July 7, 2000, in *FBIS Daily Report – China* (FBIS-CHI-2000-0707) (July 7, 2000).
44. "National Public Work Conference Held in Beijing," *Xinhua* (New China News Agency), Domestic Service, April 3, 2001, in *FBIS Daily Report – China* (FBIS-CHI-2001-0403) (April 5, 2001).
45. Ibid.
46. Chen Fang, "Xinjiang Party Secretary Addresses Meeting on Public Order," *Xinjiang Ribao* (Xinjiang Daily), April 16, 2001, in *FBIS Daily Report – China* (FBIS-CHI-2001–0521) (May 21, 2001).

47. Ibid.
48. Ibid.
49. "PRC to Intensify 'Strike Hard' in Xinjiang," *Xinjiang Ribao* (Xingiang Daily), May 29, 2001, in *FBIS Daily Report – China* (FBIS-CHI-2001-0618) (June 18, 2001).
50. Ibid; "Xinjiang Prefecture Mounts Crackdown on Separatists, Terrorists, Extremists," *Zhongguo Xinwen She* (China News Service), January 3, 2002, in *FBIS Daily Report – China* (FBIS-CHI-2002-0103) (January 3, 2002).
51. Wang Xinhong, Zhong Xiuling, "Urumqi City Public Security Bureau Scores Initial Results in 'Strike Hard' Campaign" *Xinjiang Ribao* (Xinjiang Daily), May 29, 2001, in *FBIS Daily Report – China* (FBIS-CHI-2001-0618) (June 18, 2001).
52. "China Rejects Prominent Xinjiang Businesswoman's Jail Appeal," *Hong Kong Agence France Presse*, December 11, 2000, in *FBIS Daily Report – China* (FBIS-CHI-2000-1211) (December 11, 2000).
53. Tianjin Municipal Minorities Affairs Commission, *Xin shiqi chengshi minzu gongzuo zhengce fagui xuanbian* (Collection of policies and laws on urban minorities work in the new era) (Beijing: Nationalities Press, 2004), 96–7.
54. "China Sentences Son of Nobel Nominee," *The Times of India*, April 17, 2007, http://timesofindia.indiatimes.com/Top_Headlines/China_sentences_son_of_Nobel_nominee/articleshow/1918800.cms
55. State Nationalities Affairs Commission, *Zhongguo gongchandang guanyu minzu wenti de jiben guandian he zhengce* (Basic viewpoints and policies of the Chinese Communist Party on nationalities issues) (Beijing: Nationalities Press, 2002), 164–5. See also, William Neilson and Ding Lu, eds, *China's West Region Development* (Singapore: World Scientific Publishing, 2004).
56. Tianjin Municipal Nationalities Affairs Commission, "Quanguo minwei 'shi wu' qijian jingji gongzuo guihua," (Economic work plan for nationalities commissions across the country during the Tenth Five Year Plan) in Tianjin Municipal Minorities Affairs Commission, *Xin shiqi chengshi minzu gongzuo zhengce fagui xuanbian* (Collection of policies and laws on urban minorities work in the new era) (Beijing: Nationalities Press, 2004), 163–70; Y. M. Yeung, "Introduction," in *Developing China's West: A Critical Path to Balanced National Development,* ed. Yue-Man Yeung and Shen Jianfa (Hong Kong: The Chinese University Press, 2004), 1–25; Shi Shengtan, *Xibu kaifa zhengce* (Policies on China's western development) (Lanzhou: Gansu People's Press, 2001).
57. Qing Jue *et al.*, "Xinjiang jingji shehui fazhan dui minzu guanxi de yingxiang," (Effects of economic and social development on nationalities relations in Xinjiang) in *Xinjiang yanjiu wenlun xuan – di yi ji* (Collection of selected essays on the study of Xinjiang – Vol. 1), ed. Tie Muer and Mao Gangning (Beijing: Nationalities Press, 2003), 196–224); Ma Dazheng, *Guojia liyi gaoyu yiqie* (National interests precede everything else), 138–42.
58. Y. M. Yeung and Shen Jianfa, eds, *Developing China's West: A Critical Path to Balanced National Development* (Hong Kong: The Chinese University Press, 2004), Part I; June Teufel Dreyer, "Ethnicity and Economic Development in Xinjiang," *Inner Asia* 2 (2000): 137–54. Also, see general listing of priorities in chapter headings of Gao Zhaoping, Liu Zhong and Chen Shaoxue, *Zhongguo xibu dakaifa zhanlue yanjiu* (Study of China's western development strategy) (Xining: Qinghao People's Press, 2000).
59. Wang Luolin et al., *Zhongguo xibu dakaifa zhengce* (China's western development policy) (Beijing: Economic Management Publishing, 2003), 7–18.
60. Christian Tyler, *Wild West China: The Taming of Xinjiang* (New Brunswick, NJ: Rutgers University Press, 2004), 214–21.
61. Sun Yu, Guo Chenjie and Liu Hongbi, *Zhongguo xibu diqu fazhi huanjing yanjiu* (Study of the legal system environment in China's western regions) (Chongqing: Chongqing Press, 2001), 204–8.
62. Ibid., 190–2.

63. Bu He, "Jiaqiang minzu fazhi jianshe, cuzin ge minzu gongtong fanrong," (Strengthen establishment of minority legal system, promote the wellbeing of all nationalities) in *Minzu gongzuo wenzhai xuanbian 1990–2002* (Collection of documents on nationalities work – 1990–2002), ed. State Nationalities Affairs Commission and CPC Central Archives (Beijing: Beijing Central Archives Press, 2003), 98–111; Liu Zhun *et al.*, "Xinjiang guanche luoshi dang de minzu zhengce de qingkuang ji duice," (Situation and countermeasures concerning full implementation of party nationalities policies in Xinjiang), 275–78.
64. Sun Yu, Guo Chenjie and Liu Hongbi, *Zhongguo xibu diqu fazhi huanjing yanjiu* (Study of the legal system environment in China's western regions), 204–8.
65. Ibid.
66. H. V. Savitch, "Global Challenge and Institutional Capacity: Or How We Can Refit Local Administration for the Next Century," *Administration and Society* 30 (1998): 248–73.
67. William Blomquist and Elinor Ostrom, "Institutional Capacity and the Resolution of the Commons Dilemma," in *Polycentric Governance and Development: Readings from the Workshop in Political Theory and Policy Analysis,* ed. Michael D. McGinnis (Ann Arbor, MI: University of Michigan Press, 1999), 60–73.
68. P. Healey, "Building Institutional Capacity Through Collaborative Approaches to Urban Planning," *Environment and Planning* 30 (1998): 1531–46; Lisa L. Martin and Beth A. Simmons, "Theories and Empirical Studies of International Institutions," *International Organization* 52 (1998): 729–57.
69. S. Dougherty and R. McGuckin, "Federalism and the Impetus for Reform in China," *China Law and Practice* 15 (2002): 30–4; S. Dougherty, R. McGuckin, and J. Radzin, "How Federalism – Not Just Privatization – Is Driving China's Economy," *Mei-Zhong jingji pinglun* (USA-China Business Review) 2 (January 2002): 115–17, or www.china-review.org/news/manage/image/45161534.doc
70. Susan Shirk, *The Political Logic of Economic Reform in Chin*a (Berkeley, CA: University of California Press, 1993), Ch. 5.
71. Ma Dazheng, *Guojia liyi gaoyu yiqie* (National interests precede everything else), 28–9.
72. Ibid., 175–6; Xinjiang weiwuer zizhiqu minzu shiwu weiyuan hui, (XUAR Minorities Affairs Commission) "Xinjiang weiwuer zizhiqu minzu guanxi jiben qingkuang," (Basic situation of relations among nationalities in Xinjiang Uighur Autonomous Region) in *Xinjiang yanjiu wenlun xuan – di yi ji* (Collection of selected essays on the study of Xinjiang – Vol. 1), ed. Tie MuEr and Mao Gangning (Beijing: Nationalities Press, 2003), 183–95.
73. Ma Dazheng, *Guojia liyi gaoyu yiqie* (National interests precede everything else), 92–100.
74. Ling Jun, "Xitong yanjiu he zhengque xuanquan Xinjiang de lishi, wei Xinjiang de wending he fazhen fuwu," (Systematic research and precise propaganda on Xinjiang's history serve stability and development in Xinjiang) in *Xinjiang yanjiu wenlun xuan – di yi ji* (Collection of selected essays on the study of Xinjiang – Vol. 1), ed. Tie MuEr and Mao Gangning (Beijing: Nationalities Press, 2003), 43–51.
75. Song Caifa, ed., *Minzu quyu zizhifa tonglun* (General Survey on the Law on Autonomy in Minority Areas) (Beijing: Nationalities Press, 2003), 291–5.
76. Shi Shengtan, *Xibu shengtai huanjing* (The ecology and environment of the West) (Lanzhou: Gansu People's Press, 2001), 147–8.
77. See priorities reflected in chapter headings of Zeng Peiyan, ed., *Guojia xibu kaifa baogao* (Report on national western development) (Beijing: Water Publishing, 2003).
78. Shi Shengtan,. *Xibu shengtai huanjing* (The ecology and environment of the West), 149–53.

79. Thomas Gold, Doug Guthrie and David Wank, eds, *Social Connections in China* (Cambridge: Cambridge University Press, 2002); Alan Smart, "Gifts, Bribes and *Guanxi*: A Reconsideration of Bourdieu's Social Capital," *Cultural Anthropology* 8 (1993): 388–408.
80. Jose Tomas Gomez Arias, "A Relationship Marketing Approach to *Guanxi*," *European Journal of Marketing* 32 (1998): 145–56; Hui Chin and George Graen, "Guanxi and Professional Leadership in Contemporary Sino-American Joint Ventures in Mainland China," *Leadership Quarterly* 8 (1997): 451–65.
81. Catherine R. Xin and Jane L. Pearce, "Guanxi: Connections as Substitutes for Formal Institutional Support," *Academy of Management Journal* 39 (1996): 1641–58.
82. Lai Bangfan, ed., *Xibu kaifa zhengfu guanli yanjiu* (Study of government administration in China's western development) (Beijing: National Administration Institute, 2002), 30.
83. "Li Peng Joins Xinjiang NPC Delegation's Deliberation," *Xinhua* (New China News Agency) Domestic Service, March 14, 2002, in *FBIS Daily Report – China* (FBIS-CHI-2002-0314) (March 18, 2002).
84. Xinjiang CPC Propaganda Department, *'Si ge rentong' duben* (Reader on 'four identities') (Urumqi: Xinjiang People's Press, 2004), 4–5.
85. Sun Yi *et al.*, "Xinjiang peiyang shaoshu minzu ganbu ji shaoshu minzu daibiao renshi wenti," (Issues in training minority cadres and minority representatives in Xinjiang) in *Xinjiang yanjiu wenlun xuan – di yi ji* (Collection of selected essays on the study of Xinjiang – Vol. 1), ed. Tie Muer and Mao Gangning (Beijing: Nationalities Press, 2003), 285–310; Wu Shimin, *Zhongguo minzu zhengce duben* (Reader on China's nationalities policy) (Beijing: Central Nationalities University Press, 1998), 162, 252–3.
86. State Nationalities Affairs Commission, *Zhongguo gongchandang guanyu minzu wenti de jiben guandian he zhengce* (Basic viewpoints and policies of the Chinese Communist Party on nationalities issues), 169–71.
87. Ibid., 191–2.
88. Tian Weijiang, Chen Chao and Ma Pinyan, *Zhengque chanming Xinjiang lishi, Xinjiang minzu shi, Xinjiang yisilanjiao shi* (Correctly explaining Xinjiang history, Xinjiang ethnic history, and Xinjiang Islamic history) (Urumqi: Xinjiang People's Press, 2001), 2.
89. Central Party School Nationalities and Religious Theory Office, *Zhonggong zhongyang zuzhi bu, Zhonggong zhongyang tongzhanbu, Guojia minwei guanyu jinyibu zuohao peiyang xuanba shaoshu minzu ganbu gongzuo de yijian* (Opinion of the CPC Organization Dept., CPC United Front Work Dept., and State Nationalities Ministry on continuing to do well the work of training and selecting minority cadres) (Beijing: Central Party School Nationalities and Religious Theory Office, 1998), 138–9.
90. Sun Yi *et al.*, "Xinjiang peiyang shaoshu minzu ganbu ji shaoshu minzu daibiao renshi wenti," (Issues in training minority cadres and minority representatives in Xinjiang) in *Xinjiang yanjiu wenlun xuan – di yi ji* (Collection of selected essays on the study of Xinjiang – Vol. 1), 285–310.
91. Ma Dazheng, *Guojia liyi gaoyu yiqie* (National interests precede everything else), 80.

Part VII

Juries, regulation and renovation in Japanese courts

18 Japan's new criminal trials

Origins, operations and implications

Kent Anderson and David T. Johnson

Introduction

In May 2009, Japan will start a new trial system for serious criminal cases in which six lay persons will sit with three professional judges to adjudicate guilt and determine sentence. This lay judge system (裁判員制度: *saiban-in seido*) will place citizen participation at the centre of Japanese criminal trials – and criminal justice – for the first time since 1943, when the nation's original jury law was suspended. This chapter explains the rationales for and the political origins of Japan's new trial system, describes briefly how that system will operate in practice, and assesses its significance for Japan and other Asian nations.

In May 2004, Japan enacted a law introducing lay judges into its criminal justice system, and courts and citizens were given five years to prepare for its advent.[1] Two years later, Kent Anderson co-wrote an interim report on Japan's preparations for the new system that focused on the domestic political debate leading up to enactment of the 2004 law and on the public relations efforts that Japan's government was undertaking in an attempt to convince a sceptical public about the virtues and viability of the new system.[2] That report concluded by suggesting that though there was reason for optimism about the system in light of the preparations being made by courts, prosecutors and citizens, Japan's private lawyers appeared ill-prepared for the changes the new system would thrust upon them.

With the new trial system still half a year away at the time of this writing, the present chapter can be considered a second interim report on Japan's road to the most consequential criminal justice reform since the Occupation ended in 1952. At the most basic level, we aim to introduce the structure of this new model of lay participation in criminal law to a wider audience. Before that, however, we explore some of the political and jurisprudential reasons given for instituting this reform. The final section of this chapter asks whether Japan's model of lay participation has something instructive to say to the rest of Asia and the world. We believe it does.

Rationality, power and reform

Japan's justice system reform movement (司法改革運度: *shihō kaikaku undō*) is an effort to improve the quality of Japanese law and democracy by increasing the size of the legal profession and the availability of legal services, improving the quality of legal services through reforming legal education, and instituting other 'huge' and 'extensive' reforms that 'relate to the very foundation of all aspects of the justice system'.[3] Of the 'other' reforms now being pursued, the lay assessor system is widely regarded as the most significant.

This section begins by introducing two rationales – better justice and greater civic engagement – that have been put forward to justify lay participation in Japan's criminal system. These rationales are important, because they provide a yardstick against which the *saiban-in* system may be assessed. The section then explores two reform puzzles: Why are the police – the most powerful and problematic actor in Japanese criminal justice – not included in reforms that are meant to be comprehensive? And, given the resistance to court reform that until quite recently characterized all of the most powerful institutions in Japanese criminal justice – the police, the procuracy and the judiciary – why was there any reform at all?

Rationales

Japan's lay assessor system is a hybrid of the classic common law jury and the civil law mixed court. The rationales for the new system are both multiple and ambitious. On the one hand, the designers of the new system hoped to improve the quality of Japanese criminal justice by widening the experience of trial decision-makers and thereby reducing the elitism of the small corps of professional judges who have had the last word in criminal trials since 1943, when Japan's pre-war *Jury Act* was suspended.[4] The designers also believed the new system would foster greater civic participation in Japan's polity and society. Evidence from other countries suggests that both goals are reasonable and feasible in some situations, but what remains to be seen is whether the law in action will foster or obstruct the realization of these aims in the Japanese context.

To assess the significance of the lay assessor system, it is essential to identify the goals of increasing lay participation. But this is difficult to answer, because a variety of constituencies have asserted competing and contradictory objectives for the system. Discussions of the lay assessor reform have also taken place in terms of wider debates about the appropriate supply of legal professionals and the aims and methods of legal education, thus making it nearly impossible to disentangle the justifications for different judicial reforms. Nonetheless, it is possible to identify the core principles that proponents inside and outside of Japan have given for wanting to introduce lay participation into the heart of Japan's criminal trial system.

Most of the reasons advanced outside of Japan in support of juries and lay participation have also been reflected in Japan's own debate about judicial reform. Many Japanese commentators contend that increasing citizen participation is necessary because of the high conviction rate that prevails in criminal cases and more generally the low level of citizen involvement in the government system. Interestingly, these motives do not include promotion of defendants' rights, which the Justice System Reform Council explicitly excluded as a rationale for reform.[5]

In reality, however, many of the persons pushing for reform share the view expressed by Professor Ryuichi Hirano, the dean of Japanese criminal justice studies, who claimed that rights are so marginal and trials so ritualistic that Japan's criminal process must be deemed 'abnormal', 'diseased', and 'really quite hopeless'.[6] Although we do not agree with all of Hirano's diagnosis,[7] we do acknowledge that the perception of real problems in the Japanese criminal justice – the length, intensity, and intrusiveness of interrogations, the procedural rules that systematically favour state interests, the bias and discrimination against foreign suspects and female victims, the wrongful convictions and other miscarriages of justice, and a serious shortage of transparency and accountability in the criminal process – has motivated many reformers to pursue major change.

In broadest terms, Japan's new criminal trial system is meant to ameliorate these problems by (1) producing a higher quality of criminal justice, and (2) promoting a more democratic society through greater civic engagement.

Better justice

The primary justification for more lay participation in Japan's criminal process is the belief that it will produce better justice by ensuring that verdicts and sentences better reflect common citizens' experiences and common sense. This assertion rests on two corollary claims. The first is the conviction that because lay people have collectively a wide range of practical experiences, they are well prepared to evaluate factual allegations of criminal conduct and to decide the appropriate responses to them. The second conviction is that professional judges are handicapped as decision-makers in criminal cases because they have narrower life experiences, are over-represented by educational and cultural elites, and are likely to possess or develop a bias in favour of governmental interests (because they are employed by and beholden to the Japanese state).

Although these claims are not unique to Japan, some of them – especially those related to professional judges – have particular resonance there. For example, because of the historical difficulty of passing Japan's bar exam (until reforms to legal education took effect in 2004, the bar pass rate was less than 3 per cent),[8] Japanese judges have been better educated and richer than their non-lawyer peers. Similarly, the rotating career judge system in Japan may limit the scope of social experience.

Critics of the present system often argue that judges' disconnection and isolation from society makes the judiciary partial towards the police and prosecution. If there is a tilt, it probably derives from some combination of the personality characteristics of elites who self-select into the judicial profession, their socialization to the dominant norms within the judicial bureaucracy, and the politics of recruitment and promotion. Whatever the precise mix of causes, many analysts believe that lay people who do not possess elite backgrounds, and who are not subject to socialization and control within the career judiciary, will be more inclined to hand down decisions against state interests, including those of the police and prosecutors.[9] In this way, the new lay assessor system is supposed to improve the quality of Japanese justice by expanding the narrow focus and tempering the pro-state bias of professional judges through the perspectives of ordinary citizens.

Greater civic engagement

The second reason often offered as justification for increasing lay participation in Japan's judicial system is the belief that jury-like institutions will promote the development of Japanese civic engagement. There are both positive and cynical versions of this view. The positive argument is that when ordinary citizens are called for duty, they will learn more about and become more interested in the judicial system, and this will translate into a legal system that will be more responsive to, and reflective of, the needs of society. On this view, lay participation will promote grassroots democratic involvement, albeit through conscription. Others suggest lay participation is being introduced so that the public shares ownership of the outcomes of the criminal process. And sometimes it is cynically suggested that this serves the judiciary's interest by insulating its decisions from criticisms for being too lenient or too out of touch with public sensibilities.

Power

Rationality is the major means for making law and democracy work in modern societies.[10] But when it comes to reform, what is counted as rational frequently depends on context, and the most critical context of rationality is usually *power*. This section shows that in Japan's justice system reform movement, power has sometimes blurred the dividing line between rationality and rationalization by ensuring that some subjects that should have been reform imperatives – such as the power and accountability of the police – were left off the reform agenda. The section then briefly explores a different puzzle about power and reform in Japanese criminal justice: how was the lay judge system introduced against the resistance of powerful institutions such as the police, the procuracy and the judiciary, who believed that greater lay participation would reduce their control of the criminal process?

Where are the police?

In Japan's justice system reform movement, the police appear to be missing in action – and for no principled reason. As has been documented elsewhere,[11] Japanese police are hugely powerful (perhaps more powerful than police in any other democracy); they misuse their power; and they are neither transparent nor accountable. In some central respects, they constitute the primary impediment to the 'rule of law' that is aspired to in Japan's justice system reform movement. If these premises are correct, then an important inference follows: The police should have been a central focus of Japan's justice system reform.[12]

It would have been rational to place police squarely at the centre of Japan's criminal justice reforms, but that did not happen, largely because the police did not want it to. In particular, the police did not want their status – much power and little accountability – to change, and on the surface, at least, they seem to be getting what they want. This may seem an odd conclusion, for police were far less active in reform deliberations than were lawyers, prosecutors and judges. In this sense, the police exercised little power. But power has a second face that can be more important than direct participation in deliberative decision-making, and this face is evident when an actor is able to limit the scope of the political process to public consideration of only those issues that are innocuous to the actor. In Japan's justice system reform movement, the police have largely succeeded in keeping certain key issues – their power, performance, and unaccountability, especially in pre-indictment interrogations and investigations – outside the realm of public discussion. Their success at this agenda-setting illustrates another important political truth: that power has the capacity to define reality by producing knowledge that is conducive to the policies it wants to pursue and by suppressing knowledge for which it has no use.

But the triumph of power over rationality may not be the bottom line, and police dominance over the pre-indictment process might not endure as long as the foregoing account suggests. One inescapable truth about legal reform is that changes implemented in one part of a system – such as trial – frequently stimulate, or indirectly result in, changes elsewhere in the system. In Japan, lay judge trials have not yet started, but already actors in the criminal justice system are modifying their standard operating procedures in anticipation of the change. Greater provisions have been made for the legal representation of indigent suspects in the crucial pre-charge period.[13] The right to discovery is expanding. Trial processes are being simplified and trial issues focused. Defendants are more often being released on bail. Victims are being given more voice in the criminal process, including the authority to directly question defendants during trials, and to state their sentencing preferences to the courts. Courts are restricting the admissibility of overly developed dossiers drafted by police and prosecutors. Prosecutors and defence lawyers are learning new methods of presentation and styles of performance that they will need to undertake in the new trial system.[14] During investigations, prosecutors have started to experiment with electronically recording interrogations, and police seem likely to follow.[15] And at trial, defendants are being allowed to wear more ordinary clothes and to sit next to their defence lawyers rather than being separated from them.[16] In all of these ways (and more), the forthcoming reforms to the criminal trial are casting a shadow over many other aspects of the criminal process.[17] The net effect may well be to shift the fulcrum of a balance of power in Japanese criminal justice that has long favoured the police and prosecutors' interests in securing confessions and convictions.

Why so much reform?

If power tends to get its way in legal reform, how was the creation of a new trial system even possible when so many powerful institutions opposed it? With one of the world's highest conviction rates, prosecutors profit considerably from the predictably of the present system of criminal adjudication by professional judges.[18] Similarly, the police have nothing to gain and much to lose by permitting a shift in the locus of decision-making away from the pre-indictment investigation processes that they currently control. And judges, who have long had the last word in Japanese trials, were less than enthusiastic about sharing their monopoly decision-making authority with ordinary citizens. More theoretically, in legal systems of all kinds, nothing is quite as imbedded as the procedures for proof and trial, because most of what a legal system does is to decide matters of proof.[19] Yet between 2001 and 2004, Japan designed a new court system that, in fairly rapid order, fundamentally changed the procedures for proof and trial. How did this happen?

Our answer is complex, incomplete, and somewhat speculative. The extant accounts of the slow birth of Japan's new trial system sheds little light on how this baby was conceived in the context of so many powerfully prophylactic institutions. But some parts of the story can be told.[20]

The first step is recognizing that Japan's lay judge reform is part of a much broader effort to change fundamentally the country's justice system. Ultimately, the main aim of justice system reform is to strengthen popular sovereignty by pursuing three main purposes: satisfying public expectations for a system that is easy to use, easy to understand and reliable; strengthening the legal profession by increasing its size and improving its quality; and establishing a popular base for the justice system by allowing for more popular participation in legal processes.[21] In turn, these purposes of judicial reform are linked to three other broad shifts in Japanese government, all of which have been aimed at enhancing popular sovereignty: electoral and other reforms in the political sphere that are intended to strengthen political leadership; the deregulation of Japan's much-discussed administrative state, which long has relied on the advance control of 'administrative guidance'; and the promotion of greater transparency and accountability in a variety of governmental sectors. In some respects, justice system reform in Japan is riding a much larger wave of 'path-breaking change', which breaks from the more 'gradualist' approach to reform that characterized Japan in previous decades.[22]

In addition to these domestic contexts of change, however, at least five other factors helped create momentum for wide-ranging justice system reform. First, some problems in Japan's justice system had festered for so long that 'they could no longer be ignored'.[23] Indeed, in 1962 – nearly four decades before Japan's current reforms started – a different reform council proposed recommendations for legal change that resembled in many salient respects the reform recommendations that emerged in 2001 (especially concerning the size of the legal profession and access to legal services). Second, Japan's long recession during the 'lost decade' of the 1990s undermined confidence in many aspects of Japan's standard operating procedures, and this perception of failure created openness to new ways of doing things.[24] Third, while there was little direct foreign pressure on Japan to change its justice system, the general impacts of internationalization did generate considerable demand for new legal services, especially among business elites who came to appreciate the roles that legal professionals could play in an increasingly globalized world, and therefore became one of the strongest supporters of thorough justice system reform.[25] Fourth, legal reform became a high priority among key leaders, especially hugely popular Prime Minister Junichiro Koizumi (2001–6), one of the most aggressive and effective reformers in Japan's post-war political history. Fifth, the salience of justice system reform in Japanese political circles resulted in the creation of reform commissions and advisory committees that were *not* dominated by the three main branches of the legal profession – the bar, the procuracy, and the judiciary – that had controlled and curtailed efforts at reform in previous years. This time, Koizumi and other political elites treated legal change as a matter of pressing public importance, and the agents of change they appointed to key committees and commissions included actors from *outside* the institutions that could be expected to resist significant reform. In the end, two key groups – politicians and business leaders – supported the general goals of legal and administrative reform, and once it became clear that justice system reform would be regarded as an object of debate among a wide range of constituencies (not just the legal professions), 'the door was opened for wide-reaching reforms' that included lay participation.[26]

As for the more specific processes of change that led to the lay judge system, when the Justice System Reform Council released its recommendations in 2001, Japan was the only advanced nation that did not significantly involve the public in its judicial process. Throughout modern Japanese history, international norms have often stimulated change in law and policy, and this seems to be another instance where such norms made a difference.[27] Partly as a result of the perception – correct or otherwise – that Japan was an unjustifiable outlier in the developed world, the Reform Council reached a general agreement that Japanese citizens should be more involved in criminal trials, while leaving open the precise form that public participation should take. It was here that the main institutions of criminal justice made their preferences clear. The Japan Federation of Bar Associations favoured reintroducing a common law-style jury system in which lay persons would deliver verdicts independent of professional judges.[28] In contrast, the Japanese Supreme Court proposed giving citizens a chance to express their opinions to judges at criminal trial, but only in an 'advisory' manner.[29] The Ministry of Justice, which is largely run by prosecutors, took an intermediate position between the bar and the bench, opposing a genuine jury system but allowing citizens to discuss cases with judges and to decide verdicts and sentences together with them (as currently occurs in many European nations).[30] Prosecutors and judges seemed to regard some kind of lay participation as all but inevitable, and their perception was probably sound considering the overwhelming support that the *Lay Assessor Act* later received in the Diet.[31] Given their perception that some kind of lay participation would be implemented, these institutions – the procuracy and the judiciary – worked hard to avoid the outcome they both deemed least desirable: a pure jury system. In the end, and after several serious conflicts and impasses among key stakeholders about the form the new court should take, the lay judge system that emerged – three professional judges sitting with six lay assessors in serious criminal cases that are contested – can be construed as a compromise between the more liberal position taken by the bar and the more conservative stances of the procuracy and the judiciary.

If the foregoing answer helps dispel some of the mystery surrounding our second puzzle about power and justice system reform in Japan, it does not eliminate it. A more persuasive account of the political struggles that produced Japan's new trial system remains to be written.

Operations

The previous sections briefly explained Japan's most important criminal justice reform of the past half-century. This section explains how Japan's lay judge system is likely to work in practice, since it began to operate in May 2009. It addresses six core questions: What kinds of criminal cases will lay judges hear? How will lay judges be selected? What will be the composition of these mixed panels? What powers and duties will lay judges have? How will verdicts and sentences be determined? And what protections and penalties will govern lay judges?

Cases heard by lay judges

The *Lay Assessor Act* provides that the new courts will hear two types of serious crimes: those punishable by death or imprisonment for an indefinite period or with hard labour, and those in which the victim has died due to an intentional criminal act.[32] The law does not give defendants the right to waive a lay assessor panel, but it does grant discretion to the court to determine that a case that qualifies for a *saiban-in* trial might nonetheless be heard by a traditional judicial panel.[33] Based on crime statistics for 2007 and the definition of crimes that are justiciable by lay judges, the Ministry of Justice expects there to be about 3600 lay judge trials in the first year.[34] By comparison, in 2006 the Australian state of Victoria, with a population of just over five million, had 553 jury trials, while it is estimated that the United States had roughly 98,000 criminal jury trials in state and federal courts.[35] But since Japanese prosecutors will retain great discretion about whether and what to charge, they will be the gatekeepers who determine how many cases proceed to lay judge trial.[36]

Selection of lay judges

Selection of lay judges is to be by lots from the electoral rolls within the municipal jurisdictional divisions.[37] Thus, the single positive criterion for becoming a lay judge is one's eligibility to vote in Diet elections, for which Japanese citizens must be at least 20 years of age. This definition also means that permanent residents of Japan, including the large numbers of Korean and Chinese descendents, will not be eligible to serve.

From citizens who are eligible, the law precludes some people from serving. First are those who have not completed compulsory education through to year nine and those who have been imprisoned.[38] Lawyers, quasi-lawyers such as tax attorneys and patent agents, and politicians are also precluded from service.[39] Currently enrolled students, people 70 years or older, and persons who have served as a lay judge or alternate in the past five years may decline to serve.[40]

Besides these general exemptions, two flexible exemptions are available. First, courts will have broad discretion to disqualify persons whom they deem unable to act fairly at trial.[41] This is expected to be a rarely employed exemption for people who have conflicts of interests or relationships with others who will participate in the trial. It remains to be seen, however, how expansively this provision will be applied. Second, courts may excuse persons for reasons of serious illness or injury; family, childcare, or nursing responsibilities; important work obligations; or unavoidable social obligations such as attendance at a parent's funeral.[42] The open-ended nature of these categories raises concerns that *saiban-in* panels may take on a less representative nature if many exemptions are granted, as is the case in some American jurisdictions. Japanese court officials say, however, that these exceptions will be used sparingly.

Composition of mixed panels

The *Lay Assessor Act* provides for either panels of three judges and six lay assessors, or panels of one judge and four lay assessors.[43] The full panels are the default option, while the smaller panels are to be deployed when the issues are undisputed.[44] Given the historical high rate of confessions in Japan, it will be interesting to see how often prosecutors and the defence seek the smaller panels. At present, judges indicate that they will not freely grant requests for the smaller tribunals (authors' interviews), but considering the concerns about efficiency that seem central to many Japanese courts, reality may turn out differently.[45]

Powers and duties of lay assessors

The *Lay Assessor Act* stipulates that judges and lay assessors should reach a verdict based on their recognition of the facts and application of the relevant laws and ordinances, and then they should sentence accordingly.[46] Only professional judges are authorized to interpret the law and make decisions on litigation procedure, though lay assessors will be allowed to comment on such issues.[47] Lay assessors also may directly question witnesses, victims and defendants.[48]

Method of deciding verdicts

The law and regulations leave the most critical stage – how the professional and lay judges work together to come to decisions – largely undefined. The traditional jury requirement of unanimity is not present; instead, there will be a more complex formula for a modified majority rule. Decisions are to be based on the majority opinion of the members of the panel, but at least one judge and one lay judge must agree with the majority view.[49] This gives professional judges a veto by precluding the possibility of a five- or six-person majority that is not joined by at least one professional judge. For decisions about sentence, if a majority consensus cannot be reached, the opinion(s) in favour of the harshest sentence will be added to those for the next harshest opinion until a majority is reached.[50]

Protections and penalties

Lay judges are specifically protected from adverse treatment in their employment due to *saiban-in* service, disclosure of information about them, and being contacted about the trial by outsiders.[51] The Act also provides sanctions against those who threaten, solicit, or leak information about lay assessors.[52] Lay assessors, moreover, may be held criminally liable for leaking secrets, making false statements during questioning, or failing to appear.[53] Researchers and the mass media are concerned that these rules will make it difficult, if not impossible, for lay Judges to perform their roles well. Critics contend that these confidentiality requirements, combined with the fact that the professional judges are solely responsible for the written judgment, will render Japan's new trial system too opaque and unaccountable.[54]

Implications

Lay participation in criminal trials is a cornerstone of justice in many parts of the world, yet its absence or weakness in some countries with strong democratic and legal cultures suggests that it is not an essential precondition for democracy or the rule of law to flourish.[55] Starting in 2009, however, Japan's new criminal courts will start to operate, and one practical question is whether this change will help produce the hoped-for benefits. Time will tell, for research shows that academic 'experts' like us are not much better than 'dart-throwing monkeys' at predicting the future.[56]

But some of the early signs are promising. Even before lay judge trials started, Japan's criminal justice system had been making adjustments that mitigate some of the more serious problems that have afflicted it for years: from the difficulty of obtaining release on bail for defendants who do not confess, to access to defence lawyers in the crucial pre-charge period.[57] There is reason to believe that trial reform will stimulate even more changes in the pre-indictment process, after that reform has actually taken effect, and the involvement of ordinary citizens in deciding criminal verdicts and sentences may well change the system's outputs as well. It might well reduce Japan's famously high conviction rate (which is partly a product of the high predictability of verdicts issued, solely by professional judges in the former system), and it also could alter the established 'going rates' for criminal sentences that are imposed on those defendants who are found guilty. More broadly, the lay judge system is meant to be 'the linchpin' that ties together a much broader set of interrelated reforms in the Japanese justice system. If the new courts work as intended, they should facilitate change in some fundamental features of the present system, from excessively low levels of adversarial contestation,[58] to an excessive reliance on written records (調書:: *chōsho*) that contradicts the principle that trials should be decided based on the direct evaluation of oral evidence presented in open court.[59]

While some of the signs are promising, there are also reasons to wonder how deep the changes will be. The received wisdom is that Japan's pre-war jury system was handicapped by cultural sensibilities that preferred judgment by professionals rather than by fellow citizens, and some observers suggest that these sensibilities have not changed enough to eradicate the risk of a recurrence. On this view, 'the hierarchical nature of Japanese society, the high level of trust for authority figures in Japanese society, Japanese group consciousness, and the desire to maintain harmony' will make it difficult for Japan's new mixed court system to function effectively.[60] Similarly, on current estimates, only about 20,000 citizens will serve on mixed courts in the first year – about one Japanese in every 6,000 – while polls suggest that up to 70 per cent of Japanese adults do not want to serve at all.[61] Is that enough civic participation in what Tocqueville called 'Little Parliaments' to produce a significantly more vibrant democracy than the one that presently exists?

There are also difficult questions about what Japan's new system of concentrated trial will do to the supply of decent defence lawyering. In the present system of discontinuous trials presided-over by professional judges, a trial session occurs every month or two until a verdict is reached, making it possible for defence lawyers to juggle a large and varied case-load if they schedule their trial appearances accordingly. But in the new lay judge system, when trials will proceed continuously from start to finish, lawyers will need to be available continuously, for a day or two in simple cases to two weeks or more in more complicated ones. The new trial system will thus require major adjustments in the way Japanese lawyers organize their work lives. For at least some lawyers in a society that hardly has a surplus of enthusiastic and experienced defence lawyers, the new system may create incentives to avoid criminal defence work altogether. Beyond the questions of the quantity of defence lawyers, there are also concerns about the quality of their practice. In contrast to prosecutors who have the resources of the state behind them for the necessary retraining, private defence lawyers who lack financial means may come into the new system with limited training.

The final question about the implications of Japan's new criminal court is what effects it will have on the death penalty.[62] Japan is, with the United States, one of only two developed democracies in the world to retain capital punishment, and continues to conduct executions on a regular basis. In Asia, Japan is one of only two nations where executions have increased in recent years, the other being Pakistan.[63] On some views, the use of lay assessors in capital cases will decrease death sentences by forcing Japanese citizens to confront directly difficult questions about the propriety of state killing, and it may even create momentum for Japan to abolish the ultimate sanction altogether.[64]

But the advent of lay assessors might also stimulate some surprising changes. Among supporters of capital punishment – around 80 per cent of Japanese citizens in recent surveys[65] – one anxiety is that the more lay judges learn about the particular circumstances of a capital case, the more reluctant they will become to impose a sentence of death (there is some evidence that this is the case with capital jurors in America).[66] Among death penalty opponents, by contrast, there is a strong desire to stop the ongoing surge in death sentences and executions, even if the death penalty cannot soon be eliminated. In 2008, these two constituencies came together in the Japanese Diet to propose the creation of a 'life without parole' (LWOP) sentence that would reduce the gap between the death penalty and the next most severe sanction that currently exists – a life sentence with the possibility of parole. If LWOP is enacted, it may make the lay judge role in capital trials a little easier to perform. But if the introduction of LWOP in the United States is any indication, LWOP in Japan may well have little effect on the volume of death sentences or executions, while substantially increasing the terms of imprisonment imposed on many criminal defendants in non-capital cases.[67] Those are not outcomes most abolitionists desire.

This possibility raises a broader issue: Will Japan's new trial system increase criminal punishments by deepening the country's present trend towards 'penal populism'? We believe it could, for one condition of Japanese criminal justice that promoted leniency in punishment before the shift towards penal populism started in the late 1990s is the insulation that criminal justice professionals enjoyed from the more punitive sentiments of the general public.[68] That insulation has been eroding for several years, and the participation of lay judges in criminal sentencing could deepen the trend. On the other hand, ordinary citizens helped generate more lenient outcomes in Japan's pre-war jury system, and that also seems to be one effect of South Korea's new jury system.[69]

If these are some of the central questions concerning the future of Japan's new criminal trial system, what, if anything, does the new system mean for other nations in Asia and the world? Robert Precht, co-director of the Juries and Democracy Program at the University of Montana, has argued that Japan's 'democratic experiment' with lay participation has 'important consequences for the rest of Asia'.[70] Rudy Monteleone, the Juries Commissioner for the Australian state of Victoria, has stated that Japan's *saiban-in* experiment is crucial, because the rest of Asia will be watching how it goes, to determine whether similar reforms are feasible and desirable.[71]

Yet direct lay involvement in criminal justice is hardly an international standard, and Asia seems to have in practice fewer direct roles for lay participants than many other parts of the world.[72] Hong Kong and Sri Lanka do maintain jury institutions for some kinds of major crimes, but several other Asian jurisdictions have moved away from lay participation at trial. India abolished criminal jury trials after a high-profile murder case in Maharashtra ended in acquittal in 1959.[73] Singapore abolished jury trials for most criminal cases in 1959 and for all criminal cases in 1969.[74] As in India, the elimination of jury trials in Singapore stemmed, in part, from a high-profile acquittal but in this case, Prime Minister Lee Kuan Yew – the prime mover against the jury – was himself the defence lawyer who had secured the acquittals that later led to his 'grave doubts about the practical value of the jury system' in his country.[75] In Brunei, two lay assessors participated in criminal trials at the High Court until 1988, but since then capital trials have been heard by two professional judges, and all other criminal trials have been heard by a single judge. Also in Southeast Asia, Malaysia – a common law country strongly influenced by English jurisprudence – abolished both jury trials and the use of lay assessors when it amended its *Code of Criminal Procedure* in 1995.[76]

Notwithstanding the theme of this publication – new courts in Asia – there is no widespread movement in the region towards more lay participation at trial, at least in the sphere of criminal justice. Indeed, in some Asian jurisdictions, the association of lay participation with colonial injustices of the past, together with contemporary concerns about case-processing efficiency, may mitigate against the reintroduction of lay participatory systems. So might the perception that jury and lay judge systems are difficult to implement in racially diverse and divided societies, of which Asia has many.[77] For these and other reasons, there is little reason to believe that Asia is on the verge of a reform stampede towards new criminal courts.

Nevertheless, Japan's reform does deserve watching, not least because other nations in the region are doing just that. Korea's ongoing experiment with an advisory jury system has been stimulated and informed by the perceptions of reform developments across the Sea of Japan, or East Sea, and there have also been high-level discussions of increasing lay participation in the criminal trial systems of Taiwan and the People's Republic of China[78]. Stephen Landsman and Jing Zhang, "A Tale of Two Juries: Lay Participation Comes to Japanese and Chinese Courts," *UCLA Pacific Basin Law Journal* 25 (2008): 1790. Historically, jury and lay judge systems have often emerged in periods of democratic development, sometimes waning with the rise of more authoritarian forms of government. [79] If democracy continues to spread in the Asia region, different forms of lay participation could spread too, not only because of domestic dynamics, but also because 'nothing spreads adoption of new ideas like other actors doing the same'.

One of the main motivations for introducing the *saiban-in* system into Japan is the desire to improve the quality of Japanese criminal justice, which some observers will measure by whether there is a change to the system's famously high conviction rate. On this view, the success of the new system partially depends on whether it will make criminal trials less predictable. By some standards, criminal courts in Japan have served the rule of law well, at least as measured by careful, consistent, and predictable decision-making that is largely insulated from the kinds of corruption that undermine legal institutions in many other Asian countries.[80] Yet some analysts worry that Japanese criminal justice has been so consistent and predictable that trials have been rendered 'empty shells' and 'meaningless rituals'.[81] By injecting the common sense of lay people into the criminal process, Japanese reformers hope that trials will become more meaningful venues for substantive decision-making, instead of merely forums for the ratification of decisions that are made long before the trial even starts. Where trial systems face similar problems of overly predictable outcomes – as, perhaps, in South Korea, China, Taiwan, Mongolia, Singapore, Malaysia, Thailand, and Vietnam – similar solutions may look attractive.

Another reason for increased lay involvement in Japan's legal process is the desire to improve the standing of the judiciary in the eyes of the public. This need for legitimacy has been forcefully advanced by many legal scholars and professionals, including Chief Justice James Spigelman of the Supreme Court of New South Wales, who noted that if people are perceived to have a significant role in administering justice, the judiciary will be insulated from criticisms that it is remote or out of touch.[82] This belief is also one reason why Japan's own Supreme Court became willing to promote a *saiban-in* system that reduces the authority of professional judges. Where trial systems suffer from similar concerns about legitimacy, as appears to be the case in many parts of Asia, lay participation may help repair the reputation of courts and raise public regard for judicial decision-making.[83]

Finally, since lay participation in criminal trials puts powerful pressure on the state to behave properly, it can lead to better governance and to the promotion of more civic engagement and popular sovereignty. The chairperson of Japan's Justice System Reform Council, Professor Koji Sato, proposed the *saiban-in* system because he believed Japanese people were too accustomed to being ruled from above and not sufficiently engaged with the democratic institutions of a modern liberal state.[84] Similarly, other participants and observers have made arguments that 'rule *by* law' rather than 'rule *of* law' characterizes Japan's legal system. Some research suggests that higher order ideals of democracy and the rule of law can be facilitated through jury participation.[85] In the United States, for example, the voting rates of former jurors are significantly higher than those of persons who have not participated in Tocqueville's 'Little Parliaments'.[86] If this finding is found elsewhere, then reformers in the emerging democracies of Asia might want to consider the potential civic and political benefits of introducing or expanding systems for lay participation.

In the end, Japan's hybrid system for criminal trials may be one attractive option for some developing states in Asia without much history of lay participation in criminal justice. Notably, Japan's new system is neither a foreign nor a Western imposition, and Japan itself is unlikely to aggressively market this model elsewhere in the region.[87] But since globalization means (among other things) the exchange of information across national borders, evidence about how Japan's new criminal trials are doing may be as interesting to reformers in Bangkok and Kuala Lumpur as it is in Sendai and Fukuoka. For this reason – and because Japan's new criminal courts are the most important institutional reform in Japanese criminal justice in more than half a century – we, too, will continue watching how this institution develops.[89]

Notes

1. *Saiban'in no sanka suru keiji saiban ni kansuru hôritsu* (*The Act Concerning Participation of Lay Assessors in Criminal Trials*), *Law No. 63/2004*; translated at Kent Anderson and Emma Saint, "Japan's Quasi-Jury (*Saiban-in*) Law: An Annotated Translation of the Act Concerning Participation of Lay Assessors in Criminal Trials," *Asian-Pacific Law and Policy Journal* 6 (2003): 233. Hereinafter *Lay Judges Act*.
2. Kent Anderson and Leah Ambler, "The Slow Birth of Japan's Quasi-Jury System (saiban-in seido): Interim Report on the Road to Commencement," *Journal of Japanese Law* 21 (2006): 55.
3. Justice System Reform Council, *Recommendations of the Justice System Reform Council – A Justice System to Support Japan in the 21st Century 2001* (2001), ch. V, pt 1.
4. Anna Dobrovolskaia, "The Jury System in Pre-War Japan: An Annotated Translation of 'The Jury Guidebook' (Baishin Tebiki)," *Asian-Pacific Law and Policy Journal* 9 (2008): 231–2.
5. Justice System Reform Council, *Recommendations of the Justice System Reform Council – A Justice System to Support Japan in the 21st Century 2001*, ch. IV, pt 1(4).
6. Ryuichi Hirano, "Diagnosis of the Current Code of Criminal Procedure," trans. Daniel H. Foote, *Law in Japan: An Annual* 22 (1989):129.
7. David T. Johnson, *The Japanese Way of Justice: Prosecuting Crime in Japan* (New York: Oxford University Press, 2002), 279.
8. Mark J. Ramseyer and Minoru Nakazato, *Japanese Law: An Economic Approach* (Chicago, IL: University of Chicago Press, 1999), 7.
9. Mark J. Ramseyer and Eric B. Rasmusen, *Measuring Judicial Independence: The Political Economy of Judging in Japan* (Chicago, IL: The University of Chicago Press, 2003), 170.
10. See generally, Bent Flyvbjerg, *Rationality and Power: Democracy in Practice* (Chicago, IL: The University of Chicago Press, 1998).
11. David T. Johnson, "Nihon ni okeru Shiho Seido Kaikaku: Keisatsu no Shozai to Sono Juyosei," (Justice System Reform in Japan: Where Are the Police and Why It Matters) *Horitsu Jiho* 76 (2004): 8.
12. David T. Johnson, "Above the Law? Police Integrity in Japan," *Social Science Japan Journal* 6 (2003): 19–27; Johnson, "Nihon ni okeru Shiho Seido Kaikaku: Keisatsu no Shozai to Sono Juyosei," (Justice System Reform in Japan: Where Are the Police and Why It Matters) 8–15; David T. Johnson, "Chohoki teki Sonzai: Nihon no Keisatsu ga Shiho Seido Kaikaku kara Hazusareta Riyu," (Above the Law: Why the Japanese Police Were Omitted from Justice System Reform) *Causa* March (2004): 39–44; David T. Johnson and Satoru Shinomiya, "Rights Reforms and Missing Rights in Japanese Criminal Justice," in *Emerging Concepts of Rights in Japanese Law*, ed. Harry N. Scheiber and Laurent Mayali (Berkeley, CA: The Robbins Collection, 2007), 23–48.
13. Satoru Shinomiya, "Saibaninho wa Keiji Jitsumu no Genba ni Nani o Motarashite Iru ka," (What Does the Saiban-in Law Bring to the Prosecutors' Actual Place of Practice) *Hogaku* 644 (2008): 1.
14. Anderson and Ambler, "The Slow Birth of Japan's Quasi-Jury System (saiban-in seido): Interim Report on the Road to Commencement," 76.
15. David T. Johnson, "Kazemuki o Shiru no ni Otenki Kyasuta wa Iranai: Nihon ni okeru Torishirabe Rokuon-Rokuga ni tsuite Gasshukoku to Kankoku kara Manabu koto," (You Don't Need a Weather Man to Know Which Way the Wind Blows: Lessons from the United States and South Korea for Recording Interrogations in Japan) *Ho to Shinri* 5 (2006): 76.

16. Shinomiya, "Saibaninho wa Keiji Jitsumu no Genba ni Nani o Motarashite Iru ka," (What Does the Saiban-in Law Bring to the Prosecutors' Actual Place of Practice) 1.
17. Ibid.
18. Johnson, *The Japanese Way of Justice: Prosecuting Crime in Japan*, 47.
19. John H. Langbein, "Torture and Plea Bargaining," *The University of Chicago Law Review* 46 (1978): 19.
20. Daniel H. Foote, *Na mo Kao mo Nai Shiho: Nihon no Saiban wa Kawaru no ka*, trans. Masayuki Tamaruya (Tokyo: NTT, 2007); Akira Goto, "Saibanin Seido o Meguru Tairitsu wa Nani o Imi Shite Iru ka," (What Do the Conflicts Over Japan's Lay Judge System Mean?) *Sekai* 779 (2008): 90–100.
21. Justice System Reform Council, *Recommendations of the Justice System Reform Council – A Justice System to Support Japan in the 21st Century 2001*, ch. I, pt 3(1).
22. Daniel H. Foote, "Justice System Reform in Japan," http://www.reds.msh-paris.fr/communication/docs/foote.pdf, 1.
23. Foote, "Justice System Reform in Japan," http://www.reds.msh-paris.fr/communication/docs/foote.pdf, 7; Hiroshi Fukurai, "The Rebirth of Japan's Petit Quasi-Jury and Grand Jury Systems" (paper presented at the Citizen Participation in East Asian Legal Systems Symposium, Ithaca, New York, September 22, 2006).
24. Luke Nottage, Leon Wolff and Kent Anderson, *Corporate Governance in the 21st Century: Japan's Gradual Transformation* (Cheltenham, UK: Edward Elgar, 2008), ix. Symbolically, the shift from the Showa to the Heisei era and the start of the twenty-first century may also have created more openness to change than had previously existed (Foote, "Justice System Reform in Japan," http://www.reds.msh-paris.fr/communication/docs/foote.pdf, 8).
25. Setsuo Miyazawa, "Politics of Judicial Reform in Japan: The Rule of Law at Last?," *Asian-Pacific Law and Policy Journal* 2 (2001): 103.
26. Foote, "Justice System Reform in Japan," http://www.reds.msh-paris.fr/communication/docs/foote.pdf, 10.
27. Eric Feldman, "The Culture of Legal Change: A Case Study of Tobacco Control in 21st Century Japan," *Michigan Journal of International Law* 27 (2005–6): 744–5.
28. Anderson and Ambler, "The Slow Birth of Japan's Quasi-Jury System (saiban-in seido): Interim Report on the Road to Commencement," 59.
29. Ibid.
30. The Japanese police sensed that they were unlikely to do themselves much good by weighing in on a matter – criminal trial procedure – in which they were widely perceived to be secondary participants, and they seemed satisfied that legal reform would not directly challenge many of their investigatory prerogatives. They therefore adopted no clear position on the shape that lay participation should take (Johnson, "Nihon ni okeru Shiho Seido Kaikaku: Keisatsu no Shozai to Sono Juyosei," [Justice System Reform in Japan: Where Are the Police and Why It Matters] 8). As explained later in this chapter, they may have miscalculated.
31. In April 2005, Japan's Lower House unanimously approved the *Lay Assessor Act, Law No 63/2004* and one month later the Upper House approved it by a vote of 180 to 2 (Anderson and Ambler, "The Slow Birth of Japan's Quasi-Jury System (saiban-in seido): Interim Report on the Road to Commencement," 61).
32. *Lay Judge Act* art. 2(i)(ii).
33. *Lay Judge Act* art. 3(1).
34. "Top Court Seeks Lay Judge Budget," *Japan Times*, August 27, 2008, http://search.japantimes.co.jp/cgi-bin/nn20080827a6.html.
35. Supreme Court of Victoria, "2006–7 Annual Report," http://www.supremecourt.vic.gov.au/wps/wcm/connect/Supreme+Court/resources/file/eb8cb54f3b77f77/

Supreme%20Court%20of%20Victoria%20Annual%20Report%202006–7.pdf, 27; National Centre for State Courts, "State of the State Survey of Jury Improvements," http://www.ncsconline.org/D_Research/cjs/pdf/SOSCompendiumFinal.pdf, 7 (noting there are estimated 148,558 jury trials in the United States in 2006 with 66 per cent being criminal).

36. Johnson, *The Japanese Way of Justice: Prosecuting Crime in Japan*, 13.
37. *Lay Judge Act* art. 20.
38. *Lay Judge Act* art. 14.
39. *Lay Judge Act* art. 15.
40. *Lay Judge Act* art. 16.
41. *Lay Judge Act* art. 41.
42. *Lay Judge Act* art. 16(vii).
43. *Lay Judge Act* arts 2(2)–(3).
44. *Lay Judge Act* arts 2(2)–(3).
45. Ramseyer and Rasmusen, *Measuring Judicial Independence: The Political Economy of Judging in Japan*, 103; John Owen Haley, *Authority without Power: Law and the Japanese Paradox* (New York: Oxford University Press, 1991), 125.
46. *Lay Judge Act* art. 6(1).
47. *Lay Judge Act* art. 6(2).
48. *Lay Judge Act* arts 56–59.
49. *Lay Judge Act* art. 67.
50. *Lay Judge Act* art. 67(2).
51. *Lay Judge Act* arts 71–73.
52. *Lay Judge Act* arts 77–78, 80.
53. *Lay Judge Act* arts 79, 82–83.
54. Japan's secrecy provisions seem to be more extreme than those in other jury and lay judge systems, and they have drawn at least five criticisms. First, both lay and professional judges are required to maintain confidentiality, but only the former are subject to criminal punishment for breaking the obligation. Second, lay judges in Japan may experience 'vicarious traumatization' from listening to some of life's most troubling stories, yet the law allows no exception for them to speak to counselors, judges, or family members about what they have experienced. Third, there is no outlet for lay judges to report the illegal or inappropriate actions of fellow assessors (such as consulting the Internet or flipping a coin) or the overbearing behavior of professional judges. Fourth, the secrecy provisions may impede public understanding of the judicial system, which is ostensibly one of the main purposes of the lay judge reform. And fifth, Japan's information controls may contradict the Constitutional principles of media freedom (Article 21) and open criminal trials (Article 34). See Mark Levin and Virginia Tice, "Secrecy of *Saiban-in*: Potential Pitfalls of Japan's New Lay Assessor System," *Asia-Pacific Journal* 19–6–09 (May 9, 2009), 1–15.
55. Neil Vidmar, ed., *World Jury Systems* (New York: Oxford University Press, 2000), 447.
56. Philip E. Tetlock, *Expert Political Judgment: How Good Is It? How Can We Know?* (Princeton, NJ: Princeton University Press, 2005); Nassim Nicholas Taleb, *The Black Swan: The Impact of the Highly Improbable* (New York: Random House, 2007).
57. Shinomiya, "Saibaninho wa Keiji Jitsumu no Genba ni Nani o Motarashite Iru ka," (What Does the Saiban-in Law Bring to the Prosecutors' Actual Place of Practice) 1.
58. Daniel H. Foote, "Reflections on Japan's Cooperative Adversary Process," in *The Japanese Adversary System in Context: Controversies and Comparisons*, ed. Malcolm M. Feeley and Setsuo Miyazawa (New York: Palgrave Macmillan, 2002), 29.
59. Foote, "Justice System Reform in Japan," http://www.reds.mshparis.fr/communication/docs/foote.pdf, 24.
60. Lester W. Kiss, "Reviving the Criminal Jury in Japan," in *World Jury Systems*, ed. Neil Vidmar (New York: Oxford University Press, 2000), 378; Dobrovolskaia,

"The Jury System in Pre-War Japan: An Annotated Translation of 'The Jury Guidebook' (Baishin Tebiki)," 277.

61. Robert E. Precht, "Japan, the Jury," *New York Times*, December 1, 2006, http://query.nytimes.com/gst/fullpage.html?res = 9801E2DC1E3EF932A35751C1A9609C8B63#
62. There are, of course, other important questions that we cannot engage here. Will professional judges dominate lay assessors during the deliberation process, as apparently occurs in some of the mixed courts of Europe? (Kent Anderson and Mark Nolan, "Lay Participation in the Japanese Justice System: A Few Preliminary Thoughts Regarding the Lay Assessor System from Domestic Historical and International Psychological Perspectives," *Vanderbilt Journal Transnational Law* 38 [2004]: 935.) Will the selection of lay judges and the new trial procedures be so time-consuming and cumbersome that they will generate incentives to avoid contested trials through plea-bargaining-like practices? Will the greater unpredictability of lay judge trials cause prosecutors to relax their charging standards, thus leading to more acquittals? (Johnson, *The Japanese Way of Justice: Prosecuting Crime in Japan*, 271.) Will the need for evidence to be presented in open court at lay judge trials produce more transparency in pre-indictment interrogations and investigations? Will the public's seemingly lukewarm reaction to the lay judge reform endure and, if it does, will it affect how the system operates?
63. David T. Johnson, "Parole Debate Misses the Central Question," *International Herald Tribune*, August 8, 2008, 22. In the six years between 2001 and 2006, Japanese District Courts imposed 81 death sentences, nearly triple the number (28) they imposed in the previous six years (1991–6). And in the 18 months that started on 25 December 2006, Japan carried out more hangings – 23 – than it performed in the previous nine years (David T. Johnson and Franklin E. Zimring, *The Next Frontier: National Development, Political Change, and the Death Penalty in Asia* [New York: Oxford University Press, 2009], 69).
64. Leah Ambler, "The People Decide: The Effect of the Introduction of the Quasi-Jury System (Saiban-in Seido) on the Death Penalty in Japan," *Northwestern University Journal of International Human Rights* 6 (2007–8): 1–23.
65. Johnson and Zimring, *The Next Frontier: National Development, Political Change, and the Death Penalty in Asia*, 302.
66. Scott E. Sundby, *A Life and Death Decision: A Jury Weighs the Death Penalty* (New York: Palgrave Macmillan, 2005), 161ff.
67. Johnson, "Parole Debate Misses the Central Question," 22.
68. David T. Johnson, "Japanese Punishment in Comparative Perspective," *Hanzaishakaigaku Kenkyu* 33 (2008):.
69. Su-Hyun Lee, "Suwon Journal: Justice Is Swift for Novice Korean Jurors," *New York Times*, July 17, 2008, http://www.nytimes.com/2008/07/17/world/asia/17jury.html?partner = rssnyt&emc = rss. In April 2007, South Korea's National Assembly enacted the *Act for the Civil Participation in Criminal Trials*. This introduced a quasi-trial-by-jury system into Korea's criminal process, 'the first substantial change to [Korean] criminal trials, investigations, and indictments' since 1954 (Sung-woo Park, "Korea's First Jury Reaches a Verdict," *JoongAng Daily*, February 13, 2008, http://joongangdaily.joins.com/article/view.asp?aid = 2886143). In the new Korean system: (1) five, seven or nine jurors hear cases (depending on the seriousness of the charge) along with three professional judges; (2) the jury's decision must be unanimous, and when jurors cannot reach unanimity on their own, they meet with the judges to deliberate further, though the judges are not allowed to vote on the verdict; (3) the jury's decision does not bind the judges with respect to verdict or sentence; and (4) the defendant has the right to choose whether to have the case heard by judges or by a jury. More than 100 criminal cases will be tried under the new system in 2008, and the early returns suggest that 'jury trials appear to be leading to a higher rate of

acquittals, as jurors debate and question prosecutors' assumptions' (Lee, "Suwon Journal: Justice Is Swift for Novice Korean Jurors," http://www.nytimes.com/2008/07/17/world/asia/17jury.html?partner = rssnyt&emc = rss). But there are also complaints that the new system is generating judgments that are too fast and rough (Lee, "Suwon Journal: Justice Is Swift for Novice Korean Jurors," http://www.nytimes.com/2008/07/17/world/asia/17jury.html?partner = rssnyt&emc = rss). South Korea will continue to experiment with its jury trial system until 2012, when a decision will be made about whether to make it permanent.

70. Precht, "Japan, the Jury," http://query.nytimes.com/gst/fullpage.html?res = 9801E2DC1E3EF932A35751C1A9609C8B63#
71. Rudy Monteleone, "Australian Experience with Lay Participation and its Relevance to Jury Reform in Japan" (paper presented at Australian Network for Japanese Law (ANJeL) Conference, Canberra, July 6, 2007).
72. Vidmar, *World Jury Systems*, 435. Worldwide, at least 55 countries and dependencies have 'pure' jury systems, while mixed tribunals of professional and lay judges exist in many other places (Vidmar, *World Jury Systems*, 3).
73. Vidmar, *World Jury Systems*, 435.
74. Ibid.
75. Lee Kuan Yew quoted in Chris Lydgate, *Lee's Law: How Singapore Crushes Dissent* (Melbourne: Scribe Publications, 2003), 38.
76. Vidmar, *World Jury Systems*, 437.
77. Ibid., 447.
78. Ibid.
79. Lawrence W. Sherman, "Evidence-Based Crime Prevention: A Global View from the US to Japan," *Hanzai Shakaigaku Kenkyu* 29 (2004): 91. See also Malcolm Gladwell, *The Tipping Point: How Little Things Can Make a Big Difference* (New York: Little, Brown & Co., 2000).
80. Haley, *Authority without Power: Law and the Japanese Paradox*, 13–14; John Owen Haley, *The Spirit of Japanese Law* (Athens, GA and London: The University of Georgia Press, 1998), 115; John Owen Haley, "The Japanese Judiciary: Maintaining Integrity, Autonomy, and the Public Trust," in *Law in Japan: A Turning Point*, ed. Daniel H. Foote, (Seattle, WA and London: University of Washington Press, 2007), 99, 112. For a more critical account of judging in Japan, see Ramseyer and Rasmusen, *Measuring Judicial Independence: The Political Economy of Judging in Japan*, and for a summary of different assessments of the Japanese judiciary, see Frank K. Upham, "Political Lackeys or Faithful Public Servants? Two Views of the Japanese Judiciary," *Law and Social Inquiry* 30 (2005): 421–55.
81. Johnson, *The Japanese Way of Justice: Prosecuting Crime in Japan*, 6.
82. Chief Justice James Spigelman quoted in Kent Anderson and Mark Nolan. "Reintroducing a Criminal Jury in Japan: Reform Lessons for Us All?," *Reform* 90 (2007): 47.
83. For a classic discussion of the functions and conditions of 'legitimacy' in different stages of legal development, see Philippe Nonet and Philip Selznick, *Law and Society in Transition: Toward Responsive Law* (New York: Harper & Row, 1978).
84. Carol Lawson and Simon Thornley, "Translation: 'Perceptions of the Current State of the Japanese Legal System': Interview with Kōji Satō, Chairman of Japan's Judicial Reform Council," *Australian Journal of Asian Law* 4 (2002): 80.
85. Jeffrey Abramson, *We, The Jury: The Jury System and the Ideal of Democracy* (New York: Basic Books, 1994); Vidmar, *World Jury Systems*.
86. John Gastil, E. P. Deess and P. J. Weiser, "Civic Awakening in the Jury Room: A Test of the Connection between Jury Deliberation and Political Participation," *Journal of Politics* 64 (2002): 585–95.

87. Foote, "Justice System Reform in Japan," http://www.reds.msh-paris.fr/communication/docs/foote.pdf, 8.
88. For analysis of Japan's first two lay judge trials, which occured in August 2009, see David T. Johnson, "Early Returns from Japan's New Criminal Trials," *The Asia-Pacific Journal* Vol 36–3–09, 7 September 2009, available at http://www.japanfocus.org/-David_T_-Johnson/3212

19 Dollars to donuts

Japanese courts' new role as corporate regulator

Veronica L. Taylor

Introduction

Within the last decade or so, many new and specialized courts have emerged throughout Asia. Japan represents the counter-factual example: a highly developed, unitary court system that has been largely preserved since World War II.[1] The unity of Japan's court system has been underscored by a systemic emphasis on judicial consistency: a single cohort of career judges, uniformly educated, socialized to uphold high professional standards and concerned with producing predictable outcomes.[2] For the most part – at least in relation to civil and commercial cases – Japan's courts are not slow, do not lack competence and do not lack resources. Japan's prolonged economic stagnation after the collapse of the 'bubble' economy in 1989, however, provoked a legitimacy crisis for most of the government sector, and the courts were not immune from this. The Justice System Reform Council, established in 1998, delivered wide-ranging reform prescriptions for the courts in 2001,[3] targeting in particular areas of perceived weakness, such as intellectual property dispute processing and the opacity of criminal procedure. The reforms in these areas are described in the chapters by Shigenori Matsui, and Kent Anderson and David Johnson, respectively.

This chapter traces an equally important but more subtle systemic shift – the combination of regulatory influences that have caused Japan's courts, in their ordinary civil and commercial jurisdiction, to emerge as assertive regulators of large corporations. While this gradual shift in court posture is less dramatic than the creation of a separate, specialized court of the kind found elsewhere in Asia, it represents a controversial development within Japan, and for outside observers, an example of remarkable judicial capacity to respond to a range of new economic, political and social pressures.[4]

Through a case-study of a recent set of shareholder derivative suits concerning directors' duties, this chapter looks at the response of the civil and commercial jurisdiction of the Osaka District and High Courts and considers two questions raised in the Introduction to this book: What do we mean by a 'new' court? and How do we evaluate 'new' court performance?

The case-study discussed in this chapter is a pair of shareholder derivative suits commenced in the Osaka District Court in the early 2000s against the large

Japanese corporation Duskin, parent company of the Japanese fast-food franchise 'Mr Donuts'. In *Duskin*,[5] directors and auditors of both Mr Donuts and Duskin were sued on behalf of the company for corporate losses that occurred when the Mr Donuts chain knowingly sold Chinese-manufactured food products that contained an additive not approved for use in Japan.

The Osaka District Court award of US$97 million in this case became the second-highest initial award against corporate directors and auditors following the decision in *Daiwa Bank* – an initial award of US$775 million, later reduced to US$2 million, as part of a settlement that preserved the findings of liability against the directors and auditors.[6] The shareholder derivative suit in *Daiwa Bank* sought damages from the bank's directors and statutory auditors for, *inter alia*, failure to supervise a New York-based local hire, whose illegal trades resulted in multi-million dollar losses and ultimately the cancellation of Daiwa's banking licence in the United States. The finding of director liability in *Daiwa Bank* was based in part on clear statutory breaches of the relevant federal and New York State banking laws, but also on the failure to institute a system of internal corporate controls, and on corporate cover-up, concealment of facts from regulators and a failure to stem losses arising from the employee's illegal acts. In *Duskin*, as we will see, the courts at both the first instance and appellate levels unambiguously expand the scope of directors' duties quite dramatically beyond *Daiwa Bank*, making *Duskin* the current 'high-water mark' in corporate accountability and risk management in Japanese corporate law.[7]

The hypothesis of this chapter is simple: that the courts reached this result in *Duskin* not through any formal restructuring or changes to the general commercial law jurisdiction, but in response to changes in the surrounding regulatory environment that induced the courts to consolidate their role as corporate regulators after *Daiwa Bank*. The new factors, clearly visible in *Duskin*, include: prolonged economic recession; greater media scrutiny of large corporations and their management failures; the institutionalization of civil shareholder suits as predictable consequences of statutory breach by large corporations; the emergence of lawyer and non-governmental organization (NGO) shareholder bodies as corporate monitors through shareholder suits; a public regulatory discourse involving much greater awareness of risk management; procedural reforms since 1993 allowing more suits to be filed against large corporations; and the continued filtration of United States corporate governance concepts into Japanese corporate law, illustrated in the watershed directors' duties decision in *Daiwa Bank*.[8] These elements have combined to create a new regulatory climate in Japan, within which the courts are both able to – and expected to – take on a more assertive role in responding to illegal, negligent or reckless acts by large corporations. The result has been, I suggest, a 'new' role for existing courts, evidenced in the style of court decision in the important decision in *Duskin*. This presents a new opportunity for us to evaluate Japanese courts' responsiveness to multiple stakeholders – national and local government, NGOs, the media, and shareholders – as they define their role as corporate regulators. In this chapter I test that hypothesis in three parts below.

In the first part, I briefly describe the Japanese court system and some of the key structural and procedural reforms that have occurred within it since 1989, the collapse of Japan's asset bubble economy, and the introduction of the Justice System Reform Agenda.[9] In the second part, I illustrate the courts' response to a changed regulatory environment by analysing the decision in *Duskin*. In the third part, I discuss the regulatory significance of *Duskin* and *Daiwa Bank*, which seem to recast the courts' role in relation to business in Japan. This is most obvious in the blunt language of the decisions, which includes lengthy criticism of the parties and is clearly intended to mark out the 'shadow of the law' for other corporate actors in Japan. Both *Duskin* and *Daiwa Bank* represent record damages awards within a system with no punitive damages. *Duskin*, like *Daiwa Bank* before it, resonated in business circles in Japan for this reason.[10] Finally, *Duskin* can be read as courts reflecting the policy directions of the executive in the Justice System Reform process, where the overarching intent was to shift Japan's regulatory style from an administrative model of *ex-ante* problem-avoidance to an *ex-post facto* reliance on remedies.[11] For these reasons, it seems likely that the new style of decision-making for Japanese courts evidenced in *Daiwa Bank* and now confirmed in *Duskin* is one that is likely to continue.

Structural change within a single court hierarchy

Japan's court system

Japan's modern courts sit within a constitutional framework developed as part of the post-war Occupation reforms.[12] The 1947 *Constitution of Japan* (*Constitution*) confirmed Japan as a unitary state with a single court hierarchy, within which the Supreme Court controls judicial training and appointment and is the final court of appeal for all Summary, District and High Courts. From District Court level and above, all courts have general jurisdiction (including judicial review of constitutionality).[13] All cases are entitled to an automatic appeal on the facts and the law, and a second appeal on questions of law.[14] The 1947 *Constitution* provided for the establishment of one special court – the Family Court – which operates in parallel with District Courts, but is staffed and overseen by the Supreme Court in the same way as courts of general jurisdiction.

Japan belongs to the civil law tradition: its statutory codes are European-influenced, and judges are career appointees who, in theory, interpret the codes and special-purpose legislation, rather than making law through cases. In practice, Japan's legal system is significantly hybridized; much of the late twentieth century Japanese borrowing of legal concepts and doctrines has been from both American and European Union models and no legal scholar or practitioner today doubts that Japanese judges, and the case-law that they make, are as significant as statutory provisions as a source of law. The needs of a modern regulatory state have also shifted the system firmly towards case-law as a means of responding to new and complex social and economic questions.[15] Equally important has been the shift in legal *mentalité* towards Anglo-American law, as large numbers of young judges, prosecutors, attorneys and legal scholars are dispatched annually to the United States by the Supreme Court, Prosecutors' Office, law firms and universities for research and credentialing.

Japan's courts are also characterized by a professionalized, elite judiciary.[16] The standard path is completion of a law degree, selection through the national bar exam and a period of practical training at the Supreme Court Judicial Research and Training Institute, in company with classmates who will become prosecutors and attorneys.[17] The incidence of judicial misconduct and corruption is extraordinarily low and this is usually explained with reference to judges' high social status and in the very tight institutional control exercised by the Supreme Court Personnel Secretariat.[18] This section of the Court arranges the routine rotation of judges through rural and urban postings, promotion and – rarely – disciplinary action. Judges are expected to act as a uniform cohort of public servants and to be somewhat anonymous.[19]

Until Japan introduced graduate-level law schools in 2004, judges' pre-appointment education was generally limited to the discipline of law and/or politics. This would typically be an undergraduate degree in a faculty of law,[20] followed directly by passing the national bar exam and entry to, and completion of, the Supreme Court Judicial Training and Research Institute. Appointments to the bench from other branches of the profession were extremely rare, except in the case of the Supreme Court. At the Supreme Court level, in addition to judges who are promoted through the court hierarchy, the 1947 *Court Organization Law* (Article 41) permits the appointment of persons 'of broad vision and extensive knowledge of law', of whom at least ten must be drawn from the ranks of judges, public prosecutors, lawyers and professors or assistant professors of law in universities. As a matter of convention, Supreme Court appointees include distinguished former attorneys and prosecutors as well as non-lawyers in addition to career judges. The appointments are notable for their lack of partisanship.[21]

Japanese judges' exposure to business and/or legal practice is minimal and was seldom remarked upon during Japan's sustained economic growth period (the 1960s to the early 1990s), when courts were not a preferred venue for business disputation.[22] Courts' low profile was also, John Haley argues, a result of government deliberately limiting the size of the judiciary and tightly controlling court resources and, thus, access.[23]

This is not to say that courts were not used: Japanese courts have long been important as spaces for public protest. In the 1970s and 1980s, protest litigation forced the government along a path of statutory reform in fields such as the environment, mass torts, civil rights for minorities and gender equality.[24] That pattern was repeated during the 1990s in litigation arising from government regulatory failure which left blood transfusion patients in Japan infected with the HIV virus[25] and is now evident in the surge of cases involving medical malpractice.[26] This tension between the courts as government-controlled organs of the state and as venues for citizen mobilization of law is not unique to Japan. In the 1990s it manifested as a scholarly debate about the degree of political 'independence' enjoyed by judges.[27]

By the late 1990s, however, policy-makers in Japan were concerned not about any lack of court independence, but rather about their accountability. Government bureaucrats concerned with Japan's trade performance were expressing dissatisfaction with Japan's capacity to handle cross-border disputes in new technical fields such as intellectual property[28] and competition law, while domestically criticism was mounting that a country as affluent as Japan still lacked an equitable distribution of legal services.[29]

The government response to these pressures was not to create new, special courts, but instead to carry out thoroughgoing reforms of the existing judicial system. The policy blueprint developed was the 'Justice System Reform' package, a planning process commenced under the Obuchi cabinet of 1998, when fundamental changes to the courts, provision of legal services and legal education were mooted.[30] These were then finalized in a Justice System Reform package in 2001.[31] The final set of reforms was enacted in a wave of special legislation[32] carried out vigorously under the Koizumi administration (2001–6)[33] and then, with less intensity, by its successors, the Abe (2006–7) and Fukuda (2007–8) administrations, and currently by the embattled Aso administration (2008 –present). Viewed against the pace of legal reform between World War II and 1990, the policy and reform prescriptions that it contained were both comprehensive and surprisingly swift.

The 1990s structural reforms and court responses

In this chapter we focus exclusively on the legal and regulatory changes, including the policy package that impacted corporate actors in Japan. The first of these were structural reforms to the justice system. These included:

1. new, specialized divisions in the Tokyo and Osaka District Courts for hearing cases arising under new bankruptcy laws;
2. the adoption of a national intellectual property and technology strategy and the creation of specialized intellectual property courts in Tokyo and Osaka;[34]
3. the revision of the *Arbitration Law* and the development of new, consolidated alternative dispute resolution legislation; and
4. the expansion of professional jurisdictions of both foreign lawyers and non-attorney legal service providers (breaking the litigation monopoly of attorneys).[35]

More controversially, the reform agenda required the complete redesign of legal education and mandated a dramatic increase in the number of candidates permitted to pass the national bar examination and then become judges, prosecutors and attorneys.[36]

A second cluster of changes was procedural. These predated, or ran in parallel to, the Justice System Reform agenda. So, for example, in 1993 an important barrier to shareholder actions against management was removed, when the filing fees for shareholder derivative suits were reduced to a nominal flat-fee amount.[37] In 1996, Japan overhauled its *Code of Civil Procedure*, updating its archaic language and streamlining its provisions. The *Code of Civil Procedure* reforms, which became effective in 1998, also introduced a modified system of pre-trial discovery and created a new small claims procedure that operated as a continuous hearing rather than the periodic hearings which were then standard in other civil and criminal litigation.[38] New consumer protection statutes were introduced that streamlined product liability claims, whether advanced through alternative dispute resolution or through litigation.[39]

These changes responded to concerns about the efficient processing of disputes in Japan. Bureaucrats, with the support of some peak business bodies, had promoted the perception that business was not well served by the courts in Japan. However, many observers did not regard processing times for filed cases in Japan as particularly slow and indeed, beyond the civil procedure reforms of 1998, no dramatic reform to the handling of civil and commercial cases occurred under the Justice System Reform agenda. Recent data from Tokyo District Court (Division 8), which handles corporate governance, bankruptcy, and competition litigation, for example, confirms the efficiency of Japanese courts: the average time from filing to conclusion for commercial cases is 8 months, in a system that uses discontinuous hearings.[40] Significantly, only 48 per cent of cases proceed to a decision – many cases conclude more quickly. Of those that do, 52 per cent are withdrawn, or are settled, or use court-annexed conciliation.[41] Similarly, the Court's disposition rate for new cases is improving annually (in 2006 only 8 per cent of cases remained unresolved).[42]

By contrast, delays in Japanese litigation do occur at the appellate level. The automatic right to appeal from decided cases leads to a second full hearing of the case if it is appealed. Perhaps for this reason, courts continue to regard settled outcomes as desirable. What is new in the Tokyo District Court data above is the court's own analysis – explicit and repeated references to the need to be responsive to the 'relevant parties', and the need to both create and show newly improved/introduced procedures, such as those introduced for bankruptcy after the passage of the 2000 *Civil Rehabilitation Law*.[43] Moreover, the need to show – rather than simply to assert – competence is underscored by the court. The Tokyo District Court characterizes its decision to provide three judges hearing cases as a panel (where a single judge at District Court level is not uncommon) as a way to maintain institutional memory and 'know-how' for commercial litigation within a system of national judicial rotation.[44]

A third group of commercial legal reforms since 1990 has been substantive. The tempo of corporate law reform changed dramatically as Japan's economic downturn deepened. *Commercial Code* reforms from 1996 onwards became extensive, annual and in some cases politically, rather than bureaucratically, led.[45] The reforms focused first on strengthening corporate organs, borrowing and adapting the Anglo-American concept of 'corporate governance'. This is well illustrated in the 2002 *Commercial Code* reforms that allowed corporations to adopt United States-style committee structures for organizing their management.[46] Then, effective in

May 2006, a new *Companies Act* was introduced, which provided a wide-ranging menu of corporate forms and governance structures – including the committee structure – for small, medium and large-scale businesses.[47]

The combined effects of these structural, procedural and substantive reforms can be seen in the increased civil and commercial litigation in the period 1986–2001, particularly in the civil divisions of the District Courts in Tokyo and Osaka.[48] Glen Hoetker and Tom Ginsburg view the procedural reforms as a key driver in the rise of civil litigation in Japan, which to them signals the repudiation of an earlier cultural 'reluctance' to litigate.[49] This, however, assumes that litigation involves choice, whereas some types of proceedings – for example, insolvency – may be financially induced and procedurally necessary, but not a first choice strategy of either party.[50]

Certainly the composition and subject-matter coverage of commercial cases in the 1990s changed. Insolvency cases are a prime example, but other kinds of cases also map the unravelling of transactions that underpinned the Japanese economy during the 1980s and 1990s. Examples include final attempts to recover debts from insolvent or near-insolvent transaction partners; attempts to enforce personal guarantees by owner/directors of corporations; non-payment of insurance claims by failing insurance companies; and claims against builders/developers by property owners who were promised fixed (or stable) rates of return on redeveloped and leased property, so-called 'sub-lease' cases.[51]

While the conventional wisdom in Japanese law until the early 1990s was that large corporations neither sued nor appeared as named parties in litigation, the last decade shows civil and commercial case reports peppered with the names of well-known Japanese corporations.[52]

Shareholder representative litigation (derivative suits) against management, in particular, have increased markedly after the 1993 reduction in filing fees.[53] After an initial surge, derivative suits have settled into a fairly stable pattern of filings at the rate of 20–30 cases per year.[54] A typical pattern is for large-scale torts, fraud, or illegal acts (such as payment of political contributions or payment of bribes to organized crime) by large corporations to be prosecuted as criminal acts or statutory breaches initially and then to be re litigated as civil derivative suits. While there is no doubt that shareholder derivative suits in Japan are generally mobilized by attorneys, the legitimacy of this type of litigation was helped by the fact that many plaintiffs were backed by NGO watchdogs set up specifically for the purpose of shining light on corporate malfeasance, and adding impetus to government policies promoting transparency and accountability.[55] The possibility of such suits also pushed many corporations to restructure their governance systems, develop compliance departments and pay much closer attention to the direct application of regulatory law to their operations. A push-back statutory reform following the *Daiwa Bank* case in 2000, in turn, allowed corporations to cap the liability of their directors and corporate officers.[56] Taken together, however, the changes represented a regulatory environment from the 1990s onwards that became far less tolerant of banks, insurance companies, trading companies and other large corporations' management failures.

How did the courts respond to this climate of heightened regulatory awareness and increases in commercial litigation? The next section explores those court responses in relation to the latest case on directors' duties arising from a shareholder representative action: *Duskin*.

The *Duskin* case[57]

Facts

The *Duskin* case comprises a series of related decisions between 2005 and 2007 arising from the same facts.[58] The parent corporation in this case, Duskin, is a large listed corporation with headquarters in Osaka, Japan.[59] It is a multinational conglomerate business with five different business divisions and numerous affiliated and subsidiary companies. One of these is 'Mr Donuts', a franchised chain that currently has 1,300 retail food outlets.[60] In Japan, Mr Donuts was originally known for its cheap coffee and tasty donuts. In 1992, the company decided to add Chinese dim sum to the menu.[61] As a culinary combination, coffee, iced donuts, wontons and steamed pork buns seems dubious, but market competition may have been a driver.[62]

The decision to add the dim sum items led Mr Donuts into complex supply chain arrangements and some subcontracted production in China. From a risk management standpoint, Mr Donuts was exposed on three fronts: managing quality assurance in the supply chain; reliance on imported products from a developing country; and as a food retailer, the need to maintain food safety and public trust.[63]

The Japanese market is very sensitive to food safety issues. Food imports from China, particularly, have become politically charged because of fears about national food security and the economic threat of imported products claiming market share. Chinese food products have also been the target of Japanese consumer fears about food product safety.[64] Consumer fears are justified, in light of a long line of corporate scandals and mass torts in Japan to date involving food contamination, production and packaging.[65] The result has been that even the smallest production problem concerning food receives intense media scrutiny within Japan.

Mr Donuts' troubles began with the addition to its menu of a line of large steamed pork buns (*dainikuman*: 大肉まん).[66] This product was initially subcontracted to one supplier, with another supplier under consideration for a contract if they could meet the product quality level. At a tasting event, two industry insiders – actually competing suppliers who were themselves transacting with Duskin – pointed out to Duskin managers that the current supplier of this product was known to be using a non-approved additive. The additive in question was TBHQ,[67] which acts as an antioxidant in oils and as an anti-spoiling agent. Although widely used in the United States and other countries and not regarded as toxic in the minute amounts used in fast food products, it was not approved under Japan's *Food Sanitation Law*.[68] Between the start of production and the point at which Duskin stopped distributing the product, Mr Donuts' stores had sold tens of millions of pork buns with the non-approved additive.[69]

At no stage were there any consumer complaints or reports of consumers suffering ill-effects from Mr Donuts' pork buns. However, upon becoming aware of the additive problem on or around 8 December 2001, Duskin's Senior Managing Director at the time (Director B),[70] who was responsible for the Food Service Group, and Director A, Duskin's Manager responsible for the Mr Donuts' franchise business, decided to sell all of the remaining inventory. At the same time, Director A paid their informants a total of JPY63,000,000 (approximately US$583,000) for reasons that appeared to have no legitimate business basis. Sometime later, these facts were leaked to regulators.[71] The Ministry of Health Labour and Welfare issued Duskin with a notice and on 15 May 2002 conducted a site inspection of eight Mr Donuts' outlets in Osaka. The press was alerted and on 20 May 2002 Duskin held a press conference and made the facts public. The next day, the story of the use of the non-approved additive, the continued sales of the product, the corporate cover-up and the 'hush money'[72] paid were extensively covered in media reports.[73]

What had been a relatively minor problem in production, with no ill-effects on consumers, then spiralled into significant economic loss for the company. Duskin lost an estimated JPY10,561,000,000 (approximately US$97,290,957) between the time the problem became public and the end of that financial year (March 2003), largely attributable to a sales slump in Mr Donuts' chain stores.[74] The amount of losses claimed was calculated as:

- compensation for five months of lost profits by chain stores, resulting in reduced royalties JPY5,752,000,000 (US$52,740,320);
- advertising campaign costs JPY2,016,000,000 (US$18,510,400);
- additional support mechanisms for chain stores JPY1,700,000,000 (US$15,735,860);
- newspaper coverage and advertising aimed at restoring business confidence, including posters and advertising inserts JPY684,000,000 (US$6,553,830); and
- changing the dim sum menu, destroying inventory and destroying inventory past its 'use-by' date JPY346,000,000 (US$2,776,780).[75]

These losses then led to a series of shareholder representative actions (derivative suits), filed by plaintiff shareholders against Duskin management. The targets of the litigation were Duskin's current and former directors and statutory auditor(s).[76] Of these, four directors were principally involved in shaping the events leading to the losses and two of those four had first-hand or early knowledge of the problem and were the primary decision-makers in the corporate response. Accordingly, the shareholder actions proceeded in parallel against these two directors and then against a further eleven directors and statutory auditor(s).

The first case, *Duskin Case No. 1* was filed 4 April 2003 in the Osaka District Court; a second case, *Duskin Case No. 2* was filed 2 May 2003.[77] *Duskin Case No. 1* and *Duskin Case No. 2* were then consolidated in the same court on 11 June 2003. These consolidated cases were subsequently separated on 2 June 2004 into the case concerning two defendant directors and the case concerning 11 defendant directors and statutory auditors.

The Osaka District Court gave its decision in the action against the two directors on 9 February 2005,[78] finding them liable for the full amount of damages claimed JPY10,561,000,000 (approximately US$97,290,957). On appeal by the two defendants (*kōso*, 控訴 or first appeal), in its decision of 18 January 2007, the Osaka High Court upheld the District Court's findings of liability against the two defendants, but reduced the damages award against them by 50 per cent.[79] The plaintiffs filed a *jōkoku* (上告 or second) appeal to the Supreme Court.

The Osaka District Court gave its decision in the action against the 11 defendants on 22 December 2004, finding liability on the part of one director but not others.[80] The plaintiffs and that director appealed to the Osaka High Court (a *kōso* or first appeal). The appellate decision was given on 9 June 2006, where the Osaka High Court then found all 11 original defendants liable, but apportioned the damages against them.[81] Both plaintiffs and defendants filed a *jōkoku* (or second) appeal to the Supreme Court. (The findings of liability on appeal and the damages awards in both sets of decisions are set out in Table 19.3).

Like all complex litigation, *Duskin* features a large cast of characters. In addition to the multiple past and present directors and statutory auditor(s) there was also a long tail of suppliers and subcontractors, many of whom had potential claims and counter-claims against each other and Duskin. In this chapter, we focus only on the management players and summarize their profiles in Table 19.1. Different reports of the decisions and commentary in Japanese code the multiple defendants differently; in this chapter, I have re-labelled and unified all the references to the defendants as Directors A, B, C, D and 'others' to be consistent with Table 19.1.

The decisions at first instance

At each stage of this parallel litigation the overarching question was whether the directors, individually and together, had breached their duties to the corporation. In Japanese corporate law the 'fiduciary duties' of directors broadly divide into two related branches:

a *Duty of care.* Directors have a duty to the company as a mandatory (or agent), as defined in *Commercial Code* Article 254, paragraph 3. This provision is interpreted as importing the general obligation of mandatories from the *Civil Code*[82] Article 644: '[a] mandatory is obligated to manage the

Table 19.1 'Who's who?' in the Duskin case[1]

Director A	Jun 2000	Appointed Director, Mr Donuts Franchise Chain Business Head Office
	Dec 2001	Steps down
Senior Managing Director B	Jun 1994	Appointed Director, Production Division
	Apr 1997	Appointed Managing Director responsible for management of Head Office Business (*jōmu torishimariyaku*: 常務取締役)
	Apr 1999	Appointed Senior Managing Director (*senmu torishimariyaku* : 専務取締役) responsible for Food Business Division
	Jun 2001	Steps down; appointed advisor (*komon* : 顧問)
	Dec 2001	Contract as advisor terminated
Senior Managing Director C Later, (new) company president	Jun 1994	Appointed Director, Mr Donuts Division
	Apr 1997	Appointed Director Production Division
	Jun 2000	Appointed Managing Director Production Division (*senmu torishimariyaku* : 専務取締役)
	Apr 2001	Appointed Representative Director (*daihyō torishimariyaku* : 代表取締役) and Company President
	Nov 2002	Steps down
Director and President D	Jun 1994	Appointed Representative Director (*daihyō torishimariyaku* : 代表取締役) and Company President
	Jun 2000	Appointed Chair of Representative Directors' Committee and Company President
	Jun 2001	Steps down

Source: 1 Tracking the directors, what they knew and when they knew it, is complex; even the Japanese commentaries have mistakes and cross-references to different coding in the court reports. This summary table is adapted from Akira Takeuchi, "Dasukin jiken kōsai hanketsu de torishimariyaku ni hatasareta shinraikaifuku gimu: Osaka kōsai han heisei 18.6.9 ni miru kuraishisumanejimento no arikata," (The duty to restore trust imposed on directors in the Duskin High Court decision: What the 9 June 2006 Osaka High Court decision tells us about crisis management) *NBL* 860 (2007): 31.

entrusted affairs with *the care of a good manager* in accordance with the tenor of the mandate'.[83]

b *Duty of loyalty*. The directors' duty of loyalty to the corporation requires that '[t]he directors shall comply with law, ordinances and the provisions of the articles of incorporation, as well as resolutions adopted at the general meeting, and shall perform their duties faithfully on behalf of the company'.[84]

The duties are conceptually distinct (the duty of loyalty, for example, most obviously applicable in cases of director's self-dealing) and they date from different points in the evolution of Japanese corporate law; the duty of loyalty was imported from the United Sates in 1950.[85] In practice, as is obvious from the language of the provisions, there can be overlap in the scope of the two duties and a breach of one quite often involves a breach of the other, and so courts quite often treat the duties as running together and the consequences of breach as identical.

In this case, the two directors with direct knowledge of the additive problem, and those to whom they reported were, prima facie, in breach of their duty of loyalty to comply with the law and with the company's articles of incorporation. In *Duskin* the articles of incorporation did create an express duty to report serious problems to the company's officers. The same analysis can be applied to the hush-money payments, which were clearly expenditures made in violation of company accounting policy and the articles of incorporation.

The second level of analysis in the each of the cases was whether the acts taken (or not taken) constituted breaches of the duty of care – whether, as they learned of the problem, individual directors and statutory auditor(s) had exercised 'the care of a good manager' by making an appropriate discretionary decision – the equivalent of the United States 'business judgment rule'.[86]

The directors' individual and collective actions are easier to evaluate if we look at the chronology of key actions in the cases, as shown in Table 19.2.

In the case at first instance against the Directors A and B (see Table 19.1), the Osaka District Court found for the plaintiffs in relation to all claims.[87] On the question of breach of the duty of loyalty, in the form of compliance with law, the answer was clear. Prior to the litigation, Duskin Ltd submitted a report acknowledging the breach of the *Food Sanitation Law* and outlining the corporate sanctions (salary cuts and demotions) applied to all of the directors involved.[88] Similarly, the hush-money payments had no business basis that court found persuasive or legitimate, and so these too, were acts in violation of the duty of loyalty.

The earlier *Daiwa Bank* case had already established a duty to have in place an internal control system for the corporation. In Duskin's case the corporation had in place a rather elaborate internal system for risk management that included:

- a company-wide risk management checklist with clear lines of report and decision-making, including a legal response team and a product liability response team;
- articles of incorporation that mandated serious problems involving customers, stores, factories and transactions to be reported to the management committee;[89]
- employee training on the company's own internal manuals and procedures, which included trouble-shooting and reporting protocols; and
- a detailed risk management seminar on 13 July 2002 run by the advisor to Fuji Fire and Marine Insurance that focused on the (then) recent losses suffered by the Snow Brand Milk Company when problems at its Osaka production plant were discovered and made public.[90]

Table 19.2 Chronology of actions by management in the *Duskin* case[1]

May 2000	Test sales of pork buns (400,000 units monthly). Of two suppliers at the time, one is using a non-approved additive
6 Oct 2000	Sales expanded nationally (5,000,000 units monthly)
30 Nov 2000	At a taste test meeting, supplier M points out that the competing supplier's products have the non-approved additive; potential supplier N is also present at the meeting. This is reported to Director A, who acknowledges the information
2 Dec 2000	The supplier using the additive voluntarily ceases production of the pork bun (at this point sales of product with non-approved additive total 13,140,000 units), issues a formal apology to Duskin and asks to be reinstated as a supplier. Director A reports on the illegal additive problem to Senior Managing Director B, who acknowledges the information
8 Dec 2000	Directors A and B decide to sell the remaining inventory of pork buns
13 Dec 2000	Director A pays M JPY8,000,000
15 Dec 2000	Director A pays M JPY25,000,000
20 Dec 2000	Sales of pork bun inventory are completed
29 Dec 2000	Potential supplier N reports to Managing Director C about the additive problem; C acknowledges the information. C demands an explanation from A and accepts the explanation
18 Jan 2001	A pays M JPY30,000,000 in the presence of N
8 Feb 2001	N reports to President D about the non-approved additive; D acknowledges the information. President D demands an explanation from A and B and accepts the explanation
July 2001	Other directors request details from A; the process to date comes to light and other directors acknowledge the detailed information
18 Sep 2001	At the instigation of an outside director, an internal corporate investigation committee is formed
28 Oct 2001	An outside director sends an urgent action memo to the (new) company President, President C
6 Nov 2001	The internal corporate investigation committee submits its report without touching on whether it should be made public. (New) President C consults with senior corporate officers and they decide to take no positive action to make the issues public
29 Nov 2001	At the Board of Directors meeting the investigation committee's report is released. A and B are sanctioned and the Board concurs with the decision to take no positive action to make the issues public
15 May 2002	Company receives a directive from Ministry of Health Labor and Welfare; eight retail outlets in Osaka are subjected to site inspections
20 May 2002	The media reports pick up the events; Duskin Ltd holds a press conference and makes public the facts to date
21 May 2002	Reports escalate and include details of the deliberately continued sales, the hush money payments and the deliberate internal cover-up
31 May 2002	Osaka Metropolitan government issues an administrative order banning Mr Donuts from selling or restocking pork buns manufactured in China
4 September 2003	Directors A and B and Duskin are fined for (criminal) breaches of the *Food Sanitation Law*[2]

Source: 1 Akira Takeuchi, "Dasukin jiken kōsai Hanketsu de torishimariyaku ni hatasareta shinraikaifuku gimu: Osaka kōsai han heisei 18.6.9 ni miru kuraishisumanejimento no arikata," (The duty to restore trust imposed on directors in the Duskin High Court decision: What the 9 June 2006 Osaka High Court decision tells us about crisis management) *NBL* 860 (2007): 31.

2 Japan's *Food Sanitation Law* was extensively amended and a new *Food Safety Law* introduced in May 2003.

Duskin's risk management also extended to its suppliers and subcontractors, who were selected, vetted and monitored in a rigorous process, which included site visits to their manufacturing facilities and independent testing of their products prior to releasing them for sale. In fact, one of the business issues that Directors A and B had been wrestling with around the time of the additive problem was management of this supply chain. Recurrent scandals in Japan where food was discovered to contain foreign matter, plus the fact that all of Duskin's suppliers for this food line were manufacturing in China, had added some pressure to the contractual problem of managing competing suppliers. One of these was N, the aspiring supplier who had so helpfully pointed out the non-approved additive in his competitor's product. N was being held at arm's length because his company's manufacturing facilities did not meet Duskin's exacting standards. Directors A and B later revisited that decision and N was hurriedly given a one-year supply contract in 2000 to commence in January 2001. He was later terminated in October 2001, whereupon he sued Duskin.[91]

Since Duskin's risk management system was demonstrably in place, the case then turned on the actions of the directors post-discovery of the additive. In particular, the court looked at the question of whether the acts of Directors A and B, in covering up the breach, continuing to sell the product, and making hush-money payments to the informants were causally linked to the losses suffered by the corporation. On this question the court found a clear causal link, because in essence Director A and B's actions had forestalled an opportunity for management to take a business decision at an early stage of the problem.

The court reasoned that:

> [I]n this case, knowing that they had breached the *Food Sanitation Law* the defendants decided to continue with sales and so there was a possibility that for some reason, or in some way, consumers would discover those facts. Consequently, regardless of whether Duskin's other directors decided to make public the fact of the sales – and irrespective of when that decision would be made – there was a possibility that consumers would come to know of the sales and become anxious and uncertain about the safety of Duskin's food products, resulting in loss of trust in the company and reduction of sales with financial losses inflicted on the company.
>
> Certainly, in relation to the losses in this case, [the outcome would be influenced by] for example, decisions such as whether to stop sales of pork buns that did not contain TBHQ; how much advertising would be necessary to restore confidence in the corporation; what support would be necessary for loss of sales by member stores, so not all of these [resulting losses] were caused solely by the fact of the continued sales.
>
> Nevertheless, determining the total amount of these losses was a matter requiring a decision based on the situation in which Duskin was placed and with full consideration of the circumstances. Because the directors at the time had a broad discretion, in the absence of evidence to the contrary, [one]

> could have anticipated a process of [deliberation], and a result from business decision-making by the directors [and thus] at law, the causal relationship between the defendants' acts and the losses in this case cannot be denied.[92]

In the claim against the remaining 11 defendants at first instance, the key question was whether these other directors and statutory auditor(s) were liable for breaching their duties to exercise 'the care of a good manager', once they knew of the problem. The plaintiff claimed that inaction by these directors had resulted in Duskin losses in the amount of JPY10,561,000,000 (approximately US$97,290,957), plus the hush-money payment of JPY63,000,000 (approximately US$583,000).

The court found against Duskin's then Senior Managing Director (Director C) for becoming aware of the problem on or about 29 December 2000, but not communicating this to Director D (then Representative Director and President) or to the Board of Directors. However, the court at first instance imposed no liability on Director D, who had no direct knowledge of the sales, nor on the other Defendants (Directors and Statutory Auditors), who became aware of the problem after July 2001.[93]

That decision was appealed to the Osaka High Court by the plaintiffs and Managing Director C. The Osaka High Court set aside the District Court's finding, instead determining that *all* the Directors and Statutory Auditor(s) were liable, albeit it in differing degrees.

The decisions on appeal

Both decisions of first instance were appealed. As with other civil and criminal cases in Japan, the first appeal is of right and both the facts and law of the case are subjects of the appeal.

In relation to the two defendant directors, the Osaka High Court reduced the damages award against the defendant-appellants by 50 per cent, to JPY5, 343,500,000 (approximately US$51,134,487).

In reaching that decision, the court followed much of the District Court's reasoning and accepted the plaintiff-respondents arguments that the defendant-appellants had in fact breached their directors' duties. In calculating the causality between the defendant-appellants acts and the corporation's losses, the court accepted all the heads of loss claimed by the plaintiff-appellee, but then continued:

> If we accept these [losses], the amount of damage suffered as a result of the causal relationship between the appellants' breach of duty of care and the cost of Duskin restoring confidence in the corporation, considering the JPY10,561,000,000 claimed, we should recognize the losses that would have occurred as a result of expenditure to restore corporate confidence, even if the defendants had fully exercised their duty of care.

When considering what amount of loss would have been suffered in order to restore confidence in the corporation, even if the appellants had fully exercised their duty of case, it is difficult to readily calculate a concrete figure. However, pursuant to our finding ... above,

i if we compare the significant social criticism of Snow Brand Milk's posture of concealment, the flight of consumers and the resulting drop in its sales, with the Santen Pharmaceuticals public announcement [of a problem with foreign matter in an eye solution] and their product recall, which did not attract strong outcry, and the facts determined in this case, where there was a cover up of the additives to the food product; continued sales and then intense media coverage, particularly of Duskin's deliberate continued sale of pork buns in breach of the *Food Sanitation Law*; the fact that hush money in the amount of JPY630,000,000 was paid and that further, the (then) President gave instructions that the matter be covered up, and that it was the target of criticism [for these acts] and

ii [then] on the other hand, [consider] that TBHQ is used in the US and more than 10 other countries; that the WHO does not classify it as toxic; that in the quantities in which it was used in the pork buns it would have no effect on health; that there are other additives not permitted in Japan that are deemed to be acceptable elsewhere; that there was information to the effect that had permission been sought for the additive it is likely that it would have been granted; that had the appellants exercised their duty of care and stopped sales immediately, recalled the product, made public the facts, and apologized, it would have been possible to limit the loss of confidence in the corporation and the drop in sales, with the strong possibility that the outlays necessary for supporting the member stores and for lifting their sales and for advertising campaigns could have been limited;

it is reasonable to assess that these losses would not have amounted to more than half of the actual JPY10,561,000,000 losses that occurred.

Accordingly, we find that it is reasonable to assess the causal relationship between the appellants' acts in breaching their duty of care and continuing sales and related acts to Duskin's loss of corporate confidence and the costs of restoring this as being at least half of the claimed amount of JPY10,561,000,000, being JPY5,280,500,000.[94]

The appeal by the plaintiffs against the 11 other defendants, on the other hand, divided broadly into two issues: (1) the duty of the directors who had direct knowledge of the non-approved additives and their actions immediately afterwards; and (2) the duty of the directors who discovered the facts later and their (in)action upon receiving the information.

The claim by the plaintiffs was that the directors' duty of care included a duty to make public the problem. In response, the defendants argued a business judgment rule defence – that they had not breached the duty of care, in part because they had considered the problem and made a decision. Their decision was that, since there was no evidence of the additive causing a health problem, and since it was impossible to recall the products in question, alerting consumers to the problem after the fact would – conversely – cause confusion and contribute to a loss of confidence in the company. For these reasons they decided not to take positive action to announce the problem.

The detailed chronology of facts in Table 19.2 makes this a somewhat difficult argument for the defendant directors to sustain, since the more they deliberately concealed the problem, the more likely the negative response when it was eventually revealed. The directors seemed to be acting in the earnest hope that that concealment would succeed. This is not at all an unusual posture in corporate problems in Japan: the last decade is replete with media reports of corporate scandals and attempts to conceal negligence from regulators and the public, with greater or lesser success in each case. What is puzzling in *Duskin* is that Directors A and B decided on concealment in December 2000 and the other directors acquiesced, immediately following the September 2000 Osaka District Court in *Daiwa Bank* on director liability.[95]

On appeal by the plaintiffs and Director C, the Osaka High Court found that the total damages claimed for losses arising from acts by the plaintiffs, including continued sales of the tainted products and failure to disclose the problem, could be attributed to multiple factors. However, the court viewed key contributing facts as being the cover-up by Directors A and B, who had direct knowledge of the problem *and* the subsequent inaction by the other directors upon discovering the problem.

On the question of whether there was breach by the directors who had no direct knowledge of the problem, but learned of it later, the Osaka High Court found in the affirmative, stating:

> [In a climate where] the mass media posture and public option are very sensitive to corporate malfeasance and cover-ups [*inpei taishitsu* or 隠蔽体質], and where a small scale malfeasance or cover-up is frequently blown up [when discovered] and then pursued and escalates, it is clear from previous cases that this results in loss of confidence, which damages the corporation. Moreover, if we add a situation where – as in this case – there is the provision of JPY63,000,000 for an undisclosed purpose that appears to be a deliberate act of cover-up, and that [the facts relate to] food product safety, it must be said that the fact that this would result in a crisis of existence for the corporation [*kigyōni totte wa zonbō nokiki* or 企業にとって存亡の危機] should have been clearly foreseeable.
>
> Consequently, it is clear that what was required of the managers was to actively consider a strategy to limit, to the minimum degree, the damage from loss of confidence in Duskin corporation resulting from a significant legal act that had already occurred and the likelihood of the situation [we have just described].

> However, ... the defendants did not actively consider such a strategy at the Board of Directors meeting, but rather elected to 'not actively disclose ourselves' and to adopt a see-how-things-go approach [*nariyukimakase no hōshin* or 成り行き任せの方針], [eventually] silently acknowledging the reality in an ambiguous, procedural fashion. This, fundamentally, is not a 'business decision'.[96]

The court elected to analyse the causality of the directors' failure to disclose the problem on an individual basis and apportion damages accordingly. It found Director D (then Representative Director and President) and Director C (then a Senior Managing Director) liable for 5 per cent of the claimed damages and the other nine named defendants each liable for 2 per cent of the claimed damages. Although this is not clear from the reported decision, the latter group presumably includes the external director who raised the matter with the new Company President and insisted on an internal review of the matter (see Table 19.2).

The final apportionment of liability after the two cases at first instance and the two appeals is shown in Table 19.3.

Duskin is not the first case in which director liability has been apportioned among different management actors, but Japanese commentators have debated this aspect of the award.[97] The first question concerns the role of the court in reducing the damages awarded, given that shareholder representative litigation (derivative suits) are themselves an element of internal corporate governance. The new *Corporations Act* provides shareholders with the option of releasing directors from liability for breach of duty through the mechanism of the shareholders' meeting.[98] A second question is whether the basis for the apportionment of liability was clear enough in this case.

The apportioned liability represents a significant increase of penalties on appeal: recall that the court of first instance found insufficient causality between the (in)actions of Director D and the other directors and the loss of trust in the corporation that led to the financial losses sustained.

What was not clear until *Duskin* was whether (in)action by other directors – such as in this case – is a breach of duty once a problem is discovered, whether or not an internal compliance mechanism is in place. In *Duskin*, the directors sought to defend themselves by arguing that their actions fell within the scope of 'business judgment', since no consumers were harmed, the products could not be recalled, and production and sale of the product had ceased.

The appellate court was completely unsympathetic to this stance, with the second appellate court finding in relation to these other directors that no genuine business judgment was exercised. On the contrary, the passivity of the directors contributed to the escalation of negative perceptions of the corporation and, ultimately to the economic loss sustained. This appellate court focuses in particular on the remaining directors' duty to 'limit loss of trust' and to 'restore trust' in the corporation.[99] Part of the rationale for the finding of liability against Director and new company President C was that, at the time at which he became aware of the problem, although barely a year into his tenure, 'it cannot be said that it was

Table 19.3 Apportionment of director liability in Duskin after High Court appeals

	Director A	*Senior Managing Director B*	*Managing Director C/ (new) President*	*Director/ President D*	*Other Directors and Statutory Auditor(s)*
Addition of non-approved additive to pork buns	No	No	No	No	No
Sale of pork buns after becoming aware of non-approved additive	Yes	Yes	No	No	No
Payment of JPY63,000,000 in hush money	Yes	Yes	Partial	No	No
Point at which defendant knew about sale of pork buns with additive	30 Nov 2000	2 Dec 2000	29 Dec 2000	8 Feb 2001	July 2001
Response after acknowledging sale of pork buns with additive	–	–	Yes	Yes	Yes
Causal relationship between damage suffered by corporation and breach of duty of care	50% of claimed losses + JPY63,000,000	50% of claimed losses + JPY63,000,000	5% of claimed losses + JPY30,000,000	5% of claimed losses	2% of claimed losses

impossible to recall [the products]'.[100] On its face, this suggestion was somewhat impractical – after all, Mr Donuts is a fast food outlet. Nine days after the sale of the remaining stock is a little late to tell consumers that you need your pork buns back. What the court was pointing to, however, was a complete absence of action on the part of the company – or indeed, any attempt to fully investigate the facts, inform the company president, or strategize about alerting consumers or recovering tainted products.

The rationale for the finding against Company President D was that, having become aware of a breach of an important statute, he had an obligation to carry out a full investigation about the breach, to discover the cause and to ensure that measures were in place to avoid a re-occurrence of the breach and to consider whether and how to take *ex-post-facto* action such as communicating with the media and the relevant supervisory government agency.[101]

The regulatory significance of *Duskin*

Are the courts doing anything 'new' in *Duskin*? At one level it seems that the court decisions reviewed above build very consciously on *Daiwa Bank*, which turned in part on non-compliance with (foreign) law and the failure to create and maintain internal control systems, for which the directors were heavily penalized. In *Duskin*, there is a breach of law and a breach of directors' duties resulting from failure to comply with statute and with the company's articles of incorporation, but both problems initially appear benign and are remedied. Moreover, in contrast to the facts in *Daiwa Bank*, Duskin was a corporation with a high degree of risk awareness. Here is a Japanese corporation, well-established in its home and off-shore markets and now outsourcing production to China. As a food services retailer, Duskin's Mr Donuts business operates in a highly regulated environment with supply chain risks, food safety risks and consumer confidence risks. Duskin had in place a full set of self-regulating corporate risk management tools. Unfortunately, there was also a corporate culture lag: as soon as a minor supply chain problem surfaced, the directors fell back on the old ways – pay-offs, mutually enforced silence, pro forma internal investigation and belief in the passage of time as a cure-all. Unlike many of the banking scandals of the 1990s, Duskin's response seems not to have involved document shredding, secret rooms or document concealment. Ultimately, however, the failure to pre-emptively use self-regulation and public announcements opens the door to a whistleblower or a leak to regulators. This in turn creates an easy opening for a shareholder representative action and a role for the courts as corporate regulator.

What is interesting about the courts' response in *Duskin* is the very extended criticism of the parties and the condemnation – in unusually blunt language for judges – of the directors' performance. Here the courts, explicitly expand the scope of director's duties of care to acts and inaction *after* a damaging event is discovered and strip away the business judgment defence where they see insufficient attention to the problem. Significantly, the number of directors found guilty of breach of their duties increases, rather than decreases, in the appellate decision.[102]

In *Duskin* it is the external director who insists on an internal investigation, playing a textbook monitoring role, but with the conspicuous lack of success in persuading the internal director group to override their management peers. The results of the internal investigation are shelved. If *Daiwa Bank* was about the duty to have in place an internal control system, *Duskin* is about the directors' duty to use them. *Duskin* also clearly extends the duties of other, less directly involved directors, to restoring trust in the corporation once a problem is discovered, whether or not an internal compliance mechanism is in place.

Duskin clearly builds on *Daiwa Bank*, but is new in the sense that it uncompromisingly articulates new standards of corporate behaviour in an area where, until as recently as 2000, directors' ignorance of regulatory law was treated as a good defence.[103] Thus it becomes the latest stage in a progressive and clear articulation by the Japanese courts of new regulatory norms for large corporations. Both *Duskin* and *Daiwa Bank* suggest, contrary to some American critiques, that Japanese courts have ample institutional capacity to articulate clear commercial rules.[104]

How do we evaluate the court performance in *Duskin*? Both of the *Duskin* appellate decisions were appealed to the Supreme Court, but that second appeal is on questions of law only. Unless all the subordinate courts have made legal errors on the scope of directors' duties, *Duskin* will stand as an important regulatory signal from the courts to corporate managers.

The damages awards in these cases are also important regulatory signals. At both the first instance and first (*kōso*) appeal levels, the *Duskin* decisions represent damages awards many times larger than those in other shareholder derivative suits against directors, within a legal system with no punitive damages. The readiness of the District Court in the action against Directors A and B to award the full JPY10,561,000,000 (approximately US$97,290,957) is breathtaking by Japanese standards, in part because it shows the *Daiwa Bank* damages award at first instance (US$775 million, reduced on appeal through court settlement to US$2 million in order to preserve findings of liability against the defendants, seems not to have been an aberration.[105] Even with the 50 per cent discount on appeal, the award is highly significant and still many times larger than the final *Daiwa Bank* amount payable. On appeal, both *Duskin* awards fell short of the actual losses suffered by the corporation, but were clearly designed as very significant financial sanctions against the directors and corporate officers involved. *Duskin*, like *Daiwa Bank* before it, resonated in business circles in Japan for this reason.[106]

Despite the large damages awards in *Duskin*, the result in hindsight seemed fairly predictable after *Daiwa Bank*: it is not uncommon for Japanese court decisions in corporate and commercial litigation to 'track' previous decisions without directly citing or referring to them.[107] In this sense, *Duskin* may stand for the court consciously injecting some continuity and predictability after the dramatic *Daiwa Bank* decision, in line with their common practice of carefully calibrating damages awards, either according to an internal court-wide scale, or to what the judges determine will be socially acceptable.

Finally, *Duskin* can be read as courts reflecting the policy directions articulated by the members of the Justice System Reform Council in 1999:

> We are in the process of abolishing unclear advance control of administration through economic structural reform and administrative reform to shift to a post-watch / remedy society in order to establish a freer society. In such society, it is a natural prerequisite to establish a system in which all kinds of disputes among the people are solved properly and promptly under fair and clear legal rules ... [108, 109]

In contrast with Japan's high growth decades, when courts were tolerated as a destination of last resort in civil, administrative and economic disputes, we now see a state attempting to harness courts in the service of revitalizing the Japanese economy, and courts responding. For these reasons, at least for the present, it seems likely that this new style of decision-making for Japanese courts evidenced in *Daiwa Bank* and now confirmed in *Duskin* is one that is likely to continue.

Notes

1. Japan is a unitary (i.e. non-federated) state with a single court hierarchy that until recently had only one special purpose court, the Family Court. Shigenori Matsui describes in this book the background to the establishment of Japan's new intellectual property courts.
2. This may seem counterintuitive in a civil law tradition such as Japan's, but there is abundant empirical and anecdotal evidence of the courts formally agreeing and calibrating outcomes in areas such as torts – most recently, medical malpractice. The landmark study in English in relation to torts is Takeo Tanase, "The Management of Disputes: Auto Accident Compensation in Japan," *Law and Society Review* 24 (1990): 65. On court predictability in relation to contract, see John Owen Haley, "Rethinking Contract Practice and Law in Japan," *Journal of East Asia and International Law* 1 (2008): http://ssrn.com/abstract = 1131327
3. Justice System Reform Council, "Final Report," http://www.kantei.go.jp/foreign/judiciary/2001/0612report.html
4. For an overview of the historical foundation of the modern Japanese legal system, see John Owen Haley and Veronica L. Taylor, "Rule of Law in Japan," in *Discourses on Rule of Law in Asia*, ed. Randall Peerenboom (London: Routledge, 2004), 446. For an overview of the key systemic changes in Japan since 1989, see Daniel H. Foote, ed., *Law in Japan: A Turning Point* (Seattle, WA: University of Washington Press, 2008).
5. Note that Japanese court decisions do not assign names to the case or use party names; cases are identified by the date and the court in which the decision was given. Citation in this chapter follows that format. The cases we focus on are the shareholder suit against two of Duskin's directors: Osaka District Court (Division 4 Civil), 9 February 2005, *Shiryoban Shōjihōmu* 256 (2005): 24 and the decision on appeal in that case: Osaka High Court (Division 6 Civil), 18 January 2007, *Shiryoban Shōjihōmu* 275 (2007): 202, as well as the shareholder suit against 11 of Duskins' directors and statutory auditors: Osaka District Court, 22 December 2004, *Hanrei Jihō* 1892 (2005): 108; also reported in *Hanrei Taimuzu* 1172 (2005): 271 and the decision on appeal in that case: Osaka High Court (Division 4 Civil), 9 June 2006 reported *Jurisuto* 1332 (2007): 102.
6. Osaka District Court, 20 September 2000, *Hanrei Jihō* 1721 (2000): 3. The plaintiffs claimed against 47 current and former directors and statutory auditors of the bank, of whom 11 were ultimately found liable of breaching their directors' duties. On appeal the plaintiffs settled for a small fraction of the awarded damages amount (US$2,000,000) and contributions from each of the original 47 defendants, and the settlement preserved the findings on the directors' liability. Partially translated in Bruce E. Aronson, "Learning from Comparative Law in Teaching US Corporate Law: Directors' Liability in Japan and the US," *Penn State International Law Review* 22 (2003): 213, and discussed in Bruce E. Aronoson, "Reconsidering the Importance of Law in Japanese Corporate Governance: Evidence from the Daiwa Bank Shareholder Derivative Case," *Cornell International Law Journal* 36 (2003): 11.

7. The earlier jurisprudence on directors' duties in Japan is discussed and summarized in Mark D. West, "Why Shareholders Sue: The Evidence from Japan," Michigan Law and Economics Research Paper No. 00–010, http://papers.ssrn.com/paper.taf?abstract_id = 251012
8. Osaka District Court, 20 September 2000, *Hanrei Jihō* 1721 (2000): 3.
9. Justice System Reform Council, "Final Report," http://www.kantei.go.jp/foreign/judiciary/2001/0612report.html
10. "Dasukin kabunushi soshōhanketsu no kōgeki," (The impact of the decision in the Duskin shareholder action) *Nikkei shimbun* (Nikkei Newspaper) August 28, 2006 quoted in Akira Takeuchi, "Dasukin jiken kōsai hanketsu de torishimariyaku ni hatasareta shinraikaifuku gimu: Osaka kōsai han heisei 18.6.9 ni miru kuraishisumanejiment no arikata," (The duty to restore trust imposed on directors in the Duskin High Court decision: What the 9 June 2006 High Court decision tells use about crisis management) *NBL* 860 (2007): 30.
11. Justice System Reform Council, "The Points at Issue in the Justice Reform," http://www.kantei.go.jp/foreign/policy/sihou/singikai/991221_e.html
12. Japan has a long pre-modern tradition of formal bureaucratic administration of justice through a court system: For an authoritative summary of that history, see Dan Fenno Henderson, *Conciliation and Japanese Law: Tokugawa and Modern*, 2 vols (Seattle, WA: Association for Asian Studies / University of Washington Press, 1965). For a more recent essay on pre-modern Japanese law, see Carl Steenstrup, "New Knowledge Concerning Japan's Legal System before 1868, Acquired from Japanese Sources by Western Writers since 1963," in *Law in Japan: A Turning Point*, ed. Daniel H. Foote (Seattle, WA: University of Washington Press, 2008), 7.
13. 1947 *Constitution of Japan* art. 81.
14. The Supreme Court now exercises discretion in accepting appeals, whereas until 1998, appellate cases proceeded to that Court automatically, resulting in 'a staggering case-load': John Owen Haley, "The Japanese Judiciary: Maintaining Integrity, Autonomy and Public Trust," in *Law in Japan: A Turning Point*, ed. Daniel H. Foote (Seattle, WA: University of Washington Press, 2008), 105.
15. Reflected in the intense study of cases in Japanese law school courses and a wealth of commercial legal publishing based on both case reports and commentary on cases.
16. Elite in the sense of small numbers selected from a rigorous examination system. On the judiciary generally, see Haley, "The Japanese Judiciary: Maintaining Integrity, Autonomy and Public Trust," 105. On career preferences, see Curtis J. Milhaupt and Mark D. West, "Law's Dominion and the Market for Legal Elites in Japan," Michigan Law and Economics Research Paper No. 02–006 and Columbia Law and Economics Working Paper No. 206, http://ssrn.com/abstract = 316120.
17. Historically, the bar exam was also open to non-university graduates and this option remains, for the time being, following the reforms that created graduate level law schools from 2004.
18. Haley, "The Japanese Judiciary: Maintaining Integrity, Autonomy and Public Trust," 105.
19. The most obvious example of this is the typical inability of an average Japanese university-educated person to name any of the country's Supreme Court bench – or to be particularly concerned that they cannot.
20. Institutionally the home of both the disciplines of law and politics.
21. Haley, "The Japanese Judiciary: Maintaining Integrity, Autonomy and Public Trust," 107.
22. John Owen Haley, "The Myth of the Reluctant Litigant," *Journal of Japanese Studies* 4 (1978): 359–89.
23. Ibid.

24. Frank Upham, *Law and Social Change in Postwar Japan* (Cambridge, MA: Harvard University Press, 1987), presenting four case studies of toxic tort litigation, environmental litigation, gender discrimination litigation and litigation by the Japanese *burakumin* (部落民) (outcaste) minority.
25. Eric A. Feldman, *The Ritual of Rights in Japan: Law, Society and Health Policy* (New York: Cambridge University Press, 2000), a book-length study of the HIV-contaminated blood product scandal and litigation.
26. See, for example, Robert B. Leflar, "Medical Error, Deception, Self-Critical Analysis and Law's Impact," in *Law in Japan: A Turning Point*, ed. Daniel H. Foote (Seattle, WA: University of Washington Press, 2008), 409.
27. See J. Mark Ramseyer and Eric B. Rasmusen, *Measuring Judicial Independence: The Political Economy of Judging in Japan* (Chicago, IL: University of Chicago Press, 2003) (arguing, *inter alia*, that judges who find against the government are penalized in truncated career paths); and Haley, "The Japanese Judiciary: Maintaining Integrity, Autonomy and Public Trust," 107 (arguing, *inter alia*, that Japan has an enviable record of no direct political interference in judicial appointments and performance, particularly at Supreme Court level).
28. Toshiko Takenaka, for example, argues that United States patent owners and domestic industries have long complained about the slow and inadequate relief provided by Japanese courts in patent infringement cases. Some Japanese patent owners have even indicated that they would rather litigate in United States courts than Japanese courts, because Japanese courts have been slow to give relief, and the relief given was too small to cover their legal expenses. Responding to these criticisms, the Ministry of International Trade and Industry (MITI) and the Japanese Patent Office (JPO) announced the goal of restructuring the patent system to give quick and strong patent protection. They reviewed the possibility of creating a special court with exclusive jurisdiction over patents and other industrial property. The Supreme Court of Japan has also, for the first time, started to pay attention to whether the judicial system provides adequate protection: Toshiko Takenaka, "Comparison of US and Japanese Court Systems for Patent Litigation: A Special Court or Special Divisions in a General Court?," http://www.law.washington.edu/CASRIP/Symposium/Number5/pub5atcl6.pdf
29. See the discussion in Setsuo Miyazawa, "Law Reform, Lawyers and Access to Justice" in *Japanese Business Law*, ed. Gerald P. McAlinn (Alphen aan den Rijn, Netherlands: Wolters Kluwer, 2007), 52–3.
30. Veronica L. Taylor "Re-regulating Japanese Transactions: The Competition Law Dimension," in *Japanese Governance: Beyond Japan Inc*, ed. Peter Drysdale and Jennifer Amyx (London: Routledge Curzon, 2003), 138.
31. Justice System Reform Council, "Final Report," http://www.kantei.go.jp/foreign/judiciary/2001/0612report.html
32. In the Japanese legal system 'special' legislation refers to individual statutes dealing with specific areas of (usually new) regulation. These are contrasted with, and often override, the general legal principles governing civil, commercial and criminal matters contained in the five basic codes and the *Constitution* (together referred to as the six codes (*roppō* or 六法).
33. The Koizumi Cabinet under Finance Minister and former academic Heizo Takenaka re-regulated the banking and insurance industries, provided state-backed restructuring for failing banks, and privatized the postal system. For Takenaka's personal account see Heizo Takenaka, *The Structural Reforms of the Koizumi Cabinet* (Tokyo: Nikkeishimbunsha, 2008).
34. Discussed in Shigenori Matsui's chapter in this book.
35. The reforms also stressed the theme of citizen access to justice, and under this rubric, major changes included the introduction of a new lay jury system for serious criminal

trials and improved government and legal profession provision of improved legal aid services. See the discussion in Setsuo Miyazawa, "The Politics of Judicial Reform in Japan: The Rule of Law at Last?," in *Raising the Bar: The Emerging Legal Profession in Asia*, ed. William P. Alford (Cambridge, MA: East Asian Legal Studies / Harvard University, 2007), 121–3.

36. See, for example, Miyazawa, "The Politics of Judicial Reform in Japan: The Rule of Law at Last?," 107.
37. The *Commercial Code* provisions have since been superseded by the 2005 *Companies Act*; article 847 sets out the conditions for bringing shareholder derivative suits. The policy background to the reform is discussed in West, "Why Shareholders Sue: The Evidence from Japan," http://papers.ssrn.com/sol3/papers.cfm?abstract_id = 251012.
38. 1996 *Code of Civil Procedure* arts 368–81.
39. See, for example, Luke Nottage, "Product Liability and Safety Regulation," in *Japanese Business Law*, ed. Gerald P. McAlinn (Alphen aan den Rijn, Netherlands: Wolters Kluwer, 2007), 221.
40. Yasushi Kanokogi and Kazuhiro Yamaguchi, "Tokyo chisai ni okeru shōjijiken no gaikyo," (The general situation of commercial cases in the Tokyo District Court) *Shōjihōmu* 1796 (2007): 13.
41. Meaning either a rejection of the suit; a judgment upholding the claims; or a judgment rejecting claims.
42. Rates differ for listed and unlisted companies.
43. The introduction of the 2000 *Civil Rehabilitation Law, Law No. 225/1999* marked an increase in the number of bankruptcy filings in Japan, with the courts responding by establishing special divisions in the Tokyo and Osaka District Courts for speedy processing. The reforms and the other legislative pathways to bankruptcy and corporate reorganization are analysed in detail in Kent Anderson and Trevor Ryan, "Reorganization and Bankruptcy," in *Japanese Business Law*, ed. Gerald P. McAlinn (Alphen aan den Rijn, Netherlands: Wolters Kluwer, 2007), 595.
44. Yasushi Kanokogi and Kazuhiro Yamaguchi, "Tokyo chisai ni okeru shōjijiken no gaikyo," (The general situation of commercial cases in the Tokyo District Court) 13.
45. Gilson and Milhaupt tabulate the major *Commercial Code* changes relating to companies between 1993 and 2002 in Ronald J. and Curtis J. Milhaupt, "Choice as Regulatory Reform: The Case of Japanese Corporate Governance," ECGI-Law Working Paper No. 22/2004; Columbia Law and Economics Working Paper No. 251 and Stanford Law and Economics Olin Working Paper No. 282, http://papers.ssrn.com/sol3/papers.cfm?abstract_id = 537843
46. Ibid.
47. *Law No. 86/2005* on Company Law; translated as Companies Act at http://www.cas.go.jp/jp/seisaku/hourei/data/CA1_4.pdf.
48. This comes about procedurally because of the ceiling on the monetary value of cases brought before the lower Summary Courts, which handle small claims, and because a plaintiff suing a corporation generally is required to bring suit in the jurisdiction (court district) in which the corporation is physically located. With some notable exceptions, large corporations are overwhelmingly headquartered in Tokyo and Osaka.
49. Glenn P. Hoetker and Tom Ginsburg, "The Unreluctant Litigant? An Empirical Analysis of Japan's Turn to Litigation," Illinois Law and Economics Research Paper No. LE04–009, http://ssrn.com/abstract = 608582
50. Insolvency proceedings can be a prerequisite for installing new management or appointing a receiver. Significantly, the 1990s in Japan was also a period of record post-war levels of personal bankruptcy and corporate insolvency. New insolvency legislation created new frameworks and procedures, and the courts responded by setting up divisions equipped to handle personal bankruptcy and corporate insolvency

and educating themselves and court-appointed receivers (often attorneys) about this new practice area. See, generally, Anderson and Ryan, "Reorganization and Bankruptcy," 595.

51. Examples of cases in these categories can be found readily in the major Japanese legal reporters: *Jurisuto*, *Hanrei Jihō*, *Hanrei Taimuzu*, *NBL* and *Shōji Hōmu* as well as the commercially available electronic case database *Riigaaru Beesu* (Legal Base).
52. A useful shorthand guide to this is the *Shōjihōmu kenkyūkai* published cumulative listing of derivative suits in Japan with its case report of each new action. The table summarizes parties and cause of action. Recent listed companies that have featured include Nomura Securities, Snow Brand Milk, Mizuho Financial Group. See, for example, "Shuyōna kabunushi daihyōsoshōjiken ichiranhyō," (Major shareholder representative actions at a glance) *Shōjihōmu* 281 (2007): 136.
53. See the cumulative listing in "Shuyōna kabunushi daihyōsoshōjiken ichiranhyō," (Major shareholder representative actions at a glance) *Shōjihōmu* 281 (2007): 136.
54. Yasushi Kanokogi and Kazuhiro Yamaguchi, "Tokyo chisai ni okeru shōjijiken no gaikyo," (The general situation of commercial cases in the Tokyo District Court) 15.
55. West, "Why Shareholders Sue: The Evidence from Japan," http://papers.ssrn.com/sol3/papers.cfm?abstract_id = 251012; Curtis J. Milhaupt, "Nonprofit Organizations as Investor Protection: Economic Theory, and Evidence from East Asia," *Yale Journal of International Law* 29 (2004): 169.
56. Aronoson, "Reconsidering the Importance of Law in Japanese Corporate Governance: Evidence from the Daiwa Bank Shareholder Derivative Case," 11.
57. Japanese case reports are cited by date and the subject matter of the litigation, not by party name. Most commercial reports of the case also render the party names simply as X and Y. In keeping with that style of citation, I have called this the *Duskin* case (covering two filings at first instance and two appeals) and code the key defendants as Directors A, B, C and D.
58. In addition to the two parallel cases discussed in this chapter, cases filed against Duskin relating to these facts include *Duskin Case No.3* (claim for damages arising from company's own share buy-back; dismissed) Osaka District Court 9 November 2005 and (later appealed to the Osaka High Court) and *Duskin Case No. 4* (claim for damages) filed in the Osaka District Court in 2005 *Shiryoban Shōjihomu* 261 (2006): 233.
59. Duskin, "Kaisha gaiyō," (Corporate Overview) http://www.duskin.co.jp/company/gaiyo/index.html. Listed capital in August 2008 was JPY11,352,940,000
60. 1,100 outlets at the time of the case: "Dasukin kabunushi daihyōsoshō jiken hanketsu (hikoku 2mei bun)," (Decision in the Duskin shareholder suit: Results against two defendants) *Shiryoban Shōjihōmu* 256 (2005): 22.
61. "Dasukin kabunushi daihyōsoshō jiken hanketsu (hikoku 2mei bun)," (Decision in the Duskin shareholder suit: Results against two defendants) *Shiryoban Shōjihōmu* 256 (2005): 32.
62. Competitors and later market entrants, including Starbucks, and the refurbished Doutor coffee chains, offer multiple savoury food items in addition to coffee and pastries.
63. See the (unofficial) translation of the *Food Safety Basic Law, Law No. 48/2003*: http://www.fsc.go.jp/sonota/fsb_law160330.pdf
64. Those fears were well illustrated in January 2008 when *gyōza* or 餃子(meat dumplings) imported from China and distributed through Japanese supermarkets were found to contain toxic levels of pesticide and again in September 2008 when rice imported from China and contaminated with pesticide was sold to Japanese hospitals and nursing homes: Kyodo News, "119 hospitals in Kinki got Inedible Rice," *The Japan Times*, September 12, 2008, 1.

65. See generally, Luke Nottage, *Product Safety and Liability Law in Japan: From Minamata to Mad Cows* (London: Routledge Curzon, 2004).
66. Literally 'big meat buns' but typically the meat is pork (or pork-like).
67. Tertiary butylhydroquinone. For a link to the World Health Organization's 1975 evaluation of this additive, see World Health Organization, "Toxicological Evaluation of Some Food Colours, Thickening Agents, and Certain Other Substances," http://www.inchem.org/documents/jecfa/jecmono/v08je11.htm
68. Article 6 of the *Food Sanitation Law, Law No. 233/1947* (as amended); translated at http://www.cas.go.jp/jp/seisaku/hourei/data/fsa.pdf. See also, the *Food Safety Law, Law No. 48/2003*. For an explanation of how the Ministry of Health Labour and Welfare approves food additives in Japan, see Ministry of Heath Labour and Welfare, "Food Additives," http://www.mhlw.go.jp/english/topics/foodsafety/foodadditives/index.html
69. Between May and 20 December 2000, Mr Donuts reportedly sold 13,140,000 units.
70. Senior Managing Director is *senmu torishimariyaku* (専務取締役) in Japanese. This, along with Managing Director (*jōmu torishimariyaku*: 常務取締役) is a common designation within large companies, but these titles do not correspond to the *Commercial Code* classification of corporate officers, which provides simply for company 'directors' (*torishimariyaku*: 取締役), a board of directors and 'representative directors' (*daihyō torishimariyaku*: 代表取締役). The latter have the power to legally bind the corporation. Many large Japanese companies voluntarily moved to supplement this simple set of corporate organs and in particular those listed on the New York Stock Exchange began to adopt the committee system of corporate officers used the United States. In response to these market moves, the Japanese government revised the corporations law in 2003 to allow corporations maximum flexibility in their choice of governance structure: see Gilson and Milhaupt, "Choice as Regulatory Reform: The Case of Japanese Corporate Governance".
71. The case reports are not explicit about how the information flowed to regulators. The actual plaintiffs included former Duskin employees, but it is not clear whether the catalyst was internal whistleblowing or perhaps a leak from a disgruntled player in the supply chain.
72. In Japanese *kuchi-dome* (口止め), literally 'stop your mouth' money.
73. See the summary of the facts in "Shokuhineiseihōjōshiyōga mitomeraretiinai shokuhintenkabutsu o shiyōshita shōhin ga hanbaisaretita koto o ato kara ninshikishita torishimariyaku no kōhyōsubekigimu – dasukin kabushikidaihyō soshōjiken," (Directors' duty to make public after being informed of the sale of foodstuffs with a non-approved additive: the Duskin shareholder suit) *Jurisuto* 1332 (2007): 102.
74. See the summary of the facts in "Shokuhineiseihōjōshiyōga mitomeraretiinai shokuhintenkabutsu o shiyōshita shōhin ga hanbaisaretita koto o ato kara ninshikishita torishimariyaku no kōhyōsubekigimu – dasukin kabushikidaihyō soshōjiken," (Directors' duty to make public after being informed of the sale of foodstuffs with a non-approved additive: the Duskin shareholder suit) *Jurisuto* 1332 (2007): 102.
75. "Dasukin kabunushi daihyōsoshō jiken hanketsu (hikoku 2mei bun)," (Decision in the Duskin shareholder suit: Results against two defendants) *Shiryoban Shōjihōmu* 256 (2005): 26; Akira Takeuchi, "Dasukin jiken kōsai hanketsu de torishimariyaku ni hatasareta shinraikaifuku gimu: Osaka kōsai han heisei 18.6.9 ni miru kuraishisu manejiment no arikata," (The duty to restore trust imposed on directors in the Duskin High Court decision: What the 9 June 2006 Osaka High Court decision tells us about crisis management) *NBL* 860 (2007): 32.
76. In addition to directors, the Japanese *Commercial Code* additionally provides for 'statutory auditors' (*kansayaku* or 監査役), who are charged with oversight of the company's actions and who technically supervise the board of directors. Often, though not always, these are attorneys but seldom are qualified accountants.

The perceived failure of the statutory auditor role in monitoring corporations was one of the catalysts for the introduction of the optional committee system of corporate governance introduced in Japan in 2003.

77. Duskin is headquartered in Osaka and so the Osaka District Court is the court most proximate to the defendant's place of business.
78. Osaka District Court (Division 4 Civil), 9 February 2005, *Shiryoban Shōjihōmu* 256 (2005): 24.
79. Osaka High Court (Division 6 Civil), 18 January 2007, *Shiryoban Shōjihōmu* 275 (2007): 202.
80. Osaka District Court, 22 December 2004, *Hanrei Jihō* 1892 (2005): 108; also reported in *Hanrei Taimuzu* 1172 (2005): 271.
81. Osaka High Court (Division 4 Civil), 9 June 2006, "Shokuhineiseihōjōshiyōga mitomerareteinai shokuhintenkabutsu o shiyōshita shōhin ga hanbaisaretita koto o ato kara ninshikishita torishimariyaku no kōhyōsubekigimu – dasukin kabushikidaihyō soshōjiken," (Directors' duty to make public after being informed of the sale of foodstuffs with a non-approved additive: the Duskin shareholder suit) *Jurisuto* 1332 (2007): 102. Also reported in *Shiryoban Shōjihōmu* 268 (2006): 74.
82. *Civil Code* general provisions apply to legal acts unless displaced by special legislation: here the Commercial Code is invoking the *Civil Code.*
83. Emphasis added.
84. *Commercial Code* art. 254–3.
85. For an extended discussion of the duty of loyalty, see Hideki Kanda and Curtis J. Milhaupt, "Re-examining Legal Transplants: The Director's Duty in Japanese Corporate Law," in *Law in Japan: A Turning Point*, ed. Daniel H. Foote (Seattle, WA: University of Washington Press 2008), 437.
86. For a discussion of the classic United States cases on business judgment, see Bruce E. Aronson, "Learning from Comparative Law in Teaching US Corporate Law: Directors' Liability in Japan and the US," *Penn State International Law Review* 22 (2003): 213.
87. Osaka District Court, 9 February 2005, *Hanrei Jihō* 1889 (2005): 130; appealed.
88. Osaka District Court (Division 4 Civil), 9 February 2005 "Dasukin kabunushi daihyōsoshō jiken hanketsu (hikoku 2mei bun)," (Decision in the Duskin shareholder suit: Results against two defendants) *Shiryoban Shōjihōmu* 256 (2005): 36.
89. (*yakuin kyōgikai* or 役員協議会). This is distinct from a board of directors and usually connotes a smaller inner-circle management group.
90. Osaka District Court (Division 4 Civil), 9 February 2005 "Dasukin kabunushi daihyōsoshō jiken hanketsu (hikoku 2mei bun)," (Decision in the Duskin shareholder suit: Results against two defendants) *Shiryoban Shōjihōmu* 256 (2005): 33.
91. Ibid., 36.
92. Osaka District Court (Division 4 Civil), 9 February 2005 "Dasukin kabunushi daihyōsoshō jiken hanketsu (hikoku 2mei bun)," (Decision in the Duskin shareholder suit: Results against two defendants) *Shiryoban Shōjihōmu* 256 (2005): 38. This and all other translations of the excerpts from the cases are mine.
93. Osaka District Court, 22 December 2004, *Hanrei Taimuzu* 1172 (2005): 271.
94. Osaka High Court (Division 6 Civil), 18 January 2007, *Shiryoban Shōjihōmu* 275 (2007): 226.
95. See generally, Aronoson, "Reconsidering the Importance of Law in Japanese Corporate Governance: Evidence from the Daiwa Bank Shareholder Derivative Case," 11.
96. Osaka High Court (Division 4 Civil), 9 June 2006 "Shokuhineiseihōjōshiyōga mitomeraretiinai shokuhintenkabutsu o shiyōshita shōhin ga hanbaisaretita koto o ato kara ninshikishita torishimariyaku no kōhyōsubekigimu – dasukin kabushikidaihyō soshōjiken," (Directors' duty to make public after being informed of the sale of foodstuffs with a non-approved additive: the Duskin shareholder suit) *Jurisuto* 1332 (2007): 102.

97. For a summary of commentary and critique, see Hatada Kōmei, "Shokuhineiseihōjōshiyōga mitomeraretiinai shokuhintenkabutsu o shiyōshita shōhin ga hanbaisaretita koto o ato kara ninshikishita torishimariyaku no kōhyōsubekigimu – dasukin kabushikidaihyō soshōjiken," (Directors' duty to make public after being informed of the sale of foodstuffs with a non-approved additive: the Duskin shareholder suit) *Jurisuto* 1332 (2007): 103.
98. *Company Law* (*Kaishahō*), *Law No. 86/2005* art. 425 and following.
99. Akira Takeuchi, "Dasukin jiken kōsai Hanketsu de torishimariyaku ni hatasareta shinraikaifuku gimu: Osaka kōsai han heisei 18.6.9 ni miru kuraishisumanejiment no arikata," (The duty to restore trust imposed on directors in the Duskin High Court decision: What the 9 June 2006 High Court decision tells use about crisis management) *NBL* 860 (2007): 33.
100. Ibid., 33.
101. Ibid., 34.
102. See Table 19.3 in this chapter.
103. West, "Why Shareholders Sue: The Evidence from Japan," http://papers.ssrn.com/sol3/papers.cfm?abstract_id = 251012, 11 footnote 21, discussing the Supreme Court decision in the *Nomura Securities* case, concerning directors' illegal payments to clients to compensate for trading losses.
104. See, for example, Ronald J. Gilson, "The Poison Pill in Japan: The Missing Infrastructure," *Columbia Business Law Review* 21 (2004) quoted in Stephen Givens, "Corporate Governance and M&A," in *Japanese Business Law*, ed. Gerald P. McAlinn (Alphen aan den Rijn, Netherlands: Wolters Kluwer, 2007), 172.
105. Aronoson, "Reconsidering the Importance of Law in Japanese Corporate Governance: Evidence from the Daiwa Bank Shareholder Derivative Case," 11, 42.
106. "Dasukin kabunushi soshōhanketsu no kōgeki," (The impact of the decision in the Duskin shareholder action) *Nikkei Shimbun* (Nikkei Newspaper) August 28, 2006 quoted in Akira Takeuchi, "Dasukin jiken kōsai hanketsu de torishimariyaku ni hatasareta shinraikaifuku gimu: Osaka kōsai han heisei 18.6.9 ni miru kuraishisumanejiment no arikata," (The duty to restore trust imposed on directors in the Duskin High Court decision: What the 9 June 2006 High Court decision tells use about crisis management) *NBL* 860 (2007): 30.
107. Haley, "Rethinking Contract Practice and Law in Japan"; Veronica L. Taylor "Japanese Commercial Transactions and Sanctions Revisited: Sumitomo v. UFJ," *Washington University Global Law Review* 7 (2009): 399–425.
108. Justice System Reform Council, "The Points at Issue in the Justice Reform," http://www.kantei.go.jp/foreign/policy/sihou/singikai/991221_e.html.
109. Justice System Reform Council, "Final Report," http://www.kantei.go.jp/foreign/judiciary/2001/0612report.html

Index